CROSSOVERS 1

A Secret Chronology of the World
(Dawn of Time-1939)

CROSSOVERS 1

A Secret Chronology of the World
(Dawn of Time-1939)

by
Win Scott Eckert

A Black Coat Press Book

Dedicated, in loving memory, to Philip José Farmer and Bette Farmer

Text Copyright © 2010 by Win Scott Eckert.
Introduction © 2010 by Kim Newman.
Cover illustration Copyright © 2010 by Mark Maddox.

ISBN 978-1-935558-10-1. First Printing. May 2010. Published by Black Coat Press, an imprint of Hollywood Comics.com, LLC, P.O. Box 17270, Encino, CA 91416. All rights reserved. Except for review purposes, no part of this book may be reproduced or transmitted in any form or by any means, electronic or mechanical, including photocopying, recording, or by any information storage and retrieval system, without permission in writing from the publisher. Printed in the United States of America.

Acknowledgements

No work of this magnitude is created in a vacuum. Some researchers pick an area of "specialty." For instance, Brad Mengel is the J.T. Edson expert, but has also supplied a wide variety of other crossover information, as have Matthew Baugh, Greg Gick, and others mentioned herein. Loki Carbis is the Callahan's specialist. Dennis Power is a master at delving into otherwise hidden connections and resolving ostensibly conflicting events. Not surprisingly, Jess Nevins shared his vast knowledge regarding the penny dreadfuls and dime novels (Sexton Blake, Nelson Lee, Dixon Hawke, etc.), as well as German dime novel characters (Capitan Mors and so on), various crossovers from European literature, and Mexican crossovers. Jean-Marc Lofficier provided multiple reviews and contributed vital facts regarding French pulp characters. Vincent Mollet supplemented this information with some of his own. Don Glut very kindly reviewed crossover entries for his stories and provided indispensable feedback. Rick Lai is a wealth of expertise when it comes to the pulps and other literature, and shared his extensive knowledge on crossover references. Jay Lindsey provided many of the Stephen King shared universe crossovers. Jay, along with Chris Nigro and I. Ronald Schablotski, supplied some modern horror information, while the research and theories of Mark Brown and Chuck Loridans created the framework for the classic horror crossover data. And Art Bollmann explored the secret archives of the Illuminati to bring me those crossovers. Attempting to acknowledge each and every specific piece of data that has been sent my way over the years will lead to the Mountains of Madness, as I'll surely, if inadvertently, overlook something. So let me instead express my sincere gratitude to:

Octavio Aragão, Roberto Barreiro, Matthew Baugh, Terry Beatty, Edward P. Berglund, Art Bollmann, James "JEB" Bowman, Kevin Breen, Andrew J. Brook, Mark Brown, Loki Carbis, Christopher Paul Carey, Marc Carlson, Max Allan Collins, Steven Costa, Bill Cunningham, Peter Currane, Sean Curtin, Chris Davies, Walter C. DeBill, Jeffrey Diehl, "Dr. Hermes," "Dragonrider," Danny Dyche, Darryl Elliott, Matthew Elliott, Mark Ellis, Douglas Ethington, Ron Fortier, Jacques Garin, Greg Gick, Donald F. Glut, David A. Goodman, Ernesto Guevara, Holger Haase, Dennis Hager, Micah Harris, Jim Harmon, Andrew Henry, Mark Hodder, Cheryl Huttner, Matthew Ilseman, Kai Jansson, Tom Johnson, Roberto Lionel, Stephen A. Kallis, Jr., Tom Kane, David Kennedy, Lawrence Knapp, Rick Lai, Roman Leary, Sean Levin, Jay Lindsey, Victor Litwin, Jean-Marc Lofficier, Chuck "The Savage Chuck" Loridans, Patrick Lozito, Terry McCombs, John McDonagh, Andrew McLean, Dan McQueen, Brad Mengel, Vincent Mollet, Lou Mougin, Kevin Mowery, Bobby Nash, Adrian Nebbett, Jess Nevins, Kim Newman, Chris Nigro, Michael Norwitz, Toby

O'Brien, Ben O'Neill, Michael A. Ongsingco, Marcus Pitcaithly, Dennis E. Power, Cenate "Hooper_X" Pruitt, Curt Purcell, Patrick Reumann, Jose A. Rivera, Chris Roberson, Kurt M. Roberts, "Rtomlin2001," André-François Ruaud, Charles Rutledge, Matthew Rutsala, Doug A. Scott, I. Ronald Schablotski, Randall A. Schanze, Frank Schildiner, Emile Schwarz, Bryan Shedden, Jason Shepherd, Kadzuwo J. Shimidzu, Robert Short, B.L. Sisemore, Art Sippo, John Small, George Henry Smathers, Jr., aka "Henry Covert," "Spooky," Royce Testa, Chris Tucker, Chris Wike, and Mike Winkle.

My thanks also to David Saindon and the gang at Mile High Comics for keeping me well stocked in—cue Dr. Evil broadly making finger quote marks and slowly but emphatically intoning—"Research Materials."

Special thanks to those whose creative mythographical insights and literary archaeological theories are quoted herein. For unflagging friendship, support, scholarship, camaraderie, genial disagreements, moral support, multiple reviews of the manuscript, and many valuable suggestions, my cohorts at the NWNMS (New Wold Newton Meteoritics Society)—all of whom, not coincidentally, are already listed above.

For special services: Mike Croteau, Paul Spiteri, Keith Howell, Charles Berlin, Jason Robert Bell, Joey Van Massenhoven, and, again, Dennis E. Power.

In particular, Christopher Paul Carey has my deep appreciation for reviewing the manuscript, and for providing much valuable advice and feedback. My appreciation also goes to Jean-Marc Lofficier at Black Coat Press, publisher extraordinaire, for giving *Crossovers* an excellent home, and for all his assistance with the manuscript.

For ceaseless inspiration—Philip José Farmer. Both he and his wife, Bette Farmer, are greatly missed.

Lastly, but never least, thanks to my family for not filing a missing persons report on me while I was entrenched in research and writing—and to Lisa especially for countless mugs of Café Du Monde to keep me fully charged.

W.S.E.

Introduction

In *The Mind Robber*, a 1968 *Doctor Who* serial which remains bizarre even by the standards of the program, the Doctor and his companions were dematerialised out of normal reality and turned up in the Land of Fiction (where, of course, we had always known they lived). Here, Lemuel Gulliver, Medusa, a 21st Century superhero called the Karkus, Sir Lancelot, and Rapunzel live alongside D'Artagnan, Cyrano de Bergerac and Blackbeard (all real people, though fictionalised in this context). It wasn't an entirely new thought—John Kendrick Bangs had envisioned something similar in his houseboat on the Styx and John Myers Myers covered much the same ground in his wonderful novel *Silverlock*. However, it was the first time the notion had been put to me—and I've been pleased by it ever since.

As this odd, obsessive, useful, trivial, argumentative, fascinating book will reveal, there are all kinds of crossovers. Through a single character (Richard Belzer's Detective John Munch), the shows *Homicide: Life on the Street, The X-Files, Law and Order, The Beat, Law and Order: Special Victims Unit, The Brady Bunch* and *Gilligan's Island* can be absorbed into a single universe (the last two come in via the film *A Very Brady Sequel*); and, by extension, these shows cross over into *Chicago Hope, The Simpsons, St Elsewhere, Cheers, The Lone Gunmen, Oz, Millennium, Strange Luck, The Critic, King of the Hill, Futurama*, sundry *Law and Order* franchise offshoots and so on, with ripples still spreading. I have no problem in believing that there are regions of the Land of Fiction which look extremely like modern-day Baltimore, others where UFO abductions aren't arrant nonsense and a town full of yellow people with fewer fingers than the norm. Win Scott Eckert does, but that's what the appendices are for...

The original impulse for this sort of thing was satiric (Fielding wanted to make fun of Richardson's Pamela Andrews and so invented the character of Pamela's equally naïve brother Joseph), presumptuous (Maurice LeBlanc, wanting to big up his Arsène Lupin, brought on Conan Doyle's Sherlock Holmes and had his thief run rings around the rival author's sleuth) or the sort of inside-joke few readers would notice (H.P. Lovecraft and Robert Bloch wrote stories about caricature versions of themselves—with each writer killing off his friend in prose). Sometimes, crossovers arise (and I can testify to this from my own work) because authors are either too lazy to make up new characters or wary of just bringing on the same old stock figure under a new name. The oddest I've come across is courtesy of the prolific Peter Leslie, who turned out a stack of 1960s TV show tie-in books in the UK: he had one character (gossip columnist Trewithick Polgadden-Warr) show up in both *Deadline* (an *Avengers* novel published under the by-line of star Patrick Macnee) and *Night of the Trilobites* (an *Invad-*

ers novel in which David Vincent chases aliens in Wales). By the reasoning of this book, that brings *The Invaders* into the Crossover Universe...

Some writers like P.G. Wodehouse deliberately set out to create their own universe, with all their characters inhabiting the same space; others do so piecemeal, like Stephen King (or—ahem—me), by dropping references which tie together works that can't possibly take place in a single universe (i.e., *The Stand* wipes out the possibility of, say, *Misery*) or mapping a multiplicity of parallel worlds (like Michael Moorcock) to incorporate their entire bibliography. Occasionally, a fictional universe isn't owned by a single creator but a corporation—like the old-time pulp fiction worlds of the Shadow or Sexton Blake, or the increasingly complex multiverses operated by most comic book publishers (I still remember the frisson of Spider-Man's pathetic attempt to join the Fantastic Four). Sometimes, crossovers are basically jokes—in Evelyn Waugh's *Decline and Fall*, a particularly horrible school is located on Egdon Heath, the setting of Thomas Hardy's *Return of the Native* (I put a prison there in my " Sorcerer, Conjurer, Wizard, Witch"). Some fictions—especially TV series with attendant spinoffery—become franchises which threaten to swallow their universes. Writers are all gods in their worlds (there are even stories about this—King's "Umney's Last Case"or Ian Rankin's "Reichenbach Falls"), and mostly jealous—which means the consensus reality of any crossover universe will always be on the point of tearing apart. I'd hate to think the world of my books is going to end up as the anodyne *Star Trek* universe and am tempted to have Derek Leech (the Devil in a bunch of my stories and novels) murder everyone in Iowa named Kirk to ensure the Roddenberryverse never comes to be—if only I could be sure no time paradox story would undo my tampering.

This book takes as its mainstream reality the not-exactly-unproblematic region of the Land of Fiction colonized by Philip José Farmer in his Tarzan and Doc Savage biographies—books which were as influential on me in the 1970s as on several other authors (Alan Moore, Howard Waldrop, Warren Ellis) who are frequently mentioned in these pages. Farmer's thesis was not only that all manner of characters, from Leo Bloom (of *Ulysses*, not *The Producers*) to Kilgore Trout, live in the same world, but are part of a large, complex extended family. I've never been entirely comfortable with this. If Lois Lane was Margo Lane's sister, one or other would probably have mentioned it and Lois at least already has a well-worked-out family tree (including a sister, Lucy—though Lois's pesky niece Susie hasn't been around for years thanks to DC's ongoing spoilsport policy of squeezing any charm and fun out of their universe). It seems to me unnecessarily soap-operaish to have so many great characters collide with "Luke, I am your father" moments. An obsession with absent fathers throbs through American popular culture all the way back to Tarzan and Bruce Wayne—outside of Dickens, British heroes get by perfectly well without being traumatised orphans. Holmes and Moriarty don't have to be related to hate each other....I also feel part of the appeal of pulp adventure is the thought that we all might work hard and develop an invisibility serum or become a mental/physical marvel, without having the need to be descended from some useless titled twonk who tripped over a meteorite.

Of course, according to my grandmother, my great-great uncle did invent invisibility (in a film, at least) and my mother inspired Winston Smith to rebel against Big Brother. My father's mother was purportedly Claude Rains' cousin and my mother's name, Julia, was borrowed by George Orwell for the novel's heroine (my mother's mother typed the manuscript of *Nineteen Eighty-Four*). Through some skewed logic rising from these connections, I can now write myself into the crossover universe—compounded by an appearance in an issue ("Calliope") of Neil Gaiman's *Sandman* comic (fair enough—Neil makes a noise in my story "The Original Dr Shade" and novel *The Quorum*) which in theory gives DC Comics the right to license action figures of me (I think Susie Lane is ahead of me in that queue). Name-checks in other people's novels (Paul McAuley's *Whole Wide World*, Simon Ings's *Headlong*, Nicholas Royle's *The Director's Cut*, Iain Sinclair's *Radon Daughters*) further cement my phantasmal other self. This may be an area of worthwhile future research, since—as Farmer's *Riverworld* already proved—it means we all get to be inhabitants of the Land of Fiction eventually.

A few words to writers who might be tempted to add to this game—it's not enough to cover pages with flow-charts, family trees and speculation to establish an extended kinship between Charles Foster Kane, Kathy Kane (Batwoman), Solomon Kane, Karl Wagner's Kane, Sugar Kane (Marilyn Monroe in *Some Like It Hot* or maybe Linda Evans in *Beach Blanket Bingo*), the Reverend Kane (the *Poltergeist* sequels), Killer Kane of the 25th Century (Buck Rogers' nemesis), the other Killer Kane (William Peter Blatty's *The Ninth Configuration*), Marshal Will Kane (*High Noon*), Claire "the Clown" Kane (*Short Cuts*), Officer J.Z. Kane (Kim Basinger in *Dog and Cat*), Candy Kane (the porn movie *Blonde Ambition*), Laverne Higby Todd Kane (Park Overall in *Empty Nest*), the Kane Family of *Veronica Mars*, Adam Kane (*Mutant X*), Police Captain Fergus K. Kane (who butted heads with Marlowe in *The Lady in the Lake*), Ariana Kane (Faye Dunaway on *Alias*), Erica Kane (Susan Lucci on *All My Children*), Lucifer Kane (villain in *Rogue's Gallery*), Martin Kane Private Eye, Frank and Danny Kane (*The Paradise Club*), the John Hurt spaceman who gets impregnated by the Alien, Felix Kane (who revived the Cybernauts on *The New Avengers*), Benjamin Kane (Rob Lowe in *Wayne's World),* John Kane (Sidney Poitier in *Brother John*) and Margo Kane (villain of the first episode of *Adam Adamant Lives!*)—even if you do remember Sugar Kane from *Some Like It Hot* was born Kowalczyk and manage to square that. You also have to have a good story to put all this stuff in—and perhaps an attitude to the original material.

If you use a pre-existing fictional character, you are under the same obligation a writer of historical fiction is in using a real person—you still have to make them over to fit into your own fictional universe, and perhaps pass judgment on them (as with all those writers who decide Holmes couldn't be that smart or there's something wrong with the way Mike Hammer gets off on hurting folks). The lifeblood of the Land of Fiction remains story—the adventures, exploits, loves and deaths—not the crossovers; fun as they are, they have to come second or you get sub-par fan fiction (as opposed to outstanding fan fiction—which is what, say, Joseph Andrews is). It might get you into a future edition of this book, but it won't make anyone want to read (or reprint) the story.

Now, I hand you over to Win Scott Eckert. Without a TARDIS malfunction, he can transport you to the Land of Fiction, and guide you through one path of the labyrinth.

Kim Newman
Islington, London
June 2007

World-Building, Fictional Biographies, and Crossovers

Fictional Biographies

I've long been fascinated by the genre called "fictional biographies," in which the character is treated as if he or she were real. As one can see from the list below, the fictional biography is a fairly small, and yet intriguing, phenomena, especially when one excludes reference books or articles that commingle pure fictional biographical details with "real world details" (e.g., Doyle based the character of Sherlock Holmes on Joseph Bell, and so on).

As I stated in the Foreword to the Bison Books edition of Philip José Farmer's *Tarzan Alive: A Definitive Biography of Lord Greystoke* (University of Nebraska Press Bison Books, 2006), the fictional biography genre was birthed from

> ...*The Sherlockian tradition in which the object of the fictional biography is treated as a real person. Sherlockian biographical scholarship (commonly called the "Game") arose as a response to a myriad of discrepancies in Watson's writings of the master detective, Sherlock Holmes. In the Sherlockian Game Holmes' amanuensis, Dr. Watson, is also treated as a real person. As Dr. Watson narrates the cases, Arthur Conan Doyle is relegated to the status of Watson's "editor."*

Game players then write critical essays that resolve the chronology of the Sherlock Holmes canon and otherwise provide explanations for inconsistencies in Watson's work. Sometimes the inconsistencies are explained as resulting from Watson's carelessness, whereas in other instances we are told that Watson deliberately changed certain details, times, and names to protect innocent parties and prevent delicate information from being uncovered through his writings.

Occasionally Game players go so far as to research and write complete biographies of their subjects.

The Sherlockian Game brings us to this list of fictional biographies, which forms the basis of the continuity I call the "Crossover Universe." Some of the fictional biographies themselves have crossovers, as noted below.

- *America's Secret Service Ace: The Operator 5 Story* by Nick Carr
- *Biggles: The Authorized Biography* by John Pearson
- *Confessions of a Teen Sleuth*, an autobiography by Nancy Drew, edited by Chelsea Cain (Mega-crossover with other teen sleuths that Nancy Drew meets throughout her lifetime: Frank and Joe Hardy, the Hardy Boys; Nurse Cherry Ames; Vicki Barr, Flight Stewardess; Louise and Jane Dana, the Dana Girls; Tom Swift, Sr.; aviator Ted Scott; Bert, Freddie, and Flossie Bobbsey, from the Bobbsey Twins; Tom Swift, Jr. and his pal Bud Bar-

clay; Christopher Cool, Geronimo Johnson, and Spice Carter, TEEN agents; Foxy Belden-Frayne, daughter of Trixie Belden; Kim Aldrich, secretary at WALCO, Inc.; Judy Bolton; Donna Parker; Encyclopedia Brown; and Jupiter, Pete, and Bob, the Three Investigators)
- *Doc Savage: His Apocalyptic Life* by Philip José Farmer (Mega-crossover with countless other heroes, villains, adventurers, and detectives, as part of the Wold Newton Family Tree)
- "Edgar Rice Burroughs: A Brief Biographical Sketch" by John Flint Roy in his *A Guide to Barsoom*
- *Four-&-Twenty Bloodhounds*. Like *Sleuths* (see below), there is a mini-biography of each detective along with each short story. The detectives featured are Shadrack Arnold, Senator Brooks U. Banner, Jim Burgess, Dr. Gideon Fell, Mortimer Death, Dr. Mary Finney, Dr. Sam: Johnson, Scott Jordan, Johnny Liddell, Inspector Magruder, John & Suzy Marshall, Merlini, Miss Rachel Murdock, the Mysterious Traveler, Nick Noble, O'Reilly Sahib, Ben Pedley, Solar Pons, Ellery Queen, Mike Shayne, Henry Smith, Dr. Paul Standish, Lieut. Timothy Trent, Jeff & Haila Troy, and Hildelgarde Withers. Nearly every detective has a "Detective's Who's Who" entry provided by his creator. The only detectives who do not have entries are Ellery Queen, Mike Shayne, and the Mysterious Traveler. Ellery Queen provides a letter containing a vague summation of his life: "I was born, I have lived, and I'm going to hang on as long as I can." Mike Shayne's creator, Brett Halliday, provides a brief biography which is short on actual biographical details. The Mysterious Traveler writes Boucher a letter so disconcerting that it is unprintable, and Boucher forwarded it to the archives of Miskatonic University, thus establishing a crossover with H.P. Lovecraft's Cthulhu Mythos
- *The Flying Spy: A History of G-8* by Nick Carr
- "An Informal Biography of Conan the Cimmerian" by Clark, Miller, and de Camp in *The Blade of Conan*
- *The Great Detectives: Seven Original Investigations* by Julian Symons. Each of the investigations is a short biographical sketch in the form of a short story, first person narration, or interview. The detectives covered are Sherlock Holmes, Miss Marple, Nero Wolfe and Archie Goodwin, Hercule Poirot, Maigret, Ellery Queen(s), and Philip Marlowe
- *Holmes and Watson* by June Thomson
- *James Bond: The Authorized Biography of 007* by John Pearson
- *Jeeves: A Gentleman's Personal* Gentleman *by C. Northcote Parkinson* (Crossover with Father Brown, Hercule Poirot, and Lord Peter Wimsey)
- *John Steed: An Authorized Biography, Volume 1: Jealous In Honour* by Tim Heald (Crossover with James Bond)
- "Jonathan Swift Somers III, Cosmic Traveller in a Wheelchair: A Short Biography by Philip José Farmer (Honorary Chief Kennel Keeper)" in

Myths for the Modern Age: Philip José Farmer's Wold Newton Universe (Crossover with Edgar Lee Masters' *Spoon River Anthology*)
- *Leopold Bloom: A Biography* by Peter Costello
- *The Life and Exploits of the Scarlet Pimpernel* by John Blakeney
- *The Life and Times of Hercule Poirot* by Anne Hart
- *The Life and Times of Horatio Hornblower* by C. Northcote Parkinson
- *The Life and Times of Miss Jane Marple* by Anne Hart
- "Michael Shayne as I Know Him" by Brett Halliday in *Four-&-Twenty Bloodhounds*
- *Nero Wolfe of West Thirty-Fifth Street: The Life and Times of America's Largest Private Detective* by William S. Baring-Gould (Crossover with Sherlock Holmes)
- "The Obscure Life and Hard Times of Kilgore Trout," by Philip José Farmer in *The Book of Philip José Farmer*; reprinted in *Venus on the Half-Shell and Others*
- *The Official World of Austin Powers* by Andy Lane
- *The Private Life of Dr. Watson: Being the Personal Reminiscences of John H. Watson, M.D.* by Michael Hardwick
- *The Private Lives of Private Eyes, Spies, Crime Fighters, and Other Good Guys* by Otto Penzler. Lew Archer, Modesty Blaise, James Bond, Father Brown, Nick Carter, Charlie Chan, Nick and Nora Charles, Bulldog Drummond, C. Auguste Dupin, Mike Hammer, Sherlock Holmes, Jules Maigret, Philip Marlowe, Miss Jane Marple, Perry Mason, Mr. Moto, Hercule Poirot, Ellery Queen, The Shadow, John Shaft, Sam Spade, Dr. Thorndyke, Philo Vance, Lord Peter Wimsey, and Nero Wolfe
- *Radio's Captain Midnight: The Wartime Biography* by Stephen A. Kallis, Jr.
- *Sherlock Holmes of Baker Street: The Life of the World's First Consulting Detective* by William S. Baring-Gould (Crossover with Nero Wolfe)
- *Sherlock Holmes: My Life and Crimes* by Michael Hardwick
- *Sleuths: Twenty-Three Great Detectives of Fiction and Their Best Stories*. Each story features a short biography of the detective in the story; many biographies are by the characters' authors, providing canonicity. The twenty-three detectives are: C. Auguste Dupin, Sherlock Holmes, Martin Hewitt, Eugene Valmont, The Thinking Machine, The Old Man in the Corner, Craig Kennedy, Uncle Abner, Dr. Thorndyke, Father Brown, Astro, Philip Marsham Trent, Max Carrados, William Dawson, Mr. Reginald Fortune, Hercule Poirot, Jim Hanvey, Superintendent Wilson, Lord Peter Wimsey, Dr. Hailey, J.G. Reeder, Detective Duff, and Henry Poggioli
- *Tarzan Alive: A Definitive Biography of Lord Greystoke* by Philip José Farmer (Mega-crossover with countless other heroes, villains, adventurers, and detectives, as part of the Wold Newton Family Tree)

- *The Wimsey Family* by C.W. Scott-Giles
- *Yankee Lawyer: The Autobiography of Ephraim Tutt* by Arthur Train

The Crossover Chronology

For perhaps even longer than I've followed the genre of fictional biographies, I've been a fan of crossovers. It was originally my deep interest in Wold Newton studies which sparked these obsessions, and first led me to seek out and document crossover stories involving characters whom Philip José Farmer had placed in his Wold Newton Family Tree. The idea has since expanded well beyond that basis, leading to my idea of creating and building a consistent universe out of a chronology of crossovers.

The Crossover Chronology builds a universe using the fictional biographies listed above as its platform. Put another way, the Crossover Chronology plays a "six degrees of separation" game, with the characters from the fictional biographies as the first degree. Given the role of Sherlockian studies in this metafictional Game, it should surprise no one to learn that Sherlock Holmes is, without a doubt, the most crossed-over character in history. It is possible that Count Dracula runs a distant second. H.P. Lovecraft's Cthulhu Mythos also ranks high in the crossover count.

The Crossover Chronology also honors the basic tenant of fictional biographies, treating the universe it documents as a series of real, historical events. Of course, this universe only resembles our real world on the surface. Dig deeper, and one finds crimefighters and villains of extraordinary ability and scope, Lovecraftian entities, covered-up alien visitations, and innumerable spy and counter-spy cartels. Still, to the ordinary Joe on the street, this universe very much resembles the world outside our window.

In order to maintain the real-world appearance, crossovers are incorporated using a set of rules and guidelines. I documented these guidelines in *Myths for the Modern Age: Philip José Farmer*'s *Wold Newton Universe* (MonkeyBrain Books, 2005). Although the universe shown in these crossover events has grown many degrees beyond the original Wold Newton mythos, those original guidelines still prove instructive, and are reproduced here, with amendments and revisions.

The Crossover Chronology is a timeline of crossover stories in which two or more literary characters, situations, universes, or, in some rare cases, actual historical personages, are linked together.[1] A very good example is *The Rainbow*

---

[1] Fan fiction is not included. An exception to this policy is fiction that is written by professionally published authors, but which goes unpublished for some reason. This exception allows for the inclusion of:
- *The Final Affair* by David McDaniel (who has many other published *Man From U.N.C.L.E.* novels to his credit);
- *Tarzan on Mars* by "John Bloodstone" aka Stuart J. Byrne (not authorized by ERB, Inc. but Byrne is a professionally published science-fiction author);

Affair, which brings together Sherlock Holmes, Fu Manchu, Nayland Smith, James Bond, Miss Marple, and The Avengers, (all already in the Crossover Universe [CU], based on the list of fictional biographies), with The Men From U.N.C.L.E (Napoleon Solo and Illya Kuryakin), The Saint, Inspector West, and Department Z (all added to the CU per this crossover).

Noncanonical pastiche is the rule, not the exception. This book is not for Sherlockians who devoutly subscribe only to the Canon of the original four novels and 56 short stories by Sir Arthur Conan Doyle. Nor is it for fans of *Star Trek* who religiously restrict themselves to the televised episodes and films (and ignore *Star Trek: The Animated Series*).

Derivations from media other than the original are acceptable, as long as they do not explicitly contradict the information in the original source. If a seemingly contradictory story can be shown to fit into the continuity after all, through a scholarly essay, piece of research, or a reconciling theory, so much the better.

Again, when evaluating crossovers, I am looking for stories that involve two or more fictional characters and that do not involve contradictions (that are too difficult to resolve) with what is already included. Examples of the latter would be the otherwise enjoyable Sherlock Holmes and the Hentzau Affair, and Superman: War of the Worlds. These stories are mentioned instead in an addendum on *Alternate Universe Crossovers, Parodies, and Farces*.[2]

On Historical Figures

When I first began to catalog crossovers, I often used a fictional character meeting an historical character as a way of linking in different fictional characters. After a while, though, it became obvious that certain historical characters made this problematic, Adolph Hitler and Jack the Ripper being two prime examples. Who hasn't met them in some fictional tale? This was too easy. Therefore, I concluded that no more fictional characters should be added on that basis, although I would not retroactively exclude characters previously brought in that way. A side rule to this is that fictional descendants and/or relatives of fictionalized versions of real people can be used to make additions to the Crossover Universe, because this type of crossover is not as over-utilized as the fictional-

---

- *Farewell Pellucidar* by Allan Howard Gross (author of the ERB, Inc. authorized Sunday *Tarzan* strip and several *Tarzan* comics published by Dark Horse); and
- *Red Axe of Pellucidar* by John Eric Holmes (author of the ERB, Inc. authorized *Mahars of Pellucidar*, as well as *Mordred*, the authorized sequel to Philip Francis Nowlan's *Armageddon 2419 A.D.*).

[2] Regarding parodies, I am much more likely to include a parody that uses original characters to spoof a genre, such as Derek Flint spoofing the genre of spy films, than I am to include parodies that substantially change preexisting characters, such as those which cast Sherlock Holmes as an addle-headed bumbler, or James Bond as a cross-dresser. Nevertheless, I have doubtless bent or broken this "rule" once or twice.

character-meets-real-person scenario. An example of the fictional relative crossover is a character on the television program *Alias* who states that he is the great-nephew of Harry Houdini. Since a strongly fictionalized version of Houdini exists in the CU, this brings in *Alias*.

Furthermore, if an historical person becomes a bona fide character in a fictional series, then we are dealing with the Crossover Universe version of that person. Therefore, Peter Heck's "Mark Twain-as-a-sleuth" series of mystery books come in through Twain's meeting with Inspector Lestrade, because this is not "our" universe's Mark Twain, it's the CU version of Twain. The same goes for Harry Houdini's numerous appearances in the CU, as well as the historical highwaymen Dick Turpin, Tom King, Cartouche, John "Sixteen String Jack" Rann, and Claude Duval, versus the romanticized, fictionalized versions, and so on.

On Superheroes and Comic Book Universes

The Crossover Universe is not a superhero universe. The CU is grounded in the literary trick that everything being discussed is real and takes place in our world. If an event or characters appear outlandish in real-world terms, then perhaps the events or characters are concealed from the world-at-large, so that those of us living our day-to-day lives have no idea of the secret history occurring all around us, all the time. Or perhaps the events depicted in the story have been fictionalized and somewhat exaggerated beyond the real events.

If one accepts that the CU at least appears to be the real world, if it is not actually the real world, then one would not expect to see too many superheroes. A supposedly "real world" universe filled with superheroes is not believable. A universe containing only a few superheroes operating in secret (or not operating in secret, but nevertheless regarded as urban legends) is much more believable if one wishes to maintain the premise that, to the general observer, the Crossover Universe is the real world.

This means not only limiting the number of superheroes or "mystery men," but also that these characters must be alternate universe (AU) versions of their comic-universe selves. This is important in order to avoid importing the whole history, continuity, and character-set of the comic-universe. This applies in particular to the overly "retconned" and continuity-laden DC Comics and Marvel Comics Universes, in which extraterrestrial beings are a fact of life well known to all inhabitants of Earth in the 20th and 21st centuries, and which have a very different socio-political dynamic (Marvel's Civil War and the widespread hatred directed towards the mutants of the X-Men, to name but two examples) than the real world does. Earth-CU, to use a comic book naming convention, is not subject to alien invasions and attacks every other month, as seems to occur in the DC and Marvel Universes.

Additionally, it should be assumed across-the-board that the that Crossover Universe versions of superheroes operated for less time than as portrayed by comic book publishers, that they were much less powerful than as described in the exaggerated comics, and that their adventures were considerably less cosmic and earth-shaking. This means that there is a preference for superhero references that are set in the particular superhero's original general time frame, such as Superman in the 1930s-40s, or Spider-Man in the 1960s-70s. In a "real-world" continuum like the Crossover Universe, it is unlikely, though not impossible, that Spider-Man would still be operating in the early 21st century, absent an *elixir vitae* like Fu Manchu's. Therefore less weight will be given to superhero crossover references that take place late in a particular hero's publishing career and particularly after superhero-universe "reboots" or in the context of a superhero-universe "retcon." Obviously, viable explanations will be considered, such as interpreting the 1986 Batman/Sherlock Holmes crossover as a meeting between Batman III and Holmes.

Having thus established the necessity for limiting the inclusion of superheroes when building a universe that resembles the real world, some general Rules, Guidelines, and Exceptions follow.

The basic rule of the Crossover Universe is: Very few superheroes. This is not because I find some of the powers unbelievable (although some are), but because large numbers of high-powered superheroes would change the nature and outcome of events in this continuity. The goal of the CU is to emulate the real world. This is clearly not the goal of superhero universes such as the DC and Marvel Universes. Too many superheroes make the Crossover Universe less and less similar to the real world. And too many super-powered heroes also overshadow the other heroes like Philip Marlowe and Travis McGee.

The exception to the basic rule is: Superheroes will be admitted if they appear in a crossover with a character already in the Crossover Universe. For example: Batman appears through Tarzan and Sherlock Holmes crossovers. Captain America is in through the appearance in a Green Hornet story. Elongated Man appears through a meeting with Sherlock Holmes, and Plastic Man appears though a connection with The Spirit. Spider-Man comes in because he shared adventures with Red Sonja, King Kull, and Doc Savage.

Rule: Superheroes do not automatically bring in other superheroes through crossovers that take place within their own regular universes, especially the highly continuity-burdened DC and Marvel Universes which are overflowing with superheroes. Instead, these are taken on a case-by-case basis. This rule also applies to non-superheroes from superhero universes. Examples: The Elongated Man does not imply the existence of the Silver Age Flash in the Crossover Universe. The X-Men cannot be added just because they met Captain America. The presence of "Hop" Harrigan does not mean that all the members of the Justice Society of America are in the CU. Red Sonja's battle with Kulan Gath, an evil wizard in Marvel Comics, does not mean that other Marvel superheroes that battled Kulan Gath are incorporated into the CU. Shang Chi does not bring in the other Marvel heroes. The Prowler (who is not technically a superhero anyway) can bring Airboy (also not a superhero) into the CU, but these characters will not necessarily bring the Eclipse Comics Universe's superheroes into the CU. The Shadow's meeting with the Ghost does not necessarily bring in the rest of Dark Horse Comics' superheroes.

Rule: Appearances or cameos of a superhero's alter ego are enough to place that alter ego in the CU, but are not enough to substantiate the presence of the actual superhero. Examples: The mention of Billy Batson in "The New York Review of Bird" is not enough to bring in Captain Marvel. The appearance of Freddy Freeman in Lin Carter's *The Earth-Shaker* does not bring in Captain Marvel Jr. The mention of Donald Blake in the Doc Savage/Thing crossover does not bring in Thor. The mention of Carol Danvers in the Red Sonja/Spider-Man crossover is not sufficient to bring in Ms. Marvel. The appearance of Bruce Wayne in the Prince Zarkon novels is not enough to bring in Batman (but Batman comes in anyway through his meetings with Tarzan and Sherlock Holmes). The appearance of Clark Kent in a Green Hornet story does not suffice to link in Superman (but Superman does come in via more solid Crossover Universe links in the stories "Three Men, a Martian, and a Baby" and "War Between Two Worlds").

Exception: Even though technically only Steve Rogers appears in the Green Hornet crossover, he is definitely Captain America; otherwise, he would be portrayed as quite scrawny and emaciated.

Rule: Once a superhero is already validly included, that superhero can bring in other characters, as long as the other characters are not from an overly continuity-laden universe like the DC and Marvel Universes. Examples: A reference to the *Daily Star* newspaper from Superman is sufficient to bring in a pulp-like African-American hero, Captain Gravity. Likewise, the appearance of the *Daily Planet* newspaper in a Jon Sable comic serves to substantiate Sable's presence in the CU.

Rule: Characters such as Dracula and the Frankenstein Monster are not automatically valid crossover links; many different comic publishers (and films, for that matter) have portrayed conflicting versions of Dracula and so they must be evaluated on a case-by-case basis. Example: Although Dracula is a character in the Crossover Universe, the Marvel Comics Universe version of Dracula does not automatically bring in every Marvel superhero that Dracula ever met. If the Marvel version of Dracula meets another Marvel character who has a valid, independent link to the Crossover Universe, then that crossover can also be interpreted as valid. For example, a version of Dr. Strange exists in the Crossover Universe via a reference in a Dr. Zarnak tale, "The Deep Cellars;" since Marvel's *The Tomb of Dracula* series fits well with CU continuity, via links to Alexandre Dumas' Count Cagliostro and Robert E. Howard's King Kull, it is likely that the Dracula-Dr. Strange clash depicted in the pages of Marvel Comics also occurred in the CU.

Rule: Inter-company crossovers from independent publishers (i.e., not DC or Marvel) that are based on promotional marketing strategies will be evaluated on a case-by-case basis to determine if they mesh with or violate continuity. Example: Vampirella's promotional crossovers with characters from other publishers, such as ShadowHawk, Lady Death, Purgatori, and Shi, are taken on a case-by-case basis to ensure that they fit into continuity; many do, and many do not. The same goes for the many crossovers involving Tomb Raider, Shi, Darkchylde, Witchblade, Spawn, Cyblade, Darkness, Avengelyne, Glory, the 10th Muse, Pandora, etc.

Rule: Superhero teams, particularly from the DC and Marvel Universes, are generally excluded. There is not enough time in a realistic chronology of a hero's life to have all of his/her own adventures and have regular adventures with a formally organized superteam. Additionally, the menaces superteams face are almost always cosmic or at least earth-shattering in scope. One cannot theorize the concealment of all these events from the public in the hopes of maintaining the facade of a "real" world—the sheer numbers are too great.

Exception 1: "Family" superhero teams like the Fantastic Four are more likely. Besides the family connections and going through the origin of their superhero powers together, they tend to have most of their adventures together and not individually. Cameos of superhero teams in individual hero's comic books can be excluded as cross-promotional ploys designed to encourage readers to try other comics. This leaves out the following examples:

- The brief appearance of a Marvel Comics' superteam, The Avengers, in an Iron Man comic book which features Fu Manchu; the Iron Man/Fu Manchu connection remains intact; and
- The appearance of Scott Summers and Jean Grey (from The X-Men) in an Iron Fist comic which features Del Floria's Tailor Shop (from *The Man From U.N.C.L.E.*); the Iron Fist/U.N.C.L.E. connection remains intact.

Exception 2: A commando type of superteam, expressly brought together for one, or perhaps two missions, is more realistic—as long as the characters who are part of the team have valid, independent links into the Crossover Universe which follow the rest of these guidelines. In this way, perhaps a Crossover Universe version of the World War II team code-named "The Invaders" (comprised of Captain America, Bucky, and the Sub-Mariner, who all have valid independent CU links) performed one or two assignments, although certainly not all the ongoing missions depicted in forty-one issues of the original *Invaders* comic series from Marvel Comics. Likewise, so many Golden Age DC Comics heroes have valid connections to the CU, independent of crossovers with other DC superheroes, that one might be tempted to postulate that in the Crossover Universe they banded together and performed one or two missions under the direction of President Franklin D. Roosevelt, calling themselves the "Justice Society of America." However, the JSA as an ongoing superteam, and their intertwined continuity with the DC Universe, must be dismissed as contradictory with mainstream Crossover Universe continuity.

Rule: Multiversal connections: There are so many Cthulhu Mythos references throughout Marvel and DC comics that they cannot be treated as an automatically valid connector, or else the combined DC/Marvel Universes would subsume the CU. Therefore the Cthulhu Mythos will be treated as existing across multiple universes, when it comes to superhero crossovers from DC Comics and Marvel Comics. Likewise, there are a few Predator and Aliens stories that have strong connections to the Crossover Universe, but many tales are not in continuity. The Predators and Aliens are treated as races which exist in many parallel universes.

Any crossover that appears to be valid and passes these rules and guidelines must still pass the bar of being non-contradictory with existing Crossover Universe continuity. Therefore, even if a comic book hero meets a character from one of the listed fictional biographies, or a character in a valid crossover chain, it is not necessarily a genuine crossover for purposes of Crossover Universe continuity.

For instance, there have been several G.I. Joe/Transformers crossovers in comics. G.I. Joe is nominally in the Crossover Universe because Action Force, the European counterpart to the G.I. Joe team, met Shang Chi, and CU primary links Fu Manchu and Nayland Smith were mentioned in the story. So far, this is a valid crossover chain. However, the alien giant robots featured in the *Transformers* violate the overall guiding principle that the Crossover Universe, on the surface, must resemble the world outside our window, and thus they are excluded. As with all crossovers, the settings, characters, and time placement must harmonize with whole of the Crossover Universe.

Some might argue that the inclusion of mystical characters such as Witchblade, H.G. Wells' Martian Invasion, occult monsters like Dracula, or Lovecraftian entities violates the real world premise—that in fact they do not harmonize with the continuity of the Crossover Universe—in the same way that the inclusion of all of DC and Marvel's costumed super-powered heroes would. Granted that such creatures of the night and events are not part of our real world, inhabitants of the Crossover Universe would also maintain that such creatures are not part of their world, or are urban legends. The world at large would not know of the 1898 Martian Invasion, which was covered up or is dismissed as an event that "never really happened." It would be hard to similarly cover up or dismiss giant alien robots using Earth as a battleground for twenty years running.

Conversely, inhabitants of the DC or Marvel Universes would know about and readily report on events such as the Superhuman Registration Act in the aforementioned Civil War event from Marvel Comics. Average citizens of Earth would know that at least something was up with the multiple Crises that routinely afflict their world in the DC Universe. They would know about the worldwide devastation meted out in Marvel's World War Hulk series. The Marvel and DC

Universes are increasingly about yearly colossal, world-changing events with lasting socio-political repercussions.

Thus, seemingly unrealistic characters or events can be included in the Crossover Universe, as long as, again, the CU appears to the average Joe to be the world outside our window.

Besides, who's to say that clandestine and mystical cabals like the Illuminati and the Nine Unknown really haven't been secretly ruling the world since time immemorial?

Conjecture

As previously mentioned, sometimes crossover stories or events are included in the Crossover Universe which, on their face, appear to be mutually exclusive or contradictory. Sometimes crossover characters are included on the basis of a genealogical relationship with a prior included character, but the exact familial relationship is not mapped out. These circumstances require, or at least open the door to, a limited integration of conjecture in order to reconcile these disconnects or gaps. The conjecture is included on three bases:
- For the purpose of filling in genealogical "holes";[3]
- For reconciling seemingly conflicting information;[4] and
- For answering "burning questions" which are raised by different elements of the Crossover Universe.[5]

---

[3] As an example, the inclusion of the character Clive Reston (Master of Kung Fu comic series) left open the question of his parentage. It was established in the series that James Bond was Reston's father, and his great-uncle was Sherlock Holmes. Matthew Baugh postulated that Mycroft Holmes was Reston's grandfather, and that Mycroft Holmes had a daughter who had an affair with James Bond. As seen in the short story "The Eye of Oran" (*Tales of the Shadowmen Volume 2: Gentlemen of the Night*, Black Coat Press, 2006) I named the daughter "Shrinking" Violet Holmes, married her off to British agent Charles Reston, killed off Reston, and gave Violet and Bond a child: Clive Reston.

[4] An example of reconciliation is my explanation in the *Crossover Chronology* of the history of Professor Moriarty and Captain Nemo, and the inclusion of Rick Lai's "The Secret History of Captain Nemo" (*Myths for the Modern Age: Philip José Farmer's Wold Newton Universe*, MonkeyBrain Books, 2005). Lai views some events as completely fictional, while Prof. H.W. Starr and Philip José Farmer believe other events to be fictional. My explanation views all the recorded events as having happened, and attempts to meld them together, thus rescuing the Prince Dakkar character and the events of Jules Verne's *The Mysterious Island* from the fictional oblivion to which Starr consigned them.

[5] An example here is my answer to the burning question raised by the inclusion of H.G. Wells' Martian Invasion from his novel *The War of the Worlds* (via Sherlock Holmes and *League of Extraordinary Gentlemen* crossovers), *Superman*, and *The X-Files* (connected to the Cthulhu Mythos): if humanity has a past history of contact with extraterrestrial beings, why is Dana Scully such a disbeliever in alien life? My answer is contained herein and it is conjecture, but it is conjecture within the established facts and boundaries of the Crossover Universe.

It should be noted that conjectural theories are not used to create a crossover which is not otherwise a crossover on its face. The crossovers listed herein are from documented appearances in published media—books, comics, film, television, and so on. They are crossovers on their own merits, not constructed based on creative theorizing.[6]

Some creative mythological essays or conjectural theories are referred to as background info, in order to explain published crossovers which are contradictory. For instance, Chuck Loridans' "soul-clone" theory is cited in order to explain a multitude of contradictory Dracula crossovers which otherwise would not fit into one continuity.

Put another way, the crossovers themselves do not emanate from speculative theories; speculative theories are used to explain some of them. If the amount of speculation needed to reconcile strains believability (and believability is subjective, of course), then the crossover is listed in the Alternate Universes Addendum since it is not in mainstream Crossover Universe continuity.

There are some ambiguous references that could be interpreted either as to a fictional or pop culture figure, or to a real person within continuity. There is a preference for the latter interpretation, as it allows for more inclusions, but is usually applied regarding pop cultural references to figures or series which already have strong, valid ties to Crossover Universe continuity, such as Sherlock Holmes: "He's a regular Sherlock Holmes!"

The Latest and Greatest

Crossovers is being published in two volumes. The first encompasses the Dawn of Time to 1939, with an addendum covering a multitude of "six-degrees" television crossover links. The second volume starts in 1940 and ends up in the far future, wrapping up with an addendum surveying the Alternate Universe crossover entries that don't fit on the main timeline, another addendum covering Kim Newman's "*Anno Dracula* Universe and Character Guide," and a Selected Bibliography.

While every effort has been made to incorporate as many crossovers as possible, there are of course many stories with crossover references which the constraints of time and resources unfortunately did not allow for specific inclusion, such as Mick Farren's vampire novels, the FBI Special Agent Pendergast series by Douglas Preston and Lincoln Child, the Repairman Jack series by F. Paul Wilson, Will Thomas' Cyrus Barker novels, the Dray Prescot books by

---

[6] That said, these are my own editorial metafictional musings and dot-connectings, not necessarily an authoritative bible to the original intent of the many authors whose works I cite. For instance, Philip José Farmer took extreme care never to claim that Sahhindar, the Gray-Eyed God from *Hadon of Ancient Opar* and *Flight to Opar*, was Tarzan. In the addenda to *Hadon*, he intentionally infers that Sahhindar is the time traveler from *Time's Last Gift*, nowhere mentioning an Edgar Rice Burroughs connection.

Alan Burt Akers, Edgar Wallace's interconnected fiction, Simon R. Green's Nightside books, and numerous Cthulhu Mythos pastiches.

Additionally, the following crossover projects have been announced, but not released in time for evaluation for inclusion in the Crossover Universe:

- *War of the Independents*: A comics "mega-crossover" featuring many characters from a variety of independent publishers. The characters slated for inclusion who already have valid links to the Crossover Universe are Shi, ShadowHawk, Cassie Hack and Slash, the Badger, the Yellow Jacket, and Dawn. Other War of the Independents characters who are listed as existing in alternate universes to the CU are Liberty Girl and Mr. Monster. Given the wide variation of background stories, continuities, and characters involved, it is likely that War of the Independents takes place in an alternate universe to the CU.
- *The Darkness/Darkchylde*: Kingdom Pain, a one-shot comic by Randy Queen and Sarah Queen, Top Cow Comics. The story also features Witchblade.
- A Phantom/Captain Action crossover story by Mike Bullock and Reno Maniquis for Moonstone Comics.

As Kim Newman said in his Introduction, it's all about the story, not just the crossovers. The fascinating thing is, as one reads through the following 1500-plus crossover entries in chronological order, it becomes apparent that the individual stories and characters combine into mini story-arcs in ways that the original writers never could have foreseen. These arcs occasionally transcend the individual tales, transforming the singular crossovers into a tapestry constituting a secret meta-history, and providing a window into the rich and complex world that is the Crossover Universe.

It is all about the story.

Win Scott Eckert
Denver, Colorado
June 2010

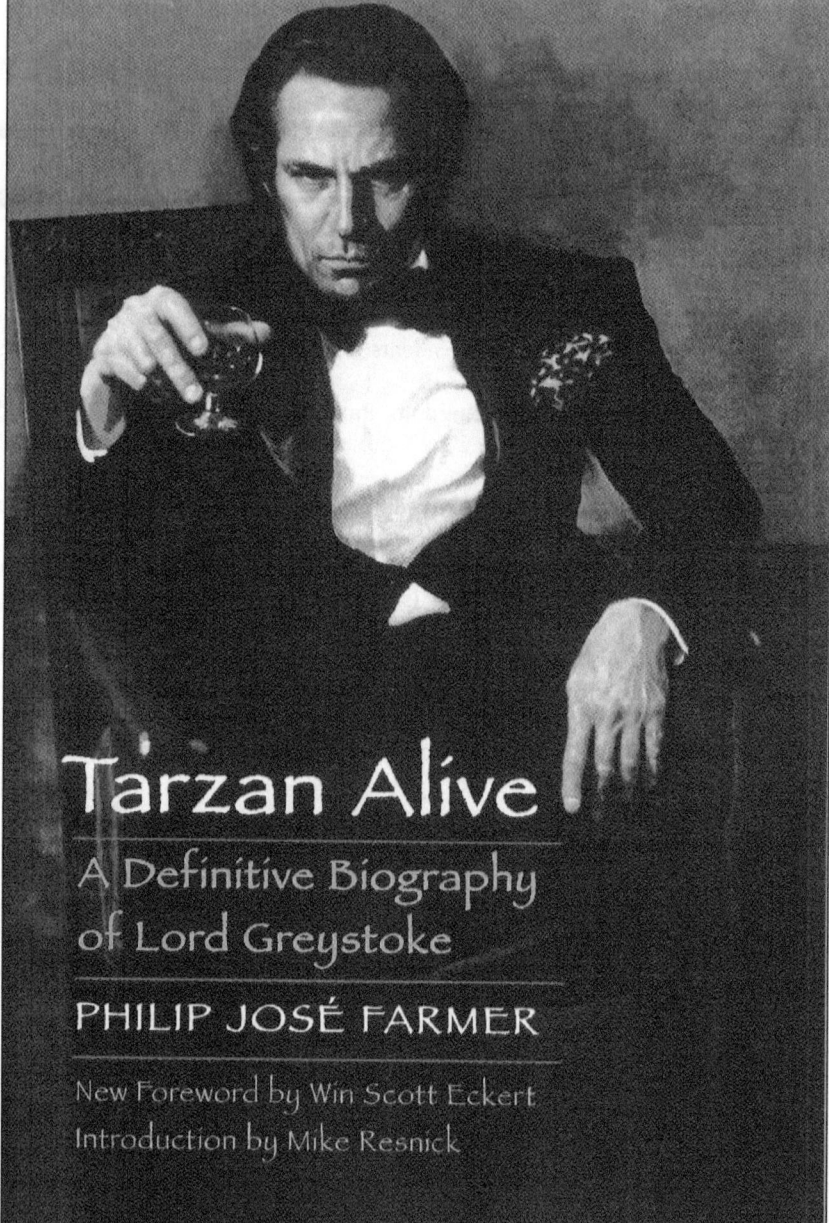

Tarzan Alive
A Definitive Biography of Lord Greystoke

PHILIP JOSÉ FARMER

New Foreword by Win Scott Eckert
Introduction by Mike Resnick

Crossovers Volume One: Dawn of Time-1939

c. 6,000,000 BCE

QUARB AND THE WAR BALL

Unnamed aliens perform an experiment in which they attempt to introduce intelligent life into Earth's ecosystem. In what will be Africa, they bathe two hominids in a strange light and then depart. Shortly thereafter, the two hominids reproduce, and the resulting child, Quarb, resembles an exceptionally hairy modern day human being. As he grows up, it becomes clear that Quarb has a genius-level IQ, coming up with many advanced inventions, as well as teaching his companions to hunt and kill with a bow and arrow. As they hunt, Quarb's companions yell "Kreegah!" and "Bundolo!" Quarb also becomes very prolific, fathering 372 children with his eighty wives. While the children are marginally more intelligent than others in the tribe, they are not nearly as evolutionarily advanced as he is, and he concludes that evolution will have to take its long, natural course. After about fifty years, Quarb realizes that he is not aging, and takes his leave of his tribe in search of further knowledge. The aliens return occasionally to check on the progress of their "experiment," but Quarb evades them each time, reasoning that their investigations might involve some invasive procedures upon his body and brain. After five centuries, the time-traveling Restin Dane (also known as "The Rook") arrives to investigate Quarb's advanced tree house, the fossilized remains of which have been found by the Leakeys in the year 1978. The unnamed aliens arrive and capture Dane, examine him, realize he is from six million years in the future, and abandon their experiment in evolution on Earth as unsuccessful. Restin then finds Quarb in his tree house, but Quarb "plays dumb," and Restin eventually leaves, reasoning that the aliens must have constructed the tree house as a lure for creatures like himself or the "dumb ape man." As the Rook departs, Quarb lights his pipe and has a good chuckle.

A story in The Rook *series by Bill DuBay and Luis Bermejo in Warren's* Eerie *magazine #98, January 1979. Quarb's tribal companions' use of the words "Kreegah!" and "Bundolo!" provides a solid linguistic connection to Edgar Rice Burroughs' Tarzan books, indicating that Quarb's tribe is likely pre-Mangani. Since Philip José Farmer established Tarzan as a member of the Wold Newton Family (WNF), Quarb also exists in the Crossover Universe (CU) in which Tarzan lives. Quarb is the ancestor of every human being on Earth, and went on to spread his genes throughout humanity during his life of six million years, taking a special interest in the McDane/Dane family.*

c. 1,000,000 BCE

THE HUNTED
Caveman Robot saves a group of pre-Mangani from a robotic wooly mammoth.

A story by Jason Robert Bell in Caveman Robot Gigantic Mega-Annual 2004, *Tetragrammatron Press. The whole story is told in the Mangani language ("Kreegah!", "Bundolo!", "Tantor," etc.), creating a linguistic connection to the Tarzan novels of Edgar Rice Burroughs. Since Tarzan is in the Crossover Universe, so is Caveman Robot. On page 93 of the* Mega-Annual 2004 *there is a caption that reads, "This comic is dedicated to the brilliant Philip José Farmer."*

c. 500,000 BCE

Aliens from the planet Yargon visit Earth and give a group of humans an evolutionary jump-start, resulting in the births of Tragg and future mate, Lorn ("Spawn of Yargon," in *Tragg and the Sky Gods* #1 by Donald F. Glut and Jesse Santos, Gold Key Comics, June 1975). As demonstrated in the first Tragg tale ("Cry of the Dire Wolf" by Glut and Santos, in *Spine-Tingling Tales* #1, Gold Key Comics, May 1975), his tribe lives in an isolated land where conditions have allowed the survival of the otherwise extinct dinosaurs. Several of these hidden, isolated pockets of these prehistoric lands will survive until at least the 20th century. Don Glut notes, "This is the same prehistoric 'universe' as in two of my Warren *Vampirella* stories, 'Scaly Death' and the later 'Devil Woman,' which, in turn, is a spin-off from my never-sold *Man-Lizard* comics series."

ANOTHER WORLD…ANOTHER TIME
Dagar the Invincible, in pursuit of his ladylove Graylin, is transported back in time from c. 20,000 BCE. He meets a primitive group of humans, and befriends one of them named Jarn.

Dagar the Invincible *#5 by Donald F. Glut and Jesse Santos, Gold Key Comics, October 1973. Glut later established Jarn as the older brother of Tragg, thus connecting Dagar to the series* Tragg and the Sky Gods. *In fact, Tragg himself makes a cameo appearance in one crowd scene.*

MASTER OF THE LIVING BONES
In an effort to prevent the caveman Tragg from siring future generations who will contest their powers, the Dark Gods intercept a meteor containing the alien sorcerer Ostellon, bring it to Earth, and set Ostellon against Tragg. Tragg, however, defeats Ostellon; his future descendants include Dagar the Invincible, and the occult investigator, Dr. Adam Spektor.

The eighth and final issue of Tragg and the Sky Gods *by Donald F. Glut and Dan Spiegle, Gold Key Comics, February 1977. (A final Tragg story appeared in* Gold Key Spotlight *#9, September 1977.) Tragg and his mate, Lorn, are distant ancestors of Dr. Adam Spektor. As such their adventures take place in the Crossover Universe. (It's probably a moot point, but since Tragg's lineage apparently lasted up to the present day, he and Lorn are the ancestors of everybody living today, not just Dagar and Spektor.) Spektor is linked to the CU through a reference in a Frankenstein novel by Donald F. Glut, and Frankenstein is in the CU through a mention of Victor Frankenstein's experiments in Philip José Farmer's* Doc Savage: His Apocalyptic Life. *Ostellon went on to battle both Dagar and Adam Spektor. The Dark Gods are part of a backstory that runs through Glut's novels and comic stories, especially* The Occult Files of Dr. Spektor. *The backstory involves a cosmic battle on Earth between the good and noble Warrior Gods and the evil Dark Gods, long before the rise of humanity. Although defeated, the Dark Gods still exist as shades and are able to exert their influence through willing servants.*

c. 491,000 BCE

The time of Thongor, a barbarian warrior of the ancient continent of Lemuria. The saga of Thongor was told by Lin Carter in a series of novels: *Thongor and the Wizard of Lemuria, Thongor and the Dragon City, Thongor Against the Gods, Thongor in the City of Magicians, Thongor at the End of Time,* and *Thongor Fights the Pirates of Tarakus*. There are also two short tales of Thongor contained in Carter's volume *Lost Worlds*: "Thieves of Zangabal" and "Keeper of the Emerald Flame." Thongor is associated with the Cthulhu Mythos. Although Cthulhu Mythos tales may occur across the multiverse, at least some of them do occur in the Crossover Universe. Philip José Farmer's *Doc Savage: His Apocalyptic Life* placed Robert Blake (from H.P. Lovecraft's "The Haunter of the Dark") in the Wold Newton Family. Farmer also wrote a tale in which Bukawai, a descendant of

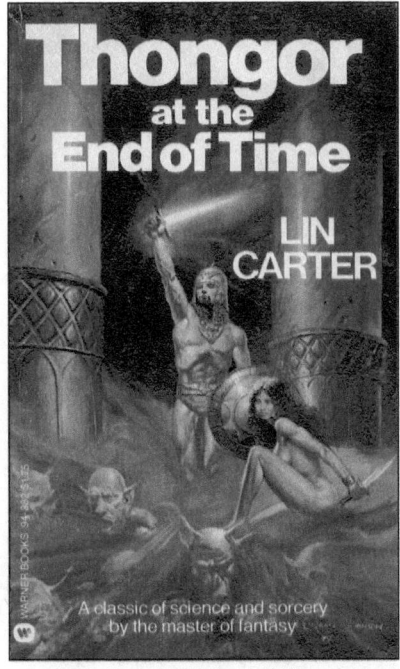

the witch doctor featured in Edgar Rice Burroughs' *Jungle Tales of Tarzan*, attends Miskatonic University, thus making a clear connection between Wold

Newton Family member Tarzan and Lovecraft's Cthulhu Mythos. Therefore, the Thongor tales take place in the CU. (Some of Lin Carter's tales of Thongor were freely adapted by George Alec Effinger, Tony Isabella, Gardner F. Fox, and Steve Gerber in *Creatures on the Loose* #22-29, Marvel Comics, 1973-1974.)

c. 400,000 BCE

In the wake of the Fall of Lemuria, many surviving Lemurians found the first empire of Atlantis. The first empire of Atlantis eventually falls, giving rise to a second empire.

c. 24,000 BCE

Time of the fall of the second empire of Atlantis, as told in *The Black Star* by Lin Carter (Dell Books, 1973). Much of Atlantis sinks.

c. 20,000 BCE

Robert E. Howard's tales of King Kull of Valusia. The remnants of the great civilization of Atlantis have deteriorated to barbarism, and Kull is a barbarian warrior from this ancient land. He goes on to become King Kull of Valusia. Most of Howard's tales of ancient warriors, including Kull, are connected with the Cthulhu Mythos, and hence are essential components of the history of the Crossover Universe. The Kull stories are collected in *King Kull*, Lancer Books, 1967, and include several fragments, which were completed by Lin Carter. The latest collection is *Kull: Exile of Atlantis*, Del Rey Books, 2006.

DAGAR THE INVINCIBLE

Dagar the Invincible battles and defeats the evil sorcerer Ostellon.

In #1: *"The Sword of Dagar,"* Dagar the Invincible *by Donald F. Glut and Jesse Santos, Gold Key Comics, October 1972. Ostellon had fought against Dagar's distant ancestor, Tragg, and later confronted his descendant, Dr. Adam Spektor. The Dagar stories take place in* the same time frame as Robert E. Howard's tales of King Kull, for reasons that are explained in a later entry.

Dagar discovers that the legendary "lobrostone" can cure werewolves of the curse of lycanthropy.

In #2: "The Beast Within." Dagar's descendant, Adam Spektor, would also seek the cure of the lobrostone after being afflicted with the curse of the werewolf.

Dagar, in pursuit of his ladylove Graylin, is transported back in time to c. 500,000 BCE, where he meets a primitive group of humans, and befriends one of them named Jarn.

In #5: "Another World...Another Time (October 1973). Glut established Jarn as the older brother of Tragg, thus providing a further connection to Tragg and the Sky Gods.

Dagar and another adventurer, Durak, battle against a wicked queen and her wizard.

In #7: "Two Swords Against Zora-Zal." (April 1974), Glut linked the barbarian adventurer Durak to Dagar. Durak, or "Duroc," who first appeared in Gold Key's Mystery Comics Digest, *and also appeared in three stories in* Dr. Spektor Presents Spine-Tingling Tales *#3, November 1975.*

Tragg appears in flashback, in which it is revealed that he was responsible for the construction of several giant stone monoliths, in an effort to construct a calendar. Later, in Dagar's time, the monolithic calendar focuses the light of the moon in such a way as to spawn a primordial ooze creature that requires a yearly human sacrifice to appease its hunger.

In #11: "It Lurks by Moonlight" (April 1975). Further links to Tragg and the Sky Gods.

Dagar once again fights alongside his friend Durak.

In #12:"Forest of Fear" (July 1975).

Dagar and Durak, along with fellow warrior Torgus, battle against a golem brought to life by the powers of the Dark Gods. At the conclusion of the battle, Durak is thought dead, but reappears telling a tale of being magically sent to another world of incredible wonders.

In #13: "The Sorcerer's Golem" (October 1975). The tale of Durak's journey is told in Occult Files of Dr. Spektor *#16.*

Although she loves Dagar, Graylin decides she can no longer tolerate the nomadic life of a mercenary warrior's mate, and leaves him.

In #15: Beware the Death Talons" (April 1976). The reason this is a crossover is revealed in "Kull: Talons of the Devil Birds."

The hermit wizard Galga-Thar is collecting a group of spells concerning demons dwelling within the nether-regions of existence. He plans to call his book *The Demonomicon.*

In #6 of Gold Key Spotlight: *"Death Flies on Scarlet Wings," the final published Dagar adventure (June 1977). Features* The Demonomicon; *which is* mentioned in many of Glut's interconnected works; "A Tour of Spektor Manor" (a text piece in The Occult Files of Dr. Spektor #20) reveals that Adam Spektor has a copy in his library.

TALONS OF THE DEVIL BIRDS

Kull, temporarily deposed from his kingship of Valusia, wanders the Thurian lands in search of a way to regain his crown. In his travels, he rescues a woman from three evil wizards. She cannot remember her name, or where she came from, although she has faint memories of a previous warrior lover. Kull dubs her "Laralei" and she agrees to accompany him in his travels, although she insists that she cannot again love a warrior. Additionally, Kull's minstrel companion, Ridondo, swears by the Dark Gods.

Kull the Destroyer #22 by Donald F. Glut, Ernie Chan, and Vong Montaño, Marvel Comics, August 1977. The amnesiac Laralei is Graylin from the Dagar the Invincible series. Laralei continues to accompany the former king in adventures chronicled through Kull #28, when she leaves him for reasons similar to those why she left Dagar. In #29, it is revealed that Kull's archfoe, the mage Thulsa Doom, was responsible for Graylin/Laralei's amnesia, as a part of a larger plot to ensnare Kull. The Dark Gods are referred to in Glut's tales of Tragg, Dagar, and Dr. Spektor, as well as Glut's Frankenstein novels, short stories, and various comics written for DC, Red Circle, and so on.

A KING COMES RIDING

In 1981, Dr. Strange tends a wounded Spider-Man. However, the only cure for Spidey's injury lies in the distant past, in the time of King Kull (c. 18,000 BCE). Strange sends Spider-Man's astral body back in time, where Spidey is able to possess bodies for a short time. He saves Kull's life, and thus winning the King's favor, Kull helps Spidey in his quest. Brule the Spear-Slayer and the ageless druid Tu also appear, as does Dr. Strange's servant, Wong.

Marvel Team-Up #112, December 1981 by J.M. Dematteis, Herb Trimpe, Mike Esposito, and Marie Severin. Since Robert E. Howard's legendary hero, King Kull, is in the Crossover Universe (through crossovers with Conan, who in turn crossed over with Solomon Kane, who was, per Farmer, a pre-meteor-strike-WNF member), a version of Spider-

Man also exists in the CU. However, this is not the Spider-Man of the Marvel Comics Universe, which has a significantly different history and continuity than that of the Crossover Universe. Therefore, the references to the superhero team, "The Defenders," are fictional, although the Crossover Universe version of Namor was active in the 1940s. Dr. Stephen Strange has also been mentioned in a Dr. Zarnak story, so it seems fairly conclusive that a version of Dr. Strange exists in the Crossover Universe.

The Great Cataclysm, a disaster that destroys much of the old world, signals the beginning of the Hyborian Age. See "The Hyborian Age," in *The Coming of Conan the Cimmerian* by Robert E. Howard, Del Rey Books, 2003.

c. 12,000 BCE

Tarzan arrives in this era from the year 2070 (*Time's Last Gift* by Philip José Farmer).

c. 10,000 BCE

CONAN THE BARBARIAN
Coincident with the end of the Hyborian Age is the time of Conan, a barbarian warrior from Cimmeria. In tales related by Robert E. Howard, L. Sprague de Camp, Lin Carter, Roy Thomas, and many others, it has been told that Conan had many great adventures, eventually becoming King of Aquilonia.

Nineteen-year-old Conan is captured by a shaman who reveals the secrets of the past and the future. Among the visions revealed is that of King Kull of Valusia.

Marvel Comics' Conan the Barbarian #1, "The Coming of Conan," by Roy Thomas and Barry Windsor-Smith; reprinted in The Essential Conan, *Marvel Comics*, 2000, and in The Chronicles of Conan, *Volume 1, Dark Horse Books, 2003*. The cross-references to Kull are so numerous throughout the Conan series, it would be redundant to note them all, and so only selected references will be listed.

The Ape-Men who capture young Conan and keep humans for slave labor all have Mangani names, perhaps pointing to the distant origin of the tribes, which survived to live in 19th-century Africa.

Marvel Comics' Conan the Barbarian *#2, "Lair of the Beast-Men," by Roy Thomas and Barry Windsor-Smith; reprinted in* The Essential Conan *and in* The Chronicles of Conan, *Volume 1. Tarzan was raised by the Mangani, as described in Edgar Rice Burroughs'* Tarzan of the Apes *and Philip José Farmer's* Tarzan Alive.

Maldiz, the finest blacksmith and goldsmith in Shadizar, tells Conan that the gold piece he forges for Conan is "not quite up to a falcon I once forged." Thus, the bird in question would be the "Maldiz Falcon."

Marvel Comics' Conan the Barbarian *#6, "Devil-Wings over Shadizar," by Roy Thomas and Barry Windsor-Smith; reprinted in* The Essential Conan *and in* The Chronicles of Conan, *Volume 1. Clearly, the origin of the fabled object known in the present day as the Maltese Falcon, featured in the novel by Dashiell Hammett, goes much farther back into ancient history than once was thought.*

Young Conan fights alongside a warrior from another dimension called Elric of Melniboné.

#14-15 of Marvel Comics' Conan the Barbarian, *"A Sword Called Stormbringer/The Green Empress of Melniboné," by Roy Thomas, Michael Moorcock, James Cawthorn, and Barry Windsor-Smith; reprinted in* The Essential Conan *and in* The Chronicles of Conan, *Volume 3, Dark Horse Books, 2003. The immortal warrior Kane would also meet Elric, verifying that the various dimensions in which Moorcock's Eternal Champion stories occur are alternate universes to the CU. The wizard Kulan Gath in this tale is the same Kulan Gath who appears in the Red Sonja/Spider-Man team-up, "Sword of the She-Devil."*

Red Sonja's exploits also take place during this time period. Her adventures are chronicled in Marvel comic books, as well as in six novels by David C. Smith and Richard L. Tierney: The Ring of Ikribu, Demon Night, When Hell Laughs, Endothor's Daughter, Against the Prince of Hell, *and* Star of Doom. *The Red Sonja collaborations by Smith and Tierney also link Smith's Attluma stories to Tierney's* Simon of Gitta.

CONAN THE BARBARIAN

While trapped during a siege in the city of Makkalet, Conan meets the amazing Red Sonja for the first time.

#23 of Marvel Comics' Conan the Barbarian, *"The Shadow of the Vulture," by Roy Thomas and Barry Windsor-Smith, freely adapted from the story by Robert E. Howard; reprinted in* The Essential Conan *and in* The Chronicles of Conan, *Volume 4, Dark Horse Books, 2004. Conan and Red Sonja went on to meet and fight together many times. For instance, the next issue, "The Song of Red Sonja," features a reference to King Kull. Only a few of the numerous Conan/Red Sonja meetings will be chronicled herein.*

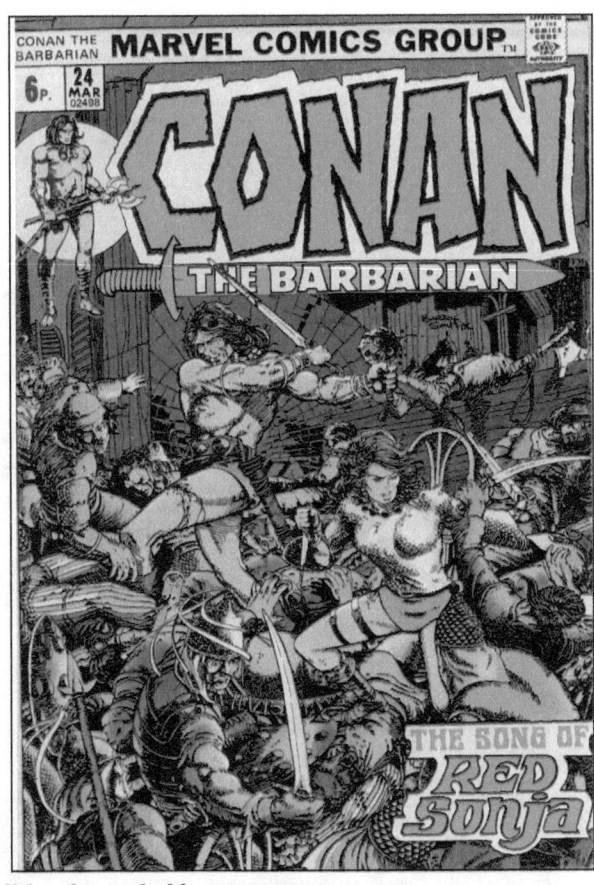

Conan battles the resurrected wizard Rotath. Rotath was first killed 10,000 years previous by Kull the Destroyer.

#37 of Marvel Comics' Conan the Barbarian, *"The Curse of the Golden Skull," by Roy Thomas and Neal Adams, inspired by the short story by Robert E. Howard; reprinted in* The Chronicles of Conan, *Volume 6, Dark Horse Books, 2004.*

Conan battles Rune, a millennia-old energy vampire from the stars.

"Conan vs. Rune: The Dark God." One-shot by Barry Windsor-Smith, Marvel Comics, November 1995. Rune was created by Windsor-Smith and is part of the Marvel Comics Universe. Following the guidelines for incorporating Marvel characters, a parallel version of Rune exists in the Crossover Universe apart from Marvel continuity.

Conan enters into a bare-knuckle boxing match with Stokosta the Seaman.

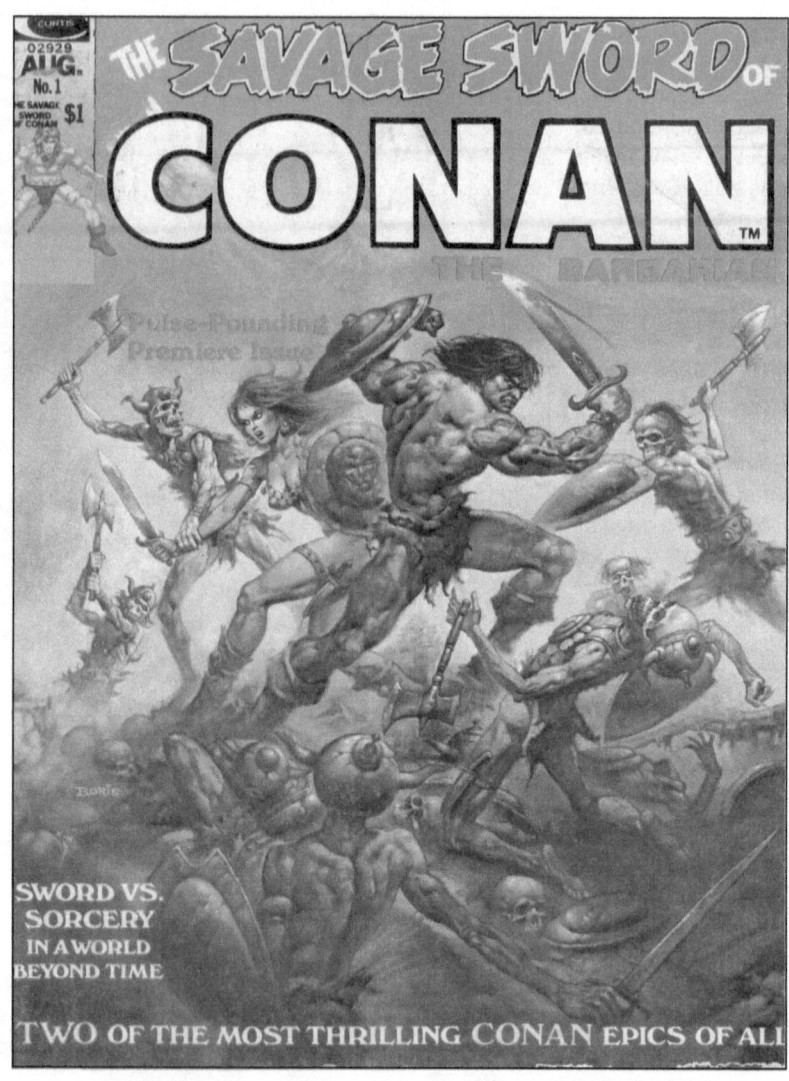

    #37 of Dark Horse Comics' Conan, "Rat's Den," by Timothy Truman, Cary Nord, and Richard Isanove, February 2007. Stokosta is depicted as wearing a red and black horizontal striped shirt, much like sailors were shown in the pulps of the early 20th century. Stokosta is clearly an homage to Robert E. Howard's boxing seaman, Sailor Steve Costigan. For Crossover Universe purposes we can assume that Stokosta is a very distant ancestor of Sailor Steve, although Matthew Baugh rightly points out that Stokosta would be an ancestor of everyone living today.

Conan and Red Sonja team to fight a wizard come back to life.

#1 of Marvel Comics' Savage Sword of Conan, *"Curse of the Un-Dead Man," by Roy Thomas, John Buscema, and Pablo Marcos; reprinted in Marvel's* Conan *#78. The story takes place between* Conan *#42 and 43.*

Conan and Bêlit vie with Red Sonja for a page torn from the sorcerous Book of Skelos. King Kull, along with his palace and his Black Warriors, are briefly transported to Conan's time.

"The Battle of the Barbarians." This tale begins in Marvel Comics' Conan the Barbarian *#66, September 1976. It continues in* Marvel Feature: Red Sonja *#6, then* Conan *#67,* Marvel Feature *# 7, and concludes in* Conan *#68. The story arc was written by Roy Thomas, with John Buscema illustrating the Conan issues, and Frank Thorne drawing the Red Sonja issues. The two Red Sonja entries are reprinted in* The Adventures of Red Sonja, *Volume 1, Dynamite Entertainment, 2005.*

Conan is traveling through Kush on his way north following the death of Bêlit when he falls prey to the sorceries of the city of Negari. He is transported to the distant past when Negari was a city of Atlantis, where he has an adventure with Solomon Kane, who has also been transported to the past.

This tale, "Death's Dark Riders," in Marvel Comics' Savage Sword of Conan *#219-220, March-April 1994, by Roy Thomas and Colin MacNeil, is a sequel to R.E. Howard's Solomon Kane story "The Moon of Skulls." Reprinted in* The Saga of Solomon Kane, *Dark Horse Books, July 2009.*

Conan enters into a bargain with the wizard Zukala to bring Bêlit back to life. However, when he discovers that Red Sonja's life is also part of the price, Conan beheads Zukala.

Marvel Comics' Conan the Barbarian, *#115, "A War of Wizards," by Roy Thomas, John Buscema, and Ernie Chan, October 1980; reprinted in* The Chronicles of Conan, *Volume 14, Dark Horse Books, 2008. Conan and Red Sonja crossed paths many more times during Marvel's run of* Conan, Savage Sword of Conan, *etc.*

RED SONJA/CLAW: DEVIL'S HANDS

Red Sonja meets Claw the Unconquered and attempts to help him overcome his curse.

Comic book miniseries by John Layman and Andy Smith, WildStorm Comics and Dynamite Entertainment, May-August 2006. This crossover brings a version of DC Comics' Claw into the CU.

WHAT IF THOR OF ASGARD HAD MET CONAN THE BARBARIAN?

While pursuing his enemy Loki through a series of caverns, the mighty Thor is mystically time-warped back to the Hyborian age. He arrives with amnesia, and has lost much of his power, due to the fact that the Norse gods don't yet exist in this time period. Thor meets and battles Conan, although they soon become allies. The god Crom, the sorcerer Thoth-Amon, and the Valusian Serpent-Men appear. In a mystically weakened state, Thor sacrifices himself in combat with Thoth-Amon. As he dies, Thor bequeaths his hammer, Mjolnir, to Conan, instructing the Hyborian barbarian to take it to Crom as "a symbol of the love that deities of a later age will share with reverent mankind."

#39 of What If? *by Alan Zelenetz, Ron Wilson, and Danny Bulanadi, Marvel Comics, June 1983. The death of the superhero Thor in this story further supports the notion that the Crossover Universe is a separate and distinct reality from the Marvel Universe; the Thor in this tale is the version from the CU, who has an alternate universe counterpart in the mainstream Marvel Universe.*

RED SONJA VS. THULSA DOOM
Red Sonja battles the evil mage who has plagued many heroes through the ages, Thulsa Doom.

Comic book miniseries by Peter David, Luke Lieberman, and Will Conrad, Dynamite Entertainment, 2006. Thulsa Doom was also a foe of King Kull and Cormac Mac Art.

CONAN THE BARBARIAN
Conan battles an evil wizard (is there any other kind?) who seeks the Book of Nameless Cults and invokes mighty Cthulhu in an attempt to hasten the coming of the Old Ones. Conan and his companions also encounter and battle the Worms of the Earth.

Conan and the Songs of the Dead, a miniseries by Joe R. Lansdale and Timothy Truman, Dark Horse Comics, 2006. The Mythos references solidify Conan's connection to the CU. The Worms of the Earth are from a Bran Mak Morn tale by Robert E. Howard.

Conan of Cimmeria and Red Sonja of Hyrkania are transported back in time, where they meet King Kull and fight against the ageless, evil wizard Rotath. Kull's shaman Gonar and fellow warrior Brule the Spear-slayer also appear, as well as a descendant or reincarnation of Gonar who lives in Conan's time, also called Gonar.

The Ravagers Out of Time, *a Marvel Comics graphic novel by Roy Thomas, Michael Docherty, and Alfredo P. Alcala published in 1992.*

Conan, Red Sonja, and the modern Gonar are drawn to a cavern containing the Mirrors of Tuzun Thune, whereupon Conan and Sonja are thrust through time once more, first to the age of dinosaurs, and then back to the era of King Kull's Valusia. Kull's Gonar then sends Sonja in search of Kull, who remains time-displaced following the events of *The Ravagers Out of Time*. Meanwhile, Conan, whom Brule the Spear-slayer admits bears a resemblance to the missing Kull, is selected to serve as a stand-in for the absent King of Valusia. Sonja arrives 500 years after the time of Kull, at the time of the Great Cataclysm, which is signaled by the sinking of Valusia and Atlantis, and which heralds in the Hyborian Age. She saves the life of Volonius, a descendant of Kull. After a battle against the evil Priest of the Black Shadow, Kull is returned to his rightful time, but Conan and Red Sonja end up three millennia short of their era, in Acheron. More combat ensues before they finally return home.

"The Many Mirrors of Tuzun Thune," a storyline by Roy Thomas, Michael Docherty, and E.R. Cruz in Marvel Comics' Savage Sword of Conan *#223-224, 226, and 229-230 (July-August and October 1994, and January-February 1995), a direct follow-up to* The Ravagers out of Time. *"The Mirrors of Tuzun Thune" is a King Kull short story by Robert E. Howard which first appeared in* Weird Tales, *September 1929.*

Conan and Red Sonja return to their rightful time, only to discover that they have been replaced by evil mirror-doubles who came through the mirrors in the cavern of Tuzun Thune when they were sent through time. The doppelgängers are accompanied by the ancient wizard Tuzun Thune himself, possessing the body of the modern Gonar. Tuzun Thune mentions that he matched wits with King Kull and was killed by Brule the Pict, but his eldritch essence lived on for centuries in the enchanted mirrors.

"Reflections of Evil," a storyline by Roy Thomas, Michael Docherty, and E.R. Cruz in Marvel Comics' Savage Sword of Conan *#231-332, March-April, 1995. Red Sonja continues to ride with Conan and his fierce Kozaks in a tale told in* Savage Sword *#233, before finally parting ways for a time.*

Conan and Red Sonja, in search of an idol, discover a lost city and battle a gibbering horror. They then set off to rescue a group of kidnapped children held in slavery, after which they part ways once more.

"The Waiting Doom," a storyline by Charles Dixon, Gary Kwapisz, Erine Chan, and Geoff Isherwood in Savage Sword of Conan *#144-145, Marvel Comics, January-February, 1988.*

Red Sonja is hired to track down an outlander who she discovers to be Conan. Conan has joined up with his old she-pirate comrade, Valeria, in search of a mountain-sized emerald. The "emerald" turns out to be simple ice, and the three end up fighting to survive in the northern wastes,

"Emerald Lust," a story by Charles Dixon and Gary Kwapisz in Marvel Comics' Savage Sword of Conan *#170, February 1990.*

In the northern reaches, Conan, Red Sonja, and Valeria encounter the swordswomen known as the Iron Damsels.

"Fury of the Iron Damsels," a story by Chuck Dixon and Gary Kwapisz in Savage Sword of Conan #179, Marvel Comics, November 1990.

King Conan encounters remnants of the lost race of Serpent-Men in a "place of once-Valusia," returns the spear which Brule's sons once bore, and takes King Kull's crown in exchange.

"They Shall Be Lords Again," #35-36 of Conan *by Timothy Truman, Paul Lee, and Dave Stewart, Dark Horse Comics, December 2006-January 2007. The past events referred to in this story are depicted in Dark Horse's* Kull *miniseries (2008-2009), specifically #4.*

HADON OF ANCIENT OPAR
FLIGHT TO OPAR
THE SONG OF KWASIN

Hadon is a warrior from the ancient city Opar, the ruins of which will be discovered in Africa by Tarzan in 1910. Hadon's giant cousin Kwasin spent much of his youth in the caves near Opar but is originally from Dythbeth. Opar and Dythbeth are but two among thirty queendoms making up the mighty empire of Khokarsa.

The novels Hadon of Ancient Opar *and* Flight to Opar *are by Philip José Farmer and were published by DAW Books in 1974 and 1976, respectively. Opar appears or is mentioned in several Tarzan books written by Edgar Rice Burroughs (*The Return of Tarzan, Tarzan and the Jewels of Opar, Tarzan and the Golden Lion, Tarzan and the Tarzan Twins with Jad-bal-ja, the Golden Lion, *and* Tarzan the Invincible*).* The Song of Kwasin, *set primarily on the island of Khokarsa as Kwasin leads the resistance against the tyrannical King Minruth, is by Philip José Farmer and Christopher Paul Carey. Khokarsa is Opar's "mother country" spoken of by La of Opar in* The Return of Tarzan *that Burroughs later mistakenly conflates with Atlantis in* Tarzan and the Jewels of Opar. *It should also be noted that the character of the Gray-Eyed God, Sahhindar, god of plants, of bronze, and of time, is in actuality Tarzan, who has traveled back in time (see the entry for* Time's Last Gift, *year 2070). The characters Paga and Lalila are meant to be Pag and Laleela from Haggard's* Allan and the Ice-Gods. *The axe crafted by Pag in that book is passed to Kwasin in* Hadon of Ancient Opar. *Farmer has also speculated on the relationship between Opar and the lost cities of H. Rider Haggard's* Allan Quatermain, *as well as other lost cities from Burroughs' Tarzan novels. The residents of the Khokarsan city of Wentisuh are meant to be ancestors of the Zu-Vendis from Haggard's* Allan Quatermain; *the populations of Wethna and Kethna are ancestors of Athne and Cathne respectively (*Tarzan and the City of Gold*); the inhabitants of Towina and Bawaku are ancestors to those living near the volcano Tuen-Baka (*Tarzan and the Forbidden City*); those from Mikawuru are ancestors of the Kavuru (*Tarzan's Quest*); and the people of Siwudawa, who worship a parrot-headed androgyne god, are forebears of the parrot worshippers of Xuja (*Tarzan the Terrible*). In the third novel in the series, the ko'bok'ul"ikadeth, "a giant three-horned, armor-cowled rhinoceros with skin as thick as iron," is possibly meant to be the gryf (triceratops) of Pal-ul-don from Burroughs'* Tarzan the Terrible. *The large double-handled amphora made of fine black clay and bearing an image of what appears to be of Sahhindar shooting an arrow at an antelope is the same vase "of very ancient manufacture" from which Horace Holly and Leo Vincey drink while among the Amahagger in Haggard's* She and Allan. *Kwasin dreams of "a winged feminine form standing balanced atop a colossal, stone-hewn sphere," which is a statue that Horace Holly observes in the innermost court of Kôr in Haggard's* She.

Hadon's scribe, Hinokly, survives what had seemed a certain death, only to be captured and tormented by Kawuru pirates aboard the infamous *Haken*. Hinokly, however, gets his bittersweet revenge.

"A Kick in the Side," a short story by Christopher Paul Carey published in The Worlds of Philip José Farmer 1: Protean Dimensions, *Michael Croteau, ed., Meteor House, 2010, taking place during the events of* Flight to Opar. *The banner flown by one of the Kawuru ships bears the symbol of a noose, the weapon of trade of the Kavuru from Burroughs'* Tarzan's Quest. *The diamond reputedly possessed by the captain of the* Haken *is the legendary diamond referred to in* The Song of Kwasin *as the Begetter of All Jewels, which may be the true Father of Diamonds from Burroughs'* Tarzan and the Forbidden City.

c. 9960 BCE

After a great catastrophe, Kohr, the son of Hadon of Opar emigrates to the south and founds the city of Kôr (see H. Rider Haggard's *She,* 1884). He carries with him a huge axe made of meteorite iron, which will eventually be passed down to Umslopogaas, the great Zulu hero, who will shatter it in the city of Zu-Vendis (Haggard's *Allan Quatermain,* 1886). Rick Lai adds: "In Haggard's *She and Allan*, Ayesha battled a fellow immortal, a giant called Rezu. This immortal took his name from an ancient sun god worshipped in Kôr. In Farmer's Hadon novels, the cult of Rezu (the spelling is changed to Resu) is identified with Opar's cult of the Flaming God from the Tarzan novels. The physical description of Rezu in Haggard's novel fits Hadon's cousin, Kwasin."

c. 3400 BCE

The events of the feature films *The Scorpion King* and *The Scorpion King 2: Rise of a Warrior*, which take place in the CU as prequels to the 1999 film *The Mummy* and its sequel *The Mummy Returns*.

c. 3000 BCE

J.-H. Rosny Aîné's "Les Xipéhuz," in which primitive humans encounter non-humanoid aliens, reprinted in *The Navigators of Space and Other Alien Encounters*, translated by Brian Stableford, Black Coat Press, March 2010.

1302 BCE

SEVEN STARS PROLOGUE: IN EGYPT'S LAND
At the time of Exodus, Pai-net'em, a councilor and Pharaoh's scribe to Meneptah, meets his fate.

Seven Stars *by Kim Newman consists of this prologue and seven chapters, all of which take place at different times throughout history, and involve different characters. This prologue takes place during the reign of Meneptah II. Pai-net'em was a real historical figure whose mummy was discovered in 1881. Although I tend to avoid using real historical figures to connect stories within the CU, subsequent chapters of* Seven Stars *involve established CU personages, as well as incorporate some new characters.* Seven Stars *(which can be found in* Dark Detectives, *edited by Stephen Jones, Fedogan & Bremer, 1999, and in the U.K. anthology* Seven Stars, *Pocket Books, 2000) also incorporates characters and the jewel from Bram Stoker's* The Jewel of Seven Stars, *1903.* Seven Stars *picks up again in June 1897 with "Seven Stars Episode One: The Mummy's Heart."*

c. 500 BCE

DUAR THE ACCURSED
In this tale of the kingdom of Ygoth, there is a reference to "the terrible white apes of the hills of Barsoom." The apes originate in Sorjoon, a place full of cliffs and crags.

Short story by Clifford Ball, Weird Tales, *May 1937; reprinted in* New Worlds for Old, *Lin Carter, ed., Ballantine Books, 1971. Rick Lai notes, "Ball wrote sword and sorcery in imitation of Robert E. Howard. He created a group of fictional kingdoms, centering on a fictional nation named Ygoth, in a series of three stories. Two of the stories featured a Conan-type hero named Rald." The references to Barsoom place the Ygoth/Rald series in the Crossover Universe.*

THE THIEF OF FORTHE
A half-human having at least four arms is the offspring of a woman who was raped by one of the Barsoomian apes.

Short story featuring Rald by Clifford Ball, Weird Tales, *July 1937; reprinted in* Savage Heroes, *Eric Pendragon, ed., Star Books, 1977, and* The Barbarian Swordsmen, *Sean Richards, ed., Star Books, 1981. The apes from Edgar Rice Burroughs' stories had six arms.*

THE GODDESS AWAKES
Ygoth and its surrounding territories are adjacent to historical kingdoms on Earth. Rald sees idols of Buddha during his travels, and the cult of Bast from the river Nile takes over a kingdom near Ygoth.

Short story by Clifford Ball, Weird Tales, *February 1938; reprinted in* Realms of Wizardry, *Lin Carter, ed., Doubleday Books, 1976. Rick Lai adds, "Clifford Ball's historical references make it difficult to reconcile his Ygoth series with the real world. Buddha lived around 563-483* BCE, *and there surely would be some historical records of Ygoth if it existed on Earth around that time. My theory is that Ygoth exists in another dimension with doorways into both Earth and Burroughs' Barsoom. A group of white apes must have migrated through the dimensional opening from Barsoom into Sorjoon, a territory near Ygoth."*

c. 380-335 BCE

The events of Ayesha's autobiographical tale, entitled *Wisdom's Daughter* by its editor, H. Rider Haggard. The final chapter carries Ayesha's story through the year 1902. Further entries in the saga are *She and Allan*; *She*; *King of Kôr, Or, She's Promise Kept,* (by Sidney J. Marshall); *Ayesha: The Return of She*; and *The Vengeance of She* (by Peter Tremayne).

c. 200 BCE

The events of *Miles Gloriosus*, *Pseudolus*, and *Mostellaria* by Plautus, collectively retold as *A Funny Thing Happened on the Way to the Forum.*

55 BCE

TROS MUST BE CRAZY!
Tros of Samothrace receives a bit of help from a druid and his super-strong companion, against the Wyrms of the Earth.

Short story by G.L. Gick in Tales of the Shadowmen Volume 5: The Vampires of Paris, *Jean-Marc and Randy Lofficier, eds., Black Coat Press, 2009; reprinted in French in* Les Compagnons de l'Ombre (Tome 5), *Jean-Marc and Randy Lofficier, eds., Rivière Blanche, 2009. Tros of Samothrace is an adventurer featured in a series of novellas by Talbot Mundy, originally published in the 1920s in the pages of the pulp magazine* Adventure. *The druid is Panoramix and and his companion is Astérix, the recipient of super-strength due a potion the druid has brewed. Both are from the French comic series* The Adventures of Astérix *(Astérix le Gaulois) by René Goscinny and Albert Uderzo. The Wyrms of the Earth are Robert E. Howard's* Worms of the Earth.

27-50 CE

Exploits of Simon of Gitta, as told by Richard L. Tierney in tales collected in the volume Scroll of Thoth. These adventures are associated with the Cthulhu Mythos, and therefore with the CU.

32

January
THE BLADE OF THE SLAYER
Simon of Gitta meets Kane, the immortal slayer.
This short story by Richard L. Tierney, in the volume Scroll of Thoth *(Chaosium, 1997), brings Karl Edward Wagner's Kane into the Crossover Universe.*

34

Spring
THE SOUL OF KEPHRI
This Simon of Gitta tale mentions "the sword of the Aquilonian king" and also refers to the phantom sage Epimetrius.
This short story by Richard L. Tierney is also in the volume Scroll of Thoth. *The first reference is to R.E. Howard's Conan tale, "The Phoenix on the Sword." Epimetrius also comes from the Conan stories of Robert E. Howard, L. Sprague de Camp, and Lin Carter.*

37

Spring
THE RING OF SET
This Simon of Gitta tale refers to the Ring of Set.

This is another short story by Richard L. Tierney, in Scroll of Thoth. *The Ring of Set* appeared in the Conan tale, "The Phoenix on the Sword." The Ring would surface again in 1934, as seen in Howard's John Kirowan tale, "The Haunter of the Ring."

Autumn
THE WORM OF URAKHU
The Worm Shai-urt-ab destroys Simon of Gitta's Roman pursuers.
This short story by Richard L. Tierney, in Scroll of Thoth, *links the Dune universe into the Cthulhu Mythos. The tale indicates that Shudde-M'ell (from Brian Lumley's Mythos tales) came from a planet called Urakhu (Arrakis), and its race is also known as Shai-urt-ab (similar to Shai-Hulud, the name for Arrakis' sandworms). The giant desert worms in this story produce a "worm-dust" similar to the Dune sandworms' "spice." Perhaps Arrakis is a planet in the CU, but Frank Herbert's Dune series either takes place in an alternate universe, or in the far-flung future.*

41

January
THE SCROLL OF THOTH
Simon pursues the Book of Thoth, the scroll of Thoth-Amon, who was Conan's old adversary. There are also references to Pain Lords, whom Red Sonja encountered 12,000 years ago.
A short story by Richard L. Tierney, in the collection Scroll of Thoth.

206-210

The adventures of Pict warrior Bran Mak Morn, as related in tales by Robert E. Howard, the novel *Legion from the Shadows* by Karl Edward Wagner, and the novel *For the Witch of the Mists* by David C. Smith and Richard L. Tierney.

206

WORMS OF THE EARTH
Bran Mak Morn's quest for the mystical Black Stone leads him to the ghastly and foul half-human creatures of the underground, called the Worms of the Earth.

"Worms of the Earth" is by Robert E. Howard, and has been reprinted in: Bran Mak Morn, *Baen Books, 1996;* Cthulhu: The Mythos and Kindred Horrors, *Baen Books, 1987; and* Bran Mak Morn: The Last King, *Del Rey Books, 2005. It has been adapted into graphic format by Roy Thomas, Tim Conrad, and Barry Windsor-Smith, Cross Plains Comics, 2000. The creatures featured in this tale are the same beings seen in Howard's "The Children of the Night" and "People of the Dark." The Black Stone is also featured in "People of the Dark."*

207

KINGS OF THE NIGHT
Bran Mak Morn summons Kull of Atlantis, king of Valusia. The ancient wizard Gonar (of England) also appears in this tale and communicates with his ancestor, Gonar (of Valusia). It is revealed that Bran Mak Morn is descended from Kull's compatriot Brule the Spear-slayer.

R.E. Howard links two of his creations, Kull and Bran Mak Morn, in this story, published in Bran Mak Morn, *Baen Books, 1996, and* Bran Mak Morn: The Last King, *Del Rey Books, 2005. Baen Books published the King Kull stories as* Kull, *1995, sans the completed fragments by Lin Carter. The most recent collection is* Kull: Exile of Atlantis, *Del Rey Books, 2006.*

208

Spring
LEGION FROM THE SHADOWS
Bran Mak Morn again sees Kull, Brule, and Gonar in a vision. The Children of the Night (aka Worms of the Earth, aka the People of the Dark) and the Black Stone also appear.

Further evidence linking Bran Mak Morn and Kull, in this novel by Karl Edward Wagner, Baen Books, 1988. The novel takes place after "Worms of the Earth."

c. 410s

THE PILLAR IN THE MIST
Kerak, a soldier and son of both Rome and Britannia, faces a spectral warrior. Kerak mentions his father speaking of the Old Ones and their cruel rites.

Short story by Ardath Mayhar in the anthology Cross Plains Universe: Texans Celebrate Robert E. Howard, *a joint publication of MonkeyBrain Books and FACT, Inc. (Fandom Association of Central Texas), edited by Scott A. Cupp and Joe R. Lansdale, 2006. The Old Ones are from Lovecraft's Cthulhu Mythos.*

470s-490s

The exploits of Cormac Mac Art, as originally told by Robert E. Howard, and expanded upon by Andrew J. Offutt, Keith Taylor, Richard L. Tierney, and David Drake.

Late 480s

THE TEMPLE OF ABOMINATION
Kull, Atlantis, and the Old Ones of the Cthulhu Mythos are mentioned in this Cormac Mac Art adventure.
By Robert E. Howard and Richard L. Tierney, in the volume Tigers of the Sea, *Zebra Books, 1975. Links Cormac Mac Art, Kull, and the Cthulhu Mythos.*

490

THE UNDYING WIZARD
THE SIGN OF THE MOONBOW
Cormac Mac Art encounters the ageless druid Tu, who was also an advisor to Kull, and it is revealed that Cormac is the reincarnation of Kull, as well as Conan. Cormac then battles Kull's ancient enemy, the mage Thulsa Doom.
Andrew J. Offutt's Cormac Mac Art novels link with Conan and King Kull. Both are linked to the Cthulhu Mythos, which in turn is part of the CU. These are books #6 and 7 in the Cormac Mac Art cycle, published by Zebra Books in the 1970s and reprinted by Ace Books in the 1980s. The other books in the series are: #1: The Mists of Doom *by Offutt; #2:* The Tower of Death *by Offutt and Taylor; #3:* When Death Birds Fly *by Offutt and Taylor; #4:* Tigers of the Sea *by Howard and Tierney; and #5:* Sword of the Gael *by Offutt. The original R.E. Howard material has also been reprinted in* Cormac Mac Art, *Baen Books, 1995, with an original story and fragments of Howard's work completed by David Drake.*

c. 650

First known exploit of Chinese sage Li Kao and his redoubtable assistant Number Ten Ox. (*Bridge of Birds* by Barry Hughart.)

c. 1017

THE DARK MAN
The statue containing Bran Mak Morn's soul is seen in this Turlogh O'Brien story.
Short story by Robert E. Howard, Weird Tales, *December 1931; reprinted in* Bran Mak Morn: The Last King, *Del Rey Books, 2005. The story brings Turlogh O'Brien into the CU. The statue is seen again in Howard's "Children of the Night." Turlogh O'Brien is an 11th-century outlaw warrior also known as Turlogh Dubh ("Black Turlogh").*

Late 1100s

The adventures of Robin Hood.

1194

Sir Walter Scott's *Ivanhoe*. Descendants of characters from *Ivanhoe* are mentioned in J.T. Edson's western novels, which also incorporate or relate to other members of Farmer's Wold Newton Family.

c. 1240s-1250s

The events of Edgar Rice Burroughs' *Outlaw of Torn*. Philip José Farmer has postulated that Norman of Torn (aka John Caldwell, aka Richard Plantagenet) was later known as John Carter, Warlord of Mars. This theory was explained and expanded upon by Dennis E. Power and Dr. Peter M. Coogan's "John Carter: Torn from Phoenician Dreams" in *Myths for the Modern Age: Philip José Farmer's Wold Newton Universe*, Win Scott Eckert, editor, MonkeyBrain Books, 2005.

An action-packed novel of swordplay and chivalry by the creator of TARZAN and PELLUCIDAR.
Complete & Unabridged

1300

ARMY OF DARKNESS
After being sucked back through time, Ashley "Ash" Williams once again finds himself involved with the book of

evil known as the Necronomicon Ex Mortis.

The third feature film in the Evil Dead *series, 1993. The* Necronomicon Ex Mortis *that appears in this series and the film* Jason Goes to Hell *does not appear to be the* Necronomicon *of the mad Arab Abdul al-Hazred, which features prominently in the Cthulhu Mythos of H.P. Lovecraft.*

1310s

Events of *La Tour de Nesle* by Alexandre Dumas père, in which Queen Marguerite de Bourgogne orders the deaths of her illegitimate sons.

1327

Brother William of Baskerville is embroiled in a series of murders and intrigue in *The Name of the Rose*, as related by Umberto Eco. William must be an ancestor of that family which was brought to fame in the Sherlock Holmes case, *The Hound of the Baskervilles*.

1348

The events of Sir Nigel, as told by Sir Arthur Conan Doyle. In *Doc Savage: His Apocalyptic Life*, Philip José Farmer placed Sir Nigel Loring as an ancestor of several modern Wold Newton Family members.

1366

The further adventures of Sir Nigel Loring are told in *The White Company* by Sir Arthur Conan Doyle.

1416

The vampire Geneviève Dieudonné is born. Dieudonné appears in several novels by Kim Newman, which take place in several different alternate universes. In the Crossover Universe, Dieudonné will meet private detective Philip Marlowe ("The Gumshoe") in 1942; Marlowe is a Wold Newton Family member, per Farmer's *Doc Savage*.

1476

December. Undeath of Vlad Tepes, the Impaler. Farmer, in *Doc Savage*, made a passing reference to a member of the Van Helsing family, implying the existence of Dracula in the CU. Dracula will also cross paths with many Wold Newton Family members, such as Sherlock Holmes.

December
DRACULA VS. KING ARTHUR
Immediately following Dracula's undeath, Lucifer sends him back to the days of Camelot to battle King Arthur.
Miniseries by Adam Beranek, Christian Beranek, Chris Moreno, and Jay Fotos, Silent Devil Productions, 2005-2006.

1477

The events of *Dracula Unborn* (aka *Bloodright: Memoirs of Mircea, Son to Dracula*), as related by Peter Tremayne.

1481

The events of Victor Hugo's *Notre-Dame de Paris*.

1492-1499

Young Kit Walker serves as cabin boy to Christopher Columbus, then explores the New World and discovers the desert mesa which will be known as "Walker's Table" (Lee Falk's *The Phantom* comics strip).

Early 1500s

Raphael Hythloday's voyage to the New World land of Utopia, as told by Sir Thomas More. In *Doc Savage*, Farmer placed Raphael Hythloday as an ancestor of several modern Wold Newton Family members.

1516

Birth of Kit Walker's son, who will become the first Phantom.

1520

First known adventure of Italian mercenary Luigi Caradossa. ("Red is the Blade" by F.R. Buckley.)

1535

Death of Captain Kit Walker in a pirate raid; his son, also named Kit, the sole survivor, washes up on a remote Bangalla beach and is rescued by pygmies. Kit swears an oath on the skull of the pirate who killed his father that he and his descendants will fight pirates and evildoers all over the world. He becomes The Phantom. Scholar Dennis E. Power adds: "In Addendum 3 of Farmer's *Tarzan Alive*, he states: 'Tarzan is descended from a number of huge and powerful men. Hrolf the Ganger, or Walker, was so called because no horse was big enough to carry his gigantic body.' Perhaps this may have been the originator of the Walker family, although his descendants were a bit smaller."

1549

Solomon Kane is born to a prosperous Puritan family in Devonshire, England. According to Farmer's Wold Newton genealogy, several modern Wold Newton Family members are descended from Solomon Kane.

c. Mid-Late 1500s

The events of Sir Walter Scott's *Kenilworth*, which takes place in the CU through references in J.T. Edson's works.

c. 1566

Solomon Kane embarks on his adventures, as related by Robert E. Howard.

1572

Dracula is destroyed by the wizard Cristaldi. (*Santo y Blue Demon Contra Drácula y el Hombre Lobo* [*El Santo and Blue Demon vs. Dracula and the Wolfman*], feature film, 1973.) These events continue in 1972.

Researcher Chuck Loridans has constructed a theory to account for the multiple variants of Dracula seen in a range of stories and films. Under Loridans' theory, the Dracula seen here is actually Dracula-prime's Mexican "soul-clone." As Loridans states:

"The soul-clone theory is based upon events recorded in the Hammer film, The Legend of the 7 Golden Vampires. *In this film's 1804 opening, Kah, a Chinese wizard, travels to Transylvania to seek Dracula's aid in reviving seven evil vampires. Kah's wish is to be the master of these vampires himself, so that he may hold a reign of terror over China. What he soon learns is that you can't cut deals with the Prince of Darkness. Dracula is intrigued with the idea of ruling an army of vampires, even if it is not in his native country. Dracula proclaims the wizard a fool, and grabs him by his throat. A swirling mist envelopes them both, and when we next see Kah's body, he has the mind and voice of Dracula. When Kah departs, Dracula is nowhere to be seen. We next see Kah in 1904 China. He is destroyed by Lawrence Van Helsing, but before he turns to ashes, he reveals what Van Helsing already knew, that Kah was indeed Count Dracula. From this information, one might assume that Dracula used his shape-shifting abilities to transform himself into the wizard, travel to China, and rule the seven vampires. But if Dracula, in Kah form, was in China from 1804 to 1904, Dracula's confrontations with Abraham Van Helsing, and later his son Lawrence Van Helsing, are impossible. Abraham fought Dracula in the year 1887 (Bram Stoker's novel* Dracula*), and Lawrence, from 1895 to 1910 (see Hammer Films'* Dracula *series). In* Legend of the 7 Golden Vampires, *Van Helsing and Dracula acknowledge that they have met before. So the 'soul-clone' theory was born.*

"*Why does Dracula make soul-clones? It is shown time and time again that Dracula is strongest when surrounded by the soil of his native Transylvania, and is in peril if he does not have a supply of it nearby. From this one can assume that this soil is one of his sources of strength, fuel, if you will. Nowhere can a greater supply of this soil be found than in Transylvania itself. My theory is that the longer the Prince of Darkness rests in this soil, the stronger he becomes. Lying in the dirt for extended periods of time, however, is not helpful, when one plans to rule the world. He needs field agents with great power to traverse the globe, setting his plans into motion. So he makes soul-clones, beings with powers almost equal to his. Living (or unliving) puppets, which Dracula exists through, hears through, sees through, and drinks through, all while his original body lies sleeping, gathering power.*"

The soul-clone theory is supported by several passages from Paul Féval's **Vampire City**, *a novel which predates Stoker's* Dracula *by about thirty years* (published 1875, although evidence indicates it was written in the mid 1860s; translated by Brian Stableford, Black Coat Press, October 2003). These passages describe the dividuality of the vampire race: "Each vampire is a collective, represented by one principal form, but possessing other accessory forms of indeterminate number." "Each subsidiary form, like the dominant form, also has the ability to duplicate itself." "This bundle of beings, singular and plural at the same time—which seems to be the most blatant realization of the most incomprehensible mysteries of our Christian era—was not created all of a piece. It was aggregated and rounded out by conquest, like the winnings in a game of cards, or a rolling snowball. The infamous Monsieur Goetzi, having drunk the blood of all the inhabitants of the Ale and Amber, had incorporated them all into himself. You will readily appreciate that this facility was extremely convenient." For more on Loridans' theory, see his MONSTAAH website.

1574

CASTLE OF THE UNDEAD

Count Dracula saves Solomon Kane's life. When Kane learns of Dracula's true vampiric nature, they battle, and Kane nearly wins. However, Dracula reminds Kane of his life debt, and Kane spares the Count's life, leaving Transylvania.

Farmer has proposed that Kane was a distant ancestor of many Wold Newton Family members. Dracula's existence in the Crossover Universe is confirmed in this story in #3 of Marvel's black-and-white *Dracula Lives* magazine (by Roy Thomas and Alan Weiss), October 1973; reprinted in *The Saga of Solomon Kane*, Dark Horse Books, July 2009. For information on Dracula's inclusion in the CU, see the Holmes-Dracula encounter of 1887. Although Marvel published this story, the Marvel Comics universe is not part of the Crossover Universe. The complete Solomon Kane stories by Robert E. Howard have been compiled in *Solomon Kane*, Baen Books, 1995, and *The Savage Tales of Solomon Kane*, Del Rey, 2004.

1575

THE DRAGON AT CASTLE FRANKENSTEIN

Solomon Kane comes to Nieder-Beerbach where Castle Frankenstein sits on the northern edge of Magnet Mountain. The castle was erected in 1250 and houses the local baronial family, currently ruled by Baron Hans von Frankenstein (implicitly an ancestor of the famous Victor Frankenstein).

Story by Donald F. Glut and Sonny Trinidad in Marvel Comics' Savage Sword of Conan *#22, September 1977; reprinted in* The Saga of Solomon Kane, *Dark Horse Books, July 2009. The 1531 date referenced in the story must be discounted in light of research that places Kane's adventures in the latter half of the 16th century, rather than the first half.*

1576

THE ANTI-POPE OF AVIGNON

Solomon Kane clashes with Fausta. Gaston de Rochefort also appears, as does one of the Horla. Goody Cloyse is mentioned as having fled Devonshire for the New England colonies.

Short story by Micah Harris in Tales of the Shadowmen Volume 4: Lords of Terror, *Jean-Marc and Randy Lofficier, eds., Black Coat Press, 2008; reprinted in French in* Les Compagnons de l'Ombre *(Tome 5), Jean-Marc and Randy Lofficier, eds., Rivière Blanche, 2009. Solomon Kane is Robert E. Howard's Puritan hero. Fausta is Michel Zevaco's anti-heroine from the series of swashbuckling novels featuring the indomitable Chevalier de Pardaillan. The Horla is from Guy de Maupassant's short story of the same name. Gaston de Rochefort is an ancestor of the Rochefort in Dumas'* The Three Musketeers. *Goody Cloyse is from Nathaniel Hawthorne's story "Young Goodman Brown." According to Harris, "Her deal with the devil involved her receiving some kind of extension of days, as Kane was acquainted with her as a child in the 1500s, and Hawthorne's story takes place in the late 17th century."*

1587

RETRIBUTION IN BLOOD
   Having previously spared Count Dracula's life, Solomon Kane's guilty conscience spurs him to return to Transylvania for a rematch. Kane defeats and kills Dracula with a sharpened, jewel-encrusted wooden crucifix. However, thieves later come upon the scene of the battle, with the implication that they will remove the crucifix from the Count's corpse, thus reviving him.
   A story by Donald F. Glut, with art by David Wenzel and Marilitz, in Marvel's black-and-white Savage Sword of Conan #26; *reprinted in* The Saga of Solomon Kane, *Dark Horse Books, July 2009.*

1588

THE KNIGHT OF LA MANCHA
   The 2nd Phantom participates in the events of Don Quixote.
   #1037 of The Phantom, *Frew Publications, Australia, bringing the events of Miguel de Cervantes' classic into the Crossover Universe.*

1588-1594

   The Sea-Hawk, as told by Rafael Sabatini.
   The Sea-Hawk*'s Sir Oliver Tressilian is an ancestor of Lord Greystoke as described in Farmer's* Tarzan Alive.

1599

   Birth of Percy Blake (aka the Laughing Cavalier), later known as Sir Percy Blakeney (*The Laughing Cavalier* by Baroness Emmuska Orczy).
   Farmer placed Percy's descendant, the Scarlet Pimpernel, at the Wold Newton meteor event in December 1795.

c. 1600

ZORRO CONTRO MACISTE
   The first Zorro versus the heroic strongman Maciste.
   1963 feature film, released in English as Samson and the Slave Queen. Zorro contro Maciste *establishes Maciste as a part of the Crossover Universe. Maciste is either an immortal or else a descendant of the Maciste who first appeared in the Italian film* Cabiria, *1914. This Zorro is not Don Diego Vega, but rather is a poet named Ramon; the complete background for this crossover is provided in Matthew Baugh's "The Legacy of the Fox: Zorro in the Wold New-*

ton Universe," Myths for the Modern Age: Philip José Farmer's Wold Newton Universe, *Win Scott Eckert, ed., MonkeyBrain Books, 2005.*

1610

DEATH'S DARK RIDERS

Solomon Kane is abducted from Devon by magical riders from Negari and taken to that city, now a part of Africa. He is transported to the distant past when Negari was a city of Atlantis, where he has an adventure with Conan, who has also been transported to the past.

This tale by Roy Thomas and Colin MacNeil in Marvel Comics' Savage Sword of Conan *#219-220, March-April 1994, is a sequel to R.E. Howard's Solomon Kane story "The Moon of Skulls" reprinted in* The Saga of Solomon Kane, *Dark Horse Books, July 2009.*

1615

Birth of D'Artagnan.

1619

Birth of Cyrano de Bergerac.

c. 1620

ZORRO E I TRE MOSCHETTERI

Spain is at war with France and agents of Cardinal Richelieu gain an advantage in the conflict by capturing Isabella, the cousin of the King of Spain. The young Count of Seville travels to Spain to trade Spanish military secrets for Isabella's release. Actually this is a ruse, enabling the Count to don the mask of Zorro and to rescue Isabella. Richelieu's enemies, Athos, Porthos, and Aramis, join with Zorro in this adventure.

This 1963 film was released in English as Mark of the Musketeers. *Matthew Baugh, speculating that this Zorro is the son of Ramon from* Zorro contro Maciste, *states that "The fact that D'Artagnan is not present suggests that this adventure takes place before the events of Alexandre Dumas' novel,* The Three Musketeers. *The connection between Ramon of* Zorro contro Maciste *and the Count in this film is speculative but makes sense given their proximity in time."*

1623

January. The first Sir Percy Blakeney's first chronicled adventure, *The Laughing Cavalier*, as told by Baroness Orczy.

1624

March. The events of *The First Sir Percy*, as related by Baroness Orczy.

1625-1635

Events of Paul Féval's *Bel Demonio*, a precursor to the Black Coats saga.

1625-1628

Events of *The Three Musketeers*, chronicling the adventures of Athos, Porthos, Aramis, and D'Artagnan, as told by Alexandre Dumas. Sequels by Dumas are *Twenty Years After* and *The Vicomte de Bragelonne: Ten Years Later*, but some of their other subsequent adventures are documented in the Diaries of Monsieur D'Artagnan, retold for a modern audience by Sarah D'Almeida as *Death of a Musketeer*, *The Musketeer's Seamstress*, *The Musketeer's Apprentice*, *A Death in Gascony*, and *Dying by the Sword*.

1626

THE VANISHING DIAMONDS
The Time Traveler goes back in time from 1898 and becomes embroiled in D'Artagnan's mission to retrieve the Queen's diamonds.
Short story by Sylvie Miller and Philippe Ward in Tales of the Shadowmen Volume 2: Gentlemen of the Night, *Jean-Marc and Randy Lofficier, eds., Black Coat Press, 2006; reprinted in French in* Les Compagnons de l'Ombre (Tome 1), *Jean-Marc and Randy Lofficier, eds., Rivière Blanche, 2008. Note that while H.G. Wells obviously used the British spelling for the character (The Time Traveller), most of the pastiches are by American authors and for the sake of convenience and consistency the Americanized spelling (The Time Traveler) is adopted herein.*

1627

ALL FOR ONE, ONE FOR ALL
Batman and Robin travel back in time from the 1940s. They arrive in France, during the reign of Louis XIII and meet D'Artagnan, Aramis, Athos, and

Porthos, otherwise known as the Three Musketeers, defying the schemes of Cardinal Richelieu and Milady De Winter to help protect Queen Anne.

Batman *#32, DC Comics, December 1945-January 1946. According to Aaron Severson's online Golden Age Batman Chronology "This story probably takes place midway through the events of the novel [*The Three Musketeers*], probably before the assassination of the Duke of Buckingham, which occurred on August 22, 1628." In* World's Finest *#82 (May-June 1956), Bruce Wayne (Batman), Dick Grayson (Robin), and Clark Kent (Superman) travel back in time to 1696 to fill in as the Three Musketeers and help D'Artagnan free the Man in the Iron Mask. The Musketeers don't recognize Batman and Robin from their prior adventure together; this fact, plus the chronological difficulties (*The Man in the Iron Mask *occurs in 1661), lead to the conclusion that this story is fictional in relation to the Crossover Universe.*

c. 1630

The events of *Shogun*, as related by James Clavell. Other novels in Clavell's "Asian Saga" include *Tai-Pan, Gai-Jin, King Rat, Noble House, Whirlwind,* and *Escape*.

c. 1630s

LOS MOSQUETEROS PEQUEÑOS
Three young musketeers have a series of adventures in France, on their own and in the company of Athos, Porthos, Aramis, and D'Artagnan.
From the Spanish pulp Los Mosqueteros Pequeños *#1-9*.

THE DAGGER
A brave musketeer for Queen Anne, known as "the Dagger of the Queen," has adventures in England and France, on his own and with Athos, Porthos, Aramis, and D'Artagnan.
From the Spanish pulp El Puñal del Rey *#1-20*.

FLORIAN, EL CADETE DE LA REINA
Florian, a Spanish boy in the court of Queen Anne, has a variety of cape-and-epee adventures, on his own and alongside Athos, Porthos, Aramis, and D'Artagnan.
From Hugo Reyd's Florian, el Cadete de la Reina, Aventuras de un Muchacho Español en la Corte de Francia *#1-16, 1931*.

LOS MOSQUETEROS DE QUINCE AÑOS
A trio of fifteen-year-old musketeers has a series of cape-and-epee adventures, on their own and with Athos, Porthos, Aramis, and D'Artagnan.

From the Spanish pulp Los Mosqueteros de Quince Años *#1-50.*

1632

Birth of Robinson Crusoe.

1639

AVENGELYNE/SHI

The angel Avengelyne saves the female Japanese warrior called Shi (Yuri Ishikawa) from a demon lord called Akuma, but Akuma is only banished to a nether realm and vows vengeance.

Avengelyne/Shi *#½ by Robert Lugibihl, Sean Shaw, and Robert Jones, Avatar Comics, November 2001. Shi (or rather her distant descendant Ana Ishikawa) is connected to the Crossover Universe by a story where Ana meets Vampirella in 1996. Vampirella, in turn, is linked in via Dracula. This tale brings in Avengelyne (who has not yet become a fallen angel).*

1645-1646

The events of Sir Walter Scott's *A Legend of Montrose.*

1648-1649

Twenty Years After by Alexandre Dumas.

Mid 1600s

Two rival extraterrestrial races, the Eridaneans and the Capelleans, crash on Earth. Over the centuries, both races, which are very long-lived, will covertly continue their rivalry while living amongst humans. Many humans will be secretly inducted into the ranks of both the Eridaneans and the Capelleans, in furtherance of the conflict. These humans will be given an elixir allowing them to live at least one thousand years, barring accidental death. (*The Other Log of Phileas Fogg* by Philip José Farmer.)

1650

As a young man the Dutch portraitist Schalken loses the love of his life. ("Schalken the Painter" by J. Sheridan Le Fanu.)

c. 1650s

THE PALACE OF THE BLOODSUCKING WOMAN
Hattori Hanzō III and his Iga ninjas investigate a series of murders in Edo (the future Tokyo). A woman, the agent of a satanic monk, seduces men and drugs them with fatal doses of wolfsbane and opium. She tells one of her victims to dream of Shangri-La.

Episode of the first Shadow Warriors *television series. The reference to Shangri-La from James Hilton's* Lost Horizon *places the events and characters featured in this story in the Crossover Universe. In Quentin Tarentino's film* Kill Bill, *Hattori Hanzō is a swordsmith played by Sonny Chiba. The character in* Kill Bill *is an homage to Chiba's role as Hattori Hanzō in the television series* Kage no Gundan; *the ancient Hattori Hanzō is an ancestor of the one seen in* Kill Bill, *thus linking that film and the rest of Tarentino's interconnected films into the Crossover Universe.*

1651

September 1. Beginning events of Daniel Defoe's *Robinson Crusoe*.

1652

Birth of Peter Blood, who Farmer postulated was an ancestor of many modern Wold Newton Family members.

1655

Autumn
CYRANO AND THE TWO PLUMES
The sorcerer Alcandre sets Cyrano de Bergerac against the Musketeer Charles de Batz de Castlemore, Count d'Artagnan, who was once the companion of Porthos, Athos, and Aramis. De Bergerac's friend Ragueneau also appears.

Short story by John Shirley in Tales of the Shadowmen Volume 4: Lords of Terror, *Jean-Marc and Randy Lofficier, eds., Black Coat Press, 2008; reprinted in French in* Les Compagnons de l'Ombre (Tome 3), *Jean-Marc and Randy Lofficier, eds., Rivière Blanche, 2009. Cyrano de Bergerac and Ragueneau are historical, but also from Edmond Rostand's play* Cyrano de Bergerac.

D'Artagnan is historical, and also from Alexandre Dumas' The Three Musketeers and sequels. The magician Alcandre is from Jean de Rotrou's play La bague de l'oubli *(1628)*.

1660

Spring. Birth of Lemuel Gulliver.

Summer. Claude Duval begins his career as a "knight of the road," a gentleman highwayman. (James Rymer's *Claude Duval, the Dashing Highwayman: A Tale of the Road* #1-201, 1854.)

Summer
WOMEN, FOOLS AND SERPENTS
Izak van Helsing, captain of the *Sémillante*, and his vampire pirate companion Scarlet Lips, encounter a sea monster. They agree to next tackle a giant white whale.

Short story by Jean-Marc Lofficier in the Club Van Helsing series, included with The Katrina Protocol, *Black Coat Press, May 2008; reprinted in the Lofficiers' collection* Pacifica, *Black Coat Press, 2010. Izak van Helsing is part of the American branch of the famous vampire hunting family. Scarlet Lips is a character seen in the French comics* Dragut *and* Black Lys. *The giant white whale is a reference to Herman Melville's* Moby Dick.

1660-1667

The Vicomte de Bragelonne: Ten Years Later by Alexandre Dumas, including: *The Vicomte de Bragelonne, Louise de la Vallière,* and *The Man in the Iron Mask.*

1661

Isaac Newton attends Cambridge University, where he meets Daniel Waterhouse, setting in motion events which change the world. (*The Baroque Cycle*, a trilogy by Neal Stephenson.)

1662

Izak van Helsing marries Robin Whitby, one of the Slayers. (*Crépuscule Vaudou* aka *The Katrina Protocol* by Jean-Marc Lofficier. The American branch of the Van Helsing family as documented in Lofficier's *Crépuscule Vaudou* is distinguished from the various European branches by the lowercase "van" rather than uppercase "Van.")

1664

Birth of Micah Clarke, an ancestor of several Wold Newton Family members, per Farmer's *Doc Savage*.

1665-1666

THE SKELETON HORSEMAN
Claude Duval teams with Paul Peril, the Red Hand, the Red Avengers, and the Skeleton Horseman to defeat the Black Band and England's King Charles II. Duval then assists Peril in running away with Nell Gwynne.

The Skeleton Horseman, 1866. Claude Duval is in the Crossover Universe via the story Black Bess, *which takes place 1737-1739. The Skeleton Horseman brings Paul Peril, the Red Hand, the Red Avengers, the Skeleton Horseman, and the Black Band into the CU. Perhaps Dr. Cornelius Kramm, several centuries hence, named his Red Hand criminal syndicate after the illustrious Red Hand.*

1666

The Blazing World is psychically charted by the Duchess of Newcastle.

1671

October
BLACK SAILS
Pirate Captain Miguel Estacado, current bearer of power of "the Darkness," fights the woman who currently has the mantle of the Magdalena, Benedetta Maria Ferro.

One-shot by Ron Marz and Keu Cha, Top Cow Comics, March 2005. Estacado's descendant, Jackie Estacado, and the Magdalena both have good independent links to the Crossover Universe via Vampirella, and thus it is likely that the meeting between Miguel Estacado and this earlier Magdalena also takes place in the CU.

1673

Captain Robert Owemuch discovers The Floating Island, Scoti Moria.

1680

LEYENDAS MACABRAS DE LA COLONIA
Luchadores Mil Máscaras, Tinieblas, and El Fantasma Blanco travel back in time to the year 1680, to fight the mestiza witch Luisa, El Monje Loco, and La Llorona.

Feature film, 1973. Mil Máscaras and Tinieblas are in the Crossover Universe via various crossovers with El Santo and Blue Demon. This film links in El Fantasma Blanco, El Monje Loco, and La Llorona. El Monje Loco was a Mexican comics horror host in the 1940s and '50s. Tinieblas and El Fantasma Blanco teamed up again in Las Momias de San Angel, *1973.*

1682-1683

The first League of Extraordinary Gentlemen, comprised of Prospero, Caliban, Ariel, Captain Robert Owemuch, and Christian, sails on a fateful expedition to The Blazing World, as told by Alan Moore and Kevin O'Neill in "The New Traveller's Almanac, Chapter One: The British Isles" in *The League of Extraordinary Gentlemen II*.

1685

Summer. Captain Blood by Rafael Sabatini. Further adventures of Captain Peter Blood were told in *Captain Blood Returns* and *The Further Adventures of Captain Blood*. Izak van Helsing dies fighting alongside Captain Blood. (*Crépuscule Vaudou* aka *The Katrina Protocol* by Jean-Marc Lofficier.)

Late 1680s

The Phantom battles pirate and Wold Newton Family ancestor Captain Peter Blood, thus placing the multi-generational Phantoms in the Crossover Universe.

c. Late 1600s

The events of *Lorna Doone: A Romance of Exmoor*, as related by Richard Doddridge Blackmore. According to Philip José Farmer's *Tarzan Alive*, one of the descendants of Lorna Doone and John Ridd was Lorena Ridd of Exmoor. Lorena Ridd was the mother of Hugh "Bulldog" Drummond and John "Korak" Drummond.

1690

The University of Cosmopoli is established in England. (*The Purple Sapphire*, a collection of short stories by Edward Heron-Allen.)

1692

Raziel van Helsing marries Laurel Doone, a cousin of Lorna Doone. (Jean-Marc Lofficier's *Crépuscule Vaudou* aka *The Katrina Protocol*).

1694

The main events of John Barth's *The Sot Weed Factor* begin with Ebenezer Cooke's appointment as Poet Laureate of Maryland by Lord Baltimore. Ebenezer Cooke is an antecedent of a branch of the Wold Newton Family, as seen in Farmer's *Doc Savage*.

GULLIVER'S TRAVELS
JONATHAN SWIFT

1699

May 4. Lemuel Gulliver embarks on his various strange voyages, as told in Gulliver's Travels by Jonathan Swift.

Autumn. Raziel van Helsing vanishes while sailing with Lemuel Gulliver. (*Crépuscule Vaudou* aka *The Katrina Protocol* by Jean-Marc Lofficier).

Autumn. First recorded exploit of French adventurer Henri Lagardère. (*Le Bossu* by Paul Féval.)

Autumn. French author Mlle. de Scudery solves a crime and saves an innocent man from death. ("Mademoiselle de Scudery" by E.T.A. Hoffmann.)

c. 1700

Winter. Wandering Chinese storyteller Kai Lung uses his wits to get himself out of many difficulties. (*The Wallet of Kai Lung*, a collection of short stories by Ernest Bramah.)

Spring. A feud brews between two Hungarian families. ("Metzengerstein" by Edgar Allan Poe.)

c. Early 1700s

The Life, Adventures, and Pyracies of the Famous Captain Singleton as recounted by Daniel Defoe. Farmer's *Tarzan Alive* refers to Defoe's tale.

Events of Antoine François Prévost's (the Abbé Prévost) novel *Manon Lescaut* (*Histoire du chevalier des Grieux et de Manon Lescau*t).

1709

September 18. Birth of Dr. Sam: Johnson, detective in tales recounted by Lillian de la Torre.

1710

Jeremiah van Helsing clashes with James Boon, founder of Jerusalem's Lot (*Crépuscule Vaudou* aka *The Katrina Protocol* by Jean-Marc Lofficier.)

1710-1721

LE ROI DES BANDITS

Inspired by Claude Duval's exploits, Louis-Dominique Bourguignon takes to the roads of France and becomes known as the highwayman Cartouche.

Artheme Fayard's Le Roi des Bandits *#1-38, 1907-1908. Jess Nevins adds, "Cartouche is explicitly described as having been inspired by Duval's example. It is not widely known is that Cartouche ventured into England and carried out various gallant acts there."*

1715-16

Events of Sir Walter Scott's *Rob Roy.*

1718

Casca: The Pirate: Casca sails the high seas with Blackbeard and other dread buccaneer chieftains. (*A novel by Barry Sadler. The 5th Phantom battled*

Blackbeard, among other pirates, ing Wold Newton Family ancestor Captain Blood.)

1719

Birth of Nathaniel "Natty" Bumppo. Philip José Farmer's Doc *Savage: His Apocalyptic Life* placed Bumppo in the Wold Newton Family Tree. According to Jean-Marc Lofficier, Bumppo's mother is Mazhira van Helsing (*Crépuscule Vaudou* aka *The Katrina Protocol*).

c. 1724

BLUE DWARF
Sapathwa, "the Blue Dwarf," is actually Baron Mountjoye. He gathers several thieves, including Dick Turpin, Rob Roy, Tom King, the Mohicans, and Jonathan Wild, at the Maypole Inn.

A serial by Percy B. St. John. Jess Nevins notes, "The Maypole Inn appears in Charles Dickens' Barnaby Rudge. *The dating on* Blue Dwarf *(the 1874-1875 revision of the original 1860-1861 penny dreadful) is theoretical, as the dreadful includes not just Dick Turpin, but also Rob Roy, Jonathan Wild, and Mohicans, and fitting all of them into the same time frame is tricky because of the various characters' lifespans. Turpin is treated in the story as a notorious thief, but he didn't get his true notoriety until later." Rob Roy is in the CU via the appearance of Sir Hector Osbaldistone, a descendant of Sir Francis Osbaldistone from Sir Walter Scott's* Rob Roy, *in Philip José Farmer's* The Other Log of Phileas Fogg. *Thus,* Blue Dwarf *brings Sapathwa, Dick Turpin, the Mohicans, Tom King, Jonathan Wild, and Dickens'* Barnaby Rudge *into the CU.*

1726

TALES OF AN ANTIQUARY
Ptolemy Horoscope is a London astrologer who is visited by Dick Turpin, although Turpin ends up with Horoscope's assistant, Titus Parable, who poses as Horoscope.

Story by Richard Thomson, 1828, placing Ptolemy Horoscope in the Crossover Universe.

1729

Birth of Christopher Syn.

1731-1736

BLUESKIN
Joe Blake, known as "Blueskin," is a retired thief who works for crime lord Jonathan Wild. Blake helps young Jack Sheppard enter Wild's organization, but eventually Wild is hanged, while Blake and Sheppard escape to France.
Story by Edward Viles, 1866-1867, linking Blueskin and Jack Sheppard into the CU.

1732

RED RALPH
Highwayman Red Ralph's friends and companions are Lucy Lockit and Polly Peachum, associates of Macheath; Elizabeth "Edgeworth Bess" Lyon and Poll Maggot, friends of Jack Sheppard; and the highwaymen Dick Turpin, John "Sixteen String Jack" Rann, Tom King, and Blueskin.
Story by Percival Wolfe, 1866, bringing Red Ralph, Lucy Lockit, Polly Peachum, Macheath, Elizabeth "Edgeworth Bess" Lyon, Poll Maggot, and Sixteen String Jack Rann into the Crossover Universe.

1735

Yakob van Helsing marries Cassandra Wentworth, granddaughter of the witch Melinda Warren. (Jean-Marc Lofficier's *Crépuscule Vaudou* aka *The Katrina Protocol*).

1736

EDITH THE CAPTIVE
While Jack Sheppard and Blueskin are still working for Jonathan Wild, Dick Turpin helps in the reformation of highwayman Captain Heron, who then marries Edith Tarleton, and becomes the new Earl of Whitcombe.
Story by James Malcolm Rymer, 1860, placing Captain Heron in the CU.

1737-1739

BLACK BESS
Highwayman Dick Turpin continues his career, assisted through the years by Sixteen String Jack Rann, Tom King, Blueskin, Claude Duval, and Captain

Hawk. In 1738, Turpin accidentally shoots Tom King during a robbery. In 1739, Turpin is captured and hanged for his crimes.

Edward Viles' Black Bess, #1-254, 1863-1868. This crossover links Captain Hawk into the Crossover Universe. The accidental shooting of gentleman highwayman Tom King by Turpin is a real historical event. Claude Duval—the Crossover Universe version of Duval, that is—must be quite elderly by now.

WILD WILL, OR THE PIRATES OF THE THAMES

Claude Duval and Sixteen String Jack Rann assist Wild Will in his career as a pirate on the Thames.

Story by Charles H. Ross, 1865, placing Wild Will in the Crossover Universe.

1739

Summer
THE BLACK HIGHWAYMAN

After Dick Turpin's death, body snatchers attempt to steal his body. Captain Hawk rescues the body and, after giving it a proper burial, goes on to several adventures.
Story by Edward Viles, 1868-1869.

Probable birth of Colonel Bozzo-Corona (Fra Diavolo) of the Black Coats.

1740

Natty Bumppo's stories, *The Leatherstocking Tales*, by James Fenimore Cooper, begin here. They are: *The Deerslayer* (1740-1745), *The Last of the Mohicans* (1757), *The Pathfinder* (1760), *The Pioneers* (1793), and *The Prairie* (1804).

1743

Birth of Joseph Balsamo (Alexandre Dumas' *Joseph Balsamo*). In *Doc Savage*, Farmer placed Balsamo/Count Cagliostro as an ancestor of one branch of the Wold Newton Family.

1745-1755

MANDRIN, ROI DES VOLEURS
Inspired by the escapades of Claude Duval and Cartouche, Louis Mandrin operates as a highwayman. Mandrin also had adventures in England.
Mandrin, Roi des Voleurs *#1-16, 1925. Both Duval and Cartouche are mentioned by name in the story.*

1749

The events of *Fanny Hill, Or, Memoirs of a Woman of Pleasure,* as told by John Cleland.

1751

The events of *Kidnapped* and *Catriona*, as recounted by Robert Louis Stevenson.

1753

THE TRUE STORY OF WILHELM STORITZ
The Time Traveler arrives in 1753 and is captured by Otto Storitz. The Traveler happens to have Griffin's (The Invisible Man's) notebooks with him, and Storitz researches them, passing on their secrets to his corrupt son, Wilhelm Storitz. The Time Traveler mentions that he originally got the notebooks from an innkeeper in Port-Stowe named Marvel, who eventually moved to Kansas and became a traveling fortune-teller called Professor Marvel.
A short story Michel Pagel in The Mammoth Book of New Jules Verne Adventures, *Mike Ashley and Eric Brown, eds., Carroll & Graf, 2005. The story explains the source of Wilhelm Storitz's invisibility in Jules Verne's* Le Secret de Wilhelm Storitz, *1910. Professor Marvel is the traveling circus fortune-teller whom Dorothy encounters at the beginning of the film version of* The Wizard of Oz, *1939. Frank Morgan played Professor Marvel, the Wizard of Oz, and several other roles in the film.*

1754

The events of *Doctor Syn on the High Seas*, as recounted by Russell Thorndike, wherein Syn assumes the identity of the piratical Captain Clegg. Syn's further adventures were told in *Doctor Syn Returns, The Further Adventures of Doctor Syn, The Amazing Quest of Doctor Syn, The Courageous Exploits of Doctor Syn, The Shadow of Doctor Syn*, and *Doctor Syn*.

1754-55

PORTO BELLO GOLD
Robert Omerod becomes involved in a clash over treasure stolen to help further the Jacobite cause. Some of this treasure will be seen again during the events of *Treasure Island*. Besides Ben Gunn, Billy Bones, Long John Silver, and Blind Pew, every other pirate mentioned in *Treasure Island* also appears.
Novel by Arthur D. Howden Smith, third in a series chronicling the exploits of the Omerod family. The crossover with Robert Louis Stevenson's Treasure Island *places the Omerod family in the Crossover Universe. The Omerod family also features in Howden Smith's* Alan Breck Again. *Breck is from Stevenson's* Kidnapped *and* Catriona, *placing those works in the CU.*

1757

April-June. Events of Jules Verne's *Le Secret de Wilhelm Storitz*.

1760

Summer. The events of *Treasure Island*, as told by Robert Louis Stevenson. Gideon van Helsing sails with Long John Silver (*Crépuscule Vaudou* aka *The Katrina Protocol* by Jean-Marc Lofficier.) Events leading up to Stevenson's novel are told in *Flint and Silver: A Prequel to Treasure Island* by John Drake.

December 5. Birth of the second Percy Blakeney (aka the Scarlet Pimpernel), the great-great-grandson of the first Sir Percy. Sir Percy will be present at the Wold Newton meteor strike in December 1795.

1764

Birth of Fitzwilliam Darcy to Mr. George and Lady Anne Darcy. Darcy will be present at the Wold Newton meteor strike in December 1795.

1764-1770

THE EARTH WILL SHAKE

Adolescent Sigismundo Celine of Napoli, Italy believes he has discovered a famous volume of black magic that was owned by Johann Dippel von Frankenstein, but the book turns out to be a hoax. Nevertheless, the Frankensteins are regarded as an infamous family of alchemists. Sigismundo also has a ferocious infatuation with Maria Maldonado. Maria, however, marries Sir John Babcock, an English nobleman who is related to the powerful Greystoke family. In a drunken fit, Sigismundo insults the Maldonado family, fights a duel with Maria's brother, and is forced into exile. Cassanova also appears.

Volume One of the Historical Illuminatus Chronicles *by Robert Anton Wilson. The Greystokes are the ancestors of the present day John Clayton, Lord Greystoke, otherwise known as Tarzan. In Wilson's autobiography, he claims that the character of Hans Zoesser is an earlier incarnation of Wilson. In Volume Two,* The Widow's Son *(1771-1774), Sigismundo continues to brush up against secret societies in pre-Revolutionary France.*

1767

March
THE BLACK COAT AND ATHENA VOLTAIRE: BLOOD FOR WATER

The Black Coat helps a privateer fend off pirates who have attacked in search of a shipment of waters from the legendary Fountain of Youth.

One-shot comic, story by Ben Lichius, Ape Entertainment, February 2009. The story picks up a little over 150 years later with an Athena Voltaire adventure. Since Athena Voltaire's adventures take place in the Crossover Universe, so do those of The Black Coat, aka Nathanial Finch. The Black Coat is not to be confused with the criminal organization, the Black Coats.

1770

CAPTAIN KRONOS, VAMPIRE HUNTER

A member of the Karnstein family uses sorcery to transform herself into a vampire. She then uses similar magic to resurrect her late English husband as a vampire. Captain Kronos comes to England and defeats this new breed of vampire.

Feature film, Hammer Films, 1974. The Karnstein family is from Sheridan LeFanu's Carmilla. Since Carmilla is in the CU, so is Captain Kronos. Rick Lai notes that "Another Hammer movie that ties into Carmilla is Twins of Evil. The main villain is Count Karnstein. Carmilla has a brief role in the film. The Count summons his kinswoman Carmilla from her grave through a black magic ritual. She then turns him into a vampire and leaves. It's not clear if Carmilla's resurrection was only of a temporary nature, or whether she was again free to ravage the countryside."

1770-1774

The events of Dumas' *Joseph Balsamo*. In *Doc Savage*, Farmer placed Balsamo/Cagliostro as an ancestor to various Wold Newton Family villains. Further volumes in Dumas' saga are *Le Collier de la Reine* (*The Queen's Necklace*), *Ange Pitou* (aka *The Taking of the Bastille*), *La Comtesse de Charny*, and *Le Chevalier de Maison-Rouge*.

1771

Spring. Don Diego de la Vega, the son of Don Alejandro de la Vega, and the future Zorro, is born. Jess Nevins postulates that Don Alejandro had a cousin, Ebardo de la Vega. "Ebardo had married and raised a child, Maria Concepción, and she in turn had married and borne Miguel." Miguel de Vega was a dwarf who later sought revenge against the United States for dispossessing his family of their Californian land. When he fought multiple battles against Secret Service agent James West he was known as Dr. Miguelito Loveless.

Autumn. Gideon van Helsing "kills" Joseph Curwen. (Jean-Marc Lofficier's *Crépuscule Vaudou* aka *The Katrina Protocol*).

1772

Birth of Elizabeth Bennet, who will be present, along with her husband Mr. Darcy, at the Wold Newton meteor strike in December 1795.

1772; Early 1940s; 1972; 1987 (alternate); **1792**

THE LONG WET PURPLE DREAM OF RIP VAN WINKLE
Rather than merely falling into a deep slumber and waking twenty years later, Rip van Winkle is actually bounces through several time periods before things are set aright and he ends up in 1792. In the 1940s, he encounters two crimefighters named Margo and Lamont.

Short story by Philip José Farmer first printed in Puritan 7, *1981, and collected in* The Purple Book *(Tor Books, 1982) and* Riders of the Purple Wage *(Tor Books, 1992). Margo and Lamont are Margo Lane and Lamont Cranston, respectively. Lamont Cranston was an identity often used by The Shadow, although The Shadow's real identity was Kent Allard. To complicate matters, there was a real Lamont Cranston, but he mostly stayed out of New York while The Shadow was using his identity. The character seen in "The Long Wet Purple Dream of Rip van Winkle" is likely The Shadow, based on references to his .45s, and black hat and cloak. The story brings Washington Irving's 1819 short story "Rip van Winkle" into the Crossover Universe.*

1775-1780

Events of Charles Dickens' *Barnaby Rudge: A Tale of the Riots of 'Eighty.*

1775

Summer
CLOWN FISH
The crew of the pirate ship *Lady Anne* encounters one of the spawn of Cthulhu in the mid-Atlantic. One of the ship's crew is a young Delaware Indian named Hawk who had formerly sailed with Captain Clegg. Hawk mentions that Clegg had taught him to read, claiming that he had to teach at least one of Hawk's people to read scripture before he could return home.

Short story by Matthew Baugh in High Seas Cthulhu, *William Jones, ed., Elder Signs Press, 2007. Clegg and Cthulhu are solidly in the Crossover Universe.*

November
DEATH IN DOVER
Young Percy Blakeney is traveling with his father and French tutor, and is staying at a seaside inn where smuggling and murder takes place. The smugglers use scarlet pimpernel flowers as means of identifying themselves to potential customers. Percy takes one of these flowers as a souvenir. Lucie Manette appears, as does Jonathan Barrett, a gentleman buying wine from the smugglers.

Short story by P.N. Elrod in Death by Dickens, *edited by Anne Perry, Berkley Prime Crime, 2004. Lucie Manette is from Charles Dickens'* A Tale of Two Cities. *Jonathan Barrett is the protagonist of Elrod's* Jonathan Barrett, Gentleman Vampire *series; this story takes place before his conversion. Percy Blakeney should need no introduction by now, but it's worth noting that although he is portrayed as eleven years old in this story, he was almost fifteen in November 1775.*

1776-1782

NATURE'S GOD
Sigismundo Celine sojourns in the wilderness during the American Revolution. His half-brother, Giuseppe Balsamo, remains in Europe and becomes known as Count Cagliostro. Reference is again made to the relationship between the Babcocks and the Greystokes. A number of historical figures, such as Thomas Paine, George Washington, Mozart, etc., also appear in the chronicles.
Volume Three of the Historical Illuminatus Chronicles *by Robert Anton Wilson.*

1776

July 4. Birth of Horatio Hornblower. Hornblower was referred to in Philip José Farmer's *Tarzan Alive*, although the Hornblowers were not placed as Wold Newton Family members.

1779

Events of the film *Pirates of the Caribbean: Curse of the Black Pearl*.

1780

Spring
ENTER THE SCARECROW!
Jack Sparrow is an old friend of Mr. Mipps. The Scarecrow of Romney Marsh (aka Dr. Syn aka Captain Clegg) comes to the rescue when Sparrow and his ship are captured.
Story by Michael Stewart and Bret Blevins in Disney Adventures Comic Zone, *linking Captain Jack Sparrow and the events of the film* Pirates of the Caribbean: Curse of the Black Pearl *into the Crossover Universe. Philip José Farmer implied the existence of the Scarecrow/Dr. Syn in his World of Tiers series. This story occurs after the adventures told in Disney's film* Dr. Syn, Alias the Scarecrow, *which is an adaptation of* Further Adventures of Doctor Syn, *occurring in 1776-1777. Matthew Baugh notes that "In this story Mr. Mipps is pre-*

sented in a manner more consistent with the bland fellow in the Disney movie rather than the impish (and very dangerous) character from the novels. He is referred to as 'Dimity Mipps,' a name which is only used in the Disney movie. It is easy to assume that 'Dimity' was a nickname that the pirates had for Mipps."

Summer
PIRATES OF THE CARIBBEAN: DEAD MAN'S CHEST

When Jack Sparrow is forced to reveal to his crewmates the presence of the black spot on his palm, his response is "My eyesight's fine!"

Feature film, 2006. Sparrow's comment is a clear reference to Blind Pew, deliverer of the black spot in Stevenson's Treasure Island.

1780-1790

PIRATES OF THE CARIBBEAN: AT WORLD'S END

Jack Sparrow's first mate Joshamee Gibbs says, "Sweet blessed Westley."

Feature film, 2007. Westley is, of course, the real first name of the Dread Pirate Roberts. Gibbs' comment reveals some familiarity with the events depicted in the film The Princess Bride *(1987), based on William Goldman's 1973 novel.*

1785

A DUEL OF DEMONS

Count Dracula and Count Cagliostro appear in this story, in which Dracula goes to pre-Revolutionary France to offer his services to Louis XVI as an advisor. Cagliostro is already an advisor to the King and a rivalry develops. Cagliostro kills Dracula's loyal servant, whereupon Dracula attacks Cagliostro's wife, Lorenza, turning her into a vampire.

Story by Gerry Conway and Frank Springer, in Marvel's Dracula Lives *#5; reprinted in* Dracula Lives *Annual #1 and in* The Essential Tomb of Dracula, *Volume 4, 2005. In Dumas'* Memoirs of a Physician, *Altotas kills Lorenza by draining her of blood, which he plans to use in an elixir. The truth is revealed here: it was Dracula who drained Lorenza. Cagliostro thought that Altotas had* done the deed and killed him. However, per this story, Cagliostro soon discovered that Lorenza was not dead, but was undead. Cagliostro is mentioned in Philip José Farmer's Doc Savage *as an ancestor to many villains in the Wold Newton Family.*

1786

Gideon van Helsing is killed by the Headless Horseman. (Jean-Marc Lofficier, *Crépuscule Vaudou* aka *The Katrina Protocol*).

1787

The events of *The Legend of Sleepy Hollow*, as related by Washington Irving.

1787

The League of Extraordinary Gentlemen of the 18th century, whose adventures are as yet unchronicled, is comprised of a very elderly Lemuel Gulliver, Sir Percy Blakeney and wife, the Reverend Dr. Syn, Fanny Hill, and Natty Bumppo. Note that Sir Percy was *not* married to Marguerite Blakeney at this time; in fact, he did not even meet Marguerite until the later events of *The Scarlet Pimpernel*. As I stated in my "'They Seek Him There...': The Demmed Fine Blakeney Family Tree" (available on *The Wold Newton Universe* website), "Though it is possible that Sir Percy actually was married at the time, information from the biography *The Life and Exploits of The Scarlet Pimpernel (A Gay Adventurer)* by John Blakeney would tend to discount this. In 1789 Sir Percy was involved with a woman named Mary de Courcy. The courtship ended badly and Percy left for Paris. It is probable they knew each other even earlier, that the woman in the 1787 portrait was Mary de Courcy, and that Percy and Mary were forced to pose as husband and wife during the as-yet unchronicled 1787 mission, much like Allan Quatermain and Mina Murray were obliged to pose as a married couple during their 1898 adventures. Percy and Mary's 1787 mission led to a romantic entanglement, but it soon became clear that any romance was due to the adventure they had shared, and not any true passionate emotions for each other." In the early 1790s, Sir Percy, his wife Marguerite, and Miss Fanny Hill toured Europe, as related in "The New Traveller's Almanac, Chapter Two: Europe" in *The League of Extraordinary Gentlemen II*.

1788

Writer Ann Radcliffe, Merry Bones the Irishman, and faithful servant Grey Jack set out for Selene, the "Vampire City," to destroy the dreaded lord vampire

Otto Goetzi. (*Vampire City* by Paul Féval, translated by Brian Stableford, Black Coat Press, 2003.)

1789

July
SHADOW OVER VERSAILLES
Count Cagliostro and his wife have returned briefly to Louis XVI's court; however, they depart quickly, searching for a "cure" for her vampirism. Dracula, still at court, then becomes involved in the political machinations of the impending Revolution. The story concludes with the storming of the Bastille. The King asks for Dracula's assistance (with his vampiric powers) to keep order in France. Dracula refuses and departs.

By Tony Isabella, John Buscema, and Pablo Marcos, in Marvel's Dracula Lives *#6; reprinted in* Dracula Lives *Annual #1 and in* The Essential Tomb of Dracula, *Volume 4, 2005. Cagliostro was banished from Louis' court in 1786, after his involvement in the affair of Marie Antoinette's diamond necklace; my hypothesis is that he returned briefly in 1789, seeking Dracula's help in curing his wife. When Dracula refused, Cagliostro found it prudent to move on.*

1790-1800

The events of Mary Shelley's novel *Frankenstein*, in which Victor Frankenstein creates the first Creature. In the short story "Evil, Be My Good" (by Philip José Farmer, *The Ultimate Frankenstein*, iBooks, March 2003), it is revealed that Frankenstein used Dr. Krempe's brain in making the Creature. Dr. Krempe was a hated instructor of Victor's who fell into a cataleptic state and was taken for dead. After the events of Frankenstein, the Creature wandered the Arctic and Krempe's brain managed to take over just long enough to record the details of the story. There are several Dr. Frankensteins in the Crossover Universe, all of whom created their own Creatures, as Mark Brown explains in these excerpts from his essay "The House of Frankenstein," the complete text of which can be found on The Wold Newton Universe website:

"The story of Victor Frankenstein is too well known to repeat here. Victor, a descendant of that noble family of Frankenstein, Germany, was born in Geneva, Switzerland in 1772.

"His father, Alphonse Frankenstein, came from a long line of counselors and syndics. Alphonse's wife was Caroline Beaufort, whose father had been a longtime friend of Alphonse's. Victor had two younger brothers, Ernest (born 1778) and William (born 1786).

"In 1790, Victor became the first known man to create artificial life. In doing so, he triggered a series of events which would lead to the deaths of his youngest brother, his bride, his father, and his best friend. Victor would hound his creation around the globe for 10 years before dying in the Arctic in the arms of Robert Walton, who brought the story of Victor Frankenstein to the world.

"Victor's brother Ernest went on to become a farmer and did very well on the family lands. He managed to reclaim the title of Baron of Frankenstein. He married ---, daughter of Lothar von Harben, a visiting military officer from Cronstadt, Lutha. His bride wore a wreath of orange blossoms on her wedding day, beginning a tradition that lasted for three generations. His oldest son, named William after the brother who died so tragically young, was born in 1802. He married Madeleine Delacroix.

"William's son, Alphonse Victor, married a distant cousin, Felicia Saville, of America. Felicia was the second daughter of Victor Saville. According to Robert J. Myers (*The Cross of Frankenstein,* J.B. Lippincott, 1975), Victor Saville was the illegitimate son of Victor Frankenstein, fathered on a tavern girl during Victor's years of pursuit of the creature he had made. Victor II was rescued from poverty by Robert Walton, and raised by his sister, Margaret Saville. After several years of tragic adventures similar to those of his father, Victor II settled down and married, producing a daughter, Felicia. Alphonse and Felicia's son, Henry was born c. 1860.

"Henry Frankenstein began delving into the history of his family and learned of the researches of his ancestor. In the mid 1880s, Henry both married his long-time sweetheart, Elizabeth, and created a living being in a manner similar to Victor I. Henry's homunculus was more crudely made than Victor's, however, being unable to speak and capable of moving only with a shambling, lurching gait.

"In 1886, Henry, working with someone claiming to be the sinister Renaissance alchemist Dr. Pretorius, succeeded in something his forefather would not do, and created a mate for his creation. However, the mate rejected her intended spouse, and, in despair, the creature attempted to destroy them both. Henry and Elizabeth moved to England and had at least two children: Wolf, and Ludwig. Both were brilliant scientists who duplicated much of their father's work and had their own experiences with Henry's creature, Wolf in late 1919 and Ludwig in early 1921. Ludwig's daughter, Elsa (named after Wolf's wife, with whom Ludwig had secretly been in love) later had more encounters with the creature. This "Monster" was last seen in La Mirada, Florida in June of 1998.

"Wolf's son, Peter, was traumatized by the events he witnessed as a child, and tried to distance himself from the Frankenstein legacy. He began going by his middle name, Frederick, and even changed the way his surname was pronounced. But he could not escape his family's past. He too went into medicine and was tempted to create a living being. But at least he did not reject his creation, and was able to redeem his family name to some extent by helping his masterpiece find its place in the world."

There are rumors of other descendants of the Frankenstein family surviving in both Europe and America; many of these have been documented in various crossover stories, and by scholar Chuck Loridans in his "Children of the Night" timeline on the *MONSTAAH* website.

1790

THE HEART OF THE MOON

Doctor Omega, his companion Telzey Amberdon, Captain Kronos, Doctor Grost, Solomon Kane, and Maciste, fight the vampires Prince Vseslav and Yvgeny of Selene, the so-called "Vampire City." Passing through the Hungarian town of Stregoicavar, they arrive at Selene in search of a device called the Heart of the Moon, which allows Selene to remain in perpetual darkness. They battle the Lord and Lady of Selene, Baron Iscariot and Baroness Phryne. Kane has heard that vampires are a servitor race created by the Old Ones. He also refers to the lost city of Negari in Africa. Telzey refers to the architecture of Lessur. She also tells a story about three evil gods who stripped away the moon's atmosphere in order to put down a revolt. Kronos' stories of Maciste's feats remind Yvgeny of a man called Münchhausen. Kronos once did a favor for a man named Hanzo, who gave Kronos a sword made by the sword-smith Muramasa. Yvgeny refers to the vampire Ruthven. Orlock is the oldest vampire in Selene.

Short story by Yvgeny, edited by Matthew Baugh in Tales of the Shadowmen Volume 3: Danse Macabre, *Jean-Marc and Randy Lofficier, eds., Black Coat Press, 2007; reprinted in French in* Les Compagnons de l'Ombre (Tome 2), *Jean-Marc and Randy Lofficier, eds., Rivière Blanche, 2008. Kronos is not named, and Kane is only referred to as Solomon, but descriptors, such as "the Captain" and the "English Puritan," are detailed enough to confirm the identifications. Kronos and Doctor Grost are from the 1974 Hammer film* Captain Kronos, Vampire Hunter. *Robert E. Howard told the tales of Solomon Kane, who is also an ancestor of many Wold Newton Family members. Negari is also from the Kane stories. Maciste is the Hercules-like hero of a long-running series of Italian silent films, starting with 1914's* Cabiria, *and resurrected in the 1960s as another series of "sword and sandal" adventures. Kronos, Kane, and Maciste are immortal or extremely long-lived. Prince Vseslav is an historical character, a Russian prince who was thought to be a sorcerer and werewolf in life. Baron Iscariot, Baroness Phryne, and Selene are from Paul Féval's* Vampire City, *recently translated by Brian Stableford, Black Coat Press, 2003. The Old Ones are from H.P. Lovecraft's tales of the Cthulhu Mythos. Doctor Omega is from the novel of the same name by nould Galopin, adapted and retold by Jean-Marc and Randy Lofficier, Black Coat Press, 2003.* Telzey Amberdon is the telepathic heroine of a series of stories by James Schmitz. She is from the planet Orado in the far future. Here, she is Doctor Omega's companion, reinforcing the notion that Doctor Omega is Doctor Who. The story about the three evil gods destroying the Moon's atmosphere is a reference to the tale "Lost Paradise" by C.L. Moore. The story takes place in the alternate universe of Northwest Smith stories, but could easily be known to a companion of the dimension-hopping Doctor Omega. Lessur is from C.I. Defontenay's Star or Psi Cassiopeia *(*Star ou Psi de Cassiopeéa: Histoire Merveilleuse de l'un des Mondes de l'Espace, *1854)*. The Hanzo who gave Captain Kronos his sword is one of the

Hanzo Hattori characters played by Sonny Chiba on Japanese television. Muramasa is a semi-legendary Japanese sword-smith. Münchhausen is Baron Münchhausen. Stregoicavar is from the Robert E. Howard story "The Black Stone." Lord Ruthven is from John Polidori's The Vampyre. Orlock is from the silent film Nosferatu.

1791

Birth of Henri de Belcamp (John Devil).

1792

THE MAN WHO KILLED THE KING

Roger Brook, a British spy during the French Revolution and the Napoleonic Wars, proposes to Prime Minister William Pitt that a secret organization be created to rescue Frenchmen from the guillotine. Pitt responds that such an organization, the League, has already be created by a prominent member of the British nobility: "Are you perchance acquainted with Sir Percy Blakeney?" Brook mentions that he had heard of Blakeney, but never met him. Brook learns from Pitt how to contact the League inside France. After traveling to France, secret messages are conveyed by the League from Brook to Pitt during 1792-1794.

Dennis Wheatley wrote this series of historical adventures. Researcher Rick Lai notes, "Although the words 'Scarlet Pimpernel' are never uttered, there is little doubt that Wheatley is connecting his characters with Baroness Orczy's. It should be noted that the concluding chapters of The Man Who Killed the King, revolving around the fate of the Dauphin (Louis XVII), directly contradict Orczy's Pimpernel novel, El Dorado: An Adventure of the Scarlet Pimpernel."

September-October. The events of *The Scarlet Pimpernel* by Baroness Orczy. The complete series: *The Laughing Cavalier, The First Sir Percy, The Scarlet Pimpernel, Sir Percy Leads the Band, I Will Repay, The Elusive Pimpernel, The Way of the Scarlet Pimpernel, Lord Tony's Wife, Mam'zelle Guillotine, El Dorado: An Adventure of the Scarlet Pimpernel, Sir Percy Hits Back, The Triumph of the Scarlet Pimpernel, The League of the Scarlet Pimpernel, The Adventures of the Scarlet Pimpernel, A Child of the Revolution, In the Rue Monge*, and *The Pimpernel and Rosemary*. Pastiches: P.N. Elrod's "Death in Dover"; *The Blakeney Papers: Daughter of the Revolution, Such Mighty Rage*, and *Bordeaux Red* by C. Guy Clayton (the adventures of Marguerite Blakeney); and my "Is He in Hell?"

September 1792-Late Autumn 1793. The events of Jane Austen's *Pride and Prejudice* (the first draft of which was entitled *First Impressions* and was recorded by the Darcys' biographer, Jane Austen, during the years 1796-97). Elizabeth Bennet and Fitzwilliam Darcy are married in early December 1793. Thereafter, Mr. and Mrs. Darcy are present at the Wold Newton meteor strike, on December 13, 1795.

1794

June 1794-April 1798. The events of the first volume in Horatio Hornblower's biography, *Mr. Midshipman Hornblower*, as related by C.S. Forester.

Summer
NOB AND NOBILITY
   Two English nobles both claim to be the Scarlet Pimpernel. They are both obviously imposters.
   Episode of the Blackadder III *television program. It is clear from the way the other characters speak that there is a real Scarlet Pimpernel. This crossover brings all the various* Blackadder *series into the CU.*

1795-1797

   The Dashwood sisters finally settle upon appropriate husbands, as told in Jane Austen's *Sense and Sensibility*.

1795

   Summer. Don Diego de la Vega becomes El Zorro (Johnston McCully's *The Curse of Capistrano [aka* The Mark of Zorro*])*. He is one of many, although the most famous, men (and women) to don the mask of Zorro, as revealed in Matthew Baugh's "The Legacy of the Fox: Zorro in the Wold Newton Universe," *Myths for the Modern Age: Philip José Farmer's Wold Newton Universe*. Among them are Don Cesar de la Vega (*Zorro and Son* and *Don Q, Son of Zorro*); Jeff Stewart (*Son of Zorro*); Alejandro (Mesones) Murieta/Alejandro de la Vega (*The Mask of Zorro* and *The Legend of Zorro*); Juan Garza, Diego Guadeloupe, and Maria (*Three Swords of Zorro*); Joaquin Mesones de la Vega/Ken Mason (*Ghost of Zorro*); Barbara Meredith (*Zorro's Black Whip*); and Jim Vega (*Zorro Rides Again*).

November
IS HE IN HELL?
   In the guise of Rambert, Sir Percy Blakeney (The Scarlet Pimpernal) and his driver Lecoq fool Sergeant Favraux and rescue the Baron de Musard from the guillotine and evade Chauvelin. The malevolent entity Leonox reveals that he has possessed many wizards in the past, including Xaltotun of Python, Atlantes, Frestón, and Lodac. Leonox refers to a long-ago barbarian warrior king

who once defeated Xaltotun. Marguerite St. Just Blakeney and the Blakeneys' constant companion Alice make a last minute appearance with an artifact, the Heart of Ahriman, which they received from the Colonel's man Lecoq. Sir Percy's pocket watch is embossed with the constellation Eridanus.

Short story by Win Scott Eckert in Tales of the Shadowmen Volume 6: Grand Guignol, *Jean-Marc and Randy Lofficier, eds., Black Coat Press, 2010; reprinted in French in* Les Compagnons de l'Ombre (Tome 7), *Jean-Marc and Randy Lofficier, eds., Rivière Blanche, 2010. Sir Percy Blakeney (the Scarlet Pimpernel) and his wife Marguerite St. Just Blakeney are from Baroness Emmuska Orczy's* The Scarlet Pimpernel *and sequels, as is Blakeney's nemesis Chauvelin. Sergeant Favraux is an ancestor of the banker Favraux from Louis Feuillade and Arthur Bernède's silent film serial* Judex. *Rambert is an ancestor of Etienne Rambert and Charles Rambert from the Fantômas novels by Marcel Allain and Pierre Souvestre. Lecoq is Albert Lecoq, from Philip José Farmer's* Tarzan Alive. *He is the father of Leo Lecoq from Paul Féval's Black Coats saga, and the grandfather of Émile Gaboriau's Monsieur Lecoq. Baron de Musard is an ancestor of the Baron de Musard referred to in Philip José Farmer's Doc Savage novel* Escape from Loki. *Alice is Sir Percy Blakeney's future second wife, Alice Clarke Raffles, from Philip José Farmer's* Tarzan Alive. *Xaltotun of Acheron, the city of Python, the Heart of Ahriman, and the barbarian warrior king are from Robert E. Howard's Conan novel* The Hour of the Dragon. *The sorcerer Atlantes is from Ludovico Ariosto's* Orlando Furioso. *Frestón the Magician is from Miguel de Cervantes'* Don Quixote. *The wizard Lodac is from Bert I. Gordon's 1962 film* The Magic Sword. *Léonox is from the series of Léonox novels by Paul Béra (aka Paul Bérato, aka Yves Dermeze). The Colonel is Colonel Bozzo-Corona, head of the Brothers of Mercy and future godfather of the Habits Noirs, from Paul Féval's Black Coats saga. Sir Percy's embossed pocket watch is an indication that he is an Eridanean agent in the conflict described in Philip José Farmer's* The Other Log of Phileas Fogg.

December 13. Wold Newton meteor strike: Seven couples and their coachmen "were riding in two coaches past Wold Newton, Yorkshire.... A meteorite struck only twenty yards from the two coaches.... The bright light and heat and thunderous roar of the meteorite blinded and terrorized the passengers, coachmen, and horses.... They never guessed, being ignorant of ionization, that the fallen star had affected them and their unborn." *Tarzan Alive*, Addendum 2, pp. 247-248. The meteor strike was "the single cause of this nova of genetic splendor, this outburst of great detectives, scientists, and explorers of exotic worlds, this last efflorescence of true heroes in an otherwise degenerate age." Id., pp.230-231.

1796

Spring
THE FRANKENSTEIN / DRACULA WAR

While attempting to live a normal life among men, the Frankenstein Monster is blackmailed by the almost-immortal Count de Saint-Germain into attacking Count Dracula. Dracula refers to tales of a monstrous golem, in Prague. After various events, in which the Creature and Dracula almost become allies, they once again turn on each other and eventually fight to a standstill.

Comic book miniseries by Roy Thomas, Jean-Marc Lofficier, Claude St. Aubin, Allen Nunis, and Armando Gil, Topps Comics, 1995. After these events, the Monster heads back for the Arctic, with the events of "Black as the Pit, From Pole to Pole" transpiring several years later. The tale of the Golem of Prague is the story of the creation of a golem, a man, or Homunculus, crafted out of clay by a Rabbi known as the Maharal, in order to protect the 16th-century Jews of Prague from persecution.

Summer. Birth of Edmond Dantes (Count of Monte-Cristo).

Summer
RAMAGE

Lt. Ramage recalls his lack of skill at playing cards: "…He always found the game too slow, and had a bad memory. In fact his complete inability to remember the cards already played at those interminable games of whist at the Superb used to drive that fellow Hornblower mad. Yet, Ramage remembered with amusement, he sometimes won simply because he was such a bad player: even if Hornblower guessed the cards he held it was no help since his play was completely unpredictable. Nor, when Ramage won, did Hornblower like being reminded that surprise was the vital element in tactics."

The first novel in the Ramage *series by Dudley Pope. Rick Lai notes, "In 1796, C. S. Forester's Horatio Hornblower had been a midshipmen abroad two ships, the Justinian and the Indefatigable. There is no record of Hornblower (who was promoted to lieutenant in 1797) having served abroad a ship called the Superb (the ship is briefly mentioned in a totally different context in Parkin-*

son's biography of Hornblower). However, Horatio Hornblower was a skillful card player (see particularly Forester's Lieutenant Hornblower). Probably the young officers on the Superb invited officers from nearby ships to play cards there."

1797

February-May. The events of *Northanger Abbey*, as told by Jane Austen.

Spring
OLD FRIENDS AND NEW FANCIES
Some three-and-a-half years after the marriage of Fitzwilliam Darcy and Elizabeth Bennet in *Pride and Prejudice*, characters from all six of Jane Austen's biographical novels cross paths in various ways: Mr. and Fitzwilliam Mrs. Darcy, Mr. and Mrs. Charles Bingley, Miss Bingley, Mr. and Mrs. Hurst, Mr. Bennet, Kitty Bennet, Georgiana Darcy, Lady Catherine de Bourgh, Miss de Bourgh, Colonel Fitzwilliam, Mrs. Gardiner, and Mrs. Annesley (*Pride and Prejudice*); William Price, Mary Crawford, Henry Crawford, Mrs. Grant, Mr. and Mrs. Yates, and Tom Bertram (*Mansfield Park*); James Moreland, Lady Portinscale, General Tilney, Captain Tilney, and Isabella Thorpe (*Northanger Abbey*); Mr. and Mrs. Edward Ferrars, Mr. and Mrs. Robert Ferrars, Mrs. Jennings, Anne Steele, and Mr. Palmer (*Sense and Sensibility*); Captain and Mrs. Wentworth, Sir Walter Elliot, and Miss Elliot (*Persuasion*); and Mr. and Mrs. Knightley (*Emma*).

Old Friends and New Fancies: An Imaginary Sequel to the Novels of Jane Austen *is a novel by Sybil G. Brinton (1914) reprinted by Sourcebooks Landmark, 2007. It is a more faithful satire of manners, following the tenor, theme, and style of Austen's novels, than Carrie Bebris' otherwise enjoyable series of Mr. and Mrs. Darcy mysteries, which also cross-over with other Austen novels.*

Late 1790s-early 1800s

The Exploits of Brigadier Gerard and *The Adventures of Gerard* (the Napoleonic stories) by Sir Arthur Conan Doyle. In *Doc Savage: His Apocalyptic Life*, Farmer placed Gerard as an ancestor to several modern Wold Newton Family members, including James Bond.

1799

HIS FATHER'S EYES
In the wake of Dr. Victor Frankenstein's refusal to create a bride for the Monster, the Creature roams the Scottish Moor; he kidnaps and rapes young local girl Rosemary, but spares her life. Nine months later, the pregnant Rosemary

is sent to give birth in Rouen, Normandy, among her uncle's family. She dies in childbirth after seeing the baby's hideous yellow eyes—the same as his father's. The baby is christened Erik.

A short story by Jean-Mark and Randy Lofficier, collected in their adaptation of Gaston Leroux's The Phantom of the Opera, *Black Coat Press, October 2004; reprinted in French in* Les Compagnons de l'Ombre (Tome 2), *Jean-Marc and Randy Lofficier, eds., Rivière Blanche, 2008; and in the Lofficiers' collection* Pacifica, *Black Coat Press, 2010.*

1800

January
ANGEL VS. FRANKENSTEIN: THE HEIR

The vampire Angelus comes to Geneva posing as Wilhelm Frankenstein, an heir to the Frankenstein fortune. He is pursued by Victor Frankenstein's Creature, whom he has double-crossed.

One-shot written and illustrated by John Byrne, IDW Comics, October 2009. Angelus will later be known as Angel, and should not be confused with The Angelus, the sometime nemesis of Witchblade and The Darkness.

Spring. British naval captain Jack Aubrey meets Spanish doctor Stephen Maturin, and their great friendship begins. (*Master and Commander*, Patrick O'Brian.)

c. 1800-1819

BLACK AS THE PIT, FROM POLE TO POLE

Frankenstein's Creature travels through a hole in the Arctic, and thence through a series of inner worlds, before emerging at the locale of *the Mountains of Madness* in the Antarctic. Arthur Gordon Pym, Mocha Dick, Otto and Axel Lidenbrock, and Abner Perry, all either appear or are mentioned.

This story by Steven Utley and Howard Waldrop was originally published in New Dimensions 7, *Robert Silverberg, ed., Harper & Row, 1977; reprinted in* Eternal Lovecraft, *Jim Turner, ed., Golden Gryphon Press, 1998. The story links together Shelley's* Frankenstein, *Lovecraft's Cthulhu Mythos stories, Poe's* Arthur Gordon Pym, *Melville's* Moby Dick, *Verne's* Journey to the Centre of the Earth, *and E.R. Burroughs'* Pellucidar *series. The story features the original Frankenstein Monster, not the monsters that were created much later, such as that seen in a series of films from Universal Pictures.*

1801

A British captain and five of his lieutenants board a French ship and take an artifact, a bronze hand, as booty. The captain snaps off the five fingers, giving them to the lieutenants, and keeps the bronze palm for himself. The captain's name is Greystoke, and the other lieutenants are Holmes, Quatermain, Templar, Bond, and Roger Croft. (*Lara Croft: Tomb Raider: The Man of Bronze* by James Alan Gardner). The bronze hand split by Greystoke, Holmes, Quatermain, Templar, Bond, and Croft will endow their descendants with some sort of beneficial mutation. Captain Greystoke must be John William Clayton, the 3rd Duke of Greystoke. Holmes must be Dr. Siger Holmes. Both of these men were also present at the Wold Newton meteor strike in 1795. Allan Quatermain's father was a missionary in Africa, so Lieutenant Quatermain is probably Allan's uncle. Lieutenant Bond is the great-great-grandfather of British agent James Bond. Templar is a distant ancestor of Simon Templar, The Saint. Lieutenant Roger Croft is an ancestor of Lara Croft, the Tomb Raider.

ORLAK, EL INFIERNO DE FRANKENSTEIN
Dr. Carlos Frankenstein, a distant relative of Dr. Victor von Frankenstein, creates his own monster, Orlak, using his cousin's methods.
Feature film, 1960.

1802

THE WANTON PRINCESS
Roger Brook is posing as a Frenchman when Napoleon Bonaparte says to him: "You are almost as conceited as that gallant who commands the Hussars of Conflans. What's his name? Yes, Brigadier Gerrard."
Although author Dennis Wheatley spelt Gerard with an extra "r" in The Wanton Princess, *he uses the more common spelling later in* Evil in a Mask.

1803

May. The final events of *Doctor Syn: Death of Syn,* who, in his lifetime, has operated as the pirate Captain Clegg and as the night riding smuggler known as the Scarecrow of Romney Marsh.

Summer. Accountant Hickey J. Lubus retires and leaves New England for the Orient, in search of adventure. He first opens a gambling den in Japan ("The Black Demon's Sword" by Budd Lewis and Jose Ortiz, *Eerie* #87-89) before finally ending up as a pirate on the China seas ("Hickey and the Pirates" by Bill DuBay and Jose Ortiz, *Eerie* #99).

Summer
THE SECRET HISTORY OF THE PINK CARNATION
    Lord Richard Selwick follows in Sir Percy Blakeney's footsteps, albeit in a different masked identity, the Purple Gentian. Sir Percy retired as the Scarlet Pimpernel because his identity had been discovered. When the French government discovers that Selwick is the Purple Gentian, Selwick retires and the Pink Carnation founds her own organization.
    Novel by Lauren Willig, New American Library, 2005. Rick Lai notes that *"Although Chauvelin had learned Blakeney's identity in* The Scarlet Pimpernel, *set in 1792, Baroness Orczy's novels have Blakeney continuing to operate as the Pimpernel for two more years, up to the downfall of Robespierre in 1794. Since* The Secret History of the Pink Carnation *is set in 1803, it could be argued that Selwick actually succeeded Blakeney in 1794, and that Blakeney spread the false rumor that he retired two years earlier in order to make it more difficult for others to identify Selwick as the Purple Gentian."* Further books in the series are The Masque of the Black Tulip, The Deception of the Emerald Ring, The Seduction of the Crimson Rose, The Temptation of the Night Jasmine, *and* The Betrayal of the Blood Lily, *which continue to refer to Sir Percy Blakeney and the Scarlet Pimpernel.*

1804

The events of Paul Féval's *The Vampire Countess* (as translated and adapted by Brian Stableford, Black Coat Press, 2003).

1805

DRACULA VS. ZORRO
    Don Diego de la Vega, otherwise known as Zorro, fights against Count Dracula in Spain and France.
    This is a comic book miniseries/graphic novel published by Topps

Comics by Don McGregor and Thomas Yeates. The 1820 date given in the comic is inaccurate; see Matthew Baugh's "The Legacy of the Fox: Zorro in the Wold Newton Universe," Myths for the Modern Age: Philip José Farmer's Wold Newton Universe. Since Dracula is a part of the CU (see the Holmes-Dracula encounter in 1887), so too is Zorro. The Count Dracula featured here is the "real" Count or "Dracula-prime."

1805-Summer 1817

The events of Paul Féval's *John Devil* (*Jean Diable*; English translation and adaptation by Brian Stableford, Black Coat Press, 2005). *John Devil* takes place in the same continuity as Féval's Black Coats saga.

1806

CABALGANDO HACIA LA MUERTE
Don José de la Torre dons the mask of Zorro.
Feature film, 1962, also known as *L'Ombra di Zorro* (The Shadow of Zorro). Don José de la Torre is called "Zorro II," for our purposes); he is a distant descendant of the Zorros seen in Zorro Contro Maciste *and* Zorro E I Tre Moschietteri. He must have been inspired by the exploits of another man in Spanish California known as Zorro (Don Diego de la Vega).

1807

Spring
EVIL IN A MASK
British spy Roger Brook (still pretending to be a Frenchman) is captured by the Russians. One of his fellow captives is a French captain in the Hussars of Conflans. Brook remarks: "Indeed, you must be a brave fellow, since you hold that rank under such a dashing commander as Brigadier Gerard."
Rick Lai notes, "Denis Wheatley made several errors in his references to Gerard. He was a Lieutenant with the Tenth Hussars during 1802 and 1807. He first joins the Hussars of Conflans as a Captain in 1809 ('How the Brigadier Captured Saragossa'). He becomes their commanding colonel in 1810, and is promoted to a Brigadier in 1813. The cited dates are based on Jack Tracy's

chronology of the Gerard stories in the 1982 Jove paperbacks, Brigadier Gerard *and* The Return of Gerard.*"*

Summer. The Colonel establishes the Black Coats (Paul Féval's Black Coats saga.)

Summer
ZORRO AND THE MOUNTAIN MAN
American mountain man Joe Crane comes to Los Angeles and Zorro helps him out of some trouble.
Episodes #63-65 of Disney's Zorro *television series. The titles of all three episodes were: "Zorro and the Mountain Man," "The Hound of the Sierras," and "Manhunt." Joe Crane was also a regular on another Walt Disney series,* The Saga of Andy Burnett, *and actor Jeff York played Crane in both series. This crossover brings Andy Burnett into the Crossover Universe.*

1808

July 18. Birth of Prince Dakkar of India (Verne's *The Mysterious Island*), the son of Rajah Dakkar of Bundelcund, a Capellean (Farmer's *The Other Log of Phileas Fogg*). Later in his life, Prince Dakkar will call himself "Captain Nemo."

Summer
MEN AREN'T THE ONLY ONES WITH DUAL IDENTITIES
Anita Santiago goes into action as the incredible Lady Rawhide, Zorro's sometime-enemy and sometime-ally.
#3 of Topps' Zorro *series by Don McGregor and Mike Mayhew introduced the heroine Lady Rawhide to the CU. She went on to individual adventures in two comic book miniseries.*

1809

Birth of C. Auguste Dupin.

1810

OTHER PEOPLE'S BLOOD
Lady Rawhide lies bleeding and near death after various battles. One of Dracula's spawn, Carmelita Rodriguez (see Dracula vs. Zorro), is on the same ship as Lady Rawhide, and after denying her vampiric urges for so long, Carmelita can no longer resist. But in Carmelita's feeding on Lady Rawhide, she is also saving her life.

This is in the second Lady Rawhide *solo miniseries published by Topps Comics, written by Don McGregor and illustrated by Esteban Maroto, which abruptly ended mid-series with #5. Does this mean that Lady Rawhide became a vampire too? In #5, Lady Rawhide has regained her health and goes on to further battle, and there the series ends. Scholar John Small believes that she went on to become a well-known vampire, with whom Lady Rawhide shares many shapely characteristics and attributes (see "Kiss of the Vampire," Myths for the Modern Age: Philip José Farmer's Wold Newton Universe).*

1810-1811

THE ANUBIS GATES
Brendan Doyle is transported back in time from the year 1983 to London in September 1810, where his life becomes inextricably entwined with that of the somewhat obscure poet, Sir William Ashbless (1785?-1846?).
A novel by Tim Powers, Ace Books, 1983. A 20th-century William Ashbless—possibly the same person as the Ashbless in Powers' novel—figured prominently in James Blaylock's The Digging Leviathan, *which takes place in the CU through its connection to Pellucidar. Tarzan, a Wold Newton Family member, visited Pellucidar on several occasions. Although this story begins in 1983, the bulk of the action takes place in 1810-1811, so I have chosen to place it there in the timeline.*

1810-1840

Events of *Les Mystères de Londres* (*The Mysteries of London* aka *Gentlemen of the Night*) a precursor to Paul Féval's Black Coats saga.

1810s-1830

The events of William Makepeace Thackeray's *Vanity Fair: A Novel without a Hero.*

1811-1814

French general Tullius Beringheld encounters the immortal vampire-like alchemist Count Maxime Beringheld Sculdans. (*The Centenarian* by Honore de Balzac.)

Rick Lai notes that "The Centenarian briefly has a French scientist writing a letter to a fellow savant named James Gordon living in Paris. Since this letter is written during the closing years of the Napoleonic Wars, James is most likely an American. He could be the father of Gaboriau's Arthur Gordon."

December 24, 1812-Winter 1840

Events of Charles Dickens' *Great Expectations*.

1814

Summer
SHARPE'S JUSTICE
Major Richard Sharpe tangles with a young Captain of the Yorkshire militia, George Wickham.

This is a British television movie based on Bernard Cornwell's Richard Sharpe *novels. This might be the same George Wickham seen in Jane Austen's* Pride and Prejudice. *However, this tale is set in 1814, and the George Wickham seen here seems to be in his twenties or early thirties, while the George Wickham in* Pride and Prejudice *would have been about fifty by this point. Additionally, Sharpe's Wickham is still in the militia, while the Wickham in* Pride and Prejudice *takes a commission in the regular army at the end of that novel. Most likely, the Wickham seen here is George Wickham, Jr. The Wickham connection brings in Richard Sharpe, since Darcy and Elizabeth Bennet from* Pride and Prejudice *are mentioned prominently in Farmer's Wold Newton Family Tree. Richard Sharpe has at least three children; one of them appears in Cornwell's* Starbuck *series of Civil War novels, thus bringing those books into the CU.*

1815

Spring. Lord Ruthven is introduced in John Polidori's *The Vampyre*, reprinted in *Lord Ruthven, the Vampire*, Black Coat Press, 2004.

Summer. Zorro II is imprisoned (*Las Hijas del Zorro* [*The Daughters of Zorro*], feature film, 1963).

1815-1853

A VERY ENGLISH AGENT
Charlie Boylan works for British Intelligence as an agent licensed to kill under the code of "003." Captain Quex is the quartermaster and Armouror to British Intelligence. Boylan entrusts secret documents to Mr. Guppy. Inspector Bucket also appears, but he withdraws from the case to investigate a murder (the murder in *Bleak House*) and Sergeant Cuff takes over. The Darcys also appear.

Novel by Julian Rathbone. The double-0 numbering of agents is from Ian Fleming's James Bond series. Implicitly, Q-Branch (from the Bond films rather than books) is named after Captain Quex. Mr. Guppy and Inspector Bucket are from Charles Dickens' Bleak House. Bucket's surname derives from Huguenot ancestors called "Bouquet," a reference to the comedy series Keeping Up Appearances. Sergeant Cuff is the detective from Wilkie Collins' The Moonstone. The Darcys are from Pride and Prejudice. The novel concludes leaving the reader unsure if these were real events or made up out of whole cloth by Boylan; the breakup of the Darcys' marriage, in particular, is suspect.

1815-1838

The events of Alexandre Dumas' *Le Comte de Monte-Cristo* (*The Count of Monte-Cristo*).

1817

Birth of Allan Quatermain. Although not descended from those present at the Wold Newton meteor strike in 1795, Farmer's *Doc Savage* does list Quatermain as an ancestor of several prominent Wold Newton Family members.

1818

ZORRO AND THE BRUJA
Zorro faces Doña Inez, a woman known as the Bruja. Inez has a young boy named Ysidro who assists her, and an arcane golden charm known as the "Talisman of Byagoona."

Short story by Matthew Baugh in More Tales of Zorro, Richard Dean Starr, ed., Moonstone Books, 2010. Though the story does not make it explicit, the villain is the same as the character who will menace Mysterious Dave Mather in 1880.

1819

ONE FOR ALL
While in France, Zorro has an adventure with the descendants of Athos, Porthos, Aramis, and D'Artagnan.

This is a 1991 two-part episode of New World television series Zorro, *confirming Dumas'* The Three Musketeers *and related novels in the CU. Zorro scholar Matthew Baugh interprets this as an adventure of Don Diego Vega's son, Don Cesar Vega.*

1820

Summer
ZORRO'S RIVAL
Zorro meets Violette Durand, who is visiting El Pueblo de Los Angeles with her father, M. Durand, a traveling merchant.
Short story by Win Scott Eckert in More Tales of Zorro, Richard Dean Starr, ed., Moonstone Books, 2010. Violette Yvonne Durand is actually M. Durand's adopted daughter. Her real parents are Sir Percy Blakeney and his wife, Marguerite St. Just Blakeney. The tale of how and why she and her sister, Hélène, were adopted by the Durand family has yet to be told.

Autumn. Tivel van Helsing sails with Captain Ahab. (*Crépuscule Vaudou* aka *The Katrina Protocol,* Jean-Marc Lofficier).

1822

Spring. Birth of Harry Paget Flashman. Farmer's *Doc Savage* also includes Flashman in the Wold Newton Family Tree. Flashman is a character in Thomas Hughes' *Tom Brown's Schooldays,* thus incorporating that work into the CU.
Summer. Birth of Rocambole.

1823

Events of Paul Féval's *The Companions of Silence.*

1826

Corrupt English nobleman Lord Henry Seymour begins a series of crimes in France. (*The Mylord L'arsouille* series by Noel Marin.)

1827

April
EDGAR ALLAN POE ON MARS
Struggling author Edgar Allan Poe and his companion Ligeia find themselves transported to Mars' distant past, where Poe teams up with Gullivar Jones to defeat the mad necromancer Rodrik-Usher. Poe and Ligeia are also briefly

transported to 1840 Paris where they meet detective C. Auguste Dupin; in the bar of l'Epi-Scié they meet Coyatier, aka the Marchef, the Colonel's personal executioner from the Black Coats. There are also references to the Rue Morgue case. Gullivar Jones uses the incantation "Ka nama Ka lajerama." Although Gullivar Jones traveled to Mars from the 1890s, he journeyed through time to arrive on ancient Mars, millions of years ago.

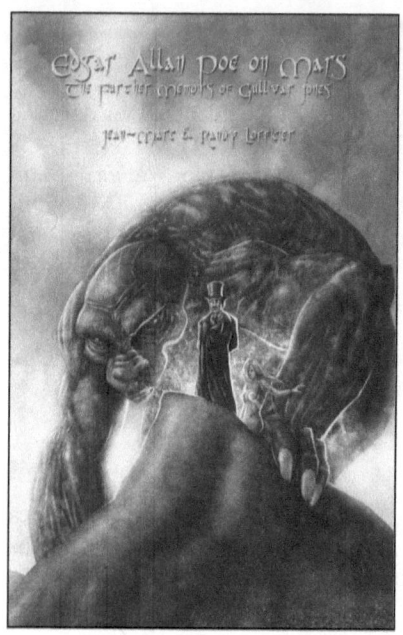

Novel by Randy and Jean-Marc Lofficier, Black Coat Press, December 2007. Note that Gullivar Jones and Edgar Allan Poe were transported to Mars (which is the same as John Carter's Barsoom) for this adventure from their respective time periods. Gullivar Jones' original trip to Mars occurred in the 1890s. Jean-Marc Lofficier adds, "The Mars action takes place in the very distant past and includes references to the Martians of Doctor Omega *(the Macrochephales and the reptilian polar Ice Warriors-type race)*, and the Ancient Mars of Leigh Brackett's Sword of Rhiannon *(Sark, Caer Dhu)*, in addition of course to references from Gullivar of Mars *(Seth, Princess Heru, Phra, etc.)*. The story explains how Mars eventually became a dead world and some of the Martians moved to Earth and became our ancestors." The incantation "Ka nama Ka lajerama" is from the works of Robert E Howard. The Epi-Scié bar is mentioned in virtually every Black Coats novel, and Coyatier is a prominent figure in the books 'Salem Street *and* The Invisible Weapon.

Summer. Events of Charles Dickens' *The Pickwick Papers*. Samuel Pickwick's landlady is named Mrs. Martha Bardell. Almost a hundred years later, Mrs. Martha Bardell served as Sexton Blake's landlady. Perhaps the latter Mrs. Bardell married a descendant of the first Mrs. Bardell.

1827-1828

The tale of Arthur Gordon Pym's expedition to the Antarctic, told by Edgar Allan Poe in *The Narrative of Arthur Gordon Pym of Nantucket* (recently reprinted in the anthology *The Antarktos Cycle*, Chaosium, 1999). Later in his career, Pym will use the alias "Captain Nemo" as a cover for his own piratical activities.

1828

Ithamar van Helsing meets Captain Obed Marsh and battles the Esoteric Order of Dagon. (Jean-Marc Lofficier, *Crépuscule Vaudou* aka *The Katrina Protocol*).

1829

March 22. Artemus Gordon is born.

Summer. Birth of Monsieur Lecoq. An ancestor of Lecoq is mentioned in Farmer's *Tarzan Alive* as one of the coachmen present at the Wold Newton meteor strike.

Summer. Birth of Aharon van Helsing to Tivel van Helsing and Rosalie Mayfair, one of the Mayfair witches. Their daughter Danya (b. 1831) will keep the maiden name Mayfair, and in 1859 will give birth to Blodgett Mayfair, the father of Andrew Blodgett "Monk" Mayfair. (Jean-Marc Lofficier's *Crépuscule Vaudou* aka *The Katrina Protocol*).

1830s-1843

Main events of Paul Féval's Black Coats saga: *The Blackcoats: 'Salem Street, The Invisible Weapon, The Parisian Jungle, Heart of Steel, The Companions of the Treasure,* and *The Cadet Gang* (all translated by Brian Stableford and available from Black Coat Press).

1831-c. 1840s

THE PASSION OF FRANKENSTEIN

Victor Hugo is accosted by Frankenstein's Creature, who demands that Hugo introduce him to Quasimodo; but Hugo cannot, as Quasimodo, even if he was real, must be dead these many hundreds of years. A few years later, Alexandre Dumas père has a vision in which it is revealed that as Esmeralda was being put to death in Notre-Dame de Paris, Count Dracula came to Quasimodo and offered to save her. Dracula and Quasimodo succeeded, apparently in exchange for future vampiric servitude to the Count. Dumas père ignores his vision as a dream. Later still, the Creature reveals that he went to Doctor Faustus, seeking the secret to travel back in time and meet Quasimodo. Hugo approaches Dumas and asks him to try to channel another vision, in order to determine what happened when the Creature traveled to the past. Dumas has another vision and reveals that the Creature arrived just as Dracula did. Thinking Dracula was attacking Quasimodo, the Creature interfered, and thus prevented Esmeralda's rescue. Cagliostro and the Comte de Saint Germain are also mentioned.

Short story by Frank J. Morlock in Frankenstein Meets the Hunchback of Notre-Dame, *Black Coat Press, June 2005. Since Frankenstein and Dracula are in the CU, so too are the events of Victor Hugo's* Notre-Dame de Paris *and Christopher Marlowe's* Doctor Faustus. *The story places the events of* Notre-Dame de Paris *in 1481.*

1832

Spring. Birth of Phileas Fogg.

Philip José Farmer's Wold Newton Family Tree in Doc Savage *places Fogg as the biological son of Sir William Clayton. Art Bollmann notes, "The 1981 Baen Books edition of Farmer's* Father to the Stars *has a blurb on the back by Phileas Fogg. The blurb treats the work as fiction but it does show that the immortal Fogg of* The Other Log of Phileas Fogg *exists in the same universe as Farmer, and is aware of his work."*

1833

Summer. The two daughter of Zorro II (Don José de la Torre), now grown, don masks and capes themselves (*Las Hijas del Zorro*).

According to the speculations of Jess Nevins, after their father is freed, Zorro II goes on to several more exploits. This is the Zorro seen in the Mexican films Zorro alla corte di Spagna *(1962),* El Zorro *(1968), and* Zorro alla corte d'Inghilterra *(1969), although biographers of Zorro II changed the names used in the fictional recounting of his exploits. One of his daughters also had a further adventure as seen in the film in* Le Sorelle di Zorro *(1966). Nevins adds, "When those daughters had children of their own, those children carried on the good fight, most as Zorro, the Fox, but one as 'El Látigo,' the Whip, from the Mexican film series* El Látigo *(1978),* El Látigo contra Satanás *(1979), and* El Látigo contra las momias asesinas *(1980), in which El Látigo fights animated mummies—in the company of the time-traveling luchador Tinieblas, who was a member of Los Campeones Justiciero along with El Santo."*

1834

Summer. Birth of Sherringford Holmes.

Summer
LE DÉTECTIVE VOLÉ: EDGAR POE ET SHERLOCK HOLMES

Using H.G. Wells' time machine, Sherlock Holmes travels to 1834 Paris, where he meets Eugène François Vidocq of the Sûreté, as well as the criminal Pierre-François Lacenaire. He then goes on to America, where he encounters Edgar Allan Poe.

Novel by René Reouven, Denoël, Paris, 1988.

1835

February 9-April 13
MAY THE GROUND NOT CONSUME THEE...

Lord Ruthven encounters Lord Wilmore (aka Edmond Dantès, aka the Count of Monte Cristo, aka Abbé Busoni), as well as Noirtier de Villefort, Renée de Saint-Meran, and Haydée. The late Ianthe also appears, inhabiting a new body.

Short story by Micah Harris in Tales of the Shadowmen Volume 5: The Vampires of Paris, *Jean-Marc and Randy Lofficier, eds., Black Coat Press, 2009; reprinted in French in* Les Compagnons de l'Ombre (Tome 6), *Jean-Marc and Randy Lofficier, eds., Rivière Blanche, 2010. The story also has flashbacks to February and April 1834. Lord Ruthven is from John Polidori's* The Vampyre; *Ianthe is a girl whom Ruthven killed. Edmond Dantès, Noirtier de Villefort, Renée de Saint-Meran, and Haydée are from Alexandre Dumas'* The Count of Monte Cristo.

Autumn. The events of Charles Dickens' Oliver Twist, which, per Farmer's *Doc Savage*, takes place in the CU.

Autumn. Birth of Colonel James Clayton Moriarty, son of Sir William Clayton and Morcar Moriarty (per Farmer's *Doc Savage*). Curiously he is the oldest of three brothers, all named James. Morcar's brother is Jerrold Moriarty. Jerrold becomes a favorite uncle and father figure to the three Moriarty brothers.

1836

February-March
OLE DEVIL HARDIN

Ole Devil Hardin is sent to collect a consignment of Caplock Rifles for the newly formed Republic of Texas. During the mission, he fights off Mexican-backed rebels led by Randolph Galsworthy and his wife Madeline de Moreau.

Young Ole Devil, *a novel in the Ole Devil Hardin series by J.T. Edson. Takes place February 18-25, 1836. Madeline de Moreau is undoubtedly related to Dr. Alphonse Moreau who will conduct strange experiments in the 1880s and 1890s.*

Ole Devil takes possession of a consignment of Caplock rifles from a friend, Beauregard Rassendyll of New Orleans.

Ole Devil and the Caplocks, *a novel in the Ole Devil Hardin series by J.T. Edson. Takes place February 26-27, 1836. Beauregard Rassendyll must be related to the Rudolph Rassendyll seen in Anthony Hope's* A Prisoner of Zenda.

Ole Devil eventually delivers the rifles to General Houston. Along the way, they have to fight off the Mexican Patrol, which is led by Major Abraham Phillipe Gonzales de Villena y Danvila, a relative of Colonel José Gonzales de Villena y Danvila.

Ole Devil and the Mule Train, *a novel in the Ole Devil Hardin series by J.T. Edson. Takes place February 28-Early March 1836. Colonel José Gonzales de Villena y Danvila faced Captain Horatio Hornblower as recorded in Chapter XIII of* Ship of the Line *by C.S. Forester.*

Autumn. Birth of Professor James Robert Moriarty, son of master criminal Dr. James Noel and Morcar Moriarty (per Farmer's *Doc Savage: His Apocalyptic Life,* with modifications to Farmer's theory by Rick Lai's "The Secret History of Captain Nemo," *Myths for the Modern Age: Philip José Farmer's Wold Newton Universe*). He is one of three men who will use the identity of "Captain Nemo."

1837

Summer. First recorded adventure of Charles O'Malley, an Irish dragoon. (*Charles O'Malley, The Irish Dragoon,* 1838, by Charles Lever.) In 1903, Nick Carter would be assisted on one case by Charles O'Malley, an Irish detective who in appearance, speech, and mannerisms is so similar to the Irish dragoon Charles O'Malley that the detective must be the grandson or great-grandson of the dragoon. (*New Nick Carter Weekly* #380, April 16, 1904.) Jess Nevins notes, "O'Malley appeared a third time, albeit under the name 'Barney O'Murphy' (but it's O'Malley, the same way that 'Aristide Dupin' is Arsène Lupin) in the 1878-1879 penny dreadful *English Jack Amongst the Afghans,* which is set in Afghanistan during the Second Afghan War (1878-1880), the same conflict in which Doctor Watson got his wound(s)."

October 20. Miguelito Loveless is born.

December 24-25. A Christmas Carol, as related by Charles Dickens.

1838

Events of the film *Nosferatu*.

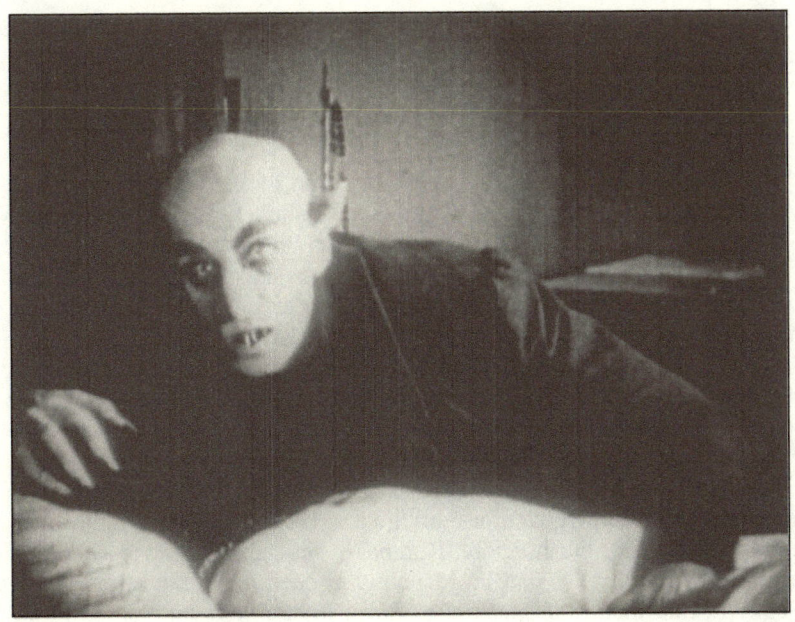

December 1839-March 1840

THE SPHINX OF THE ICE FIELDS
This adventure contains many references to Arthur Gordon Pym. Captain Nemo's conquest of the South Pole is also mentioned in a footnote.

Jules Verne's sequel to Edgar Allan Poe's The Narrative of Arthur Gordon Pym; *reprinted in the anthology* The Antarktos Cycle, *Chaosium, 1999. The cycle of stories continues in John W. Campbell, Jr.'s* Who Goes There? *and H.P. Lovecraft's* At the Mountains of Madness, *both also republished in* The Antarktos Cycle. *The mention of Nemo also ties in with Verne's own* 20,000 Leagues under the Sea.

c. 1840s-50s

Uncle Abner solves mysteries in the mountain district of Virginia. (*Uncle Abner, Master of Mysteries* by Melville Davisson Post.)

c. 1840s

EL LÁTIGO CONTRA LAS MOMIAS ASESINAS
The luchador Tinieblas travels back in time to help El Látigo against murderous mummies.
Feature film, Mexico, 1980. Since Tinieblas is in the CU via a 2004 crossover, so is El Látigo.

1840

Winter. Birth of James Douglas Henry, son of the legendary John Henry and grandson of Sir William Clayton (see Dennis E. Power's "Wold Wold West" on *The Wold Newton Universe: A Secret History* website).

Winter. Birth of James Noel Moriarty (the third Moriarty brother), the second son of Dr. James Noel and Morcar Moriarty. He will later assume the identity of his older brother, Professor James Moriarty.

Autumn. Birth of Fu Manchu. According to Farmer's *Doc Savage*, Fu Manchu is the son of Sir William Clayton and Ling Ju Hai. The birth date is derived directly from a close reading of Sax Rohmer's Fu Manchu series, wherein it is revealed that Fu Manchu served as the governor of Honan province under the Empress Dowager Tz'u-hsi. Farmer demonstrates that it is likely that Fu Manchu did not become governor until the late 1870s, when he would have been over thirty years old. Furthermore, Rohmer's *The Island of Fu Manchu*, which takes place in 1940, states that Fu Manchu has been falsifying scientists' deaths and conscripting them into his service for at least sixty years (since 1880). He had to be an adult when he began this practice.

1841-1845

C. Auguste Dupin's cases, as related by Edgar Allan Poe: "*The Murders in the Rue Morgue,*" "*The Mystery of Marie Rogêt,*" and "*The Purloined Letter.*" Farmer's *Tarzan Alive* established Dupin as a Wold Newton Family member. Michael Harrison continued the Dupin stories with seven pastiches, compiled in *The Exploits of the Chevalier Dupin*. Gérard Dôle has collected more Dupin cases in *The Adventures of C. Auguste Dupin*, which are available in both French and English. John Peel has provided another Dupin case, "The Kind-Hearted Torturer," as has Samuel T. Payne with his "Lacunal Visions," and Dennis E. Power with his "No Good Deed..." In 1849, Dupin investigated Poe's death in *The Murder of Edgar Allan Poe*, as told by George Egon Hatvary. Dupin also went on to appear in *The League of Extraordinary Gentlemen*.

December 1841-early 1842

The events of *Moby Dick*, as told by Ishmael, related by Herman Melville.

1842

Spring
THE KIND-HEARTED TORTURER
In Paris, detective C. Auguste Dupin teams up with Edmond Dantès, the Count of Monte-Cristo, to defeat a gang of nefarious Black Coats kidnappers. Marguerite Sadoulas, the Countess of Clare, also appears.

Short story by John Peel in Tales of the Shadowmen Volume 1: The Modern Babylon, *Jean-Marc and Randy Lofficier, eds., Black Coat Press, 2005; reprinted in French in* Les Compagnons de l'Ombre (Tome 1), *Jean-Marc and Randy Lofficier, eds., Rivière Blanche, 2008. The Black Coats saga was written by Paul Féval; the Countess of Clare appears in a cameo in the first volume, and has a larger role in the second. This crossover brings Edmond Dantès and the events of Alexandre Dumas'* The Count of Monte-Cristo *into the CU.*

LA MYSTÉRIEUSE ANTARCTIDE
An Antarctic expedition includes a Randolph Carter, his fiancée Audrey Jeorling, Dirk Peters, and cabin boy Jules Verne, age fourteen. When they reach the Sphinx discovered by Arthur Gordon Pym, they find that it guards a dimensional gate. Randolph, Audrey, Dirk, and the crew cross the dimensional barrier, while Verne sails back to France.

Story by Christian Vilà, a sequel to Edgar Poe's The Narrative of Arthur Gordon Pym *and Jules Verne's* The Sphinx of the Ice Fields *in* La Machine à remonter les rêves: Les Enfants de Jules Verne *(*The Dream Machine: The Children of Jules Verne*), Mnémos, 2005. Randolph Carter is obviously an ancestor of H.P. Lovecraft's Randolph Carter of Arkham, Massachusetts. Dirk Peters must have somehow survived* The Sphinx of the Ice Fields *to return one last time.*

Summer. The Duke of Gerolstein changes lives and fights evil in Paris. (Eugène Sue's *Les Mystères de Paris* [*The Mysteries of Paris*].)

1843

March 1. James T. West is born.

Summer. The events of Robert Louis Stevenson's "The Pavilion on the Links," found in the volume *New Arabian Nights*. Per Lai's "The Secret History of Captain Nemo," Bernard Huddlestone, the prominent banker in the story, is the uncle of Morcar Moriarty, and therefore the great-uncle of the three Moriarty brothers.

1844

Winter. Young Phileas Fogg, adopted son of Sir Heraclitus Fogg, an original Eridanean, undergoes a blood-sharing ceremony that enables him to become a full human-Eridanean and gives him a lifespan of one thousand years (Farmer's *The Other Log of Phileas Fogg*).
Winter. Bleak House by Charles Dickens.
Winter. Tonto is born.

1844-45

Rocambole's first recorded adventure, *L'Héritage Mystérieux* by Pierre Alexis Ponson du Terrail.

1844-1892

The historical novel *Raintree County* by Ross Lockridge, Jr., takes place in the CU as established in Farmer's *Doc Savage*.

1845

LACUNAL VISIONS
C. Auguste Dupin joins with Parisian police Sergeant Picard to solve the case of an ongoing series of thefts from watchmakers and clock repair shops. One of the watchmakers is Maître Zacharius of Verdain Street. The mysterious Doctor Omega also figures in the case.

Short story by Samuel T. Payne in Tales of the Shadowmen Volume 1: The Modern Babylon, *Jean-Marc and Randy Lofficier, eds., Black Coat Press, 2005; reprinted in French in* Les Compagnons de l'Ombre (Tome 4), *Jean-Marc and Randy Lofficier, eds., Rivière Blanche, 2009. Sergeant Paul Picard would later become Inspector Picard, as seen in William Kotzwinkle's novel* Fata Morgana. *Picard is surely an ancestor of* Star Trek: The Next Generation*'s Captain Jean-Luc Picard. Maître Zacharius is from Jules Verne's story "Maître Zacharius ou l'horloger qui avait perdu son âme" ("Master Zacharius or the clock and watch maker who had lost his heart"). "Lacunal Visions" explains how he got access to the strange time technology in Verne's tale. Doctor Omega is from a novel by Arnould Galopin, adapted and retold by Jean-Marc and Randy Lofficier.*

1847

February 12. Birth of Mycroft Holmes. As stated in Farmer's *Tarzan Alive* and *Doc Savage*, the Holmeses are prominent Wold Newton Family members.
Summer. Abner Perry is born in New England.
Summer. The events of *L'Assommoir*, as told by Emile Zola.

1848

Autumn. Events of David Copperfield, as related by Charles Dickens.
September 14. Reid is born. He will become The Lone Ranger.

1849

Spring. Wilkie Collins' *The Moonstone*.
Summer. First known exploit in America of Spanish adventurer Don César de Echagüe, "El Coyote." (*El Coyote* series by José Mallorquí.)

Summer
ROCAMBOLE: RED IN TOOTH AND CLAW
In London, Rocambole wins a bundle at the rat pit fights. The following appear or are mentioned: Café Royal, de Guéran, d'Ardeche, the Doge of Venice, a small black monkey, Gordon Street, Speed, Treadgold, Louis Froget, John Sinnat, a false declaration of war, the Countess of Clare, the Duke of Gerolstein, Emile Benoit, Albanian Brown, Sten de la Gardie, Archipelago Street, Gray's Inn Road, a priory rat, Qwghlm, the Spanish naturalist, Sumatra, "Fan...cy...friends," the Dragon, the Vulture, Snarleyyow, Miss Voyant, Coyle, Red Shadows, Abraham the Gentle, Inspector Bucket, Sergeant Cuff, Hunt, Creegan, Fitz, Tennison, and Doc Blake.
Short story by Jess Nevins in Tales of the Shadowmen Volume 4: Lords of Terror, *Jean-Marc and Randy Lofficier, eds., Black Coat Press, 2008; reprinted*

in French in Les Compagnons de l'Ombre (Tome 5), Jean-Marc and Randy Lofficier, eds., Rivière Blanche, 2009. Rocambole is from the tales by Pierre-Alexis Ponson du Terrail. The Café Royal is from Clarence Rook's "The Stir Outside the Café Royal." De Guéran is from Adolphe Belot's A Parisian Sultana. D'Ardeche is from Ralph Adams Cram's "No. 252 Rue M. le Prince," (which also brings in Cram's "The Dead Valley" and "Sister Maddelena"). The Doge of Venice is from Cutcliffe Hyne's Captain Kettle stories. The small black monkey is from J.S. Le Fanu's "Green Tea." Regarding the false declaration of war, a similar trick was later played by Zenith the Albino. Gordon Street is from the Tom Hypnos stories. Speed is Lord Speedicut, from George Macdonald Fraser's Flashman books. Treadgold is from Valentine Williams' Mister Treadgold stories. Louis Froget is from Georges Simenon's Monsieur Froget stories (Rocambole clearly knew of Froget's ancestor). John Sinnat is from S.B.H. Hurst's Bugs Sinnat stories (this is Bugs' grandfather). The Countess of Clare is a character in Féval's Black Coats saga. The Duke of Gerolstein is from Eugène Sue's The Mysteries of Paris. Emile Benoit is from Charles Robert-Dumas' Commandant Benoit's novels (Rocambole clearly knew of Benoit's ancestor). Sten de la Gardie is from M.R. James' "Count Magnus" (Rocambole obviously knew of Count Magnus' descendant). Archipelago Street was seen in Henry Hering's Mr. Psyche stories. Gray's Inn Road is from the Dixon Brett stories. The priory rat refers to H.P. Lovecraft's "The Rats in the Walls." Qwghlm is from Neal Stephenson's Baroque Cycle. The Spanish naturalist is Stephen Maturin, from Patrick O'Brian's Aubrey and Maturin novels. Sumatra is a real place, but here it refers to the Giant Rat of Sumatra, which was mentioned as an untold Holmes case in "The Adventure of the Sussex Vampire." "Fan...cy...friends": reverse the syllables of "fancy" yields "cyfan," or "Si-Fan," the implication being that Jack Black got the Sumatran rat from the Si-Fan, who are introducing the Giant Rat of Sumatra into England as an act of terrorism. The Dragon is from the stories of Robert Macaire. The Vulture is from Ben Conlon's Pete Rice stories. Snarleyyow is from Frederick Marryat's novel of the same name. Miss Voyant refers to Jack Sparling's Claire Voyant comic strip; she is an ancestor of Claire Voyant. The Coyle here is Coyle's grandfather from Hugh Pentecost's Danny Coyle novels. The reference to Red

Shadows is from the Nick Kennedy stories. Inspector Bucket is from Charles Dickens' Bleak House, *while Sergeant Cuff is from Wilkie Collins'* The Moonstone. *Hunt is Gene Hunt's ancestor from the television series* Life on Mars. *Creegan is Dave Creegan's ancestor from the television program* Touching Evil. *Fitz is Fitzgerald's ancestor, from the television series* Cracker. *Tennison is Jane Tennison's ancestor from the television series* Prime Suspect. *Doc Blake is meant to be Sexton Blake's father. Albanian Brown and Abraham the Gentle are characters original to Nevins.*

November 1849-January 1850

C. Auguste Dupin investigates the death of his friend in *The Murder of Edgar Allan Poe*, as told by George Egon Hatvary.

1850

Spring
JERUSALEM'S LOT
A copy of *De Vermis Mysteriis* appears, and the entity Yos-sothoth (Yog-Sothoth) is mentioned.
Short story by Stephen King, found in the collection Night Shift. *Both are from the Cthulhu Mythos, bringing this story into the CU, as well as the novel* 'Salem's Lot, *and, from there, most of the "Stephen King Universe." According to Mike Winkle, "If you read Robert Bloch's 'Shambler from the Stars' before 'Jerusalem's Lot,' you'll realize the sacrificed animal in 'Lot' has been sucked dry by the Shambler, which was a vampiric being from space. And 'Shambler' was the first of a trilogy, it being followed by HPL's 'Haunter of the Dark,' and that by Bloch's 'Shadow from the Steeple.'" It should also be noted that since the main Stephen King Universe is included, many of the works of Tabitha King are also linked. For instance, her novels have references to the Shawshank State Prison and Chamberlain (the town from* Carrie*). And one of Tabitha King's major female characters is hinted to be the daughter of the black psychic from* The Shining.

Spring. Birth of private detective Eugene Valmont, whose cases were recorded by Robert Barr (*The Triumphs of Eugene Valmont*). While in London from 1893-1906, Valmont also lived in the Soho district under the alias Professor Paul Ducharme. The real Paul Ducharme was the son of "Baccarat," the courtesan Louise Charmet, from Ponson du Terrail's Rocambole series. Professor Ducharme committed suicide after being dismissed from his position. Valmont took his identity upon moving to London and becoming a private detective. But before Ducharme died, he had a son who in turn fathered Louise Ducharme (b. 1902), the doctor in Guy D'Armen's *Doc Ardan: City of Gold and*

Lepers. This would also make Paul Ducharme the great-grandfather of Dr. Justine Ducharme (b. 1928), the daughter of Doc Savage ("Doctor Francis Ardan") as seen in the story "The Vanishing Devil."

c. Early-Mid 1850s

ENTRETIEN WITH A VAMPIRE
Alexandre Dumas père is threatened with financial ruin unless he agrees to forgo staging his stage play about Lord Ruthven, *Le Vampire*. The man threatening Dumas is Sir Williams, who is revealed to actually be Lord Ruthven. Sir Williams' underling, Rocambole, also appears.

Short story by Frank J. Morlock in The Return of Lord Ruthven, *Black Coat Press, October 2004. The story contradicts the established origins of Sir Williams as Andrea de Felipone. To resolve this, one must assume the real Sir Williams/Andrea died as established in the Rocambole books and Lord Ruthven just assumed the Sir Williams identity.*

1851

EL COYOTE
The Californian masked vigilante El Coyote is compared to the English adventurer Dick Turpin.
Novel by José Mallorquí, 1943.

1852

Summer. In Rome, Aharon van Helsing marries Maria Walker, granddaughter of the 15th Phantom. (*Crépuscule Vaudou* aka *The Katrina Protocol* by Jean-Marc Lofficier.)

Summer 1852-1858. Events of Paul Féval's *The Sword Swallower*, last entry in the Black Coats saga.

August 7. Birth of John H. Watson.

1853

NO GOOD DEED...

Young newsboy Jean lives at an orphanage run by Abbé Théodore Fausse-Maigre. Jean has received some tips in pickpocketing from an Englishman named Charley Bates. The young newsboy becomes involved in one of armchair detective Père Tabaret's rare failures, the conviction of tailor Césaire Derème for his wife's murder. After speaking with Père Tabaret's nemesis, Inspector Gévrol, and Derème is released, Jean is paid a visit by the Chevalier Auguste Dupin. Witnesses later describe a tall Asian with flaming green eyes or a tall, bald Asian with bright, yellow eyes.

Short story by Dennis E. Power in Tales of the Shadowmen Volume 6: Grand Guignol, *Jean-Marc and Randy Lofficier, eds., Black Coat Press, 2010; published in French in* Les Compagnons de l'Ombre (Tome 7), *Jean-Marc and Randy Lofficier, eds., Rivière Blanche, 2010. Père Tabaret, Inspector Gévrol, and Césaire Derème are from Emile Gaboriau's* L'Affaire Lerouge *(1866), which also introduced police detective Monsieur Lecoq. Jean will later become much better known as Jean Passepartout from Jules Verne's* Around the World in Eighty Days. *Charley Bates is from Charles Dickens'* Oliver Twist. *Abbé Théodore Fausse-Maigre is the author of* The Higher Common Sense, *in Stella Gibbons' 1932 novel* Cold Comfort Farm. *C. Auguste Dupin is from Edgar Allan Poe's "The Murders in the Rue Morgue" and other stories. The tall Asian with flaming green eyes might be Guy d'Armen's Doctor Natas (aka Sax Rohmer's Fu Manchu), but Doctor Fu Manchu was born in 1840. The tall, bald Asian with bright, yellow eyes could be Monsieur Ming from Henri Vernes' Bob Morane novels.*

1854

January 6. Birth of Sherlock Holmes at a farmstead in the North Riding of Yorkshire.

Summer. Birth of Martin Hewitt.

1855

Spring. Events of Anthony Trollope's *The Warden.*

Autumn. Professor Augustus S.F.X. Van Dusen (aka "the Thinking Machine") is born.

1856

Winter. Birth of Russian detective Erast Petrovich Fandorin.

Summer
ROCAMBOLE ET LE SPECTRE DE KERLOVEN (ROCAMBOLE AND THE SPECTRE OF KERLOVEN)
   Rocambole clashes with the Black Coats, now led by his former boss Sir Williams.
   Novel by Michel Honaker, 2002. The book says it takes place "around 1830," which seems impossible according to the chronology of Rocambole's other adventures. This links Rocambole to Paul Féval's Black Coats saga. Again, is the "Sir Williams" seen here really Lord Ruthven, as established in "Entretien with a Vampire"?

1857

   Spring. Birth of Lord John Roxton, a Wold Newton Family member, as stated in Farmer's *Tarzan Alive*.
   Autumn. Victor Frankenstein III creates the second Monster as seen in the film The Horror of Frankenstein. Researcher Mark Brown has proposed that there were several generations of Frankenstein doctors, resulting in the creation of several different creatures.

1858

   Summer. Twin sons are born to the first Professor James Moriarty. Throughout his long life, one twin will call himself "Wolf Larsen," "Baron Karl von Hessel," and simply "Baron Karl." The other twin is known as "Death Larsen." (For more information, see Christopher Paul Carey's "The Green Eyes Have It—Or Are They Blue?" which originated the Wolf Larsen/Moriarty/Baron Karl connection; see also Dennis E. Power's "Asian Detectives in the Wold Newton Family" and my "Who's Going to Take Over the World When I'm Gone?" All three essays are collected in *Myths for the Modern Age: Philip José Farmer's Wold Newton Universe*.)
   September 7. Birth of Irene Adler in Trenton, New Jersey.

1859

   Winter. Miguelito Loveless, Jr., is born.
   Spring. First chronological appearance of Inspecteur Lecoq in Monsieur Lecoq by Emile Gaboriau.

May 19-28
FROM MONSIEUR LECOQ, RUE JERUSALEM, PARIS, TO INSPECTOR BUCKET, SCOTLAND YARD

M. Lecoq and Inspector Bucket exchange a series of letters and involve muel Pickwick, Esq. in a dreadful misunderstanding. The Count Smorltork vouches for Pickwick.

From Andrew Lang's Old Friends, *Letter 22, 1890. M. Lecoq's tales were told by Emile Gaboriau. Lang dates the letters to 1852, seven years before Lecoq's first chronological appearance in 1859. Since this is impossible, I have changed the date to 1859. Inspector Bucket is from Charles Dickens'* Bleak House. *The Count Smorltork is an acquaintance of Samuel Pickwick from Dickens'* The Pickwick Papers. *This anecdote brings Pickwick into the Crossover Universe.*

Summer. Prince Dakkar, a Capellean like his father, begins the *Nautilus Project* on a remote Pacific island, under the instructions of his Capellean chiefs. The submarines being built will combine Capellean technology with blueprints plundered from the Nine Unknown (see Talbot Mundy's tale *Jimgrim* and *The Nine Unknown*).

Summer
A FATE CAST IN SILVER
    Elena Mason is a schoolteacher, one of whose students is young John Reid.
    Short story by John Allen Small in his collection Days Gone By: Legends and Tales of Sipokni West, *Ethan Books, 2007. Elena (Murieta) Mason is the character played by Catherine Zeta-Jones in* The Mask of Zorro, *1998 and* The Legend of Zorro, *2005. The association between the name Murieta and the Americanization "Mason" is outlined in Matthew Baugh's "The Legacy of the Fox: Zorro in the Wold Newton Universe,"* Myths for the Modern Age: Philip José Farmer's Wold Newton Universe. *John Reid is the future Lone Ranger.*

c. 1860s

    Events of *The Story of Doctor Dolittle* by Hugh Lofting, which takes place in the CU as established in Mark Brown's "From Pygmalion to Casablanca: The Higgins Genealogy," *Myths for the Modern Age: Philip José Farmer's Wold Newton Universe.*
    The Siege of the Red House by J. Sheridan Le Fanu.

1860

Spring. The events of *The Curse of Frankenstein*, in which Victor Frankenstein III creates a third Creature. Further episodic adaptations of events in Victor III's life are presented in several films. In *The Revenge of Frankenstein* he is known as Dr. Victor Stein. He also later uses the name "Dr. Franck." He also appears in *The Evil of Frankenstein* and *Frankenstein Must Be Destroyed*. Many times he is thought dead, only to somehow escape his final fate. However, in 1895 he is finally killed by one of his Creatures, leaving his daughter, Baroness Tania Frankenstein, and Victor III's latest assistant, Dr. Charles Marshall, to carry on his bizarre experiments (*Lady Frankenstein*, aka *La Figlia di Frankenstein*).

Summer. The affair of Bram Stoker's *The Lair of the White Worm*.

Summer
LES BÂTARDS DE ROCAMBOLE (ROCAMBOLE'S BASTARDS)
The following conspiracies or secret cabals are mentioned: Les Habits Noirs, Mohicans of Paris, Valets de Cœur, Ravageurs, and Etrangleurs.

Novel by Jules Cardoze, 1886. *The story is mostly about Rocambole's illegitimate children, and takes place while he is prisoner in Toulon. The references to the various criminal conspiracies are: Paul Féval's* Black Coats, *Alexandre Dumas'* Mohicans of Paris *(serialized 1854-1859), Rocambole's earlier* Valets de Cœur (Jack of Hearts) *gang, and Eugène Sue's* Ravageurs *from* Les Mystères de Paris *and the* Etrangleurs (Stranglers) *from* Le Juif Errant.

September 1-October 31
SO FAR FROM US IN ALL WAYS
In the wake of the death of his son and commitment of his wife, Dr. Abraham Van Helsing takes a medical position in China. While escorting the corpse of another Westerner back to Tianjin, Van Helsing meets a young Manchurian scholar named Fu Zheng Lei. When their convoy is mysteriously attacked, only Fu and Van Helsing survive. They are rescued by a Taoist priest named Master Xi, who explains that the last of seven undead warrior brothers pursues them. Fu

and Van Helsing finally defeat the undead creature, although Master Xi does not survive.

A short story by Chris Roberson in the anthology The Many Faces of Van Helsing, *Jeanne Cavelos, editor, Ace Books, April 2004. Fu Zheng Lei is the man who will later be known to the world by the more familiar appellation "Dr. Fu Manchu." The seven Undead warriors are a reference to the 1974 Hammer film* The Legend of the 7 Golden Vampires. *According to the film's version of events, in 1804 a Chinese priest named Kah went to Castle Dracula to seek the Count's help in reviving seven vampires in China. Perhaps Master Xi, Fu, and Abraham Van Helsing were not as successful as they thought, since the film then jumps ahead to 1904, showing how Lawrence Van Helsing and his son Leyland team up with seven brothers and one sister, all mighty martial artists, to fight against the seven golden vampires.*

1860-1861

MISSISSIPPI RAIDER

Vincent Boyd catches Alfred Higgins while the latter is trying to rob Roger de Bois Gilbert. After Vincent finishes a fox hunt with his daughter Belle and several others, including Phillipe Fronte de Boeuf, his manor Baton Royale is attacked by Northern supporters and burnt to the ground. Vincent and his wife Electra are killed. It is revealed that the Front De Boeufs are all descended from Sir Reginald Front De Boeuf. Captain Alexandre Dartagnan also appears.

A novel in the Civil War series by J.T. Edson. While not explicitly stated, it appears that Roger is descended from Brian de Bois-Guilbert from Ivanhoe *by Sir Walter Scott. The reference to Sir Reginald Front De Boeuf makes the connection to* Ivanhoe *explicit. The Front de Boeufs appear in many other of Edson's works. Edson also states that Belle Boyd was the great-aunt of Jane Porter of Baltimore, who married Tarzan. Dartagnan is descended from the famous Gascon swordsman of similar name (D'Artagnan).*

1861

February 10-15
PROWL UNCEASING

Dr. Abraham Van Helsing meets the Indian Captain Dakkar, and both survive a harrowing adventure together while guests of the White Raja of Sarawak, Sir James Brooke. Sandokan, the Tiger of Malaysia, is mentioned.

A short story by Chris Roberson in the anthology Adventure, Vol. 1, *Chris Roberson, editor, MonkeyBrain Books, 2005. Dakkar was later known as the notorious Captain Nemo. Sarawak, Sir James Brooke, and Sandokan are all from the Sandokan series by Emilio Salgari, placing that series in the Crossover Universe.*

Spring. Aharon van Helsing and his wife travel with Captain Nemo; they meet Aharon's distant cousin Abraham Van Helsing. (*Crépuscule Vaudou* aka *The Katrina Protocol*, Jean-Marc Lofficier.)

c. 1861-1862

The main events of George Bernard Shaw's *An Unsocial Socialist*, which chronicles the life of John Clayton, the fifth duke of Greystoke, Tarzan's grandfather (see Farmer's *Tarzan Alive*).

1861-1865

Gone with the Wind by Margaret Mitchell. Rhett Butler was mentioned by Farmer in *Tarzan Alive*.

December 1861-June 1862

THE REVENGE OF DRACULA

Upton Welsford, of the British Foreign Office, is committed to a sanatorium after a horrific experience with Count Dracula. Welsford records his experience in a manuscript, which finds its way into the hands of Dr. Hugh Strickland, the head of a mental health clinic near Guildford in Surrey. A poem is recited: "Even he who is pure at heart / And says his prayers at night / May become a wolf when the wolfbane blooms / And the moon is full and bright."

Dr. Hugh Strickland provided the manuscript to Peter Tremayne in 1977, whereupon it was published by Dell Books, 1980. Dr. Strickland, shortly after turning over the manuscript, went on to be a major player in The Vengeance of She. *Since the* She *novels take place in the Crossover Universe, so does* The Revenge of Dracula, *which in turn brings in two other Dracula novels by Tremayne:* Dracula Undead *(aka* Bloodright*), and* Dracula, My Love. *The Dracula featured in these books is "Dracula-prime." Also of note, the female protagonist of* The Revenge of Dracula *is a woman named Clara Clarke. Clarke is a name that is not* unknown in the annals of Wold Newton genealogy. Her father is named as Colonel George St. John Clarke of the Egyptian Rifle Brigade. Her mother is an Egyptian Princess named Yasmini. The poem is a variant on that recited in Curt Siodmak's classic film The Wolf Man. Tremayne's epilogue to this tale, "Dracula's Chair," is found in The Mammoth Book of Vampires, Stephen Jones, ed., Carroll & Graf, 1992.

1862

Spring. Events of *Alice's Adventures in Wonderland* and *Through the Looking-Glass (and What Alice Found There)*, as related by Lewis Carroll. There are more Alice stories in *Fantastic Alice: New Stories from Wonderland*, Margaret Weis, editor, Ace Books, 1999.

Summer. Samuel Clemens is a reporter in Virginia City, and writes editorials for the *Territorial Enterprise*. One of his first subjects is a politician who is trying to steal the Cartwright's Ponderosa Ranch. ("Enter Mark Twain," first season episode of the television program *Bonanza*, which takes place in the CU through the appearance of some Cartwright family members in the *Star Trek* novel *Ishmael*.)

Summer. The events of *Five Weeks in a Balloon*, as recounted by Jules Verne.

Autumn. Birth of Urania Caber Moriarty, daughter of Professor James Robert Moriarty and Emily Caber. (The character Urania Moriarty was proposed by Farmer in *Doc Savage*.) By this time, Professor Moriarty has been inducted into the secret ranks of the Capelleans.

Autumn. Birth of Professor George Edward Challenger, father of Enid Challenger and grandfather of Lew Archer. (Farmer established the genealogical relationship between Challenger and Archer in *Doc Savage*.) Late in his life, Professor Challenger must have had a son, who in turn had a daughter, Titania "Doc" Challenger.

1863

June
JOURNEY TO THE CENTRE OF THE EARTH
There are references to the events of *Five Weeks in a Balloon* and *The Adventures of Captain Hatteras*.
A novel told by Axel Lidenbrock and edited by Jules Verne. Lidenbrock is referred to in The League of Extraordinary Gentlemen, *and therefore these events take place in the CU.*

THOR'S HAMMER

The 16th Phantom is involved in the events of *Journey to the Centre of the Earth*. The expedition in *Journey* consisted of Professor Otto Lidenbrock, his nephew Axel, and their guide Hans. Here, they are also accompanied by Jules Verne, with The Phantom following the quartet intent on stopping them. The Phantom ultimately reveals himself and forbids the group to go any further, because the Phantoms are protectors of Thor's Hammer, which was put at the Earth's center by Thor long ago. After more adventures, it is agreed to let Verne publish his account, deleting all references to Verne and Thor's Hammer.

The Phantom #1145, Frew Publications, Australia. *1861 is incorrectly given as the date of* Journey.

Summer. Birth of Rudolf Rassendyll. Farmer proposed Rassendyll as a Wold Newton Family member in *Doc Savage*.

Summer. An English antiquarian awakens something nasty in an expedition to Scandinavia. ("Count Magnus," a short story by M.R. James.)

Autumn. Charles Dickens and his son-in-law, Charles Collins (brother of Wilkie Collins) solve a murder with the help of *The Moonstone*'s Sergeant Cuff ("The Passing Shadow" by Peter Tremayne in the anthology *Death by Dickens*).

Autumn. Prince Dakkar is indirectly responsible for the death of Professor Moriarty's wife and two of their twin children, James and Emile Caber. Only their other twin children, "Wolf Larsen" and "Death Larsen," and their fifth child, Urania Moriarty, survive. Vowing revenge, Moriarty encourages Rajah Dakkar of Bundelcund, the Prince's father, to go renegade from the Capelleans. In turn, Prince Dakkar also becomes persona non grata with the Capelleans. However, Prince Dakkar continues with the submarine project on his own.

Autumn

THE ADVENTURES OF CAPTAIN HATTERAS AKA THE FIELD OF ICE

The opening leading to the Center of the Earth is mentioned.

The Adventures of Captain Hatteras *is a novel by Jules Verne. Since the events of* Journey to the Centre of the Earth *take place in the CU, so do the events of this novel.*

1864

Winter. Plantagenet Palliser's first appearance, in *The Small House at Allington*, as told by Anthony Trollope.

Winter. Hercule Poirot is born in Belgium.

Spring. In accordance with his own plans, the first Professor Moriarty (the second Moriarty brother) is ordered by the Capelleans to infiltrate Prince Dakkar's group and begin working for the Prince on the secret construction of the two atomic submarines, adding his own genius to Capellean technology. Both of these underwater craft will be named the *Nautilus*. Following orders which comport exactly with his personal need for revenge against Prince Dakkar, Professor Moriarty stages a rebellion, steals one sub, and sabotages the second sub, severely injuring Prince Dakkar with radiation poisoning. However, Dakkar overcomes his illness and succeeds in repairing the remaining *Nautilus*.

May 26
A ROOT THAT BEARETH GALL AND WORMS

Appearing or mentioned are: De Peyrac; Elle Le Loup, d'Argouges; Dr. Miguel de Vega; giant lizards, in a few subterranean settings, or in isolated valleys in Texas and Mexico, or on secluded plateaus in Brazil; albino giants who exist in Mercia, in England; their cousins in the American west; the Thibetan variety with an appetite for iron; Monsieur Lecoq and Père Tabaret; Carot; the colleagues Moreau, Klotz, and van Ouisthoven; "one end had an oval bump with a pair of antennae protruding from it"; the explorer Paturel; Migvegaphala; Vegamorpha; Scottish legends of deadly worm-men; "And with the negligible help of Morgan of Oxford I have discovered a method for directing and manipulating this facial alteration"; the Chevalier de Trélern; Hector Ratichon; Don Alejandro de la Vega; a dwarf woman in Finland who has borne Loveless a son; Jules Poiret; Flashman; Butler; British Hidalgo; M. Parent; Fernand; the first Zorro, Ramon de la Torre; El Latigo; El Coyote; Khlit; Isadore Persano; de Lobo; the Hualpai; Elena de la Torre, great-granddaughter of Ramon de la Torre; Montabania; a man with a "z" scar left by a Spaniard; the Black Moon café in Paris; the explosion of Vesuvius; the Brotherhood and Count Fosco; and cousin Antonio.

Short story by Jess Nevins in Tales of the Shadowmen Volume 5: The Vampires of Paris, *Jean-Marc and Randy Lofficier, eds., Black Coat Press, 2009; reprinted in French in* Les Compagnons de l'Ombre (Tome 6), *Jean-Marc and Randy Lofficier, eds., Rivière Blanche, 2010. De Peyrac is from Anne Golon's "Angelique" novels. Elle Le Loup is from Maurice Druon's "Les Rois Maudits" novels. d'Argouges is from Pierre Naudin's "D'Argouges" novels. Dr. Miguel de Vega is better known as Dr. Miguelito Loveless from the television series* The Wild Wild West, *here going by his original, birth name. The subterranean reference is to Edgar Rice Burroughs'* Pellucidar. *The Texas ref-*

erence is to the film Valley of the Gwangi. *The Mexico reference is to the film* El Monstruo de la Montana Hueca. *The Brazil reference is to Doyle's Professor Challenger novel* The Lost World. *The albino giants in Mercia, in England are from Bram Stoker's* Lair of the White Worm. *Their cousins in the American west are from the film* Tremors *and various sequels. The Thibetan variety with an appetite for iron is from "Worms of Doom" in the British comic* Wizard, *1934-1936. Monsieur Lecoq and Père Tabaret are from Emile Gaboriau's classic detective stories. Carot is Maurice Landay's Raphaël Carot. According to Nevins, "Carot was created by Maurice Landay and appeared in twenty-five novellas in* Le Livre Populaire *(October 1911-October 1913). Carot is a faithful agent of Napoleon during the French Revolution and works for him, fighting the wicked enemies of France from the shadows. Carot is a particularly lethal swordsman, hence his nickname 'coupe-tête' (or 'the decapitator')." The colleagues Moreau, Klotz, and van Ouisthoven are from, respectively,* The Island of Dr. Moreau, *Edgar Fawcett's* Solarion, *and Sterling Lanier's "A Father's Tale." "...One end had an oval bump with a pair of antennae protruding from it": what Loveless has created is the ancestor to the Crossover Universe version of Captain Marvel's opponent Mister Mind. The explorer Paturel is the father of Monsieur Paturel, from Arnould Galopin's* Les Aventures de Monsieur Paturel *(1928-1930). Migvegaphala is the Ceti Eel, from* Star Trek II: The Wrath of Khan. *Vegamorpha is the worm species from the film* Slither. *The Scottish worm-men are from Robert E. Howard's "Worms of the Earth." Morgan of Oxford is the man who gave Phil Flash, "the Man of a Thousand Faces," his face-changing ability, from the "Man of a Thousand Faces" stories in various British comics, 1912-1931. According to Nevins, "The Chevalier de Trélern was created by 'Jean d'Agraives,' the pseudonym of Frédéric Causse, and appeared in* L'Aviateur de Bonaparte *#1-22 (1926). In the late 18th century the Chevalier de Trélern is a brilliant, patriotic French inventor. Although he is an émigré, living in Austria, he is devoted to Napoleon's cause, and so creates for Napoleon a flying machine, the* Vélivole, *a propeller-driven dirigible." Per Nevins, "Hector Ratichon was created by the Baroness Orczy and appeared in seven stories which were collected in* Castles in the Air *(1921). Once, Hector Ratichon was among the best confidential agents of the French government, whether for Robespierre, Napoleon, or King Louis." Don Alejandro de la Vega was otherwise known as Zorro, although not the first to fight for justice under that guise (feature films* The Mask of Zorro *and* The Legend of Zorro, *starring Antonio Banderas). Loveless's son by a dwarf woman from Finland is Ilmari Erko, a dwarf genius and inventor from the Jonas Fjeld novels by Øvre Richter Frich. Nevins tells us, "Jules Poiret was created by Frank Howel Evans and appeared five stories in* The New Magazine *in 1909 and 1910, beginning with the October, 1909 issue; the stories were collected in* The Murder Club *(1924). Jules Poiret, aka 'Old Pawray,' is a French detective currently living in London. He is a former member of the French Secret Service who retired after a 'most dis-*

tinguished career.'" Flashman is George MacDonald Fraser's Harry Flashman. Butler is Rhett Butler from Gone with the Wind. British Hidalgo is from Avram Davidson's Limekiller stories. Per Nevins, M. Parent is from "Jules Lermina's M. Parent stories, published in French newspapers from 1869. Parent is an armchair detective. Three of the stories were published in Three Exploits of M. Parent (1894)". Fernand is the Man in Grey. According to Nevins, he "was created by Baroness Orczy and appeared in The Man in Grey (1918). The Man in Grey is Monsieur Fernand, a self-described 'secret agent' and officer of His Imperial Majesty Napoleon I. Fernand works in a rural province in western France in 1809, enforcing Napoleon's law and bringing justice to murderers and thieves. Fernand dresses all in grey, and is a good, insightful detective, with a keen eye for detail and both determination and intelligence in abundance. He has no objections to killing in the pursuit of justice." Ramon de la Torre, the first Zorro, appeared in the Mexican film Zorro contro Maciste. His son appeared in the Mexican film Zorro e i tre moschettieri. An American de la Torre Zorro appeared in the Mexican Zorro film Cabalgando hacia la muerte. The idea that a Zorro was active in Spain in the 1840s is from the Mexican films Zorro alla corte di Spagna (1962) and Zorro alla corte d'Inghilterra (1969). El Látigo appeared in the Mexican Zorro rip-off films. Per Nevins, "El Coyote was created by 'Carter Mulford,' the pseudonym of José Mallorquí, and appeared in almost two hundred short stories from 1943 to 1953, beginning with 'El Coyote' (Novelas del Oeste #9, 1943); El Coyote also appeared in a comic strip and two films. The Coyote is a masked vigilante modeled on Zorro who was popular enough to take on a life of his own." Khlit was created by Harold Lamb. He appeared in Adventure from 1917 to 1926. Isadore Persano is mentioned in Doyle and Watson's Holmes story "The Problem of Thor Bridge." Although the Holmes tale gives the first name as Isadora, it is seen in many pastiches as Isadore. Per Nevins, "Señor Lobo was created by Erle Stanley Gardner and appeared in twenty-three stories in Detective Fiction Weekly from 1930 to 1934." The Hualpai are a native tribe appearing in Gianluigi Bonelli's Tex Willer stories, one of the greatest of the Italian comic strips. Elena de la Torre is from the Mexican Zorro films Las Hijas del Zorro (1963) and Le Sorelle di Zorro (1966). Montabania appears in the radio series Chandu the Magician. The man with a "z" scar is Zigomar. According to Nevins, "Zigomar was created by Léon Sazie and first appeared in a serial

in Le Matin *(1909); he later appeared in the pulps* Zigomar *#1-28 (1913) and* Zigomar contre Zigomar *#1-8 (1924) as well as in another serial, "Un Nouveau Coup de Zigomar" (*Le Petit Parisien, *1938). Zigomar also appeared in four silent films from 1910 to 1912, including* Zigomar contre Nick Carter *(1911) in which Zigomar jousts with Nick Carter. Zigomar is a masked crime lord, similar to but anticipating Fantômas, who was deliberately modeled on Zigomar." Per Nevins, "The Black Moon appeared in a number of stories in* Bullseye *in 1932, beginning with "The Mark of the Black Hand" (*Bullseye, *April 9, 1932). The Black Moon is a famous café in Paris, high up on the hill of Montmartre. The Black Moon is a favorite with visitors, who flock to it to hear the unusual stories of Emil Lupin, formerly the most mysterious man in all of France. The owner of the Black Moon is Madame Zola, a patriot who always successfully conspires to defeat those who would harm France." The explosion of Vesuvius is a reference to the Vesuvius Club, of Mark Gatiss' Lucifer Box novels. The Brotherhood is a Black Coats-like conspiracy in Wilkie Collins'* The Woman in White. *Count Fosco is also from* The Woman in White. *Cousin Antonio is Guy Boothby's Dr. Nikola. Nevins' tale resolves the many stories of Isadora/Isadore Persano in the Crossover Universe: "Isadore Persano used Loveless' worm to create other men who thought they were Isadore Persano, and acted like it. The real Persano did this to hide himself from Count Fosco, but the result is that many of the untold Holmes stories about Isadore Persano and the 'worm unknown to science' are true. There is no one Isadore Persano; there are many. So the various contradictory Persano stories can all take place in the CU."*

Summer. Birth of Arthur J. Raffles.

Summer 1864-March 1865. The events of Jules Verne's *The Children of Captain Grant* (aka *In Search of the Castaways* aka *Les enfants du Capitaine Grant*). Toward the end, in March 1865, a villain named Ayrton is stranded on a desert island.

1865

Winter. Babette Hersant gains fame as the greatest chef, male or female, in Paris. ("Babette's Feast" by Isak Dinesen.)

Spring. The events of E. Harcourt Burrage's Broad Arrow Jack.

Spring. Carmelita Loveless, daughter of Dr. Miguelito Loveless, is born.

Summer. Prince Dakkar creates the identity of "Captain Nemo" and launches his submarine *Nautilus*. Upon being apprised of this intelligence by a Capellean spy whom Professor Moriarty left in Dakkar's camp, Moriarty launches his own *Nautilus*, also going by the name "Captain Nemo." Moriarty's goal is to commit as many heinous, reprehensible, and criminal acts as possible, all the while having them attributed to Dakkar. Young Phileas Fogg is placed among Moriarty-Nemo's crew as a spy for the Eridaneans; he is ultimately successful in sinking Moriarty-Nemo's second *Nautilus* in 1868. It is also possible that Moriarty-Nemo's first sons, Wolf Larsen and Death Larsen, serve as cabin-boys on this *Nautilus*.

Autumn. Captain Cyrus Smith and other Union soldiers are stranded on Lincoln Island (*The Mysterious Island*). Shortly thereafter, Cyrus Smith and his friends rescue Ayrton (from Verne's *The Children of Captain Grant*), who says that he's been living on the island for twelve years; obviously this is a bit of an exaggeration, as he was stranded in March 1865.

October
BACK TO THE BLOODY BORDER
Six months after the end of the Civil War, Belle Boyd foils a plot by General Caillard to form his own nation. Belle joins the United States Secret Service.

A novel in the Civil War series by J.T. Edson. Edson reveals that Caillard is the grandson of Colonel Jean-Baptiste Caillard seen in the Horatio Hornblower novel Flying Colours *by C. S. Forester.*

FROM THE EARTH TO THE MOON/ROUND THE MOON
The members of the Baltimore Gun Club finance the first recorded attempt to reach the Moon. On board the capsule is Michel Ardan.

Novels by Jules Verne. The Gun Club was also mentioned in Verne's The Purchase of the North Pole *and Rosny & Farmer's* Ironcastle. *Michel Ardan may be related to Flash Gordon's girlfriend, Dale Arden, as postulated in the article "The Amazing Lanes" on the Wold Newton Chronicles website.*

November
TWENTY THOUSAND YEARS UNDER THE SEA
Captain Nemo vs. mighty Cthulhu. One of Nemo's crewmen aboard the Nautilus is named Suydam.

Short story recorded by Professor Arronax and edited for publication by John Peel in Tales of the Shadowmen Volume 4: Lords of Terror, *Jean-Marc and Randy Lofficier, eds., Black Coat Press, 2008; reprinted in French in* Les Compagnons de l'Ombre (Tome 3), *Jean-Marc and Randy Lofficier, eds., Ri-*

vière Blanche, 2009. *The tale takes place before Arronax and Ned Land came aboard the* Nautilus *as recounted in Jules Verne's* 20,000 Leagues under the Sea. *Cthulhu and Suydam are from the stories of H. P. Lovecraft.*

Mid 1860s

Aharon van Helsing clashes with Dr. Miguelito Loveless, duels Rhett Butler, and helps the Wizard of Oz escape from Barnum in a balloon. (*Crépuscule Vaudou* aka *The Katrina Protocol* by Jean-Marc Lofficier.)

1866-1868

20,000 LEAGUES UNDER THE SEA (VINGT MILLE LIEUES SOUS LES MERS)

"Captain Nemo" is actually the Indian Prince Dakkar, as revealed in the sequel *The Mysterious Island*. Ned Land refuses to believe the events of Journey to the Centre of the Earth. He states, "The common man still believes in super-comets crossing outer space, in prehistoric monsters thriving in the interior of the earth, but neither geologists nor astronomers believe such myths." The first *Nautilus* submarine appears to sink into the Maelstrom in 1868, but Professor Aronnax and Ned Land survive. Dakkar-Nemo also survives the incident, but radiation sickness continues to plague him, and he retreats with the *Nautilus* to remote Lincoln Island to recover.

20,000 Leagues under the Sea *is a novel by Jules Verne, as is* Journey to the Centre of the Earth, *which featured the prehistoric monsters. Verne would later deal with super-comets in* Hector Servadac. *Professor H.W. Starr, in his article "A Submersible Subterfuge, or, Proof Impositive," included in Farmer's* The Other Log of Phileas Fogg, *viewed the events of Verne's* 20,000 Leagues *sequel,* The Mysterious Island, *as completely fictional. However, while Starr was correct in asserting that Moriarty used the Nemo identity first created by Dakkar, he did not realize that most of the events of* The Mysterious Island *were true, that Prince Dakkar was not a fictional person, and that Dakkar was the true Captain Nemo.*

1866

April
THE YSABEL KID
   The Floating Outfit meets Cheyenne Bodie.
   The first novel in the Floating Outfit series by J.T. Edson. The Floating Outfit is comprised of Dusty Fog, Mark Counter and Loncey Dalton "Ysabel Kid" Ysabel. Dusty Fog is a relative of the English Foggs, and thus is a Wold Newton Family member. Cheyenne Bodie is from the television series Cheyenne.

   Autumn. Upon hearing of the mysterious exploits of another submarine, and its master, Captain Nemo, Arthur Gordon Pym also begins calling himself "Captain Nemo," and begins plundering ships worldwide. In the course of his adventures, this third Captain Nemo encounters the square-jawed, self-righteous Dick Lightheart and his boys, the water-logged survivors of an encounter with a "sea-monster." The sea monster turns out to actually be the third Nemo's submarine, the *Enigma*. Pym-Nemo regales Lightheart and the boys with a fictional autobiography, calling himself "Harold Duggan." As "Duggan," he weaves a false tale of his history as a Confederate veteran whose fiancée, convinced that he was dead, married someone else. For this "Nemo" has sworn vengeance, sinking ships and generally causing havoc on the high seas. Having his destructive exploits attributed to the real Nemo is an added benefit. (See Bracebridge Hemyng's *Dick Lightheart; or, the Scapegrace at Sea*.)

   Autumn. French gamine Cigarette dies in North Africa. (*Under Two Flags* by Ouida.)

1866-1886

   John Carter makes his first trip to Barsoom (Mars). However, before he reaches Barsoom, he is diverted to an astral plane where he meets several other cosmic explorers (Alan Moore's *Allan and the Sundered Veil*). After this adventure, Carter resumes his journey to Barsoom and the events of Edgar Rice Burroughs' *A Princess of Mars* ensue. The remainder of the series consists of: *The Gods of Mars, The Warlord of Mars, Thuvia, Maid of Mars, The Chessmen of*

Mars, *The Master Mind of Mars, A Fighting Man of Mars, Swords of Mars, Synthetic Men of Mars, Llana of Gathol,* and *John Carter of Mars*. Carter also appears in *The League of Extraordinary Gentlemen, Volume II*, as well as the short stories "Mars: The Home Front" (by George Alec Effinger) and "A Princess of Earth" (by Mike Resnick).

1867

Summer. The events of Nana, as related by Emile Zola.
Summer. Births of Fantômas and Juve.

August
QUIET TOWN
Dusty Fog arrives in Quiet Town and is offered the position of Sheriff. He accepts when he is told that the town has already tried Wild Bill Hickok, Matt Dillon, and Dan Troop.
A novel in the Floating Outfit series by J.T. Edson. Matt Dillon is from the television series Gunsmoke. *Dan Troop is from the television series* The Lawman.

September 1867-January 1868. Spock of Vulcan, trapped in his past and stricken with amnesia after being subjected to a Klingon Mind-Sifter, spends several months with his human ancestor, Aaron Stemple, in the town of Seattle, Washington (*Ishmael*, as told by Barbara Hambly). Stemple and a few others realize that Spock is not of this world, but nevertheless protect and care for him. Stemple's experiences with Spock give him the means to successfully deal with another alien contact in 1873.

1868

Winter. U.S. Secret Service agents James West and Artemus Gordon begin working under the direct orders of President Grant. ("The Night of the Inferno," the first episode of the 1960s television series *The Wild Wild West*. For further information and a list of episodes, see *The Wild Wild West: The Series* by Susan Kesler, Arnett Press, 1988.)
Spring. Dr. Martin Hesselius, a German psychic physician, narrates the case of the "Green Tea" (as edited for publication by J. Sheridan Le Fanu in the 1872 collection *In a Glass Darkly*).

Summer
VOYAGE AU CENTRE DU MYSTÈRE
The Black Coats send Fantômas to Paris, where he meets Moriarty, another member of the society.

A novel by René Reouven, Paris, Denoël, 1995. In this novel, Fantômas and his twin brother Juve are the illegitimate children of Jules Verne and Verne's cousin and mistress, Marie Duchesne. Fantômas is raised as Robert Urbain Duchesne and will also be known as Robur the Conqueror. *The only way this scenario can work is if the Fantômas in Reouven's novel is not "the" Fantômas, but rather an inspiration for the later, but better-known Fantômas who terrorized Paris in the early 20th century. According to French pulp expert Jean-Marc Lofficier, the Black Coats (Les Habits Noirs) saga, written by Paul Féval from 1863-1875, concerned an international band of criminals. The Moriarty crossover reference brings the Habits Noirs saga and Fantômas into the CU. This story must take place after the sinking of the second* Nautilus, *after which Moriarty had temporarily given up at passing himself off as "Captain Nemo."*

1869

Spring. The Lone Ranger (John Reid) and Tonto ride into action.

Spring. Birth of Arronaxe Land, daughter of Ned Land, named after Ned's friend Professor Aronnax.

Spring
THE MYSTERIOUS ISLAND

Prince Dakkar reveals himself to Cyrus Smith and the others who have been stranded on his island for three years. Captain Robert Grant and Ayrton appear, and there are references to the events of Five Weeks in a Balloon, The Adventures of Captain Hatteras, and Around the Moon.

Jules Verne's The Mysterious Island *takes place from 1865-1869, but is placed here in the Chronology in order to put the events involving Dakkar in context. Regarding the dating, Dennis E. Power postulates, "In 1865, Dakkar was wounded by radiation poisoning, and in the same year the American soldiers landed on the island he was using as a secret base. He aided the soldiers. The following year, the events of* 20,000 Leagues *began. There were times, not depicted in* 20,000 Leagues, *when Dakkar returned to Lincoln Island, times when Aronnax and company were not allowed*

to know where they were headed. These visits lasted only a day or so, while Dakkar dropped off supplies to the American soldiers. Why did he not rescue them? He could not take the chance that they had somehow discovered his secret base, yet he did not want them to die from want." The novel serves as a sequel to both Verne's 20,000 Leagues under the Sea *and* The Children of Captain Grant *(aka* In Search of the Castaways*).* Five Weeks in a Balloon, The Adventures of Captain Hatteras, *and* Around the Moon *must also take place in the Crossover Universe. Jules Verne did fictionalize the ending of* The Mysterious Island, *in that Dakkar did not die and the Nautilus was not destroyed. Rick Lai's essay, "The Secret History of Captain Nemo," was an invaluable resource in resolving the question of Dakkar-Nemo and Moriarty-Nemo and the two submarines called Nautilus. However, I respectfully disagree with Rick Lai's dismissal in "Secret History" of* The Other Log of Phileas Fogg, The Return of Moriarty, *and* The Revenge of Moriarty *as completely fictional.*

Summer. Secret Service agents James Douglas Henry and Barton Swift defeat the evil plans of Dr. Arliss Loveless, a relative of the equally evil Dr. Miguelito Loveless (1999 feature film *Wild Wild West*). Records of the conflict were altered and the victory was attributed to agents Jim West and Artemus Gordon. The reason for the alteration was either (1) based purely on racist motivations or (2) the result of a grand plot, which is better explained by reading Dennis E. Power's "Wold Wold West" at *The Wold Newton Universe: A Secret History* website.

Summer. Bartholomew Aloysius Lash, otherwise known as Bat Lash, is born.

Summer. The first Professor James Moriarty, who has abandoned the "Captain Nemo" identity, uncovers the diabolical plans of an Anglo-Egyptian named Rathe, who formerly called himself Ahtar. Abetted by his masterful abilities of disguise, Moriarty kills Rathe and takes his place as an instructor at a school in London. He serves as young Sherlock Holmes' tutor (see *The Infernal Device*) and fencing instructor (see *Young Sherlock Holmes*).

Summer
THE LAND OF FURS
A character named Hobson mentions Captain Hatteras. There is also a reference to a total eclipse in the Canadian North.

The Land of Furs *(aka* The Fur Country *aka* Seventy Degrees North Latitude) *is a novel by Jules Verne. Since Captain Hatteras is in the CU, so are the events of this novel. The eclipse in question took place on August 7, 1869.*

Autumn. The events of Charles Dickens' unfinished novel, *The Mystery of Edwin Drood.*

1870s

Scarlett by Alexandra Ripley, a sequel to *Gone with the Wind.*

1870-1889

The events of Oscar Wilde's *The Picture of Dorian Gray.*

1870

Winter. The possible first meeting of Holmes and Watson (*Young Sherlock Holmes* by Watson, Alan Arnold, ed.; Watson's account was made into a 1985 feature film). Holmes and Watson expose Rathe's evil plans, but Rathe kills Holmes' young love, Elizabeth. Holmes thinks Rathe dead, but unknown to Holmes, Rathe survives and retreats to his true identity, Moriarty. In 1881's *A Study in Scarlet*, Watson describes in detail his first meeting with Holmes, and makes no reference to their prior adventure in 1870. Therefore, Watson either (1) had reasons for suppressing the account of *Young Sherlock Holmes*, (2) did not mention the events of *Young Sherlock Holmes* in order to keep the narrative of *A Study in Scarlet* moving, (3) forgot, or (4) the story of *Young Sherlock Holmes* is apocryphal.

Summer. The events of *Dracula, My Love*, as told by Peter Tremayne.
July 4. John Evelyn Thorndyke, M.D., is born.
Summer. The events of Jules Verne's *Une fantaisie du Docteur Ox (A Fantasy of Dr. Ox* aka *Dr. Ox's Experiment*).
Autumn. Birth of Jules de Grandin. A de Grandin was briefly mentioned in Farmer's *Tarzan Alive.* This reference has been expanded upon in Cheryl Huttner's "Name of a Thousand Blue Demons," *Myths for the Modern Age: Philip José Farmer's Wold Newton Universe.*

1871-1875

Events of *Hondo*, as related by Louis L'Amour. Elsewhere, I have suggested that Hondo Lane was the antecedent of one branch of a larger Lane family, many of whose members' exploits take place in the CU (see "The Amazing Lanes" on *The Wold Newton Chronicles* website).

1871-1876

The events of Jules Verne's *The Begum's Millions* (aka *The Begum's Fortune* aka *Les cinq cents Millions de la Bégum*). Herr Schultze's projectile is launched in 1876; in 1886 scientists would mistakenly suspect Robur's ship of being Herr Schultze's projectile.

1871

Winter. Main events of the tale of "Carmilla," as chronicled by J. Sheridan LeFanu.

Spring. The events of Susan Coolidge's *What Katy Did*. Sequels are *What Katy Did at School* and *What Katy Did Next*.

Spring. First recorded case of Italian consulting detective John Siloch. (*John Siloch, the Greatest Policeman in the World* series by Antonio Quattrini.)

Summer
THE JAMES BOYS
 Clint Adams witnesses Marshal Reuben "Rooster'" Cogburn handle a group of toughs by riding into their midst, reins in teeth and guns blazing.
 The Gunsmith *novel #200 by J.R. Roberts, Jove Books, September 1998. Since The Gunsmith is linked into the Crossover Universe, so are the characters of Charles Portis' novel* True Grit *and subsequent film sequels.*

DECISION FOR DUSTY FOG
 There is a reference to Matt Dillon. Lord James Roxton, father of Lord John Roxton, also appears. Roxton says, "I wish I had that Hottentot 'Ventvogel' of Quatermain's."
DIAMONDS, EMERALDS, CARDS AND COLTS
 Lord James Roxton, the father of John Roxton, again appears with the Floating Outfit and Sir John Unglow Ramage.
THE CODE OF DUSTY FOG
 The Floating Outfit encounters Edmund Fagin and Sir John Unglow Ramage, the youngest son of Sir Nicholas Ramage.
 Three novels in the Floating Outfit series by J.T. Edson. Matt Dillon is from the television series Gunsmoke. *Edmund Fagin is the grandson to the Fagin from Dickens'* Oliver Twist. *The* Hottentot Ventvogel *is from the Allan Quatermain novel* King Solomon's Mines *by H. Rider Haggard. Sir John Unglow Ramage is the youngest son of Sir Nicholas Ramage, from the* Ramage *series by Dudley Pope. Lord John Roxton is a Wold Newton Family member, who would*

accompany Professor Challenger to *the Lost World. The use of a first name in conjunction with a title is indicative that the individual is the younger son of an Earl, Marquess, or Duke; the title is honorary and dies with the holder. Thus, the elder Roxton would be more properly addressed as "James Roxton, Lord Roxton." In Farmer's family tree in* Doc Savage: His Apocalyptic Life, *the elder Roxton (aka "Wentworth") is listed as a Baron.*

Autumn. The events of *The Coming Race* by Edward Bulwer-Lytton.

1872

Winter-Spring
THE GREAT DETECTIVE AT THE CRUCIBLE OF LIFE; OR, THE ADVENTURE OF THE ROSE OF FIRE

On expedition in Africa with Allan Quatermain, Sir Richard Burton, Professor Maria Mitchell, Will Scott, Thomas Huxley, Sergeants Danny Dravot and Peachey Carnehan, Richard Holmes, Sergeant Cuff, and Axel Lidenbrock, the latter two of whom die on the adventure.

From a memoir by Allan Quatermain, recorded by Doctor John H. Watson, and edited by Thos. Kent Miller, Wildside Press, 2005. "Will Scott" is actually a young Sherlock Holmes, while "Thomas Huxley" is his older brother Sherringford. However, the theory that Sherringford Holmes went on to become Professor Moriarty—and Jack the Ripper—is not workable with the rest of Crossover Universe continuity. Richard Holmes might be a distant relation to Sherlock and Sherringford. Dravot and Carnehan are from Rudyard Kipling's "The Man Who Would Be King," while Cuff is from Wilkie Collins' The Moonstone. *Axel Lidenbrock is from Verne's* Journey to the Centre of the Earth, *and Quatermain should need no further introduction.*

January
THE HIDE AND HORN SALOON

Madam Bulldog takes over the Hide and Horn Saloon and starts a series of high stakes poker games. Invited guests include Madam Moustache, Poker Alice, Abraham "Pappy" Maverick, and Ben "Pappy" Maverick.

A novel in the Calamity Jane series by J.T. Edson (not the historical Calamity Jane). It appears that after a certain age all of the Maverick men are re-

ferred to as "Pappy" Maverick. Beauregard Maverick, the father of Brett, Bart, and Brent Maverick, is oddly absent from this list. His brother Bentley, father of Beau Maverick and grandfather of Ben Maverick (see The New Maverick *and* Young Maverick*) must be the Ben Maverick mentioned. Abraham Maverick is unusual, as all known Mavericks have first names that start with "B." Perhaps he was known as Bram Maverick and Edson gave the correct and more formal name.* The New Maverick *was the pilot for the* Young Maverick *television series. Poker Alice appeared in* The New Maverick *and later had a pilot film of her own.*

Spring. Laura de Guéran travels to Africa in search of her husband, the missing explorer Baron de Guéran. (*La Sultane Parisienne* [*A Parisian Sultana*] by Adolphe Belot, 1879.)

Summer. Moriarty prepares to use the "Nemo" identity once more (see Farmer's *The Other Log of Phileas Fogg*). During this time period, Moriarty also remarries, to a woman named Donleavy, thus providing his daughter Urania with a stepmother, and eventually half-sister, Patricia Donleavy (see *The Beekeeper's Apprentice* by Mary Russell Holmes, edited by Laurie R. King).

Summer
SLOCUM'S SLAUGHTER
John Slocum is an ex-Major of the Confederate States of America. After the Civil War, he served in the United States Cavalry in the American West. He recalls his former mathematics tutor, Professor Moriarty. Despairing of any success in teaching the boy John, Moriarty returned to England to take a position with a prominent family named "Homes, or some such."
Novel by Jake Logan, Playboy Press, August 1980, placing John Slocum in the CU. Professor James Robert Moriarty's stint in the Antebellum South must have taken place in the late 1850s.

October-December. The events of Jules Verne's *Around the World in Eighty Days.*

October-December
THE OTHER LOG OF PHILEAS FOGG
In this companion novel to Jules Verne's *Around the World in Eighty Days*, it is revealed that the first Professor James Moriarty once posed as "Captain Nemo." Moriarty-Nemo has several Capellean assistants: Colonel James Moriarty (the very tall dark man with a heavy stoop); Colonel Sebastian Moran; and a man named Vandeleur. It is also divulged that Phileas Fogg, in disguise, was a crewman aboard the Nautilus who was working against Moriarty-Nemo during 1865-1868, and that Fogg was ultimately responsible for the sinking of the Nautilus. One of the henchmen of Moriarty-Nemo is "the dissolute wenching

young baronet, Sir Hector Osbaldistone." At one point in the past, Passepartout was instructed to get hired as a valet for Lord Windermere. With the death of the last Old One (an original alien Eridanean or Capellean), this adventure marks the end of the secret conflict between the Eridaneans and the Capelleans.

Novel by Philip José Farmer, DAW, 1973; Tor Books, 1982. In it, Farmer builds on the theory that Professor Moriarty and Captain Nemo were the same person. Farmer has also proposed that Moriarty and Fogg were Wold Newton Family members. Vandeleur appeared in Robert Louis Stevenson's short story "The Rajah's Diamond," which appeared in the volume New Arabian Nights. *Moran was the first Professor Moriarty's lieutenant and appeared in Doyle and Watson's Sherlock Holmes story "The Adventure of the Empty House." Colonel Moriarty is the Professor's elder half-brother. Regarding the theory, adopted* here, that there were two Professor James Moriartys (as well as an older brother, Colonel James Moriarty), please refer to *The Return of Moriarty* and *The Revenge of Moriarty, both by John Gardner, Berkley Books, 1981. The author is the same John Gardner, incidentally, who continued to write the James Bond series of books in the 1980s and '90s. Sir Hector Osbaldistone is a descendant of Sir Francis Osbaldistone from Sir Walter Scott's* Rob Roy. *Lord Windermere is probably the husband of Lady Windermere of* Lady Windermere's Fan: A Play About a Good Woman *by Oscar Wilde. Sir Hector took after the villainous side of the family. The Rajah Dakkar of Bundelcund, a renegade Capellean who is killed in this adventure, is not the Prince Dakkar of Verne's* The Mysterious Island, *but rather must be the Prince's father. After these events, the first Professor Moriarty permanently gave up on the "Captain Nemo" identity and laid low for several years, before resuming his criminal career under his own name.*

December
FOGG BOUND
Paladin meets Phileas Fogg during the events of *Around the World in Eighty Days*, as Fogg travels through America. Paladin escorts Fogg, Passepartout, and Aouda from San Francisco to Nevada.

1960 episode of television series Have Gun, Will Travel. *Evidently neither Verne nor Farmer knew of this particular incident.*

1873

Winter. Bancroft Stoneham Pons is born to Asenath Pons and Roberta McIvor.

March
NEW ORLEANS FIRE
Secret Service agent James West asks Clint Adams, aka "The Gunsmith," to accept a courier mission for President U.S. Grant.

The Gunsmith #10 *series by J.R. Roberts (pseudonym for Robert J. Randisi), Ace/Charter Books, October 1982. Since agent James West, from the television program* The Wild Wild West, *is in the Crossover Universe, so is Clint Adams, "The Gunsmith." Adams also met with thinly disguised versions of western series characters Edge, Adam Steele, and Jim Sundance in* The Gunsmith #34: The Night of the Gila.

Summer. Throughout this time period, the Karsid Empire is in power in this quadrant of the galaxy. The Karsids have built their Empire primarily on economic infiltration of less advanced worlds, eventually leading to total dependence and subjugation, rather than military invasion. When the Karsids, disguised as humans, make first contact with the U.S. government, Congressman

Aaron Stemple, addressing a secret Congressional committee, argues vehemently against any dealings with them. Fortunately for Earth, his arguments carry the day (*Star Trek:* Ishmael *by Barbara Hambly*).

Summer
SHE AND ALLAN

Allan Quatermain goes on a quest to find the legendary White Witch, also known as Ayesha, She-who-must-be-obeyed.

Novel by Allan Quatermain, edited by H. Rider Haggard. Ayesha also appeared in Wisdom's Daughter, She, Ayesha: The Return of She, *and* The Vengeance of She. *Since Allan Quatermain appears in Farmer's Wold Newton Family genealogy, Ayesha must also exist in the CU.*

September
MYSTERIOUS DAN'S LEGACY

Dan Hawkins arrives in Arkham from Kansas to collect his later father's legacy, while some nefarious characters, members of the cult of Starry Wisdom, attempt to prevent him from doing so. Jasper Thorne picks up Dan at the train station. Mr. Pumblechook tells him about a pirate cult of the winged octopus that Dan's father encountered on the island of Ral. Reverend Woolcot summons a "hunter." There is also a reference to Miskatonic University.

Short story by Matthew Baugh in Arkham Tales: Legends of the Haunted City, *William Jones, ed., Chaosium, 2006. Mr. Pumblechook is a relative of Uncle Pumblechook in Dickens'* Great Expectations, *and is also (like the famous Marsh family) cross-bred with a Deep One. The pirate cult of the winged octopus that Dan's father encountered on the island of Ral is the cult of the Feathered Octopus from the Doc Savage pulp novel* The Feathered Octopus. *Jasper Thorne is an ancestor of John Thunstone's enemy Rowley Thorne. The Starry Wisdom cult is from Lovecraft's "The Haunter of the Dark," while Arkham and Miskatonic are staples of the Cthulhu Mythos. The creature that Reverend Woolcot summons is one of the hunting horrors of Nyarlathotep.*

Autumn. First recorded adventure of Jonah Hex (*All-Star Western* #10, DC Comics).

Autumn
RIO GUNS

Dusty Fog is compared to Gil Favor, while the Ysabel Kid is considered the best scout including Cheyenne Bodie and Bronco Layne.

Novel by J.T. Edson. Gil Favor is the trail boss from the television show Rawhide. *Cheyenne Bodie is from the show* Cheyenne, *while Bronco Layne is from* Bronco, *a spinoff of* Cheyenne.

1874

Winter. Birth of Richard Hannay. Per Farmer's *Doc Savage*, Hannay's uncle, William Drummond, is the grandfather of Hugh "Bulldog" Drummond and John "Korak" Drummond-Clayton. Hannay's maternal grandmother is Oread Butler, a cousin of Rhett Butler (*Gone with the Wind*).

Winter. Birth of Arsène Raoul Lupin. Farmer's *Tarzan Alive* states that an ancestor of Lupin was one of the coachmen present at the Wold Newton meteor strike.

February
THE COLD COMES SOUTH

Mysterious Dave Mather encounters Ithaqua on the Staked Plains of Texas. Dave also mentions that he is acquainted with the Tsichah Indians.

Short story by Matthew Baugh featured in the magazine In Lovecraft's Shadow, *#1. Ithaqua is one of the Great Old Ones from the Cthulhu Mythos. Dave Mather is a historical gunfighter. This is the fictional version of the character. It also bears noting that Mysterious Dave Mather and Mysterious Dan Hawkins (from Baugh's tale "Mysterious Dan's Legacy") are meant to be the same character. The Tsichah are a fictional people who appear in the John Thunstone and David Return stories of Manly Wade Wellman.*

Spring
THE QUEST FOR BOWIE'S BLADE

The Ysabel Kid encounters Octavius Xavier "the Ox" Guillemot who states that he learned of the whereabouts of Bowie's blade from the first Professor James Moriarty, who in turn learned of it while perusing the family library of Squire Holmes of Yorkshire. After losing the knife, the Ox leaves Mexico for Europe in search of the Maltese Falcon.

THE SCHOOL TEACHER

Dusty Fog reveals that Mark Counter is a relative of Bret Maverick.

COMANCHE BLOOD

Near the Mexican border, the Ysabel Kid encounters a man calling himself El Zorro. The Kid figures out that he is actually a local man named Diego.

Three more Western entries from writer J.T. Edson. "Comanche Blood" is a short story found in The Hard Riders. *Bret Maverick is from the television series* Maverick. *Note that Warren's* The Rook *series establishes Bishop Dane as the owner of Bowie's blade.*

Summer. Birth of Randolph Carter, whose tales were chronicled by H.P. Lovecraft in such classics as "The Statement of Randolph Carter," "The Dream Quest of Unknown Kadath," and "The Silver Key."

Summer

THE REMITTANCE KID

Calamity Jane works with Lt. Ed Ballinger, Belle Boyd, and Capt. Patrick Reeder.

Thanks to the research of Philip José Farmer, J.T. Edson reveals in this Calamity Jane novel that Ed Ballinger is the grandfather of Lt. Frank Ballinger, the head of M Squad. M Squad's adventures were made into a television series, which appeared from 1957 to 1960. Belle Boyd is revealed to be the great aunt of Jane Clayton, née Porter, and Patrick Reeder is the uncle to J. G. Reeder, Edgar Wallace's famous detective.

Autumn. Jules Verne's *Michel Strogoff: The Courier of the Czar.*

Autumn

THE KIDNAPPERS

Mark Counter meets his cousin Beau and lends him $1000 to play in a poker game. Beau is highly successful and repays Mark $2000.

Short story by J.T. Edson in Troubled Range. *Beau speaks with a British accent and is most likely Beau Maverick.*

WANTED! BELLE STARR (aka OKLAHOMA OUTLAW)

Belle Starr cons Armand Chauvelin.

Novel by J.T. Edson. While not specifically stated, it's likely that the Chauvelin seen here is a descendant of Chauvelin from Baroness Orczy's The Scarlet Pimpernel.

November 5-November 6, 1875. Tragedy on Egdon Heath. (*The Return of the Native* by Thomas Hardy, 1878.)

1875

April
HOMUNCULUS

In a prologue, which takes place in 1870, scientist Langdon St. Ives is in a curio shop searching after rumors of a crystal egg, which supposedly contains visions of the Martian landscape. One of the main characters, Bill Kraken, carries around a volume on philosophy by William Ashbless. The evil hunchback Dr. Ignacio Narbondo also appears. St. Ives' man Hasbro mentions that a Scotland Yard investigator named Koontz was once involved in the Isadora Persano affair, "the business with the worm and the inside-out pouch of tobacco."

Novel by James P. Blaylock, Ace Books, 1986, reprinted by Babbage Press, 2000. The crystal egg appeared in H.G. Wells' tale of the same name, which also served as a prologue to the Martian Invasion in the pastiche Sherlock Holmes's War of the Worlds. Ashbless was a major character in Tim Powers' novel The Anubis Gates. Dr. Narbondo later played a role in Blaylock's Lord Kelvin's Machine. A modern-day William Ashbless, the California Cahuenga poet, also appeared in The Digging Leviathan, although uncertainties remain regarding whether he might have actually been the original Ashbless. St. Ives also appears in Lord Kelvin's Machine, The Ebb Tide, and the short stories "The Ape-Box Affair," "Two Views of a Cave Painting," and "The Idol's Eye." The Persano affair refers to a Sherlock Holmes case that was never documented by Dr. Watson (see Doyle and Watson's "The Problem of Thor Bridge"). Harry "Bunny" Manders eventually revealed the details of the case (see "The Problem of the Sore Bridge—Among Others" edited by Philip José Farmer). However, the timing is problematic, as it is unlikely that either Holmes or Manders' partner Raffles could have been involved in such a case before the 1875 events of Homunculus. Additionally, Manders' manuscript of the case is dated to 1895. There must have been another case involving an earlier Persano, perhaps a father or an uncle.

Spring
SLAUGHTER ROAD

In San Francisco, Josiah "Edge" Hedges meets detectives Samuel Spade, Phil Marlow, and Lou Archer. All three are part of the same firm. Spade mentions that he once worked on a case involving a statue of a black bird. The group is later joined by two more detectives: Hammer (from New York) and a redhead named Shayne from Florida. Edge asks for the spelling of the latter name, and Hammer replies, "S-H-A-Y-N-E." "Didn't think he was that one," says Edge in response.

Novel by George C. Gilman (pseudonym for British writer Terry Harknett), Pinnacle Books, 1977. The private detective firm of Spade and Archer (from The Maltese Falcon*) may be older than first thought. The Samuel Spade seen here must be Sam Spade's (again,* The Maltese Falcon*) grandfather. Per Philip José Farmer, Samuel Spade was a policeman, so Samuel must have quit as a private detective and joined the police some time after this case. If Samuel Spade was really involved in a case about a statue of a black bird—the Maltese Falcon— sometime before 1875, then the Falcon must have some strange, unrevealed attraction to the Spade family: Sam Spade was involved with the statue in 1928, while his son, Sam Spade, Jr., was mixed up with the black bird in 1974. Although Lew Archer is descended from Professor Challenger (Lew is Enid Challenger's son), Lew Archer may be descended from Lou Archer on his (Lew's) father's side. Lou may also be an ancestor of Sam Spade's partner in* The Maltese Falcon, *Miles Archer. Phil Marlow is an ancestor of Los Angeles detective Philip Marlowe. Hammer is an ancestor of private dick Mike Hammer. Shayne is an ancestor of private detective Mike Shayne. When Edge replies that he "Didn't think he was that one," he is likely referring to Shane from the 1953 film.*

Spring. Birth of Kimball O'Hara (Rudyard Kipling's *Kim*; also see *The Game* by Mary Russell Holmes and Laurie R. King).

July 1875-Late 1876
THE MUSGRAVE VERSION

Sherlock Holmes and Reginald Musgrave cross paths with Dr. Fu Manchu at Cambridge. Musgrave then recounts that he and Holmes spent several months as Fu Manchu's captives in China, subsequently took a "mad voyage" aboard the submarine Nautilus, and encountered the maniacal Dr. Moreau, before finally making their way back to England. Reginald Musgrave also refers to his son, Miles Musgrave.

A short story edited by George Alec Effinger, from a manuscript by Reginald Musgrave (from Doyle and Watson's "The Adventure of the Musgrave Ritual"). The story is found in the anthology Sherlock Holmes in Orbit, *DAW, 1995. The* Nautilus *mentioned here would be Prince Dakkar's submarine. The* reference to Dr. Moreau (from H.G. Wells' The Island of Dr. Moreau) places Moreau in the CU. Rick Lai points out that "In Sir Walter Scott's A Legend of Montrose, a cavalier named Sir Miles Musgrave was fighting for Charles I during 1645-46. In 'The Musgrave Ritual,' Reginald Musgrave's ancestor was a cavalier, Sir Ralph Musgrave, who accompanied Charles II into exile. Sir Miles was probably Sir Ralph's father." The Miles Musgrave mentioned in Effinger's tale provides a direct link to Scott's A Legend of Montrose.

Late July-October
THE ADVENTURE OF THE CELESTIAL SNOWS
Reginald Musgrave expands upon the tale of his and Holmes' clash with Fu Manchu, although this time Musgrave states that while Holmes had met the insidious doctor at Cambridge, his own first meeting with Fu Manchu was at the latter's London headquarters. In any event, Musgrave fills in the details of their adventure in China, in which Fu Manchu requires Holmes to solve a mystery in exchange for their freedom. The Doctor does not appreciate Holmes' solution and they barely escape with their lives. Thirty-three years later, in 1908, Fu Manchu contacts Holmes, admitting that Holmes' solution was the correct one, and Holmes is suitably rewarded.
A short story edited by George Alec Effinger, from a manuscript by Reginald Musgrave, in My Sherlock Holmes, *Michael Kurland, ed., St. Martin's Press, 2003. Interestingly, this tale also illustrates that Fu Manchu was the one responsible for Holmes' introduction to the use of cocaine and other substances. Although the story states that it runs through December 1875, the December date conflicts with the date for* Enter the Lion, *and thus I have chosen interpret this tale as concluding in October 1875. Dennis E. Power's "The Problem of Reginald Musgrave, or, The Musgrave Version of History" (*The Wold Newton Universe: A Secret History *website) reconciles "The Musgrave Version" and "The Adventure of the Celestial Snows."*

Summer. Birth of amateur detective Dr. Eustace Hailey. Hailey's cases will be chronicled by Anthony Wynne.

Summer
EL VAMPIRO SANGRIENTO
José Balsamo, the grandson of the original Count Cagliostro, kills the vampire Countess Eugenia Frankenhausen, wife of Count Siegfried von Frankenhausen. Anna Cagliostro, the daughter of José Cagliostro, also appears.
Feature film, 1962. Philip José Farmer made the original Count Cagliostro a member of the Wold Newton Family. Count Frankenhausen returned in La Invasión de los Vampiros *(1963). Of the two films, Rick Lai notes, "In the Mexican horror films* The Bloody Vampire *and* The Invasion of the Vampires, *one of the characters is Count Cagliostro, the grandson of the original. The films*

take place in the 19th century. They seem to transpire with a gap of ten years between them. I base this assertion on that fact that the actress who plays the vampiric Count Frankenhausen's wife in the first film plays her daughter in the second. The first film ended with Frankenhausen turning his wife into a vampire. The daughter was an offstage character living with her human grandfather in the first. We can speculate that Countess Frankenhausen was 30 years old in the first film, and her daughter was 20 years old in the second. I would put the first film around 1875, and the second around 1885. These facts were revealed about the grandson of Cagliostro: (1) He is known as both José (The Bloody Vampire) and Alejandro (The Invasion of the Vampires). Here it should be  noted that the original Cagliostro was called both Joseph and Alexander. This Cagliostro recently moved to Mexico. (2) He has a daughter named Anna. She appears to be in her twenties. (3) He seems to have an immortality elixir that prolongs his life. (4) The original Count Cagliostro had a second wife who was transformed into a vampire by the ancestor and namesake of Count Frankenhausen. This Countess Cagliostro was burned at the stake. The story of the attack on Cagliostro's second wife seems to be the inspiration for the Dracula vs. Cagliostro story in Marvel Comics. (5) According to his grandson in El Vampiro Sangriento, the original Cagliostro suffered a fatal accident in prison. This is somewhat distorted version of the death of the historical Cagliostro. Alexandre Dumas implied that Cagliostro faked his prison demise in The Countess de Charney. However, Dumas advanced Cagliostro's 'death' by a few years. (6) Count Cagliostro II, as we might call him, does not actually appear in The Invasion of the Vampires, but is mentioned by a doctor who trained with him."

STURMVOGEL
Alaska Jim, a trapper in the West of America and Canada and an agent for the Canadian national police, encounters the heroic Apache Storm Bird, aka "Sturmvogel."
Story in Alaska Jim #199 by Fritz & Lisa Barthel-Winkler, published in 1939.

November
ENTER THE LION: A POSTHUMOUS MEMOIR

The death of Professor Moriarty's beloved uncle and father-figure, Jerrold Moriarty, adds fuel to the Holmes/Moriarty feud. Fighting ships such as the more recent four-deckers of Nelson and Hornblower are mentioned.

Novel by Mycroft Holmes, edited by Michael P. Hodel and Sean M. Wright, Playboy Press, September 1980. Of course, given Sherlock's experiments with Royal Jelly bee pollen in the 1920s, the "Posthumous" of the title is highly questionable. This is the first time that Holmes becomes acquainted with the first Professor Moriarty in his true identity; Holmes had literally crossed swords with Moriarty five years earlier when Moriarty was posing as Rathe, but Moriarty's disguise was so brilliant that Holmes did not make the connection. Additionally, although Jerrold Moriarty as referenced as the father of Professor Moriarty, conflicting information in the Wold Newton Family Tree forces the speculation that he was an uncle instead. The Hornblower reference is to a real naval figure, confirming that this adventure takes place in the CU.

1876

February 29. Max Carrados, blind criminologist, is born. His cases will be chronicled by Ernest Bramah.

Spring. The first Professor James Robert Moriarty begins to build his vast criminal empire. Over the years, many will serve with the Professor, including his daughter Urania; his younger brother, James Noel Moriarty; Colonel Moran; and John Clay.

Spring. Birth of Carthoris of Helium, son of John Carter and Dejah Thoris.

Autumn. Sherlock Holmes has a "brief but notable" stint on the New York stage billed as "Mr. William Escott." Holmes goes on tour and is involved in several mysteries while on tour. (*Sherlock Holmes and the Hands of Othello* by Alexander Simmons. This reference explains Holmes' reputation at the time of "The Suicide Club." Additionally, Holmes used the "William Escott" many times throughout his career. Indeed, as Baring-Gould states in Sherlock Holmes of Baker Street, his birth name was William Sherlock Scott Holmes.)

1877

Winter
HOLD THE PRESS: PALADIN VS. DILLON

In Dodge City, Paladin is hired to protect a newspaperman. After the mission is completed, Marshal Matt Dillon runs Paladin out of town.

Short story by Martin Grams, Jr., in It's That Time Again 3: Even More New Stories of Old-Time Radio, *Jim Harmon, ed., BearManor Media, 2006. Dillon is from the radio and television show* Gunsmoke, *while Paladin is from the radio and television series* Have Gun, Will Travel.

OFF ON A COMET (HECTOR SERVADAC)
Hector Servadac is trapped on a comet and journeys throughout the Solar System. The events of *Black Indies* are mentioned.
Novel by Jules Verne.

BLACK INDIES (THE UNDERGROUND CITY)
There is a reference to the events of *Hector Servadac*.
Black Indies (aka *Les Indes Noires* aka *The Underground City* aka *Child of the Cavern*) is a novel by Jules Verne.

Summer. Sherlock Holmes visits C. Auguste Dupin in Paris, to seek Dupin's assistance in recovering a jewel-encrusted golden hawk, which will later be known as the Maltese Falcon. ("The Incident of the Impecunious Chevalier," edited by Richard A. Lupoff from a manuscript by Dupin's nameless amanuensis, in *My Sherlock Holmes*, Michael Kurland, ed., St. Martin's Press, 2003; reprinted in Lupoff's *The Universal Holmes*, Ramble House, 2007.) The 1877 date fits, as it is shortly after the end of the Second Carlist War in Spain in 1876. (References to Queen Isabella II as still holding the Spanish throne are inaccurate, as she was deposed in 1868; Holmes would have been only fourteen in 1868. References to Ramón Cabrera continuing the Carlist struggle in Catalonia are also inaccurate, as these events concluded in 1840, fourteen years before Holmes' birth. Thus, it is more likely that references to Queen Isabella are really to the effective continuation of the Isabelline monarchy by her son, King Alfonso XII.) In this tale, Holmes is exhibiting strong signs of drug dependency; this also fits the 1877 date well, in that it is shortly after Holmes' introduction to cocaine by the insidious Dr. Fu Manchu in late 1875.

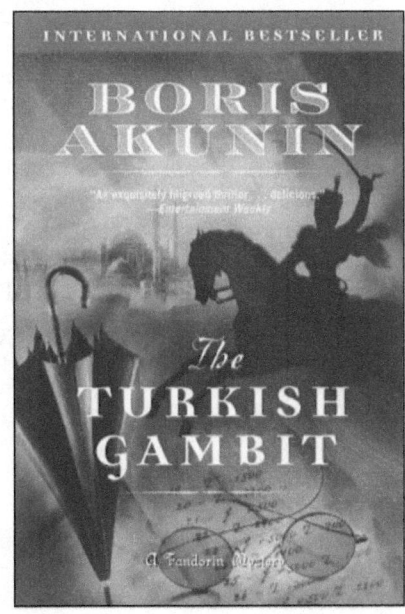

July 14, 1877-March 10, 1878
THE TURKISH GAMBIT
Russian diplomat, secret agent, detective, and all-around genius Erast Petrovich Fandorin is involved in intrigue during the Russo-Turkish War of 1877-78. Count Zurov, recounting a previous exploit, mentions going down on his knees and praying in the language of Corneille and Rocambole.
Novel by Boris Akunin (pseudonym for Grigory Chkhartishvili) first published in Russian in 1998; the English translation was published by Random House in

2005. Pierre Corneille was a 17th-century French dramatist. Pierre Alexis Ponson du Terrail's Rocambole is a mainstay of the Crossover Universe; this tale links in the brilliant Fandorin.

August
THE CISCO KID: GUNFIRE AND BRIMSTONE
The Cisco Kid escapes from the "Masked Ranger," a vigilante lawman who uses silver bullets. The Ranger's partner is an unnamed Indian. As the Cisco Kid escapes, he meets another fugitive who turns out to be Billy the Kid. Billy the Kid asks, "Who was that masked man?"
Comic book miniseries by Len Cody and Dennis Calero, Moonstone Comics, 2005. The "Masked Ranger" and his partner are obviously the Lone Ranger and Tonto. O. Henry's Cisco Kid was also seen in the 1909 adventure "The Rook: Master of the World." However, the version of the Kid seen in the 1909 story differs so greatly from this Cisco Kid that I am led to speculate that perhaps the later Kid is the son of the first, or merely took his name.

Autumn. Birth of Jean de Sainte-Claire, aka Léo Saint-Clair, aka the Nyctalope.
Autumn. Birth of J.G. Reeder, detective in cases chronicled by Edgar Wallace.

1878

Spring. The events of Robert Louis Stevenson's "The Suicide Club," found in the volume entitled *New Arabian Nights*. The story's Prince Florizel of Bohemia also appeared in the same volume's "The Rajah's Diamond" and would be seen again in Watson's/Doyle's "A Scandal in Bohemia." The "celebrated detective" who is indirectly involved in these events is clearly Sherlock Holmes. And the tall man with a heavy stoop who declines to assist the Prince is Colonel James Moriarty. Finally, as Rick Lai demonstrated in his article, "The Secret History of Captain Nemo," Dr. Noel, the retired master criminal who assists in the case, is the father of the first Professor, James Robert Moriarty, and the second Professor, James Noel Moriarty. (See Edgar W. Smith's "A Scandal in Identity" in the volume *Profile in Gaslight*, Simon & Schuster, 1944; see also Jack Tracy's "Some Thoughts on the Suicide Club" in *The Baker Street Journal*, New Series, v22, n2, June 1972.)

Spring
RAWHIDE KID: SLAP LEATHER
The Rawhide Kid (Johnny Bart) rides into the town of Wells Junction, where Miss Laura "Ingulls" is the schoolteacher. The town of Lonesome Dove is mentioned, as are "Woodrow Caul" and "Augustus McRay." Other Western

figures such as Kid Colt, the Lone Ranger, Two-Gun Kid, and Kid Shaleen are mentioned. Later on several characters apply for the position of town deputy, including "Bernard Phife the First," and brothers "Haus and Little Jo Cartrite." "Lew Grant" is the town's newspaperman. Will Kane's stunt of trying to rally townsfolk against outlaws is mentioned.

Comic book miniseries by Ron Zimmerman and John Severin, Marvel Comics, 2003. Laura Ingalls is from the Little House on the Prairie books. Lonesome Dove, Augustus McCrae and W.F. Call are from Lonesome Dove *by Larry McMurtry. "Phife" must be an ancestor of The* Andy Griffith Show*'s Barney Fife. Hoss and Little Joe Cartwright are from the series* Bonanza. *Since* Bonanza *and* The Lone Ranger *take place in the CU, so does* Rawhide Kid: Slap Leather. *Perhaps Lew Grant is the ancestor of the Lou Grant seen on the* Mary Tyler Moore Show *and* Lou Grant. *Will Kane is from* High Noon. *Kid Colt and the Two-Gun Kid appeared in the pages of Marvel Comics. Kid Shaleen is from the film* Cat Ballou.

Summer. The Lone Ranger helps out Robert Walker, the son of lawman called "Six Gun" Walker. "Six Gun," who died in 1872, left his land and property to Robert. (Television episode of The Lone Ranger entitled "*Six Gun's Legacy*.") Researcher Chuck Loridans postulates that "Six Gun" Walker is actually the 16th Phantom, also called the Masked Cowboy. The 16th Phantom operated during the 1840s-60s and he died sometime after 1867. It is possible that 16th Phantom and his wife, Texan Annie Morgan, had another child, born several years after the twins Kip (the 17th Phantom) and Julie (according to some the 18th Phantom), named Robert. The 16th Phantom died in 1872, and his younger son, who would not receive the Phantom birthright, did inherit his father's land in Texas, and returned to permanently settle there. Perhaps he is an ancestor of a modern-day kickboxing Texas Ranger, as well as Los Angeles policewoman Darcy Walker, better known as The Black Scorpion.

Summer. Birth of William Dawson, Scotland Yard inspector and Secret Service agent. Dawson's cases were recounted by Bennet Copplestone.

Summer
ANGELS OF MUSIC

Christine Daaé, Trilby O'Ferrall, and Irene Adler are the titular Angels, performing missions for their mysterious boss, Erik, the Opera Ghost. Trilby had a former mesmerist-tutor before working for Erik. The Angels' task this time is to discover the reason's behind the newly eccentric behavior of influential men, such as Cardinal Tosca and Brigadier Gerard. All the men are under the influence of much younger women, and met them through the Countess Josephine Balsamo (the Countess Cagliostro). The other men in the "Marriage Club" are the Duke of Omnium, the Chevalier Lucio del Gardo, Simon Cordier, Aristide Saccard, Georges Duroy, and Walter Parkes Thatcher. Other candidates are Count Ruboff, Baron Maupertuis, and Black Michael Elphberg. Erik's agent "The Persian" and Irene attend the Countess' Summer Ball as Rhandi Lal, the Khasi of Kalabar, and Princess Jelhi. Basil, a homosexual painter, also attends the Ball. Christine and Trilby break into the establishment of M. Coppélius and Sig. Spalanzani, and discover the true origins of one of the Countess' women, Olympia. Cochenille is Spalanzani's assistant. Ruritania is mentioned.

Story by Kim Newman in Tales of the Shadowmen Volume 2: Gentlemen of the Night, *Jean-Marc and Randy Lofficier, eds., Black Coat Press, 2006; reprinted in French in* Les Compagnons de l'Ombre (Tome 1), *Jean-Marc and Randy Lofficier, eds., Rivière Blanche, 2008. Christine Daaé and Erik are from Leroux's* Phantom of the Opera. *Trilby's former mesmerist-tutor is Svengali; both are from George Du Maurier's* Trilby. *Irene Adler is from Doyle and Watson's Sherlock Holmes tale "A Scandal in Bohemia." Cardinal Tosca's sudden death is an unchronicled case mentioned in Doyle and Watson's "The Adventure of Black Peter." Baron Maupertuis is from Doyle and Watson's Sherlock Holmes tale "The Reigate Puzzle." Brigadier Gerard is a Wold Newton Family member whose exploits were told by Arthur Conan Doyle. Josephine Balsamo, the Countess Cagliostro, is from Leblanc's Arsène Lupin stories. The Duke of Omnium is from Anthony Trollope's* The Prime Minister *and* Dr. Thorne. *The Chevalier Lucio del Gardo is from the play "The Face at the Window" by F. Brooke Warren. Simon Cordier is from Guy de Maupassant's story "The Horla," made into the film* Diary of a Madman. *Walter Parkes Thatcher is from Orson Welles'* Citizen Kane. *Aristide Saccard is from Emile Zola's* L'Argent, La

Fortune des Rougon, *and* La Curée*)*. *Georges Duroy is from* Bel Ami *by Guy de Maupassant. Rhandi Lal and Princess Jelhi are from the British action comedy film* Carry On…Up the Khyber *(1968). Count Ruboff is from the 1925 film version of* The Phantom of the Opera. *Black Michael Elphberg and Ruritania are from Anthony Hope's* A Prisoner of Zenda. *Basil is Basil Hallward* from Oscar Wilde's The Picture of Dorian Gray. *Coppélius, Spalanzani, Cochenille, and Olympia are from the opera* Les Contes d'Hoffmann *by Jacques Offenbach. The whole story is a riff on the 1970s television program* Charlie's Angels, *as if it had taken place in 1870s Paris.*

FOOL'S GOLD
Mysterious Dave Mather and Wyatt Earp encounter the mysterious "sand dwellers."

Short story by Matthew Baugh in Hell's Hangmen: Horror in the Old West, *edited by Ron Shiflet, Tenoka Press, 2006. The sand dwellers are from the Cthulhu Mythos tale "The Gable Window" by H.P. Lovecraft and August Derleth.*

1879

SNAKE OIL
In northern New Mexico, Mysterious Dave Mather meets one of the ancient serpent people. He also sees the terrible Yig, the Father of Serpents. A character gives an account of people who lived in the Americas before the Indians. He mentions the Shonokins, Sand Dwellers, Deep Ones, and the Serpent People.

Short story by Matthew Baugh in Frontier Cthulhu, *William Jones, ed., Chaosium Books, 2007. Yig is one of the Great Old Ones created by H.P. Lovecraft. He first appeared in the story "The Curse of Yig" by Lovecraft and Zealia Bishop. The serpent people are from Robert E. Howard's King Kull stories. The Shonokins are from the works of Manly Wade Wellman. The Deep Ones are from Lovecraft's "The Shadow over Innsmouth." The Sand Dwellers are from the story "The Gable Window" by Lovecraft and Derleth.*

c. Late 1870s. The events of *The Bostonians*, as chronicled by Henry James.

1880

Winter. Birth of Miss Rachel Murdock, amateur criminologist in cases recounted by D.B. Olsen.

Winter. Birth of Joseph Jorkens, a Wold Newton Family member, as stated in Farmer's *Doc Savage*.

Winter
UNTER CHINGAGOKS WAFFEN
Winoga, the "last of the Mohicans," discovers the weapons of Chingachgook.
From Winoga *#86. Chingachgook was Natty Bumppo's companion in James Fenimore Cooper's* The Last of the Mohicans. *Bumppo is a Wold Newton Family ancestor. This crossover brings Winoga into the CU.*

THESE OUR ACTORS
In a flashback set in 1880, Spike (or William, as he was then known) goes to the theatre a few nights before he becomes a vampire, and sees a performance of *A Midsummer Night's Dream*. The actor playing Oberon is a Scotsman named Hamish Bond.
A Buffy the Vampire Slayer *novel by Ashley McConnell and Dori Koogler. Bond's appearance is described as if one were to describe James Bond actor Sean Connery. Loki Carbis theorizes that this Hamish is an older brother of Campion Bond from* The League of Extraordinary Gentlemen.

June 18. Birth of Superintendent Henry Wilson of Scotland Yard. Wilson's cases will be chronicled by G.D.H. and M.I. Cole.
June 1880-October 1883. Bel Ami by Guy de Maupassant.
Summer. Sherlock Holmes works with Theodore Roosevelt. (*The Adventure of the Stalwart Companions, a novel written by Theodore Roosevelt, edited by H. Paul Jeffers, Harper & Row, 1978.*)

Late July-Early August
THE WEEPING MASKS
Dr. John Watson relates the tale that he never dared tell his friend, Sherlock Holmes: In the wake of the Battle of Maiwand, Watson and his orderly, Murray, took refuge in a relatively friendly Afghan village. There, while Watson was recovering, sinister priests in weeping masks preyed upon him and other sick Afghan villagers. The Weeping Ones were in the service of "He Who Is Not to Be Named."
Dr. Watson records these events sometime during the Great Hiatus of 1891-1894, when he thought Holmes dead. Watson's manuscript was edited by James Lowder, and appears in the Holmesian/Lovecraftian anthology Shadows Over Baker Street, *Michael Reaves and John Pelan, eds., Del Rey Books, 2003. The Battle of Maiwand took place on July 27-28, 1880. "He Who Is Not to Be Named" is the Great Old One Hastur, who is associated with a dark star near Aldebaran in the constellation of Taurus. After Watson's escape, he spent further time recuperating and being tended to by an Afghan woman, Miriam Shah (see "The Adventure of the Arab's Manuscript"), before finally returning home to England in October 1880.*

November. Solar Pons is born in Prague to Asenath Pons, consular official for Great Britain, and Roberta McIvor.

December
TRAIL OF THE BRUJO
Mysterious Dave Mather tracks an immortal sorcerer named Don Ysidro, also called the brujo, to Dallas. It is revealed in the story that the brujo is actually a man who made a bargain with the entity Byagoona centuries ago. Any time his current body dies, the brujo's spirit is transferred to a new body by the mystical "Talisman of Byagoona."

Short story by Matthew Baugh in Tales from the Cauldron, *Rhiannon Frater, ed., Library of the Living Dead Press. Though not explicitly stated, it is clear that Don Ysidro is another manifestation of the villain who met Zorro in 1818. Byagoona, the Faceless One, was worshipped in the ancient civilization of Altuas and may be an avatar of Nyarlathotep. It first appeared in the story "The Bane of Byagoona" by James Ambeuhl.*

1881

January-March
A STUDY IN SCARLET
Sherlock Holmes and John Watson meet and take rooms at 221B Baker Street. Holmes formally begins his consulting detective practice. During a conversation in which Watson learns more about Holmes' penchant for the science of detection, Holmes makes belittling comments about his predecessors Dupin and Lecoq.

This is the first Sherlock Holmes novel by Watson, edited by Sir Arthur Conan Doyle. According to Farmer, Sherlock Holmes is a Wold Newton Family member. C. Auguste Dupin's cases were recorded by Edgar Allan Poe. Lecoq's exploits were recorded by Emile Gaboriau. Of note, Farmer also posited that Dupin and M. Lecoq were Wold Newton Family members.

Winter. The events of Gaston Leroux's *The Phantom of the Opera*.

Winter. Events of *The Severed Hand* by Fortune du Boisgobey.

Early March. Colonel Sebastian "Basher" Moran returns to London from Afghanistan and begins a profitable term in the employ of Professor James Moriarty. ("A Volume in Vermillion" by Kim Newman, *Sherlock Holmes Mystery Magazine,* Vol. 1, #3, Marvin Kaye, ed., Winter 2009-2010.)

Spring. Birth of journalist/detective Philip Marsham Trent, whose cases were chronicled by E.C. Bentley.

May 1881-January 1882. The events of Jules Verne's *The School for Robinsons* (aka *The School for Crusoes*).

July 20. Birth of detective Astrogon "Astro" Kerby. (*Astro, Master of Mysteries* by Gelett Burgess.)

Summer. The events of the Allan Quatermain adventure King Solomon's Mines, as related by H. Rider Haggard. The general reading order of Haggard's series is: *Allan's Wife, Marie, Child of Storm, A Tale of Three Lions, Maiwa's Revenge; or, The War of the Little Hand, Hunter Quatermain's Story, Long Odds, Allan and the Holy Flower, Heu-Heu; or, The Monster, She and Allan, The Treasure of the Lake, The Ivory Child, Finished, King Solomon's Mines, The Ancient Allan, Allan and the Ice-Gods,* and *Allan Quatermain.* The time period covered by *Allan's Wife* actually spans the events of *Marie* and *Child of Storm.* A related novel of the great warrior Umslopogaas is Haggard's *Nada the Lily.* Umslopogaas' uncle Mopo appears in *The Ghost Kings.* The story of Quatermain's life continues in Alan Moore's *Allan and the Sundered Veil* and *The League of Extraordinary Gentlemen.*

Summer. Birth of Edward "Ned" Malone.

Summer
JOURNEY THROUGH THE IMPOSSIBLE

In Denmark, George Hatteras (the son of Captain Hatteras) dreams of becoming an adventurer and emulating his father as well as Lidenbrock, Captain Nemo, and Michel Ardan, the French member of the Gun Club Expedition. Dr. Ox gives George a potion designed to drive George insane. Consequently, George seems to gain the ability to teleport himself and his companions through time and space. They visit the center of the Earth, the *Nautilus*, and the Gun Club, as well as ancient Atlantis and another planet. In these journeys, Volsius combats Dr. Ox by assuming the identities of Lidenbrock, Nemo, Ardan, and others. While supposedly teleporting to Italy, George and his companions pick up another Danish citizen, Axel Valdemar. Eventually returning to Denmark, Volsius and George's fiancée, Eva, help George regain his sanity and Dr. Ox is defeated.

Play by Jules Verne linking together several of his creations, Prometheus Books, 2003. Rick Lai proposes the following theory: "In 'Dr. Ox's Experiment,' Dr. Ox invented a gas that caused hallucinations. Ox really submitted everyone to his gas, and this whole journey was one huge illusion. Ox used power of suggestion to manipulate his victims' perceptions. The Dane Valdemar was never in Italy, but in Denmark all the time. The only evidence that the journey transpired is a diamond that supposedly was found in the center of the Earth. This jewel could have be a fake planted by Ox. Although the 'real' Lidenbrock, Nemo, and Gun Club don't appear in this adventure, their existence is acknowledged."

Autumn
A FATHER'S TALE

Brigadier Donald Ffellowes relates a tale of his father's encounter with a man called only "Mr. Verner." The encounter occurred in the Autumn of 1881 off the coast of Sumatra, and involved a group of man-rat creatures called the Folk, who were created by the Moreau-like experiments of a scientist called Cornelius Van Ouisthoven.

A short story by Sterling E. Lanier, in Sherlock Holmes Through Time and Space, *edited by Isaac Asimov, Martin Greenberg, and Charles Waugh, Bluejay Books, 1984. "Verner" is obviously Sherlock Holmes, and this tale relates the story otherwise known as the "Giant Rat of Sumatra." Another "Giant Rat" story takes place in 1886, but its events are unrelated to this one, save that "Matilda Briggs" must have been a popular ship name in the 1880s. This story brings Lanier's Brigadier Ffellowes into the CU.*

1881-1903

A STAR FALLS, A ROSE BLOOMS…

Two former government agents are recruited by former sheriff Jess Harper to stand up against the villainous John Fain: Jeff Cable and Jeremy Pike. Chris Larabee, Griff King, and Lulu McQueen also appear, while Nellie Oleson is mentioned as having grown up to become a prostitute.

Short story by John Allen Small in his collection Days Gone By: Legends and Tales of Sipokni West, *Ethan Books, 2007. John Fain was the villain portrayed by Richard Boone in the 1971 John Wayne film* Big Jake. *This particular* incident is said to have occurred in 1886; Big Jake *occurs in 1906 and ends with Fain's death. Jeff Cable was the undercover agent played by William Shatner in the short-lived 1970s series* Barbary Coast. *Jeremy Pike, as portrayed by Charles Aidman, was a temporary replacement for an ailing Ross Martin, who played Artemus Gordon, during the final season of* The Wild Wild West. *(Small also speculates that Jeremy Pike was an ancestor of* Star Trek's *Captain Christopher Pike.) Chris Larabee is from the television version of* The Magnificent Seven—*the role originated by Yul Brynner and portrayed in subsequent sequels by George Kennedy and Lee Van Cleef, and later played in the television series by Michael Biehn. Griff King was one of the ranch hands shown in later episodes of* Bonanza, *while Lulu McQueen was one of several members of a lost wagon train seen in the 1973-74 series* Dusty's Trail. *Snobby little Nellie Oleson is from the television series* Little House on the Prairie.

1882

Spring
THE INCIDENT OF THE IMPECUNIOUS CHEVALIER

C. Auguste Dupin complains to his unnamed raconteur about Sherlock Holmes' disparaging comments in *A Study in Scarlet*. Dupin then relates the details of his 1877 case, in which he and Holmes sought the legendary Maltese Falcon.

A short story edited by Richard A. Lupoff from a manuscript by Dupin's nameless amanuensis, in My Sherlock Holmes, *Michael Kurland, ed., St. Martin's Press, 2003; reprinted in Lupoff's* The Universal Holmes, *Ramble House, 2007. The Maltese Falcon would figure later in a celebrated case involving Sam Spade, whom Philip José Farmer has stated was also a Wold Newton Family member, along with Dupin and Holmes.*

April 1882-November 1885
LORD KELVIN'S MACHINE

William Ashbless' *Account of London Scientists* includes several accounts of Langdon St. Ives' successes and adventures.

A novel by James P. Blaylock, Ace Books, 1992. Ashbless was a major character in Tim Powers' novel The Anubis Gates. *This semi-sequel to* Homunculus *also features the evil Dr. Narbondo (also known as Dr. Frost). Frost is connected to Dr. Frosticos, from Blaylock's* The Digging Leviathan, *which takes place in the CU through a connection to Edgar Rice Burroughs' Pellucidar series.*

July
TIGER! TIGER!

In India, a terrible man-eating flaming tiger stalks a hunting party, which includes Irene Adler and Colonel Sebastian Moran. Moran's prisoner, an Arab, summons the creature with the invocation, "Iä! Iä Hastur cf'ayah 'vugtlagln Hastur!"

A short story by Elizabeth Bear in the Holmesian/Lovecraftian anthology Shadows Over Baker Street, *Michael Reaves and John Pelan, eds., Del Rey Books, 2003. Hastur is one of the Great Old Ones from the Cthulhu Mythos tales of H.P Lovecraft and others.*

Summer
NO FINGER ON THE TRIGGER
Waxahachie Smith encounters Donald Garfew Beech, Head of the U.S. Secret Service. Beech's grandson, Orville Garfew "Fluency" Beech would later meet Doc Savage. Lord Maidstone, the son of Horatio Hornblower, is also mentioned.

Novel by J.T. Edson confirming the Hornblowers in the CU. Smith is an associate of the Floating Outfit and a former Texas Ranger. Orville Garfew "Fluency" Beech is from Red Snow *by Kenneth Robeson (Lester Dent).*

IT CRAWLS
Wu Chan, a mentor of The Lone Ranger and Tonto, loans his protégés two books to assist in their quest to defeat an Aztec Mummy, who is really a brain-damaged visitor from the stars. One of the books is a copy of the Necronomicon.

A Lone Ranger and Tonto comic book miniseries written by Joe R. Lansdale and published by Topps Comics. The Cthulhu Mythos link places The Lone Ranger (John Reid) and Tonto in the CU. Note that The Green Hornet (Britt Reid) would cross paths with Wold Newton Family member The Shadow in 1942, solidifying the place of the Reids in the CU.

Autumn. A.J. Raffles' earliest criminal exploit, as told by Raffles himself, in "Le Premier Pas" (edited by E.W. Hornung, and appearing in *The Amateur Cracksman*).

1883

Winter. Birth of Dr. Caber, son of John Clay (see Watson's/Doyle's "The Adventure of the Red-Headed League") and Urania Moriarty, grandson of the first Professor James Moriarty, as established by Farmer in *Doc Savage: His Apocalyptic Life.* Dr. Caber would become the nemesis of Wold Newton Family member Joseph Jorkens. Lord Dunsany related their tales in three stories: "The Invention of Dr. Caber" (found in *Jorkens Has a Large Whiskey*), and "The Strange Drug of Dr. Caber" and "The Cleverness of Dr. Caber" (both in The Fourth Book of Jorkens).

Winter. An English academic finds something nasty in a church in France. ("Canon Alberic's Scrap Book" by M.R. James.)

April
THE ADVENTURE OF THE OLD RUSSIAN WOMAN
Holmes and Watson endeavor to locate an artist named Vukcic, whose subject matter for the painting at the heart of this case is a farmwoman in Montenegro. Holmes also refers to a "mastermind" behind the mystery, whose name he knows as well as his own, but Holmes declines to name the man at this time.

Short story by H. Paul Jeffers, in the anthology The Confidential Casebook of Sherlock Holmes, *Marvin Kaye, ed., St. Martin's Press, 1998. One of Holmes' twin sons would later answer to the name Marko Vukcic, perhaps hinting that Holmes had a deeper relationship with the painter than is otherwise indicated. Both Marko Vukcic and his twin brother, Nero Wolfe, had close ties to Montenegro. The unnamed mastermind is Sherlock's brother, Mycroft Holmes.*

Spring. Denis Nayland Smith is born. Philip José Farmer stated in *Tarzan Alive* that Smith is the son of Sherlock Holmes' sister, Sigrina Holmes, and thus is the nephew of Holmes. Nayland Smith shares an interesting characteristic with another British detective, Solar Pons, namely, the habit of tugging on the left earlobe in times of stress or deep thought. Brad Mengel, in "Watching the Detectives, Or, The Sherlock Holmes Family Tree" (*Myths for the Modern Age: Philip José Farmer's Wold Newton Universe*), proposes that Nayland Smith and Solar Pons are distant cousins, related through Pons' mother, Roberta McIvor.

Spring. Old Broadbrim's first recorded case. ("Old Broadbrim, the Quaker Detective; or, The Strangest Trail of Crime on Record," *Old Cap Collier Library* #92, May 2, 1884. Written by "Jack Howard.")

Summer
A STORY OF DRACULA, THE WOLFMAN, AND FRANKENSTEIN
Dr. Vincent von Frankenstein, a nephew of the previous Baron Frankenstein, and his fiancée, Ericka, are lured to Dracula's castle. The Count takes Ericka hostage and forces Dr. Frankenstein to build another Monster who will

serve Dracula's will. Through an unforeseen series of events, Ericka becomes a werewolf, and a monster mash-up results. The familiar folk poem is quoted: "Even a man who's pure of heart / And says his prayers at night / May become a wolf when the wolfbane blooms / And the moon is full and bright."

A recorded story on the album House of Terror!, *Parade Records, 1975, with accompanying comic insert story illustrated by Neal Adams. The recorded story was also issued as a standalone record from Power Records. The Adams comic story was expanded to graphic novel format and released as* Neal Adams Monsters, *Vanguard Productions, 2003. The revised version changed the date of the story to 1912, but the original 1883 date is being used for this crossover entry. The tale adds yet another member to the extended family of Frankenstein doctors who have constructed their own Monsters. The "old folk poem" was written by Curt Siodmak for Universal Pictures' Wolf Man films.*

Summer 1883-1885. The events of *She*, as narrated by Ludwig Horace Holly, and transcribed by H. Rider Haggard. Holly, a scholar and African explorer, is the guardian of Leo Vincey, the reincarnated love of She-who-must-be-obeyed, of the lost valley of Kôr. Holly is also a Wold Newton Family member, as stated in Farmer's *Tarzan Alive*. The date is derived from *Ayesha: The Return of She*.

October 1883-March 1885. The events of R.L. Stevenson's *The Strange Case of Dr. Jekyll and Mr. Hyde.*

October 1883-March 1885
DR. JEKYLL AND MR. HOLMES

In this companion novel to Robert Louis Stevenson's *Dr. Jekyll and Mr. Hyde*, Sherlock Holmes and Dr. John Watson encounter Dr. Henry Jekyll and his alter ego, Edward Hyde.

This Holmes/Jekyll novel is by mystery writer Loren D. Estleman, published by Penguin Books in 1980.

Winter
ABBOTT AND COSTELLO MEET DR. JEKYLL AND MR. HYDE

"Slim" and "Tubby" are American cops in London to study police tactics. After ending up in jail, they are bailed out by Dr. Jekyll. Jekyll has been murdering fellow doctors who laugh at his experiments, and has more murders in mind. At one point, the serum that turns Jekyll into the murderous Hyde gets injected into Tubby.

This film takes place during the events of Robert Louis Stevenson's book. These two bumblers later met Larry Talbot and Frankenstein's Monster, although they were using different names. See Dennis E. Power's "Hyde and Hair" on The Wold Newton Universe: A Secret History *website for a further explanation of these events in the Crossover Universe. Power has also provided the solution to the mystery as to why these fellows appear to be so long-lived in his essay "Immortal Befuddled," also on his* Secret History *website.*

1884

Winter. Birth of detective Reginald Fortune, whose cases were told by H.C. Bailey.

Winter. Kathryn Koluchy conducts her nefarious activities, as detailed in *The Brotherhood of Seven Kings* by L.T. Meade and Robert Eustace.

Spring. Birth of Joseph Josephin, aka Rouletabille.

Summer. Publication of Colonel Sebastian Moran's *Three Months in the Jungle.*

August
THE DORRINGTON RUBY SEAL (R. HOLMES & CO)
Sherlock Holmes first encounters the "amateur cracksman," A.J. Raffles, who had stolen the Dorrington Ruby Seal seven months earlier, in January 1884. Holmes marries Raffles' sister Marjorie, resulting in the eventual birth of Raffles Holmes.

R. Holmes & Co. *is a collection of interconnected short stories by John Kendrick Bangs. It is speculated that Raffles Holmes was born in May 1885 and that Marjorie died in childbirth. Since it is doubtful that A.J. Raffles was old enough in 1884 to have a daughter of marrying age, Marjorie was more probably A.J. Raffles' sister, rather than his daughter as stated in* R. Holmes and Co.

Autumn. Dr. Gideon Fell is born.

Autumn. American painter Penniel achieves revenge, even though he is dead. ("A Stray Reveler" by Emma Dawson.)

Late December 1884-Late March 1885. The events of *The List of Seven,* as recounted by Mark Frost, in which Jack Sparks and his friend Dr. Arthur Conan Doyle (Watson's literary agent) break up an occult cabal known as the Seven.

1885

Winter

BUCK MASON LOSES HIS HORSE
Cowboy Buck Mason rides into town, intent on keeping an appointment with Orrin Sackett and Dusty Fog; the three are to ride up to Kansas and assist in the manhunt for the Ringo Kid, who has broken out of prison to search for Luke Plummer and his boys, who murdered Ringo's father and brother. While in the town's saloon, someone steals Buck's horse, but he convinces the culprit to return it.

Short story by John Allen Small in his collection Days Gone By: Legends and Tales of Sipokni West, *Ethan Books, 2007. Buck Mason is the father of Buck Mason in Edgar Rice Burroughs'* The Deputy Sheriff of Comanche County. *There are references to the Western novels of Louis L'Amour and J.T. Edson (the mentions of Orrin Sackett and Dusty Fog, respectively). The hunt for the Ringo Kid follows the basic plot of both the classic 1939 John Wayne film* Stagecoach *and its 1966 remake.*

Mid-March. A.J. Raffles and Bunny Manders begin working together in "The Ides of March" (edited by E.W. Hornung, and appearing in *The Amateur Cracksman*).

March-May
THE INFERNAL DEVICE
Benjamin Barnett, a member of the first Professor Moriarty's crime family, has a secretary named Cecily Perrine, who describes her father as a man who is a student of languages and dialects, and who can place someone within two blocks in London after listening to them speak. Cecily's father is a Professor whose first name is Henry, and whom Sherlock Holmes expresses an interest in meeting. Holmes and Watson actually find themselves working on the same side as Moriarty. Writers Oscar Wilde and Bernard Shaw are also mentioned, as is a statue of Lord Hornblower.

This Professor Moriarty novel is by Michael Kurland, Signet Books, 1978. Hornblower is from C.S. Forester's nautical novels. Although Cecily's father is named as Henry Perrine, this is clearly a pseudonym for Professor Henry Higgins. George Bernard Shaw told the story of Professor Higgins in Pygmalion, *also known as* My Fair Lady.

Summer. Birth of John Duff, private detective in cases told by Harvey J. O'Higgins.

Summer. Arronaxe Larsen, Doc Savage's mother, is born. As stated in Farmer's *Doc Savage*, she is the daughter of Wolf Larsen and Arronaxe Land.

Summer
CURE THE TEXAS FEVER
Waxahachie Smith works with the Floating Outfit and Theodore Roosevelt to protect those who can cure the Texas fever.
Novel by J.T. Edson. The CU version of Roosevelt worked with Sherlock Holmes and would also meet Indiana Jones.

A SHAMBLES IN BELGRAVIA
Irene Adler hires Professor Moriarty and Colonel Moran to retrieve some incriminating photographs of herself and Black Michael Elphberg of Ruritania from Colonel Sapt, chief of the Ruritanian Secret Police. Moran refers to "a run-of-the-mill safe-breaker like that cricket-playing fathead."
Short story by Colonel Sebastian Moran, edited by Kim Newman, on the BBC Cult website, 2004; included in The Best British Mysteries 2006, *Maxim Jakubowski, ed. Irene Adler, Professor Moriarty, and Colonel Moran are from the Sherlock Holmes stories, while Black Michael, Colonel Sapt, and Ruritania are from Anthony Hope's* A Prisoner of Zenda. *The cricket-playing fathead is E.W. Hornung's Raffles.*

Summer 1885-1886. Upon their return to England, the spirit of the "late" Ayesha begins to manifest itself to Leo Vincey and Ludwig Horace Holly in various manners, finally instructing them to return to Kôr. Vincey's subsequent death is greatly exaggerated, given Haggard's own sequel, Ayesha: The Return of She. (*King of Kôr, Or, She's Promise Kept*, a sequel to H. Rider Haggard's novel *She*, narrated by Ludwig Horace Holly, and transcribed by Sidney J. Marshall, 1903.)

Summer 1885-1887. Events of Rudyard Kipling's "The Man Who Would Be King."

Summer. Dr. Henry Frankenstein recreates his ancestor's experiments, as seen in the feature film Frankenstein. The full cycle of adventures of this particular Frankenstein Monster is as follows: *Frankenstein, Bride of Frankenstein, The Son of Frankenstein, The Ghost of Frankenstein, Frankenstein Meets the Wolf Man, The House of Frankenstein, House of Dracula, Abbott and Costello Meet Frankenstein, Return of the Wolf Man* (a novel by Jeff Rovin), *The Devil's Brood,* and *The Devil's Night* (both novels by David Jacobs).

Summer 1885-1886. Events of Allan Quatermain, which features the title character's purported death, as related by H. Rider Haggard. Actually, Quatermain fakes his own death. Speaking of the events of Allan Quatermain, he states, "Only my demise was sham, a ruse to grant me freedom from my suffocating reputation." (Alan Moore's *Allan and the Sundered Veil*.)

September-October 1885. The *Jekyll Legacy*, a sequel to *Dr. Jekyll and Mr. Hyde*, as told by Robert Bloch and Andre Norton, in which Dr. Jekyll's niece, Hester, is involved in some terrifying events. The murderous culprit of the tale was obviously lying when elucidating on the theft of Mr. Hyde's corpse from its grave, since, unbeknownst to many, Jekyll/Hyde still lived at the conclusion of *Dr. Jekyll and Mr. Hyde* (see *The League of Extraordinary Gentlemen* and *Tooth and Nail*).

Autumn. Publication of Hendrik Van Helsing's *Hollow Dark Places* (Zoondt, Amsterdam, 1885).

October 12. Birth of Craig Kennedy, the "Scientific Detective."

November
DICKENS OF THE MOUNTED
Harry Flashman has a cameo appearance in this history about a real-life son of Charles Dickens.

Novel by Eric Nicol, linking George MacDonald Fraser's Harry Flashman to the younger Dickens, who had an actual career as an incompetent member of the Mounties.

November 1885-Autumn 1896
THE LADY IN THE BLACK GLOVES
Josephine Balsamo meets with Mrs. Noel Moriarty at the Villa Corbucci in Naples; both women are former students at Madame Fourneau's College for Young Women. Mrs. Moriarty is otherwise known as Madame Koluchy of the Brotherhood, a branch of the Black Coats. Madame Koluchy's father is an unnamed Italian Count. Her attendants are Mary Holder and Helen Lipsius. Noel Moriarty's late brother is James. By 1896, Irina Putine goes to work for the Chupin Detective Agency and is investigating a series of unexplained murders; the victims are all models of the painter Jacques Salliard, who is later revealed to be Isadora Klein. Doctor Maubeuge is the director of an asylum called La Maison de Repos at the Ville-d'Avray. Dr. Brion, the Royal Palace Hotel, Dr. Anatole Cerral, Arsène Lupin, and *L'Écho de France* are all mentioned. The po-

lice discuss sculptor Boris Yvain. The late artist and killer Gaston Morrell, also known as Bluebeard, is mentioned as the brother of the late Madame Fourneau. Inspector Lefevre investigated the Bluebeard murders in 1878. The Duke of Carineaux's art collection is mentioned. Louis Fourneau masquerades as Inspector Maurice d'Andresy. Van Klopen's dressmaking shop was sold in 1892 to the House of Crafts, a London firm owned by Madame Koluchy.

Short story Rick Lai in Tales of the Shadowmen Volume 3: Danse Macabre, *Jean-Marc and Randy Lofficier, eds., Black Coat Press, 2007; reprinted in French in* Les Compagnons de l'Ombre (Tome 6), *Jean-Marc and Randy Lofficier, eds., Rivière Blanche, 2010. Josephine Balsamo is Arsène Lupin's nemesis from Maurice Leblanc's* La Comtesse de Cagliostro *and* La Cagliostro se venge. *Madame Fourneau's College for Young Women is from the Spanish film* La Residencia *(aka* The House That Screamed*). The Villa Corbucci is the home of Count Corbucci from E.W. Hornung's Raffles stories. Madame Koluchy's father is meant to be Corbucci. Koluchy and the Brotherhood are from* The Brotherhood of Seven Kings *by L.T. Meade and Robert Eustace. Her relationship with Noel Moriarty is outlined in Rick Lai's "The Secret History of Captain Nemo" (*Myths for the Modern Age: Philip José Farmer's Wold Newton Universe*). Noel's brother James is Professor Moriarty. The Black Coats are from Paul Feval's* Habits Noirs *saga. Boris Yvain is from "The Mask" by Robert W. Chambers. Helen Lipsius is from Arthur Machen's* The Three Impostors, *although in that book, she is only called Helen. She works for the mysterious Dr. Lipsius. By giving Helen the surname of her superior, Lai raises the speculation that she is the doctor's mistress (like Carl and Irma Peterson). Mary Holder is from Sir Arthur Conan Doyle's Sherlock Holmes tale "The Adventure of the Beryl Coronet." Irina Putine is really Irene Tupin/Chupin, the niece of Victor Chupin; she is also derived from* The House That Screamed, *as is Louis (Luis) Fourneau. Victor Chupin (also known as Toto Chupin) is from Emile Gaboriau's Monsieur Lecoq series. Gaston Morrell, Inspector Lefevre, and the Duke of Carineaux are from the 1944 film* Bluebeard, *starring John Carradine. The asylum at the Ville-d'Avray is from Maurice Leblanc's "The Lady with the Hatchet." Doctor Maubeuge is really Doctor Mabuse, from the series of German films by Fritz Lang, and from fiction by Norbert Jacques. Dr. Brion and the Royal Palace Hotel are from the first Fantômas novel. Arsène Lupin and* L'Écho de France *are from Maurice Leblanc's stories. Van Klopen is a recurring character in Emile Gaboriau's Monsieur Lecoq series. Krafthaus ("the House of Crafts") is from John Buchan's* The Power-House. *Jacques Salliard is from E.W. Hornung's Raffles stories, while Isadora Klein is from Doyle's Holmes story "The Adventure of the Three Gables." Dr. Anatole Cerral is the father of the scientist in Maurice Renard's* The Hands of Orlac, *and played a prominent role in Lai's "Dr. Cerral's Patient" (*Tales of the Shadowmen Volume 2: Gentlemen of the Night*).*

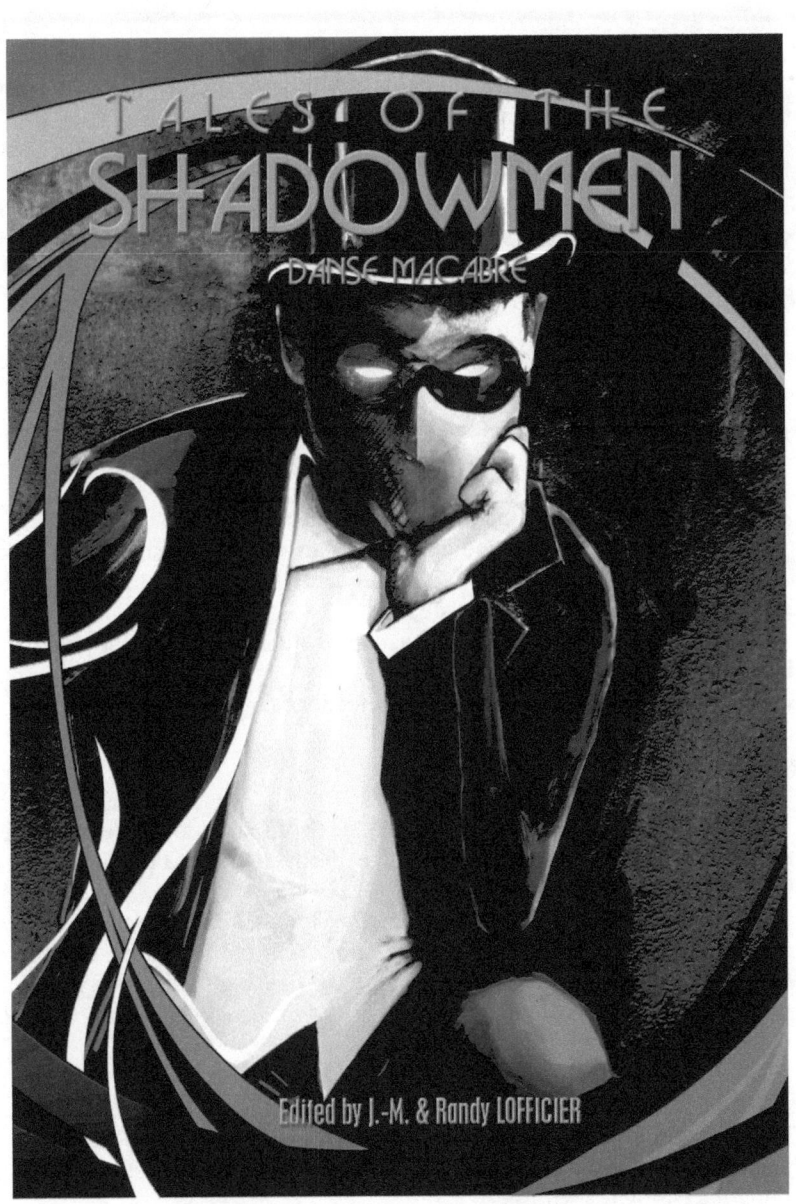

December 1885-October 1886
THE PURCHASE OF THE NORTH POLE
 The members of the Baltimore Gun Club buy the North Pole at an international auction. The events surrounding the previous auction of a Pacific island are also mentioned, as well as the events of *Hector Servadac* and *The Adventures of Captain Hatteras*.
 The Purchase of the North Pole *(aka* Topsy Turvy*) is a novel by Jules Verne. The Gun Club was also mentioned in Verne's* From the Earth to the Moon *and Rosny & Farmer's* Ironcastle. *The Gun Club members are now twenty years older since the Moon project. The previous auction of the Pacific island occurred in Verne's* The School for Robinsons *(aka* The School for Crusoes*).* Hector Servadac *and* The Adventures of Captain Hatteras *are also novels by Jules Verne.*

1886

 Winter. Events of the film *Bride of Frankenstein*.
 Winter. Mycroft Holmes is appointed head of the British Secret Service, thus becoming the first modern "M." Subsequent "M"s will include Admiral Sir Miles Messervy and Barbara Mawdsley.
 Winter. Birth of Dominick Medina, son of James Noel Moriarty and Kathryn Koluchy.
 Winter. Birth of amateur detective Philo Vance.

Winter
SEXTON BLAKE AT SCHOOL
 Sexton Blake, as a schoolboy, investigates a threat to his life and the peculiar and sinister actions of his guardians. He discovers that his real birth name is "Ronald Blakeney."
 Story by John Garbutt in Pilot *#75, March 6, 1937. Jess Nevins notes that "This late retelling of Blake's origin is different (but not ultimately contradictory) with previous versions of Blake's origin. And with a birth name like Blakeney I can only conclude that he is a part of the Blakeney [Sir Percy Blakeney, aka the Scarlet Pimpernel] family tree."*

March
THE GIANT RAT OF SUMATRA
 Holmes is retained by Professor August Belknap for assistance in a case involving the Cthulhu Mythos.
 Short story edited by Paula Volsky, from a manuscript by H.P. Lovecraft, based on the notes of Dr. John Watson, contained in the volume Resurrected Holmes, *Marvin Kaye, ed., 1996; reprinted in* Eternal Lovecraft, *Jim Turner,*

ed., 1998. August Belknap must be a relative of H.P. Lovecraft associate and fellow writer Frank Belknap Long.

Spring
ROBUR THE CONQUEROR

There are references to the cities Franceville (aka France-Ville) and Stahlstadt, as well as to the power source of Captain Nemo's Nautilus. Scientists also mistakenly suspect Robur's ship of being Herr Schultze's projectile.

Robur-le-Conquérant (*aka* Clipper of the Clouds*), like many of Jules Verne's stories, contains cross-references to his other novels, indicating that most if not all Verne stories take place in the CU. Franceville, Stahlstadt, and Herr Schultze's projectile are from* The Begum's Millions *(aka* The Begum's Fortune*), while Nemo is from* 20,000 Leagues under the Sea.

May-June 1886. Three men encounter a haunted house in Paris. ("No. 252 Rue M. le Prince," a short story by Ralph Adams Cram.)

May 19, 1886. Birth of Shadrack Arnold, private detective in cases told by Verne Chute.

Summer
THE ADVENTURE OF THE RARA AVIS

Holmes and Watson pursue the fabled Maltese Falcon, consulting an amateur Egyptologist named Basil Blakeney. Along the way, Herr Professor Hans-Josef Gutman is murdered, and they run afoul of the shady Greek, Aristophanes Cairo.

Short story by Carolyn Wheat in Murder, My Dear Watson, *edited by Greenberg, Lellenberg, and Stashower, Carroll & Graf, 2002. Blakeney may be a member of the family made famous by Sir Percy Blakeney. Gutman and Cairo must be ancestors of Caspar Gutman and Joel Cairo from Hammett's* The Maltese Falcon. *Holmes recovered the Black Bird in 1889, but it must have once again left his possession sometime thereafter.*

RAFFLES AND THE SHERE KHAN POUCH (aka MADAME BLAVATSKY'S TEACUPS)

Early in their partnership, Raffles and Manders are in Simla, the summer capital of the Viceroy of India. They become involved in intrigue surrounding a diplomatic pouch, and along the way they meet young journalist Rudyard Kipling and Madame Helena Petrova Blavatsky. At the conclusion of the adventure, Raffles and Manders observe Kipling meeting a young boy named Kim.

A short story by Barry Perowne in Ellery Queen's Mystery Magazine, *January 1977 (reprinted as "Madame Blavatsky's Teacups" in the anthology* Raffles of the M.C.C., *St. Martin's Press, 1979). Twenty-year-old Kipling was in Simla in the summer of 1886. He went on to write about the young boy he met in his seminal novel* Kim.

Summer. *The Old Detective's Pupil*, Nick Carter's first case, by John Russell Coryell and Ormond Smith. Since Nick Carter's adventures take place in the CU, many other penny dreadful and dime novel heroes can be included. According to scholar Jess Nevins, these are: Ted Strong, Old Broadbrim, Miss Amelia Butterworth, Charles O'Malley, Nic-Stop, Charlot, Jack Franklin, the Master Detective, and Joseph Petrosino, the hero of an Italian dime novel series. Nevins adds, "There are also grounds for concluding that Prince Wu Ling and the Brotherhood of the Yellow Beetle fought both Sexton Blake and Nick Carter. Further, there is an uncanny similarity between Sexton Blake's bloodhound Pedro—given to him, remember, by one 'Mr. Nemo'—and Nick Carter's bloodhound Pedro, and so some relation between the two can be inferred."

August. Leo Vincey and Ludwig Horace Holly set out for Central Asia on a quest to locate Ayesha; they will not succeed until 1903 (*Ayesha: The Return of She*).

August
THE NIGHT ORCHID (CONAN DOYLE IN TOULOUSE)
Arthur Conan Doyle is summoned to France by his paleontologist friend, Professor Frédéric Picard, to help solve a mysterious death. Although Doyle and Picard's "mutual friend" is otherwise occupied, Doyle does bring along young Professor George Challenger to assist. Opera singer Irène Ader is also involved in the case, ostensibly the victim's wife.

A short story by Jean-Claude Dunyach in the anthology The Night Orchid, *Black Coat Press, 2004. The mutual friend is mentioned several times and is clearly implied to be Sherlock Holmes. This case would inspire Challenger's later fabled expedition to the Lost World. There is more to "Irène Ader" than meets the eye, as she is clearly intended to be Irene Adler, "the Woman" from the Holmes tale "A Scandal in Bohemia." It is doubtful that she is really the sister of another character in the story, Clément Ader, or that she was married to the victim. It is more likely that she was undercover in Toulouse for some undisclosed reason. This story takes place before "Bohemia," which Baring-Gould places in May 1887. Therefore I have altered Dubyach's placement of "The Night Orchid" from 1890 to 1886. Professor Picard could very well be a distant ancestor of 24th-century space explorer Jean-Luc Picard.*

Autumn
THE SINGULAR ADVENTURE OF THE GENTLEMAN CRACKSMAN
Holmes and Watson versus Raffles and Manders.
Short story by Gareth Tilley in It's That Time Again 3: Even More New Stories of Old-Time Radio, *Jim Harmon, ed., BearManor Media, 2006.*

December. The events of *Sherlock Holmes and the Hands of Othello*, as related by Alexander Simmons. Holmes helps Amanda Aldridge, the black actress and daughter of the famous "Negro Tragedian," the late Ira Aldridge. Holmes is hired by Thomas Kane (Amanda's suitor) to investigate a strange series of events. Holmes also fights Phillipe Moreau, an assassin hired to kill Amanda Aldridge. The first duel between Moreau and Holmes ends in a draw. In the second duel, a sword fight, Holmes kills Moreau. (Further genealogical research may reveal a distant connection between Dr. Alphonse Moreau and Phillipe Moreau.)

December. "The Adventure of the Red Leech," in which Holmes and Watson foil the first Professor Moriarty's plan to assassinate Queen Victoria (*Detective Comics* #572).

1887

January
DEATH BY GASLIGHT
The first Professor Moriarty concocts a scheme involving Her Majesty's Battleship Hornblower. Colonel Sebastian Moran continues to be a sometime operative for Moriarty. Holmes and Watson also appear, as does the eighty-year-old Duke of Denver.
Michael Kurland's Professor Moriarty novel (Signet, 1982) most likely takes place in January, not the March date listed, since the good Professor is otherwise occupied in February-April 1887. The ship is named after nautical hero Horatio Hornblower, thus confirming Hornblower in the Crossover Un-

iverse. The Duke of Denver seen here is probably the 14th, making him Lord Peter Wimsey's grandfather, George Wimsey. Kurland indicated that another Moriarty novel, The Murder Trust, was in the works; apparently it was never published.

February-April
ALL-CONSUMING FIRE

In which Holmes and Watson encounter a mysterious traveler known as the Doctor (Who, that is, the Seventh incarnation) and together battle Azathoth, the Blind Idiot God of the Cthulhu Mythos. Mycroft Holmes, Sherringford Holmes, Professor Moriarty and Professor Challenger's associate, Lord John Roxton, also appear, as does Inspector Cribb. Fu Manchu's Si-Fan criminal organization, Professor Challenger, and Kolchak the Night Stalker are mentioned.

A Doctor Who *novel by Andy Lane, part of* The New Doctor Who Adventures *series, Doctor Who Books, 1994. Given the differences between the history of Doctor Who's universe and that of the Crossover Universe, it is probable that the Doctor in* All-Consuming Fire *is a parallel version to the Doctor of an alternate universe which we can call the Doctor Who Universe. It is also confirmed that the Cthulhu Mythos is associated with the CU. This novel brings in Peter Lovesey's detective, Inspector Cribb. Also of interest, Kim Newman's character from the* Anno Dracula *series, the British agent Charles Beauregard who works for the Diogenes Club (British Secret Service), is mentioned in* All-Consuming Fire *in the same role. This is a case of Newman's own practice of "borrowing" characters in reverse. However, the Anno Dracula Universe is a parallel reality to the CU.*

Winter
A DRUG ON THE MARKET

In the wake of the events of Dr. Jekyll and Mr. Hyde, a group a speculators attempts to profit from the "Jekyll Tonic." An opera singer who "conducted a famous amour with a Ruthenian Prince" is mentioned. Richard Enfield is the administrator of the late Utterson's estate.

Short story by Kim Newman, Dead Travel Fast, *Dinoship Books, 2005. The opera singer is Irene Adler. Richard Enfield = R. Enfield = Renfield. It is un-*

clear how this Richard Enfield relates to the Renfield seen in Bram Stoker's Dracula.

Winter. The first recorded exploits of French Inspector Tony, as he fights against German spies. (*The Mysteries of the Heart of Berlin*, pulp by Gabriel Bernard.)

Winter. The events of H.G. Wells' *The Island of Dr. Moreau*.

Winter. Birth of Charlie Chan. According to Dennis E. Power's "Asian Detectives in the Wold Newton Family" (*Myths for the Modern Age: Philip José Farmer's Wold Newton Universe*), Chan is the son of Fu Manchu.

April. The events of Anthony Hope's *The Prisoner of Zenda*.

Spring
MY LADY'S MONEY: AN EPISODE IN THE LIFE OF A YOUNG GIRL

The slovenly detective Old Sharon reads a book that describes a French detective who is very much like Père Tabaret.

Novella by Wilkie Collins first published in the 1887 Christmas Number of the Illustrated London News. *In fact, researcher Jess Nevins is convinced that this is an intentional reference to Gaboriau's Père Tabaret, unofficial member of the French police and mentor to Inspector Lecoq, thus placing Old Sharon in the Crossover Universe.*

May-November. The events of Bram Stoker's *Dracula*.

June. Paterson Erskine Guthrie takes a position as the confidential secretary to British spymaster Mycroft Holmes, essentially playing a Victorian Archie Goodwin to Holmes' Nero Wolfe (*Against the Brotherhood* by Guthrie, edited by Quinn Fawcett, Tor Books, 1998).

Summer. Samuel Clemens meets The Lone Ranger and Tonto. ("Gold on the Mississippi," a story found in Pure Imagination Comics' reprinting of Lone Ranger comic strips. Clemens, while in 1893 San Francisco, was accidentally transported to the U.S.S. *Enterprise*-D in the year 2368 [Star Trek: The Next Generation episode "Time's Arrow"]).

Summer. Birth of Jules Amedée François Maigret.

Summer. Birth of Arthur Hastings.

Summer
HOLMES AND THE LOSS OF THE BRITISH BARQUE *SOPHY ANDERSON*

Holmes takes a case involving Lieutenant Richard Hornblower, great-grandson of Admiral Viscount Horatio Hornblower.

Short story edited by Peter Cannon, from a manuscript by C.S. Forester, based on the notes of Dr. John Watson. Contained in volume entitled Resurrected Holmes, *Marvin Kaye, ed., 1996.*

August-November
SHERLOCK HOLMES VS. DRACULA OR THE ADVENTURE OF THE SANGUINARY COUNT

Holmes and Watson fight against Count Dracula in this companion novel to Bram Stoker's *Dracula*.

The Holmes/Dracula novel is by Watson, edited by mystery writer Loren D. Estleman, published by Penguin Books in 1979. Dracula's encounter with Holmes confirms Dracula in the Crossover Universe. Therefore, Zorro is also in the CU through his battle with the Count in 1809. The Count Dracula featured here is the "real" Count, Dracula-prime, as opposed to one of his many "soul-clones." Although Watson dated these events in 1890, further research reveals that Dracula-prime was once again present in England in 1888, just prior to the Ripper murders (see entry for Dracula: The Suicide Club). Dracula: The Suicide Club *also makes it clear that the events of Stoker's* Dracula *took place one year previous, i.e., 1887.*

August-November; May 1891
SCARLET IN GASLIGHT

Contemporaneously with the events of Dracula, Professor Moriarty controls the Lord of the Vampires during his stay in London, planning to use Dracula's blood to save his dying daughter, Agatha. Meanwhile, Holmes and Watson investigate the mysterious illness and subsequent death of Lucy Westenra, who was being treated by Dr. Abraham van Helsing. Mycroft Holmes and Col. Moran also appear, along with actress Sarah Bernhardt, Sir Henry Irving, and Bram Stoker himself. In the 1891 postscript at Reichenbach Falls, Moriarty injects himself with a vial of Dracula's blood to insure against possible defeat by Holmes. However, after Moriarty falls to his apparent death and Holmes departs, Dracula arrives to exact a final vengeance upon Moriarty.

Graphic novel by Martin Powell and Seppo Makinen, Malibu Comics, 1988. As with Sherlock Holmes vs. Dracula, *this story takes place during the events of Stoker's novel. Sarah Bernhardt, Sir Henry Irving, and Bram Stoker are real historical figures, of course. Although 1891 is given as the date in the story, for purposes of the Crossover Universe chronology, the date must be changed to 1887. Although it seems that Dracula kills Moriarty in the 1891* postscript, perhaps Moriarty's plan worked after all, since the first Professor Moriarty has many post-1891 appearances in various Crossover Universe stories.

September
THE DROWNED GEOLOGIST

This case takes place in Whitby, and the ship *Demeter* is mentioned, as is the Phoenician god Dagon.

A short story by Caitlín R. Kiernan in the Holmesian/Lovecraftian anthology Shadows Over Baker Street. *The locale Whitby and the ship* Demeter *are from Bram Stoker's* Dracula, *during which the events of this story take place. In the Lovecraftian Mythos, Dagon is the head of the Deep Ones who in turn serve Cthulhu. This tale appears to reconcile the Phoenician Dagon and the Lovecraftian Dagon.*

November-May 1888
MINA: THE DRACULA STORY CONTINUES

Mina (Murray) Harker, conducting an investigation in London, wonders, "What would Detective Holmes do?"

Novel by Marie Kiraly (pseudonym for Elaine Bergstrom). Although the novel also refers to the Holmes stories as being written by Doyle, everyone knows that Holmes was a real person and that Doyle served as Dr. Watson's editor and literary agent.

December
QUINCEY MORRIS, VAMPIRE

In the aftermath of the events of *Dracula*, Quincey Morris becomes a vampire himself, although of a different breed—one with a soul. Morris mentions that he and Arthur Holmwood had hunted tigers in India with Colonel Sebastian Moran. Moran had bagged a twelve-foot man eater with one shot. In remembrance of this incident, Moran gave both Morris and Holmwood a carven humidor.

Novel by P.N. Elrod. The Dracula described in this book is probably not "Dracula-prime," but rather a soul-clone, perhaps the same one seen in Dracula books by Fred Saberhagen. This book takes place in the same continuity as Elrod's other books, such as the Lord Richard d'Orleans series, the Jonathan Barrett series, and the Jack Fleming, Vampire P.I. series.

1888

Winter. Birth of Theodore Marley "Ham" Brooks, one of Doc Savage's five assistants.

Winter. Birth of Tara of Helium, daughter of John Carter and Dejah Thoris.

April-May 1888; August 1898; November 1897-August 1898
THE SPACE MACHINE

Edward Turnbull and Amelia Fitzgibbon use Sir William Reynolds' combination Time/Space Machine. They initially travel to August 1898 and witness a Great Britain devastated by the Martian Invasion. Escaping back in time, they are accidentally deposited on Mars, approximately ten months before the August 1898 arrival of the Martian Invaders on Earth.

A novel by Edward Turnbull, edited by Christopher Priest, Popular Library, 1978, combining elements of H.G. Wells' The Time Machine *and* The War of the Worlds. *On Mars, Turnbull and Fitzgibbon encounter red-skinned humans who are enslaved by the invaders. Therefore it is likely that Turnbull and Fitzgibbon were deposited on Barsoom, which exists in a universe parallel to the Crossover Universe. The Martian Invasion on Earth was launched from Barsoom, as seen in "Mars: The Home Front" and* The League of Extraordinary Gentlemen II. *The 1903 date attributed to the Martian Invasion in Turnbull's account is inaccurate. For more on Sir William Reynolds and the various time travelers, see Loki Carbis' "Travels in Time,"* Myths for the Modern Age: Philip José Farmer's Wold Newton Universe.

May-October
BLOOD TO BLOOD: THE DRACULA STORY CONTINUES
Arthur Holmwood, Lord Godalming, refers to Sherlock Holmes and his Baker Street Irregulars.

Novel by Elaine Bergstrom, a sequel to Mina: The Dracula Story *Continues. Although the novel's events are dated to 1891, and there are references to the Jack the Ripper murders of late 1888, the larger Dracula chronology dictates setting these events in May-October 1888.*

Summer. Birth of Michael Lanyard, the Lone Wolf.
Summer. Publication of Sir William Clayton's three-volume memoir, *Never Say Die*.
Summer. Birth of detective Harry Allan Dickson, "the American Sherlock Holmes," in New York. Dickson is the son of a stage magician, Edgar Arthur

Dickson, and an Australian woman. Later in his career, Dickson will work with armchair detective Mr. Mortimer Triggs, thus also placing Triggs in the Crossover Universe.

Late August-September
DRACULA: THE SUICIDE CLUB
Dracula has become the President of London's Suicide Club. Sherlock Holmes, Dion Fortune, and Sir John Chandos also have roles in this case. A journalist named Milverton also briefly appears.
Comic book miniseries published in 1992 by Adventure Comics, written by Steven Phillip Jones and illustrated by John Ross. The Suicide Club is derived from Robert Louis Stevenson's New Arabian Nights. *Holmes makes an unnamed appearance, but the appearance is clear. There was a real English occultist and author named Dion Fortune, but she was born in 1890 and her true name was Violet Mary Firth; perhaps the Dion Fortune seen in this story is her mother, or at least an influence. (Interestingly, she studied occultism under Dr. Theodore Moriarty.) Milverton is probably not Charles Augustus Milverton, as seen in Watson's/Doyle's* "The Adventure of Charles Augustus Milverton" *(the descriptions do not match), but is almost certainly a relative. Sir John Chandos is undoubtedly a descendant of Sir John Chandos (from Jean Froissart's* Chronicles, *as well as Sir Arthur Conan Doyle's* Sir Nigel *and* The White Company*). Researcher Brad Mengel has also proposed a relationship between the first Sir John Chandos and Richard William Chandos of Dornford Yates'* Chandos *series. This Dracula appears to be Dracula-prime, and not one of his "soul-clones." This exploit concludes just as the Jack the Ripper murders are beginning.*

Early September
THE ADVENTURE OF THE ARABIAN KNIGHT
Sherlock Holmes embarks to recover a stolen document on behalf of his client, Captain Sir Richard Francis Burton.
Story by Loren Estleman in Murder in Baker Street, *2001. Sir Richard Francis Burton translated the* Arabian Nights *and the* Kama Sutra *into English, and discovered the source of the Nile. He also figures largely in Philip José Farmer's Riverworld series, which is related to the CU through a reference to* Moby Dick *(Ezekiel Hardy is a character in Farmer's* The Magic Labyrinth *and he was also mentioned in* Moby Dick*).*

September-November
A STUDY IN TERROR
Sherlock Holmes solves the Jack the Ripper slayings.
A novelization of the Holmes film, written by Dr. Watson and supplemented by Ellery Queen (Manfred B. Lee and Frederic Dannay), Lancer Books,

1966. After reading Watson's manuscript in 1966, Ellery Queen had his own take on the Ripper case. But in 2265, Captain Kirk and the crew of the Enterprise *would encounter the energy being truly responsible for the murders, the life-form known as Redjac.*

Autumn. Birth of Henry Poggioli, psychologist and detective whose cases were recounted by T.S. Stribling.

Autumn
THE ADVENTURE OF THE GRINDER'S WHISTLE
Ned Malone becomes a member of the Baker Street Irregulars, and meets Holmes and Watson during their investigation of the Ripper murders. Of the Ripper murders Malone writes, "Some thought him a butcher gone mad, or to be like old Sweeney Todd, the Demon Barber; of Fleet Street some years ago."
A short story by Edward Malone, edited by Howard Waldrop, and appearing in Waldrop's collection Night of the Cooters, *Ace Books, 1993; originally published in* Chacal *#2, Spring 1977. Edward "Ned" Malone later became a newsman and had adventures with Professor Challenger. The Sweeney Todd reference places the Demon Barber in the CU, although Sweeney Todd is based on real events and a real Sweeney Todd who was born in 1748. In the introduction to the story, Waldrop reveals the story was originally written at the behest of Philip José Farmer, who was organizing a fictional-author anthology: "Like most things from the Seventies, this is Philip José Farmer's fault... If you don't like it, don't write me. Write Philip José Farmer."*

November 22. Tarzan, Lord Greystoke (the future eighth duke of Greystoke), is born after his parents, Alice and John Clayton (the son of the fifth duke), are stranded in the jungle of French Equatorial Africa (Gabon). Authorized books in Edgar Rice Burroughs' Tarzan series are: *Tarzan of the Apes, The Return of Tarzan, The Beasts of Tarzan, The Son of Tarzan, Tarzan and the Jewels of Opar, Jungle Tales of Tarzan, Tarzan the Untamed, Tarzan the Terrible, Tarzan and the Golden Lion, Tarzan and the Ant Men, Tarzan, Lord of the Jungle, Tarzan and the Lost Empire, The Tarzan Twins, Tarzan at the Earth's Core, Tarzan the Invincible, Tarzan Triumphant, Tarzan and the City of Gold, Tarzan and the Lion Man, Tarzan and the Leopard Men, Tarzan's Quest, Tarzan and the Tarzan Twins with Jad-bal-ja, the Golden Lion, Tarzan and the Forbidden City, Tarzan the Magnificent, Tarzan and the Foreign Legion, Tarzan and the Madman, Tarzan and the Castaways, Tarzan and the Valley of Gold* by Fritz Leiber, *Tarzan: The Lost Adventure* by E. R. Burroughs and Joe R. Lansdale, and *The Dark Heart of Time: A Tarzan Novel* by Philip José Farmer. (There are many other Tarzan pastiches listed in this Chronology.)

Late November-December 25
THE TANGLED SKEIN

Holmes and Watson once again meet Dr. Abraham Van Helsing. Van Helsing enlists their aid in tracking down Dracula, who has returned to England. Stapleton, the villain who attempted to terrorize Sir Henry Baskerville, also makes an appearance.

Novel by Dr. John H. Watson, edited by David Stuart Davies, 1992. The novel, a sort-of sequel to Doyle and Watson's The Hound of the Baskervilles, *treats this as the first encounter between Holmes, Van Helsing, and Dracula. It even recounts the facts of Dracula's arrival in England aboard the* Demeter. *This would lead one to assume that the events of this case would parallel those related in Bram Stoker's* Dracula, *as does Watson and Estleman's* Sherlock Holmes vs. Dracula. *However, this is not the case, as none of the remaining events recounted in* The Tangled Skein *parallel those in* Dracula. *Therefore, these events can be seen as a subsequent meeting of Holmes and Dracula, rather than the initial one. Watson must have had his own reasons for confusing the facts of this case, one for which, of course, "the world is not yet prepared."*

1889

January
THE ADVENTURE OF THE VOORISH SIGN

Sherlock Holmes' latest case involves the dreaded Voorish Sign.

A short story by Richard A. Lupoff in the Holmesian/Lovecraftian anthology Shadows Over Baker Street; *reprinted in Lupoff's* The Universal Holmes, *Ramble House, 2007. The story takes place in wintertime, shortly after the introduction of Emile Berliner's gramophone (1887). The Voorish Sign is from H.P. Lovecraft's "The Dunwich Horror."*

February
A CASE OF ROYAL BLOOD

Sherlock Holmes and H.G. Wells investigate the case of an apparent poltergeist which is plaguing Holland's royal family. In the course of the investigation, Holmes finds copies of the *Necronomicon* and Von Juntz's *Nameless Cults*. There are also references to Yog-Sothoth and the Shoggoth.

A short story by H.G. Wells, edited by Steven Elliot-Altman, in the Lovecraftian anthology Shadows Over Baker Street. *The editors assign this tale to 1888. However, references to Wells' recently published story, "The Chronic Argonauts," (1888; this story formed the basis for Wells' later novel* The Time Machine), *make an 1889 date more likely.*

Spring
UN RIVAL DIABOLIQUE (aka A DIABOLICAL RIVAL)

Rocambole meets Princess Sonia Danidoff.

1960s Rocambole *comic, #13. Princess Sonia Danidoff is from the Fantômas series, confirming that Rocambole's and Fantômas' exploits all take place within the CU.*

THE MADNESS OF COLONEL WARBURTON

Sherlock Holmes receives the Maltese Falcon as a gift for successfully concluding this case. The Maltese Falcon will become the object of great pursuit in forty years, embroiling San Francisco detective Sam Spade in much intrigue.

Short story edited by Carole Buggé, from a manuscript by Dashiell Hammett, based on the notes of Dr. Watson. In the volume Resurrected Holmes, *Marvin Kaye, ed., 1996.*

UN PIÈGE DIABOLIQUE (aka A DIABOLICAL TRAP)

Rocambole disguises himself as his "rival" Sherlock Holmes.

1960s Rocambole *comic, #17.*

ALLAN AND THE SUNDERED VEIL

Allan Quatermain ingests the narcotic taduki and enters a state akin to the Dreamlands, a land where linear time does not exist. Indeed, there he meets the astral projection of Randolph Carter, who has come from the early 20th century. He also meets Randolph's great-uncle, John Carter, who, on his way to Barsoom from the Arizona cave where he lay dying in 1866, has been diverted to this realm. At the end of the second chapter, as the three are about to be attacked, The Time Traveler appears to rescue them. It is also revealed that the Morlocks of the far future are related to the Mi-Go of the Cthulhu Mythos.

Novella by Alan Moore serialized in the six issues of the comic book miniseries, The League of Extraordinary Gentlemen. *Allan Quatermain was established as part of the Wold Newton Family by Philip José Farmer, as was H.G. Wells' Time Traveler (aka Bruce Clarke Wildman). For additional information on The Time Traveler, please read "Travels in Time"* (Myths for the Modern Age: Philip José Farmer's Wold Newton Universe) *by Loki Carbis. This crossover confirms that E.R. Burroughs' John Carter was originally an inhabitant of the Crossover Universe, before he took up permanent residence in the dimension containing the planet Barsoom. It also relates John Carter to H.P. Lovecraft's*

Randolph Carter, who appeared in such classics as "The Statement of Randolph Carter," "The Dream Quest of Unknown Kadath," and "The Silver Key."

June 26. Detective and criminologist Jim Hanvey is born. His cases will be recounted by Octavus Roy Cohen.

Summer. Events of Rudyard Kipling's *Soldiers Three.*

Summer. Birth of Carl Peterson, archenemy of Bulldog Drummond. According to Philip José Farmer's *Doc Savage*, Peterson is the second son of John Clay and Urania Moriarty, making him the grandson of the first Professor James Moriarty and the brother of Dr. Caber.

Summer
RITE OF PASSAGE
Kyle Shore, Shalako, Sam Hollis, and Stony Brooke appear together, as does the town of Hendersonville.

Short story by John Allen Small in his collection Days Gone By: Legends and Tales of Sipokni West, *Ethan Books, 2007. This story incorporates two more references to the works of Louis L'Amour, specifically the inclusion of the character Kyle Shore from the novel* The Skyliners, *and the title character from* Shalako. *Sam Hollis was portrayed by Dean Martin in a comedic Western film entitled* Texas Across the River. *Stony Brooke was the character portrayed by both John Wayne and Bob Livingston in the old "Three Mesquiteers" film series of the 1930s and '40s. Hendersonville refers to Edgar Rice Burroughs' Western novel* The Bandit of Hell's Bend. *John Small adds, "While not a crossover, there's also an almost tacky sort of in-joke in this story; I named the villains after four of the best-known Western movie heroes of their day—Gene, Roy, Lash, and Durango. I guess I just wanted to see if anyone noticed."*

August-September
THE RED PLANET LEAGUE
After a scientific rival, Sir Nevil Airey Stent, decimates Professor Moriarty's *The Dynamics of an Asteroid* in public, Moriarty sets about upon his course of revenge. Mentioned are: the Si-Fan; the Lord of Strange Deaths in Limehouse; the Maracot Bell; Ogilvy; a crystal egg; C. Cave; the publisher Jedwood; Professor Pierre Arronax; the Bishop of Brichester; and the director of Purfleet Asylum.

Story by Kim Newman in Gaslight Grimoire, *J.R. Campbell and Charles Prepolec, eds., Edge Science Fiction and Fantasy Publishing, 2008. The Lord of Strange Deaths in Limehouse is Dr. Fu Manchu. The Si-Fan is the worldwide criminal organization from Rohmer's Fu Manchu books. "The Red Planet League" shows that Moriarty called upon Fu Manchu's diabolical services from time to time, but by late in the following decade, they were enemies (see* The League of Extraordinary Gentlemen*). The Maracot Bell is a reference to Sir Ar-*

thur Conan Doyle's The Maracot Deep, *although Maracot's practical application of his technology with an expedition to Atlantis is still some thirty-five years hence. Ogilvy is from H.G. Wells'* The War of the Worlds, *while the Crystal Egg and C. Cave are from Wells'* "The Crystal Egg." *The publisher Jedwood is from George Gissing's* New Grub Street *(1891). Professor Pierre Arronax is, of course, from Jules Verne's* 20,000 Leagues under the Sea. *The director of Purfleet Asylum is Dr. John Seward from Bram Stoker's* Dracula. *Brichester is a town from Ramsey Campbell's Cthulhu Mythos stories.*

August 1889-1892
SÂR DUBNOTAL VS. JACK THE RIPPER

Sâr Dubnotal, the "Napoléon of the Intangible," and his assistants, the beautiful Italian medium Gianetti Annunciata and young Rudolph, confront and defeat the evil Russian nobleman and mystic hypnotist Tserpchikopf, who turns out to have been behind the Jack the Ripper murders.

Five linked novellas of the Sâr Dubnotal *series (1909-1910) adapted by Brian Stableford, Black Coat Press, 2009. Tserpchikopf appears to be a Ripper copycat. The novellas are: "Le Manoir Hanté de Creh'h-ar-Vran" (The Haunted Manor of Creh'h-ar-Vran), Sâr Dubnotal's first recorded case; "Tserpchikopf, the Bloody Hypnotist;" "The Quartered Woman of Montmartre;" "Jack the Ripper;" and "Posthumous Hatred."*

September. Pilar Ana Maria Reina de la Vega is the daughter of a Gypsy circus fortune teller. She works with the Baker Street irregulars and Holmes calls her a "little Irene Adler." (*The Fall of the Amazing Zalindas*, the first book in the Sherlock Holmes and the Baker Street Irregulars series by Tracy Mack and Michael Citrin, Orchard Books, 2006. Pilar is possibly the granddaughter of Don Cesar de la Vega, one of the men to don the mask of Zorro.)

November 14, 1889-January 25, 1890
RACE AGAINST DEATH

When her brother Kit Walker is injured, Julie Walker dons the garb of The Phantom and shadows intrepid reporter Nellie Bly on her trip around the world, shielding Bly from harm. A placard at Bly's departure reads: "Nellie! Beat Phileas Fogg!" and Fogg's trip around the world in eighty days is referred to as a real historical event.

Julie Walker is…The Phantom *one-shot by Elizabeth Massie and Paul Daly, Moonstone Comics, 2010.*

November 21. Upon the death of the fifth duke of Greystoke, his brother, William Cecil Clayton, becomes the sixth duke.

December
A CHRISTMAS TOGETHER

A member of a Native American tribe, the Manowacks, appears.

Short story by John Allen Small in his collection Days Gone By: Legends and Tales of Sipokni West, *Ethan Books, 2007. The Manowacks are a fictional tribe first created by Joe R. Lansdale for his Batman novel* Captured by the Engines *(Warner Books, 1991).*

c. Late 1880s-early 1890s. The events of *Kim,* as related by Rudyard Kipling.

Early 1890s. Criminal exploits of Paul Finglemore/Colonel Clay, as told by Grant Allen in *An African Millionaire.* Colonel Clay was also the John Clay seen in Watson/Doyle's "The Red-Headed League," per Farmer in *Doc Savage: His Apocalyptic Life.*

1890

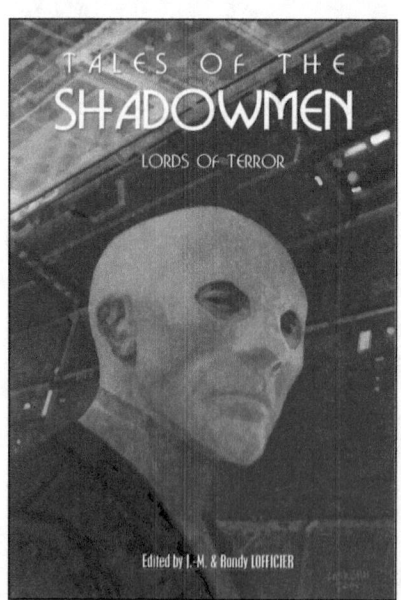

Winter 1890-1900
LONG LIVE FANTÔMAS

Over the course of a decade, Jack the Ripper continues his bloody work, aided by the recently unearthed Stone of Priam, and pursued by Signor Saladin and Enrico Gioja of the Black Coats, as well as the Sûreté agent called M. Clampin (aka "Pistolet"). The Ripper becomes known as "Fantômas," and is eventually revealed as the British Lord Edward Beltham. Beltham's protégé, Gurn, turns on his master under the pay of the Black Coats. In 1900, when Gurn kills Beltham (in the course of being caught bedding the Lord's wife, Lady Maud Beltham), the eldritch powers of the Stone of Priam change Gurn into Beltham/Fantômas. Fantômas, the Loup-Garou of Paris, and the Phantom of the Opera are called urban legends. Claudius Bombarnac, the late Professor, Paterson, Doctor Krampft, the Colonel who never died, Madame Doulenques, and Father Rodin all appear or are mentioned.

Short story by Alfredo Castelli in Tales of the Shadowmen Volume 3: Danse Macabre, *Jean-Marc and Randy Lofficier, eds., Black Coat Press, 2007; reprinted in French in* Les Compagnons de l'Ombre (Tome 4), *Jean-Marc and Randy Lofficier, eds., Rivière Blanche, 2009. Signor Saladin, Enrico Gioja, the Black Coats, the Colonel (Colonel Bozzo-Corona), and Pistolet/Clampin are all from the Black Coats saga by Paul Féval. Lord Edward Beltham, Lady Maud Beltham, and Fantômas/Gurn are from the Fantômas series by Marcel Allain and Pierre Souvestre. Doctor Krampft is from Allain's* The Yellow Document, or, The Fantômas of Berlin *(1919). Madame Doulenques is from the Fantômas television miniseries (1980). The Loup-Garou of Paris is from the film* An American Werewolf in Paris *(1997). The Phantom of the Opera is from the novel by Gaston Leroux. Claudius Bombarnac is a reporter from Jules Verne's novel of the same name. The late Professor is Sir Arthur Conan Doyle's Professor Moriarty. Reports of his death are probably exaggerated. Paterson is from Pierre-Alexis Ponson du Terrail's* Les Démolitions de Paris *(*The Demolitions of Paris*), also known as* Rocambole en Prison *(*Rocambole in Jail*), and* La Corde du Pendu *(*The Hanged Man's Rope*). Father Rodin is from Eugène Sue's* Le Juif Errant *(*The Wandering Jew*). The concept of the Ripper/Beltham/Fantômas moving and taking up residence in Gurn's body is reminiscent of the* Star Trek *episode "Wolf in the Fold," and is very consistent with the history of the Ripper in the Crossover Universe.*

Winter
SHERLOCK HOLMES i LIVSFARE

A.J. Raffles, in London, steals a pearl necklace, only to be apprehended by Sherlock Holmes. Raffles, piqued, appeals to Professor Moriarty to have Holmes eliminated.

Danish silent film, 1908, aka Sherlock Holmes in Danger of His Life.

IN MEMORIAM

A group of the late Dorian Gray's friends stage a performance of *The King in Yellow* in his honor.

Short story by Roger Johnson and Robert M. Price in Rehearsals for Oblivion, Act I: Tales of the King in Yellow, *edited by Peter A. Worthy, Dimensions Books, 2006. The crossover with Oscar Wilde's* The Picture of Dorian Gray *places Robert W. Chambers'* The King in Yellow *in the Crossover Universe. There is actually a passage in Wilde's* Dorian Gray *where Gray reads a rather odd book whose description matches fairly well with the book* The King in Yellow.

February 4-March 14
THE EMPRESS OF INDIA
   The Duke of Denver is briefly mentioned. One of the criminals goes by the sobriquet "The Artful Codger."
   A Professor Moriarty novel by Michael Kurland, St. Martin's Minotaur, February 2006. The Duke of Denver mentioned here is probably Lord Peter Wimsey's grandfather, George Wimsey. The Artful Codger may be Dickens' Artful Dodger from Oliver Twist, all grown up.

   Winter. Sinister murderer Branscom terrorizes many people in California. ("The Death of Halpin Frayser" by Ambrose Bierce.)
   Winter. Birth of Wold Newton Family member Lord Peter Wimsey.

March 1890-June 1898
THE GYPSIES IN THE WOOD
   Charles Beauregard of the Diogenes Club and reporter Kate Reed investigate the strange disappearances of a brother and sister. Beauregard meets young Dickie Riddle, who will soon go on to a detective career of his own. Mycroft Holmes is mentioned, as is his brother and John Watson. Beauregard's house is on Cheyne Walk. He keeps a copy of *Vermis Mysteriis* in his library. Sgt. Beale appears, as does "publicist" Billy Quinn.
   Novella by Kim Newman in the anthology The Fair Folk, *Marvin Kaye, ed., Science Fiction Book Club, 2005; reprinted in Newman's collection* The Secret Files of the Diogenes Club, *MonkeyBrain Books, 2007. Mycroft Holmes and the Diogenes Club are from Doyle and Watson's Sherlock Holmes stories. Kate Reed is a "deleted" character from Stoker's* Dracula; *she has a vampire counterpart in the Anno Dracula Universe* (ADU). *Beauregard also serves the Diogenes Club in the ADU. Dickie (Richard) Riddle also appeared in Newman's short story "Richard Riddle, Boy Detective, in 'The Case of the French Spy.'" The occult investigator Carnacki also lives on Cheyne Walk. The Vermis Mysteriis is an occult tome related to the Cthulhu Mythos. Sgt. Beale may be an ancestor of Detective Sgt. Beale from the 1971 British film* Assault, *based on Kendal Young's novel* The Ravine. *Alternatively, Sgt. Beale may be an ancestor of the Sgt. Beale seen in the 1957 British film* Town on Trial. *Or both. Advertising agent Quinn previously appeared in Newman's "A Drug on the Market."*

June
DR. CERRAL'S PATIENT
   Dr. Anatole Cerral is a surgeon at the Countess Yalta Memorial Hospital in Avignon, where Parisian private detective Victor Chupin is due to arrive. Victor's older sister Victoire appears and their father Polyte Chupin is mentioned. Victoire also cares for a sixteen-year-old boy, Raoul d'Andresy. Victor was

once a member of the Mascarot blackmail ring, and thereafter a protégé of the wealthy Champdoce family. The Dreux-Soubise family and Raoul's mother, Henriette d'Andresy are mentioned. Henriette (d'Andresy) Lupin was the estranged wife of Théophraste Lupin. Irene, Victoire's daughter, used to attend Madame Fourneau's College for Young Women, until Fourneau's son went on a killing spree. Teresa Grévin was one of the victims. Irene becomes a patient of Dr. Cerral, and later moves to an English nursing home called the Sanctuary Club. Detective C. Auguste Dupin is mentioned, as are Dr. Moreau, Ballmeyer, and John Clay.

Short story by Rick Lai in Tales of the Shadowmen Volume 2: Gentlemen of the Night, *Jean-Marc and Randy Lofficier, eds., Black Coat Press, 2006; reprinted in French in* Les Compagnons de l'Ombre (Tome 5), *Jean-Marc and Randy Lofficier, eds., Rivière Blanche, 2009. Dr. Anatole Cerral is the father of the scientist in Maurice Renard's* The Hands of Orlac. *Victor Chupin (also known as Toto Chupin) is from Emile Gaboriau's Monsieur Lecoq series, especially* Les Esclaves des Paris *(published in English as two volumes:* Caught in the Net *and* The Champdoce Mystery*) and* La Vie Infernale *(published in English as two volumes:* The Count's Millions *and* Baron Trigault's Vengeance*). Polyte Chupin, Victor's father, appeared in* Monsieur Lecoq. *Mascarot the blackmailer and the Duke of Champdoce are also from* Les Esclaves des Paris. *From Maurice Leblanc's Arsène Lupin stories: Arsène's father Théophraste is mentioned in* La Comtesse de Cagliostro *(translated into English as* The Memoirs of Arsène Lupin*). Henriette d'Andresy appeared in "The Queen's Necklace," as did the Dreux-Soubise family. Arsène Lupin uses the alias of Raoul d'Andresy in both* La Comtesse de Cagliostro *and "The Queen's Necklace." Victoire Chupin, Arsène Lupin's nurse, first appeared in the play* Arsène Lupin *by Leblanc and Francis de Croisset. Irene and Teresa, as well as Madame Fourneau and her son, come from the Spanish film* La Residencia *(aka* The House That Screamed*). Here, Irene is the daughter of Victoire Chupin, and thus the niece of detective Victor Chupin. It is also implied that Irene is the illegitimate daughter of Theophraste Lupin, making Irene the half-sister of Arsène. The Countess of Yalta is derived from Fortune du Boisgobey's* The Severed Hand *(1882). At the conclusion of the novel, there are plans to construct a hospital in Yalta's memo-*

ry somewhere in France. L.T. Meade and Robert Eustace's The Sanctuary Club (1900), is the source for the English nursing home. Dupin is from Edgar Allen Poe's stories. Dr. Moreau is from The Island of Dr. Moreau by H. G. Wells. Ballmeyer is from Gaston Leroux's The Mystery of the Yellow Room, while John Clay is from Dr. Watson and Sir Arthur Conan Doyle's "The Adventure of the Red-Headed League."

October. The events of Anthony Hope's *Rupert of Hentzau*. Death of Rudolf Rassendyll.

Autumn. First appearance of "Thomas Edison, Jr." in *Tom Edison, Jr.'s Sky-Scraping Trip; or Over the Wild West Like a Flying Squirrel*.

Autumn
THE MORIARTY EXPERIMENT
Dr. Eustace Moriarty, enamored of The Phantom's aunt, Julie Walker, follows her to Bengali and experiments upon native children. After Dr. Moriarty kidnaps Julie, The Phantom follows them to Bachenreik Falls where he and Moriarty tussle and fall over the edge. The Phantom attempts to find Moriarty, but cannot and presumes him dead. Three months later, Dr. Eustace Moriarty is shown presenting himself at 221B Baker Street, inquiring after Sherlock Holmes.

Story shown in flashback in #1443 and 1453 of Frew Publications' The Phantom, *2006. It remains unknown whether "Eustace" Moriarty is one of the three known Moriarty brothers, or another relative entirely.*

Autumn 1890-1891
THE BEAUTIFUL WHITE DEVIL
Alie Dunbar is a female pirate in the Pacific, of the Robin Hood variety. A man named Benwell appears briefly.

Novel by Guy Boothby. Benwell was also minor character in Guy Boothby's novel Dr. Nikola, *thus linking this novel to the Nikola books. Nikola is in the Crossover Universe through references to Lecoq and Sherlock Holmes, and an appearance in the Doc Savage comic book miniseries* Doom Dynasty.

1891

Winter. Birth of Richard Wentworth (The Spider), son of Lord John Roxton, who is, in turn, a descendant of Lord Byron. (See Farmer's *Doc Savage* for complete information.)

Winter. Keith Hilary Pursuivant is born in Pursuivant Landing, Kentucky.

Winter. Malachi van Helsing assists John Reid against the Black Arrow. (*Crépuscule Vaudou* aka *The Katrina Protocol*, Jean-Marc Lofficier.)

Winter
THE COFFIN OF DRACULA
When his uncle dies, Lord Adrian Varney inherits Dracula's coffin. Opening the coffin, Dracula possesses Varney, and Dracula-Varney then kidnaps Mina Harker. Jonathan Harker enlists Dr. Abraham Van Helsing and Dr. John Seward to help save his wife once more.

Story by Archie Goodwin and Reed Crandall in Creepy #8-9, *Warren Publishing, April-June, 1966. Lord Adrian Varney is undoubtedly a relation of Sir Francis Varney from James Malcolm Rymer's* Varney the Vampyre; or, The Feast of Blood. *The Varney family could tend toward vampirism, making Lord Adrian Varney more susceptible to possession by Dracula. This tale provides yet more evidence in support of Chuck Loridans' "soul-clone" theory, which is fully described elsewhere in this Chronology and on his* MONSTAAH *website. Following Loridans' theory, the Dracula who possesses Varney is Dracula-prime. Within two years, Dracula would return to full-bodied life, as seen in the tale "Places for Act Two!"*

March-April
THE GREAT GAME

The first Professor Moriarty is described as being either the head of a vast criminal network, or the head of the British Secret Service, or both. Of course he denies it. A Fat Man named Gottfried Kaspar appears, and another man is seen posing as a priest named Father Ugarti. One of the amateur spies playing at the "Great Game" is named Charles Bredlon Summerdale, who is the second son of a duke. Although she does not appear "on-screen," it is mentioned that Summerdale has a sister named Lady Patricia Templar. She is described as being married to "an energetic young prelate destined someday to become an archbishop, or even, if he had his way, a saint."

A Professor Moriarty novel by Michael Kurland, St. Martin's, 2001. Gottfried Kaspar is obviously based on Sydney Greenstreet's Caspar Gutman from John Huston's cinematic version of The Maltese Falcon. *For our purposes, we may postulate that the man in* The Great Game *is the father of Caspar Gutman. The variations on the name "Caspar" can be viewed as a series of aliases used by this father and son throughout their shady careers. Ugarti is the name of Peter Lorre's character in* Casablanca. *Again, it can't be the same man, but is likely his father. Thus, there are crossover connections between this novel,* The Maltese Falcon, *and* Casablanca.

Researcher Dennis E. Power postulates that Summerdale's sister and her husband, Mr. Templar, must have emigrated to South Africa sometime between 1891 and the Boer War. The young prelate, Mr. Templar, died in the Boer War in 1899. His widow, Mrs. Templar, took up with a cousin of Mr. Templar, A.J. Raffles, and bore a child, giving him the name Simon Templar. However, I further speculate that A.J. Raffles himself is descended from a Templar, the Lieutenant Templar, who, during the Napoleonic Wars, captured a bronze artifact which had an undefined but beneficial influence upon his descendants. Thus, Simon Templar's line of descent from Lieutenant Templar is preserved.

Moriarty denies being the head of the British Secret Service, but if his denial is false, it certainly dovetails nicely with the events revealed in The League of Extraordinary Gentlemen *and also fits in with a theory of layers upon layers within the British Secret Service. In* The Great Game, *the British Secret Service in 1891 is practically nonexistent. A high British official says that since Britain is not training and fielding real agents, many young men of idle means have stepped up to become "amateur" agents in foreign lands, operating with the knowledge of Britain, but without a truly official sanction. That's the first layer.*

I would postulate that the second layer is the group headed by Mycroft Holmes and sometimes headquartered at The Diogenes Club. This is the same operation seen at work in the Quinn Fawcett books, as well as in Andy Lane's All Consuming Fire *and in Kim Newman's* Seven Stars *and his Diogenes Club stories. Charles Beauregard is also a part of this group. This operation is fairly secret and is not widely known even among most high British officials. Hence the British official's contention in* The Great Game *that Britain is fielding only amateur agents.*

Next is the third layer, which is the ultra top secret "black ops" Secret Service group controlled by the first Professor Moriarty, as seen in The League of Extraordinary Gentlemen. *Before 1891, Moriarty never had any offices in any official British building and operated out of his home on Russell Square, as seen in* The Great Game *(as well as many more secret lairs). Before 1891, he was both a criminal mastermind and in charge of the British black ops group. After 1894, Moriarty moved into the offices at Whitehall (seen in* The League of Extraordinary Gentlemen*) and his activities became more open, so that by 1898, Mycroft Holmes knew of Moriarty's role in the Secret Service, although he was powerless to do anything about it.*

May 1891-April 1894. The Great Hiatus: Both Holmes and the first Professor Moriarty are erroneously believed dead after their encounter at Reichenbach Falls (see Doyle and Watson's *"The Final Problem"*). Holmes travels the world during this period. Meanwhile, the third Moriarty brother (James Noel Moriarty, herein referred to as the second Professor Moriarty) has recruited followers from his not-so-late elder brother's criminal organization for his own purposes.

Summer. Birth of Perry Mason.

Summer. The affair of Jules Verne's *Le Château des Carpathes (The Castle of the Carpathians)*.

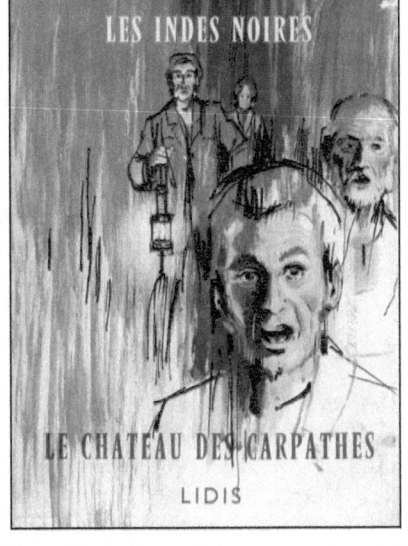

Summer 1891-Spring 1893
IN STRANGE COMPANY

John Macklin, an English albino dwarf, commits a series of crimes throughout the world. Count de Panuroff of Thursday Island also appears.

Novel by Guy Boothby. Count de Panuroff was mentioned by a character in Boothby's Nikola novel A Bid for Fortune, *placing the events of this novel in the same continuity as Nikola, and thus in the Crossover Universe.*

Summer
ZAMBRA THE DETECTIVE

Sebastian Zambra, an English consulting detective of some repute and many similarities to Sherlock Holmes, investigates a murder case involving a "Suicide Club." The Club is likely the successor to the Suicide Club of thirteen years previous.

Story by Headon Hill, a pseudonym for Francis Edward Grainger. The Suicide Club link places Sebastian Zambra in the CU.

RAFFLES AND THE ARTFUL DODGER

Raffles and Manders help out an elder member of Raffles' club, General Sir Giles Bamford. Sir Giles is being blackmailed by his manservant, who also happens to be the real-life "Artful Dodger" upon whom Dickens modeled Jack Dawkins in *Oliver Twist*.

A short story by Barry Perowne in Ellery Queen's Mystery Magazine, *June 1980.*

September
THE CANARY TRAINER

Sherlock Holmes, while living in Paris during the Great Hiatus and using his "Sigerson" identity, matches wits with Erik, the Opera Ghost. Irene Adler also appears in this case. The detective Auguste Dupin is mentioned, as is the Marquis de Saint-Evremonde. A footnote adds, "This aristocratic family was hunted to the brink of extinction during the Terror (1793), but survived in an offshoot who called himself Darnay. One of Darnay's descendants (he married the daughter of a Bastille prisoner and produced children by her) evidently reassumed the family name and title."

A novel by Nicholas Meyer. Meyer also "edited" The Seven-Percent Solution, *a Holmes novel and film wherein Moriarty was not a villain, but was an innocent unjustly persecuted by Holmes. I discount Meyer's references to the events of* The Seven-Percent Solution, *following scholar Mark Brown's theory that Meyer was fooled by the* Seven-Percent *manuscript, which was a hoax perpetrated by the second Professor Moriarty. The events of* The Canary Trainer *also appear to be a sequel or "copycat" incident of some sort, since the original case of* The Phantom of the Opera *took place in 1881. Following these events, Holmes pursued Irene Adler to Montenegro, a decision that would culminate in the birth of twins Nero Wolfe and Marco Vukcic the next year. Dupin, by now, needs no further explanation. Darnay is Charles Darnay, from Charles Dickens'* A Tale of Two Cities.

December
SHERLOCK HOLMES ON THE ROOF OF THE WORLD, or, THE ADVENTURE OF THE WAYFARING GOD

During the Great Hiatus, Ludwig Horace Holly and Leo Vincey are conducting research in the monasteries of Tibet, when they meet another European, a Norseman by the name of Sigerson (Sherlock Holmes' identity during this time period). Sigerson solves the murder of the head librarian of one of the monasteries.

A novella by Leo Vincey, edited by Thomas Kent Miller. Per Farmer's genealogies, Holly (from H. Rider Haggard's She*) and Holmes are Wold Newton Family members, and this manuscript confirms that they actually knew each other.*

1892

Winter. Birth of Bruce Hagin Rassendyll (G-8), who will later use the identity Jim "Red" Albright (Captain Midnight). G-8 is the brother of Kent Allard (The Shadow) and the half-brother of Richard Wentworth (The Spider). G-8 and The Shadow's father, Ralph Rassendyll, is the cousin of Rudolf Rassendyll (from The Prisoner of Zenda and Rupert of Hentzau). Farmer established all of these genealogical relationships in *Doc Savage*, with the exception of the theory that G-8 was the same person as Captain Midnight. That theory is derived from Jim Harmon's article "The Life Story of King Kong."

Winter
DER NAPOLEON DES VERBRECHENS

Tom Shark picks up the pursuit of Professor Moriarty and his organization after the death of Shark's "master," Sherlock Holmes.

Tom Shark, der König der Detektive *#623*. *This story brings detective Tom Shark into the Crossover Universe.*

WATER FROM THE MOON
Sherlock Holmes, still using the Arne Sigerson identity, is in Chiang Mai, Siam, and meets Louis Leonowens, the son of Anna Leonowens, who served as the royal tutor. A Siamese policeman, Sergeant Taed Chutima, admires Vidocq and Dupin, but respects Holmes most of all.

Short story by Carolyn Wheat in the anthology Sherlock Holmes: The Hidden Years, *Michael Kurland, ed., St. Martin's Minotaur, November 2004. Anna Leonowens was a real person who spent 1862-1867 in Siam. She wrote her account* The English Governess at the Court of Siam *in 1870, followed in 1872 by* The Romance of the Harem. *Long afterwards, Margot Landon combined the two books into a new book called* Anna and the King of Siam. *Regarding the detectives, Holmes actually met Vidocq through the miracle of time travel, and expressed his disdain of Dupin in* A Study in Scarlet.

March. Occult detective Flaxman Low's first recorded case, "The Story of the Spaniards, Hammersmith," by "E. and H. Heron," *Pearson's Magazine* (January 1898).

April 13. Birth of Henry Smith, insurance salesman and criminologist in cases told by Fredric Brown.

Spring. First documented appearance of *Arsène Lupin*, as told by Maurice Leblanc. Other Lupin books are *Arsène Lupin, Gentleman-Cambrioleur*; *Arsène Lupin Versus Herlock Sholmes*; *The Hollow Needle: The Crystal Stopper; Countess Cagliostro*; *813*; and many others. As established by Farmer, Lupin was a Wold Newton Family member.

Summer
THE LONG ARM OF THE LAW
The Gunsmith, Longarm, and Slocum meet in Denver.

The Gunsmith *#300 by J.R. Roberts, Jove Books, December 2006. The Gunsmith and Slocum are already linked into the Crossover Universe. This novel brings in the Western character Longarm.*

July
DEAR MR. HOLMES
Cowboy-turned-detective Gustav "Old Red" Amlingmeyer, a fan of Sherlock Holmes, writes a letter to Holmes in care of *The Strand Magazine*.

Short story by Steve Hockensmith in Ellery Queen's Mystery Magazine, February 2003. *This tale is the start of series featuring Old Red and his brother, Otto "Big Red" Amlingmeyer. Greg Gick adds, "At a glance it seems that the characters only think Holmes exists, but in the 2006 novel* Holmes on the Range *we find Holmes does exist in the Amlingmeyers' world. So Big Red and Old Red are part of the CU."*

Summer. Holmes meets seventeen-year-old Kimball O'Hara (*The Game* by Mary Russell Holmes and Laurie R. King).

Summer. Birth of twin brothers Nero Wolfe (aka John Hamish Adler aka Auguste Lupa) and Marko Vukcic (aka Scott Adler). Their parents are Sherlock Holmes and Irene Adler.

Summer. Birth of Mary Finney, doctor, missionary, and mystery-solver in cases recounted by Matthew Head.

Autumn. A comical character attempts to travel around the world in 37 days, as told by Jules Verne in *Claudius Bombarnac*.

Autumn. Alexander Waverly is born in Northampshire, England.

Autumn
FRANK READE, JR.'S CATAMARAN OF THE AIR; OR, WILD AND WONDERFUL ADVENTURES IN NORTH AUSTRALIA
Frank Reade, Jr., and his crew of adventurers travel to Northwest Australia, where they find three races of subterranean peoples. While there, they encounter the evil "Shunokins."

Story by Luis Senarens in The Boys of New York, *April 15-June 17, 1893. The "Shunokins" may possibly be a link to the Shonokins in the works of Manly Wade Wellman.*

TOO MANY STAINS (THE ADVENTURE OF THE SECOND STAIN)
Sherlock and Mycroft Holmes go up against international criminal Adolphus Zecchino. A.J. Raffles also appears in the case under the alias "Mr. Maturin."

This short story is edited by Marvin Kaye, from a manuscript by Rex Stout, based on the notes of Dr. Watson, and can be found in the anthology Resurrected Holmes, *Marvin Kaye, ed., 1996. It takes place during The Great Hiatus. Adolphus Zecchino went to America and continued his criminal career as Arnold Zeck. Holmes' son Nero Wolfe clashed with criminal mastermind Zeck for several years before Zeck's death in 1950 (Rex Stout's novel* In the Best Families). *E.W. Hornung told the tales of Raffles, who Farmer established as a Wold Newton Family member. Raffles did not put his "Maturin" alias into regular use until 1895 or 1896; this incident must constitute a very early use of the identity.*

October 31, 1892-April 30, 1895
ALL PREDATORS GREAT AND SMALL

Appearing or mentioned are: Dracula, Josephine Balsamo, the Black Coats (who are only interested in "treason, revenge and extortion"), Claude Dupont-Verdier (aka Satanas), the Frankenhausens, Hildegarde Einem (aka Frau Hildegarde), José Alejandro Balsamo, Ricardo and Anna Peisser, Grost, Ludvig Prinn, the Great Old Ones, Slidith (aka Draco), Count Szandor, Baron Kralitz, the Durwards, Joseph Bridau, Urania Caber (aka Urania Moriarty), Mrs. Jillian Blake (aka Jill Fagin), Gorcha the Vourdalak, Henri de Belcamp (aka Serge Dolgolruki), Sara Balsamo (aka Madame Sara), Madame Koluchy, Larry Parker, Jacob Dix, Madame Delhomme (aka Elodie Vaucogne), Aguilar, Captain Thompson, Irma Vep, Sabine Balsamo (aka Dr. Absalom), Szandra (aka Countess Dracula), Charles Maurice Loridan, Boneport, St. Swithin's Medical School, Akivasha's Tear (aka Dracula's Tear), and Medjora diphtheria.

Short story by Rick Lai in Tales of the Shadowmen Volume 5: The Vampires of Paris, *Jean-Marc and Randy Lofficier, eds., Black Coat Press, 2009; reprinted in French in* Les Compagnons de l'Ombre (Tome 7), *Jean-Marc and Randy Lofficier, eds., Rivière Blanche, 2010. Dracula is from Bran Stoker's classic vampire novel. The main action takes place September-October 1893, during Dracula's return sojourn to London. (In this timeline, the events of* Dracula *occur in 1887; as with Bradley H. Sinor's story "Places for Act Two!" Lai's tale necessitates a conjectural second London incursion by Dracula in 1893.) Josephine Balsamo is a villainess in Maurice Leblanc's Arsène Lupin tales. The Black Coats are Paul Féval's legendary criminal organization. The reference to the Black Coats' interest in treason, revenge and extortion suggests a connection between the Black Coats and SPECTRE from Ian Fleming's James Bond novels. Claude Dupont-Verdier is the real name of Satanas in the English version of Louis Feuillade's French serial* The Vampires. *Irma Vep is also from* The Vampires.*The Frankenhausens, Hildegarde Einem (aka Frau Hildegarde), José Alejandro Balsamo, and Ricardo and Anna Peisser are all from the Mex-*

ican films The Bloody Vampire *and* The Invasion of the Vampires. *Frau Hildegarde's surname of Einem suggests a family relationship with Hilda von Einem, Richard Hannay's adversary in John Buchan's* Greenmantle. *Grost is from film* Captain Kronos, Vampire Hunter, *as is the Durward family.* Baron Kralitz is from Henry Kuttner's "The Secret of Kralitz." *Draco is from Peter Tremayne's trilogy of prequels to Stoker's classic:* Dracula Unborn *(also known as* Bloodright)*,* The Revenge of Dracula *and* Dracula, My Love. *In all these novels, Dracula worships Draco, a dragon god. Richard Tierney's* The House of the Toad *implied that Draco was one of H.P. Lovecraft's Great Old Ones. Draco is conflated with Slidith, the Lord of Blood worshipped by the Red Druids in Lin Carter's* Thongor of Lemuria *novels. Ludvig Prinn's* The Mysteries of the Worm *is from Robert Bloch's "The Shambler from the Stars." Count Szandor is from Paul Féval's* The Vampire Countess. *Joseph Bridau is from Honore de Balzac's* A Bachelor's Establishment. *He appears in other "Human Comedy" novels as well. Larry Parker is meant to be Colonel Moran's henchman from Doyle and Watson's "The Adventure of the Empty House." Madame Koluchy is from* The Brotherhood of the Seven Kings *by Meade and Eustace. Madame Sara Balsamo is meant to be the immortal Madame Sara from* The Sorceress of the Strand *by the same writers. Jacob Dix is from Fergus Hume's* Hagar of the Pawnshop. *Henri de Belcamp is an alias of the title character in Paul Féval's* John Devil. *Prince Serge Dolgolruki is from Leblanc's* La Comtesse de Cagliostro *(the English version is* The Memoirs of Arsène Lupin)*. Gorcha the Vourdalak is from "The Family of a Vourdalak" by Alexis Tolstoy. The story was filmed with Boris Karloff as part of the anthology film* Black Sabbath. *Urania Caber is Urania Moriarty from Philip José Farmer's* Doc Savage: His Apocalyptic Life. *Lai's short story "Urania's Children" (in* Farmerphile *#12) explains why she prefers to use her mother's maiden name. The genealogy in Farmer's book also cites a Jill Fagin who may have been married to a man named Blake. This is the basis for Jillian Blake. In Emile Zola's* La Terre, *a brothel in Chartres was inherited by Elodie Vaucogne after she married Ernest Delhomme. Aguilar is the villain of the spaghetti western* The Stranger in Town. *Captain Thompson is from William Hope Hodgson's "The Haunted* Jarvee," *a story featuring Carnacki the ghost finder. Medjora diphtheria: Dr. Medjora was the scientific murderer from Rodriguez Ottolengui's* A Modern Wizard. *St. Swithin's Medical School is from the "Doctor in the House" books by Richard Gordon. The ruby called Akivasha's Tear is meant to be the jewel called Dracula's Tear in the Lupin III episode "The Case of the Risible Dirigible," in which the Gabriel family of Austria owned the jewel for generations. Akivasha is the female vampire encountered by Conan in Robert E. Howard's* The Hour of the Dragon. *Charles Maurice Loridan's* L'Essence du Dragon *is Lai's invention. The name of the fictional author is derived from Chuck Loridans whose theories about Dracula and soul-clones are used in Lai's story with Loridans' permission. Ditto for the Loridan surname. Boneport, Louisiana, is from Loridans' unpublished* Diary of an

Evil Henchman. *Sabine Balsamo (aka Dr. Absalom) and Szandra (aka Countess Dracula) are also Lai's creations.*

December. Birth of Allard Kent Rassendyll (aka "Kent Allard" aka The Shadow,) brother of G-8 and half-brother of Richard Wentworth (The Spider). Farmer's genealogy in *Doc Savage* places The Shadow in the Wold Newton Family.

1893

Winter. First recorded exploit of Dr. Nikola, *A Bid for Fortune, Or, Dr. Nikola's Vendetta*, as recounted by Guy Boothby. Other books in the series are: *Dr. Nikola Returns, The Lust of Hate, Dr. Nikola's Experiment,* and *Farewell, Nikola!*

Early May
THE BUGHOUSE CAPER

During the Great Hiatus, Sherlock Holmes is in San Francisco, where he assists detectives John Quincannon and Sabina Carpenter in solving a series of burglaries and a locked-room murder.

Short story by Bill Pronzini in Sherlock Holmes: The Hidden Years, *edited by Michael Kurland, St. Martin's Minotaur, November 2004. Carpenter and Quincannon are Old West detectives created by mystery writers Bill Pronzini and Marcia Muller. There are three books so far:* Quincannon *(1985),* Beyond the Grave *(1986), and* Carpenter and Quincannon: Professional Detective Services, *a 1998 anthology of short stories. This crossover brings them into the CU.*

Early June
CROSS OF GOLD

During the Great Hiatus, Sherlock Holmes is in New York and clears a young immigrant, Tadeusz Jan Fortunowski, of a trumped up murder charge. Fortunowski is P.I. Dan Fortune's grandfather.

Short story by Dan Fortune, edited by "Michael Collins" *(pseudonym for Dennis Lynds), in* Sherlock Holmes: The Hidden Years, *edited by Michael Kurland, St. Martin's Minotaur, November 2004. The story places Collins' detective*

Dan Fortune in the CU. The time of year is given as "spring"; it is likely that Holmes came directly to New York from San Francisco, where he was in May during "The Bughouse Caper." This also fits in with Holmes' knowledge of certain current events in California which pertain to the mystery in "Cross of Gold."

Summer. During the Great Hiatus, Sherlock Holmes visits a realm known in this world only as "Wonderland" ("The Case of the Detective's Smile" by Mark Bourne).

Summer. English gemologist Bernard Sutton solves a number of jewel-related mysteries. (*Jewel Mysteries I Have Known*, a collection of short stories by Max Pemberton.)

Summer. Martin Hewitt's first recorded case, "The Lenton Croft Robberies," by Arthur Morrison.

Summer. Events of *The Sea Wolf* by Jack London. As suggested by Farmer in *Doc Savage,* Wolf Larsen is the father of Mr. Moto and the grandfather of Doc Savage.

Summer. First recorded case of detective Sexton Blake, *The Missing Millionaire,* as related by Hal Meredith (pseudonym for Harry Blyth). Blake was mentioned in Farmer's *Doc Savage,* although not specifically as a Wold Newton Family member (although there was a coachman, Arthur Blake, at Wold Newton in December 1795; see *Tarzan Alive*). It should be noted that Blake's presence in the CU implies the presence of many other dime magazine and penny dreadful heroes and villains, with whom Blake teamed up or confronted over his long career. These include: Nelson Lee, Dixon Hawke, Dixon Brett, Waldo the Wonder Man, Marko the Miracle Man, Arthur Stukeley Pennington, Sir Richard "Spots" Losely, Lobangu (a Zulu detective who in turn teamed up with detective Gordon Keith), Jeff Clayton (who actually teamed up with Blake's bloodhound, Pedro), Detective-Inspector Will Spearing, Captain Christmas, Ferrers Lord, the solicitor Havlock Preed, Mademoiselle Yvonne, and of course Zenith the Albino.

Summer. Lobangu begins assisting Sir Richard Losely among the Etbaia Zulus. As time goes by Lobangu begins adventuring on his own and leads the

Etbaia Zulus without Sir Richard's help. Eventually he is solving crimes internationally and befriends Sexton Blake. (*Union Jack Library* #8, June 23, 1894.)

Summer
BOILERPLATE
The mechanical man Boilerplate is unveiled in Machinery Hall at the World's Columbian Exposition in Chicago. Kate Reade is present for the unveiling.

Boilerplate Unpublished: The Graphic Novel That Never Was by Paul Guinan, 2005. Kate Reade is the daughter of Frank Reade, Jr. The famous Reade clan also includes Frank Reade and Frank Reade III. Since the Reades are in the CU, so is Boilerplate.

PLACES FOR ACT TWO!
Dracula is back in London, where he appears in Gilbert & Sullivan's *The Pirates of Penzance* and becomes embroiled in a plot to trap terrorists seeking to assassinate Prince Albert. Mycroft Holmes appears, making an allusion to Col. Sebastian Moran and referring to his "late" brother. Dr. Watson and A.J. Raffles are also mentioned as being in attendance at the Opera.

Short story by Bradley H. Sinor collected in Dracula in London, *P.N. Elrod, ed., Ace Books, November 2001. Although the conceit of the anthology is that all the short stories take place during Bram Stoker's novel* Dracula *and show what the Count was doing "off-screen" during other events of that novel, the timing here does not work. This story explicitly takes place during the Great Hiatus of Sherlock Holmes (May 1891-April 1894), and* Dracula, *at least in the CU, does not take place during that period. However, other sources have shown that the Count survived the events depicted in Stoker's novel, and so this tale must take place during one of his return visits to London.*

THE SHADOW OF FRANKENSTEIN
Henry Frankenstein and his wife Elizabeth travel to London to escape persecution in their homeland. Unbeknownst to them, the still-living Creature that Henry created follows them. When a new series of Ripper murders begins, Henry is the prime suspect. Seward's asylum is mentioned several times.

Novel by Stefan Petrucha, DH Press, July 2006. Seward's asylum is from the Universal film version of Dracula. *Although the book purports to take place in an ambiguous 1930s, the slight references to that time period are easily ignored, and must be to fit the novel into the larger timeline for the Universal Frankenstein films. Likewise the statement that the book's events begin directly after the film* Bride of Frankenstein. *The storyline that Jack the Ripper is half a century old and needs to procure certain organs to maintain his longevity can also be dismissed as a fictionalization, as the Ripper needs no such motivation to murder. A resurgent Ripper in the mid 1890s is consistent with Alfredo Cas-*

telli's short story "Long Live Fantômas," which accounts for the Ripper's doings during that decade.

September
TAMMERS' DUEL

Count Julowski, a German-Polish aristocrat and an expert duelist, challenges Tammers to a duel on the island of Jersey. Anson, Tammers' second, arranges the duel with his counterpart, a Frenchman named de Boivet, and observes: "I had, like the late Sherlock Holmes, deduced so much from the behavior of de Boivet."

Novel by "E. and H. Heron," pseudonym of Hesketh V. Prichard and Kate O'Brien Ryall Prichard, 1898. "The late Sherlock Holmes" refers to Holmes' supposed death at the hands of Professor Moriarty at the Reichenbach Falls.

Autumn. Samuel Clemens makes a brief excursion to the future and visits the U.S.S. Enterprise NCC 1701-D. In San Francisco, Lt. Commander Data of the Enterprise encounters Jack London, who chronicled the exploits of several Wold Newton Family members (the events of the *Star Trek: The Next Generation* episode "*Time's Arrow*").

Autumn. First appearance of Nelson Lee in "A Dead Man's Secret" by "Maxwell Scott," a pseudonym of Dr. John Staniforth (*The Halfpenny Marvel* #46, September 19, 1894).

November
THE SCOTTISH PLOY

Mycroft Holmes refers to his contemporary, Professor Challenger.

This is the fourth in a series of books about British spymaster Mycroft Holmes. The adventures were recorded by Holmes' confidential secretary, Paterson Erskine Guthrie, and edited for publication by Quinn Fawcett.

1894

January-February. Doc Savage's great-uncle, Bruce Clarke Wildman, begins his strange adventures through time (*The Time Machine*, as related to H.G. Wells; *Doc Savage: His Apocalyptic Life* by Philip José Farmer; for more information, read Loki Carbis' "Travels in Time," *Myths for the Modern Age: Philip José Farmer's Wold Newton Universe*). Pastiche continuations of The Time Traveler's story are (in no particular order): *The Return of the Time Machine* by Egon Friedell, *Morlock Night* by K.W. Jeter, *The Space Machine* by Christopher Priest, *The Time Ships* by Stephen Baxter, "The Case of the Inertial Adjustor" by Stephen Baxter (in *The Mammoth Book of New Sherlock Holmes Adventures*), "The Richmond Enigma" by John DeChancie (in *Sherlock Holmes in Orbit*), *Allan and the Sundered Veil* by Alan Moore and Kevin O'Neill (in *The League of Extraordinary Gentlemen)*, *Die Unter Und Uber Der Erde* by Robert Heymann (in *Wunder Der Zukunft* #3, 1909), and *The Rook* comic series.

Winter
A PRINCE OF SWINDLERS

Simon Carne, a clever criminal, adopts the identity of private detective Klimo, and is soon lauded by the British public as being "as great as Lecocq, or even the late lamented Sherlock Holmes." The Earl of Amberley also appears.

Collection of interconnected short stories by Guy Boothby, also published under the title The Viceroy's Protégé. *The Holmes reference is in the tale "The Duchess of Wiltshire's Diamonds." Of course this reference is made during the time that Holmes is still thought dead. Lecocq is meant to refer to Emile Gaboriau's detective Lecoq. Per Philip José Farmer, both Holmes and Lecoq are in the CU, so this reference brings in Carne/Klimo. The Earl of Amberley was also seen in Boothby's first Dr. Nikola novel,* A Bid for Fortune, *thus connecting Carne/Klimo to Nikola.*

February-April
FLASHMAN AND THE TIGER

The "brawl" in Baker Street: Harry Flashman goes up against Colonel Moran. The final events of this conflict occur concurrently with Watson's "The Adventure of the Empty House."

Novel by G.M. Fraser. Apparently Flashman and Moran had also previously met briefly in Flash for Freedom!

Spring. Events of Rudyard Kipling's *The Jungle Book*.

Spring. Captain Kettle does right by his ship's owners and lets his ship sink, embarking on a strange series of adventures. ("The Giant Sea Swindle," a serial by C.J. Cutcliffe Hyne.)

Spring. Birth of Mr. Moto, a Wold Newton Family member per Farmer's *Doc Savage*.

April. Holmes returns to England (Doyle and Watson's "The Adventure of the Empty House"*)*. The second Professor Moriarty masquerades as the first Professor Moriarty and rebuilds his elder brother's criminal empire, while at the same time coming to terms with Holmes and creating a truce of sorts. However,

the second Professor is quickly driven out of England (see John Gardner's *The Return of Moriarty*). Unbeknownst to all, the first Professor Moriarty also survived Reichenbach Falls and spends several years recovering from the fall (see *Sherlock Holmes in New York, The League of Extraordinary Gentlemen,* and *The Earthquake Machine)*; he allows his younger brother to continue with his own criminal escapades as Professor Moriarty in order to confuse and confound Holmes. This is in conflict with the younger Moriarty's falsified accounts in the so-called "Moriarty Journals," in which the second Professor describes his 1888 murder of his entirely innocent and somewhat downtrodden older brother, the original Professor Moriarty. The second Professor was also responsible for other fabrications in the two published volumes of the "Moriarty Journals" (*The Return of Moriarty* and *The Revenge of Moriarty*, edited by John Gardner), such as his account of the incident at Reichenbach Falls.

May 1894-August 1896. The second Professor Moriarty (James Noel Moriarty) is in America, plotting his return to England (*The Revenge of Moriarty*). During this period, in the year 1895, the second Professor Moriarty and Kathryn Koluchy establish their own criminal league/terrorist cult, the "Circle of Life" (see *The Second War of the Worlds*). Over the years, this organization will evolve and come to be known as Krafthaus (see *The Power-House*), and later THRUSH (see *The Dagger Affair*).

May
THE MYSTERY OF THE WORM
   Holmes meets Dr. Nikola and learns of the latter's quest for an immortality Elixir Vitae. Nikola also refers to his colleague of Asian descent who has discovered an Elixir of Life. One of Nikola's henchmen is *Isadora* Persano.
   A short story by John Pelan in the Holmesian/Lovecraftian anthology Shadows Over Baker Street, *taking place some weeks after "The Adventure of the Empty House." The colleague of Asian descent is Dr. Fu Manchu; however, Fu Manchu did not complete his Elixir until 1929 (see Sax Rohmer's* The Mask of Fu Manchu). *Perhaps Fu Manchu has discovered a part of the formula by this point. Nikola also refers to Fu Manchu as being an Egyptian Pharaoh, thou-*

sands of years old. Perhaps this is what Fu Manchu wants Nikola to believe. Nikola also refers to Royal Jelly as an ingredient in the formula. In later years, Holmes will pursue this line in his attempts to create his own age-delaying elixir. This must be a different Persano than that seen in Farmer's "The Problem of the Sore Bridge—Among Others."

STAGECOACH
Brisco County Jr., transports a British female espionage agent to Mexico for a prisoner exchange. The woman's name is Emma Steed. An American agent named Ashenden also appears.
Episode of The Adventures of Brisco County, Jr. *Emma Steed and Ashenden are most likely ancestors or relatives of British secret agent John Steed (*The Avengers*) and W. Somerset Maugham's* Ashenden, *respectively, both of whom are already in the Crossover Universe. This crossover places Brisco County Jr., in the CU.*

Spring. Birth of Senator Brooks U. Banner, criminologist in cases recounted by Joseph Commings.
Spring. The events of *Lieut. Gullivar Jones: His Vacation* (aka *Gullivar of Mars*) as related by Edwin L. Arnold, in which Gullivar Jones is carried to Mars, braves several adventures, and eventually marries a Martian princess. (Lieut. Gullivar Jones was freely adapted by Roy Thomas, Gerry Conway, and George Alec Effinger in *Creatures on the Loose* #16-21, Marvel Comics, 1972-1973.) Jones would later meet John Carter in *The League of Extraordinary Gentlemen, Volume II*, confirming that Jones' Mars is the same as Carter's Barsoom.

June
SHERLOCK HOLMES AND THE BOULEVARD ASSASSIN
Holmes is on the Continent, investigating the assassination of the President of France. He works with Monsieur Dubuque of the Paris police, and crosses paths with the infamous thief "Arsène Jupin."
Novel by Watson, edited by John Hall, Breese Books, 1998. Dubuque was first introduced in Watson's/Doyle's "The Second Stain" (not to be confused with "Too Many Stains [The Adventure of the Second Stain]"), and Holmes would work with him again during the case of The Pandora Plague. At first blush, one would think that "Arsène Jupin" is in fact Arsène Lupin. However, 1894 would be too early for Lupin to be well known as a thief. Furthermore, Holmes and "Jupin" have clashed twice before and "Jupin's" career was well established even back in 1891, when Lupin was but seventeen years old. Rick Lai has proposed that perhaps "Jupin" is a younger brother of Victor "Toto" Chupin from the Gaboriau novels, such as Monsieur Lecoq, *named Arsène Chupin. Furthermore, there was no presidential assassination in France in 1894; we must assume that part to be fictionalized. Perhaps Holmes' role was*

even deeper than revealed here, and he prevented an assassination, since he dealt with a "Boulevard Assassin" once more in October 1894 in "The Adventure of the Parisian Gentleman."

Mid June
ART IN THE BLOOD
 Sherlock and Mycroft Holmes consult on a case involving the Elder Gods, with references to Nyarlathotep, Cthulhu, and Azathoth. It is also stated that the Diogenes Club has a "hidden agenda," once again implying a connection to the British Secret Service.
 A short story by Brian Stableford in Shadows Over Baker Street. *The 1892 date assigned by the editors is not viable, as this would be during the Great Hiatus of 1891-1894. A character in this story, Chevaucheux, states that he first met Watson in India thirteen years ago. Dr. Watson is not currently in medical practice at the time of this tale. Watson sold his practice in May 1894. Watson traveled to India in late 1878, but by the spring of 1880, he was in Afghanistan. Chevaucheux must have been mistaken; he and Watson must have met in India in 1879, fifteen years ago.*

June 25-26
TIME PATROL
 Manse Everard of the Time Patrol encounters Sherlock Holmes, Dr. Watson, and Inspector Lestrade, as Holmes investigates the Addleton tragedy, and the singular contents of the ancient British barrow.
 Short story by Poul Anderson in The Time Patrol, *Tor Books, 1991, making the Time Patrol series one possible future of the CU. The Addleton tragedy was referred to in Doyle and Watson's "The Adventure of the Golden Pince-Nez," collected in* The Return of Sherlock Holmes. *However, this is the second "Addleton tragedy" that Holmes has investigated; the first was "The Adventure of the Rara Avis." Everard's adventure starts in 1954, and this exploit brings him to the Oligocene Era, 1894, c. 860s, 1944, and back to 1954.*

Summer
THE CASE OF THE LOST FOREIGNER
 Lawyer-turned-private investigator Martin Hewitt makes reference to the mind reading scene in "Murders in the Rue Morgue" when deciphering the drawings of a traumatized anarchist: "Do you remember the feat of Dupin in Poe's story, 'The Murders in the Rue Morgue'—how he walks by his friend's side in silence for some distance, and then suddenly breaks out with a divination of his thoughts, having silently traced them from a fruiter with a basket, through paving stones, Epicuris, Dr. Nicholas, the constellation Orion, and a Latin poem, to a cobbler lately turned actor?"

A short story in Arthur Morrison's The Chronicles of Martin Hewitt, *first published in June 1895 in* The Windsor Magazine.

THE STORY OF MR. FLAXMAN LOW
Flaxman Low fights a duel in France with his archenemy, Dr. Kalmarkane. Count Julowski is Kalmarkane's second.
Short story by "E. and H. Heron," pseudonym of Hesketh V. Prichard and Kate O'Brien Ryall Prichard from The Experiences of Flaxman Low, *1899. Since Count Julowski is in the Crossover Universe, so is Flaxman Low.*

THE CURIOUS CASE OF MISS VIOLET STONE
Miss Violet Stone, who has been ill, bed-ridden, and has not eaten for three years, asks her brother to secure for her a copy of the *Necronomicon*. Instead, he consults Sherlock Holmes. The Great Ones are also mentioned.
A short story by Poppy Z. Brite and David Ferguson in the Holmesian/Lovecraftian anthology Shadows Over Baker Street.

Summer. Scientist Abednego Danner creates a serum designed to give great strength to human beings, and tests it on his unborn son (Philip Wylie's *Gladiator*). Danner's son, Hugo, will grow up to have powers similar, although lesser, to those of Clark Kent; however, eventually Danner will become a social outcast, turning to crime, going into seclusion, and finally meeting death by lightning in South America.

Summer. Birth of Andrew Blodgett "Monk" Mayfair, one of Doc Savage's fabulous five. Per Farmer, Monk is the nephew of Professor George Edward Challenger.

August. Birth of Damian Adler, the third son of Sherlock Holmes and Irene Adler (*The Language of Bees* by Mary Russell Holmes and Laurie R. King).

August 20-23
THE ADVENTURE OF THE ANTIQUARIAN'S NIECE
Holmes consults with Thomas Carnacki in this tale which features references to Cthulhu, Shub-Niggurath, and Yog-Sothoth.

A short story by Barbara Hambly in the Holmesian/Lovecraftian anthology *Shadows Over Baker Street*. *Occult detective Thomas Carnacki, the "ghost finder," was created by William Hope Hodgson.*

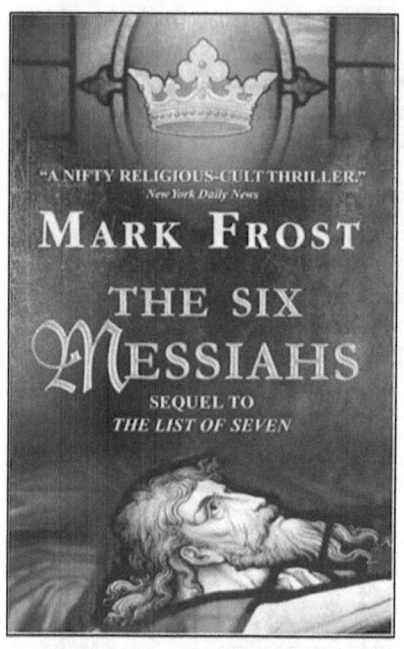

September. Arthur Conan Doyle and his sometime partner, Jack Sparks, share an adventure in America in *The Six Messiahs*, as told by Mark Frost.

Autumn
THE ADVENTURE OF THE YELLOW SIGN
   Sherlock Holmes battles a madman who tries to conjure the Yellow King.
   Short story by G. Warlock Vance in Rehearsals for Oblivion, Act I: Tales of the King in Yellow, *edited by Peter A. Worthy, Dimensions Books, 2006. The story confirms the Yellow King in the Crossover Universe.*

SHERLOCK HOLMES AND THE PANAMANIAN GIRLS
   Holmes enlists the assistance of American safe-cracker Jimmie Valentine.
   Novel by Frank Thomas, Xlibris, 2004. O. Henry (William Sydney Porter) wrote "A Retrieved Reformation," a short story featuring Jimmy (or "Jimmie") Valentine, the criminal with a heart. The short story was turned into a successful Broadway play, Alias Jimmy Valentine.

October
THE ADVENTURE OF THE PARISIAN GENTLEMAN
   Discussing the Great Hiatus, Watson states, "I knew that Holmes had spent considerable time in Paris. Much of that period was spent investigating the curious affair of the Opera Ghost. My friend knew every twist and turn of the fabled Paris Opera House."
   Short story by Doctor Watson, edited by Robert Weinberg & Lois H. Gresh in The Mammoth Book of New Sherlock Holmes Adventures, *Mike Ashley, ed., Carroll & Graf, 1997. Holmes did indeed face the Opera Ghost during this time period, as told in Nicholas Meyer's The Canary Trainer.*

October-November. Holmes first discovers that the first Professor Moriarty is still alive and is resuming his criminal activity, as told in *The Star of India* by John H. Watson, edited by Carole Buggé.

December 22, 1894-December 24, 1895
THE DISAPPEARANCE OF EDWIN DROOD

Mr. John Jasper consults Sherlock Holmes regarding the disappearance of his nephew, Edwin Drood. In Cloisterham, Dr. Watson drops that they are visitors from Baker Street, and the news quickly spreads that Sexton Blake is in town.

A novel by Watson, edited by Peter Rowland, Constable Crime Books, 1991. This novel is a follow-up to Charles Dickens' incomplete novel, The Mystery of Edwin Drood. *Although Watson dismisses Sexton Blake as a fictional creation, we know better. Even though this case takes a year to solve, Holmes is involved in many different unrelated cases during this time period.*

1895

January
NECROPOLIS

London private detective Clyde Beatty works on a mystery involving stolen gold bullion. He tells Inspector Lestrade not to take Mr. Holmes' jibes too seriously. Beatty looks out the window of his London residence and recognizes two passersby, Holmes and Watson.

Novel by Basil Copper, Arkham House, 1980, bringing detective Clyde Beatty into the CU.

THE TREASURE OF THE UBASTI

In India, Sâr Dubnotal, Dr. Henry Jones, Sr., and Captain Hood arrive deep in the jungle aboard Banks' Behemoth, a steam-powered elephant. Hiking deeper into the jungle in their quest, they encounter Mowgli, and danger in the form of the Cult of Ubasti.

Short story by Travis Hiltz in Tales of the Shadowmen Volume 6: Grand Guignol, *Jean-Marc and Randy Lofficier, eds., Black Coat Press, 2010; reprinted in French in* Les Compagnons de l'Ombre (Tome 7), *Jean-Marc and Randy Lofficier, eds., Rivière Blanche, 2010. Sâr Dubnotal is anonymously created French psychic detective. Dr. Henry Jones, Sr. is the father of Henry "Indiana" Jones, Jr., Captain Hood, Banks, and the Behemoth are from Jules Verne's* The Steam House. *Mowgli is from Rudyard Kiping's* The Jungle Book. *The Cult of Ubasti is from the 1934 film* The Return of Chandu.

February
THE CASE OF THE WAVY BLACK DAGGER

Holmes and Watson are very briefly in New York, on a mission to return an important relic—a keris—to its rightful owner, so that she may perform a ceremony which will keep a denizen of the Old Ones, the Eater of Souls (also called the Devourer of Children or simply the Black Naga), at bay for another thousand years.

A short story by Steve Perry in the anthology Shadows Over Baker Street, *Michael Reaves and John Pelan, eds., Del Rey Books, 2003. Although the editors assign a date of 1884 to this wintertime tale, references to Holmes' encounter with Irene Adler in "A Scandal in Bohemia," combined with the "late" Professor Moriarty, dictate a placement in 1894 or later.*

March. On the trail of a murderer, Holmes and Watson cross paths with many London luminaries, including George Bernard Shaw, Oscar Wilde, actress Ellen Terry, Gilbert (of Gilbert and Sullivan), and Bram Stoker. (*The West End Horror,* a novel by Watson, edited by Nicholas Meyer.) It is interesting to note that several of the authors Holmes met were historians who brought to light many remarkable people and events of the Crossover Universe.

Spring
THE FOUR DETECTIVES
One of the four detectives is "Arséne Pupin," the finest detective of the Sûreté Francaise, and the chief official of the "Cordon Bleu Soceite Internacionale Des Chefs Culinaries." "Pupin" frequently refers to "ze gray cells."

A novella by Frank Thomas in The Secret Files of Sherlock Holmes. *At first glance, one might think "Pupin" could be equated with Leblanc's Arsène Lupin; however, these details do not match up with those of Lupin. "Pupin" is more likely the famous detective Hercule Poirot; the description here as the finest detective of the Sûreté Francaise is a slight exaggeration, as Poirot's time with the Belgian police force was a few years off. (This tale could have been placed in the early 1900s when Poirot was actually with the police, but a reference in Frank Thomas'* Sherlock Holmes and the Sacred Sword *makes this impossible.)*

May
THE PROBLEM OF THE SORE BRIDGE—*AMONG OTHERS*
Sherlock Holmes again crosses paths with the notorious thief (and his former brother-in-law), A.J. Raffles, on the trail of a "worm unknown to science."

This is a short story by Raffles' partner, Harry "Bunny" Manders, edited by Philip José Farmer, found in Riverworld and Other Stories, *published by Berkley Books, 1979;* Sherlock Holmes Through Time and Space, *edited by Isaac Asimov, Martin Greenberg, and Charles Waugh, Bluejay Books, 1984; and* Venus on the Half-Shell and Others, *edited by Christopher Paul Carey, Subterranean Press, 2008. See also the 1918 entry for Farmer's* Escape from Loki.

Spring. John Kirowan is born. Rick Lai has suggested that John Kirowan is descended from Turlogh Kirowan. Turlogh, who fled Ireland for France at the time of Cromwell's atrocities, was seen in an obscure Robert E. Howard story called "The Ghost in the Doorway," an historical ghost story set in 1650.
Spring. Events of the film *The Catman of Paris.*

Spring
THE POLITICIAN, THE LIGHTHOUSE, AND THE TRAINED CORMORANT
Holmes, in the course of solving this mystery, evinces knowledge of a race of "Great Apes" (Mangani) of Africa and hints that during The Great Hiatus he observed Mangani capable of raising a human being from infancy.

Apparently Holmes has some knowledge of the details of Tarzan's birth. Short story edited by Craig Shaw Gardner, from a manuscript by Edgar Rice Burroughs, based on the notes of Dr. Watson, in the volume entitled Resurrected Holmes, *Marvin Kaye, ed., 1996.*

SHERLOCK HOLMES AND THE SACRED SWORD
Watson refers to Holmes' previous dealings with "Arséne Pupin," the pride of the Sûreté Francaise, and their previous acquaintance in the case of "The Four Detectives."

Novel by Frank Thomas, Pinnacle Books, 1980. As established earlier, "Pupin" is probably Hercule Poirot. A reference to General Kitchener preparing for the reconquest of the Sudan places this case in 1895.

Summer
URANIA'S BABYSITTER
Urania Moriarty seeks a sitter for her two sons, Jimmy Caber and Claude Darrell Caber, so she can attend a meeting at London's North Umberland Hotel to help decide the course of her late father's criminal organization. Antonio Nikola arrives with two more children in tow, Henry Peters, Jr., and Dominick

Damien Moriarty (the son the third Moriarty brother, Noel Moriarty). Finally the sitter, Milady Nevermore, arrives with yet another child, the seemingly harmless Lili Bugov. Not appearing, but mentioned, are: Gabrielle Tuke; Josephine Balsamo; Sabine Balsamo; Urania's hated half-sister Patsy Moriarty; Julius Pavia; and Henry Peters, Sr.

Short story by Rick Lai in Farmerphile: The Magazine of Philip José Farmer *#12, Paul Spiteri and Win Scott Eckert, eds., April 2008. Urania Caber (Moriarty) is the daughter of the first Professor James Moriarty from Philip José Farmer's Wold Newton genealogy in* Doc Savage: His Apocalyptic Life. *Moriarty is from Sir Arthur Doyle's Sherlock Holmes stories. The North Umberland Hotel is where THRUSH was born in David McDaniel's U.N.C.L.E novel* The Dagger Affair. *Gabrielle Tuke is a character meant to be sister of Tuke, the sinister butler in John Buchan's* The Power-House. *Josephine Balsamo is from Maurice Leblanc's Arsène Lupin stories. Sabine Balsamo is from Rick Lai's* Tales of the Shadowmen *story "All Predators Great and Small." Patsy Moriarty is meant to be Patricia Donleavy from Laurie R. King's* The Beekeeper's Apprentice. *Julius Pavia is an alias for Andrew Lumley (Noel Moriarty, referred to in this chronology as James Noel Moriarty, aka the second Professor Moriarty) in John Buchan's* The Power-House. *Antonio Nikola is Guy Boothby's* Dr. Nikola. *Dominick Damien Moriarty is meant to be Dominick Medina from John Buchan's* The Three Hostages. *Henry Peters, Sr., is from Sir Arthur Conan Doyle's "The Disappearance of Lady Frances Carfax." Henry Peters, Jr., is Henry Lakington, Carl Peterson's lieutenant in Sapper's* Bulldog Drummond. *Jimmy Caber is Lord Dunsany's Dr. Caber. Claude Darrell Caber combines Claude Darrell from Agatha Christie's* The Big Four *with Carl Peterson. Milady Nevermore is from Rick Lai's* Tales of the Shadowmen *story "Corridors of Deceit." Lily Bugov is from Farmer's authorized Doc Savage novel* Escape from Loki. *Lily is seven years old in 1895. Since she was at least eighteen before the start of World War I, she has to be at least twenty-two in* Escape from Loki *(set in 1918); an 1888 birth year makes her thirty in* Loki. *Note that the first Professor Moriarty may not be as late as some think, but must have reasons for not revealing himself to various friends and family.*

HOW DON Q FOUGHT FOR THE VALEDEREJOS
Don Q fights a duel with Count Julowski, and gravely wounds the Count, making it impossible for him to fight any more duels.
Short story by "E. and H. Heron," pseudonym of Hesketh V. Prichard and Kate O'Brien Ryall Prichard from The New Chronicles of Don Q, *1906. The Julowski is connection brings Don Q into the Crossover Universe.*

October
THE TRIAL OF SHERLOCK HOLMES
Sherlock Holmes is accused of the murder of a prominent Scotland Yard assistant commissioner. Lord Godalming's name is tossed out at a banquet at Buckingham Palace.
Five-issue comic book miniseries by Leah Moore, John Reppion, and Aaron Campbell, Dynamite Entertainment, 2009. Godalming is from Bram Stoker's novel Dracula.

THE ADVENTURE OF THE INERTIAL ADJUSTOR
Writer H.G. Wells brings the murder of an innovative scientist to Sherlock Holmes' attention.
Short story by Stephen Baxter in The Mammoth Book of New Sherlock Holmes Adventures, *Mike Ashley, ed., Carroll & Graf, 1997. The date given is 1894. However, Holmes is familiar with Wells' account of* The Time Machine, *first published in 1895; therefore, I have adjusted the date to 1895.*

October-November
THE HOUSE OF THE WOLF
Dr. John Coleridge, an American professor of folklore, leads a search for a werewolf in Hungary. Dr. Abercrombie, a Scotsman, shows Coleridge a copy of the London Times which tells the story of Clyde Beatty's solution of the mystery of the stolen gold bullion.
Novel by Basil Copper, 1983, referring back to the events of the novel Necropolis, *which takes place in the CU through connections to Sherlock Holmes.*

Late November
SHERLOCK HOLMES, DRAGON-SLAYER (THE SINGULAR ADVENTURES OF THE GRICE PATERSONS IN THE ISLAND OF UFFA)
James Jorkens and Sherlock Holmes share an adventure together.
Short story edited by Darrell Schweitzer, from a manuscript by Lord Dunsany, based on the notes of Dr. Watson. In the anthology Resurrected Holmes, *Marvin Kaye, ed., 1996. The narrator of this story must be the father of Joseph Jorkens, a Wold Newton Family member.*

1896

Winter. "The Adventure of the Mulberry Street Irregular": Holmes is in New York, and works once more with Teddy Roosevelt. (Play by Frank J. Morlock, collected in *Sherlock Holmes: The Grand Horizontals*, Black Coat Press, January 2006.)

Winter. Events of Pierre Benoit's *L'Atlantide* (1919), wherein two French soldiers happen upon the secret city of the cruel Queen Antinea in the Hoggar Mountains of the Sahara; published in English as *The Queen of Atlantis*.

Winter
THE DYNAMICS OF AN ASTEROID
Doctor Omega and his companions, Denis Borel, Fred, and Tiziraou, travel in the *Cosmos* to Reichenbach Falls on May 4, 1891, and pluck Professor Moriarty from certain death. After enlisting one more companion, Zephyrin Xirdal, they return to outer space in the year 1896, with the intent of consulting Moriarty on the matter of an asteroid which will impact the earth, in Russia, on June 30, 1908. After Moriarty inevitably betrays them, the Doctor proposes dropping him on Pitcairn Island in the year 1750.

Short story by Denis Borel, edited by John Peel, in Tales of the Shadowmen Volume 5: The Vampires of Paris, *Jean-Marc and Randy Lofficier, eds., Black Coat Press, 2009; reprinted in French in* Les Compagnons de l'Ombre (Tome 5), *Jean-Marc and Randy Lofficier, eds., Rivière Blanche, 2009. Doctor Omega, Borel, Fred, and Tiziraou are from novel* Doctor Omega *by Arnould Galopin, adapted and retold by Jean-Marc and Randy Lofficier. Zephyrin Xirdal is from Jules Verne's* The Chase of the Golden Meteor *(*La Chasse au Météore*). Professor Moriarty is Sherlock Holmes' nemesis. After his apparent demise, Moriarty's brother, James Noel Moriarty, impersonated him, calling himself "Professor Moriarty" and taking over his "late" brother's criminal organization; he is referred to herein as the second Professor Moriarty. This tale explains how the first Professor Moriarty survived the incident at Reichenbach Falls, although a mystery remains regarding his escape from Pitcairn Island in 1750 and his return to London, circa late 1894. The asteroid impact in Siberia on June 30, 1908 is known as the Tunguska event.*

March
THE RICHMOND ENIGMA
Sherlock Holmes investigates the disappearance of his distant relative, the Time Traveler.

Short story by John DeChancie in anthology Sherlock Holmes in Orbit, *DAW, 1995. For more information on the Time Traveler, please see "Travels in Time" by Loki Carbis,* Myths for the Modern Age: Philip José Farmer's Wold Newton Universe.

April 7. Birth of Hildegarde Withers, spinster schoolteacher and criminologist in tales by Stuart Palmer.

Spring. Birth of Hans von Hammer (*Enemy Ace: War Idyll, Enemy Ace: War in Heaven*).

Spring. Birth of Nick Noble, L.A. wino-detective in cases recounted by Anthony Boucher.

Spring. Birth of Fah Lo Suee, daughter of Fu Manchu and an unnamed Russian woman.

Spring
THE ADVENTURE MERLIN'S TOMB
The newly ordained Father Brown comes to Baker Street to consult with Sherlock Holmes and Dr. Watson about strange goings-on in the wake of the discovery of an ancient tomb in the Father's Church.

This short play by Frank J. Morlock, collected in Sherlock Holmes: The Grand Horizontals, *Black Coat Press, January 2006, takes place as Easter 1896 approaches. This must have been the first true meeting between Holmes and Father Brown, despite the information provided in the novel* Night Watch.

THE ADVENTURE OF THE BENEFICENT VAMPIRE
Count Dracula, with the help of Sherlock Holmes, Dr. Watson, and Father Brown, exposes Lord Ruthven's scheme to farm homeless English girls for their blood.

Short story by Frank J. Morlock in Lord Ruthven, the Vampire, *Black Coat Press, October 2004. This story cannot feature Dracula-prime, as this Dracula works in concert with Holmes (at least for a time) and they have not previously met. It is also probably not the "Vlad Dracula" seen in Fred Saberhagen's tales, as this Dracula reveals his own nefarious plans at the conclusion of the story. Additionally, Holmes would not meet "Vlad Dracula" until June 1897. "The Beneficent Vampire" must feature another "soul-clone" of Dracula. This story could have been placed earlier, but for the presence of Father Brown, who must be extremely young in this tale; there are also allusions to the previous Holmes/Brown story, "The Adventure of Merlin's Tomb."*

DEMONS ARE MADE...NOT BORN
Occult bookseller Solyomi finally gets a copy of *The Chronicles of Satan*, but is murdered by his partner, Ludwig Kruzz. Kruzz wants the book for himself so he can summon and command demons, but things don't work out quite as he planned. Several other books, including the *Demonomicon* and the *Ruthvenian*, are seen in Solyomi's musty bookshop.

Story by Donald F. Glut and Quico Redondo in DC Comics' House of Mystery *#227, October-November 1974. The presence of the* Demonomicon *and the* Ruthvenian *indicate that this tale occurs in the CU.*

BULLETS OVER BOMBAY
Captain John Good meets Docteur Mystère, his teenaged sidekick, Cigale, and Sandy Arbuthnot.

Short story by Captain John Good, RN, edited by David A. McIntee, in Tales of the Shadowmen Volume 3: Danse Macabre, *Jean-Marc and Randy Lofficier, eds., Black Coat Press, 2007; reprinted in French in* Les Compagnons de l'Ombre (Tome 4), *Jean-Marc and Randy Lofficier, eds., Rivière Blanche, 2009. Captain John Good is from H. Rider Haggard's novels* King Solomon's Mines *and* Allan Quatermain. *Philip José Farmer's* The Adventure of the Peerless Peer *indicated that Good remained in Zu-Vendis and had a family after the 1885-1886 events of* Allan Quatermain. *If so, he left Zu-Vendis long enough for a brief visit to India as seen in this tale. Sandy Arbuthnot is from John Buchan's Richard Hannay novel* Greenmantle; *as Arbuthnot was born in 1882, he'd only be fifteen in this story.*

CLASH OF THE VAMPIRES
Dracula and Holmes team once more against Lord Ruthven, but perhaps all is not as it seems.

Play by Frank J. Morlock, collected in Sherlock Holmes: The Grand Horizontals, *Black Coat Press, January 2006. The story is a sequel to "The Adventure of the Beneficent Vampire." After these events, Ruthven and his vampire sister Diana fled to Southern California, where they were staked in 1897, as seen in the film* Countess Dracula's Orgy of Blood.

EN DANSK LECOQ
Axel Johnson begins a successful career as a police officer in Copenhagen, Denmark. He is described as a "Danish Lecoq."

Story by C. Andersen, 1897.

THE IRREGULARS...IN THE SERVICE OF SHERLOCK HOLMES
Sherlock Holmes' Baker Street Irregulars play a large role in this case. Professor Challenger appears, and there is a reference to Seward's sanitarium. A man named Erich also appears, as does an evil talisman, the Hand of Ahirman.

Graphic novel by Steven Elliot-Altman, Michael Reaves, and Bong Dazo, Dark Horse Books, February 2005. *Seward's sanitarium is a nod to Bram Stoker's novel* Dracula, *which took place in 1887. At a minimum,* The Irregulars *cannot have occurred in 1885, as stated in the graphic novel. Changing the year to 1896 presupposes that the first Professor Moriarty didn't die at Reichenbach, or else* The Irregulars *features the second Professor Moriarty. Rick Lai notes that "There is a disguised connection to a Conan story, 'The Hand of Negral' by Robert E. Howard and Lin Carter. The Hand of Ahirman in* The Irregulars *appears to be the same evil talisman as the Hand of Negral encountered by Conan since the Hand of Ahirman is opposed by a good Heart talisman. The Irregulars calls the other talisman the Heart of Omhrazad, but it was called the Heart of Tammuz when Conan encountered it. The Heart of Tammuz should not be confused with the Heart of Ahriman, a talisman that is featured in Howard's* Hour of the Dragon/Conan the Conqueror. *Erich is supposed to be Lovecraft's Erich Zann, and the 'the Black King' is meant to be an alias for Nyarlathotep. I am also wondering if the shape-shifting Jack Springer is meant to some sort of version of Spring-Heeled Jack."*

Summer. Birth of private eye Sam Spade.

Summer. The events of H.G. Wells' *The Invisible Man,* featuring scientist Dr. John Hawley Griffin, who sometimes goes by Jack Griffin.

Summer
THE HONOUR OF A SPORTSMAN

Although Sherlock Holmes knows the famous cricketer A.J. Raffles to be the infamous "Amateur Cracksman," in this case Holmes knows Raffles to be innocent and strives to clear him.

Short story by Barrie Roberts in The Strand Magazine, *February-May, 2007.*

A MATTER WITHOUT GRAVITY

Holmes and Watson are called to Devon by Edward, Lord Beltham to investigate strange happenings. Holmes reveals that he would have gone anyway, as a high-ranking Minster had expressed concern over socialist writer Herbert George Wells, also of Devon. Arriving at Wells' residence, they meet Wells himself as well as others named Bedford, Cavor, and a third called only the Traveler.

Short story by Alain le Bussy in Tales of the Shadowmen Volume 5: The Vampires of Paris, *Jean-Marc and Randy Lofficier, eds., Black Coat Press, 2009; reprinted in French in* Les Compagnons de l'Ombre (Tome 5), *Jean-Marc and Randy Lofficier, eds., Rivière Blanche, 2009. Lord Beltham is from Marcel Allain and Pierre Souvestre's Fantômas series. Bedford and Cavor are from Wells'* The First Men in the Moon, *while the Traveler is from* The Time Machine.

August
PREDATOR: NEMESIS
    Mycroft Holmes and the ruling cabal of the Diogenes Club recruit Captain Edward Soames to track down and eliminate a serial killer prowling London. In the course of the case, Soames also works with Inspector Lestrade. The London newspapers refer to the killer as "Spring-Heeled Jack," but the Diogenes Club covers up the true nature of the murderer.
    Miniseries by Gordon Rennie and Colin MacNeil, Dark Horse Comics, 1997. The Diogenes Club, Mycroft Holmes, and Inspector Lestrade are all from the Sherlock Holmes stories. This case further solidifies the notion that the Diogenes Club was a secret arm of the British government. The alien hunters called Predators have been crossed-over with so many different comic characters and universes, that they must be deemed "multiversal." Therefore, only crossovers that work within Crossover Universe continuity, such as Tarzan vs. Predator at the Earth's Core, *will be listed here. Another way of saying this is that Soames encountered the CU version of the Predators.*

Mid August-Early September
SHERLOCK HOLMES AND THE SEVEN DEADLY SINS MURDERS
    Sherlock Holmes and Dr. Watson become involved in a series of murder in which there have already been two victims, with five remaining potential victims. The seven victims each had taken the role of one of the seven deadly sins while in college. One of the five remaining potential victims is Holmes' brother Mycroft, while two others are Professor George Edward Challenger and Challenger's longtime nemesis, Professor Summerlee. Ostensibly the murderer's quest is for the stolen *Book of Kor*, but this is merely a cover for the true motive of revenge.
    A novel by Dr. John H. Watson, edited by Barry Day, published by Second Option, Inc., 2002. Professors Challenger and Summerlee are from Arthur Conan Doyle's Professor Challenger series. The Book of Kor *is not related to the Kôr of Haggard's* She *books, despite Watson several times comparing the female protagonist in* The Seven Deadly Sins Murders *to his imagined vision of Ayesha from his reading of Rider Haggard's books. Regarding dating this adventure, the information provided by Watson is subject to his customary confusion regarding such matters, with the contradictory possibilities including 1888,*

1889, or post-Reichenbach (after 1894). I have chosen the latter for placement in this chronology. Furthermore, a significant question remains as to how Mycroft Holmes (b. 1847) and Professor Challenger (b. 1863) could have been student contemporaries at Christ Church College, Oxford; at a bare minimum, Watson's narrative is incorrect in stating that they were both part of the class of 1867.

September 1896-May 1897. The second Professor Moriarty has returned to England and once again has turned his attention toward rebuilding the Moriarty crime empire (John Gardner's *The Revenge of Moriarty*). However, the involvement of Irene Adler in these proceedings is another falsehood perpetrated by the second Professor.

Autumn. Writer and sleuth Samuel Clemens (Mark Twain) settles his family in Tedworth Square in London for the winter, quickly becomes involved in a new mystery, and works with Inspector Lestrade. Lestrade, of course, is from the Sherlock Holmes mysteries by Watson/Doyle. This novel, *The Guilty Abroad*, does not feature the "real" Twain, the Mark Twain of "our" universe, but rather the fictional character Twain of the Crossover Universe. Following the death of his daughter Susy, Twain and his family secluded themselves in the Tedworth Square abode in the Autumn of 1896. In this mystery by Peter J. Heck, Berkley Books (1999), Susy is alive and well.

October
FOOTSTEPS IN THE FOG

Sherlock Holmes and Professor George Edward Challenger team to solve a mysterious string of killings. The deaths are tied to a green fog, which arose after a strange meteor crashed in Regent's Park. Meanwhile, Colonel Sebastian Moran has escaped from prison and means to avenge himself upon Holmes and Watson by hunting them down and killing them. Professor Summerlee and McArdle, a reporter for the *Daily Gazette*, also appear.

This is a novella by Dr. John Watson, and edited by Kel Richards, in the volume Footsteps in the Fog and Other Stories, *Beacon Books, 1999. It takes place two years after "The Empty House." Summerlee, Challenger, and McAr-*

dle are from Arthur Conan Doyle's Professor Challenger series; McArdle is Ned Malone's editor in the Challenger stories. Since Holmes and Watson first met Challenger in The Seven Deadly Sins Murders, *this story must take place after that one, despite Watson's claim here that this is their first meeting.*

November
THE ADVENTURE OF THE HEADLESS MONK
Sherlock Holmes is consulted by Mortimer Harley, a supernatural detective. Harley refers to his colleague Carnacki.
Written by Ken Greenwald in The Lost Adventures of Sherlock Holmes, *Mallard Press, 1989. The story is based on the original Sherlock Holmes radio plays by Denis Green and Anthony Boucher, which in turn were based on Dr. Watson's notes. Thomas Carnacki, the "ghost finder," is an occult detective created by William Hope Hodgson, and this crossover confirms his presence in the CU.*

CORRIDORS OF DECEIT
Appearing or mentioned are: The Black Coats, Kaitlin de Winter (aka Kitty Winter), Baron Gruner, Berenice Fourneau (aka Blythe Furnace), the White Lodge, Catarina Koluchy (aka Mrs. Moriarty), Count Corbucci, Antonio Nikola, Madame Sara, Josephine Balsamo, Marguerite Chavain, Maude North Lady Maud Beltham, Irene Chupin/Tupin (aka Irina Putine), Victor Chupin, Rosette Trevor, Eva Relli, the Institution-Bachelard, the Countess Yalta, Purity Parker, the Pallid Mask, the Pendulum, Sebastian Medina, Roget Vollin, Anna Beringer, Porky Shinwell (aka Shinwell Johnson), Mary Holder, the Old Fellow, Dr. Mabuse, Juan North (aka Fantômas), and Richard Vollin.
Short story by Rick Lai in Tales of the Shadowmen Volume 4: Lords of Terror, *Jean-Marc and Randy Lofficier, eds., Black Coat Press, 2008; reprinted in French in* Les Compagnons de l'Ombre (Tome 7), *Jean-Marc and Randy Lofficier, eds., Rivière Blanche, 2010. The Black Coats are from Paul Féval's saga of novels about the criminal organization. Count Corbucci is from the works of E. W. Hornung. Kitty Winter, Baron Gruner, and Shinwell Johnson are from Doyle's "The Adventure of the Illustrious Client." May Holder is from "The Adventure of the Beryl Coronet." The Old Fellow appeared in* Le Pendu de Londres, *the seventh Fantômas novel. Maude North is the unnamed Boer wife of Fantômas alluded to in* The Daughter of Fantômas. *Her real name of Hendrika Pienaar suggests that she is related to Peter Pienaar from John Buchan's Richard Hannay novels.* The Daughter of Fantômas *mentioned that the master criminal's wife was dead by the time of the Boer War, but the text doesn't specifically say when she perished. Juan North was an alias used by Fantômas before the Boer War. The Pallid Mask and the Phantom of Truth are mentioned in* The King in Yellow *by Robert W. Chambers. The White Lodge is the residence of Andrew Lumley in Buchan's* The Power-House. *Lumley is Noel Moriarty (aka*

the second Professor Moriarty). "Steel-Skin" is the term used to describe the invincibility technique of an unnamed "White-Eyebrow Monk" in a 1974 Shaw Brothers film, Shaolin Martial Arts. *Although the Monk does not physically appear in the film, he is clearly Pai Mei, the villain of numerous other Kung Fu films and* Kill Bill, Volume 2. *The Iga and Koga ninja clans have an historical basis, but their rivalry formed the basis of the various television incarnations of* Shadow Warriors *in which Sonny Chiba played various Iga chieftains. Marguerite Chavain is based on a reference to Madame Fourneau's prize student, a botanist, in* La Residencia. *The Golden Ram crest of the Cagliostro family is from the Lupin III animated film,* The Castle of Cagliostro.

Rosette Trevor is the mother of Gertrude Trevor from Guy Boothby's Farewell, Nikola! *Eva Relli is the mother of E. Varelli, the sinister architect from Argento's* Inferno. *Varelli worked for the Three Mothers, and his mother is employed by three "Godmothers." The Insitution-Bachelard is a school mentioned in Zola's* Pot-Bouille. *Countess Yalta is from du Boisgobey's* La Main Coupee *(The Severed Hand). Purity Parker is intended to be the sister of Colonel Moran's henchman from Doyle's* "The Adventure of the Empty House." *Like Madame Koluchy, Anna Beringer is from* The Brotherhood of the Seven Kings *by Meade and Eustace. Madame Sara is from* The Sorceress of the Strand *by the same writers. Sebastian Medina and his son were played by Vincent Price in the film version of* The Pit and the Pendulum. *Richard Vollin was the Poe-obsessed surgeon played by Bela Lugosi in* The Raven. *The Espionage Hotel is an earlier version of the hotel from Fritz Lang's* The Thousand Eyes of Dr. Mabuse.

November 17-18
THE REPULSIVE STORY OF THE RED LEECH
    Holmes refers to Professor Challenger's recent monograph, which "has quite exploded the claims of the spirit mediums."
    A short story by David Langford in the anthology The Mammoth Book of New Sherlock Holmes Adventures, *Mike Ashley, editor, Carroll & Graf, 1997. This is the second Holmes tale concerning a repulsive red leech, the first taking place in December 1886.*

November
A CASE OF BLIND FEAR

Sherlock Holmes, Dr. Watson, and Professor Challenger fight against the Invisible Man. Colonel Sebastian Moran, Irene Adler, and Irene's estranged husband Godfrey Norton also appear.

This Sherlock Holmes miniseries, later collected as a graphic novel published by Malibu Graphics, was written by Martin Powell and illustrated by Seppo Makinen. It also serves as a sequel to H.G. Wells' The Invisible Man. *The date given is 1894; however, for purposes of the Crossover Universe, an 1896 date is more probable. The Invisible Man's first name is given as Murray, and he is equated with the orderly Murray who saved Watson's life at the Battle of Maiwand during the Second Anglo-Afghan War of 1878-1880 (see Doyle and Watson's* A Study in Scarlet). *Given that the original Invisible Man has been reconciled as Dr. John Hawley Griffin, aka Jack Griffin (see* The League of Extraordinary Gentlemen, *as well as Dennis E. Power's article, "The Invisibles," at* The Wold Newton Universe: A Secret History *website), the Murray Griffin seen in* A Case of Blind Fear *must be a sibling of John Hawley Griffin who has stolen his brother's invisibility formula for his own nefarious ends. This solution also reconciles the death of the Murray Griffin Invisible Man in* Blind Fear *with the death almost two years later of John Hawley Griffin in* The League of Extraordinary Gentlemen II.

1897

January
SHADOW OF DRACULA/WHEN WAKES THE DEAD

Vampirella and Dracula are both sent back in time from 1970 to 1897 where they meet Abraham Van Helsing and Abraham's brother, Boris Van Helsing, who lives in Maine. Dracula appears to attempt to reform. Mina and Jonathan Harker are also in Maine. Together they resurrect Lucy Westenra, but only briefly. Dracula's "reformation" is short-lived and he ends up attacking Mina before being defeated once again.

Vampirella *magazine #19-20, Warren Publishing, by T. Casey Brennan and José Gonzalez. We can presume that Mina and Jonathan Harker divorced shortly after these events, per* The League of Extraordinary Gentlemen, *in which Mina still bears Dracula's bite marks from this attack. Boris Van Helsing is the ancestor of Conrad Van Helsing and Conrad's son Adam, both of whom are regulars in Warren's Vampirella series. Vampirella has encountered Dracula many times in her career. Vampirella also has been crossed-over with many other comic book creations. In order to maintain Crossover Universe continuity, these will be taken on a case-by-case basis. For a complete explanation of Vampirella's true origin in the Crossover Universe, please read John A. Small's*

"Kiss of the Vampire," Myths for the Modern Age: Philip José Farmer's Wold Newton Universe.

February-June
THE CASE OF THE FAITHFUL RETAINER

Holmes mentions fellow investigator and master-chef M. Auguste Didier several times in this adventure.

Short story by Amy Myers in The Mammoth Book of New Sherlock Holmes Adventures. *Myers also writes the Didier mysteries, which take place contemporaneously with the Holmes stories.*

March. Events of *Enter the Nyctalope* (*L'Assassinat du Nyctalope*) as told by Jean de La Hire, translated and adapted by Brian Stableford, Black Coat Press, 2009.

March 19. Birth of Inspector John Magruder, detective in cases recounted by Jerome and Harold Prince.

Spring. Simon Carne's first recorded exploit, *A Prince of Swindlers*, as told by Guy Boothby.

Spring. The events of "The Lizard," as *related* by C.J. Cutcliffe Hyne.

Spring. Respected private detective Horace Dorrington is revealed to be a murderer. ("The Narrative of Mr. James Rigby" by Arthur Morrison.)

Spring. Kathryn Koluchy is blinded in a fire and becomes known as the "Blind Spinner."

Spring
THE PRISONER OF BLACKWOOD CASTLE

Harry Challenge, of the Challenge International Detective Agency, is in the kingdom of Orlandia, trying to get back with the local princess who doesn't want him. In this adventure, he is found "...attempting to concentrate on the front page of the morning paper. There was political unrest in Ruritania, a severe earthquake had struck the farmlands of Graustark, there'd been an assassination attempt in Valeria."

Novel by Ron Goulart. The Ruritania reference connects to Hope's The Prisoner of Zenda. *Since* Zenda *takes place in the CU, so do these events. Fol-*

lowing the chain, the Graustark novels of George Barr McCutcheon also occur in the CU.

THE CURSE OF THE OBELISK
   The villain, Zaytoom, is an immortal Egyptian whose longevity comes from the extinct tana plant. Challenge's ally, the Great Lorenzo, shouts "El Carim Zanzibar Zatara!" as a diversion. Lorenzo also utters, "Lando Zambini Marvelo!" Ruritania and Graustark are mentioned again.
   The second Harry Challenge novel by Ron Goulart. The tana plant reference is from Universal's Mummy films. El Carim, Master of Magic, is a magician seen in the pages of Master Comics. *El Carim's name spelled backwards is "miracle." Zanzibar (*Mystery Men*), Zatara (*Action Comics*), Zambini the Miracle Man (*Zip Comics*), Lando, Man of Magic (*World's Best Comics*), and Marvelo, Monarch of Magicians (*Big Shot Comics*) are also Golden Age comic book magicians.*

EL HOMBRE INVISIBLE CONTRA FU MANCHU (THE INVISIBLE MAN VS. FU MANCHU)
   The Invisible Man vs. Fu Manchu!
   A Spanish comic, #34 Editorial Rialto, Colección Diamante negro, 1944. As Dennis E. Power notes, "We know that Hawley Griffin faked his death at the end of the The Invisible Man, *and other than hiding out at Rosa Coots' Academy, we do not knowwhat he was up to. Although Fu Manchu was governor of the Honan province in 1895-1900, we also know that he spent some time in England around this time, due to the events of* The League of Extraordinary Gentlemen, *in which Moriarty went up against the Devil Doctor. The chronological placement of this entry is highly speculative since we do not have access to the original material."*

May
THE MYSTERY OF THE HANGED MAN'S PUZZLE
   Holmes investigates a case involving Obed Marsh, Innsmouth, and the Deep Ones.
   A short story by Paul Finch in the Holmesian/Lovecraftian anthology Shadows Over Baker Street.

NIGHT OF THE JACKASS
   An illicit drug called Hyde 25(m) is spreading throughout England. The drug is taken by those who are poor, homeless, downtrodden, and have no hope. It turns them into unstoppable monsters who go on killing sprees, "jackassing," for a period of twenty-four hours before they expire. Several survivors of previous jackassing incidents, one of them named Bishop, band together to halt the episodes and find an antidote to the drug.

Four short "Jackass" tales by Bruce Bezaire and José Ortiz were collected in Warren's Eerie #115, October 1980. A connection to the drug used in Robert Lewis Stevenson's Dr. Jekyll and Mr. Hyde is implied by the name of the jackass drug, Hyde 25(m). A 1990s miniseries from Harris Comics, Hyde-25: Return of the Jackass, featured the great-great grandson of Bishop, and made the Jekyll connection explicit.

June 10-22
THE HOLMES-DRACULA FILE

Sherlock Holmes and Vlad Dracula cross paths while working against a group intent on unleashing a plague upon London during the Queen's Jubilee.

Novel by Fred Saberhagen, Ace Books, 1978, based on the memoirs of Vlad Dracula and an unpublished manuscript of John Watson. This is another adventure that Watson referred to as the "Giant Rat of Sumatra," the first occurring in 1886; obviously, Watson was enamored of the phrase. The Dracula encountered here is not the same as that encountered by Holmes and Watson in 1887 (see Watson's Sherlock Holmes vs. Dracula, or, The Adventure of the Sanguinary Count*). For a full explanation of Vlad and his relationship to the true Count, please read Dennis E. Power's "Best Fangs Forward" on The Wold Newton Universe: A Secret History website; the essay also covers the truth behind the "familial relationship" between Holmes and Vlad, and is based upon research by Brad Mengel. It is revealed that Mina Harker, still married to Jonathan Harker, is Vlad Dracula's lover. This is understandable in light of the fact, as established in The League of Extraordinary Gentlemen II, that Jonathan refused to have anything to do with Mina following the January 1897 events of Shadow of Dracula. It must be presumed that Jonathan discovers the relationship shortly after the conclusion of this case, for, by May of 1898, Mina Harker is known as Mina Murray.*

June
VAN HELSING: THE LONDON ASSIGNMENT

Monster hunter Gabriel Van Helsing battles Mr. Hyde in London.

The London Assignment *is an animated prequel to the* Van Helsing *feature film. The immortal Gabriel Van Helsing must be the progenitor of the vampire-hunting family made famous by Dr. Abraham Van Helsing in Bram Stoker's novel* Dracula. *Although the story is said to take place during Queen Victoria's Golden Jubilee (1887), the internal chronology for Mr. Hyde in the CU makes the Diamond Jubilee (1897) more likely.*

SEVEN STARS EPISODE ONE: THE MUMMY'S HEART
    Charles Beauregard is an agent of the Diogenes Club (a front for the British Secret Service), reporting to Mycroft Holmes. His current assignment involves investigating a series of murders connected to the discovery of the Jewel of Seven Stars, found within the mummy of Pai-net'em. Professor Abel Trelawny also appears, as do Inspector Lestrade, Henry Wilcox, and Sir Joseph Whemple. Reporter Kate Reed is involved in this adventure, and the mad Arab, Al-Hazred, is mentioned. Beauregard also consults with Thomas Carnacki, the "ghost finder," and with Machen.
    This chapter of Seven Stars *by Kim Newman confirms that the Charles Beauregard of the Anno Dracula Universe has a counterpart in the Crossover Universe. Abel Trelawny is borrowed from Stoker's* The Jewel of Seven Stars. *Inspector Lestrade, Mycroft Holmes, and the Diogenes Club are from Doyle and Watson's Sherlock Holmes stories. Henry Wilcox is from E.M. Forster's* Howards End. *The Whemple in this story must be the father of the Whemple in 1932's* The Mummy, *bringing the events of that film into the CU. Kate Reed is a "deleted" character from Stoker's* Dracula; *this Kate Reed has a vampire counterpart in the Anno Dracula Universe. Al-Hazred is from Lovecraft's Cthulhu Mythos stories. Carnacki* the "ghost finder" *is an occult detective created by William Hope Hodgson; this story confirms him in the CU. Machen is supernatural writer Arthur Machen (1863-1947). The serial continues in February 1922 with "Seven Stars Episode Two: The Magician and the Matinee Idol."*

THE ADVENTURE OF THE ANGEL'S TRUMPET
    Barrister Kevin O'Bannion, an ancestor of Patrick Butler, comes to Holmes for assistance in clearing his client of murder charges.
    John Dickson Carr's Patrick Butler appeared first in Below Suspicion *with Dr. Gideon Fell. He then appeared in his own novel,* Patrick Butler for the Defense. *This short story is by Carolyn Wheat, in* Holmes for the Holidays, *Greenberg, Lellenberg, & Waugh, eds., Berkley Books, 1996.*

Summer. The unsinkable liner Titan sinks, as told in Morgan Robertson's novel *The Wreck of the Titan, Or, Futility.*

Summer
HOUSE OF THE VAMPIRE, LONDON, ENGLAND, 1897

Slayer Angelique Hawthorne and her watcher Peter Van Helsing (brother of Abraham Van Helsing) chase Spring-Heeled Jack, or at least a demon posing as him. When Van Helsing asks if a detective named Peasbody looked for fingerprints, Peasbody implies that Van Helsing should discuss such crackpot ideas with the detective on Baker Street who works with Lestrade. A scene in a wax museum displays Dr. Jekyll and Mr. Hyde, Jack the Ripper, and Lizzie Borden. Angelique and Van Helsing tangle with Dracula. Angelique Hawthorn mentions being trained in the martial art of Baritsu.

Short story by Michael Reaves in Tales of the Slayer, Volume II, *Pulse, January 2003. The Van Helsing, Dracula, Sherlock Holmes, and Dr. Jekyll connections in this story confirm that* Buffy the Vampire Slayer *is part of the Crossover Universe. Sherlock Holmes is the only known practitioner of Baritsu. It should be noted that by "Season 8" of Buffy as seen in Dark Horse Comics, the occult, monsters, and Slayers become widely known to the world at large; this is incompatible with the Crossover Universe and is not included in CU continuity.*

June 1897; 1917; 2100
WHEN THE SLEEPER WAKES

Mr. Graham falls asleep in Mr. Isbister's kitchen in Boscastle, England and doesn't awake for 203 years. Twenty years after finding Graham, Mr. Isbister discusses the coma with Graham's friend Mr. Warming, and all the events that have occurred: "And there's been the War," said Isbister. "From beginning to end." "And these Martians."

Novel by H.G. Wells, 1899; revised as The Sleeper Awakes, *1910. Mr. Graham slips into his coma shortly before Queen Victoria's Diamon Jubilee (June 20, 1897). The Martian reference is to Wells'* The War of the Worlds, *which occurred in 1898. The novel is the loose basis for the Woody Allen film* Sleeper *(1973).*

September
WOLFMAN OF DARTMOOR

Sherlock Holmes and Dr. Watson again work with *Daily Gazette* reporter James McArdle. At the adventure's conclusion, McArdle suggests that in the future he will pursue a series of stories about strange happenings, parts of which cannot be explained. He would label these stories "X" for unknown, and would keep them in a special file.

This is a novella by Dr. John Watson, and edited by Kel Richards, in the volume Footsteps in the Fog and Other Stories, *Beacon Books, 1999. McArdle was Ned Malone's editor in Sir Arthur Conan Doyle's Professor Challenger stories. McArdle's statement about keeping a file of file of strange, unexplained events marked "X" is more of an in-joke than a real connection to* The X-Files.

Autumn
THE DIME MUSEUM MURDERS

Young magician Harry Houdini and his brother, Dash Hardeen, solve a series of murders in New York City. Houdini attempts to emulate his hero, Sherlock Holmes, and quotes Holmes several different times. Houdini and Dash also (erroneously) compare a criminal leader to Professor Moriarty, and there is a reference to the master thief, Raffles.

Novel narrated by Dash Hardeen, and edited by Daniel Stashower, Avon Books, 1999. Houdini met Holmes in 1900 and several times thereafter. This is not a crossover involving the "real" Houdini of "our" universe, but rather the fictional character Houdini of the Crossover Universe. Interestingly, Harry and Dash refer to Holmes' final encounter with Moriarty at Reichenbach, but don't refer to Holmes' return to London in 1894; this is undoubtedly because the story of Holmes' survival was not widely publicized until the publication of "The Empty House" in 1903.

FROM THE TREE OF TIME

Sherlock Holmes briefly consults with his "cousin" Vlad Dracula on a case involving another vampire.

Short story by Fred Saberhagen in the anthology Saberhagen: My Best, *Baen Books, May 1987. This is the same Vlad Dracula that Holmes first encountered in Saberhagen's* The Holmes-Dracula File, *not to be confused with the much more sinister Count of Bram Stoker's novel.*

December 23-24
THE ADVENTURE OF THE EXTRAORDINARY LODGER

The jade necklace owned by Theodore Hartnell is the same necklace for which Los Angeles private eye Philip Marlowe will hunt in the late 1930s.

A short story by Dr. Watson, edited by Matthew J. Elliott, in the U.K. magazine Sherlock #52, *Christmas 2002. Elliott also writes for the U.S. radio series* The Further Adventures of Sherlock Holmes. *The story ran on radio under the title "The Blackmailer of Lancaster Gate." The necklace was seen in Raymond Chandler's* Farewell, My Lovely.

1898

January
THE CASE OF THE DETECTIVE'S SMILE
Holmes receives a visit from Alice Liddell and they discuss their respective sojourns to the dimension known as Wonderland.

Short story by Mark Bourne in the anthology Sherlock Holmes in Orbit, *DAW, 1995, bringing Alice Liddell into the CU. Wonderland is an alternate realm, or a "pocket universe," to the Crossover Universe.*

January-February. Harry Houdini and his brother, Dash Hardeen, assist the "Dean of American magicians," the Great Kellar, and solve another murder along the way in *The Floating Lady Murder* by Dash Hardeen, edited by Daniel Stashower.

Winter. First recorded exploit of German-American reporter Count Leo V. Hagen. ("In a Zeppelin around the World" by Robert Kraft.)

Winter
THE YOUNG LORD PETER CONSULTS SHERLOCK HOLMES
Young Lord Peter Wimsey consults the Great Detective upon the matter of a missing kitten. It is also revealed that the Wimsey family is distantly connected with that of Reginald Musgrave.

Lord Peter himself narrates this short tale, which can be found in the book Sayers on Holmes: Essays and Fiction on Sherlock Holmes *by Dorothy L. Sayers, Mythopoeic Press, 2001.*

March. The events of H.G. Wells' "The Crystal Egg."
Spring. Twins Jimmy and Constance "Nan" Christopher are born in China.

Spring
THE HOUDINI SPECTER
This murder mystery featuring Harry Houdini and his brother, Dash Hardeen, features several references to the great detective, Sherlock Holmes, as well as the celebrated Dr. Thorndyke.

Novel narrated by Dash Hardeen, and edited by Daniel Stashower, Avon Books, 2001. Although it is not explicitly stated that Holmes and Thorndyke are real people in relation to Houdini and Hardeen's world, it is also not explicitly stated that they are fictional characters. Since there are many other references placing a version of Houdini in the Crossover Universe, we may interpret these as allusions to the real detectives, Holmes and Thorndyke.

VAN HELSING
Gabriel Van Helsing battles Mr. Hyde in Paris.
Feature film written and directed by Stephen Sommers, Universal Pictures, 2004. The Van Helsing *novelization is by Kevin Ryan. This first part of the film, detailing Van Helsing's confrontation with Hyde in Paris, takes place before* The League of Extraordinary Gentlemen. *The remainder takes place afterward, in October 1898.*

VAN HELSING: FROM BENEATH THE RUE MORGUE
Immediately after his confrontation with Mr. Hyde, Van Helsing is sent to investigate the brutal murders of two women. He is drawn to the sewers of Paris, where he encounters an invisible beast created by Dr. Moreau. Moreau used Griffin's formula to bestow invisibility on his creature. Moreau mentions the murder, this very night, of his acquaintance Dr. Henry Jekyll. Van Helsing replies that he had come to Paris stop the murderous Edward Hyde. During their conflict, Moreau escapes, ruminating to himself that he should leave civilization and set himself up on a South Seas island where he can work in peace.
Van Helsing *#1 by Joshua Dysart and J. Alexander, Dark Horse Comics, April 2004. This story takes place in between the Hyde and Dracula events in the film* Van Helsing. *Dr. Moreau's original headquarters was on a tropical island, as seen in H.G. Wells'* The Island of Dr. Moreau, *which took place in 1887. After his conflict with Van Helsing, Moreau did not set himself up with another tropical island headquarters. Instead, he was headquartered by the British Secret Service deep in the forests of England (see* The League of Extraordinary Gentlemen II*). Van Helsing's report of Jekyll's/Hyde's death was premature, as Hyde would also soon be recruited by the BSS (see* The League of Extraordinary Gentlemen*). H.G. Wells' Invisible Man Griffin would also go on to become a League member; the events of* The Invisible Man *take place in 1897, necessitating the placement of this story slightly thereafter.*

May-August
THE LEAGUE OF EXTRAORDINARY GENTLEMEN
Allan Quatermain, Dr. Henry Jekyll/Mr. Hyde, Captain Nemo (Prince Dakkar), The Invisible Man (Hawley Griffin), and Mina Murray (formerly Mina Harker), are pitted against the Devil Doctor who controls London's Limehouse. The Devil Doctor is clearly Fu Manchu, and the conflict is part of a larger battle

between Fu Manchu and the first Professor Moriarty for control of London's underworld. C. Auguste Dupin, Campion Bond, and Mycroft Holmes also appear, as does Sherlock Holmes, albeit in a flashback to the incident at Reichenbach Falls. The tale concludes as the Martian Invasion begins.

The League of Extraordinary Gentlemen *comic book miniseries was written by Alan Moore, with art by Kevin O'Neill, America's Best Comics, 1999-2000. For supplemental information on Victorian characters and stories, please refer to Jess Nevins'* The Encyclopedia of Fantastic Victoriana, *MonkeyBrain Books, 2005. The "main" crossovers are with Haggard's Quatermain, Doyle's Holmes brothers and James Moriarty, Poe's Dupin, and Rohmer's Fu Manchu, all of whom are Wold Newton Family members. Presumably Campion Bond is as well; he is most likely a relative of Fleming's James Bond, and I have identified him as Bond's great-uncle (*The League of Extraordinary Gentlemen: Black Dossier *identifies Campion as James Bond's grandfather, but this is not compatible with the genealogical information from Farmer's* Doc Savage: His Apocalyptic Life *and John Pearson's biography* James Bond: The Authorized Biography of 007*). Mina Murray is from Stoker's* Dracula*; Griffin is from Wells'* The Invisible Man*; Nemo is from Verne's* 20,000 Leagues under the Sea *and* The Mysterious Island*; and the Martian Invasion is that depicted by Wells in* The War of the Worlds.

Note that most of the main characters in League *believe that Sherlock Holmes is dead, not realizing that he returned to London in 1894. (His brother, Mycroft, is, of course, tellingly silent on the matter.) Holmes would encounter this same problem during his 1900 meeting with Harry Houdini, which continued until Watson finally got around to publishing his account of "The Adventure of the Empty House," which chronicled Holmes' "return to life" after his battle to the death with the first Professor Moriarty at Reichenbach Falls.*

Please refer to Jess Nevins' Heroes and Monsters: The Unofficial Companion to *The League of Extraordinary Gentlemen (MonkeyBrain Books, 2003), which provides much of the information on the less obvious crossovers, characters, and references in* League, *listed here in general order of appearance: Emile Zola's* L'Assommoir *and* Nana*; Rosa Coote, Miss Flaybum, "The Correctional Academy for Wayward Gentlewomen," and The Yellow Room; Ishmael* *from Melville's* Moby Dick *(Ishmael would be about 72 or 73 years old at this time); Harry Blyth's detective Sexton Blake; Inspector Dick Donovan; Verne's* Robur the Conqueror; *Reverend Septimus Harding from Anthony Trollope's* The Warden; *Plantagenet Palliser from Trollope's* Palliser/Parliamentary *novels; Dickens'* David Copperfield; *Wells'* Lavelle of Java *and* War of the Worlds; *Olive Chancellor of Henry James'* The Bostonians; *Katy Carr from Susan Coolidge's* What Katy Did *and sequels; Becky Randall from Kate Douglas Wiggin's* Rebecca of Sunnybrook Farm *and* More About Rebecca *(although the timing is problematic); Eleanor H. Porter's* Pollyanna *(again the timing may be problematic); Lord and Lady Pokingham; Ayesha, aka "She-who-must be-obeyed," from H.R. Haggard's books; Jonathan Swift's* Gulliver's Travels; *Cooper's Natty Bumppo; Orczy's Sir Percy Blakeney; Thorndike's Dr. Syn; John Cleland's* Fanny Hill; *Captain Mors; Verne's* Journey to the Centre of the Earth; *Professor Selwyn Cavor from Wells'* The First Men in the Moon; *Quong Lee from Thomas Burke's* Limehouse Nights: Tales of Chinatown, The Song Book of Quong Lee of Limehouse, *and* The Pleasantries of Old Quong; *Jim Hawkins, Long John Silver, and Robert Louis Stevenson's* Treasure Island; *E. Harcourt Burrage's* Broad Arrow Jack; *Guy Boothby's Klimo, aka Simon Carne; Guy Boothby's Dr. Nikola; Morgan Robertson's novel* Futility *(aka* The Wreck of the Titan*); Jules Verne's Phileas Fogg; Samuel Ferguson from Verne's* Five Weeks in a Balloon; *the Artful Dodger, from Dickens'* Oliver Twist; *Charles Ross and Marie Duval's* Ally Sloper, F.O.M.; *Tom Browne's Weary Willy and Tired Tim; Edward S. Ellis'* The Huge Hunter, or, the Steam Man of the Prairies; *and H.G. Wells' story* "The Purple Pinaeum."

Here are a few references from the hardcover edition of *The League of Extraordinary Gentlemen (not repeating those references already identified), listed in general order of appearance: Basil Hallward and Dorian Gray from Oscar Wilde's* The Picture of Dorian Gray; *H.P. Lovecraft's* "Pickman's Model"; *The Cabinet of Dr. Caligari; Thomas More's* Utopia; *Zenda; Flatland; Vril-ya, from Edward Bulwer-Lytton's* The Coming Race; *Sir Arthur Conan Doyle's* The Lost World; *Wonderland, from Lewis Carroll's* Alice in Wonderland; *Jules Verne's* The Steam House; *Sapathwa, aka the penny dreadful villain The Blue Dwarf; Bracebridge Hemyng's* Jack Harkaway's Schooldays; *Sir Francis Varney, from James Malcolm Rymer's* Varney the Vampyre, or, The Feast of Blood; *and Count Allamistakeo, from Edgar Allan Poe's* "Some Words With A Mummy."

Here are additional references from *The Game of Extraordinary Gentlemen, listed in general order of appearance. While these don't appear in the story proper, they are obviously intended by the authors to be a part of the* League *universe, and thus are part of the Crossover Universe. Again, many thanks to Jess Nevins for his annotations: Spring-Heeled Jack; Charles Dickens' unfinished* The Mystery of Edwin Drood; *Sweeney Todd; Professor Gibberne from H.G. Wells'* "A New Accelerator"; *Fan Chu Fang, the Wizard Mandarin, the Chinese archenemy of Dixon Brett; Prince Wu-Ling, the Fu Manchu-like enemy* of Sexton Blake; *Wu Fang*; Rudyard Kipling's Gunga Din; Wilkie Collins' The Moonstone; *Mowgli from Rudyard Kipling's* The Jungle Book; *Hugh Lofting's Dr. John Dolittle*; Edgar A. Poe's "The Black Cat"; Charles Dickens' Great Expectations; Edgar Allan Poe's "The Premature Burial"; Alexandre Dumas' The Man in the Iron Mask; Frank Norris' McTeague; Wardon Curtis' The Monster of Lake LaMetrie; *adventurer Nick Carter, who first appeared in* The Old Detective's Pupil; *Cthulhu; Charles Hamilton's Billy Bunter*; E. W. Hornung's Raffles; Mary Shelley's Frankenstein; J. Sheridan LeFanu's "Carmilla"; *Hank Morgan from Mark Twain's* A Connecticut Yankee in King Arthur's Court; *Mr. Kurtz from Joseph Conrad's* Heart of Darkness; *Frank Reade, Jr.; Washington Irving's* The Legend of Sleepy Hollow; A. E. W. Mason's The Four Feathers; Jules Verne's From the Earth to the Moon; Jules Verne's Un Express de L'Avenir; Charles Maturin's Melmoth the Wanderer; *Maurice Leblanc's Arsène Lupin*; H.G. Wells' The Island of Dr. Moreau; *Lulu from Frank Wedekind's* Earth-Spirit *and* Pandora's Box; *Henry Hobson from Harold Brighouse's* Hobson's Choice; *Mr. Cave from H.G. Wells'* "The Crystal Egg"; *Severin from Leopold von Sacher-Masoch's* Venus in Furs; *Pere Ubu from Alfred Jarry's* Ubu Roi; *Harry Flashman, who first appeared in Thomas Hughes'* Tom Brown's Schooldays *and then in George Macdonald Fraser's* Flashman *novels;* Richard Marsh's "The Beetle"; *and Fred M. White's* "The Purple Terror."

Summer
THE FURY OF A FIEND
The original Frankenstein Monster vs. Count Dracula.

Story by Gary Friedrich, John Buscema, and John Verpoorten in Marvel Comics' The Frankenstein Monster #7-9; *reprinted in* The Essential Monster of Frankenstein, Volume 1, *2004, and* The Essential Tomb of Dracula, Volume 4, *2005.*

August. The events of H.G. Wells' *The War of the Worlds.* Pastiche continuations of *The War of the Worlds* are (in no particular order): *The League of Extraordinary Gentlemen, Volumes I and II* by Alan Moore and Kevin O'Neill, *Sherlock Holmes' War of the Worlds* by Manly W. Wellman and Wade Wellman, *The Space Machine* by Christopher Priest, *Invasion of Mars* (aka *Edison's Conquest of Mars*) by Garrett P. Serviss, the various short stories in *War of the Worlds: Global Dispatches*, Kevin J. Anderson, ed.,

The Second War of the Worlds by George H. Smith, and *The Case of the Missing Martian*.

August
SHERLOCK HOLMES'S WAR OF THE WORLDS
In this companion novel to H.G. Wells' *The War of the Worlds*, Sherlock Holmes, Dr. John Watson, Lord John Roxton, and Professor George Edward Challenger fight against the Martian Invasion. Professor Challenger's assistant, Morgan, is revealed to be the son of Colonel Moran.

This is a novel by Challenger's biographer, Edward D. Malone, and Holmes' biographer, Watson, edited by Manly W. Wellman and Wade Wellman, Warner Books, 1975. For the reason why the editors added a purely fictional romance between Holmes and his landlady, Mrs. Hudson, please read Dennis E. Power's article, "The Kissable Mrs. Hudson" (available at The Wold Newton Universe *website). The 1901-1902 dates given are unlikely, and have been changed to 1898 for this Chronology. Although the prelude revolving around the Crystal Egg begins in March 1898, Holmes is involved in many different unrelated adventures during the six-month period of March-August 1898. The events of the Martian Invasion and the main events of this novel take place during August of 1898. The epilogue takes place in October 1898.*

Sir Arthur Conan Doyle edited many stories about Professor Challenger, such as The Lost World *and* The Poison Belt*. Challenger is also the uncle of Doc Savage's aide, Monk Mayfair. Regarding the red planet, Challenger was correct in his conclusion that the invaders did not come from Mars—at least not our Mars, since Mars in our universe is (supposedly) a dead planet. Challenger may have been correct in stating that they came from beyond our solar system. However, they did so via a Mars that exists in a dimension parallel to our own, that containing John Carter's Mars, otherwise known as Barsoom. For more information on the theory that Barsoom exists in a parallel universe to Earth, see John Flint Roy's* A Guide to Barsoom, *Ballentine Books, 1976.*

THE VANISHING DIAMONDS
At a Club in London, Joseph Jorkens regales his fellow members Allan Quatermain, Nemo, Lord Baskerville, Hareton Ironcastle, Griffin (admitted to the Club only at M's insistence), and The Time Traveler (sponsored by Challenger) with a story of D'Artagnan and Cardinal Richelieu. When The Time Traveler defends the truth of Dumas' story of the Queen's diamonds, he is dared to travel back in time and return with proof. The Time Traveler accepts the challenge and journeys back to 1626 in order to secure photographic proof. Ironcastle mentions a bet with Zephyrin Xirdal. The Time Traveler, who knows Doctor Omega, returns with the photographs. Unbeknownst to all, it is revealed that Dumas learned of the tale of the Queen's diamonds from Isaac Laquedem, the Wandering Jew, in 1843.

Short story by Sylvie Miller and Philippe Ward in Tales of the Shadowmen Volume 2: Gentlemen of the Night, *Jean-Marc and Randy Lofficier, eds., Black Coat Press, 2006. Jorkens, age eighteen, must have been barely old enough to join the Club. Joseph Jorkens, Allan Quatermain, Nemo, The Time Traveler, and Professor Challenger are all members of Philip José Farmer's Wold Newton Family. Lord Baskerville is doubtless related to the family made famous in Doyle and Watson's* The Hound of the Baskervilles. *Hareton Ironcastle is from J.-H. Rosny aîné's* L'Étonnant Voyage d'Hareton Ironcastle *[The Amazing Journey of Hareton Ironcastle] (1922), which was translated and revised by Philip José Farmer for publication in English as* Ironcastle *(DAW Books, 1976). Griffin is from H.G. Wells'* The Invisible Man. *D'Artagnan and Cardinal Richelieu are from Alexandre Dumas'* The Three Musketeers. *The only time that Nemo, Quatermain, and Griffin could conceivably come together in this setting is between the events of the first two* League of Extraordinary Gentlemen *graphic novels. Following League continuity, M is first, Moriarty, and second, Mycroft Holmes. Zephyrin Xirdal is from Jules Verne's* The Chase of the Golden Meteor *(*La Chasse au Météore*), linking that story to the CU. Doctor Omega is a fellow time traveler from Arnould Galopin's novel. The Wandering Jew is from Dumas'* Isaac Laquedem, *1853, although Eugène Sue and Paul Féval also wrote about the Wandering Jew.*

August-September
THE LEAGUE OF EXTRAORDINARY GENTLEMEN, VOLUME II

On Mars (Barsoom), John Carter, the Barsoomian Green Martians, the Séroni, and Gullivar Jones of Mars join together in battle, with the unintended consequence of driving the Martian Invaders toward Earth. Allan Quatermain, Dr. Henry Jekyll/Mr. Hyde, Captain Nemo (Prince Dakkar), The Invisible Man (Hawley Griffin), and Mina Murray (formerly Mina Harker) again join forces, this time against the Martian Invasion. They continue to take their orders from Campion Bond, who in turn serves a new "M," presumably Mycroft Holmes. As the fight against the Invasion continues, Quatermain and Murray are instructed to seek out the services of a scientist, Dr. Alphonse Moreau. As the Invasion concludes, Hyde kills traitor Griffin before sacrificing himself in battle against the Martian tripods.

The League of Extraordinary Gentlemen, Volume II *comic book miniseries was written by Alan Moore, with art by Kevin O'Neill, America's Best Comics, 2002-2003. The prologue depicting the united forces of Mars (Barsoom) battling against the Martian Invaders and finally driving some of them off Barsoom and toward Earth, takes place in July 1898. The final details of this battle are related in* "Mars: The Home Front."

The "main" crossovers are: Haggard's Quatermain is a Wold Newton Family member, per Philip José Farmer's Doc Savage. *It is likely that Campion Bond is also. The marks upon Bond's walking stick spell out "007" in Morse Code, solidifying his connection to Fleming's James Bond, and thus I have identified Campion as James Bond's great-uncle. Mina Murray is from Stoker's* Dracula; *Griffin is from H.G. Wells'* The Invisible Man; *Nemo is from Verne's* 20,000 Leagues under the Sea *and* The Mysterious Island; *and the Martian Invasion is depicted by Wells in* The War of the Worlds. *Mycroft Holmes, of course is from Doyle and Watson's Sherlock Holmes tales. For a bit more on Mycroft's (and Professor Moriarty's) role as "M," see the entries for* The Great Game *and* Son of Holmes. *Lieut. Gullivar Jones: His Vacation (aka* Gullivar of Mars) *was written by Edwin L. Arnold. John Carter, of course, is the hero of Edgar Rice Burroughs' Martian series. The Séroni are from C.S. Lewis' Space Trilogy (*Out of the Silent Planet, Perelandra, *and* That Hideous Strength). *Dr. Moreau is from H.G. Wells'* The Island of Dr. Moreau; *it is revealed here that British Intelligence faked his death in 1887 and set him up in a hidden headquarters in England to continue his gruesome experiments. Moreau's creatures reveal the true story behind the anthropomorphized British animals, such as Jumbo the Elephant, Tiger Tim, Mary Tourtel's Rupert the Bear, and Kenneth Grahame's The Wind in the Willows. Although this appears to be the definitive death of Hawley Griffin, Hyde somehow survived, as he resurfaced to battle Tarzan in 1909 New York.*

Please refer to Jess Nevins' A Blazing World: The Unofficial Companion to The League of Extraordinary Gentlemen, Volume II *(MonkeyBrain Books, 2004), for annotations on the less obvious crossovers, characters, and references in League II, listed here in general order of appearance: the "Hither People" from* Lieut. Gullivar Jones: His Vacation; *"Varnal, the Green City"* *from Michael Moorcock's Mars series (*Warriors of Mars, Blades of Mars, *and* Barbarians of Mars, *featuring Michael Kane, a physics professor transported to Mars' distant past, written under the pseudonym of Edward P. Bradbury); "The Crystal Egg" by H.G. Wells (which also features in* Sherlock Holmes' War of the Worlds *as a reconnaissance device for the invading Martians); Guy Boothby's Dr. Nikola; Reverend Harding, from Anthony Trollope's* The Warden; *The Bleak House inn, from Charles Dickens'* Bleak House; *Major Henry Blimp, the future Colonel Blimp; the straight razor in the museum with the plaque "Kettlewell, Yorkshire, Mr. W.C. Cording" refers to "The Lizard" by Charles John Cutcliffe Hyne; Teddy Prendrick is from* The Island of Dr. Moreau; *Percy Greg's* Across the Zodiac; *the Baltimore Gun Club, from Jules Verne's* From the Earth to the Moon *and* Round the Moon; *Augustus Bedloe from Edgar Allan Poe's "A Tale of the Ragged Mountains"; George Griffith's "A Visit to the Moon"; Edwin L. Arnold's The Wonderful Adventures of Phra the Phoenician; the White Rabbit from Lewis Carroll's* Alice's Adventures in Wonderland; *Edwin L. Arnold's Lepidus the Centurion; Edgar Allan Poe's poem "The Raven"; Charlton Lea's* Spring-Heeled Jack, the Terror of London; *Aladdin's Lamp; Mark Twain's* A Connecticut Yankee in King Arthur's Court; *Robert Cromie's* A Plunge into Space; *Karl Friedrich Hieronymus, Baron von Münchhausen; Dorian Gray, from Oscar Wilde's* The Picture of Dorian Gray; *Russell Thorndike's* Doctor Syn; *the Wolf of Kabul from the British comics* Wizard *and* Hotspur; *Baroness Emmuska Orczy's* The Scarlet Pimpernel; *Richard Marsh's* The Beetle; *Arnould Galopin's* Le Docteur Oméga; *Rudyard Kipling's "The Brushwood Boy"; Jonathan Swift's* Gulliver's Travels; *E. Harcourt Burrage's Broad-Arrow Jack; Ally Sloper and Weary Willy; Maleva, the Romany woman whose werewolf son Bela bit Larry Talbot in Universal's* The Wolf Man; *Rudyard Kipling's story ".007"; and W.H. Hudson's* A Crystal Age.

The references in The League of Extraordinary Gentlemen II: *"The New Traveller's Almanac" are so extensive that one is better served by referring to Jess Nevins' annotations in* A Blazing World, *rather than repeating them all here. Furthermore, some of them are so fanciful that one must question whether they are all viable CU references. Clearly many of these references are "real" in the context of the CU, but equally many of them may be part of an elaborate misdirection on Miss Murray's part. I lean toward the latter theory, given the other events described in the Almanac concerning "Allan Quatermain Jr." In any event, some of the references to historical Leagues are included in this Chronology.*

August
MARS: THE HOME FRONT

John Carter of Mars relates to Edgar Rice Burroughs his involvement in defeating the Martian Invasion of Earth by the evil Sarmaks of Barsoom.

A short story edited by George Alec Effinger, from a manuscript by Edgar Rice Burroughs, in the anthology War of the Worlds: Global Dispatches, *Bantam, 1996, Kevin J. Anderson, ed. Establishes that the invaders' Mars and Barsoom are one and the same (although, per* Sherlock Holmes's War of the Worlds *and* The League of Extraordinary Gentlemen II, *the Sarmaks may not be natives of Barsoom). Barsoom is located in an alternate universe to the Crossover Universe (see also* The Second War of the Worlds*).*

SOLDIER OF THE QUEEN
During the Martian Invasion, Rudyard Kipling meets Mowgli; Kim; Learoyd, Mulvaney and Ortheris; and Gandhi.

A short story edited by Barbara Hambly, *from a manuscript by Rudyard Kipling, in the anthology* War of the Worlds: Global Dispatches, *Bantam, 1996, Kevin J. Anderson, ed. The level of destruction and the political results arising therefrom are overstated in Kipling's account. Mowgli is from* The Jungle Book. *Kimball O'Hara is from* Kim. *Learoyd, Mulvaney and Ortheris are from* Soldiers Three. *Gandhi is self-explanatory. For more on Mowgli, please read Dennis E. Power's* "Jungle Brothers, Or, Secrets of the Jungle Lords," Myths for the Modern Age: Philip José Farmer's Wold Newton Universe.

TO MARS AND PROVIDENCE
During the Martian Invasion, eight-year-old Howard Phillips Lovecraft has an unusual experience and discovers a connection between the Martian Sarmaks and the Elder Gods.

A short story edited by Don Webb, *from a manuscript by H.P. Lovecraft, in the anthology* War of the Worlds: Global Dispatches, *Bantam, 1996, Kevin J. Anderson, ed.*

THE TRUE TALE OF THE FINAL BATTLE OF UMSLOPOGAAS THE ZULU
During the Martian Invasion, Winston Churchill witnesses the Allan Quatermain's companion Umslopogaas battling Martians.

A short story edited by Janet Berliner, *from a manuscript by Winston Churchill, in the anthology* War of the Worlds: Global Dispatches, *Bantam, 1996, Kevin J. Anderson, ed. Churchill places these events from November 1899-April 1900, during the Boer War, which began in October 1899. However, Dennis E. Power has postulated that Churchill was actually in Africa a year earlier, for reasons that he was unable to reveal. Since he was not allowed to disclose his presence in Africa in August 1898, he fictionalized the time frame when he prepared this account. Umslopogaas is the warrior featured in H. Rider Haggard's* Nada the Lily, She and Allan, *and* Allan Quatermain. *The explanation for his appearance in 1898 so many years after his death is revealed in the story.*

Early October
THE ADVENTURE OF THE ARAB'S MANUSCRIPT
Holmes takes a case involving the Kitab al-Azif, which was the original version of the text which later became known as the *Necronomicon* of Abdul al-Hazred, described as the most dangerous book in the world because it instructs the reader in the ways of summoning the Old Ones and Elder Gods.

A short story by Michael Reaves in the Holmesian/Lovecraftian anthology Shadows Over Baker Street.

Late October
VAN HELSING
Monster hunter Gabriel Van Helsing, along with his friend Friar Carl, Anna Valerious, and one of the Frankenstein Creatures, battles "Count Dracula" and his vampire brides. The poem "Even a man who's pure of heart..." is recited.

Feature film written and directed by Stephen Sommers, Universal Pictures, 2004; novelization by Kevin Ryan. Some of the events depicted in the Van Helsing *film took place earlier in 1898. The Dracula seen in this film cannot be the "Dracula-prime" of Stoker's novel. Rather, it must be a Dracula-variant, or "soul-clone." The Victor Frankenstein seen in the film's prologue is probably really Henry Victor Frankenstein from the original 1930s Universal films* Frankenstein *and* Bride of Frankenstein. *The portion of the prologue featuring Dracula's patronage of Henry Victor Frankenstein takes place in 1884, before the events of the original* Frankenstein *film. The latter portion of the prologue, featuring Henry's making of another Creature and his subsequent murder at the hands of his benefactor Dracula, takes place in early 1897. The poem is from Universal's* The Wolf Man. *The final battle takes place on October 31. Researcher Henry Covert has concluded, "Since he's 2,000 years old, Gabriel Van Helsing must be the progenitor of the whole monster-hunting Van Helsing clan."*

Late October-November
SPIKE VS. DRACULA
In an attempt to frame Count Dracula and set an angry mob after him, the vampire Spike goes to a pub and kills a girl. The pub is called *The Slaughtered Lamb*.

Spike vs. Dracula #1, *a miniseries by Peter David and Joe Corroney, IDW Publishing, February 2006.* The Slaughtered Lamb *pub is from the film* An American Werewolf in London.

November
THE DISAPPEARING MAN
  Stage magician Merlin the Magnificent (whose real name is Harry Price) and reporter Grace Stewart solve a magic-based mystery. Holmes, Watson, and Inspector Gregson all briefly appear. Holmes once asked Merlin about stage magic.
  Short story by Scott Flinders in Sherlock! #5, 2003.

November 24. Birth of John "Korak" Drummond-Clayton. Farmer's *Tarzan Alive* establishes that Korak's older brother is Captain Hugh "Bulldog" Drummond, and that his great-grandmother is Oread Butler, a cousin of Rhett Butler (Gone with the Wind).
  December. The mad Dr. Caresco's crimes, as told in *Le Mal Nécessaire* (*The Necessary Evil*) by André Couvreur. Dr. Caresco went on to appear in *Caresco Surhomme* (1904) and several other novels.
  Late 1898-Early1899. Dorothy Gale makes her first trip to the alternate reality called Oz (L. Frank Baum's *The Wizard of Oz*).

1899

January
NO GHOSTS NEED APPLY
  Consulting detective Cecil Barker and his journalist friend Nash are present, but hidden, when notorious London blackmailer Charles Augustus Milverton is shot by one of his victims. As Barker and Nash flee across the Heath from Milverton's burning house, they are chased by constables but saved by the intervention of a mysterious benefactor. The next day, Inspector Lestrade asks the Great Detective (who unbeknownst to Lestrade was also present with his doctor friend, neither of whom who knew that Barker and Nash were also present) to investigate Milverton's death, but he declines, as does Nash. Barker smokes Red Apple cigarettes. Barker and Nash's benefactor visits, and is re-

vealed as The Phantom, who in his youth served as Barker's page. Barker's current page is a young boy named Dickson. The Phantom divulges that he's been working on a blackmail case regarding possible survivors of an African shipwreck over ten years ago, and Barker explains that he learned that Milverton was working for Colonel Moran. Later, Barker and Nash shadow their rival detectives and learn the identity of the woman who shot Milverton. On their way to Moran's current headquarters at Carlow Castle, which is allegedly haunted by the ghost of Lord William Marshall, the dark-maned and grey-eyed 1st Earl of Pembroke, Barker speaks disparagingly of occult detectives Morris Klaw, Low, and Carnacki. Moran and his goons capture Barker and Nash, and The Phantom affects a rescue, during which Moran is viciously run through with an ancient pike, ostensibly belonging to the late Lord William Marshall. The pike embeds in solid stone, and Barker notes that he "...heard of something similar once, when Patrick Cairns harpooned Black Peter Michael Carey." Moran's attacker was either Marshall's ghost, an explanation Barker rejects, or perhaps a hireling of the woman who shot Milverton...a woman who happens to be a Duchess now due to the fact that her husband's noble relatives are missing and presumed dead in the aforementioned African shipwreck.

A short story by Win Scott Eckert in The Phantom Chronicles, Volume 2, *Joe Gentile, ed., Moonstone Books, 2010. The Phantom, of course, is Lee Falk's multi-generational comic-strip hero. The case begins as the Sherlock Holmes tale "The Adventure of Charles Augustus Milverton" concludes. Barker is Sherlock Holmes' friend and rival from "The Retired Colourman." Colonel Moran Professor Moriarty's chief from "The Empty House." Red Apple cigarettes are from various films including* Kill Bill. *Dickson is Harry Dickson, "the American Sherlock Holmes." Morris Klaw is Sax Rohmer's supernatural sleuth from* The Dream Detective; *this crossover places him in the Crossover Universe. Low is Flaxman Low, from stories by E. and H. Heron. Carnacki is William Hope Hodgson's Thomas Carnacki, the ghost finder. According to Philip José Farmer, the woman who pulled the trigger on Milverton is the Duchess of Holdernesse, from the Holmes tale "The Adventure of the Priory School," and she was apparently motivated only by revenge and to prevent Milverton from victimizing others in the future. "No Ghosts Need Apply" reveals a possible additional motive...as Farmer's theory also clarifies that in fiction, the Duchy of Holdernesse has also been called the Duchy of Greystoke. And yet the Duchess could in no way be capable of the attack upon Moran. Only a hireling, and one of prodigious strength, could possibly pull it off. Or else Marshall's ghost. Of course the Jungle Lord himself could be motivated by revenge against Moran for using his family in a blackmail scheme, and certainly would be capable of the physical feat described herein, but at this point in time Tarzan was only a shade over ten years old, and his survival in Africa still had not been discovered. Likewise Tarzan had an excellent motive for the attack on Black Peter Michael Carey (see the Holmes case "The Adventure of Black Peter," which takes place in 1895;*

Farmer has suggested that Black Peter was the same person as Black Michael, the chief mutineer on the Fuwalda who was ultimately responsible for marooning Tarzan's parents, as well as murdering Tarzan's grandfather). However, creative mythographer Christopher Paul Carey (note the shared family name) has rightfully pointed out that the murder Black Peter took place in 1895, when Tarzan was five, and still stranded in Africa. There is no logical way to—ahem—pin this attack on the Jungle Lord.

Of course, any resemblance between Lord William Marshall and Tarzan is purely coincidental.

March
A CASE OF INSOMNIA
Holmes investigates a plague of insomnia afflicting the northern town of Inswich. The Mad Arab's text (the *Necronomicon*) is mentioned.

A short story by John P. Vourlis in the Holmesian/Lovecraftian anthology Shadows Over Baker Street.

Spring. The events of *A Portrait of the Artist as Young Man* by James Joyce. The artist, Stephen Dedalus, will later meet Wold Newton Family member Leopold Bloom.

Spring
THE TERROR OUT OF TIME
Sherlock Holmes and Professor Challenger investigate murders involving the mysterious idol of M'tollo. Aleister Crowley figures peripherally in the case, and Holmes refers to the "oceanologist" Marracott.

A novel by Ralph E. Vaughan, Gryphon Books, 2002. "Marracott" is probably from Sir Arthur Conan Doyle's The Maracot Deep, *in which Maracot is a scientist who has written books on oceanic phenomenon. He will lead a scientific expedition in search of Atlantis in 1926.*

May. Birth of air ace James "Biggles" Bigglesworth.

May. Doctor Julius No, the grandson of Dr. James Noel, is born (see my "Who's Going to Take Over the World When I'm Gone?" *Myths for the Modern Age: Philip José Farmer's Wold Newton Universe*).

May
THE SECRET OF THE SCARAB
Harry Challenge discusses a trip to Ruritania to investigate a haunted castle. Professor Moriarty is still the most dangerous criminal in England. The Egyptian Pharaoh Ibis II is mentioned.

Story by Ron Goulart, Fantasy & Science Fiction, *April 2005. Ibis II may possibly be the son of Fawcett Comics' Ibis the Invincible and Taia. Whether*

Ibis revived in the 1940s in the Crossover Universe is debatable, but even if so, this crossover does not automatically import the remainder of the Fawcett characters into the CU.

Summer
THE MAGICIAN'S NEPHEW

It is stated that the Sherlock Holmes mysteries are happening concurrently with these events in Narnia: "In those days Sherlock Holmes was still living in Baker Street and the Bastable children were looking for treasure in the Lewisham Road."

Novel by C.S. Lewis. Since Narnia is clearly not part of the Crossover Universe, it must be another parallel reality that people travel to from the CU. Rick Lai adds: "Oswald Bastable was the creation of children writer E. Nesbitt. He appeared with a group of siblings in a trilogy, The Story of the Treasure Seekers *(1899),* The Wouldbegoods *(1901), and* The New Treasure Seekers *(1904). Michael Moorcock used Oswald Bastable in his Multiverse stories. Moorcock reveals that Oswald Bastable traveled through time and parallel dimensions starting in 1902. Oswald is the main character in* The Warlord of the Air, The Land Leviathan, *and* The Steel Tsar. *In novels from other series, he meets Elric and the time travelers at the End of Time. In the introduction to* A Nomad of the Time Streams, *a collection of the three Bastable novels, Moorcock acknowledges that his Bastable is supposed to be the same character as Nesbitt's. However, due to chronological issues, the Oswald Bastable of Moorcock's books can't be the same person as Nesbitt's character. Moorcock's Oswald is an adult in 1902 while Nesbitt's Oswald is 13 or 14 in 1900. The two Oswalds must be cousins. Moorcock's version was an officer in India in 1902. Nesbitt's Oswald has a great-uncle from India. The uncle doesn't seem to have any children of his own, but maybe he's a widower. Moorcock's Oswald could be the son or grandson of the 'Indian Uncle' from Nesbitt's books."*

Summer 1899. George Bernard Shaw's *Pygmalion*, aka *My Fair Lady*.
July 1, 1899. Birth of Henry "Indiana" Jones, Jr.

October
THE RANGOON JADE
Sherlock Holmes mentions that one of two men who could have cracked a particular safe is Jimmie Valentine, but that he is in America.
A short story by Frank Thomas in The Secret Files of Sherlock Holmes, *Xlibris, 2002.*

THE FIVE FISTS OF SCIENCE
Nikola Tesla, Baroness Bertha von Suttner, and Mark Twain team up to force peace upon the world's nations with a scientific weapon. They are opposed by J.P. Morgan, Thomas Edison, Andrew Carnegie, and Guglielmo Marconi, who are building the Innsmouth Tower in New York City, and have a captured Migou at their disposal.
Graphic novel by Matt Fraction and Steven Sanders, Image Comics, 2006. The Innsmouth Tower channels mystic forces, and must be related to the town of Innsmouth, Mass. The Migou is a yeti, better known in the Cthulhu Mythos as the Mi-Go.

October 31
THE PHANTOM HIGHWAYMAN
Detective Harry Challenge calls Dr. Grimshaw, "The second cleverest criminal mastermind in Europe." Grimshaw replies that if it wasn't for that Professor Moriarty, he'd be number one. Challenge's sidekick, the magician known as the Great Lorenzo, claims to have sampled an inferior vintage of Ruritanian champagne.
A short story by Ron Goulart in The Ultimate Halloween, *Marvin Kaye, ed. This reference confirms the Harry Challenge stories in the CU.*

Autumn
THE ADVENTURE OF THE HONOURABLE CRACKSMAN
During the course of a murder investigation, Sherlock Holmes encounters A.J. Raffles, Bunny Manders, Dr. Litefoot, and Mycroft's agent Ibbetson.
Short story by M.J. Elliott in Sherlock #63. *Ibbetson is from the film* The Private Life of Sherlock Holmes *along with the novelization by Michael and Mollie Hardwick. The police surgeon, Litefoot, is from the* Doctor Who *episode "The Talons of Weng-Chiang." As noted in the Addendum covering Alternate*

Universes, the inclusion of all Doctor Who *continuity in the Crossover Universe is problematic. The Litefoot seen here must be a parallel universe counterpart to the Litefoot who met the Doctor in the alternate Doctor Who Universe.*

1899-1900. The events of *The First Men in the Moon,* as told by H.G. Wells.

December. Charles Fort, with the assistance of young H. P. Lovecraft, investigates a strange series of disappearances in New York City. Governor Theodore Roosevelt also appears in the story. *(Fort: Prophet of the Unexplained,* a comic book miniseries by Peter M. Lenkov and Frazer Irving, Dark Horse Comics, 2002. The story involves the Crossover Universe versions of Fort, Lovecraft, and Roosevelt.)

December 31
THE PRISONER OF THE TOWER, OR A SHORT BUT BEAUTIFUL JOURNEY OF THREE WISE MEN
When a French nobleman is subject to extortion by Arsène Lupin, he sends for help from both Sherlock Holmes and Erast Fandorin.
Novella by Boris Akunin in the collection Jade Rosary Beads, *2006. The story is dedicated to Maurice Leblanc and his novel* Herlock Sholmes Comes Too Late. *The tale is told from the points of view of both Dr. Watson and Masa, Fandorin's Japanese servant.*

1900

January 5. James W. Gordon is born. Concurrent with his position as Gotham City's youngest ever Police Commissioner, he will work as the masked vigilante The Whisperer in the 1930s (see Arn McConnell's "The Case of Commissioner James Gordon," *The Wold Atlas,* v1, #3, Fall 1977, reprinted on *The Wold Newton Chronicles* website).

January
SHERLOCK HOLMES AND THE BIZARRE ALIBI
Holmes is recruited by French police official "Arsène Pupin" to help on a case. Safe-cracker Jimmie Valentine also appears.
Novel by Frank Thomas, Xlibris, 2004. "Pupin" is probably the famous detective Hercule Poirot, although Poirot was a Belgian detective. This case cites many different contradictory dates, but the case hinges on the Boer War, so I have placed it during that period.

THE FINISHING STROKE
Holmes and Watson pass A.J. Raffles and Bunny Manders in a dark alley. Later, Watson mentions Professor Challenger.

Story by M.J. Elliott in Gaslight Grimoire, *J.R. Campbell and Charles Prepolec, eds., Edge Science Fiction and Fantasy Publishing, 2008. Raffles, Manders, and Challenger should need no further introductions at this point.*

Winter. Hamilton Cleek (aka "the man of Forty Faces"), an exiled king of the small European kingdom of Maurevania, begins his career as a master criminal in Europe. Due to a genetic abnormality Cleek is able to rearrange his facial features and appear to be nearly anyone, hence his nickname. ("The Man of Forty Faces" by Thomas W. Hanshew.) Cleek soon gives up his illicit business and becomes a consulting detective.

Winter. Birth of the mysterious Wu Fang.

February
THE LAST VENDETTA

Arthur Gordon and many others attend an "assassin's auction" of rare and valuable weapons in New Orleans. The auction is being run by Josephine Balsamo, assisted by Aguirre. Josephine's decent from Count Cagliostro and his activities during the French Revolution are described. One of Gordon's former wives was Hermine de Chalusse of Paris. The other was Francine Xavier of Austin, Texas. Gordon receives a letter from Ignacz Djanko, alias the Undertaker. Lee Bailey's machine guns are mentioned, as are the Red Scarf Gang, General Santilla, and Stanley Corbett (aka "Count Corbucci"), the dime novel writer. Count Corbucci's publisher is Pickman and Sons. One item for sale is the Mute Shootist's Mauser Pistol. The inventions of the Red Circle and the Brotherhood of the Seven Kings are mentioned. Josephine's brief love affair with Ballmeyer is also mentioned; some of the items they amassed include the weapons of the Butcher and the seven idols of Professor Malaki. Another of Josephine's suppliers is Dr. Nikola. Josephine attended the Marie Gilbert School in Paris, followed by the Fourneau College for Young Women. The arms dealer Peterson is mentioned, as is the Bookkeeper, a member of the Ten Killers of the Underworld. Another of the weapons offered for sale, the Flying Guillotine, was used by a blind assassin. Kegan Van Roon's book *Secrets of the Shaolin Temple's Thirty-Sixth Chamber* is mentioned; the book's publisher is Golden Goblin Press. Two of the auction attendees are Hong Chen and Huan Tsung Chao, emissaries of Dr. Natas, the alias adopted by the powerful governor of the Chinese province of Honan. Huan Tsung Chao tells the story of Shogun Ietmitsu of Japan, who was beheaded by one of his own Yagyu assassins. Gordon meets Count Bielowsky, who now serves Queen Antinea. Bielowsky is at the auction to bid against Oliver Haddo for items from the tomb of the wizard Surama. Gordon tells Bielowsky the history of some of the weapons, and makes reference to Gunsight Eyes and the Rojos Brothers. Other attendees include a Japanese woman in a white kimono, who complains that a large wood baby cart filled with concealed muskets is a fake. Also attending are a man named Adam Saxon, and a man called "Nine

Fingers." More items for sale include the knives of Manuel Sanchez, Doc Holliday's revolver recently found in Clifton, Arizona, and a banjo containing a Winchester rifle inside it. Another arms dealer in attendance is named Washburn, who has a brother named John, and mentions a client in Africa called Killer. Accompanying Washburn is Monsieur Satanas of Paris, and the ensuing conversation mentions Professor Schultz's cannon. Mabuse are also mentioned.

Short story by Rick Lai in Tales of the Shadowmen Volume 1: The Modern Babylon, *Jean-Marc and Randy Lofficier, eds., Black Coat Press, 2005; reprinted in French in* Les Compagnons de l'Ombre (Tome 3), *Jean-Marc and Randy Lofficier, eds., Rivière Blanche, 2009. Arthur Gordon, Hermine Chalusse, and Wilkie Gordon are from Emile Gaboriau's* La Vie Infernale. *The implication of Gordon's marriage to Francine Xavier is that Robert E. Howard's adventurer Francis X. Gordon (aka "El Borak") is the grandson of Arthur Gordon. Ignacz Djanko (alias the Undertaker) is from Sergio Corbucci's 1966 film* Django *and the official 1987 sequel,* Django 2: Il Grande Ritorno, *aka* Django Strikes Again. *Major Jackson's followers wear red scarves in the film, but are never called the Red Scarf Gang. Lee Bailey is from the 1971 film* Hannie Caulder. *Count Corbucci is the archenemy of Raffles; his career as a dime novelist Stanley Corbett is an in-joke based on that fact that Italian director Sergio Corbucci was sometimes credited under that name in Italian Westerns. Josephine Balsamo, Leonard, and Théophraste Lupin are from Maurice Leblanc's* La Comtesse de Cagliostro *and* La Cagliostro se venge. *The portrayal of Count Cagliostro is consistent with Alexandre Dumas' novels of the French Revolution. The Mute Shootist is Silence from Sergio Corbucci's* The Great Silence. *Aguirre is Loco from the same film. The Red Circle is from Conan Doyle's "The Adventure of the Red Circle," while the Brotherhood of Seven Kings is from L. T. Meade and Robert Eustace's* The Brotherhood of Seven Kings. *Ballmeyer is Rouletabille's father from Gaston Leroux's* Le Mystère de la Chambre Jaune *and* Le Parfum de la Dame en Noir. *The Butcher of Baltimore is from the 1966 film* Chamber of Horrors, *while Professor Malaki is from the film* Dark Intruder. *Dr. Nikola is from Guy Boothby's* A Bid for Fortune. *The Marie Gilbert School is from the film* Madeline *(1998). The name for the Paris Girls' school is derived from the character Marie Gilbert (Lady Covington) who owns the school in this film. It was supposedly started by her grandmother.*

Since the movie is set in present day, it is unlikely that the school from the film is the same that Josephine Balsamo attended, but another member of the Gilbert family could have started a similar school. The school is never named in the children's books by Ludwig Bemelmans. The Fourneau College for Young Women is the school run by Madame Fourneau in the 1969 film La Residencia. Mademoiselle Tupin is the character Irene. Peterson is from Sergio Corbucci's Compañeros; *in this story, Yodlaf Peterson is Django's/Djanko's illegitimate son. The Bookkeeper is from the 1980 film* The Spearmen of Death. *The Flying Guillotine weapon is from the films* Flying Guillotine *(1974), and* Flying tine 2 *(1978). The blind assassin is from* Master of the Flying Guillotine *(1975). Kegan Van Roon is from Sax Rohmer's* The Return of Dr. Fu Manchu. *Golden Goblin Press is from Robert E. Howard's "The Black Stone." Hong Chen and Dr. Natas are from Guy d'Armen's novel* La Cite de l'Or et de la Lepre *(*City of Gold and Lepers*). Natas as an alias for the governor of Honan is an implication that Natas could be Fu Manchu, a connection first proposed in Jean-Marc and Randy Lofficier's English translation of d'Armen's novel. Huan Tsung Chao is from Sax Rohmer's* Shadow of Fu Manchu. *The story about the Shogun's assassination is from the 1978 film* Shogun's Samurai: The Yagyu Conspiracy. *Count Bielowsky and Queen Antinea are from Pierre Benoit's 1919 novel* L'Atlantide. *Surama is from H. P. Lovecraft and Adolph de Castro's "The Last Test." Oliver Haddo is from Somerset Maugham's* The Magician. *The Japanese woman in a white kimono is from the films* Lady Snowblood *(1973), and* Lady Snowblood 2: Love Song of Vengeance *(1974). The baby cart with muskets is from the Japanese comic series* The Lone Wolf and Cub, *created by Kazuo Koike. Sanchez is from the films* The Big Gundown *(1966) and* Run, Man, Run *(1968). General Santilla is also from* Run, Man, Run. *The banjo is from the 1970 film* Sabata; *in this story, Sabata becomes Zapata. The Rojos brothers are from the 1964 film* A Fistful of Dollars. *Clifton, Arizona is from the 1968 film* Day of Anger *(aka* Day of Wrath*). Gunsight Eyes is meant to be Colonel Mortimer combined with Sabata (both played by Lee Van Cleef) from 1965's* For a Few Dollars More. *John Washburn is from* Compañeros, *while the Washburn brother attending the auction is meant to be Curly from the 1968 film* A Professional Gun *(aka* The Mercenary*). The Washburn brothers are earlier versions of Curly and his twin brother from* City Slickers *and* City Slickers 2. *Actor Jack Palance played all four roles. The man in Africa named Killer is Harry Killer, from Jules and Michael Verne's* L'Étonnante Aventure de la mission Barsac. *Satanas is from the 1915 serial* Les Vampires. *The publisher Pickman and Sons is a tip of the hat to Nancy Collins' "Hell Come Sundown" (Collins refers to Pickman's Illustrated Dime Novels, a homage to Lovecraft's "Pickman's Model"). Professor Schultz is from Jules Verne's* Les Cinq cents millions de la Bégum. *Adam Saxon is from the 1972 film* The Grand Duel. *Nine Fingers is Clyde from the 1971 film* Return of Sabata. *"The Indian" is El Indio from* For a Few Dollars More. *The "Black Indian" is from the 1971 film* Adios, Sabata *(aka* Indio Black*). Dr. Mabuse is* *from the series of German films started by Fritz Lang, although Mabuse first appeared in fiction by Norbert Jacques.*

March. Josephine Balsamo has an affair with Malachi van Helsing. (Jean-Marc Lofficier's *Crépuscule Vaudou* aka *The Katrina Protocol*).

May 1900. A.J. Raffles is thought dead at Mafeking during the Boer War. ("The Knees of the Gods" in *The Black Mask* by E.W. Hornung and *The Return of Raffles* by Peter Tremayne). Harry "Bunny" Manders is wounded, returns home to England, and eventually marries ("The Last Word" in *A Thief in the Night* by E.W. Hornung and *The Return of Raffles* by Peter Tremayne).

March
INCIDENT IN THE BOER WAR

Raffles writes a letter to General Beltham confessing his crimes but also relating that the secret society Camorra is part of a larger evil which also encompasses the Red Hand, the Brotherhood of Seven Kings, and the Black Coats. Raffles' note also mentions Noel Moriarty (aka Julius Pavia), and Dr. Nikola. The Black Coats have set assassin Juan North on Raffles' trail for three years; North is an aficionado of the notorious play *The King in Yellow*. After delivering the letter, Raffles is shot in the back by Sergeant Gurn (aka Juan North, and from this point forward to be known as Fantômas).

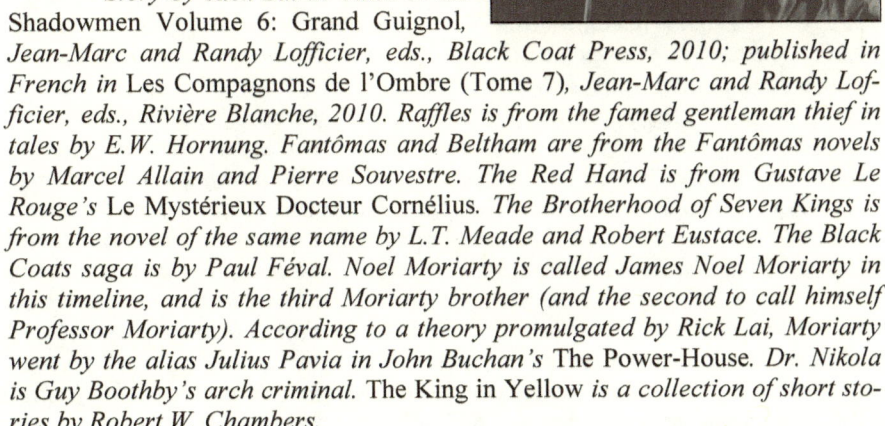

Story by Rick Lai in Tales of the Shadowmen Volume 6: Grand Guignol, *Jean-Marc and Randy Lofficier, eds., Black Coat Press, 2010; published in French in* Les Compagnons de l'Ombre (Tome 7), *Jean-Marc and Randy Lofficier, eds., Rivière Blanche, 2010. Raffles is from the famed gentleman thief in tales by E.W. Hornung. Fantômas and Beltham are from the Fantômas novels by Marcel Allain and Pierre Souvestre. The Red Hand is from Gustave Le Rouge's* Le Mystérieux Docteur Cornélius. *The Brotherhood of Seven Kings is from the novel of the same name by L.T. Meade and Robert Eustace. The Black Coats saga is by Paul Féval. Noel Moriarty is called James Noel Moriarty in this timeline, and is the third Moriarty brother (and the second to call himself Professor Moriarty). According to a theory promulgated by Rick Lai, Moriarty went by the alias Julius Pavia in John Buchan's* The Power-House. *Dr. Nikola is Guy Boothby's arch criminal.* The King in Yellow *is a collection of short stories by Robert W. Chambers.*

April. Zephyrin Xirdal causes a golden meteor to fall to the Earth (Jules Verne's *La Chasse au Météore*).

May 20. Birth of detective Albert Campion.

June. Birth of Philip Marlowe, son of Arronaxe Land and half-brother of Arronaxe Larsen, as established by Farmer in *Doc Savage*.

June. The Old Man in the Corner's first case, "The Fenchurch Street Mystery" by Baroness Orczy, *The Royal Magazine*, May 1901.

Summer
EL RETORNO DE WALPURGIS (CURSE OF THE DEVIL)

Waldemar Daninsky falls prey to a curse of lycanthropy placed on his family centuries ago, after his ancestor Irineus Daninsky wiped out a coven of witches, including, apparently Elisabeth Bathory. Daninsky's castle is near Borgo Pass.

Spanish feature film, 1973, directed by Carlos Aured, with story and screenplay by Jacinto Molina (aka Daninsky actor Paul Naschy). Borgo Pass is a real location and Elisabeth Bathory was a real person. Nevertheless, the Borgo Pass reference is clearly intended to evoke Bram Stoker's Dracula*. Although a real historical figure, there is a CU version of Bathory. Her death in this film is questionable, given her numerous appearances in vampire fiction, such as Peter Tremayne's novel* Dracula, My Love, *Harry Kümel's film* Les Lèvres Rouges *(*Daughters of Darkness*), and Donald F. Glut's film* Blood Scarab.

July 4-5
RAFFLES AND AN AMERICAN NIGHT'S ENTERTAINMENT

A.J. Raffles, Bunny Manders, Sherlock Holmes, Dr. Watson, and Mark Twain become involved in the theft of an emerald necklace.

Barry Perowne's short story appeared in Ellery Queen's Mystery Magazine, *March 1983. A.J. Raffles and Holmes had met in the early 1880s, and yet here it appears they meet for the first time. Additionally, A.J. Raffles was thought dead in action in the Boer War in May 1900. The Raffles seen here cannot really be A.J. Raffles. Jon L. Breen's pastiche-parody, "Ruffles versus Ruffles" (Ellery Queen's Mystery Magazine, June 1980), makes the case that the Raffles (or "Ruffles") seen in Perowne's pastiches of Hornung's original tales is actually A.J. Raffles' brother, R.J. Raffles. R.J. is assisted by Bunny Manders' cousin, Benny. Breen makes this claim in order to explain the subtle but sometimes significant differences between Hornung's version and Perowne's version. R.J. Raffles is more of a Robin Hood character, stealing with a greater purpose or goal in mind. A.J. is just in it for the swag. With that distinction in mind, I will occasionally note in these annotations where a case might actually belong to R.J. Raffles rather than A.J. Raffles. Brad Mengel's "The Incredible Raffles Clan" (available at* An Expansion of Philip José Farmer's Wold Newton Universe *website*) *also makes use of Breen's theory in expanding the Raffles family tree. Even if this is really a tale of R.J. Raffles, and even if Holmes had never met R.J., Holmes and R.J. must have known of each other, for Holmes was once briefly married to R.J.'s and A.J.'s sister Marjorie. Perowne wisely and discreetly leaves this fact out of his tale.*

July 1900. Holmes and Watson briefly meet magician and escape artist Harry Houdini, who evinces surprise that Holmes is alive, having thought him dead after the incident at Reichenbach (*The Pandora Plague*). Holmes dismisses Houdini's shock as a common occurrence among the public, as Watson's account of "*The Empty House*" has not yet been released.

August
THE MARK OF KANE (ANGELS OF MUSIC II)

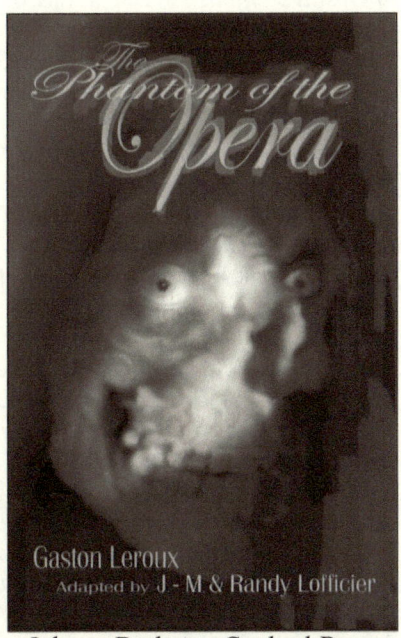

Erik's current Angels are sent on a mission at Royale-les-Eaux. Appearing or mentioned are: the Minister; Charles Foster Kane; Gilberte "Gigi" Lachaille (aka "Irma Vep"); the Persian; Elizabeth Eynsford Hill née Doolittle; Riolama (aka Rima); Théophraste Lupin; Favraux; Haghi; Percy Bennett; Madame Sara; Dunston Gryme; Simon Carne; Dr. Materialismus; Abijah K. Jones; Wanda Stielman; Ballmeyer; Baron Maupertuis; Dr. Jack Quartz; the wizard Whateley; Professor Fate; Sir Cuthbert Ware-Armitage; the Assassination Bureau, Ltd.; the Black Coats; Raymond Owen; Voltaire; Henry F. Potter; William Boltyn; Hattison; Gurn; General Guy Sternwood; Joseph Harrison Paine; Julian Karswell; Natasha Natasaevna di Murska; the Face; Emeric Belasco; Johnny Barlowe; Gaylord Ravenal; Colonel Sebastian Moran; Jimmy Valentine; Freddy Eynsford-Hill; and Bret Maverick. The former Angels are: Christine Daaé, Irene Adler; Trilby O'Ferrall; Loveday Brooke; Unorma; Grunya Constantine; Marahuna; Anna Franklyn; Hagar Stanley; Geneviève Dieudonné; Mother Gin Sling's in Shanghai; and Yuki Kashima.

Short story by Kim Newman in Tales of the Shadowmen Volume 4: Lords of Terror, *Jean-Marc and Randy Lofficier, eds., Black Coat Press, 2008; reprinted in French in* Les Compagnons de l'Ombre (Tome 3), *Jean-Marc and Randy Lofficier, eds., Rivière Blanche, 2009. Erik is Gaston Leroux's Opera*

Ghost. The Persian is also from Leroux's The Phantom of the Opera. *Royale-les-Eaux is the setting of Ian Fleming's James Bond novel* Casino Royale. *The Minister is based on the controller from* Mission: Impossible. *Charles Foster Kane is from the film* Citizen Kane. *Gilberte "Gigi" Lachaille (aka "Irma Vep") is from the film* Gigi. *Elizabeth Eynsford Hill née Doolittle and Freddy Eynsford-Hill are from George Bernard Shaw's* Pygmalion. *Riolama (aka Rima the Bird Girl) is from W. H. Hudson's novel* Green Mansions: A Romance of the Tropical Forest. *Théophraste Lupin is from the Arsène Lupin stories by Maurice Leblanc. Favraux is from the French serial film* Judex. *Haghi is from Fritz Lang's film* Spione. *Percy Bennett, also known as the Clutching Hand, is from the detective Craig Kennedy serial* The Exploits of Elaine. *Madame Sara is from Meade and Eustace's* The Sorceress of the Strand. *Sir Dunston Gryme appeared in Gustave Linbach's* The Azrael of Anarchy; *Simon Carne's tales were told by Guy Boothby. Dr. Materialismus is the title character of a story by Frederic J. Stimson. Abijah K. Jones is from George Lippard's* The Quaker City; or The Monks of Monk Hall: A Romance of Philadelphia Life, Mystery and Crime. *Wanda Stielman is a German agent from Jean de La Hire's Nyctalope tales. Ballmeyer is the father of Gaston Leroux's Rouletabille. Baron Maupertuis is from Doyle's Sherlock Holmes tale "The Reigate Puzzle." Dr. Jack Quartz is one of the arch-enemies of Nick Carter. The wizard Whateley is from H. P. Lovecraft's "The Dunwich Horror." Professor Fate is from the Blake Edwards film* The Great Race. *Sir Cuthbert Ware-Armitage is from the film* Monte Carlo or Bust! The Assassination Bureau, Ltd. *is a novel started by Jack London and completed by Robert L. Fish. The Black Coats are a criminal organization from novels by Paul Féval. Raymond Owen is from the 1914 serial* The Perils of Pauline. *Voltaire is Dr. Loveless' henchman from the television series* The Wild Wild West. *Henry F. Potter is from Frank Capra's film* It's a Wonderful Life. *William Boltyn is from Gustave Le Rouge's* La Conspiration des Milliardaires. *Ned Hattison is from Le Rouge's* L'Amerique des dollars et du crime. *Gurn is otherwise known as the notorious Fantômas. General Guy Sternwood is from Raymond Chandler's Philip Marlowe novel* The Big Sleep. *Joseph Harrison Paine is from the film* Mr. Smith Goes to Washington. *Julian Karswell is from M.R. James' "Casting the Runes." Natasha Natasaevna di Murska is from* The Angel of the Revolution *by George Chetwynd Griffith Jones. The Face is the nemesis of Adam Adamant from the British television series* Adam Adamant Lives! *Emeric Belasco is from the film* The Legend of Hell House, *based on Richard Matheson's novel* Hell House. *Johnny Barlowe is from the play* The Man Who Broke the Bank at Monte Carlo *by Ilya Surguchev and Frederick Albert Swan. Gaylord Ravenal is from Edna Ferber's novel* Show Boat *and the musical play of the same name. Colonel Sebastian Moran is Professor Moriarty's second-in-command in Doyle's Sherlock Holmes tales. Jimmy Valentine is from O. Henry's (William Sydney Porter) "A Retrieved Reformation." Bret Maverick is from the television series* Maverick. *Christine Daaé is from Leroux's* Phantom of the Opera. *Irene Adler is from the Holmes tale "A Scandal in Bohemia." Trilby O'Ferrall is from George Du Maurier's* Trilby. *Loveday Brooke is from* Loveday Brooke, Lady Detective *by Catherine Louisa Pirkis. Unorma is from F. Marion Crawford's* The Witch of Prague: A Fantastic Tale. *Grunya Constantine is from* The Assassination Bureau, Ltd. *Marahuna is from H. B. Marriott-Watson's* Marahuna: A Romance. *Anna Franklyn is from the Hammer film* The Reptile. *Hagar Stanley is from Fergusson Wright Hume's* Hagar of the Pawn-Shop, The Gypsy Detective. *Geneviève Dieudonné is a vampiress in Kim Newman's tales across several alternate universes. Mother Gin Sling's in Shanghai is from the 1942 film* The Shanghai Gesture. *Yuki Kashima is also known as Lady Snowblood from the Japanese film* Shurayukihime.

September-October
SHERLOCK HOLMES AND THE COPYCAT MURDERS

Sherlock Holmes, Dr. Watson, and Mycroft Holmes foil Graf von Bork's plot against Great Britain. Along the way, they receive help from a French Deuxième Bureau agent posing under the name "Aristide Nemo." Nemo is really Hercule Poirot. Budding Scottish writer John Buchan also lends a hand. Apparent death of the eldest Moriarty brother, Colonel James Moriarty.

Novel by Barry Day, Second Opinion, Inc., 2000. Poirot is not named, but references to his side career as a consulting detective and the "little grey cells" are enough to positively identify him. Buchan served as the biographer of a prominent Wold Newton Family member, Richard Hannay. It has been speculated elsewhere (my "Who's Going to Take Over the World When I'm Gone?" Myths for the Modern Age: Philip José Farmer's Wold Newton Universe*), that Col. James Clayton Moriarty immigrated to America late in life and started an American branch of Moriartys. If this is the case, then Col. Moriarty must have somehow faked his death in* The Copycat Murders.

Autumn
THE PROBLEM OF THE MISSING WEREWOLF

It is said that, "Everyone has heard of the Camorra and the Si-Fan…"

A Harry Challenge story by Ron Goulart in the November 2007 issue of H.P. Lovecraft's Magazine of Horror.

1901

January
THE SECOND WAR OF THE WORLDS
In this sequel to Wells' *The War of the Worlds*, Holmes and Watson help fight against a second Martian invasion on the planet Annwn, Earth's counterpart in a parallel universe. It is revealed that the invasion of Earth two years ago did indeed originate from a different universe, that in which Annwn is located. This time, the Martian invaders stick to their own dimension. The Circle of Life cult, led by the second Professor Moriarty, collaborates with the Martians in this second invasion, based on the cult members' belief that the Martian invaders are completely superior and should be the natural rulers of humanity.

This novel by George H. Smith was published by DAW Books in 1976. The Island Snatchers, Smith's follow-up Annwn novel sans Holmes, Watson, or Martians, was published by DAW in 1978. Annwn resides in the same parallel universe in which Barsoom is located and would be known as "Jasoom" to Barsoomian natives (see The League of Extraordinary Gentlemen II *and "Mars: The Home Front," which covered John Carter's role in helping to defeat the Martian invaders, the "Sarmaks of Barsoom"). The second Professor Moriarty is the brother of the first Napoleon of Crime; his full name is James Noel Moriarty.*

Winter. Following the Sarmaks' betrayal of the Circle of Life collaborators on *Annwn*, and the Circle's decimation under the heat-rays of the invaders, any mention of extraterrestrial life, Martian or otherwise, becomes an embarrassment for the second Professor Moriarty. Although he ran the Circle of Life from a distance, and was planning on using the Circle cult members and the events of the Second Invasion with an eye toward eventually ruling Annwn himself, Moriarty now realizes that he needs to distance himself from those events. He taps the remaining infrastructure of the Circle of Life organization on Earth, renames the group "Krafthaus," and assigns Krafthaus members what seems a daunting task: the complete eradication of any substantial evidence of the existence of extraterrestrials. Moriarty's goal is that within fifty years, no one on Earth will believe in alien life or that the War of the Worlds really happened. (However, even Moriarty could not have predicted the 1947 Roswell Incident and the resurgent interest in extraterrestrials.)

Over the next several decades, and even beyond the second Professor Moriarty's death, his organization, now known as THRUSH, mounts a massive disinformation campaign, reducing the events of the Martian Invasion to mere mythology. Overall, the second Professor Moriarty's plan is successful, and by the latter half of the 20th century, most people regard the events of *The War of the Worlds* as mere fiction. Of course, throughout Earth's history there have been countless extraterrestrial contacts, such as the Eridaneans and the Capelleans, an orphaned infant from the planet Krypton, and visitations as described in the annals of the Cthulhu Mythos, *Star Trek,* and *The X-Files.* However, all records and knowledge of those contacts remain secret, unsubstantiated, or lost in the mists of ancient times.

In the late 20th century, those who consider themselves to be rational and scientific, such as Dr. Dana Scully, refuse to believe, without substantial scientific proof, that alien life-forms have visited Earth. Thanks to the second Professor Moriarty's efforts, as well as the post-1947 machinations of the Consortium (see *The X-Files*), which is an offshoot of THRUSH, such proof no longer exists. Those who do continue to believe in extraterrestrials, such as Fox Mulder, are regarded as kooks and spooks.

Winter
LES EXPÉRIENCES ÉROTIQUES DE FRANKENSTEIN (LA MALDICIÓN DE FRANKENSTEIN)

Dr. Matius Artur Frankenstein succeeds in giving his Creature a brain, only to be murdered (along with his assistant, Morpho) immediately thereafter by a minion of Count Cagliostro, who takes control of the Creature. Frankenstein's daughter, Dr. Vera Frankenstein, arrives for her father's funeral and is befriended by Dr. Seward.

Feature film (France, Spain, and Portugal) directed by Jesus Franco, 1972; alternate titles are The Erotic Rites of Frankenstein *and* The Curse of Frankenstein. *The Cagliostro-Frankenstein crossover places these events in the Crossover Universe. Although the same actors played Dr. Frankenstein (played by Dennis Price) and Dr. Seward (played by Alberto Dablés) in Franco's* Drácula Contra Frankenstein *(aka* Dracula, Prisoner of Frankenstein*), they are not the same characters, and the two films occur in different time frames. It is not clear whether or not the Dr. Seward seen here is the same one who participated in the 1887 events of Bram Stoker's novel* Dracula. *If not, then he is a close relative. The film states that Count Cagliostro is reincarnated from time to time over the centuries. If so, then the Cagliostro seen in* Les Expériences Érotiques de Frankenstein *could be the same person as Count Cagliostro II from the film* El Vampiro Sangriento, *reincarnated from the* *original Count Cagliostro, although* El Vampiro Sangriento *states that Cagliostro II is the grandson of the original.*

March-April. Sherlock Holmes in New York, as told by Watson, D.R. Bensen, ed., in which the first Professor Moriarty attempts to strike at Holmes through abducting his nine-year-old son (Scott Adler, aka Marko Vukcic). The events surrounding Holmes' relationship with Irene Adler in Montenegro in 1891 are also mentioned. Curiously, there is no mention of Scott's twin brother, John Hamish Adler, the man who would later be known as Nero Wolfe. There is also no mention of Scott Adler's older half-sister, Irene Adler's daughter, Nina Vassilievna; or of Scott and John Hamish Adler's younger brother, Damian Adler.

April. In Africa, Allan Quatermain and Mina Murray search for the lost kingdom of Ayesha and the "Fire of Life." Regrettably, when they find the kingdom of Kôr, the Fire of Life has no rejuvenating effects. Moving on to Zu-Vendis, Quatermain dies. However, shortly before his death they expediently discover his long-lost son, Allan Quatermain, Jr. Leaving Zu-Vendis, Mina Murray takes up with Quatermain Jr., and they continue to travel Africa together before returning home to England. (As told by Alan Moore and Kevin O'Neill in "The New Traveller's Almanac, Chapter Four: Africa and The Middle East" in *The League of Extraordinary Gentlemen II*.)

May. Clark Savage, Sr., the illegitimate son of William Cecil Clayton, the sixth duke of Greystoke, is implicated in the kidnapping of his younger half-brother, the legitimate son of the sixth duke, as described by Watson and Doyle in the Sherlock Holmes story "The Adventure of the Priory School." After these events, Savage and his wife Arronaxe Larsen flee England; a guilt-ridden Savage vows to dedicate his life and that of his unborn child to fighting evil.

May. Birth of Irma Peterson, daughter of Dr. Caber and Madame Olivier. Thus, she is the niece of Carl Peterson. (Farmer, in *Doc Savage*, has proposed that Irma really was the daughter of the archvillain Carl Peterson. However, Rick Lai makes a convincing argument for an alternate genealogy. (See Lai's "A Brief Biography of Dr. Caber [1883-1945?]" and "Partners in Crime: Fu Manchu and Carl Peterson," both on *The Wold Newton Universe* website.) If Lai is correct, then Carl Peterson still committed incest by marrying his niece, thus making the Carl Peterson, Jr. who appears in the 1960s Bulldog Drummond films both the son and great-nephew of the original Carl Peterson.

Spring 1901-January 1902
FANTÔMAS

The madman known as Fantômas begins his Parisian reign of terror. A magistrate states: "In every age, there have been bands of dangerous creatures, led by men such as Vidocq, Cartouche and Rocambole."

Serial novel by Marcel Allain and Pierre Souvestre. As Rick Lai notes, Vidocq and Cartouche are historical characters, but Rocambole is not, thus linking Fantômas and Rocambole together in the CU.

Summer
THE GOLD BAT
Two students on the public school Wrykyn boxing team are named Moriarty and Drummond.
A novel by P.G. Wodehouse. Rick Lai writes: "First, let's establish The Gold Bat as part of the CU. Wodehouse's Jeeves stories are part of the CU. The first story in Carry on Jeeves is about Bertie Wooster's uncle writing his scandalous memoirs. The memoirs mentioned Lord Emsworth of Blandings Castle, the setting

of a different series of novels by Wodehouse. In Leave It to Psmith (pronounced "Smith"), Blandings Castle was visited by R. Psmith, who was the protagonist of his own series of novels, Mike (sometimes published in two volumes, Mike at Wrykyn and Mike and Psmith), Psmith in the City and Psmith, Journalist. Psmith's best friend, Mike Jackson, went to Wrykyn. The title character of Sam the Sudden also went to Wrykyn. Sam was once employed by Lord Tilbury (also known as George 'Stinker' Pyke), the owner of the Mammoth Publishing Company. His Lordship visited Blandings Castle in Heavy Weather. As you can see, all roads lead to Blandings Castle in the Wodehouse Universe." Lai goes on to theorize that "Moriarty" in this case is James Caber, the grandson of Professor Moriarty (as established by Philip José Farmer). Drummond is in fact Hugh "Bulldog" Drummond, who became the enemy of Caber's brother, Carl Peterson. Lai concludes his literary archaeological expedition into creative mythography with the following unearthed letter, which explains why Caber never assisted Carl Peterson against his greatest enemy:

Dear Stinker,
Since I don't know whether you are using the alias of Claude Darrell or Carl Peterson these days, I am referring to you by the charming nickname that I bestowed upon you when we were boys. Your request for a poison to be used against Hugh Drummond is hereby denied. Old Bulldog and I were teammates on the Wrykyn boxing team together, and I make it a rule never to be an accomplice in the murder of an old school chum.
Your brilliant brother, Jim

P. S. Give my love to my daughter. I understand she calls herself Irma these days as a sort of tribute to the defunct Vep female. I still feel that you are both too overly affectionate for an uncle and a niece.

Summer. Birth of Simon Templar: The Saint.

Summer. First recorded adventure of French private detective Eugene Villiod. (*Memoirs of Villiod* pulp series.)

August
RICHARD RIDDLE, BOY DETECTIVE, IN "THE CASE OF THE FRENCH SPY"

Young Dick Riddle fancies himself a detective. Together with his friend Violet and her cousin Ernest, they discover a fish-man of Dagon being held captive and rescue it. There are references to Captain Nemo and R'lyeh.

A short story by Kim Newman in the anthology Adventure, Vol. 1, *Chris Roberson, editor, MonkeyBrain Books, 2005; reprinted in Newman's collection* The Secret Files of the Diogenes Club, *MonkeyBrain Books, 2007. Young Dick Riddle met Charles Beauregard of the Diogenes Club a few years previous. Nemo is from Verne's* 20,000 Leagues under the Sea, *while Dagon and R'lyeh are from the works of H.P. Lovecraft.*

Autumn
SHERLOCK HOLMES AND THE POIROT CONNEXION

Holmes and Watson encounter a man posing as the chef of M. Calamy, a French diplomat. It is strongly implied that the undercover chef is none other than Hercule Poirot.

A short story narrated by Dr. Watson, found among the papers of Poirot's friend, Captain Arthur Hastings. The story was edited for publication by Julian Symons in The Illustrated London News, *April 1987. It appeared in* Ellery Queen's Mystery Magazine, *December 1987, under the title "Did Sherlock Holmes Meet Hercule-?".*

November 12. Clark "Doc" Savage, Jr., is born on the schooner *Orion* in a cove off the northern tip of Andros Island, Bahamas. Doc's parents are Clark Savage, Sr. and Arronaxe Larsen. Doc's maternal grandparents are the notorious

Wolf Larsen (*The Sea Wolf*) and Arronaxe Land, who is the daughter of Ned Land (*20,000 Leagues under the Sea*). As part of his training to combat crime and evil, Clark, over the years, will study various disciplines with Sherlock Holmes, Arsène Lupin, Richard Wentworth, Dr. John Thorndyke, Craig Kennedy, Kent Allard, Harry Houdini, and Tarzan (per Farmer's *Doc Savage*).

December 24
THE ADVENTURE OF THE THREE GHOSTS
Sherlock Holmes assists Timothy Cratchit, Lord Chislehurst, in discovering the source of ghostly nighttime visitations.
A short story by Loren D. Estleman, which is sequel to Charles Dickens' A Christmas Carol, *in* Holmes for the Holidays, *Greenberg, Lellenberg, & Waugh, eds., Berkley Books, 1996. There are two other Holmes/Christmas Carol sequels: "The Adventure of the Christmas Ghosts," by Bill Crider, in* Holmes for the Holidays, *and "The Case of the Rajah's Emerald," by Carolyn Wheat, in* More Holmes for the Holidays. *Each could be a valid crossover and sequel to Dickens' tale, but for the fact that each reveals a different fate for "Tiny Tim" Cratchit. "The Adventure of the Three Ghosts" was my favorite.*

1902

Winter. Birth of Simone Desroches, the future Belphégor.
Winter. Birth of Lawrence Stewart Talbot, the Wolf Man.

Winter
THE TRAVELS OF LAO CAN
Wandering physician Dr. Lao Can moves about the Chinese countryside solving crimes and righting wrongs with the help of a group of "knights errant." The narrator of the novel refers to him as "the Chinese Sherlock Holmes."
From Liu E.'s The Travels of Lao Can *(1903-04).*

Spring
THE THINGS THAT SHALL COME UPON THEM
Holmes meets occult detective Flaxman Low for the first time, on a case involving the estate of the late Julian Karswell, who was previously responsible for the death of John Harrington and a murder attempt against Edward Dunning. Other detectives of the era mentioned are Max Carrados and Inspector Beedel, Dyer's Detective Agency, Martin Hewitt, Paul Beck, Eugene Valmont, Miss Myrl, and a blind man who solves crimes while sitting at the A.B.C. teashop.
Story by Barbara Hambly in Gaslight Grimoire, *J.R. Campbell and Charles Prepolec, eds., Edge Science Fiction and Fantasy Publishing, 2008. Karswell, Harrington, and Dunning are from M.R. James' "Casting the Runes" (1911). Max Carrados and Inspector Beedel's cases were told by Ernest Bra-*

mah. Dyer's Detective Agency is from The Experiences of Loveday Brooke, Lady Detective *(1894) by Catherine Louisa Pirkis. Martin Hewitt's cases were chronicled by Arthur Morrison. M. McDonnell Bodkin wrote about Paul Beck, as well as Dora Myrl, the Lady Detective. Robert Barr documented Eugene Valmont's cases. The blind man at the A.B.C. teashop is Baroness Orczy's The Old Man in the Corner.*

Summer. Birth of Richard Henry Benson, great-nephew of Phileas Fogg (*Around the World in Eighty Days*; *The Other Log of Phileas Fogg*). Benson will become known as The Avenger and found Justice, Inc., in the late 1930s.

Summer 1902-1903. The main events of *Ayesha: The Return of She*, as told by Ludwig Horace Holly (edited by H. Rider Haggard), in which Leo Vincey is reunited with Ayesha.

July
SHERLOCK HOLMES ARRIVES TOO LATE
Sherlock Holmes' first encounter with the elusive master criminal Arsène Lupin.

A short story by Maurice Leblanc in the volume Arsène Lupin, Gentleman-Cambrioleur. *The story has been retranslated by* Jean-Marc and Randy Lofficier *and is presented in* Arsène Lupin vs. Sherlock Holmes: The Hollow Needle, Black Coat Press, 2004. *Lupin is also a Wold Newton Family member. Due to copyright issues, Leblanc was unable to secure permission to write about Holmes. Consequently, the story was published under the title* "Holmlock Shears Arrives Too Late." *I have taken the liberty of restoring to the Great Detective his proper name. Jess Nevins adds an interesting footnote to the Holmes-Lupin rivalry:* "In 1925, the Chinese master thief who calls himself 'Lu Ping' begins a correspondence with Arsène Lupin. Lupin is encouraging to the Shanghai-based Lu Ping, who is successful immediately and becomes known as the 'Oriental Arsène Lupin.' (Sun Liaohong's Lu Ping stories, beginning in 1925.) In a coincidental repetition of the Lupin-Sherlock Holmes duels of two decades before, Lu Ping repeatedly jousts with Huo Sang, 'the Oriental Sherlock Holmes,' who has (like Lu Ping) corresponded with his Western counterpart and received encouragement and advice from him. (Cheng Xiaoqing's Huo Sang stories, beginning with 'Dengguang renying,' 1914)."

August
SHERLOCK HOLMES AND THE CLOWN PRINCE OF LONDON
Holmes enlists Arsène Lupin to perform a bit of thievery for a just cause.
Comic story by Joe Gentile and Rich Gulick, Moonstone Comics, 2001.

THE GRANTCHESTER GRIMOIRE

Sherlock Holmes and Dr. John Watson team with occult detective Thomas Carnacki.

Story by Chico Kidd and Rick Kennett in Gaslight Grimoire, J.R. Campbell and Charles Prepolec, eds., Edge Science Fiction and Fantasy Publishing, 2008. The tale purports to recount the first meeting of Holmes and Carnacki, but in fact that occurred several years prior.

Late September-October
THE PANDORA PLAGUE
Sherlock Holmes and Harry Houdini are involved in the evil machinations of a hideously sinister plot. Dr. Thorndyke makes a cameo appearance, as does Monsieur Dubuque of the Paris police.

This account was written by Dr. Watson and edited by Lee A. Matthias, Leisure Books, 1981. R. Austin Freeman wrote the accounts of Thorndyke's cases. Dubuque and Holmes also met during the cases of "The Second Stain" and "The Boulevard Assassin."

Autumn. A young man named Harry Wilson saves Old Broadbrim's life. Old Broadbrim adopts Wilson as his partner, and Wilson becomes Young Broadbrim. (*Young Broadbrim Weekly* #52, September 26, 1903.)

Autumn. Rouletabille's first case, *Le Mystère de la Chambre Jaune* (*The Mystery of the Yellow Room*) by Gaston Leroux, translated as *Rouletabille and the Mystery of the Yellow Room* by Jean-Marc and Randy Lofficier, Black Coat Press, October 2009.

Autumn
DEATH DID NOT BECOME HIM
Holmes and Watson investigate a case involving reanimation of the dead. The Mad Arab al-Hazred is mentioned, as is a mad scientist named Dr. Caresco.

A short story by David Niall Wilson and Patricia Lee Macomber in the Lovecraftian anthology Shadows Over Baker Street. Dr. Caresco is from Le Mal Nécessaire *(*The Necessary Evil*)* and Caresco Surhomme by André Couvreur.

December 24, 1902-Early 1903

NIGHT WATCH
Sherlock Holmes investigates a murder at a secret ecumenical conference in London. A young Father Brown also becomes involved in the case. It is also stated that Father Brown went on to visit Holmes many times thereafter.
Novel by Stephen Kendrick, from a manuscript by John H. Watson, Pantheon Books, 2001. This book gives Father Brown's first name as "Paul" whereas in his 1967 appearance in The Rainbow Affair, *he is named "John." Perhaps his full name is John Paul Brown.*

1903

Winter. The second Professor Moriarty (James Noel Moriarty) quietly establishes a new identity for himself, that of Andrew Lumley, a respected philanthropist (see Buchan's *The Power-House*).

Winter 1903-1913. David Innes and Abner Perry make the trip to Pellucidar and the rest of the events of E.R. Burroughs' *At the Earth's Core* follow. The remaining authorized books in Burroughs' Pellucidar series are: *Pellucidar, Tanar of Pellucidar, Tarzan at the Earth's Core, Back to the Stone Age, Land of Terror, Savage Pellucidar,* and *Mahars of Pellucidar* (the latter by John Eric Holmes).

Winter. Lord Palmure, Rocambole's grandson, fights the Indian Thuggees led by Kacya, son of Feringhea. (*Le Testament de Rocambole/Olivia Contre Rocambole*, novels by Frédéric Valade, Tallandier, 1931.) Kacya, son of Feringhea, appeared in Eugène Sue's *Le Juif Errant* (serial, 1844-1845; the action is situated in 1832). Feringhea the Thuggee is an historical figure, but the character depicted by Sue is quite different, and can be considered the Crossover Universe version of Feringhea.

Spring
THE ADVENTURE OF THE LADY ON THE EMBANKMENT
Holmes meets ancestors of characters from the 30th century Vorkosigan series.

A short story by Lois McMaster Bujold relating to her Vorkosigan series, in the volume Dreamweaver's Dilemma. *This makes the Vorkosigan series one possible alternate future of the CU.*

Spring. Ted Strong's first recorded adventure. ("Ted Strong's Rough Riders; or, The Boys of Black Mountain," *Rough Rider Weekly* #1, April 23, 1904.)
Spring. Events of *The Bobbsey Twins; or, Merry Days Indoors and Out* by Laura Lee Hope.
Summer. Events of Jules and Michael Verne's *L'Étonnante Aventure de la mission Barsac* (*The Barsac Misson*).

July
SÉANCE FOR A VAMPIRE
Holmes and Watson again work with Vlad Dracula. Inspector Merrivale and Rasputin also appear. Vlad ruminates upon Rasputin, "But I believe I smiled, because the Russian word *rasputin* carries strong connotations of sexual debauchery; rather as if an Englishman or American were to introduce himself as Gregory Porno, or Ephraim Smut."
Novel by Fred Saberhagen, Tor Books, 1994. This is not the "real" Count Dracula, whom Holmes and Watson encountered in 1887 (see Watson and Estleman's The Adventure of the Sanguinary Count). *For a full explanation of Vlad and his relationship to the true Count, see Dennis E. Power's "Best Fangs Forward" on The Wold Newton Universe: A Secret History website. Inspector Merrivale was later known as Sir Henry Merrivale, whose cases were chronicled by Carter Dickson (aka John Dickson Carr). Rasputin, as revealed in* Rasputin's Revenge, *is the son of the first Professor James Moriarty. From Vlad's ruminations, on page 288, we know that Ephraim Tutt is a real person in the CU, that Vlad has encountered or heard of him, and that Vlad, here, is playing upon his name. Writer Arthur Train featured lawyer Ephraim Tutt in more than eighty short stories, most of them published in the* Saturday Evening Post *between 1919 and 1945.*

Autumn. Adam Adamant, an adventurer, expert swordsman, and sometime agent of the Diogenes Club, disappears without a trace.
Autumn. Sir Arthur Conan Doyle meets Harry Houdini for the first time, and together they investigate the debauched occultist Maximillian Cairo. (*What Rough Beast*, a novel by Sir Arthur Conan Doyle, edited by H.R. Knight, Leisure Books, February 2005.)

Autumn
THE ADVENTURE OF THE MOCKING HUNTSMAN

Holmes and Watson's investigation carries them to the towns of Norborough and Mithering, the sites of some adventures of John Steed and Emma Peel in the mid 1960s.

A short story by Watson, edited by Matthew J. Elliott, in Sherlock #55. Norborough is from The Avengers television episode "A Funny Thing Happened on the Way to the Station," while Mithering is from the episode "Dead Man's Treasure."

Late November
THE SINGULAR CASE OF THE ANEMIC HEIR
Count Dracula attempts to exact revenge upon Sherlock Holmes, but Holmes outwits him, at least for the time being.

Comic story by Will Richardson, Kevin Duane, and Anton Caravana, in The Rook #10, Warren Publishing, August 1981.

December 1903-October 1904
THE BLONDE PHANTOM
Sherlock Holmes once again works in opposition to Arsène Lupin. Holmes does not become involved, and the two do not actually meet, until a final series of episodes in October 1904.

A series of interconnected tales by Maurice Leblanc: Arsène Lupin Versus Herlock Sholmes. *Once again, the detective has been restored to his proper name. The story has been retranslated by* Jean-Marc and Randy Lofficier *and is presented in* Arsène Lupin vs. Sherlock Holmes: The Blonde Phantom, Black Coat Press, 2005. *Another episode in this volume, "The Jewish Lamp," chronicles a later Lupin/Holmes encounter in 1908.* Arsène Lupin Versus Herlock Sholmes *was filmed as a five-part German serial,* Arsène Lupin Contra Sherlock Holmes, *in 1910.*

1904

January 1904-June 1905
ARSÈNE LUPIN ARRIVES TOO LATE
Jeanne Darcieux writes a series of letters to "Paul Daubreuil," an alias for Arsène Lupin. The young Lady Strongborough/Jeanne Darcieux is accused of

her husband's murder. Her lawyer is Sir Edward Leithen, the prosecutor is Mr. Erskine-Brown, and the judge is Mr. Justice Wargrave. The warders where Jeanne is imprisoned are called George Bulman, Derek Willis, and Kavanagh. The prison Governor is Lt. Col. Venables, the prison chaplain is Reverend Fergusson, the prison's Under Sheriff is named Regan, and the Head Turnkey is Mr. Daley. A Constable Barnaby also appears. Lupin cannot come to save Jeanne, but calls upon Sherlock Holmes, who solves the mystery and prevents Jeanne's execution. The real murderer is Ballmeyer, Rouletabille's father. A Belgian policeman named Poirot is mentioned.

Short story by Jean-Marc and Randy Lofficier in Arsène Lupin vs. Sherlock Holmes: The Blonde Phantom, *Black Coat Press, 2005; reprinted in French in* Les Compagnons de l'Ombre (Tome 1), *Jean-Marc and Randy Lofficier, eds., Rivière Blanche, 2008; in the Lofficiers' translation of Gaston Leroux'* Rouletabiulle and the Mystery of the Yellow Room, *Black Coat Press, October 2009; and in the Lofficiers' collection* Pacifica, *Black Coat Press, 2010. The main events of the story take place after "Sherlock Holmes Arrives Too Late" and "The Blonde Phantom," but before "The Jewish Lamp." Holmes' involvement in the case occurs in March and April, 1905. This story provides a firm link placing Rouletabille in the CU. Lady Strongborough is mentioned as having been helped by Lupin at the end of "The Jewish Lamp." Jeanne Darcieux is the stepdaughter of Paul Darcieux, Baron Maupertuis, from Doyle's Sherlock Holmes tale "The Reigate Puzzle." Additionally, the Leblanc short story in which Jeanne appears ("La Mort qui Rôde" in* Les Confidences d'Arsène Lupin*) says that she lives at Castle Maupertuis, so it is easy to connect the two Maupertuis families. Wargrave is from Agatha Christie's play* Ten Little Indians, *adapted in prose as* And Then There Were None. *The Belgian policeman is Agatha Christie's Hercule Poirot. Leithen is from John Buchan's* The Power-House. *Mr. Erskine-Brown is doubtless an ancestor of Claude Erskine-Brown from the British television series* Rumpole of the Bailey. *George Bulman is an ancestor of George Bulman, a policeman and private detective who appeared in the British film* The XYZ Man, *and then went on to appear in two television series,* The Strangers *and* Bulman. *Likewise, the warder Derek Willis must be an ancestor of the Derek Willis who appeared in* The Strangers. *Kavanagh is an ancestor to James Kavanagh from the British program* Kavanagh QC. *Venables is an ancestor of the Governor Venables seen in the British sitcom* Porridge. *Regan is an ancestor of Inspector Regan, the hero of the British television series* The Sweeney. *Daley is an ancestor of Arthur Daley from the British television series* The Minder. *Constable Barnaby is the ancestor of Detective Chief Inspector Tom Barnaby from the books and television series* Midsomer Murders. *All of these British television programs are added to the CU by this crossover. Finally, Reverend Fergusson is an ancestor of Reverend Clare Fergusson from Julia Spencer-Fleming's mystery novels.*

Winter. Robur the Conqueror returns in Jules Verne's *Master of the World*.

Winter. The first recorded case of Danish policeman Asbjørn Krag. ("Mordet i D...Gade 63" by Sven Elvestad.)

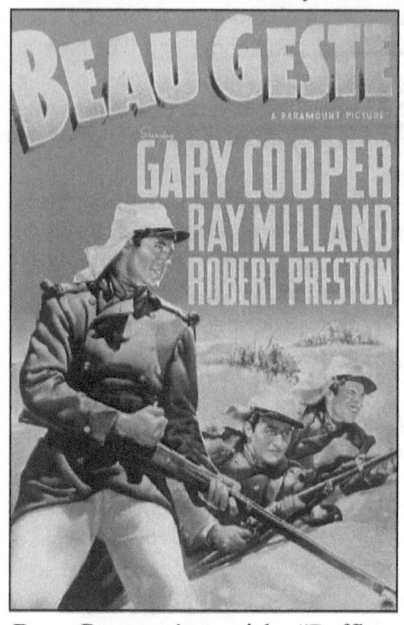

Spring. Main events of *Beau Geste*, as told by Percival Christopher Wren, taking place in the CU via a reference in Farmer's *Doc Savage: His Apocalyptic Life*.

Spring
GENOPTRYKT SOM EN DANSK SHERLOCK HOLMES
Detective Axel Johnson is now described as a "Danish Sherlock Holmes."
Story by C. Andersen, 1905.

Early June. A.J. Raffles returns to England after being thought dead four years ago in the Boer War. After a botched return to amateur cracksmanship, Raffles and Manders are recruited by the British Secret Service (*The Return of Raffles* by Peter Tremayne). Interestingly, Barry Perowne's pastiche "Raffles and the Box 4 Drama" (*Ellery Queen's Mystery Magazine*, January 1981) also makes Raffles and Manders BSS members, but not until the Great War in early 1915. This difference between the Tremayne and Perowne pastiches reinforces Jon L. Breen's theory that the Perowne stories were really describing A.J.'s brother R.J. and his adventures with Manders' cousin Benny. (See Breen's "Raffles vs. Ruffles," *Ellery Queen's Mystery Magazine*, June 1980.)

June 15
ULYSSES
Wold Newton Family member Leopold Bloom encounters artist Stephen Dedalus.
Novel by James Joyce.

Summer. Birth of Yitzik Baline (aka Rick Blaine) in New York City.

Summer. The main events of the film *The Legend of the 7 Golden Vampires*.

Summer
SEXTON BLAKE'S FIRST CASE

Blake, recollecting his first case, quotes his "great master, the Prince of Detectives," followed by a statement made by Monsieur Lecoq.

From Union Jack *#69, February 4, 1905. The Monsieur Lecoq quote comes from Emile Gaboriau's* Le Dossier No. 113 *which takes place in 1866. Jess Nevins notes, "Chronologically this is possible; two stories published in 1896 put Blake's birthdate in 1859, although a story in 1904 says that Blake is around thirty years old, thus moving his birth date ahead by at least a decade. (The latter date would jibe with "Sexton Blake at School," set in 1886.) I'm not going to try to reconcile these, but either way, Lecoq is alive into the 1890s (per his mention in the first Simon Carne story) and so could function as Blake's tutor in detection."*

Summer. Miss Mina Murray visits a master detective-turned-bee-keeper in Fulworth, Sussex, as related by Alan Moore and Kevin O'Neill in "The New Traveller's Almanac, Chapter One: The British Isles" in *The League of Extraordinary Gentlemen II*.

1905

January
THE JADE BUDDHA

Arsène Lupin, traveling the world in the guise of the Duke of Charmerace, is in Saigon where he meets Major de Beaujolais and they observe the enigmatic Hanoi Shan as he's assisted by one of his Dacoits. Afterwards, they decide to look up an old Legionnaire, Thibaut Corday, who regals then with Shan's history and tales of a Jade Buddha which Shan has acquired. De Beaujolais recites a tale of three brothers, a stolen jewel, and an African outpost named Fort Zinderneuf. Nikola is mentioned, as well as the Si-Fan and the Shin Tan. Lupin resolves to steal the Jade Buddha but instead ends up rescuing a prisoner of Hanoi Shan, a policeman named Denis Nayland Smith.

Short story by David L. Vineyard in Tales of the Shadowmen Volume 5: The Vampires of Paris, *Jean-Marc and Randy Lofficier, eds., Black Coat Press, 2009; reprinted in French in* Les Compagnons de l'Ombre (Tome 5), *Jean-Marc and Randy Lofficier, eds., Rivière Blanche, 2009. Lupin is the gentleman thief from the classic tales by Maurice Leblanc. Major Henri de Beaujolais is from P.C. Wren's* Beau Geste. *The story of the jewel, three brothers, and Fort Zinderneuf plaes this tale after the* Beau Geste *events. Hanoi Shan is from H. Ashton-Wolfe's* Warped in the Making: Crimes of Love and Hate. *The story follows Philip José Farmer's theory, proposed in his biography* Doc Savage, *that Hanoi Shan was Dr. Fu Manchu. Denis Nayland Smith and the Si-Fan are from Sax Rohmer's tales of Fu Manchu. Thibaut Corday is the protagonist of five tales by Theodore Roscoe which appeared in* Argosy *in the 1930s. Nikola is Guy Boothby's Dr. Nikola. The Shin Tan are from In Henri Vernes' Bob Morane sto-*

ries, Monsieur Ming, aka the "Yellow Shadow," an Asian megalomaniac bent on world domination, is the leader of the Shin Tan (Old Asia) cult.

February
A STOLEN LEGACY (aka SHERLOCK HOLMES)
　　Sherlock Holmes fights Dr. Mors, who is called "a proper Professor Moriarty."
　　Play by Ferdinand Bonn, 1906. Bonn's play was adapted as the German silent film Sherlock Holmes Contra Dr. Mors *(1914), in which Bonn was also part of the film's cast. Dr. Mors battled the mystic Jens Rolf in 1922.*

March-August
DOCTOR OMEGA (LE DOCTEUR OMEGA-AVENTURES FANTASTIQUES DE TROIS FRANÇAIS DANS LA PLANETE MARS)
　　Doctor Omega and his comrades travel to the Mars of several million years ago. After many adventures, they return to Earth's present, bringing with them a native Martian called Tiziraou. The Duke of Charmerace is mentioned, as well as the mad Doctor Caresco.
　　A novel by Arnould Galopin, adapted and retold by Jean-Marc and Randy Lofficier, Black Coat Press, September 2003. The "Duke of Charmerace" is Arsène Lupin. While this alone would be enough to place the events of Doctor Omega *in the CU, Doctor Omega is also referenced in* The League of Extraordinary Gentlemen, Volume II, *and in that same series Tiziraou is seen with Les Hommes Mystérieux in 1913. Dr. Caresco is a mad scientist from 1899's* Le Mal Nécessaire *(*The Necessary Evil*), written by André Couvreur. This reference places him in the CU. Of significance, the Lofficiers note that "...the Greek letter Omega is also used as a symbol of Ohm, a unit of electrical resistance... And we all know what we get when OHM is turned upside down..."*
　　Greg Gick adds, "More than likely, the Doctor Who of the Crossover Universe calls himself Doctor Omega. This actually has more connections than the Lofficier's retelling would suggest. The First of the Time Lords was a being named Omega, whom the Doctor told he admired. When the townspeople called him Doctor Omega, he took it as an honorific upon the first true Time Lord. We can assume, then, that Doctor Omega's career parallels Doctor Who's in his

own universe (the Doctor Who Universe), possibly even with the same companions every so often, while other companions (such as the ones in the Doctor Omega *novel) are completely unique.*

March 6-10
ANNUS MIRABILIS

Doctor Omega reads Albert Einstein's scientific review discussing Professor Welligham's panergon, and sensing something horribly wrong, goes to meet Einstein in person, leaving his assistant Borel in charge. They discuss Professor Mirzabeau's "violent flame," Henry R. Cortlandt's paper on apergy, and the *vril*. Based on their discussions, the Doctor deduces that Earth is under attack. He makes contact with the Xipéhuz, a race of multi-dimensional beings who are trying to establish a foothold on Earth, and convinces them to remain in their own dimensions, whereupon the normal laws of physics seem to reassert themselves.

Short story by Chris Roberson in Tales of the Shadowmen Volume 2: Gentlemen of the Night, *Jean-Marc and Randy Lofficier, eds., Black Coat Press, 2006; reprinted in French in* Les Compagnons de l'Ombre (Tome 2), *Jean-Marc and Randy Lofficier, eds., Rivière Blanche, 2008. Doctor Omega (and his assistant Borel) is from the novel by Arnould Galopin, adapted and retold by Jean-Marc and Randy Lofficier. "Annus Mirabilis" takes place between chapters two and three of* Doctor Omega. *Professor Welligham and the miraculous energy source panergon are from "Skelton Kuppord"'s (pseudonym of British author Sir John Adams)* A Fortune from the Sky *(1902). Professor Mirzabeau's violent flame is from Fred T. Jane's* The Violent Flame: A Story of Armageddon and After *(1899). Henry R. Cortlandt is from John Jacob Astor's* A Journey in Other Worlds: A Romance of the Future *(1894). Percy Greg created apergy, an anti-gravitational energy, in his novel* Across the Zodiac *(1880). The* vril *energy is from Edward Bulwer-Lytton's* The Coming Race. *The Xipéhuz are from J-H. Rosny Aîné's "Les Xipéhuz" (1887). There are other isolated instances in the history of the CU of events which violate the normal laws of physics, both in the years leading up to 1905, and after. It is my theory that although the 1905 Xipéhuz invasion was the ultimate source of these incidents, the events themselves manifest throughout the years book-ending 1905, with 1905 as the crescendo. This accounts for pre- and post-1905 manifestations of the* vril, *and further otherwise unexplainable events.*

Spring. Mark Sampson and Jack Darrow's first adventure, in which they travel *Through the Air to the North Pole; or, The Wonderful Cruise of the Electric Monarch*, as told by "Roy Rockwood" (pseudonym for Howard R. Garis).

Spring
SEXTON BLAKE IN AFRICA

Sexton Blake meets Matthew Quin, "Wild Beast Agent."

Story by William Murray Graydon in Union Jack #112, *December 2, 1905. Mark Hodder, webmaster of Blakiana: The Sexton Blake Resource, notes that "This marks the first appearance in the Blake saga of [Graydon's character] Matthew Quin, 'Wild Beast Agent.' Outside of the Blake canon, the character dates back as far as May 1898. There's also an 1894 Graydon tale that, while not naming the principal character, has all the attributes of a Quin story. In the novel* Jungles and Traitors *(Good News, 1895; S&S ed. 1902; Shaw ed. UK 1905), Quin doesn't appear but his frequent assistant Carruthers does, as well as his archenemy the Portuguese animal trapper Antonio Silva. There is also in this novel a panther-boy similar to the one in the Blake tale 'The Jungle Boy' (*Union Jack #85, 1905*), although this one controls only one panther, and is a feral child as opposed to a teenager who took to the jungle." Hodder, in turn acknowledges Dr. Georges T. Dodds for the information.*

THE MILKMAN COMETH

Rouletabille is in Russia, while Sherlock Holmes, in disguise and on the run in Boiberik, Ukraine, is rescued and taken in by Tevye and Golda Milkhiker. Also appearing or mentioned are: the King of Bohemia, Ivan Dragomiloff, Lieutenant Konstantin Vassily Illyavitch Couriakine, Charlemagne Solon, Waverly, General Mikhail Strogoff, Israel Di Murska, Leonid Zattan, Konrad von Siegfried, Nat Pinkerton, Fandorin, Reb Mendel and Yentl, Motl Komsoyl, Menakhem-Mendl, Kasrilevke, Yehupetz, Moisei Moiseyevich, Boris Badenov, Sylvia Di Murska (aka Natasha), General Trepoff, Stanislaus Wojciehowicz, and Andrei Sipowicz.

Short story by Stuart Shiffman in Tales of the Shadowmen Volume 5: The Vampires of Paris, *Jean-Marc and Randy Lofficier, eds., Black Coat Press, 2009; reprinted in French in* Les Compagnons de l'Ombre (Tome 5), *Jean-Marc and Randy Lofficier, eds., Rivière Blanche, 2009. Rouletabille is the intrepid reporter from the works of Gaston Leroux. Tevye and Golda Milkhiker are from the musical* Fiddler on the Roof, *from Sholem Aleichem's book* Tevye's Daughters *and play* Tevye der Milkhiker. *Motl Komsoyl, Menakhem-Mendl, and the locales of Kasrilevke, Boiberik, and Yehupetz are also from the works of Sholem Aleichem. The King of Bohemia and General Trepoff are from Doyle and Watson's Holmes tale "A Scandal in Bohemia." Ivan Dragomiloff is from Jack London's* The Assassination Bureau, Ltd. *Lieutenant Konstantin Vassily Illyavitch Couriakine and Charlemagne Solon are early versions of Illya Kuryakin and Napoleon Solo from* The Man From U.N.C.L.E. *Waverly is possible the father of U.N.C.L.E.'s Alexander Waverly. General Mikhail Strogoff is from Jules Verne's* Michael Strogoff: The Courier of the Czar. *Israel Di Murska and Sylvia Di Murska are from George Chetwynd Griffith's* The Angel of the Revolution. *Leonid Zattan is the nemesis of the heroic Nyctalope. Konrad von Siegfried must be an ancestor of the spy from the series* Get Smart. *Nat Pinkerton is a dime novel her, the "King of Detectives." Erast Petrovich Fandorin is Boris*

Akunin's detective, "the Russian Sherlock Holmes." Reb Mendel and Yentl are from the film musical Yentl, *adapted from Isaac Bashevis Singer's "Yentl the Yeshiva Boy." Moisei Moiseyevich is from Anton Chekhov's* The Steppe. *Boris Badenov and Natasha are from Jay Ward's classic cartoon* The Adventures of Rocky and Bullwinkle. *Stanislaus Wojciehowicz is an ancestor of Detective Stan Sipowicz from the television comedy* Barney Miller, *while Andrei Sipowicz is an ancestor of Andy Sipowicz from the television cop show* NYPD Blue.

June. Holmes takes a case for Franklin D. and Eleanor Roosevelt. *("Our American Cousins," a short story by Roberta Rogow in* The Game is Afoot, *Marvin Kaye, editor, 1995. Holmes once worked with the Roosevelts' relative, Theodore Roosevelt, in 1880. Young Indiana Jones met Theodore Roosevelt in 1909.)*

Summer
THE LABOUR EXCHANGE MYSTERY
Sexton Blake, pursuing a thief in Paris, meets up with "the Prefect of Police, an elderly, stern-visaged man." The Prefect is stern but fair with criminals, having had some experience with the criminal system from the other side. The prefect's name is Monsieur Jean Valjean. Nobody remarks on Valjean having the same name as the protagonist of *Les Miserables*.

Story by William Murray Graydon in Union Jack *#346, May 28, 1910. Pedro and Tinker are both in the story, which means it has to happen no earlier than 1905, the year of Pedro's debut. Valjean is probably the son or grandson of Jean Valjean from Victor Hugo's classic* Les Miserables.

THE SIAMESE TWIN OF A BOMB-THROWER
Eugene Valmont says, "In my own time I often hearkened to narratives regarding the performances of Lecocq with a doubting shrug of the shoulders."

Story by Robert Barr in The Triumphs of Eugene Valmont. *"Lecocq" is clearly meant to be Gaboriau's Lecoq.*

Autumn. Gordon Keith sets up shop as a consulting detective at Baker Street in London. (*Brave and Bold* #163, February 10, 1906.)

Autumn. A wave of child abductions plagues Paris; it is eventually discovered that Dr. Flax, the noted German surgeon who is heading the commission to solve the kidnappings, is actually behind the abductions. (Louis Forest's "On Vole Les Enfants à Paris" ["Someone is Stealing the Children of Paris"], *Le Matin,* 1906.)

Autumn. Events of *The People of the Pole* by Charles Derennes.

1906

Winter
R. HOLMES & CO.
   In this collection of short stories following the exploits of Raffles Holmes, it is revealed that Sherlock Holmes had a son with the sister of notorious thief A.J. Raffles.
   Stories by John Kendrick Bangs, Otto Penzler Books, 1906. The original Raffles stories by E.W. Hornung can be found in The Collected Raffles Stories, Oxford University Press, 1996. Apparently Holmes got around a bit for a man who professed to dislike the company of women. This story claims that Raffles Holmes' mother was A.J.'s daughter, but the chronologies of the various characters make it more likely that she was in fact A.J.'s sister.

DEN RØDE LYGTE
   In Norway, Sherlock Holmes and Dr. Watson work with Asbjørn Krag and Thomas Ryer on a case.
   Story by Bjarne Nielsen, 1991, linking Asbjørn Krag into the Crossover Universe.

Spring. The first recorded case of the vigilante group The Four Just Men, as revealed by Edgar Wallace (although, with the death of one of the members in 1902, there are now only Three Just Men).
   Spring. Britt Reid, son of Dan Reid, Jr., and great-nephew of The Lone Ranger, is born. He will become the first Green Hornet. (The familial relationship between the Ranger and the Hornet is not literary archaeological speculation. It was established in a 1947 radio episode of *The Green Hornet.* George W.

Trendle of WXYZ developed both shows and Fran Striker wrote for both *The Lone Ranger* and *The Green Hornet*.)

Spring
SHERLOCK HOLMES IN OZ
Holmes and Watson are transported to Oz by magic in order to solve a mystery there.
Story found in the collection The Game is Afoot, *Marvin Kaye, editor, 1995. In this short story by Ruth Berman, it is clearly stated that Oz is an alternate universe to the reality from which Holmes has come and that he may stay as long as he likes, because he can be returned to his reality (the Crossover Universe) at exactly the same time that he left. The date is conjecture, but must take place after Doyle's Holmes adventure, "The Blue Carbuncle," in 1887. Oz chronologists place this tale in a parallel Oz universe separate from the mainstream Oz timeline.*

THE MURDERS OF PROFESSOR FLAX
Sherlock Holmes fights against the evil Dr. Flax.
Story in Detektiv Sherlock Holmes *#26, 1907, bringing the notorious German archcriminal into the CU.*

Summer. First adventure of Ferrers Lord, the "Mad Millionaire," in *Wolves of the Deep* (*Boys' Friend Library* #32, 1907) by Edgar J. Murray (who wrote under the pseudonym of Sydney Drew). Lord was a wealthy inventor of two submarines, the Victoria and the Britannia.
Summer. Birth of Michael Traile, "The Man Who Never Sleeps."

Summer
MANOLESCU
Nat Pinkerton tangles with Manolescu, the "Prince of Thieves." It is revealed that Manolescu is John Kling's father.
From Neue Kriminal-Bibliothek *#46, 1907. Since Pinkerton and Kling are in the CU, so is Manolescu.*

Autumn. Fu Manchu (aka Hanoi Shan) sets up criminal operations in Paris, as related in two short stories, "The Suicide Room" and "The Scented Death," found in H. Ashton-Wolfe's *Warped in the Making: Crimes of Love and Hate*.
Autumn. Events of the film *Horror Express*.

October
THE EARTHQUAKE MACHINE
Sherlock Holmes, Mycroft Holmes, Dr. Watson, Professor Moriarty, Colonel Moran, Winston Churchill, Czar Nicholas, and Rasputin are all featured in

this novel. Nina Vassilievna, the daughter of Irene Adler and the King of Bohemia, is introduced. Holmes fakes his permanent retirement to Sussex. Deaths of Colonel Sebastian Moran and the first Professor James Moriarty.

Written by Austin Mitchelson and Nicholas Utechin, Belmont Tower Books, 1976. Nina Vassilievna is the half-sister of Nero Wolfe and Marko Vukcic. Rasputin, as revealed in Rasputin's Revenge, *is the son of the first Professor Moriarty. When in Sussex, Holmes works on scientific research designed to protect humanity in the event of another Martian Invasion (see* The Case of the Missing Martian). *The death of Moran must be exaggerated, as he appears again in Martin Powell's "Sherlock Holmes in the Lost World" (taking place in 1915) and is mentioned as finally meeting his end in 1935 in Kim Newman's "The Man Who Got Off the Ghost Train."*

Autumn
SHERLOCK HOLMES VS. FANTÔMAS

Fantômas comes to London, leading to his first clash with the Great Detective, Sherlock Holmes. Holmes is assisted by a young aspiring detective, Harry Dickson. Fantômas' lieutenant, Vachard, is a member of the Black Coats. Holmes' niece Emily is the daughter of Holmes' brother Sherrinford. One of Fantômas' underlings calls him a "new John Devil."

A play adapted by Frank J. Morlock, Black Coat Press, 2009. The original stage play was The Murder of Herlock Sholmes, or, Bandits in Black Coats *by Pierre de Wattyne and Yorril Walter (1914). The Black Coats are from the series of novels by Paul Féval. Féval's* John Devil *is about another master criminal and takes place in the same continuity as the Black Coats saga.*

1907

February 19. Birth of science-fiction writer Kilgore Trout. Some biographical details of Trout's life have been furnished by Kurt Vonnegut, Jr., in *God Bless You, Mr. Rosewater, Slaughterhouse-Five, Breakfast of Champions,* and others. According to Farmer's *Doc Savage,* Trout is the grandson of Johnny Shawnessy (*Raintree County*) and is also a distant descendant of both Natty

Bumppo (*The Leatherstocking Tales*) and Ebenezer Cooke (*The Sot Weed Factor*).

Winter
SHERLOCK HOLMES II (AKA RAFFLES FLUGT FRA FAENGSLET)
Raffles escapes from prison, set on revenge against Sherlock Holmes. In the end, Holmes triumphs and Raffles is captured again.
Danish silent film, 1908.

April
THE GRAND HORIZONTALS
Sherlock Holmes and Fantômas joust, though they never meet face-to-face, in a case involving the murder of the Duke of Graustark.
Play by Frank J. Morlock, collected in Sherlock Holmes: The Grand Horizontals, *Black Coat Press, January 2006. The story indicates that Holmes and Fantômas did previously meet in person; this would have been in* Sherlock Holmes vs. Fantômas. *This crossover confirms the Graustark novels of George Barr McCutcheon in the CU.*

Spring. Solar Pons opens his private inquiry practice at 7B Praed Street in London. (Solar Pons stories by August Derleth.)

Spring. First known case of French policeman Martin Numa. (Martin Numa, the King of Detectives series by Leon Sazie.)

Spring. Bingham Harvard, also known as "The Night Wind," is framed by a corrupt New York police inspector. (*Alias "The Night Wind"* by Varick Vanardy [pseudonym for Frederick Van Rensselaer Dey], originally published in 1913, reprinted by Wildside Press, 2007.)

Spring
PROFESSOR FLAX, DER MASSENMORDER
Sherlock Holmes battles the murderous Professor Flax again.
Story in #84 of Aus Dem Geheimakten.

HOLMES AND RAFFLES
Holmes and Raffles joust once more.
Melodrama by Gonzalo Jóver and Emilio González. The second part of "Holmes and Raffles" is "The Claw of Holmes," presented June 15, 1908 at the Theater Martín in Madrid.

Summer. French surgeon Dr. Cordat makes contact with Spiridon, a giant intelligent ant. (*Spiridon the Mute* by Andre Laurie.)

Summer. Dr. John Silence's first recorded case, "A Psychical Invasion," by Algernon Blackwood.

Summer
CHERITERA KECHURIAN LIMA MILLION RINGGIT (TALE OF THE THEFT OF FIVE MILLION DOLLARS)
"John C. Sinclair" versus Nick Carter and "Mr. Baxter."
1922 novel by Muhammad bin Muhammad Said. "John C. Sinclair" was the name under which the thief Lord Lister was known in France. John Sinclair's Scotland Yard antagonist is Inspector Baxter. Lord Lister and Nick Carter fought again in Lord Lister Contro Nick Carter, *volumes 1 (1934-1935), 2 (1938-1939), and 3 (1945-1946).*

August
AND THE OTHERS...
The entire print run of the September 1907 issue of *Hogbine's Illustrated Monthly* is destroyed in the Great Hurricane of 1907. The now-defunct magazine ran a monthly feature entitled "As They Knew Him," and the September issue was to have featured comments upon Sherlock Holmes by various acquaintances, such as Inspector Giles Lestrade. In July 1952, the Continental Enquiry and Protective Services Agency, Ltd. (the British branch of the Continental Detective Agency in the U.S.), buys the Hogbine Building and discovers, in a boarded-up closet, the complete galley proof for the September 1907 issue.
A short piece by C.D. Ewing, in My Sherlock Holmes, *Michael Kurland, ed., St. Martin's Press, 2003. Dashiell Hammett's nameless detective, the Continental Op, works for the Continental Detective Agency, thus linking the Continental Op into the CU.*

Autumn. Dr. John Thorndyke's first documented case, *The Red Thumb Mark*, as told by R. Austin Freeman.

Autumn. The events of *Le Docteur Lerne, Sous-Dieu (Doctor Lerne, Subgod)* by Maurice Renard, translated and adapted into English by Brian Stableford as *Doctor Lerne* (Black Coat Press, February 2010).

Autumn
DOCTOR WATSON AND THE INVISIBLE MAN

With Holmes out of London, Watson takes a case on his own, assisting friend Langdale Pike to avoid a murder charge. They investigate the true circumstances of how the Invisible Man (John Hawley Griffin) achieved his feat of invisibility, and their inquiry takes them down the path of the occult. In the course of their search, they meet Arthur Machen and Aleister Crowley, and at one point turn to Mycroft Holmes for assistance. Sherlock Holmes appears at the conclusion of the case, and it is revealed that while he does own property in Sussex, he has not yet been able to bring himself to completely retire from his rooms in Baker Street.

Novel by Noel Downing, Ian Henry Publications, 1991. Griffin does not appear in this adventure and the question is never raised that he might still be alive. Supernatural writer Arthur Machen (1863-1947) also appeared in Kim Newman's "Seven Stars Episode One: The Mummy's Heart."

1908

January
BARANABAS, QUENTIN, AND DR. JEKYLL'S SON

Henry Jekyll, Jr. meets Barnabas Collins in London, and travels with Barnabas to Collinsport to seek a cure for vampirism. At the conclusion of these events, it appears that Henry Jr. will marry Emily and become the local doctor in Collinsport.

Dark Shadows *novel #27 by Marilyn Ross (pseudonym for Dan Ross), Paperback Library, 1971. According to this novel, the Jekyll/Hyde affair was thoroughly covered in American newspapers. Hyde is described as a short man, consistent with Stevenson's novel. The major inconsistency with Stevenson is with Henry Jr. Henry Sr. was a bachelor in Stevenson's novel. Most likely, Henry Jr. was illegitimate, but was ashamed to admit this fact to Emily.*

Winter
MISS BOSTON, LA SEULE DETECTIVE-FEMME DU MONDE ENTIER
In Miss Ethel Boston's first adventure, she solves the murder of "Sherlock Holmes."

Miss Boston, la seule détective-femme du monde entier #1-20, 1908-1909. Jess Nevins explains this crossover: "It obviously can't be Holmes, though the story says it is. But in the Italian reprint of the Miss Boston stories, the first story is rewritten and changed, and 'Nick Carter' becomes the murder victim. Again, it can't be Nick Carter, so I began looking for a Nick Carter-wannabe. However, the cover of the Italian reprint was lifted from a John Siloch story, with a panel about the murder of the 'celebrated detective' in peril beneath a picture of Siloch himself. So, clearly the murder victim wasn't Nick Carter—that was a little fudging by Miss Boston's biographer. The murder victim was the 'celebrated detective' shown on the cover of the story: John Siloch. So, since Siloch is in the Crossover Universe via Holmes, so is Miss Boston."

LA CAPTURA DE RAFFLES, O EL TRIUNFO DE HOLMES
Sherlock Holmes succeeds in capturing Raffles.

Melodrama written by Luis Millà and G.X. Roura, held at the Teatro Moderno (Barcelona-Gracia) on November 20, 1908. The second part of the capture of Raffles, "Nadie más fuerte que Sherlock Holmes" was held on February 27, 1909.

Spring. A French newspaper reporter describes (in exaggerated terms) a European-Asian conflict. (*The Infernal War* series by Pierre Giffard and Albert Robida.)

Spring. First recorded exploit of French mad scientist Professor Tornada. (*The Invasion of Macrobes* by André Couvreur.)

Spring. The first recorded adventure of *Captain Mors der Luftpirat, The Ruler of the Ocean of the Air*. Mors links to several other characters, including Alaska Jim, Frank Allan (a world-traveling German adventurer and vigilante), and Jörn Farrow. Frank Allan, in turn, once worked with Inspector Doodle of Scotland Yard.

Spring. Jeff Clayton's first recorded case, as he chases after "Jesse James." (*Adventure Series* #42, 1909. Written by "William Ward.") Jess Nevins notes, "Given that Jesse James' death was well documented and occurred in 1882, the 'Jesse James' which Jeff Clayton, among many others (including the Merriwells and Nick Carter), chased can only have been an imitator, an individual suffering from FIS, Famous Individual Syndrome."

April. Events of Marcel Allain & Pierre Souvestre's *The Daughter of Fantômas*, translated and adapted by Mark P. Steele, Black Coat Press, August 2006.

May
THE CASE OF THE MISSING MARTIAN
The final episode of the Holmes/Martian invasion trilogy. Professor Challenger and Mycroft Holmes are featured and Sigmund Freud is mentioned as an acquaintance of Holmes. Death of the second Professor Moriarty?
A Sherlock Holmes comic book miniseries by Doug Murray and Topper Helmers, published by Eternity Comics, 1990. The three episodes chronicling Holmes' battles against the Martians establish that Wells' The War of the Worlds *is part of the Crossover Universe. Of course, Holmes supposedly met Freud in Nicholas Meyer's popular novel,* The Seven Per-Cent Solution. *However, that novel was based on a false manuscript, probably a hoax perpetrated by the second Professor Moriarty. The second Professor Moriarty's motive for stealing the last remaining Martian war machine from the British Museum appears to be merely the accumulation of power. However, his true motive, not revealed in the story, was his continuing fanatical crusade to obliterate of all evidence pertaining to extraterrestrial life, a crusade he began after* The Second War of the Worlds.

May. Young Indy meets Lawrence of Arabia. ("Young Indiana Jones and the Curse of the Jackal," episode of *The Young Indiana Jones Chronicles.* Duncan MacLeod met Lawrence of Arabia in 1916.)

May 28. Ernst Stavro Blofeld, son of "Wolf Larsen"/"Karl von Hessel," is born in Gdynia. (See my "Who's Going to Take Over the World When I'm Gone?" *Myths for the Modern Age: Philip José Farmer's Wold Newton Universe.*)

June
THE JEWISH LAMP
Arsène Lupin and Sherlock Holmes clash once more.

A tale by Maurice Leblanc in *Arsène* Lupin Versus Herlock Sholmes, *retranslated and presented in* Arsène Lupin vs. Sherlock Holmes: The Blonde Phantom, *Jean-Marc and Randy Lofficier, Black Coat Press, 2005.*

Summer. Publication of Campion Bond's *Memoirs of an English Intelligenser*.

Summer. Birth of teen-detective Frank Hardy.

Summer. Joseph Petrosino begins fighting the Black Hand and the Mafia in Italy. (*Giuseppe Petrosino, Il Sherlock Holmes D'italia* #1, July 1909.) Joe Petrosino was a New York City cop who moved to Italy to fight the Mafia. He also fought against the notorious Dr. Flax.

Summer. Mr. Psyche, purveyor of ghosts and spectres, opens his business in London. ("Psyche's Treasure Quest: A Romance of Hidden Treasure," a short story by Henry A. Hering, *Cassell's Magazine*, July 1909.)

Summer. Professor Challenger and Lord John Roxton's expedition to The Lost World, as related by Edward Malone (edited by Arthur Conan Doyle). Malachi van Helsing accompanies Challenger and Roxton on the expedition, as told in Jean-Marc Lofficier's *Crépuscule Vaudou* aka *The Katrina Protocol*. Canonical stories in the Professor Challenger series are: *The Poison Belt*, *The Land of Mist*, "The Disintegration Machine," and "When the World Screamed." Professor Challenger's adventures continued in *Professor Challenger in Space* (edited by S.W. Theaker), Nicholas Nye's *Return to the Lost World*, and several other crossovers listed on this chronology.

Summer. Fu Manchu rewards Holmes' prior service with the almost-complete formula for an immortality elixir. The missing ingredient is a particular honey, made by bees from the nectar of an unidentified flower. ("The Adventure of the Celestial Snows," edited by George Alec Effinger, from a manuscript by Reginald Musgrave, in *My Sherlock Holmes*, Michael Kurland, ed., St. Martin's Press, 2003.) Given that Holmes had already begun to dabble in beekeeping, he may have suspected the true nature of the formula, but not had the other ingredients. Holmes would perfect his Royal Jelly bee pollen life-extension elixir in 1921 (see *"The Adventure of the Notorious Canary Trainer"*).

Summer
THE ADVENTURE OF THE NOTORIOUS CANARY TRAINER
Holmes refers to his colleague Dr. John Thorndyke and mentions that they worked together the previous year on the Red Thumb Mark case.
Short story in The Lost Adventures of Sherlock Holmes, *adapted by Ken Greenwald from the Sherlock Holmes radio scripts of Anthony Boucher and Dennis Green, Mallard Press, 1989. This case is not to be confused with a case of similar name,* The Canary Trainer, *which took place in 1891.*

July-December
THE UNKINDEST CUT
Holmes pursues Lupin through London while Lupin tries to defeat a plot of the nefarious Dr. Flax (the untold "Case of the Silver Knight"). Lupin is staying at Bertram's Hotel in London. At a Christmas Ball, Watson penetrates Lupin's disguise; Lupin is attendance with Irene Adler. Watson never discovers whether Holmes knows of Irene's association with Lupin.
Short story by Dr. Watson, edited by Jean-Marc and Randy Lofficier in Arsène Lupin vs. Sherlock Holmes: The Blonde Phantom, *Black Coat Press, 2005; reprinted in French in* Les Compagnons de l'Ombre (Tome 1), *Jean-Marc and Randy Lofficier, eds., Rivière Blanche, 2008; and in the Lofficiers' collection* Pacifica, *Black Coat Press, 2010. If Holmes did know of Irene's association with Lupin, it could account for Holmes' later antipathy toward Lupin as seen in* The Hollow Needle; *although always very competitive, the intense dislike was not in evidence in their prior encounters. Bertram's Hotel is from the Miss Marple novel by Agatha Christie,* At Bertram's Hotel. *Dr. Flax is from the Harry Dickson series.*

September. Young Indiana Jones meets Pablo Picasso. ("Paris, September 1908," episode of *The Young Indiana Jones Chronicles.* Tarzan met Picasso in 1909.)

Autumn
MAN OF MEDICINE, DOCTOR OF DESPAIR
Holmes again crosses swords with the notorious Arsène Lupin, in the course of their conflict as described in "The Unkindest Cut."
A short comic story by Joe Gentile in the volume of Sherlock Holmes stories called Soul of the Dragon, *Northstar Press, 1995.*

AZEFF THE ANARCHIST
Sexton Blake battles Evno Azef (aka Eugene Azeff), an anti-czarist anarchist/terrorist, and a band of English anarchists.
Story in Union Jack *volume 11, #286, April 3, 1909.*

HOLMES AND RAFFLES DECEIVED
Holmes and Raffles meet once more.
Melodrama by Miguel Sierra published in 1916.

DER LUFTPIRAT VON OGLIVIE (THE SKY-PIRATE OF OGLIVIE)
Alaska Jim, in the Oglivie Mountains of Canada's Yukon, encounters Der Luftpirat, Captain Mors.
Story in Alaska Jim *#5 by Willi Richard Sachse, published in 1935. This brings Alaska Jim and Sturmvogel into the Crossover Universe. Jess Nevins notes, "I can't positively state that the Luftpirat in question was Captain Mors—but given how popular Captain Mors was when it was published, and given the general consciousness of other authors' works that the German heftoman ("he-ro-novel") authors showed, I can't believe it was anything but a deliberate crossover. That begs the question of dating, however, since Captain Mors' stories pretty much have to start in 1908. Luckily, though, the Alaska Jim stories, though certainly starting in the American Old West, are in a generic Western environment which is also very rural, so that the Oglivie Mountains of the 1870s, when most of Alaska Jim's adventures take place, are really not much different from the Oglivie Mountains of 1908. So, I think it's really set in 1908 and really about Captain Mors."*

November. Indiana Jones meets Sigmund Freud. ("Vienna, November 1908," episode of *The Young Indiana Jones Chronicles.* Sherlock Holmes met Freud in this year also.)

1909

January. Gaston Max, an investigator with uncanny abilities at disguise and mimicry, battles an unseen drug kingpin known as Mr. King, and solves his first case in *The Yellow Claw,* as told by Sax Rohmer. In Rohmer's *Yu'an Hee See Laughs,* Yu'an Hee See is an Asian master criminal who controls a huge drug-smuggling empire under the alias of Mr. King. Rick Lai observes that "Gaston Max's adversary supposedly drowned in the Thames, but his body was never found. Either the two Mr. Kings are the same person, or Yu'an Hee See has borrowed the alias of the earlier mastermind."

January
A DANCE OF NIGHT AND DEATH
Fantômas stops Irma Vep, who has just joined the Vampires gang, from burgling Lady Beltham's Parisian residence. Arsène Lupin is mentioned, and Satanas, the Great Vampire, appears.

Short story by Travis Hiltz in Tales of the Shadowmen Volume 3: Danse Macabre, *Jean-Marc and Randy Lofficier, eds., Black Coat Press, 2007 reprinted in French in Les Compagnons de l'Ombre (Tome 2), Jean-Marc and Randy Lofficier, eds., Rivière Blanche, 2008. Irma Vep, the Vampires gang, and Satanas are from the French serial* Les Vampires. *Fantômas and Lady Beltham are from the pulp series by Pierre Souvestre and Marcel Allain. Arsène Lupin's stories were told by Maurice Leblanc. Rick Lai notes, "The story is set in 1909 before the events of* The Vampires. *At the conclusion of 'A Dance of Night and Death,' Irma Vep reports to the Great Vampire who is identified as Satanas. The physical appearance of this character is not given. In* The Vampires, *Irma's first boss is known solely as the Great Vampire. He gets killed by a crook named Moreno, who becomes Irma's lover. Suddenly a character appears who claims that he is the true Great Vampire. This character identifies himself as Satanas. It is revealed that the late Great Vampire was merely a subordinate of Satanas. Moreno and Irma are forced to accept the domination of Satanas." Jean-Marc Lofficier responds, "It is easy to assume that Irma knew of Satanas' existence and secret overlordship of the Vampires all along (unlike Moreno) and was just lying to Moreno. The so-called Great Vampire (number two to Satanas) knew too, but since Moreno killed him, no one else but Irma knew of Satanas' existence. So the Satanas in Hitlz's story would be the 'real' Satanas. Irma does not recognize Satanas when he first appears in the film, but she might be play-acting for the benefit of other. Or Satanas is a master of disguise, as Rick Lai hinted, and looks different every time he appears."*

Winter
DEATH IN OUTER SPACE
Captain Mors is described thusly: "And just as Verne's mysterious Captain Nemo once ruled the seas, Captain Mors now rules the air with his mysterious air ship."

#102 of Captain Mors der Luftpirat.

TIP WALTER, LE PRINCE DES DETECTIVES
Tip Walter opens his consulting detective practice in Paris. He is described as "the equal of Nick Carter, Arsène Lupin, and Sherlock Holmes."

Marcel Priollet's Tip Walter, le prince des détectives *#1-55, 1910-1911.*

1909 during this adventure.

Late April-December
L'AIGUILLE CREUSE (THE HOLLOW NEEDLE)

Arsène Lupin's wife, Raymonde de Saint-Veran, is accidentally killed during his battle with Sherlock Holmes. Lecoq is mentioned. A young detective, Isidore Beautrelet, also figures in the case.

Novel by Maurice Leblanc. The best translation is by Jean-Marc and Randy Lofficier, Black Coat Press, 2004. The Lofficiers, French pulp experts, have identified Beautrelet as a pastiche of Gaston Leroux's detective Joseph Josephin, aka "Rouletabille." However, they agree that, unfortunately for the purposes of metafictional theorizing, the two characters are not one and the same. Holmes chronologists should note that Holmes was Lupin's captive for the period of June-October

Spring
MARTIN WILLÉNS UNDERLIGE HÆNDELSER

Danish consulting detective Martin Willéns deliberately copies the appearance, mannerisms, and investigative methods of C. Auguste Dupin.

Astrid Ehrencron-Kidde's Martin Willéns novels, beginning with Martin Willéns Underlige *Hændelser, 1910.*

May. Supposed death of Prince Dakkar, also known as the first Captain Nemo. (As told by Alan Moore and Kevin O'Neill in "The New Traveller's Almanac, Chapter Three: The Americas" in *The League of Extraordinary Gentlemen II*.)

Summer. Birth of teen-detective Joe Hardy.

Summer. Howards End, as recounted by E.M. Forster.

Summer
L'EFFRAYANTE AVENTURE (THE FRIGHTFUL ADVENTURE aka PANIC IN PARIS)

An English detective and French reporter investigate a mysterious case which leads them to a vast network of caverns under Paris inhabited by prehistoric monsters, and involves utilizing *vril*-force to create a "vriliogyre," a *vril*-powered flying machine.

Novel by Jules Lermina (published as L'Effrayante Aventure, *1910), translated by Brian Stableford, Black Coat Press, 2009. The* vril *is from Edward Bullwer-Lytton's* The Coming Race *(1871).*

L'AFFAIRE AZEFF-POLOUKHINE (THE AZEFF-POLOUKHINE CASE)

Sâr Dubnotal, the French psychic detective known as *"Napoléon of the Intangible,"* spars with Eugene Azeff (aka Evno Azef).

Story in Sâr Dubnotal *#16, June 1910. Since both Sexton Blake and* Sâr Dubnotal *have clashed with Azeff,* Sâr Dubnotal *exists in the Crossover Universe.*

AZEFF, LE ROI DES AGENTS PROVOCATEURS (AZEFF, THE KING OF THE AGENTS PROVOCATEURS)

Sâr Dubnotal and Eugene Azeff go head-to-head once again.

Story in Sâr Dubnotal *#19, July 1910.*

THE ROOK: MASTER OF THE WORLD

The Rook (Restin Dane) travels back in time from 1980 to 1909, where he teams up with Sir Arthur Conan Doyle, Jules Verne, William Sydney Porter (O. Henry), the Cisco Kid, "Poncho" Hernandez, and Sherlock Holmes against Robur the Conqueror.

Warren Publishing's The Rook *#4-6, August-December 1980, by Budd Lewis and Lee Elias. Time traveling Restin Dane is the grandson of H.G. Wells'* The Time Traveler *(known variously as Bruce Clarke Wildman or Adam Dane). This is discussed in more detail in a 1977 entry for The Rook in this Chronology. Dane's "home-base" time period is from 1977-1983. This crossover brings the Cisco Kid and Poncho into the Crossover Universe, although "Poncho" is more normally spelled "Pancho." Jules Verne, in our universe, died in 1905. However, this is the Crossover Universe version of Verne, or perhaps it is really Verne's son. The villain in this story is called "Robar," but is clearly Robur, of Verne's two novels* Robur the Conqueror *(aka* Clipper of the Clouds) *and* Master of the World. *This story supposedly takes place a few months after the Tunguska explosion in Siberia in the summer of 1908. However, it would have taken Robur longer than that to gather his new army, build his new ship, and construct a par-*

tial robot body, so I have placed this story a year later, in 1909. Regarding Robur, he claims to be a refugee from an alien space war. It is more likely that this is the same Robur seen in Verne's tales, experimenting with space flight, and that his ship crashed in Siberia.

The Tunguska incident on June 30, 1908, seems to be a focal point in the Crossover Universe. A young Clark Savage was involved in the event (The Asteroid Terror, DC Comics' Doc Savage, volume 2, #22-24), which had later repercussions as detailed in several episodes of The X-Files. According to the latest Shang-Chi: Master of Kung Fu miniseries, 2002, Nikola Tesla, in his quest for a new energy source, was responsible for the Tunguska explosion. Tesla's connection to the Tunguska event is also mentioned in Spider Robinson's "Callahan's Key." It is also implied that the master criminal Dorje caused the event in Talbot Mundy's Jimgrim. Fu Manchu claims that the incident was the result of a Russian experiment in Cay Van Ash's The Fires of Fu Manchu, while Joseph Jorkens states that he discovered the remains of the meteor responsible for the incident in Lord Dunsany's "A Large Diamond" from The Travel Tales of Mr. Joseph Jorkens.

HELLON SALAISUUS
The Finnish detective, Max Rudolph, is compared to Sherlock Holmes; Rudolph also alludes to the exploits of Nick Carter and Arsène Lupin.
Novel by Rudolf Richard Ruth, 1910.

THE BLACK HAND
World famous American detective Nat Pinkerton fights against a Mafia-like crime organization, The Black Hand, in New York City and Chicago. Near the end of the story, at a loss for what to do, Pinkerton wires London and receives advice from Sherlock Holmes.
This tale is from a Greek Nat Pinkerton *issue, lifting most of a Nick Carter "Black Hand" story and using Nat Pinkerton instead of Nick Carter. Perhaps both Pinkerton and Carter were really involved in these events. In any case, the Holmes connection brings Pinkerton into the CU. Jess Nevins notes that "Nat Pinkerton, also had run-ins with Inez Navarro and Dazaar, both enemies of Nick Carter, in stories in the Russian* Nat Pinkerton—Korol' Syshchikov *(Nat Pinkerton, the King of Detectives) #10 and 14 (1908). The names, in the original*

issues, were 'Iness Navarro' and 'Datsar,' but the figures of the villains are the same, and the difference in names is obviously due to faulty translation from English to Russian and back to English. Dazaar is a beautiful criminal mastermind who had six other people, all her twins, commit crimes in her name, as a way to confuse the law and Nick Carter. Inez Navarro is the 'beautiful demon' (the title of the Iness Navarro story is 'Iness Navarro—Beautiful Demon'), a psychotic Spanish beauty who was lethal and quite, quite unhinged."

August-November. The latter events of *Tarzan of the Apes*.

August. "Le Monstre": Tarzan meets Pablo Picasso in Paris. Indy met Picasso as a child and again as a young adult in May 1917 (*The Young Indiana Jones Chronicles*). Tarzan met the artist while he was in Paris during the events of *Tarzan of the Apes* in this story published by Dark Horse Comics, *Tarzan* #11 and 12, written by Lovern Kindzierski and illustrated by Stan Manoukian and Vince Roucher. Consequently, Indy exists in the same universe as Tarzan. These events appear to be a sort of "copycat" case, mirroring the 1891 events of *The Phantom of the Opera/The Canary Trainer*.

September 13-18
THE MODERN PROMETHEUS

While Tarzan is in New York, he meets John Watson's editor, Sir Arthur Conan Doyle; Nikola Tesla; Thomas Edison; and Frankenstein's Monster.

This story also occurs during the events of Tarzan of the Apes *and is published by Dark Horse Comics,* Tarzan *#13 and 14, written by Lovern Kindzierski and illustrated by Stan Manoukian and Vince Roucher. Indiana Jones would later also meet Conan Doyle and Thomas Edison. The monster is the first Creature, from Mary Shelley's novel* Frankenstein, *as opposed to later Monsters, such as that seen in the Universal film versions.*

September
TOOTH AND NAIL

Tarzan is still in New York, where he encounters Dr. Jekyll/Mr. Hyde.

Again, this story occurs during the events of Tarzan of the Apes *and is published by Dark Horse Comics,* Tarzan *#15 and 16, written by Lovern Kindzierski and illustrated by Stan Manoukian and Vince Roucher. Sherlock Holmes* and John Watson went up against the good doctor and his nasty counterpart in 1885. Contrary to The League of Extraordinary Gentlemen, Volume II, *Mr. Hyde* must have survived the events of the Martian Invasion in 1898.

September. "British East Africa, September 1909": Indiana Jones meets Theodore Roosevelt. (Episode of *The Young Indiana Jones Chronicles*. Sherlock Holmes also knew Roosevelt.)

Autumn.The first recorded case of scientific detective Craig Kennedy, "*The Silent Bullet*," as told by Arthur B. Reeve.

Autumn
BÉBÉ APACHE
A Parisian child adventurer and would-be detective, Bébé, helps capture a gang of apaches. At one point he is advised by Nick Carter.

This brings Bébé, who starred in sixty five French films in the 1910s, into the Crossover Universe. Jess Nevins proposes that "Given the difference in looks, attitude, and manner between Nick Carter and the 'Nick Carter' who appears here, it is likely that the 'Nick Carter' who met Bébé is the same 'Nick Carter' who fought Zigomar in Zigomar contre Nick Carter: Chick Carter, Nick's adopted son, using disguises and an alias."

OKA-YUMA, DER JAPANISCHE SPION
Nat Pinkerton fights Oka-Yuma, perhaps the foremost of Japan's spies.

A story in Nat Pinkerton, Der König Der Detectivs *(Nat Pinkerton, the King of Detectives) #26, 1910. This brings Oka Yuma into the Crossover Universe.*

November 1909-September 1910
THE RETURN OF TARZAN
Tarzan's first visit to Opar.

This novel records Tarzan's early adventures in Opar and was written by Edgar Rice Burroughs. It relates back to Hadon's adventures in Opar 12,000 years ago. The date is derived from Farmer's chronology in Tarzan Alive.

1910

January. While in Egypt, master illusionist and escape artist Harry Houdini has an adventure with Lovecraftian overtones. ("Imprisoned with the Pharaohs," short story by H.P. Lovecraft and Harry Houdini, *Weird Tales*, May 1924; *The Transition of H.P. Lovecraft: The Road to Madness*, Del Rey, 1996. Houdini also worked with both Sherlock Holmes and Conan Doyle.)

January
NICK CARTER VS. FANTÔMAS

Detective Nick Carter vs. a criminal mastermind, "Mr. Melvil," who is none other than the villainous Fantômas!

A play by Alexandre Bisson and Guillaume Livet, 1910, translated and adapted by Frank J. Morlock for Black Coat Press, October 2007. Although Fantômas is not named, Jean-Marc Lofficier, in his Afterword, makes an excellent case for "Melvil" being Fantômas.

Winter. Tom Swift's first adventure, Tom Swift and His Motor Cycle, *or, Fun and Adventure on the Road* by Victor Appleton. According to a theory advanced by Dennis E. Power, Tom's father, inventor Barton Swift, was once a U.S. Secret Service agent.

Winter
LA DERNIERE ENQUETE DE SHERLOCK HOLMES, OU LA SEQUESTREE

Lord Lister meets up with Sherlock Holmes, Fu Manchu, and Moriarty.

Story by Yves Varende in Lord Lister, Le Mystérieux Inconnu, *bringing the Raffles-like character Lord Lister into the CU. In France, Lord Lister was known as "John C. Sinclair." After this case, Holmes and Lister entered into a prolonged duel, as documented in the Polish pulp* Senzaca.

AVENTURAS DE LORD JACKSON

Lord Jackson begins work as a consulting detective in Madrid. Later in the year he jousts with Sherlock Holmes.

The Lord Jackson stories, 1911.

THE WINGED TERROR

Nelson Lee is marked for death by an ex-convict armed with a flying suit. Sexton Blake learns of the threat and helps Lee solve the case.

Story published in Boys Herald, *1910. Farmer mentioned detective Sexton Blake in* Doc Savage: His Apocalyptic Life. *This crossover brings detective Nelson Lee into the CU.*

March 17. Birth of Terrence Patrick O'Reilly, aka "O'Reilly Sahib," New York police officer and from 1936-1941 the Marshal of Personal Safety to His Highness Vinayak Rao Bahadur, Maharajah of Zarapore, Central India. (The O'Reilly Sahib series by Lawrence G. Blochman.)

April. Sherlock Holmes and Harry Houdini solve a case together. (*The Adventure of the Ectoplasmic Man,* novel by Daniel Stashower, Penguin Books, 1986. Although this case takes place after *The Pandora Plague,* Watson probably wrote it up first; thus his assertion that this was the first meeting of Holmes and Houdini. Houdini also had a Lovecraftian adventure, "Imprisoned with the Pharaohs." He met Holmes again in 1922, as well as working with Watson's editor, Sir Arthur Conan Doyle, on several cases.)

Spring. Birth of private detective Archie Goodwin.

Spring. Nancy Drew, daughter of Carson Drew, is born.

Spring

IL SEGRETO DELLA CASSAFORTE (THE SECRET OF THE SAFE)

Doctor Riccardo de Medici opens shop as a consulting detective in Rome. He is known as "the Italian Sherlock Holmes."

Umberto Cei's Doctor Riccardo de Medici novellas, beginning in 1911. "The Italian Sherlock Holmes," was a title formerly held by the late John Siloch.

INCIDENT AT VICTORIA FALLS

Sherlock Holmes, on a case to protect an African diamond, the Star of Africa, meets Stanley I. Bullard, the manager of a South African Hotel. Bullard is revealed to be A.J. Raffles, who faked his death in the Boer War.

One of two episodes in the Sherlock Holmes: The Golden Years *television miniseries, 1991, starring Christopher Lee as Holmes and Patrick Macnee as Watson.*

Summer. The Egyptian mummy Kharis is revived and wreaks havoc, as told in the film *The Mummy's Hand.* Sequels are *The Mummy's Tomb, The Mummy's Ghost,* and *The Mummy's Curse.*

Summer. Events of Owen Johnson's *Stover at Yale.*

Summer

THE INCOMPLETE ASSASSIN

Rouletabille and his amanuensis, Sainclair, are enlisted by Michel Strogoff to investigate a murder in a Russian ballet company. Dr. Génessier participates in Rouletabille's scheme to expose the murderer. The Phantom of the Opera is mentioned.

Short story by John Peel in Tales of the Shadowmen Volume 2: Gentlemen of the Night, *Jean-Marc and Randy Lofficier, eds., Black Coat Press, 2006; re-*

printed in French in Les Compagnons de l'Ombre (Tome 2), *Jean-Marc and Randy Lofficier, eds., Rivière Blanche, 2008. Rouletabille and Sainclair are from the stories by Gaston Leroux, who also wrote* The Phantom of the Opera. *Michel Strogoff is from Jules Verne's* Michel Strogoff: The Courier of the Czar. *Dr. Génessier is from Jean Redon's novel* Les Yeux Sans Visage, *filmed as 1959's* Eyes without a Face.

ZIGOMAR (aka ZIGOMAR THE EELSKIN)
Detective Nick Carter makes a cameo appearance.
A 1911 serial, in which Carter is played by Charles Krauss. Krauss reprised the Nick Carter role in the 1912 serial Zigomar contre Nick Carter, *about which more below.*

September. Tarzan and Jane get married (*The Return of Tarzan*). Birth of Jean Raoul de Coude, son of Tarzan and the Countess Olga Rokoff de Coude (*The Return of Tarzan* by Edgar Rice Burroughs; *Tarzan the Warrior* by Mark Wheatley, Neil Vokes, and Marc Hempel, Malibu Comics, 1992).

Autumn. The events of John Buchan's *The Power-House*, wherein British politician Edward Leithen exposes the treacherous activities of Andrew Lumley (aka the second Professor Moriarty, who evidently did not die at the conclusion of "The Case of the Missing Martian") and the Krafthaus organization. Lumley-Moriarty dies at the conclusion of this affair, and Krafthaus begins its evolution into the criminal network/"secret nation" known as THRUSH.

Autumn

THE NYCTALOPE ON MARS (aka THE MYSTERY OF THE XV)

The villain Oxus, master of the secret society of the Fifteen, tries to conquer Mars and engages in a plan to breed a new race of supermen with young girls kidnapped from Earth. However, he fights against the Martians, and is eventually defeated by the Nyctalope (Leo Saint-Clair). It's also said that Leo Saint-Clair shows himself to be an amateur detective worthy of comparison with the great Sherlock Holmes.
Novel by Jean de La Hire, 1911; translated by Brian Stableford and reprinted by Black Coat Press, 2008. The Martians are from H. G. Wells' The War of the Worlds, *this linking the Nyctalope to*

the CU, although the Mars seen here must be Barsoom, which is in the Edgar Rice Burroughs Alternate Universe.

THE ADVENTURE OF THE LOST WORLD
Holmes and Watson investigate a series of gruesome and bloody murders on Hampstead Heath, ultimately tracing them to a rampaging megalosaurus which Professor Challenger brought back from his Amazonian expedition two years back. Edward Malone, Roxton, and Summerlee are also mentioned. Watson also refers to the recent Ruritanian Abdication Crisis.

Short story by Doctor Watson, edited by Dominic Green, on the BBC Cult *website, 2004. Challenger, Malone, Roxton, and Summerlee are from Doyle's* The Lost World, *while Ruritania is from Hope's* A Prisoner of Zenda. *The dates that Watson provides in the story are incorrect; Challenger's expedition took place in 1908, not 1916.*

WHERE THE SHADOWS BEGAN
On the train to Paris, Inspector John Raymond Legrasse meets Michel Ardan and they recall an earlier adventure together. Legrasse reads the paper *Echo de France*. Later in Paris, they meet again and Legrasse reveals he's been invited by the Hastur Company to a one-time showing of the notorious play *Le Roi en Jaune* (*The King in Yellow*). *The King in Yellow* played in New Orleans, one night only, two years back and the audience was massacred, so Legrasse has a special interest, and Ardan tags along to investigate. Ardan mentions the Gun Club and the Diogenes Club, and claims to have visited Opar, Shangri-La, and Maple White Land. Ardan also mentions consulting his grandson Francis in New York.

Story by Bradley H. Sinor in Tales of the Shadowmen Volume 6: Grand Guignol, *Jean-Marc and Randy Lofficier, eds., Black Coat Press, 2010; published in French in* Les Compagnons de l'Ombre (Tome 7), *Jean-Marc and Randy Lofficier, eds., Rivière Blanche, 2010. The* Echo de France *is from Maurice Leblanc's Arsène Lupin tales. Inspector John Raymond Legrasse is from H.P. Lovecraft's "The Call of Cthulhu." Michel Ardan and the Gun Club are from Jules Verne's* From the Earth to the Moon. *The play* The King in Yellow *is from Ro-*

bert W. Chambers' collection of short stories. The Diogenes Club is from Doyle and Watson's Sherlock Holmes stories. Ardan may have visited Shangri-La, from James Hilton's Lost Horizon. It's barely possible he visited Maple White Land, which was discovered in 1908 by Professor Challenger (Doyle's The Lost World); perhaps Ardan actually was a member of Challenger's expedition who Ned Malone and his editor, Doyle, did not mention in the book. Ardan's claim of visiting Opar, however, is suspect; Tarzan only discovered the lost African city less than a year ago, and kept its existence secret (Edgar Rice Burroughs' The Return of Tarzan). Perhaps Ardan has heard vague rumors of this lost city, without knowing that Tarzan had actually discovered it, and is slightly embellishing his adventurous resume. Michel Ardan's reference to his grandson Francis Ardan is somewhat problematic. Francis Ardan, Jr., has been equated with Clark Savage, Jr., aka Doc Savage. Ardan Jr./Savage Jr. is not quite nine years old at the time of this case. It is doubtful Ardan would consult with a child on this matter; he must have been referring to Francis Ardan, Sr., aka Clark Savage, Sr. (the man Philip José Farmer, in his Doc Savage biography, called James Clarke Wildman, Sr.). Wildman Sr.'s genealogy was established by Farmer and Michael Ardan is not his grandfather. The solution to this conundrum lays in the story "The Vanishing Devil" (Tales of the Shadowmen Volume 1: The Modern Babylon), which mentions Ardan Jr./Savage Jr.'s great-aunt Michelle. Michelle Ardan's birth name was Michelle Chauvelin-Land; she was the sister of Ardan Jr./Savage Jr.'s maternal grandmother, Arronaxe Chauvelin-Land. After Michelle was widowed in her first marriage, she remarried to Frenchman Michel Ardan. So Michel Ardan is actually Ardan Jr./Savage Jr.'s great-uncle by marriage. The statement that he is child Francis Ardan Jr.'s grandfather is a bit of exaggeration; if he intended to refer to the adult Francis Ardan, Sr., then his declaration is even more of an overstatement.

Late December
DURKHEIM IS DEAD!
At a sociologists' conference, Sherlock Holmes solves the mystery of a stolen jewel, involving Marianne Weber, Emile Durkheim, Max Weber, Sigmund Freud, Georg Simmel, V.I. Lenin, W.E.B. Du Bois, Beatrice Potter, Sidney Webb, Lady Cecily Bracknell, and Algernon "Ernest" Moncrieff.
Novel by Arthur Asa Berger, AltaMira Press, 2003. Lady Cecily Bracknell (Cecily Cardew) and Algernon "Ernest" Moncrieff are from Oscar Wilde's play The Importance of Being Earnest (1895).

1911

Spring. Denis Nayland Smith and Dr. Petrie's first recorded battle with Dr. Fu Manchu (Petrie and Rohmer's *The Insidious Dr. Fu Manchu*). Nayland Smith is the nephew of Sherlock Holmes. The complete series by Sax Rohmer, unless otherwise noted, is: *The Insidious Dr. Fu Manchu, The Return of Dr. Fu Manchu, The Hand of Fu Manchu, The Terror of Fu Manchu* (by William Patrick Maynard), *Ten Years Beyond Baker Street* (by Cay Van Ash), *The Fires of Fu Manchu* (by Cay Van Ash), *The Daughter of Fu Manchu, The Mask of Fu Manchu, The Bride of Fu Manchu, The Trail of Fu Manchu, The Drums of Fu Manchu, The Island of Fu Manchu, The Shadow of Fu Manchu, Re-Enter Fu Manchu, Emperor Fu Manchu,* and *The Wrath of Fu Manchu.* Nayland Smith also appeared in several solo stories: "The Blue Monkey" in The Haunting of Low Fennel, "The Mark of the Monkey" in *Tales of East and West* (British edition only) and "The Turkish Yataghan" in *Tales of East and West.*

Spring. First recorded case of G.K. Chesterton's Father Brown in *The Innocence of Father Brown.*

Spring. Events of *The Monster Men* by Edgar Rice Burroughs, in which Professor Arthur Maxon strives to create the perfect man (first published as *A Man without a Soul*, The All-Story, November 1913).

Spring
EL CORREO DEL NORTE
The lucahador Sombra Venagadora travels back in time and teams up with the cowboy vigilante El Zorro Escarlata and the Mexican revolutionaries.

Feature film, 1960. Sombra Vengadora is in the Crossover Universe, therefore so is El Zorro Escarlata. They teamed up again in 1961's La Mascara de la Muerte.

ETHEL KING, LE NICK CARTER FEMININ
Ethel King, a successful female detective in France and Germany in the years before World War I, comes to the public's attention when she is recommended to Jean Petithuguenin, King's fictional biographer, by Nick Carter himself.

From the publisher's notes to Ethel King, Le Nick Carter Feminin *#1, 1912. According to Jess Nevins, "There was a German version of Ethel King which actually preceded Petithuguenin's version, but the German version lacked the textual link to the CU." Nevins adds that there was a Portuguese pulp,* "Eva Nina, la Unica Rival de Sherlock Holmes, *#1-15 (1913). It's a translation of the German pulp* Ethel King, Ein Weiblicher Sherlock Holmes, *except the translator has renamed Ethel King as 'Eva Nina.' The stories themselves haven't changed, though."*

June. Birth of Charlotte Clayton, daughter of Tarzan and Jane (speculation based on *The Man-Eater* by Edgar Rice Burroughs).

Summer. Jimmie Dale goes into action as the Gray Seal, in exploits related by Frank L. Packard. The Jimmie Dale novels are: *The Adventures of Jimmie Dale* (1917), *The Further Adventures of Jimmie Dale* (1919), *Jimmie Dale and the Phantom Clue* (1922), *Jimmie Dale and the Blue Envelope Murder* (1930), and *Jimmie Dale and the Missing Hour* (1935).

Summer
THE MAN IN GREY (L'HOMME AU COMPLET GRIS)

Young American detective Harry Allan Dickson is groomed by Sherlock Holmes to take over a perilous case when it appears that Jack the Ripper has returned. Gurn is actually Fantômas, and it is revealed that he is the bastard son of Rocambole and Lady Ellen Palmure; he was raised in the Sussex village of Lyndhurst by Rev. Patterson. The *Matilda Briggs* belonging to Lord Beltham supplied the island of Dr. Moreau. Jack the Ripper was a surgically evolved Man-Ape made by Moreau, who was brought London and escaped. Holmes knew the truth but for political reasons kept it under wraps.

A novel by Arnould Galopin adapted and retold by Jean-Marc and Randy Lofficier, Black Coat Press. *The story confirms Fantômas in the CU, and also brings in Rocambole. Note that the Fantômas seen here is the "canonical" Fantômas, as opposed to the version of Fantômas appearing in René Reouven's* Voyage Au Centre Du Mystère. *This tale also adds another layer to the mystery of Jack the Ripper in the CU. In* A Study in Terror, *Holmes had a different solution to the Ripper killers, one which Ellery Queen expanded upon in the 1960s. Sâr Dubnotal confronted the evil behind Jack the Ripper in the early 1890s. It was also revealed that the non-corporeal entity of Jack the Ripper actually inhabited a Fantômas prior to Gurn. Later still, in 2265, Captain Kirk and the* Enterprise *crew would encounter the energy being called Redjac who was the driving force behind Jack the Ripper. Regarding the* Matilda Briggs, *Holmes remarked in "The Adventure of the Sussex Vampire":"'Matilda Briggs was not the name of a young woman, Watson,' said Holmes in a reminiscent voice. 'It was a ship which is associated with the giant rat of Sumatra, a story for which the world is not yet prepared.'" The story of the giant rat of Sumatra is perhaps the most-pastiched of Holmes' unrecorded adventures.*

THE WEREWOLF OF RUTHERFORD GRANGE
Harry Dickson relates a tale of his youth, referring to his mentor, the Master Detective, and his summer apprenticeship with Blake of Baker Street. Blake's Limehouse battle with a Devil Doctor is also mentioned, and Blake mentions that he'll be dining with the Becks. Blake also refers to an adventure he had with the Master Detective in the catacombs under Bayonne. There is also a reference to Blake in the "sewers of Paris searching for the secret hideout of a black-coated conspiracy." A mysterious French Duke and his allies are mentioned. Dickson also says that he never got along with S.P., and refers in passing to Triggs, Hewitt, the late Mrs. Dene, and the unassuming country priest. Sir Henry Westenra and his son Alexander also appear, and Dickson meets Lord John Roxton and Sâr Dubnotal's assistant, Miss Gianetti Annunciata. Roxton states that he hopes Sâr Dubnotal is not a "sort of second Svengali." Roxton is also compared to Allan Quatermain, and he says that the Rutherfords are related to a zoologist he knows. Roxton went to school at Brookfield, and searched for a city in the Sahara referred to as a "last outpost of Atlantis." Miss Annunciata has heard of an Australian detective named Allan Dickson, and Harry explains that his mother was Australian and that his middle name is Allan. Dickson sends a message to a reporter in Paris he knows named Joseph. In the Westenra library, Dickson sees a copy of Aronnax's encyclopedias of sea life. One of the servants in the Westenra household, Darshan, goes to see a "Little Neddy" picture at the cinema. Darshan Kritchna also talks about his great-uncle in the Philippines, who wanted him as an apprentice. Further references are: M. Solange, Madame

Sara, The Hand of Riathamus, a frog that puts on a top hat, Franklin (Dickson's nephew), cat-women, the Trans-Siberian express, Prince Zaleski, the wolf-man of Paris, the were-cat of Paris, the Opera Ghost, D'Athys, New England werewolf sightings, the Incantation of Nodens, the Devil's Gate, the Figalillys, Nick Carter, Old King Brady, a friend at Cheyne Walk, the Secret Service agent Harry's father knew, and a shape-shifting legend surrounding the Ring of the Borgias.

Short story by Harry Dickson, edited by G.L. Gick in Tales of the Shadowmen Volume 1: The Modern Babylon, *Jean-Marc and Randy Lofficier, eds., Black Coat Press, 2005; completed in* Tales of the Shadowmen Volume 2: Gentlemen of the Night, *Jean-Marc and Randy Lofficier, eds., Black Coat Press, 2006; re-*

printed in French in Les Compagnons de l'Ombre (Tome 2), *Jean-Marc and Randy Lofficier, eds., Rivière Blanche, 2008. The Harry Dickson stories were mostly by Jean Ray, and others. The Allan Dickson novel* The Man in Grey *is by Arnould Galopin, and has been adapted and retold by Jean-Marc and Randy Lofficier. The Master Detective is Sherlock Holmes. Blake of Baker Street is Sexton Blake. The catacombs under Bayonne are a reference to E. Hoffmann Price's placement of a network of fictional crypts under the real life city of Bayonne on the French-Spanish border, in the author's Pierre d'Artois series and the Lovecraft collaboration, "Through the Gates of the Silver Key." The mysterious French Duke is the Duke de Richlieu from stories by Dennis Wheatley. S.P. is Solar Pons. The Becks are from M. McDonnell Bodkin's* Paul Beck *(1897),* Dora Myrl, The Lady Detective *(1900),* The Capture of Paul Beck *(1909), and* Young Beck *(1912). The black-coated conspiracy is a tip of the hat to the Black Coats criminal organization. M. Triggs is from Jean Ray's Harry Dickson tale "Les idées de Monsieur Triggs." Hewitt is detective Martin Hewitt. The late Mrs. Dene is George R. Sims' Dorcas Dene from* Dorcas Dene, Detective *(1897), while the unassuming country priest is Father Brown. These references add Triggs and Mrs. Dene to the CU. The Devil Doctor in Limehouse may be Dr. Fu Manchu, although his conflict with Blake remains unrecorded. Henry and Alexander Westenra are related to the Westenras of Whitby seen in Bram Stoker's novel* Dracula. *Lord John Roxton and Allan Quatermain are Wold Newton Family members, as established by Philip José Farmer. The zoologist named Rutherford that Roxton knows is Professor Challenger; in Farmer's dissection of the Wold Newton Family Tree, he reveals that Challenger's real surname is Rutherford. Brookfield from is James Hilton's* Goodbye Mr. Chips. *The "last outpost of Atlantis" is from Pierre Benoit's* L'Atlantide. *Sâr Dubnotal was an anonymously created mystic. Svengali is from George Du Maurier's* Trilby, *thus bringing the events of that novel into the CU. The reporter in Paris named Joseph is Joseph Josephin, confirming Rouletabille in the CU. Aronnax's sea life encyclopedias are a reference to Verne's* 20,000 Leagues under the Sea. *"Little Neddy" is Ned Nederlander, a silent film star turned adventurer seen in the 1986 motion picture* ¡Three Amigos! *M. Solange is Solange Fontaine, created by F. Tennyson Jesse. Darshan Kritchna's great-uncle in the Philippines is Nadir, the same guru who taught Fascinax. Madame Sara was featured in Meade and Eustace's* The Sorceress of the Strand *(1903). The Hand of Riathamus is a subtle reference to the young adult horror novel* Shadowmancer *by G.P. Taylor. The frog that put on a top hat is Michigan J. Frog from the classic Chuck Jones cartoon "One Froggy Evening." Little Franklin, Dickson's nephew, is Frank Hardy of the Hardy Boys. The cat-women come from Val Lewton's* Cat People. *The Trans-Siberian express is from the Peter Cushing movie* Horror Express. *Prince Zaleski was created by M. P. Shiel. The wolf-man of Paris comes from Guy Endore's book* The Werewolf of Paris, *and the were-cat is from the 1946 movie* The Catman of Paris. *The Opera Ghost is the Phantom of the*

Opera. D'Athys is from the 1918 French serial Tih Minh *directed by Louis Feuillade. The New England werewolf sightings come from the book* The Wolf in the Garden *by Alfred E. Bill. The Incantation of Nodens indicates a Lovecraftian deity being called up. The Sâr's adventure in "The Devil's Gate" refers to the stories of Cormac FitzGeoffrey, created by Robert E. Howard. The Figalillys are the psychic eccentrics from the 1970s televisions series* Nanny and the Professor. *Nick Carter is a dime novel character, as is Old King Brady. The friend at Cheyne Walk is Carnacki. The Secret Service agent Harry's father knew is Artemus Gordon from* The Wild Wild West. *The shape-shifting legend surrounding the Ring of the Borgias is from* The Shaggy Dog *and* The Shaggy D.A., *based Felix Salten's story "The Hound of Florence."*

Autumn. First recorded exploit of Parisian boy adventurer Tintin. (*The Aerial Adventures of a Small Parisian around the World*, series by Marcel Priollet.)

Autumn. Murderous thief Tenebras terrorizes Paris. (*Tenebras the Phantom Bandit* by Arnould Galopin.)

Autumn. Dixon Hawke's first appearance in "The Great Hotel Mystery" (*The Saturday Post* #347, April 6, 1912).

Autumn. John Thunstone is born.

Autum 1911-1912. The events of *The Mad King, Part I* ("The Mad King," *All-Story Weekly*, March 21, 1914), as told by Edgar Rice Burroughs.

Autumn
ZIGOMAR CONTRE NICK CARTER (ZIGOMAR VERSUS NICK CARTER)

Zigomar and his gang wound Paulin Broquet, Zigomar's policeman nemesis. Nick Carter, who is working for Broquet, sets out in pursuit of Zigomar, chasing him across France, through Paris, Marseille, and Toulon. Carter blackmails Olga Liontef, a former member of the Z gang, into helping him, and after several setbacks, in which his skill at disguise is no use and in which he is repeatedly fooled by Zigomar, Carter and the Toulon police capture Zigomar and his gang. During the trial Zigomar is apparently poisoned by his lieutenant, Rosaria, thus escaping justice.

A 1912 film serial written and directed by Victorin-Hippolyte Jasset. Jess Nevins postulates that "Given the relative ease with which Zigomar outwits and eludes Nick Carter, and given that Carter is supposedly Broquet's 'top detective,' rather than an independent operator, it is likely that the 'Nick Carter' of the film was not Nick Carter but rather Chick Carter, Nick's adoptive son and someone who not only was a physical double of Nick Carter but masqueraded on occasion as Carter." This crossover confirms the first Zigomar's presence in the Crossover Universe. A second Zigomar met The Phantom in the late 1930s.

October 26. Birth of Cliff Secord, the future Rocketeer, on a train traveling between Gary, Indiana and Chicago, Illinois.

Mid-November. Edgar Rice Burroughs is called to London, where he meets with Dr. John Watson at the Diogenes Club. Watson offers him the story of a series of events which will later take form as Burroughs' novel *Tarzan of the Apes*. In return, Watson asks only for background on the criminal element of Chicago, for a story that Watson is planning to write. In reality, Watson has solicited the Chicago information on behalf of his friend, Sherlock Holmes, who is about to undertake an undercover mission for England at the behest of his older brother, Mycroft. The undercover mission is later described in Doyle and Watson's "His Last Bow." ("The Case of the Doctor Who Had No Business, or, The Adventure of the Second Anonymous Narrator" by Richard A. Lupoff in *The Universal Holmes*, Ramble House, 2007 [but originally written in 1966]. Lupoff also indicates that Tarzan's father, John Clayton, was a British agent and was on a mission for Mycroft when the *Fuwalda* went missing in 1888. Lupoff then equates Tarzan's father, John Clayton, with the cabdriver John Clayton seen in Doyle and Watson's *The Hound of the Baskervilles*, an early attempt to build upon on Prof. H.W. Starr's Tarzanic and Sherlockian speculations in his "A Case of Identity, or The Adventure of the Seven Claytons," *The Baker Street Journal*, January 1960. However, Starr had the cabdriver Clayton as the father of Tarzan's father, which is the theory adapted by Philip José Farmer in *Tarzan Alive*, and which is also accepted herein for Crossover Universe continuity.)

1912

January. Tarzan receives an immortality treatment from an ancient witch doctor.
Winter. Harry Houdini's stage routine sabotaged by a group of "Handcuff Kings," but Sherlock Holmes comes to his rescue. (*Auf den Spuren Houdinis*, 1916).
April 10-14. Indiana Jones meets Sir Arthur Conan Doyle aboard the ill-fated *Titanic*. (*Young Indiana Jones and the Titanic Adventure*, an original young adult novel by Les Martin published by Random House, 1993.) Tarzan met Dr. John Watson's literary editor, Conan Doyle, in 1909. Of course, both Indy and Conan Doyle survived the tragedy.

April 10-14. Aboard the *Titanic*, Jacques Futrelle, chronicler of the cases of Professor Augustus S.F.X. Van Dusen (aka "the Thinking Machine") and Futrelle's wife May, investigate a series of murders. Unfortunately, Futrelle does not survive the *Titanic* tragedy, although May does (*The Titanic Murders*, as related by Max Allan Collins).

April 1912-June 1913
813

From his jail cell, Arsène Lupin is notified that the Kaiser enlisted Sherlock Holmes to solve the mystery of "813," but the Great Detective did not solve the conundrum.
Novel by Maurice Leblanc.

Spring. First recorded adventure of French boxer and adventurer Marcel Dunot. (*The King of the Boxers*, series by Jose Moselli.)

May 20. Birth of Tarzan and Jane's biological son, John Paul Clayton.

Spring
SHERLOCK HOLMES AND THE GREYFRIARS SCHOOL MYSTERY
Holmes and Watson meet the famous overweight schoolboy, Billy Bunter, and his school companions Bob Cherry, Hurree Jamset Ram Singh, and others, at the Greyfriars School.
This novel is by Watson, edited by Val Andrews, Breese Books, 1997. Billy Bunter is the most famous character in the Boy's School genre. The stories were written under the pen name of Frank Richards and they appeared in The Magnet Library *magazine from 1910 to 1940.*

STILETTKAPPEN (THE STILETTO CANE)
Leo Carring, in his first public case in Stockholm, remarks to his friend that Sherlock Holmes was a poor detective who was sloppy in his handling of evidence and had undeserved luck in his cases.
Novel by S.A. Duse and J. Regis, 1913, the first of ten Leo Carring novels.

HERR CORPWIETH, GENTLEMAN-DETEKTIV
The Finnish detective Herr Corpwieth opens a consulting detective practice in Helsinki, having concluded his study under Sherlock Holmes.

From Holger Nohrstrom's Herr Corpwieth, Gentleman-Detektiv, *1914, and* Den Gatfulle Dubbelgangaren, *1916. Corpwieth says he studied under Holmes and models himself, his writings, and his detective approach on Holmes.*

ONE FANG

John Harris tells a man named Phillips the tale of his encounter with the serpent god Set in New Mexico.

Short story by Scott A. Cupp in the anthology Cross Plains Universe: Texans Celebrate Robert E. Howard, *a joint publication of MonkeyBrain Books and FACT, Inc. (Fandom Association of Central Texas), edited by Scott A. Cupp and Joe R. Lansdale, 2006. Rick Lai notes, "Although the name Yig is not mentioned, Set is presented like Lovecraft's serpent god. There is even a character named Phillips, but he can't be Lovecraft's fictional alter ego, Ward Phillips."*

DR. MORRISON

Dr. Morrison clashes with henchmen of Fu Manchu.

Story in Dr. Morrison *#1, 1913. According to Jess Nevins, "Dr. Morrison was a Holmesian Great Detective created by the Danish mystery writer Robert Hansen under the pseudonym 'Jens Anker.' Morrison appeared in three dime novel series, in 1913-1914, 1915, and 1942."*

ARKRIGHT'S TALE

Captain Luis Da Silva goes on a sea voyage with Arkright, who normally just listens to Carnacki's stories, and together they fight a ghost. Da Silva tells Arkright that he met Carnacki in Hong Kong in the 1890s. When Arkright mentions this to Carnacki, the ghost hunter admits to being in Hong Kong, but he doesn't remember meeting Da Silva.

A short story by Chico Kidd in No. 472 Cheyne Walk: Carnacki, the Untold Stories. *Since Carnacki is in the CU, this crossover adds Kidd's own series character, Captain Da Silva, to the CU.*

Summer. First recorded adventure of Italian gentleman thief Baron Cesare Stromboli. (*The International Gentleman*, series by Jose Moselli.)

Summer 1912-1914. Sherlock Holmes goes undercover as Mr. Altamont of Chicago (Doyle and Watson's "His Last Bow").

Early Summer
MASK OF THE MONSTER

In Paris, young policeman Jules Maigret and the vigilante Judex battle Gouroull, otherwise known as Frankenstein's Creature, when Maigret's love Louise Leonard is kidnapped. Doctor Jules de Grandin from the Faculté de Médecine also helps in the investigation. When Maigret compares de Grandin to Sherlock Holmes, de Grandin calls Holmes overrated and says he would prefer to be compared to the great Dupin. De Grandin then calls Rouletabille a "puppy" who should be flattered to be compared to de Grandin rather than the other way around. The dark-cloaked Judex is likened to a modern Rocambole, and he notes that de Grandin studied under the great Sâr Dubnotal. The creature Balaoo who terrorized the city only months ago is mentioned, as is the madman Otto Beneckendorff. The notorious Dr. Cornelius Kramm and Kramm's brother Fritz, both of the Red Hand criminal syndicate, turn out to be behind the plot. Doctor Lorde also appears.

Short story by Matthew Baugh in Tales of the Shadowmen Volume 1: The Modern Babylon, *Jean-Marc and Randy Lofficier, eds., Black Coat Press, 2005; reprinted in French in* Les Compagnons de l'Ombre (Tome 1), *Jean-Marc and Randy Lofficier, eds., Rivière Blanche, 2008. Although there are other links placing Jules de Grandin, Jules Maigret, Dupin, Rouletabille, Sâr Dubnotal, and Rocambole in the CU, this story serves to strengthen their presence. This tale also brings in Judex, Balaoo, Dr. Cornelius Kramm, and Doctor Lorde. Judex is a cloaked vigilante who appeared in the 1916-1917 French serial* Judex *and several follow-ups. Dr. Cornelius Kramm is from Gustave Le Rouge's* Le Mystérieux Docteur Cornélius. *The tragic yet murderous ape-man Balaoo was the subject of a novel by Gaston Leroux. Beneckendorff is the villain from the first Jules de Grandin adventure, "Terror on the Links." De Grandin mentioned arresting the madman in Paris before the Great War; years later he turned up in New Jersey with a murderous gorilla-man hybrid. Dr. Lorde is from Cyril-Berge's* L'Expérience du Dr. Lorde.

September. Tarzan and Jane adopt Tarzan's second cousin, the orphaned John "Korak" Drummond. John is the younger brother of Hugh "Bulldog" Drummond. (Philip José Farmer's "The Great Korak-Time Discrepancy," *Myths for the Modern Age: Philip José Farmer's Wold Newton Universe*).

Autumn. Peter ("Peter the Brazen") Moore's first recorded adventure, "Princess of Static," by George F. Worts.

Autumn
THE THREE JEWISH HORSEMEN

In Montpellier, Arsène Lupin outwits three unlikely cohorts: Sir Lionel Baskerville; Josephine Balsamo, Countess Cagliostro; and Erik, the Opera Ghost. Josephine mentions a conclave of the Black Coats in Sartene the previous year. Orfanik's machine is also mentioned.

Short story by Viviane Etrivert in Tales of the Shadowmen Volume 1: The Modern Babylon, *Jean-Marc and Randy Lofficier, eds., Black Coat Press, 2005. Josephine Balsamo is from Leblanc's Arsène Lupin stories. Sir Lionel Baskerville might be a relative of the family made famous in the Sherlock Holmes novel* The Hound of the Baskervilles. *Erik is from Leroux's* The Phantom of the Opera. *The Black Coats saga by Paul Féval relates the saga of an international brotherhood of criminals. Orfanik and his machine are from* The Castle of the Carpathians *by Jules Verne, this placing the events of that novel in the CU.*

1913

January 4. Birth of New York Fire Marshall Ben Pedley. (The Ben Pedley stories by Stewart Sterling.)

Winter. Tarzan and Sheeta the Leopard have an adventure on Mount Kilimanjaro: "The Adventure of the Very Sick Circus Horse" (*The Dark Heart of Time: A Tarzan Novel*; "The Snows of Kilimanjaro").

Winter
THE SINISTER DR. SYN

Someone disguised as "the ghost of Dr. Syn" arrives to kidnap the Greyfriars Chinese junior, Wun Lung.

Story in *The Magnet Library* volume 12, #1541, August 28, 1937, written by Charles Hamilton. Dr. Syn is discussed as if he were a real person. This confirms Billy Bunter and the Greyfriars School in the Crossover Universe.

April
TWO HUNTERS

In Paris, Nikolas Rokoff, back from the dead, approaches the corrupt banker Favraux with a scheme to kidnap Lord Greystoke's wife Jane and their child, thus forcing Greystoke to lead them to his source of wealth, the lost city of Opar. Judex notifies Tarzan of the plan, and together they defeat the plot, Tarzan killing Rokoff in the process. The Vampires gang is mentioned, as well as Alexis Paulevitch.

Short story Robert L. Robinson, Jr. in Tales of the Shadowmen Volume 3: Danse Macabre, *Jean-Marc and Randy Lofficier, eds., Black Coat Press, 2007 reprinted in French in* Les Compagnons de l'Ombre (Tome 2), *Jean-Marc and Randy Lofficier, eds., Rivière Blanche, 2008. The team-up between Judex and Tarzan, a Wold Newton Family member, solidifies Judex's place in the Crossover Universe. Rokoff and Paulevitch are from Edgar Rice Burroughs' Tarzan no-*

vels. Judex and Favraux are from the French serial Judex, *while the* Vampires *gang is from the French serial* Les Vampires. *The story cannot take place as dated in 1915, as this is during the Great War events of Burroughs'* Tarzan the Untamed. *This story must take place after Rokoff's alleged death in* The Beasts of Tarzan *(June-September 1912). April 1913 is an available slot in Philip José Farmer's timeline of Tarzan's life which fits the facts.*

Spring. Birth of Creighton Holmes (probable son of Raffles Holmes).

Spring. First recorded exploit of German adventurer/explorer Konrad Gotz. (*Konrad Gotz Der Wandervogel* pulp.)

Spring. First adventure of teenaged French aviator Fifi. (*The New Adventures of Fifi* series by Arnould Galopin.)

Spring. John Kirowan's first recorded adventure, "*Dermod's Bane,*" as recounted by Robert E. Howard.

Spring. First known exploit of Heinz Brandt, a German who joins the French Foreign Legion. (*Heinz Brandt the Foreign Legionnaire*, pulp series.)

Spring. Events of the film *The Wild Bunch*.

Spring
MISS MADELYN MACK, DETECTIVE

Miss Madelyn Mack, a brilliant American female detective, is sarcastically (though respectfully) described by a New York City cop as "Miss Sherlock Holmes at work!"

Novel by Hugh C. Weir, 1914. This comment could be taken as a comparison to Holmes as a living person rather than to a fictional character.

HELL CAT OF HONG KONG

Adventurer John Gorman meets two powerful women, the White Tigress and the Old Hag.

Written by Marc A. Cerasini and Charles Hoffman, in Risqué Stories #5 *(March 1987). The Old Hag is better known to readers of James Clavell's Asian Saga as Tess "Hag" Struan (1825-1917), matriarch of Struan and Company, the most powerful trading company in Hong Kong. Thus, Clavell's Asian Saga, which is already part of the CU through a reference in the* Star Trek *novel* Ishmael, *provides the link to bring in John Gorman. The White Tigress, a criminal adventurer, would later cause problems for Robert E. Howard's Sailor Steve Costigan. While, until now, there has not been a formal connection to Sailor Steve Costigan, we may safely assume that most, if not all, of Robert E. Howard's works are part of the Crossover Universe.*

THE SUCCESSFUL FAILURE

Detective Isidore Beautrelet, working on a case with Commissioner Guichard, gets a helping hand from a young English pilot named James. James asks

Beautrelet if he works like Sherlock Holmes. When no one can pronounce James' surname, he laughs and replies that "Biggles" is just fine.

Short story John Peel *in* Tales of the Shadowmen Volume 3: Danse Macabre, *Jean-Marc and Randy Lofficier, eds., Black Coat Press, 2007; reprinted in French in* Les Compagnons de l'Ombre (Tome 4)*, Jean-Marc and Randy Lofficier, eds., Rivière Blanche, 2009. Beautrelet is from Maurice Leblanc's Arsène Lupin novel* L'aiguille Creuse *(*The Hollow Needle*). James is of course W.E. Johns' James "Biggles" Bigglesworth. Commissioner Xavier Guichard is from Georges Simenon's Maigret stories, but he was also a real person.*

May-November
THE SON OF TARZAN

It is stated that a baffled hotel proprietor would have consulted Sherlock Holmes, had he heard of Holmes, in order to solve a mystery.

Evidence that Edgar Rice Burroughs knew that Holmes and Tarzan lived in the same world.

Summer. English adventurer Percy Stuart's first recorded exploit. (*Lord Percy of the Eccentric Club*, pulp series.) In 1929, a man named Harald Harst applies for membership in the new Eccentric Club, but withdraws after learning that one must solve a certain number of cases in order to qualify for membership.

Summer. Events of Gustave Le Rouge's *Le Mystérieux Docteur Cornélius.*

Summer
DISGRACED BY HIS FATHER!

The Greyfriars School boys want to commission Ferrers Locke to trace the missing father of Dick Russell, but when Locke is unavailable, they hire Sexton Blake and Tinker instead. Billy Bunter plays a central role in the case.

Story by Frank Richards (Noel Wood-Smith) in The Magnet Library *#818, October 13, 1923. This is the one and only time that the Blake series and the Greyfriars series crossed-over. Usually Ferrers Locke was the preferred detective, but he was on a case in Russia.*

Summer-October
THE RETURN OF DR. FU MANCHU

"My blood seemed to chill, and my heart to double its pulsations; beside me Smith was breathing more rapidly than usual. I knew now the explanation of the feeling which had claimed me when first I had descended the stone stairs. I knew what it was that hung like a miasma over that house. It was the aura, the glamour, which radiated from this wonderful and evil man as light radiates from radium. It was the *vril*, the force, of Dr. Fu Manchu."

Novel by Dr. Petrie, edited by Sax Rohmer. Bulwer-Lytton's The Coming Race *is already integrated into the CU via a reference in* The League of Extraordinary Gentlemen; *this reference to* vril *bolsters the connection.*

Autumn. Miss Mina Murray reforms the League of Extraordinary Gentlemen (the team is now comprised of Mina Murray, Allan Quatermain, Jr., Orlando, A.J. Raffles, and Thomas Carnacki) and, in the caves beneath Paris' famed Opera House, they fight their French counterparts, Les Hommes Mystérieux (aeronaut Jean Robur, the Nyctalope, Arsène Lupin, Fantômas, and Zenith the Albino). The battle was actually orchestrated by the German group, the Zweilicht-Helden (Dr. Mabuse, Dr. Caligari, and Dr. Rotwang). (As told by Alan Moore and Kevin O'Neill in "The New Traveller's Almanac, Chapter Two: Europe" in *The League of Extraordinary Gentlemen II* and *The League of Extraordinary Gentlemen: Black Dossier*).

Autumn
EINE BOTSCHAFT VOM MARS (A MESSAGE FROM MARS)
German-American detective John Spurlock, known as the "Man of a Thousand Disguises," encounters and defeats (with the help of the German police and army) another invasion attempt by Martians.

From Detektiv John Spurlock *#18 and 19. This brings John Spurlock into the CU.*

November 1913-January 1914
TARZAN AND THE JEWELS OF OPAR
Tarzan returns to Opar. In the comic book adaptation of the tale, La of Opar invokes Valka.

This novel relates Tarzan's further adventures in Opar by Edgar Rice Burroughs, and also connects back to Hadon's adventures in Opar 12,000 years ago. The date is derived from Farmer's chronology in Tarzan Alive. *Valka is an Atlantean god from Robert E. Howard's tales of King Kull. The comic book adaptation appears in Marvel Comics'* Tarzan *#1-8 and 10-11 by Roy Thomas and John Buscema. The invocation to Valka is in #3.*

December
THE TERROR OF FU MANCHU

Dr. Fu Manchu returns, and Dr. Petrie teams with master detective M. Gaston Max in Paris. Inspector Dunbar also appears. Max refers to the recent case in which he was involved, that of the Yellow Claw. The events of the *Titanic* sinking, with the nefarious arch-criminal Fantômas aboard, are also mentioned. The Vampires gang of Paris appears.

Novel by Dr. Petrie, edited by William Patrick Maynard, Black Coat Press, 2009, continuing the depredations of Sax Rohmer's Fu Manchu. Gaston Max and Inspector Dunbar are from Rohmer's The Yellow Claw, The Golden Scorpion, and others. The Fantômas stories were recounted by Pierre Souvestre and Marcel Allain. The Vampires are from the 1915 French serial Les Vampires.

DIE VERGESSENE INSEL (THE FORGOTTEN ISLAND)
After a sixteen-year-old Anglo-Indian orphan, Mike Kamala, is abducted, he travels the Atlantic Ocean and learns he is the son of Captain Nemo. He also discovers the *Nautilus* hidden under a volcanic island in the West Indies.

The first in a series of juvenile German series novels, Operation Nautilus, by Wolfgang Hohlbein. Nemo is from Verne's 20,000 Leagues under the Sea, linking Kamala into the Crossover Universe.

1914

January-April
TEN YEARS BEYOND BAKER STREET
Sherlock Holmes versus Fu Manchu. Denis Nayland Smith, Dr. Petrie, and Dr. John Watson are also featured.
Novel by Dr. Petrie, edited by Cay Van Ash, Perennial Library, 1988.

Winter. The first known case of French private detective Marc Jordan. (*Marc Jordan*, pulp by Jules de Gastyne.)

Winter. Birth of Patricia Savage, Doc Savage's cousin.

Winter. Berry Pleydell's first recorded adventure, *The Brother of Daphne*, as told by Dornford Yates.

Winter
DAS MÄDCHEN VON ATLANTIS (THE GIRL FROM ATLANTIS)
Mike Kamala and his crew join with Professor Aronnax to explore Atlantis, from which Nemo had gotten at least some of his science.

An entry in Wolfgang Hohlbein's series of juvenile German novels, Operation Nautilus. Aronnax, from Verne's 20,000 Leagues under the Sea, *must by quite elderly.*

SKINNER'S SCHEME
Detective Ferrers Locke visits Greyfriars.

Story by Charles Hamilton in The Magnet Library *#360, January 2, 1915. Since the Greyfriars School exists in the CU, so does detective Ferrers Locke.*

GULLÅREN (THE VEIN OF GOLD)
International adventurer Jonas Fjeld and his American partner, Felix Leiter, fights crime in San Francisco and the Klondike.

Story by Øvre Richter Frich, 1915. Apparently Leiter worked for, or went on to work for, Pinkerton's, and even lost an arm and a leg in his adventures with Fjeld. In the first James Bond novel by Ian Fleming, Casino Royale, *Bond meets Felix Leiter, with whom he'll go on to work on many occasions. In a repeat of events that could only happen in the Crossover Universe, Leiter loses a leg and an arm in the second novel,* Live and Let Die, *thereafter going on to work for Pinkerton's. Perhaps Fjeld's Leiter is the grandfather of Bond's.*

TURKLERIN SHERLOCK HOLMESI AMANVERMEZ AVNI
Consulting detective Avni becomes known as "the Turkish Sherlock Holmes" after solving a particularly difficult case.

From Turklerin Sherlock Holmesi Amanvermez Avni *#1, 1914, written by Ebussureyya Sami. Nat Pinkerton and Avni also worked together, and saved each other's lives on a couple occasions.*

THE BLACKMAILERS
The teenaged telegram delivery boy Barney Cook is inspired to become a detective by reading about Nick Carter's adventures.

Short story by Harvey O'Higgins. The first in the Detective Barney series of short stories, this brings Detective Barney into the Crossover Universe.

April 23-June 27
MASKS OF THE ILLUMINATI
Sir John Babcock, a descendant of Maria Babcock, becomes involved in several secret societies and a mystery involving Aleister Crowley. Albert Einstein and James Joyce help him to solve it. Carl Jung and Lenin also appear. The

connection between the Babcocks and the Greystokes is mentioned again, and reference is made to a "Mr. P.J. Farmer, genealogist."

Novel by Robert Anton Wilson in the Illuminatus! *cycle. Sir John Babcock returns in the* Schrödinger's Cat *trilogy. However, this trilogy takes place across a large number of closely related alternate universes, and the one he appears in does not seem to be the same one in which* Illuminatus! *takes place.*

May. Richard Hannay's first adventure, *The Thirty-Nine Steps*, as told by Hannay and writer John Buchan. Hannay's further exploits were recorded in *Greenmantle* (1916), *Mr. Standfast* (1919), *The Three Hostages* (1924), and *The Island of Sheep* (U.S. title *The Man from Norlands*, 1936). It should be observed that most, if not all, of Buchan's works take place in a shared "John Buchan universe," and therefore also occur in the Crossover Universe.

May
YOUNG INDIANA JONES AND THE GYPSY REVENGE
Indy is traveling in France, where he encounters the descendants of the Man in the Iron Mask, who have secretly ruled the Marseilles criminal underworld since at least 1814. The current patriarch of the family wears an iron mask to inspire fear.

Young adult novel by Les Martin, Random House, 1991. This tale is a crossover with Alexandre Dumas' The Man in the Iron Mask. *According to Rick Lai, "Supposedly, Philippe from Dumas' novel had a son before he was imprisoned with the iron mask in the conclusion of the book. This son was the forebear of a lost branch of the Bourbon family. Perhaps the various men impersonating Louis XVII in Paul Féval's Black Coat novels were descended from the son of the Man in the Iron Mask."*

May 26. John "Korak" Drummond-Clayton marries Meriem (Jeanne Jacot) following events of *The Son of Tarzan*. Meriem's parents are General Armand Jacot and Suzanne Fogg. Suzanne Fogg is the daughter of Phileas Fogg.

June-July. Brother and sister Barney and Victoria Custer of Beatrice, Nebraska, visit the Greystokes in Kenya, as related by Edgar Rice Burroughs in *The Eternal Lover* (aka *The Eternal Savage*).

Summer. Swedish gentleman thief Filip Collin's first exploit. (*The London Adventures of Mr. Collin* by Frank Heller.)

Summer. Birth of Lieutenant Timothy Trant, New York homicide detective in tales recounted by Q. Patrick.

Summer
THE MAN IN THE BLACK SUIT
There are references to Castle Rock, Maine, and environs.
Short story by Stephen King, found in the collection Everything's Eventual.

THE MYSTERY OF THE HINDU TEMPLE
Detective-Inspector Will Spearing enlists the help of Sexton Blake's assistants Tinker and Pedro.
This two-part story in The Pluck Library *#554-555 (June 12 and June 19, 1915), brings Detective-Inspector Spearing into the Crossover Universe. Mark Hodder notes that Spearing also fought the criminal Laban Creed, who later battled Sexton Blake, and that in Spearing's later adventures in Pluck, Blake and Tinker make further guest appearances. Jess Nevins adds that starting in 1913, the Will Spearing stories were reprinted in the Netherlands, in the magazine* De Avonturen van W. Spearing, Politie-Detectief.

THE HOUSE OF MYSTERY
Detective-Inspector Will Spearing works with Detective-Sergeant Plummer

Story in The Pluck Library *#561, July 31, 1915, linking Detective-Sergeant Plummer into the Crossover Universe.*

July 1914. Mrs. Clayton and daughter Charlotte visit Virginia Scott and her mother, as told by Edgar Rice Burroughs in *The Man-Eater.*

July-August. Barney Custer's continued adventure in Lutha, as told in *The Mad King, Part II* ("Barney Custer of Beatrice," *All-Story Weekly*, August 7, 14, and 21, 1915) by Edgar Rice Burroughs.

August 1914-1918. Rittmeister Hans von Hammer, the deadliest German pilot of World War I, called the "Enemy Ace," guides his Fokker Dr.1 to more than 70 kills during the course of the Great War.

August. Holmes runs the German

spy Von Bork to ground in *"His Last Bow."*

August 1914-1918. Casca: The Trench Soldier: Casca fights with British forces in World War I. He is captured by the Germans and meets Manfred von Richthofen and another German air ace, Max Immelmann. (Novel by Barry Sadler. Holmes and Watson also met von Richthofen.)

Autumn. The events of C.S. Forester's *The African Queen.*

December 1914-January 1, 1915. Holmes and Watson embark on a mission behind enemy lines and again encounter Irene Adler's daughter, Nina Vassilievna, as well as Lieutenant Manfred von Richthofen. (*Hellbirds,* a novel by Watson, ed. by Austin Mitchelson and Nicholas Utechin. The reports of the death of the German spy Von Bork must be highly exaggerated, given his appearance in *The Adventure of the Peerless Peer.* Casca, the Eternal Mercenary, also met Von Richthofen.)

1915

Winter
THE EVIL EYE

Chicago detective Jimmie Lavender refers to Sherlock Holmes thusly: "How the detectives of London must jostle in the streets! From Holmes to the latest amateur is a far cry. And New York is as bad or worse. Here in Chicago, I am less handicapped by competition."

The first story in the Jimmie Lavender series narrated by Charles "Gilly" Gilruth, edited by Vincent Starrett, in Adventure Tales #1, *John Gregory Betancourt, ed., Wildside Press, Winter 2004-2005. Holmes is referred to as a real person, placing Lavender in the CU.*

Winter. Birth of Kit Walker, the 20th Phantom.
Winter. Birth of Ikano Kato.
April. The first meeting of Sherlock Holmes and Mary Russell, as related in *The Beekeeper's Apprentice* by Mary Russell Holmes, edited by Laurie R. King.

April-May. The events of *The Lusitania Murders*, as related by "S.S. Van Dine" (Willard Huntington Wright) and edited by Max Allan Collins. Van Dine teams with Pinkerton detective Philomina Vance (perhaps the sister of Philo Vance), whose murder cases Van Dine would chronicle in ensuing years.

Spring
THE GOLDEN SCORPION

French investigator Gaston Max foils the schemes of The Golden Scorpion, a henchman of Fu Manchu, who makes an unnamed appearance during the case.

The novel by Sax Rohmer places Gaston Max in the CU.

May 7
NIGHTMARE IN WAX
During the Great War, three high-ranking British officials call upon Dr. Watson to identify the voices upon a phonograph recording found in government archives. The wax cylinders were narrated by Professor James Moriarty on November 1, 1903. In the recording, Moriarty gloats that after twenty-five years of searching, he has located a copy of the *Necronomicon*. He also refers to Old Ones such as Cthulhu, Dagon, Shub-Niggurath, Y'golonac, and Daoloth. Moriarty attempts to summon the Old Ones, but his scheme backfires. The recording continues with Holmes revealing himself and taking possession of the *Necronomicon*. On November 3, 1903, Holmes narrates that Moriarty escaped, and there the recording ends. Disturbed, Watson recalls a phone call from Holmes three weeks prior, saying that Moriarty had come into possession of the *Necronomicon* once again.

A short story by Simon Clark in the Lovecraftian anthology Shadows Over Baker Street. *This story reveals that the first Professor Moriarty did not die during the events of* The Earthquake Machine *after all.*

May
SON OF HOLMES
Auguste Lupa (later to be known by the name Nero Wolfe) is established as Sherlock Holmes' son. Dr. Watson is also featured. This novel also reveals that Sherlock's brother Mycroft Holmes was the first "M," and, as such, was the predecessor of Admiral Sir Miles Messervy, who was the head of the British Secret Service M.I.6 and was James Bond's chief from the 1950s until his replacement in 1995.

This novel by John T. Lescroart firmly establishes that Sherlock Holmes, Nero Wolfe and James Bond are all part of the Crossover Universe. The publisher is Donald I. Fine, Inc., 1986.

Summer
BEN WILSON CONTRO SHERLOCK HOLMES
New York policeman Ben Wilson has a friendly competition with Sherlock Holmes.

Issue of Le Avventure del Poliziotto Americano Ben Wilson *by Ventura Almanzi, 1916.*

September 12. Birth of Mortimer Death, mortician and amateur criminologist in cases told by Ken Crossen.

Autumn
THE MAN FROM CHINATOWN

A Greyfriars student is kidnapped, and detective Ferrers Locke sets out to rescue him.

Story by Charles Hamilton in The Magnet Library *#795, 1923. Detective Ferrers Locke was also related to Dr. Locke, the Headmaster at Greyfriars.*

NIGHT'S CHILDREN

In Paris, under orders from the Great Vampire to steal Edvard Munch's painting Vampire , Irma Vep runs afoul of the very real vampire Count Orlock.

Short story by Steven A. Roman in Tales of the Shadowmen Volume 4: Lords of Terror, *Jean-Marc and Randy Lofficier, eds., Black Coat Press, 2008; reprinted in French in* Les Compagnons de l'Ombre (Tome 4), *Jean-Marc and Randy Lofficier, eds., Rivière Blanche, 2009. Irma Vep, a member of the Vampires gang, is from the 1915 French serial* Les Vampires. *Count Orlock is from Henrik Galeen and F.W. Murnau's 1922 German film* Nosferatu.

PICK WILL, EL DETECTIVE PEQUEÑO

"Pick Will," a clever English boy detective, becomes the assistant to Sherlock Holmes.

From Pick Will, El Detective Pequeño *#1-30, 1916-1917, by "Eleme" (Luis Millà)*

1916

January
PENUMBRA

Dr. Wayne and his wife Martha of Gotham City are on an extended honeymoon. In Paris, Wayne consults with the evil banker Favraux about European investments. Intrepid reporter Philippe Guérande of *Le Mondial* has been writing about the infamous gang, the Vampires, the murder of Inspector Dural, and a figure clad in skin-tight black. Wayne wants to put up the famed Gotham Girasol, mined from the Xinca region of Guatemala, as temporary collateral in his financial dealings with Favraux, but the gem has been stolen. Another criminal named Moreno is mentioned, as is Fantômas. Judex disguises himself as Favraux's secretary, Vallières. "Celeritas" Ribaudet, Rouletabille, the Nyctalope, and Cigale Mystère are also mentioned. The aviator Allard, in jail for an attempted burglary, refers to a Russian relative named Major Kentov and also mentions a cabaret called the Veuve Joyeuse. Mrs. Wayne reveals her brief affair with the dashing aviator Allard to Judex, and that she is now with child.

Short story by Chris Roberson in Tales of the Shadowmen Volume 1: The Modern Babylon, Jean-Marc and Randy Lofficier, eds., Black Coat Press, 2005; reprinted in French in Les Compagnons de l'Ombre (Tome 1), Jean-Marc and Randy Lofficier, eds., Rivière Blanche, 2008. Dr. Wayne and his wife are the future parents of Bruce Wayne, who will grow up to don cape and cowl as the vigilante Batman. The banker Favraux and Judex are from the 1916-1917 French serial Judex. Philippe Guérande, Le Mondial, Moreno, and the late Inspector Dural are from the 1915 French serial Les Vampires. The black-clad figure is the infamous villainess Irma Vep, also from Les Vampires. "Celeritas" Ribaudet is the founder of the Celeritas Detective Agency who has died just before Judex begins. Various other references in "Penumbra" confirm that it takes place concurrently with the events depicted in Les Vampires. The girasol is the gem that will later adorn the finger of the cloaked vigilante known as The Shadow. The Xinca region takes its name from the Xinca Indians, with whom Kent Allard (The Shadow) would spend time in the 1920s. Allard's relative Kentov refers to the alias Allard used in Farmer and Watson's The Adventure of the Peerless Peer ("Colonel Kentov"). Fantômas' tales were told by Pierre Souvestre and Marcel Allain. Rouletabille is the detective Joseph Josephin. Cigale Mystère is the adapted son of the Hindu mystic Docteur Mystère, whose tales were told by Paul d'Ivoi (Paul Deleutre). Italian comics stories later revealed that Cigale Mystère was the ancestor of Martin Mystère. This reference incorporates the extended Mystère family into the CU, although not all the stories fall into CU continuity. The Nyctalope' stories were told by Jean de La Hire. The Veuve Joyeuse is from the 1934 French film La Veuve Joyeuse, filmed simultaneously in English as The Merry Widow. The implication of Mrs. Wayne's affair with Allard is that Bruce Wayne (The Batman) might be the illegitimate son of The Shadow, but the paternity is never firmly established. In any event, this may explain The Shadow's ongoing interest in Wayne from the late 1920s through the mid 1950s, as seen in several comic book crossovers.

LOST AND FOUND

Judex, in the guise of Favraux's secretary, Vallières, meets with Kaspar Gutman, and then tips off the Vampires gang about the shipment of a falcon statue.

Short story by Jean-Marc Lofficier (accompanying art by Fernando Calvi) in Tales of the Shadowmen Volume 2: Gentlemen of the Night, *Jean-Marc and Randy Lofficier, eds., Black Coat Press, 2006; reprinted in French in* Les Compagnons de l'Ombre (Tome 1), *Jean-Marc and Randy Lofficier, eds., Rivière Blanche, 2008; and in the Lofficiers' collection* Pacifica, *Black Coat Press, 2010. Kaspar Gutman and the falcon statue are from Dashiell Hammett's* The Maltese Falcon. *Judex is from the titular French serial. The Vampires gang is from the French serial* Les Vampires.

Late January 1916-1918. Kent Allard, the man who will become The Shadow, is using the name Colonel Kentov (also known as The Black Eagle), and is a great World War I aviator and spy in the service of the Czar.

February-June
THE ADVENTURE OF THE PEERLESS PEER

Featured characters are Sherlock Holmes, Dr. Watson, the German spy Von Bork, Tarzan, The Shadow (Colonel Kentov), Mycroft Holmes, Dr. Gideon Fell, Henry Merrivale, and G-8 (Wentworth). Leftenant John "Korak" Drummond and Lord John Roxton are mentioned. Tarzan, Holmes, and Watson locate the lost land of Zu-Vendis, last visited by Allan Quatermain, Sir Henry Curtis, Captain John Good, and the Zulu warrior Umslopogaas. Watson brings Nylepthah, Curtis' daughter, back to England and marries her.

Novel written by John H. Watson, M.D., edited by Philip José Farmer, hardback published by Aspen Press, 1974; paperback by Dell, 1976; reprinted in Venus on the Half-Shell and Others, *Christopher Paul Carey, ed., Subterranean Press, 2008. Most characters are referred to by name; The Shadow and G-8 are not. Allan Quatermain is the protagonist of H. Rider Haggard's novels* King Solomon's Mines, Allan Quatermain, *and* She and Allan. *G-8 is a another great pulp hero, a World War I aviator and spy. For more information on The Shadow, see* The Shadow Scrapbook

by Walter B. Gibson, HBJ, 1979, and The Duende History of the Shadow Magazine *by Will Murray (author of the continued Doc Savage novels), Odyssey Publications, 1980.* Peerless Peer *also brings in Carter Dickson's (pseudonym for John Dickson Carr) detective Sir Henry Merrivale. Gideon Fell is already in the CU. Rick Lai notes that according to Farmer, "Watson married the granddaughter of Curtis and Good in 1916. The Zu-Vendis brides of those two Englishmen could only have given birth to children no earlier than 1887. This means that the parents of Watson's wife had a child when they were both about fifteen years old, and Watson may have married a fourteen-year old girl. Maybe the Zu-Vendis language was misunderstood by Tarzan and Holmes, and Watson's wife was only the daughter of Curtis or Good." Curtis is a more likely candidate since Haggard never mentioned Captain Good marrying. For an explanation as to how Farmer's alternate version of this story,* The Adventure of the Three Madmen, *can also occur within the same continuity, please read Dennis E. Power's "Jungle Brothers, Or, Secrets of the Jungle Lords" in* Myths for the Modern Age: Philip José Farmer's Wold Newton Universe*).*

February. Young Indiana Jones is living in Princeton, New Jersey with his father and meets Thomas Edison. ("Princeton, February 1916: Race to Danger," television episode of *The Young Indiana Jones Chronicles* and its young adult novelization. Tarzan met Edison back in 1909.)

Winter. The first known adventures of Swedish newspaper reporter Maurice Wallion. (*The Blue Trail* by Julius Pettersson.)

Winter
THE BROKEN FANG
Occult detective Arnold Rhymer, quoting his mentor, a famous detective, states, "Well, when you have worn out the possible, whatever is left, however impossible, comes mighty near the truth."
Story by "Uel Key," pseudonym of Samuel Whittell Key, in Pearson's Magazine, *1917. The famous detective is, of course, Holmes.*

TRAUMA
In Paris, young Britt Reid witnesses the brutal murder of Prince Vladimir by Fantômas, and is interviewed by police Inspector Maigret.
Short story by Bill Cunningham in Tales of the Shadowmen Volume 2: Gentlemen of the Night, *Jean-Marc and Randy Lofficier, eds., Black Coat Press, 2006; reprinted in French in* Les Compagnons de l'Ombre (Tome 1), *Jean-Marc and Randy Lofficier, eds., Rivière Blanche, 2008. This incident instigated Britt to take on the mantle of The Green Hornet in the 1930s. Fantômas and Prince Vladimir are from the stories by Marcel Allain and Pierre Souvestre.*

April-June. Events of the French serial *Judex*.

May. Indiana Jones meets Winston Churchill. ("London, May 1916," episode of the television program *The Young Indiana Jones Chronicles.* Sherlock Holmes knew Churchill (see *The Earthquake Machine*), further cementing Jones' place in the Crossover Universe.)

Summer. Kal-L is born on the planet Krypton.

Summer
THE BOUNDER ON THE TRAIL!
The detective Ferrers Locke trails the second-story man Mr. Lamb, aka "Slim Jim," to the Greyfriars School.

Story in The Magnet Library *volume 16, #1666, January 20, 1940, written by Charles Hamilton. This confirms Ferrers Locke in the CU.*

DOGFIGHT DONOVAN'S DAY OFF
British pilot Dick Donovan meets German ace Gerhardt von Bek.

A short story by Michael Moorcock in the anthology Adventure, Vol. 1, *Chris Roberson, editor, MonkeyBrain Books, 2005. Members of the Von Bek family are sometimes incarnated as the Eternal Champion in Moorcock's ongoing saga which spans the Multiverse.*

Summer 1916-1917. The events of Burroughs' Caspak trilogy: *The Land That Time Forgot, The People That Time Forgot,* and *Out of Time's Abyss.*

July. Hercule Poirot's first recorded case, *The Mysterious Affair at Styles* by Agatha Christie.

October. Birth of Bruce Wayne.

October 1916-January 1917
RASPUTIN'S REVENGE: THE FURTHER STARTLING ADVENTURES OF AUGUSTE LUPA, SON OF HOLMES
Featured are Auguste Lupa (Nero Wolfe), Sherlock Holmes, and Dr. Watson. Rasputin is revealed to have been the son of the first Professor James Moriarty.

John T. Lescroart's *sequel to* Son of Holmes, *published by Donald I. Fine, Inc., 1987. Establishes Rasputin as a member of the Wold Newton Family through his relationship with Moriarty.*

November
THE BLACK FOREST

In WW I Europe, the Frankenstein Creature has been discovered in the Arctic by a German sub. British Intelligence has temporarily set up headquarters in the Chateau Meinster. The Germans get an English occult expert, Dr. Dye, to control the Monster, and Dye sets about creating an army of Monsters based on Frankenstein's process. However, Dye is missing one key component and needs to get to Castle Frankenstein in Switzerland to get the original notebooks of Victor Frankenstein. American pilot Jack Shannon and British occultist/stage magician Archie Caldwell are also in a race to Castle Frankenstein to stop Dye from getting the notebooks. As they get close to the Castle, they pass a sign labeled "Vasaria." The nosferatu Graf Orlock also appears.

Graphic novel by Todd Livingston, Robert Tinnell, and Neil Vokes, Image Comics, March 2004. This is the original Frankenstein creature, last seen battling Judex in Paris in 1912, and not to be seen again until the late 1990s in Don Glut's novels. We can hypothesize that he was taken from the Arctic by the Germans, and then somehow made his way back to the Arctic after these events, to be found by Dr. Burt Winslow in the late 1990s. Chateau Meinster is from Hammer's Brides of Dracula. *Graf von Orlock is from the 1922 German film* Nosferatu. *Vasaria is from Universal's Frankenstein films, although from this tale we can conclude it is near the original Dr. Frankenstein's castle in Switzerland. A sequel,* The Black Forest 2: Castle of Shadows, *takes place immediately after* The Black Forest.

December 2. Birth of Titus Crow in London.

December. Immortal Duncan MacLeod is sent on a mission by Lawrence of Arabia. (*Scimitar*, a *Highlander* novel. Indiana Jones also knew Lawrence of Arabia.)

1917

January. Krypton blows up and Kal-L is sent to Earth in warp capsule. He is discovered and adopted by the Kents, who name him Clark Kent and keep his alien origins a secret.

January 29. Birth of Scott Jordan, attorney at law and amateur detective in cases chronicled by Harold Q. Masur.

March-April. Watson's literary agent, Sir Arthur Conan Doyle, undertakes a critical espionage mission during the Great War. During the course of his adventure, he meets an agent-for-hire called "The Hairless Mexican." (*The Demon Device,* a novel by Arthur Conan Doyle, as communicated to Robert Saffron. The Hairless Mexican is from Somerset Maugham's *Ashenden, or The British Agent.*)

March
THREE MEN, A MARTIAN, AND A BABY
Dr. Omega, his new companion Denis, their mechanic Fred, and their Martian cohort Tiziraou are aboard Omega's ship, the *Cosmos*, when it crashes on the Moon. There, they discover that they collided with a rocket ship carrying a small baby, who is incredibly strong. Verifying that the rocket ship's original destination was Earth, they send it and its occupant safely on its way, only to come under attack by the Moon's inhabitants, the Selenites.
Short story by Travis Hiltz in Tales of the Shadowmen Volume 4: Lords of Terror, *Jean-Marc and Randy Lofficier, eds., Black Coat Press, 2008; reprinted in French in* Les Compagnons de l'Ombre (Tome 2), *Jean-Marc and Randy Lofficier, eds., Rivière Blanche, 2008. Dr. Omega and Tiziraou are from Arnould Galopin's* Doctor Omega. *The baby is Kal-L, late of the planet Krypton. The Selenites are from H.G. Wells'* The First Men in the Moon.

April 5. Birth of Robert Blake, whose exploits were recorded by H.P. Lovecraft. Blake's grandmother is Jill Fagin, whose great-great grandfather was Fagin from Oliver Twist. Blake was also a great-nephew of Phileas Fogg.

April 1917-November 1918. The aerial combat adventures of G-8 and His Battle Aces. G-8 is the full brother of Kent Allard (The Shadow) and half-brother of Richard Wentworth (The Spider). Other notable Great War aces are The Red Falcon (Barry Rand), Smoke Wade, and Sky Wolf (Bill Kennedy).

May. Indiana Jones meets Pablo Picasso again. ("Spain, May 1917," episode of *The Young Indiana Jones Chronicles.*)

Spring
THE CASE OF THE TWO FINANCIERS; OR, THE MYSTERY MILLIONAIRE
Sexton Blake and Tinker team up with Ferrers Lord, the "Mad Millionaire."
Story in Union Jack *#742, December 29, 1917.*

June-September
SHERLOCK HOLMES IN THE LOST WORLD

Sherlock Holmes and Dr. John Watson are recruited to join Lord John Roxton on an expedition to locate Professor Challenger, who returned to the Lost World almost two years previous. They are joined by the Professor's daughter, Professor Jessica Cuvier Challenger, and encounter the notorious Colonel Sebastian Moran, who meets his end. Roxton ruminates about his son Richard, fighting for the Americans in the Great War.

Story by Martin Powell in Gaslight Grimoire, *J.R. Campbell and Charles Prepolec, eds., Edge Science Fiction and Fantasy Publishing, 2008. Of course, Moran somehow survives; according to Kim Newman's "The Man Who Got Off the Ghost Train," he finally is killed in 1935. Roxton's son Richard is Richard Wentworth, The Spider, per Philip José Farmer's Wold Newton Family genealogy.*

Summer. The first recorded exploit of gentleman thief the Gray Phantom. ("Seven Signs," from the *Gray Phantom* series by Herman Landon.)

July 9. Steve Rogers, the future Captain America, is born.

Summer. The Continental Op first encounters the Whosis Kid in Boston. After a stint in the Army during the Great War, the Op rejoins the Continental Detective Agency in Chicago for a couple years, before ultimately being transferred to San Francisco. (Dashiell Hammett's "The Whosis Kid," collected in *The Continental Op*.)

Summer 1917-1918. Dr. Clark Savage, Sr., and Hareton Ironcastle mount a second expedition to The Lost World discovered by Professor Challenger and Lord John Roxton.

Summer
THE MYSTERY OF THE STANDARD SHIPS
   Sexton Blake and Ferrers Lord work together again.
   Story in Union Jack *#744, January 12, 1918.*

THE INVISIBLE PATROL
   The Red Falcon is aided by fellow fliers Smoke Wade and Bill Dawe, the Sky Devil.

Story in Dare-Devil Aces, *December 1933 by Robert J. Hogan; reprinted in* The Red Falcon: The Dare-Devil Aces Years, Volume 2, *edited by Bill Mann, Age of Aces Books, 2007. The tale adds Smoke Wade and Bill Dawe to the Crossover Universe.*

DOPE

Chief inspector Red Kerry of the C.I.D. fights against Sin Sin Wa (alias Mr. Sin), who leads a drug syndicate.

Novel by Sax Rohmer, 1919. As will be shown in a later entry, Red Kerry is in the CU, and therefore so is Mr. Sin.

THE AFFAIR OF THE PREMIUM BONDS

Sexton Blake and Ferrers Lord join forces once more.
Story in Union Jack #749, *February 16, 1918.*

DYNAMITE CARGO

General Fuller calls The Red Falcon to Paris and offers him a pardon with a place back in the service and a commission of Colonel. The General mentions that he's had good reports about The Falcon's work against the enemy from Smoke Wade, G-8, and the ace called Sky Wolf. G-8 makes a brief appearance and helps The Falcon and Sika escape.

Story in Dare-Devil Aces, *January 1935 by Robert J. Hogan; reprinted in* The Red Falcon: The Dare-Devil Aces Years, Volume 1, *edited by Bill Mann, Age of Aces Books, 2007. The Red Falcon, an air ace, also appeared several times in* G-8 and His Battle Aces. *He had been sentenced to a firing squad several months before this story takes place, for crimes he didn't commit. Later in the War, the Allies once more offered a pardon to The Red Falcon, in a story entitled "Flight of the Vultures." Smoke Wade was another air ace whose adventures where chronicled by Robert J. Hogan in the pages of* G-8 and His Battle Aces, Battle Birds, *and* Dare-Devil Aces. *The Sky Wolf was an air ace named Bill Kennedy. He appeared in tales by Harold Cruickshank in the pulp magazines* Dare-Devil Aces, G-8 and His Battle Aces, *and* Battle Aces *from 1931 through 1943. This Sky Wolf should not be confused with the almost-namesake character Skywolf who appeared in Hillman Comics and Eclipse Comics, alongside other characters such as Airboy and The Heap. Since G-8 is in the Crossover Universe via Farmer's* Doc Savage: His Apocalyptic Life, *The Red Falcon, Smoke Wade, and the Sky Wolf are also in the CU.*

FANTÔMAS IN AMERICA

An NYPD detective named Frederick Dickson appears.

Novel by David White, Black Coat Press, 2007. The novel is based on the 1920 American Fantômas serial written by Edward Sedwick and George Eshenfelder for the Fox Film Corporation. Dickson is a cousin to detective Harry Dickson.

FOR POLITICAL REASONS; OR, THE CASE OF THE KIDNAPPED PRINCE
Sexton Blake and Ferrers Lord collaborate yet again.
Story in Union Jack #757, April 13, 1918.

September-November
THE FIRES OF FU MANCHU
Drug dealer Joseph Malaglou is killed by the Si-Fan.
Novel by Dr. Petrie, edited by Cay Van Ash. Joseph Malaglou is a character in Sax Rohmer's stories "The Lady of the Lattice" and "The Secret of Ismail." Rick Lai notes that "Both of the stories featuring Malaglou also feature Sheikh Ismail al As, who may be the same Sheikh Ismail from Daughter of Fu Manchu (although no Assassin connection in mentioned concerning Sheikh Ismail Ebn al As)." "The Lady of the Lattice" features another of Rohmer's series characters, Abu Tabah, a noble Egyptian who battles criminals. Lai continues: "There is also a connection between the Abu Tabah series and two other non-series thrillers by Rohmer set in Egypt; one of the Abu Tabah stories, 'The Death-Ring of Sneferu,' features a character named Hassan es-Sugra, an Egyptian who is often employed in archaeological expeditions. He also appears as a supporting character in She Who Sleeps *and* The Bat Flies Low."

Autumn. Birth of Mike Hammer.
November. Birth of --- Watson, son of Dr. John Watson and Nylepthah (*The Peerless Peer*).

Autumn
A DEAD MAN'S HATE
Sexton Blake and Ferrers Lord team up one more time, this time at the Calcroft School, where Tinker was educated.
Story in Union Jack #760, May 4, 1918.

A GOLDEN STRATAGEM
Sexton Blake and Ferrers Lord join forces for the final time this year.
Story in Union Jack *#765, June 8, 1918. It was a banner year for Blake-Lord crossovers.*

THE MOUNT STONHAM MURDER MYSTERY; OR, THE CASE OF THE MYSTERIOUS HUNCHBACK
Sexton Blake and Nelson Lee team up again, in another of several collaborations.
Story written by Edward Searles Brooks, Union Jack *#768, June 29, 1918.*

FANGS OF THE SKY LEOPARD
G-8 calls on The Red Falcon's services at the very end of this adventure. After The Falcon and his aide, the giant African Sika, help out G-8, they fly back to their aerie high in the Vosges Mountains.
G-8 and His Battle Aces, *March 1937, by Robert J. Hogan; reprinted in G-8 #7, Berkley Books, 1965.*

THE MYSTIC CYPHER; OR, THE LONE HOUSE IN THE FOREST
THE DUAL DETECTIVES
THE FLASHLIGHT CLUE
THE CASE OF THE AMERICAN SOLDIER
Sexton Blake and Nelson Lee join forces and collaborate on four cases.
Stories written by Edward Searles Brooks, Union Jack *#771, July 20, 1918;* Union Jack *#774, August 10, 1918;* Union Jack *#777, August 31, 1918; and* Union Jack *#781, September 28, 1918.*

1918

January
TRANSYLVANIA, JANUARY 1918
Indy encounters the vampire called Vlad the Impaler, otherwise known as Count Dracula, and apparently kills him.
Television episode of The Young Indiana Jones Chronicles. *Zorro, Sherlock Holmes, and other inhabitants of the Crossover Universe also had encounters with Dracula, many of whom were also under the mi-stake-n impression that the Lord of the Vampires was dead at the conclusion of their encounters. Please see Chuck Loridans' full account of the history of Count Dracula in the CU, on the MONSTAAH website.*

Winter. Birth of Paul Janus "Kickaha" Finnegan.

Winter
THE CROOKS OF RAPID HOLLOW
THE TERROR OF TREVIS WOLD
THE STUDDED FOOTPRINTS; OR, THE CLUE OF THE BLUE DUST
THE CASE OF THE HOLLOW DAGGER
WALDO THE WONDER MAN

Sexton Blake and Nelson Lee team up again for a series of cases, culminating in the capture of Rupert Waldo, better known as "Waldo the Wonder Man."

Stories written by Edward Searles Brooks, Union Jack *#784, October 19, 1918;* Union Jack *#786, November 2, 1918;* Union Jack *#788, November 16, 1918;* Union Jack *#793, December 21, 1918; and* Union Jack *#794, December 28, 1918. Jess Nevins writes, "The pair were actually best friends and members of the same club, with Blake and his assistant Tinker paying a visit to Lee and Nipper at St. Frank's on two occasions. Lee even took on one of Blake's enemies. Dr. Huxton Rymer, an adventurer and insane surgeon, customarily fought Blake, but in three stories in 1920 Rymer challenged Lee." While it should be noted that the crossovers between Blake, Lee, and their villains continued throughout the early 1920s, enough of the team-ups have been documented here to provide a flavor of this rich, intertextual universe.*

FLIGHT OF THE VULTURES

The Red Falcon and Sika are summoned to Paris by the General of the American forces to receive full pardons and Congressional Medals of Honor. Through a series of circumstances, The Red Falcon ends up being framed again. He is arrested instead of honored. The Falcon escapes with a bit of help from G-8, and goes on to defeat the plot. However, the Allied forces still believe he is a traitor, and so he never receives his pardon. In the end, The Red Falcon tells Sika, "What do we care whether they know…[that we are innocent]…or not? We know it and G-8 knows it, and that's all I care about."

A short story by Robert J. Hogan in Dare-Devil Aces, *January 1938; reprinted in* The Red Falcon: The Dare-Devil Aces Years, Volume 4, *edited by Bill Mann, Age of Aces Books, 2008. The Red Falcon is "An American flyer who had been framed in the past by his own pals, he had escaped a firing squad to hide out in the rugged mountains and fight his own aerial war against war." Since it was apparently Rand who was framed in the past, and The Red Falcon who is called to be pardoned, it seems that the Allies know Rand and the Falcon are one and the same. If The Falcon was never pardoned at the end of the Great War, he would have been a man without a country. Perhaps he and Sika wandered Eurasia, finally ending up at K'un-L'un.*

March 31-July
ESCAPE FROM LOKI: DOC SAVAGE'S FIRST ADVENTURE

Clark "Doc" Savage, Jr., meets his friends and associates Ham Brooks, Monk Mayfair, Renny Renwick, Long Tom Roberts, and Johnny Littlejohn in the German prison camp Loki. A "worm unknown to science" is mentioned. Doc's tutor in mountain climbing, yoga, and self-defense, Dekka Lan Shan, is the grandfather of Peter the Brazen. A character named Benedict Murdstone also appears. Savage & Co. meet Abraham Cohen, who went on to gain membership in Jimmie Cordies' band of mercenaries, and an Allied prisoner named O'Brien, a soldier of Irish extraction. It is also mentioned that Doc Savage was trained by an aborigine, Writjitandel of the Wantella tribe. And Doc's Persian Sufi tutor is named Hajji Abdu el-Yezdi. Lili Bugov's father and brothers were Russian aristocrats, vicious exploiters who held manhunts. Bugov also has a huge Cossack servant.

*Novel by Philip José Farmer, Bantam Books, 1991. The "worm unknown to science" was first referred to in Watson's/Doyle's "The Problem of Thor Bridge," and was followed up on in Harry "Bunny" Manders' Raffles tale (edited by Philip José Farmer), "The Problem of the Sore Bridge—Among Others." Christopher Paul Carey demonstrated the worm's connection to the Cthulhu Mythos in "The Green Eyes Have It—Or Are They Blue? or Another Case of Identity Recased" (*Myths for the Modern Age: Philip José Farmer's Wold Newton Universe, MonkeyBrain Books, 2005*). Peter the Brazen, aka Peter Moore, was an adventurer in pulp stories written by George Worts. Of Peter the Brazen, scholar Rick Lai adds, "One of Worts' Gillian Hazeltine stories mentions a ship, The King of Asia, which also appears in the Peter the Brazen stories. Worts' Singapore Sammy story, 'South of Sulu,' mentions that Sammy was friendly with a jewel trader, De Sylva. This may be the same character as the jewel merchant, Dan de Sylva, who appears in a later Peter the Brazen story, 'The Octopus of Hongkong.'"*

Murdstone is related to the family which appears in Charles Dickens' David Copperfield. The story "The Most Dangerous Game" (1924) by Richard Connell features General Zaroff, a Russian aristocrat with a huge Cossack servant, who holds manhunts. Could Lili be the daughter of Zaroff? Perhaps Count Bugov changed his name to General Zaroff after fleeing the Russian Revolution. One possible contradiction is that the General implies the manhunt on the island is his first, but Zaroff could have lied about that. The Jimmie Cordie adventures by William Wirt are a series of twenty-one stories about a group of mercenaries in the Far East after the Great War. Rick Lai adds: "O'Brien is probably Jem O'Brien, ex-jockey, ex-convict, decorated soldier in the American army during World War I, and special assistant to the Scarlet Fox. Created by Eustace Hale Ball, the Scarlet Fox was a pulp hero who appeared in seven stories in Black Mask during 1923-24. The first six stories were published as a novel, The Scarlet Fox, in 1927."

In Arthur Upfield's novel about the Australian detective, Inspector Napoleon "Bony" Bonaparte, No Footprints in the Bush *(1940), a major character is Writjitandil (Farmer changed an "i" to an "e") of the Wantella tribe. Rick Lai writes again: "In an introduction to an edition of an Upfield novel which does not feature Bonaparte,* The House of Cain *(Dennis McMillan, 1983), Philip José Farmer speculated that Bonaparte was the illegitimate son of E.W. Hornung's A.J. Raffles. In Upfield's novels, Bonaparte is illegitimate son of an unnamed white man and an aborigine woman. Upfield's early novels suggest that Bonaparte was born in the late 1880s. Raffles was in Australia about that time according to Hornung's 'Le Premier Pas.'"*

Christopher Paul Carey points out, "Sir Richard Francis Burton (the real-life protagonist of Farmer's Riverworld series) wrote a curious book entitled The Kasîdah of Hâjî Abdû El-Yezdî. *At the time the volume was first published,*

Burton claimed to be merely the translator of the wise Sufi's work. However, the truth finally came out that Burton wrote it. While Haji Abdu El-Yezdi may be a fictional character in our world, we may only assume that he existed in flesh and blood in Farmer's mythos."

In "The Green Eyes Have It—Or Are They Blue? or Another Case of Identity Recased," Carey proposes that Captain Nemo, Professor Moriarty, Wolf Larsen, Baron von Hessel (Escape from Loki), Baron Karl (Fortress of Solitude), and Dr. Karl Linningen (Up from Earth's Center) are all the same person, and the evidence he gathers is vast. However, Moriarty's career beyond Reichenbach in the CU is well documented, which could argue against him being the same person as Wolf Larsen; see also the 1858 entry on the birth of the Larsens. (Interestingly, Dennis E. Power independently discovered the Moriarty-Larsen connection in his "Asian Detectives in the Wold Newton Family," although he proposed that it is a father-son relationship.) Nevertheless, there is nothing to argue against Wolf Larsen being the same person as Baron von Hessel and Baron Karl. In fact, Von Hessel, when revealing his age-delaying elixir to Doc, states that he was born in 1858, which is close enough to the hypothesized time frame for the birth of Larsen to be taken as accurate. That Von Hessel is actually Doc's grandfather makes the battle of wills and testing of young Clark in Escape from Loki all the more remarkable.

Spring. Master criminal Anthony Trent's first recorded exploit. (*Anthony Trent, Master Criminal* by Wyndham Martyn.)

Spring. Birth of Jim Burgess, police detective in cases told by W.T. Brannon.

Spring
GRUN-THE GREEN TERROR!
Herr Grun and Herr Doktor Krueger meet for the first time. Krueger gives Grun a new weapon to test, but it backfires in battle against G-8 and his boys. Grun is captured, but escapes, and having lost his memory, returns to Krueger's laboratory and destroys it before stumbling into Krueger's Einstein-Steinmetz-Edison time dislocator device. Moments later, Grun reappears, having regained his memory.

G-8 and His Battle Aces *one-shot by Chuck Dixon and Sam Glanzman, Blazing Comics, 1991. Grun and Krueger never met in the original G-8 pulps. This comic

is a "flip-book." The other side of the comic is The Spider's Web: Starring Web-Man *and tells the tale of Grun's sojourn in the modern era. In an unfinished sequel, Grun and Herr Krueger meet more villains, Herr Stahlmaske and Herr Razorfist. ("The Face of Time" in* Time Warrior #1, Blazing Comics, 1993). *Herr Stahlmaske was from the original G-8 pulps; Herr Razorfist was not.*

Summer
RED WINGS FOR THE DEATH PATROL
RED WINGS RAIDING
    G-8 and the ace, The Red Falcon, team up two more times.
    The first tale is by Robert J. Hogan, G-8 and His Battle Aces, *June 1940. The second was a story published in April 1944.*

    September-November. Clark Savage, Jr., meets his cousin, Lieutenant John "Korak" Drummond-Clayton, while flying during the Argonne operation.
    October. Just as his brother, Kent Allard, has been known by many different names (The Shadow, the Black Eagle, Kentov, etc.), so has the aviator and spy known as G-8, who has been going by the name Jim "Red" Albright. Near the end of the Great War, and shortly after the time of G-8's last recorded exploit, G-8 returns from a mission at the stroke of midnight and acquires the name "Captain Midnight."

Mid October
THE DARK HEART OF TIME: A TARZAN NOVEL
    Tarzan recalls his adventure with Sheeta the Leopard on Mount Kilimanjaro, and how the leopard's frozen carcass remains at the summit of Kilimanjaro. An old white trader named Horn is also mentioned.
    A novel by Philip José Farmer placing Ernest Hemingway's short story, "The Snows of Kilimanjaro," in the Crossover Universe. Alfred Aloysius "Trader" Horn was an African explorer and adventurer.

November 1918-August 1920
BEHOLD "THE NIGHT WIND"
    Katherine Harvard's trusted servant and protector, Julius, has a daughter named Rosabel who is close to graduating

from Tuskegee with honors.

Novel by Christopher R. Yates, Wildside Press, 2010. Katherine Harvard is the wife of Bingham "The Night Wind" Harvard. Rosabel is clearly the woman who later married Josh Newton. Rosabel Newton graduated from Tuskegee with honors. Rosabel and Josh Newton became trusted aides of Richard Henry Benson, otherwise known as The Avenger, in the pulp novel The Sky Walker *by "Kenneth Robeson" (Paul Ernst). This novel brings The Night Wind into the Crossover Universe. The original Night Wind novels were written by Varick Vanardy (pseudonym for Frederick Van Rensselaer Dey). They are* Alias "The Night Wind" *(1913),* The Return of "The Night Wind" *(1913),* The Night Wind's Promise *(1914), and* The Lady of "The Night Wind" *(1918).*

December 1918-May 1919
THE BEEKEEPER'S APPRENTICE, OR, ON THE SEGREGATION OF THE QUEEN

A "younger son of a Duke" is mentioned as one of Holmes' associates. The archvillain, Patricia Donleavy, a daughter of the first Professor Moriarty, is killed at the end of this case.

Autobiographical account by Mary Russell Holmes, edited by Laurie R. King. The events of O Jerusalem *occur during December-January of this time period. The "younger son of a Duke" is Lord Peter Wimsey. Patricia Donleavy is a half-sister of the daughter of Professor Moriarty that Philip José Farmer identified as Urania Moriarty.*

1919

Winter
JIMMY PINKERTON

Jimmy Pinkerton, Nat Pinkerton's son, becomes a private detective.
Jimmy Pinkerton, *1919.*

GWENDOLINE CARRS SALLSAMMA PROTOKOLL

Gwendoline Carr, claiming to be Sherlock Holmes' fourth cousin, begins solving crimes in Sweden.

From Eira Hellberg's Gwendoline Carrs Sallsamma Protokoll, *1919.*

HANS STARK DER FLIEGERTEUFEL

Hans Stark, a German teenager too young to have fought in the Great War, builds a technologically advanced airplane/submarine and uses it to adventure around the world. The source of the technology is mysterious, but ultimately derives from Captain Mors' spaceship.

Victoriana expert Jess Nevins notes that this crossover appeared in Hans Stark, the Flying Devil *#1, 1919. #1 contains more-or-less explicit hints that*

Mors was the creator of the technology which Stark uses to build his ship." Since Captain Mors is in the Crossover Universe, so too is young inventor Hans Stark. Art Bollmann proposes that Hans Stark later immigrated to the United States and is an ancestor of Tony Stark.

Winter. First recorded adventure of Captain Hugh "Bulldog" Drummond by H.C. "Sapper" McNeile (*Bulldog Drummond*). Later novels were written by Gerard Fairlie. Drummond's archenemy is the evil Carl Peterson.

Spring. Birth of future Justice Inc. agent Nellie Gray, the daughter of Tarzan and Jane.

Spring. Birth of Eel O'Brian.

Spring. Events of the film *The Son of Frankenstein*, featuring Baron Wolf von Frankenstein, the son of Dr. Henry Frankenstein.

April. Nine months after Doc Savage's escape from the prison camp Loki, a child is born to Lili Bugov, the Countess Idivzhopu. The child is raised as the son of Baron Karl von Hessel (Doc's grandfather, who will go by the moniker Baron Karl by the time of the Doc Savage novel *Fortress of Solitude*). However, given young Clark Savage's intimate encounter with the Countess Idivzhopu in July 1918, there can be little doubt as to the *true* parentage of this child, who will grow up to menace the world, not to mention his own hated father, as "John Sunlight."

Researcher Christopher Paul Carey, in his article "The Green Eyes Have It—Or Are They Blue? or Another Case of Identity Recased,*"* gathers and documents an incredible amount of evidence about the Countess, Von Hessel, and Doc's archenemy "John Sunlight." Mr. Carey concludes that John Sunlight is either Lili Bugov posing as a man, or that she underwent a sex-change operation to become Sunlight. Mr. Carey evocatively points out both Bugov's and Sunlight's unusually long fingers. Keeping in mind all the physical similarities between Bugov and Sunlight that Mr. Carey documents, as well as the behavioral differences, I am led to a different conclusion. I believe Sunlight is Lili Bugov's son.

However, if Sunlight were born in April of 1919, he would be only eighteen years old in August of 1937 (*Fortress of Solitude*). This could pose a problem, in terms of his believability as a villain. On the other hand, Baron von Hessel/Baron Karl has been mentoring him in the ways of evil for those eighteen years. And Doc made a believable hero at age sixteen, just as many other Wold Newton Family members started their careers early in life. It is stated, "He was not a young man..." but I believe this to be blatant misdirection on Lester Dent's part, in order to help Doc conceal the terrible secret of Sunlight's parentage. In short, Sunlight's age is not an insurmountable issue. (It is interesting to note that, based on textual evidence in *Fortress of Solitude*, Sunlight escaped from the Siberian gulag at approximately age sixteen or seventeen—the same age at which his father escaped from a similar inescapable prison camp.)

Further, I do not believe that Farmer would have noted the sexual encounter between Clark and Lili without reason. Sunlight, like Doc, emits a strange sound in times of excitement or stress, although Sunlight's takes the form of a low, evil growl, rather than Doc's cool, exotic trilling. Sunlight's inhuman strength, derived from unspecified sources, and his incredible stamina and will power, a result of his magnificent brain, are extensively described in *Fortress of Solitude*. The derivation of Sunlight's formidable intelligence is easily understood once it is revealed that he is of the Moriarty lineage, as well as that of the Savages-Claytons. In my estimation, the physical similarities between Countess Idivzhopu and Sunlight, coupled with Sunlight's Savage-like strength, vocal habits, and brain power, undoubtedly point to a familial relationship, one made possible by Doc's indiscretion with the Countess.

May. Dr. Lyndon Parker meets Solar Pons and agrees to share rooms at 7B Praed Street.

May. Indiana Jones is working as a translator with the American delegation at the peace talks in Paris, where he again encounters Lawrence of Arabia. (*"Paris, May 1919,"* television episode of *The Young Indiana Jones Chronicles*. Immortal Highlander Duncan MacLeod met Lawrence of Arabia in 1916.)

Spring
THE MISSING PROFESSOR
Nelson Lee, Nipper, and the "Black Wolf" battle Dr. Huxton Rymer.

Story in *The Prairie Library #51, April 2, 1920. Dr. Huxton Rymer was a recurring villain of Sexton Blake. The "Black Wolf," a costumed and masked vigilante, is revealed at story's end to be Buffalo Bill. Buffalo Bill would be long dead by now, so perhaps the Black Wolf was suffering from "FIS" (Famous Individual Syndrome).*

Summer. Following the Great War, Captain Henry Arthur Milton, late of the Royal Flying Corps, begins his vigilante career as the Ringer (Edgar Wallace's *The Gaunt Stranger*; U.S. title *The Ringer*).

Summer. Harry Dickson, the "American Sherlock Holmes," begins his consulting detective practice in London, in stories told by Jean Ray, and others.

Summer. First known adventure of gentleman thief Lord Stuart. (*Lord Stuart,*

The Great Adventurer, series by Ernst Pinkert.)

Summer. The Hands of Orlac (*Les Mains d'Orlac*) by Maurice Renard, in which a scientist replaces Orlac's hands with those of a killer.

July. Damian Adler, the third son of Sherlock Holmes and Irene Adler, succumbs to drug abuse. (As noted in *A Monstrous Regiment of Women* and *The Language of Bees* by Mary Russell Holmes, edited by Laurie R. King.)

Summer
KERRY'S KID
Zani Chada, a wealthy Eurasian, is arrested for kidnapping by Red Kerry, a British police official.

A short story by Sax Rohmer in Tales of Chinatown. *Chada's Limehouse residence figures in other interconnected tales by Rohmer.*

EL MARIDO DE LA SEÑORITA SUTTER
At the invitation of the Chilean detective Román Calvo, Sherlock Holmes and Dr. Watson travel to Santiago, Chile, and help Calvo solve the disappearance of a local engineer.

Short story by Alberto Edwards in Pacifico Magazine. *This brings Román Calvo, the Chilean Sherlock Holmes, into the Crossover Universe.*

September-October. The Arcanum: Sir Arthur Conan Doyle, Harry Houdini, Marie Laveau, and H.P. Lovecraft battle occult forces. Aleister Crowley also appears, and there are several references to the Cthulhu Mythos. (Novel by Thomas Wheeler, Bantam Books, May 2004. These are not the "real" Houdini, Lovecraft, Laveau, Doyle, and Crowley of "our" universe, but rather the versions of them that exist in the Crossover Universe.)

Autumn
FRED PINKERTON, AMERIKAS MEISTERDETEKTIV
Fred Pinkerton, son of Nat and brother of Jimmy, begins his career as a detective and adventurer.

From Fred Pinkerton, Amerikas Meisterdetektiv, *1920-21.*

1920

Winter. Birth of Namor, the Sub-Mariner. Namor is the child of the Queen of a race of undersea dwellers living in the Antarctic, under the ice floes covering the South Pole, and of Commander Leonard McKenzie, leader of an American scientific expedition. It is possible that the undersea Sub-Mariners are the last dying and mutated descendants of survivors sunken Atlantis.

Winter
DECLINE AND FALL
   Paul Pennyfeather is sent to Egdon Heath Penal Settlement.
   Novel by Evelyn Waugh, 1928. Egdon Heath is the locale of Thomas Hardy's novel The Return of the Native *(1878). Kim Newman mentions the prison on Egdon Heath in his Diogenes Club tale "Sorcerer, Conjurer, Wizard, Witch," thus placing the events of both* The Return of the Native *and* Decline and Fall *in the Crossover Universe. It bears noting that a character in* Decline and Fall*, Margot Beste-Chetwynd, becomes Lady Metroland and next appears in Waugh's novel* Vile Bodies *(1930).*

HANNIBAL BLUNT, DER SCHRECKEN DER VERBRECHERWELT
   In Germany, British detective Hannibal Blunt fights against the brief return of the same Martians who attacked London in 1898. These are the same Martians who John Spurlock defeated in 1913.
   Adrian Mohr's Hannibal Blunt, der Schrecken der Verbrecherwelt, *#1-50, 1921-1922). This story places Blunt in the Crossover Universe.*

CARETAS CONTRO ARSENIO LUPIN
   American boxing champion and world adventurer Caretas encounters the gentleman thief Lupin.
   Story by Bruno de Luca in Il Romano Poliziesco *#14, 1921, placing Caretas (who appeared in* Il Romano, *1920-1922) in the Crossover Universe.*

   Spring. Young Indiana Jones and the Mystery of the Blues: Indy is in Chicago attending college, where he meets Eliot Ness. (A *Young Indiana Jones* television movie. Ness would later meet hard-boiled detective Nate Heller in the 1930s.)

Spring
TIMM FOX, DER KONIG DER DETEKTIV
   The German detective Timm Fox meets Nick Carter.
   Timm Fox, der Konig der Detektiv *#1-48, 1921, and* Aus den Geheimakten, Eines Weltdetektivs *#1-11, 1921, placing Fox in the CU.*

OKA YUMA, DER JAPANISCHE SPION (II)
   Lukas Hull, a Hamburg detective, fights Oka Yuma.

A tale in Lukas Hull, Detektiv Abenteuer *(*Lukas Hull, Detective Adventures*) #3, 1921, bringing Lukas Hull into the CU.*

May. Immortal Duncan MacLeod waves hello to Pablo Picasso, stating that they are acquaintances. (*"*Methos,*"* episode of the *Highlander* television series. Indiana Jones and Tarzan have also both met Picasso, thus confirming the place of *Highlander* in the Crossover Universe.)

Summer. Birth of Alexander Fandorin, son of detective Erast Fandorin (Boris Akunin's *Altyn Tolobas*).

Summer
THE SAINTE-GENEVIÈVE CAPER
Arsène Lupin and Sherlock Holmes joust once more, and Lupin's archnemesis Inspector Ganimard reflects that it would be a shame if Holmes succeeded in arresting Lupin before he did.
Short story by Alain le Bussy in Tales of the Shadowmen Volume 1: The Modern Babylon, *Jean-Marc and Randy Lofficier, eds., Black Coat Press, 2005.*

THE FOOTPRINTS ON THE CEILING
Sherlock Holmes and Dr. Watson become involved in the investigation of Professor Challenger's disappearance. Also appearing are Mrs. Challenger, Edward Malone, Mr. McArdle, and Lord John Roxton.
A tale by Jules Castier.

THE SECRET ADVERSARY
Tommy and Tuppence Beresford are husband-and-wife sleuths. It is mentioned that Inspector Japp of Scotland Yard has arrived to investigate a crime.
Novel by Agatha Christie. Inspector Japp worked closely with Hercule Poirot. Since Poirot is in the CU, so are the Beresfords. It bears noting that much, if not all, of Christie's work is interconnected, and thus takes place in the CU. Other of Christie's characters in the CU are: Colonel Ephraim Pikeaway, the head of Special Branch Intelligence; Mr. Robinson, a member of a mysterious group of financiers called the Arrangers; Miss Felicity Lemon, the secretary for Parker Pyne and then Hercule Poirot; Mrs. Adriadne Oliver; Superintendent Battle; Colonel Johnny Race, a British Secret Service agent; and Mr. Satterthwaite, the associate of detective Harley Quinn.

Autumn
HUNTINGTOWER
In Dickson McCunn's first adventure, Archie Roylance also appears.
Novel by John Buchan. Roylance is also a supporting character in Buchan's novels about Richard Hannay and Edward Leithen. Rick Lai notes, "John Buchan had an opening dedication entitled 'To W.P. Ker.' Ker was a

Professor of Poetry at Oxford. Buchan mentions in this dedication that McCunn is a direct descendant of Nicol Jarvie, a fictional character from Scott's Rob Roy. *According to Buchan, Jarvies had a granddaughter who married a McCunn. One of her descendants was Dickson McCunn. The dedication also quotes 'that profound critic of life and literature' who is identified as 'Mr. Huckleberry Finn.'"*

Autumn 1920-1921
IRONCASTLE

Chronicles of explorer Hareton Ironcastle's expedition to Africa. The Baltimore Gun Club appears; this club was also connected to some interesting events in 1865. Phileas Fogg is mentioned, as is the Diogenes Club, Mycroft Holmes' club in London. Ironcastle is apparently related to the eminent Baltimore scientist, Professor Porter. Sir George Curtis appears. There is also a reference to Ironcastle's previous expedition jointly headed by Dr. Savage, a famous surgeon and explorer, which was to the Lost World first discovered by Professor Challenger. This second Lost World expedition took place in 1917, which would make the Dr. Savage referred to not Doc Savage, but his father. Finally, Ironcastle mentions that he was once in Gabon with famed explorer Joseph Jorkens.

Novel by J.-H. Rosny Aîné, translated, retold, and embellished by Philip José Farmer, DAW Books, 1976, tying together Wold Newton Family members Fogg, Holmes, Tarzan, Jorkens, Savage, and Challenger. The Baltimore Gun Club is from Verne's From the Earth to the Moon. *The late Professor Porter is, of course, the father of Jane, who married Tarzan and settled in Africa in 1910. Lord Dunsany's Joseph Jorkens is also a Wold Newton Family member. Sir George Curtis is the nephew of Sir Henry Curtis from H. Rider Haggard's Allan Quatermain novels.*

November 11. Birth of James Bond in Wattenscheid, or Vienna, to Andrew Bond and Monique Delacroix. Bond is a descendant of Brigadier Gerard on his mother's side.

December 1920-February 1921. Holmes and Russell solve the case of *A Monstrous Regiment of Women*, as told by Mary Russell Holmes, edited by Laurie R. King. Sherlock Holmes and Mary Russell marry in the spring of 1921.

1921

Winter. The Picaroon, Martin Dale, brother of Jimmie Dale, goes to work as a modern Robin Hood in New York City. His exploits were told by Herman Landon (see "The Amazing Lanes" on *The Wold Newton Chronicles* website).

Winter. German adventurer Tom Hypnos uses his powers of hypnosis to fight evil around the world and on Mars. (*Tom Hypnos, the King of the Secret Services* [*Tom Hypnos, der König der Geheimwissenschaften*] #1-13, 1921.)

Winter
LA ÚLTIMA AVENTURA DE RAFFLES (THE LAST ADVENTURE OF RAFFLES)
Raffles is defeated once more, not only by Sherlock Holmes, but also by a new foe named Horacio Katman.

Melodrama by Carlos Grau presented on January 27, 1922, at the Teatro Cómico in Madrid. The pronouncement of the adventure as the gentlemen thief's "last" was premature.

STEEL HOUSE UNDER BAKER STREET
German gentleman thief Baronet Duncan is in London, at the "Steel House under Baker Street," where he evades Sherlock Holmes.

William Harrison's Baronet Duncan, aus düsteren kellern und kaschemmen, der Kampf um 218 Millionen *#1-38, 1922-1923. Jess Nevins notes, "By this time Sherlock Holmes had married Mary Russell, so the bachelor Holmes portrayed in 'Steel House under Baker Street' could not have been Sherlock Holmes. It is possible that the 'Holmes' who Duncan eluded was a 'Great Detective Syndrome' sufferer, but it is more likely that the 'Holmes' who pursued Duncan was actually Baker Street's second-most-famous resident, Sexton Blake."*

Spring. Lord Peter Wimsey, the second son of the Duke of Denver, solves his first case, "*The Vindictive Story of the Footsteps That Ran,*" as told by Dorothy Sayers. Lord Peter's first published case was *Whose Body?* (1923).

Spring. The case of *The Three Hostages* by John Buchan, wherein Sir Richard Hannay defeats the plans of Dominick Medina and his mother, the "Blind Spinner." Medina, the son of the second, and late, Professor Moriarty, is killed at the end of this adventure.

Spring
THE ADVENTURE OF THE HAUNTED LIBRARY
Carnacki, the notable psychic investigator, refers a case to Solar Pons.

Thomas Carnacki, the "ghost finder," is one of the earliest occult detectives, and was created by William Hope Hodgson. This story is by Dr. Lyndon Parker, and edited by August Derleth, published in The Casebook of Solar Pons *(book 4), Pinnacle Books.*

JEEVES: A GENTLEMAN'S PERSONAL GENTLEMAN
Reginald Jeeves and Father Brown solve a mystery, parts of which had baffled Hercule Poirot and Lord Peter Wimsey. Jeeves also meets Wimsey's man Bunter.

A biography by C. Northcote Parkinson, St. Martin's Press, 1979. The events in question can be found in chapters 6-8.

ELDRITCH
A man named John Reynolds is shipwrecked on an island where he meets a variety of man-beasts and woman calling herself Dr. Moreau. The unfortunate ship captain named Marsh, who does not survive, mentions Shub-Niggurath. Later on, Dr. Moreau states that she serves Yog-Sothoth and the Great Old Ones.

A Cthulhu Mythos story by Brad Linaweaver and Fred Olen Ray in the anthology Disciples of Cthulhu II, *Edward P. Berglund, ed., Chaosium Books, 2003. The story is also a sequel to* The Island of Dr. Moreau *by H. G. Wells. Captain Marsh must be a relation of the Marsh family seen in Lovecraft's "The Shadow over Innsmouth."*

IL NAUFRAGIO DELL' 'ALBATROSS'
Charlot discovers the wreckage of the airship *Albatross*.

#4 of Les Aventures Comiques de Charlot Detective, *featuring the comical detective Charlot, who resembles Charlie Chaplin. According to Jess Nevins, "Charlot is a comic, bumbling detective who is described as the lieutenant of Nik Parter, a Nick Carter lift. Charlot is helped by Miss Rud and Passy, 'Parter's' other assistants. Despite his usual incompetence, Charlot nonetheless suc-*

ceeds in getting his man." The Albatross is from Jules Verne's Robur the Conqueror.

May-June
THE NYCTALOPE VS. LUCIFER
    The Nyctalope goes up against Baron Glô von Warteck, aka "Lucifer," the Lord of Castle Shwarzrock in the Black Forest, whose tremendous hypnotic powers, amplified by his diabolical "teledynamo," threatens to enslave the world. Raymond de Ciserat, the commander of the French submarine *Lampas*, tells his first officer: "Yes, my dear chap, yes. It's marvelous that you've had the same idea, wonderful! We'll do better than Nansen or Peary. Ah! It's an exploit worthy of the famous Captain Nemo! To the North Pole by submarine. The *Lampas* can do it. Why didn't we think of it sooner?"
    Novel by Jean de La Hire, 1921, translated and adapted by Brian Stableford, Black Coat Press, 2007. Leo Saint-Clair, the Nyctalope, has night vision, hypnotic powers, extraordinary senses, and an artificial heart. He's a relentless adventurer who battles the forces of evil all over the world. The reference to Jules Verne's Captain Nemo confirms the Nyctalope's presence in the Crossover Universe.

    May 7. Birth of John Armand Drummond-Clayton, son of Korak and Meriem, grandson of Tarzan.
    Summer. The events of the film *The Ghost of Frankenstein*, featuring Dr. Ludwig Frankenstein, the son of Dr. Henry Frankenstein.
    Summer. Sir Joseph Whemple (son of the Whemple seen in Kim Newman's *Seven Stars*) and his assistant find Imhotep's tomb (*The Mummy*).
    Summer. Events of the serial film *Lightning Hutch*. Newly recruited THRUSH agent Ward Baldwin is also involved in this incident (see *The Dagger Affair* by David McDaniel.)

Summer
A JEST, TO PASS THE TIME
    A mysterious personage sends the world's greatest thieves on a merry chase after the fabled Moonstone.

Story by Jess Nevins in Tales of the Shadowmen Volume 2: Gentlemen of the Night, *Jean-Marc and Randy Lofficier, eds., Black Coat Press, 2006; reprinted in French in* Les Compagnons de l'Ombre (Tome 4), *Jean-Marc and Randy Lofficier, eds., Rivière Blanche, 2009. The total characters and events that this tale adds to the CU is quite extensive, so the list is in abbreviated format: The Moonstone - from Wilkie Collins'* The Moonstone; *Bernard Sutton - from Max Pemberton's* Jewel Mysteries I Have Known; *Palais Garnier - from Gaston Leroux's* The Phantom of the Opera; *Lady Wyndham - from Maurice Dekobra's* The Madonna of the Sleeping Cars; *the correspondent for the Temps - from Gaston Leroux's Rouletabille stories; Princess Narda - from Lee Falk's Mandrake the Magician stories; Inspector Tony - from Gabriel Bernard's Inspector Tony stories; Inspector Jordan - from Jules de Gastyne's Marc Jordan stories; Flambeau - from G.K. Chesterton's Father Brown stories; Le Petit Vingtieme - from Hergé's Tintin stories; Koh-i-Tur - from Herman Landon's Gray Phantom stories; Takawaja emerald - from Wyndham Martyn's Anthony Trent stories; Cosmopoli sapphires - from Edward Heron-Allen's* The Strange Papers of Dr. Blayre; *Gola pearls - from Charles Hamilton's Ken King stories; Cailles en sarcophage and Achille Papin - from Isak Dinesen's "Babette's Feast"; Brainaire-Ducru Medoc - from Roald Dahl's "Taste"; M. Dicky - from Louis Boussenard's* Les Gratteurs de Ciel; *Bencolins - from John Dickson Carr's Henri Bencolin novels; Trissons - from Louis Forest's* On Vole des Enfants a Paris; *Lama Samdad Chiemba - from Mark Channing's Colin Gray novels; Schalken - from J. Sheridan Le Fanu's "Schalken the Painter"; Amayats - from H. De Vere Stacpoole's Mynheer Amayat stories; "Z is the life! Z is the death!" - from Leon Sazie's Zigomar stories; Wallion - from Julius Pettersson's Maurice Wallion stories; Elvestad - from Sven Elvestad's Asbjørn Krag stories; Hagen-Kander - from Robert Kraft's* In Search of the World Cure *and the anonymously written* The Adventures of Harri Kander, the Flying Reporter; *Auguste Dubois - from Pierre Nord's Colonel Dubois novels; Mirculas - from Gabriel Bernard's Miraculas stories; Styria - from J. Sheridan Le Fanu's "Carmilla"; Götz - from the Konrad Götz stories in* Konrad Götz der Wandervogel; *Wormer - from Robert J. Hogan's G-8 stories; Dunot - from Jose Morelli's Marcel Dunot stories; Countess Told - from Norbert Jacques'* Dr. Mabuse, the Gambler; *The Baron of honored lineage - Baron Stombole, from Jose Moselli's Baron Cesare Stromboli stories; Caradosso - from F.R. Buckley's Luigi Caradossa stories; Picardet - Colonel Clay, from Grant Allen's Colonel Clay stories; Troyon - the Lone Wolf, from Louis Vance's Lone Wolf stories; Etienne De la Zeur - from Neal Stephenson's* Baroque Cycle *(*Quicksilver, The Confusion, The System of the World*); De la Zeur - Horace Dorrington, from Arthur Morrison's Horace Dorrington stories; Duke of Chin - from Barry Hughart's* Bridge of Birds; *Knei Yang - from Ernest Bramah's Kai Lung stories; Metzengerstein - from Edgar Allan Poe's "Metzengerstein"; Penniel - from Emma Dawson's "A Stray Reveler"; "The Hills West of Napa Valley" - from Ambrose Bierce's "The Death of*

Halpin Frayser"; "Louvre Ghost" - Belphégor, from The Phantom of the Louvre; *"that a vampire once used them as his home" - from Balzac's* The Centenarian; *"that Masons and Rosicrucians use them now for secret rites" - from* The Phantom of the Louvre; *Duc d'Arcachon - from Neal Stephenson's* Baroque Cycle; *Mylord L'Arsouille - from Noel Marin's Mylord L'Arsouille stories; Margot - from Thomas Hanshew's Hamilton Cleek stories; "Lord of Terror" - from Pierre Souvestre's Fantômas stories; "a clever anagram" - from Louis Feuillade's* Les Vampires; *Sigono - from Edward Brooker's* Sigono Contre La Police; *Forrestal - from* Raiders of the Lost Ark; *Littlejohn - from Lester Dent's Doc Savage stories; Bermejo - from Frederic van Rensselaer Dey's Nick Carter stories; albino in tuxedo - from Anthony Skene's Zenith the Albino stories; Blanchard - from Marcel Priollet's Tintin stories; "veteran" - Gaston Dupont, from Nick Carter stories; "Loki"- from Philip José Farmer's* Escape from Loki; *Carlier - from H. van der Kallen's Inspector Carlier stories; Ténèbras - from Arnould Galopin's Ténèbras stories; Courville - from Leon Sazie's Martin Numa stories; L'Année 2000 - from Albert Robida's* La Guerre Infernale; *Dr. Cordat - from Andre Laurie's* Spiridon le Muet; *Inspector Walter - from Marcel Priollet's Tip Walter stories; Satanas - from Gabriel Bernard's* Satanas; *Professor Tornada - from André Couvreur's Professor Tornada novels; "School of Crime" - from Frederic van Rensselaer Dey's Nick Carter and Doctor Quartz stories; Daily Star - from Bellem & Ballard's Jim Anthony stories; Ruder-Ox - from Antonio Quattrini's John Siloch stories; Le Café Noir de Lune - from the Black Moon stories (*Bullseye, *1930s); "Duke of honored memory" - from Paul Féval's* Le Bossu; *Emil Lupin - from the Black Moon stories (*Bullseye, *1930s); "Rupert of Graustark" - from Anthony Hope's Zenda novels and George Barr McCutcheon's Graustark novels; "Fifi's trip to Eucrasia" - from Arnould Galopin's Fifi stories, and Andre Couvreur's* Caresco Surhomme; *"The Last Draw on the Cigarette" - from Ouida's* Under Two Flags; *Anatole - from P.G. Wodehouse's Jeeves stories; "the inmate of a hard labor camp at Toulon" - from Ponson du Terrail's Rocambole stories; Professor Pelotard - from Frank Heller's Fillip Collin stories; Villiod - from* Mémoires de Villiod, Détective Privé; *"handsome black-haired woman"/Elena Acevedo - Mademoiselle Miton, from the Nelson Lee stories; Tokay Imperial - from Verne's* From the Earth to the Moon *and* Around the Moon; *Elena Acevedo - from José Mallorquí's Coyote novels; Bertrand Charon - from Sexton Blake stories (he is Simon Carne, from Guy Boothby's Simon Carne stories); Prosper Bondonnat - from Gustave Le-Rouge's Dr. Cornelius Kramm stories; Véra Roudine - from Charles Lucieto's James Nobody stories; Maxim De Winter - from Daphne du Maurier's* Rebecca; *Lord Lister - from the Lord Lister stories; Lord Stuart - from Ernst Pinkert's Lord Stuart stories; Mlle Lazarre - from the Dixon Hawke stories; Yvonne Cartier - from the Sexton Blake stories; Percy Stuart - from the Percy Stuart stories; "the Sunken City" - from Gustav Frohlich's Heinz Brandt stories; Percy Stuart's club - from the New Eccentric Club stories; painting of King Solomon* *confronting a demon - from M.R. James' "Canon Alberic's Scrap Book"; Hallward - from Oscar Wilde's* The Picture of Dorian Gray; *fingersmiths - from Roald Dahl's "The Hitchhiker"; Raffles - from E.W. Hornung's A.J. Raffles stories; Blake - from the Sexton Blake stories; "as far away as China" - from Sun Liaohong's Lu Ping stories; René Cardillac - from E.T.A. Hoffmann's "Mademoiselle de Scudéry"; and Arsène Lupin from the stories by Maurice Leblanc. Nevins adds: "Lord Sister appeared in* Lord Sister, Il Ladro Tenebroso *#1-36 (1924-1925). He is a Lord Lister lift. Sister is a rich, young, blond, insouciant nobleman and gentleman thief who prefers to victimize evil men; as he describes himself, 'I am Lord Sister, the avenging one of many faults, the dark thief who sometimes knows the justice of God.' But he makes the mistake of sending taunting notes to Percy Stuart, who then dedicates himself to capturing Lord Sister, and succeeds in the final issue of Lord Sister."*

Summer-October 1921; September-October 1925; October-November 1928
SPADE & ARCHER

Samuel Spade quits the Continental Detective Agency in Seattle and opens his own office in San Francisco.

A novel by Joe Gores, a prequel to Dashiell Hammett's The Maltese Falcon, *Alfred A. Knopf, 2009. The Continental Detective Agency was featured in tales of Hammett's other well-known detective, the Continental Op.*

LE SECRET DE LA TÊTE DE MORT (THE SECRET OF THE DEATH'S HEAD)

Detective Harry Dickson works with Nick Carter and a young Charlie Chan.

#107 and 114 of Harry Dickson *(German series); Dutch series #78-79.*

July 19. Birth of Johnny Liddell, private eye in cases recounted by Frank Kane.

August. Harry Houdini and his Pinkerton bodyguard, Phil Beaumont, apply their skills to a locked-room murder mystery. Sir Arthur Conan Doyle also appears, but does not have much of a role in solving the mystery. (Escapade, *a novel written by Walter Satterthwait, St. Martin's, 1995. Houdini also worked with Sherlock Holmes on several occasions.)*

September. More than a decade of research pays off, as Sherlock Holmes perfects his Royal Jelly bee pollen elixir (see "The Adventure of the Notorious Canary Trainer"). The mixture not only stops the aging process, but actually reverses it somewhat, thus granting Holmes and Watson, as well as their families and descendants (see Nero Wolfe, et al.), new leases on life. Holmes undoubtedly shares the elixir with his brother Mycroft, long-time head of the British Secret Service, thus explaining British agent James Bond's lengthy career.

Autumn
THE STRANGE CASE OF THE THURLINGHAM HALL ROBBERY
   Zenith the Albino vs. Nelson Lee.
   Story in the Nelson Lee Library *#379, September 9, 1922. Zenith the Albino was the archenemy of Sexton Blake. This crossover confirms the link between Blake and Lee.*

December 24
A WOOSTER CHRISTMAS
   Jeeves and Wooster spend Christmas Eve with Bertie's Aunt Dahlia, where celebrated detective Hercule Poirot and his friend Captain Arthur Hastings are also guests for the evening. Bertie mentions that Pete Wimsey wishes to become a consulting detective. Chef Gaston Blondin and Foreign Office Official Jesmond appear.
   Short story by Xavier Mauméjean in Tales *of the Shadowmen Volume 4: Lords of Terror, Jean-Marc and Randy Lofficier, eds., Black Coat Press, 2008. Jeeves and Wooster are from the tales by P. G. Wodehouse, while Poirot and Hastings are from Agatha Christie's celebrated mysteries. Chef Gaston Blondin is from Christie's* Death on the Nile. *Jesmond is from Christie's "The Theft of the Royal Ruby." Pete Wimsey is better known as Lord Peter Wimsey, Dorothy Sayers' renowned detective.*

1922

February
SEVEN STARS EPISODE TWO: THE MAGICIAN AND THE MATINEE IDOL

Edwin Winthrop and Catriona Kaye are occult detective partners and lovers, who occasionally do contract work for Charles Beauregard, Sr., who now is in charge of the Diogenes Club. The matinee idol of the title is actor John Barrymore, who is in London to shoot location scenes for a Sherlock Holmes film.

Chapter 2 of Seven Stars *by Kim Newman. This version of Edwin Winthrop also appears in Newman's "The Big Fish." An alternate version of him exists in the Anno Dracula Universe. Though it is implied that Mycroft Holmes has passed on, of course he has not really died; he has merely gone underground in the wake of his brother's discovery of the anti-aging elixir derived from Royal Jelly bee pollen. The tale picks up again in May 1942 with "Seven Stars Episode Three: The Trouble with Barrymore."*

Spring. Birth of John Steed.
Spring. First recorded exploit of French inventor-adventurer Miraculas. (*Miraculas* series by Gabriel Bernard.)

Spring
THE EXPERIMENT OF DOCTOR MORS
Jens Rolf vs. the horrifying Dr. Mors.
Story in Jens Rolf Mystisch Abenteuerliche Erlebnisse *#4, 1923. Jess Nevins adds, "The story of Dr. Mors' escape from English prison after his capture by Sherlock Holmes in 1905 and Mors' return to Germany is an untold one. Similarly, it is not known whether Dr. Mors is related to Captain Mors, although this is doubtful."*

THE KEY OF THE TEMPLE OF HEAVEN
Madame de Medici, a beautiful Eurasian, committed a successful robbery. It is mentioned that detective Paul Harley is her enemy. Chada's Limehouse residence has passed on to Madame de Medici.
A short story by Sax Rohmer in Tales of Chinatown. *Harley and Madame de Medici later clashed in a tale called "The Black Mandarin." Since Harley is in the CU through a connection to Gaston Max, so is Madame de Medici. The connection to a previous story featuring Chada also brings in Red Kerry. Further cementing Madame de Medici's place in the CU, and also connecting to further tales by Rohmer, Rick Lai writes, "Under the variant name of Madame de Medicis, this femme fatale also appeared in 'The Treasure of Taia,' a 1926 short story reprinted in* The Wrath of Fu Manchu *(1973). In this story (which does not feature Fu Manchu), Madame stole the recently unearthed treasure of an Egyptian queen, Taia. Fu Manchu owned the mummified head of Taia in* Shadow of Fu Manchu *(1948). Taia would appear to also be the unnamed sorceress from Rohmer's supernatural novel,* Brood of the Witch-Queen *(1918). The same novel featured a fictional London newspaper, the* Planet, *that also appeared in Rohmer's* The Green Eyes of Bast *(1920), and* Moon of Madness

(where the newspaper's full name was given as the Daily Planet). In Bulldog Drummond, McNeile also used the Planet as the name for a fictional London newspaper." (Rick Lai, "Partners in Crime," The Wold Newton Universe website; Rick Lai's Secret Histories: Criminal Masterminds, Altus Press, 2009.)

AROUND THE WORLD IN EIGHTEEN DAYS
"Phineas" Fogg III, the grandson of the original Fogg, is in love with Madge Harlow, daughter of the president of an international corporation that manufactures fuel. When Mr. Harlow's plan to manufacture a cheap synthetic fuel to benefit the poor is opposed by the vice president, a proxy fight results; young Fogg, along with Madge, circles the globe in quest of proxies from the firm's scattered stockholders, experiencing a multitude of adventures but arriving back in time to swing the election.
Universal Pictures serial in twelve chapters, 1923. Although the lead character is called "Phineas," the assumption is that he is intended to be Phileas Fogg's grandson, and thus his real name would be Phileas Fogg III.

YOU'RE A TEXAS RANGER, ALVIN FOG
It is revealed that Company Z was set up on the advice of the Three Just Men.
A Company Z novel by J.T. Edson. Company Z is made up of the grandsons of Dusty Fog, the Ysabel Kid, and Mark Counter, (Alvin Fog, Mark Scrapton, and Rance Smith respectively) and is an extra-legal company of Texas Rangers. The Three Just Men refers to The Four Just Men *by Edgar Wallace.*

THE ADVENTURE OF HILLERMAN HALL, OR, HOW A HERMIT WAS DISTURBED IN HIS RETIREMENT
Sherlock Holmes assists a young and very innocent Miss Jane Marple to extricate herself from a spot of trouble.
Short story by Julian Symons, The Great Detectives: Seven Original Investigations, *Orbis Publishing, 1981; also in* The Further Adventures of Sherlock Holmes, *Richard Lancelyn Green, editor, Penguin Books, 1985.*

May-June. The adventure of *Jimgrim and the Nine Unknown* by Talbot Mundy, which follows the exploits of Jimgrim (James Schuyler Grim), Jeff Ramsden, and Chullunder Ghose.

June 23. Birth of Paul E. Standish, M.D., medical examiner in cases told by George Harmon Coxe.

Summer. Sherlock Holmes and the Houdini Birthright, Part One: Holmes and Harry Houdini again work together. Watson's editor, Conan Doyle, also appears. (Novel by Dr. Watson, edited by Val Andrews, Breese Books, 1995.) In this account, Watson places the first meeting between Holmes and Houdini in 1900, as he does in *The Pandora Plague*; Watson must have been mistaken when, writing up his notes for *The Adventure of the Ectoplasmic Man*, he placed the first meeting in 1910.

Summer. Dr. Jack Griffin, the son of John "Jack" Hawley Griffin (the original Invisible Man, seen in H.G. Wells' novel), uses his father's formula to become The Invisible Man. Sequels are *The Invisible Man Returns, The Invisible Woman, Invisible Agent, The Invisible Man's Revenge, Abbott and Costello Meet Frankenstein* (a cameo appearance), and *Abbott And Costello Meet the Invisible Man*. For more information on the various invisible men and women, please read Dennis E. Power's article, "The Invisibles," at *The Wold Newton Universe: A Secret History* website.

Summer
LE ROI DE LA NUIT (THE KING OF THE NIGHT)

The Nyctalope flies to Rhea using a spaceship patented by Dr. Cavor.

Dr. Cavor, from H.G. Wells' The First Men in the Moon, is a part of the Crossover Universe, and thus so is Jean de La Hire's hero, the Nyctalope. The Rhea in this story is a natural satellite orbiting the Earth, inhabited by winged creatures, half of whom live on the day side and half on the night side. The creatures are at war, which the Nyctalope ends. It is possible that Rhea exists in an alternate universe; when the Nyctalope launches his rocket and goes there, he really gets drawn into the alternate universe, much like Carson Napier's trip to Venus/Amtor.

ADMISSION OF WEAKNESS

Dr. Anton Zarnak sets up shop at Number 13, China Alley as a guardian of the world against dark forces.

A short story by C.J. Henderson in Lin Carter's Anton Zarnak, Supernatural Sleuth, *Marietta Publishing, 2002. Number 13 sits between Chinatown and the River, in the same locale frequented by Robert E. Howard's detective Steve Harrison. Accounts vary as to whether this is in New York City or San Francisco.*

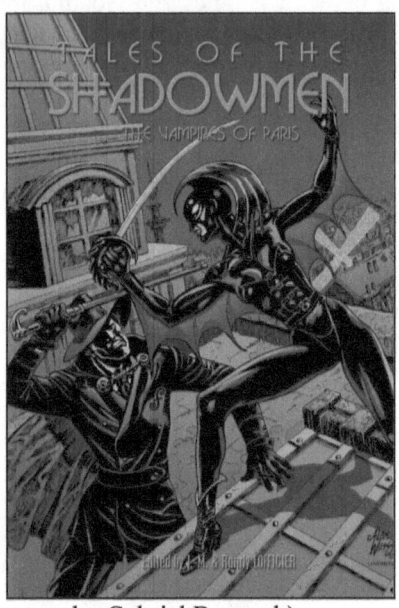

PERILS OVER PARIS

Fascinax (George Leicester, M.D.) vs. Irma Vep.

Short story by Lovern Kindzierski in Tales of the Shadowmen Volume 5: The Vampires of Paris, *Jean-Marc and Randy Lofficier, eds., Black Coat Press, 2009; reprinted in French in* Les Compagnons de l'Ombre (Tome 5), *Jean-Marc and Randy Lofficier, eds., Rivière Blanche, 2009. Fascinax is an occult investigator from the French pulps. The tale reveals that Irma Vep must not have died at the conclusion of Louis Feuillade's 1915 serial* Les Vampires, *despite all indications to the contrary.*

Autumn. French master criminal Satanas encounters a ring of telepaths. (*Satanas* by Gabriel Bernard.)

Autumn. Marko the Miracle Man commits his first recorded crime and is captured by Dixon Hawke for the first (but not the last) time. ("Marko the Miracle Man," *Dixon Hawke Library* #16, December 10, 1923.)

Autumn. Events of *The Scarlet Fox*.

Autumn
TO CAST OUT FEAR

Inspector Legrasse meets Anton Zarnak, and they are assisted by Madame La Raniella.

A short story by C.J. Henderson in Lin Carter's Anton Zarnak, Supernatural Sleuth, *Marietta Publishing, 2002. Inspector Legrasse claims that his initial contact with the Cthulhu cult was week ago. However, Lovecraft's "The Call of Cthulhu" takes place in 1907. Rick Lai explains, "One possible theory to explain the inconsistency is that Legrasse lied because he didn't know whether to fully trust Zarnak. In Henderson's story, Legrasse was expecting to find Zarnak's predecessor, Guicet, in New York. Suspicious of Guicet's sudden replacement, Legrasse fed some disinformation about his recent exploits to Zarnak." Madame La Raniella also appears in Henderson's novel* To Battle Beyond.

October 31. Karel (later Carl) Michail Kolchak is born in New York City to Janos and Fanny Kolchak.

November
WHOSE BODY?
Lord Peter Wimsey says that he is "ready to tackle Professor Moriarty or Leon Kestrel or any of 'em."

The first Lord Peter novel by Dorothy Sayers. Professor Moriarty is from Doyle and Watson's Sherlock Holmes tales. Jess Nevins notes that "Leon Kestrel was the 'Master Mummer,' a man whose skill at disguise was unmatched, and one of the most dangerous men in Europe; he even successfully impersonated Sexton Blake for a while, and was one of Blake's recurring Rogues. In context it's clear to me that Wimsey is being serious. It's not one of those 'or those chappies in stories' moments. He's talking about his contemporaries."

December
ESCAPE NOT THE THUNDERBOLT
Lupin visits Holmes in Sussex and the two come to terms with the tragic final events of *The Hollow Needle*. Lupin also mentions the young American who is almost, but not quite, as good as Holmes.

A short story by Jean-Marc and Randy Lofficier in the volume The Hollow Needle, *Black Coat Press, 2004; reprinted in French in* Les Compagnons de l'Ombre (Tome 1), *Jean-Marc and Randy Lofficier, eds., Rivière Blanche, 2008; and in the Lofficiers' collection* Pacifica, *Black Coat Press, 2010. The young American is detective Harry Dickson.*

December 23-25
YES, VIRGINIA, THERE IS A FANTÔMAS
Inspector Frederick Dickson of New York arrives in Paris claiming Fantômas is on the loose, but he's ignored by Chief Inspector Morand and Sergeant Janvier, due to a tip they received from Jules Poiret that Fantômas would come to them posing as Dickson. Tintin Blanchard and his little sister Yvonne then become embroiled in Fantômas' schemes, while the Parisian police finally start listening to Dickson when Police Commissioner Havard arrives. On Christmas Eve, Père Menou-Segrais conducts the Midnight Mass.

Short story by William P. Maynard in Tales of the Shadowmen Volume 6: Grand Guignol, *Jean-Marc and Randy Lofficier, eds., Black Coat Press, 2010; published in French in* Les Compagnons de l'Ombre (Tome 6), *Jean-Marc and*

Randy Lofficier, eds., Rivière Blanche, 2010. Fantômas and Havard are from the famed Fantômas books by Marcel Allain and Pierre Souvestre. Frederick Dickson is from the novel Fantômas in America by David White (Black Coat Press, 2007), based on the character created by Allain and Souvestre, and on Edward Sedgwick & George Eshenfelder's serial "Fantômas" (1920). Morand is from the film version of Hans Hellmut Kirst's The Night of the Generals. Janvier is from Georges Simenon's Inspector Maigret books. Jules Poiret is a detective from Frank Howel Evans' The Murder Club (1924). Tintin (who should not be confused with Herge's comic book hero) and Yvonne Blanchard are from R.M. de Nizerolles' Les Voyages aériens d'un Petit Parisien à Travers le Monde. Père Menou-Segrais is from Georges Bernanos' 1926 novel Sous le soleil de satan (Under Satan's Sun).

1923

Early 1923-Late 1924. Rick O'Connell and company fight against another mummy named Imhotep (*The Mummy*, 1999).

February-November. When a serial killer commits gruesome murders in New York City, and apparently Harry Houdini and Conan Doyle are the next targets, they team up to stop the murderer. Columnist Damon Runyon also plays a role. (*Nevermore,* novel by William Hjortsberg, St. Martin's, 1994. These events, of course, don't involve the "real" Houdini and Doyle of "our" universe, but rather the fictional characters Houdini and Doyle of the Crossover Universe.)

Spring. The events of the Universal film *Dracula* and its sequel, *Dracula's Daughter*, which features Countess Marya Zaleska. The remaining adventures in this series are told in the films *Son of Dracula, The House of Frankenstein, House of Dracula, Abbott and Costello Meet Frankenstein*, and the novels *Return of the Wolf Man, The Devil's Brood*, and *The Devil's Night*.

Spring. After crash-landing near the secret city of Shambala, Kent Allard is gifted with an age-delaying elixir used by the inhabitants of that city (DC Comics' *Blood and Judgment* by Howard Chaykin). Allard goes on to fight crime as The Shadow.

April 1-September 10, 1923
A BARNSTORMER IN OZ

Hank Stover, son of Dorothy, is transported to Oz. Glinda is described as pale and languid as one of Count Dracula's donors. An Ozian named "Sharts the Shirtless" appears. In the Author's Notes, Philip José Farmer writes that the Signal Corps project, as described in *Barnstormer*, is buried in secret government files, and "would be as difficult to find as the Ark of the Covenant, also stored by government." The brilliant scientist from the U.S. Army Signal Corps who created the green cloud gate leading to Oz is Colonel Mark Sampson. There is a group of people descended from Native Americans called the Natawey.

This novel by Philip José Farmer, Berkley Books, 1982, is a direct sequel to L. Frank Baum's The Wizard of Oz. *The note about the Ark of the Covenant being stored by the U.S. government refers to the Indiana Jones film* Raiders of the Lost Ark, *which must take place in the universe in which Hank Stover originates, the Crossover Universe. "Sharts the Shirtless" is an Oz version of Doc Savage. Hank Stover is a cousin of Dink Stover, from Owen Johnson's* Stover at Yale *(1911). Mark Sampson and his chum Jack Darrow are the two boy-heroes from Roy Rockwood's Great Marvel series (1906-1935); the orphaned boys were typically fostered by great professors or scientists, and their adventures included trips to Mars, the Moon, Venus, and the center of the Earth. The Great Marvel series was part of the famed Stratemeyer Syndicate*  which also published Tom Swift, Nancy Drew, and the Hardy Boys. "Roy Rockwood" was a Stratemeyer house pseudonym; the real name of the writer of most of the Great Marvel books was Howard R. Garis, who also anonymously wrote books in many other series, including Tom Swift, the Bobbsey Twins, the Motor Boys, the Camp Fire Girls, and Uncle Wiggily. Mark Sampson and Jack Darrow aged in real time as the Great Marvels series progressed, so that by the time of the 1920s and '30s books, they were scientists in their own right. The lost land that Kioga inhabits is called Natoway. Kioga is from a series of four books by William L. Chester, starting with* Hawk of the Wilderness.

Farmer's sequel states that the remaining Oz books by Baum and others are fictional, and that Barnstormer *tells the tale of what really happened. However, as will be seen in further crossovers, there are probably several parallel "pocket universe" versions of Oz, and Hank Stover went to a different Oz than that depicted in Baum's series. Hank's mother Dorothy, from South Dakota, may not actually be the Dorothy Gale of Kansas, since her history as given in* Barnstormer *is very different from that in the Baum books. Additionally, Farmer says that Stover's mother Dorothy first traveled to Oz in May 1890, while most chronologists place* The Wizard of Oz *in 1898-1899. There was a third Dorothy, as seen in L. Sprague de Camp's "Sir Harold and the Gnome King." Clearly a* mystery remains, which for now can be labeled "The Adventure of the Three Dorothys, Or, Too Many Dorothys."

Spring
THE LONG ARM OF LOONEY COOTE
At a Wrykyn alumni dinner there is an announcement: "...as a reward for his services in connection with the building of the new water works at Streslau, J.J. Swodger had received from the Government of Ruritania the Order of the Silver Trowel, third class (with crossed pickaxes)." Looney Coote is also a member of the Drones Club.

Short story by P.G. Wodehouse in Ukridge. *Ruritania is from Hope's* The Prisoner of Zenda. *Wrykyn is the school that appeared in Wodehouse's* The Gold Bat, *among others. The Drones Club appears in its own series of short stories as well as the Jeeves/Wooster, Mr. Mulliner, and Blandings Castle series, and several non-series novels by Wodehouse.*

THE JUSTICE OF COMPANY Z
Alvin Fog encounters Wilfred Plan.

A Company Z novel by J.T. Edson. Wilfred Plan is a descendant of Uriah Heep, from Charles Dickens' David Copperfield.

June
THE ADVENTURE OF GRESHAM OLD PLACE
Dr. Parker says that London detective Solar Pons indeed resembles the "Sherlock Holmes of Praed Street."

A Solar Pons story by Dr. Lyndon Parker, and edited by August Derleth, published in The Final Adventures of Solar Pons, *Mycroft and Moran Books, 1998.*

Summer. Birth of occultist Henri-Laurent de Marigny, son of Étienne-Laurent de Marigny.

July-August. "The Rats in the Walls," as told by H.P. Lovecraft.

August-September
A LETTER OF MARY
A young man named Peter who wears a monocle helps Mary Russell Holmes out of a spot. It is also mentioned that Peter is more than acquainted with Holmes and Russell, and is an occasional

visitor to their cottage in Sussex. When Mary is reporting the results of her investigations to her husband, she remarks that she had noted "Interesting little things. Trifles, as Sergeant Cuff would say."

It makes sense that Sherlock Holmes and his relative, Lord Peter Wimsey, as fellow detectives, would be well-known to each other, as is demonstrated in this novel by Mary Russell Holmes, edited by Laurie R. King, St. Martin's Press, 1997. Given that Mary is a student of detection under her husband, it seems likely that the methods of Cuff (from Wilkie Collins' The Moonstone) would be examined. Holmes and Russell spend the remainder of 1923 solving the cases chronicled in the novels The Moor and Justice Hall.

Mid September
THE ADVENTURE OF THE SEVEN SISTERS
Solar Pons and his associate Dr. Lyndon Parker cross paths with the evil Dr. Fu Manchu and his Si-Fan organization.
Short story by August Derleth in The Chronicles of Solar Pons *(book 2), Pinnacle Books.*

1924

January 1-February
THE GAME
Mycroft calls upon Sherlock and Mary to travel to India in search of a missing British agent, Kimball O'Hara.
A novel by Mary Russell Holmes, edited by Laurie R. King, Bantam Books, 2004. O'Hara is from Rudyard Kipling's Kim; *Holmes knew Kim for the better part of a year during The Great Hiatus.*

Winter. Birth of Manson Emmert Everard, future member of the Time Patrol.
Winter. Inspector Napoleon "Bony" Bonaparte's first recorded case, *The Barrakee Mystery*, as told by Arthur W. Upfield. Philip José Farmer has proposed that Bonaparte is the son of A.J. Raffles.
Winter. Adventuress Lady Diana Wyndham gets involved with the Great Game of espionage. (*The Madonna of the Sleeping Cars* by Maurice Dekobra.)

Winter
POVELITEL' ZHELEZA (THE SOVEREIGN OF IRON)
Mycroft Holmes has a child named Stanley, born circa 1900, who resembles Mycroft to a great degree. Sherlock and Mycroft Holmes both appear, and Sherlock proves most helpful in Stanley's assignment to help a British Minister track down Ramashandra, an Indian revolutionary.

Story by Soviet writer Valentin Katayev, 1925. While many crossovers featuring descendants of Sherlock and/or Mycroft Holmes are listed herein, just as many are not. For a more exhaustive list, please see Brad Mengel's "Watching the Detectives, Or, The Sherlock Holmes Family Tree" (Myths for the Modern Age: Philip José Farmer's Wold Newton Universe, *Win Scott Eckert, editor, MonkeyBrain Books, 2005).*

YELLOW SHADOWS
Red Kerry investigates Burma Chang's murder. Burma Chang is the possessor of the Limehouse residence formerly occupied by Zani Chada and Madame de Medici.
Novel by Sax Rohmer confirming Red Kerry in the CU. Rick Lai observes, "'The Pigtail of Hi Wing Ho,' another short tale by Rohmer, does not feature Kerry, but his assistant, Detective-Sergeant Durham, does team up with Paul Harley's assistant, Malcolm Knox. 'Tcheriapin' and 'The Dance of the Veils,' two non-series stories in Rohmer's Tales of Chinatown, *are connected to the Red Kerry series. 'Tcheriapin' mentions a Limehouse bar, Malay Jack's, which is in 'Kerry's Kid.' 'The Dance of the Veils' briefly mentions Kerry."*

April. First appearance of George Washington Tubbs II. Tubbs would meet soldier-of-fortune Captain Easy in 1929. Their adventures were chronicled by Roy Crane.
Spring. Sherlock Holmes and Mary Russell are in San Francisco, where they cross paths with writer Dashiell Hammett. (*Locked Rooms* by Mary Russell Holmes and Laurie R. King, Bantam Books, July 2005.)

Late Spring
THE MYSTERY OF THE SUPERIOR INTELLIGENCE
A bowler hat is found on the steps of 221B Baker Street, and Reginald Jeeves appears to collect it.
Story by Ernest Holman in Collectors Digest Annual 1985. *Internal dating of the story, with the full moon said to take place on March 21, places this story in 1924. In the story Jeeves and Holmes have never met before, so this must be their first meeting.*

Summer
ISLAND OF THE THIEVES
The Portuguese thief Fresquinho somehow succeeds in stealing from Fantômas, Raffles, Lord Lister, and Arsène Lupin during a congress of thieves. Fresquinho lectures the other criminals that they should target the bourgeois more often.
From Reinaldo Ferreira's serial "Ilha dos Ladroes" (ABC, January 29-April 9, 1925).

FRANK MERRIWELL VS. FRED FEARNOT
This tale features the wedding of Fred Fearnot and his sweetheart, Evelyn Olcott, as well as baseball contest between Fearnot and the great Frank Merriwell. Among the observers are: Dick Dobbs, the Millionaire detective; Tex Rickard; The Bradys; Ted Strong's Rough Riders; The Three Chums, Ben Bright, Tom True and Dot Dare; Graham McNamee; Frank Manley; Dick Daresome; and Bowery Billy. Nick Carter and Frank Reade, Jr., cannot attend, as they are busy working on case of the *Cyclops*, a ship that left port and was never seen again. Also mentioned but not in attendance are Cap'n Wiley; the late Young Klondike; the late Klondike Kit; the late Old Broadbrim; and the late Old Cap Collier.
By Ralph P. Smith. First published in Frank T. Fries "Frank Reade Library," #1-4 (September-December 1928). Since Nick Carter and Frank Reade, Jr., are already in the CU, so too are all others mentioned in this story. According to dime-novel expert Jess Nevins:
Fearnot debuted as an 18-year-old in 1898 ("Fred Fearnot; or, School Days at Avon," Work & Win, December 9, 1898, written by Harvey K. Shackleford). Frank Merriwell first appeared in Gilbert Patten's "Frank Merriwell; or, First Days at Fardale," Tip Top Weekly #1, April 18, 1896. Merriwell's adventures appeared in print through 1930, in comic strips and Big Little books through the late 1930s, in pulps in the 1940s, in comics in the 1950s, in radio serials in the 1940s, and in a movie serial in 1936. Clearly the later stories are about Frank's son, Frank Jr. (aka "Chip"). Dick Dobbs first appeared in George Marsh's "The Great Trunk Mystery; or, Dick Dobbs on a Hot Trail," Dick Dobbs Detective Weekly #1, March 20, 1909. George Lewis "Tex" Rickard (1870-1929), was a fight promoter who did much to make boxing fashionable and who was responsible for promoting Dempsey vs. Carpentier, the first one million dollar gate. The Bradys are a reference to Old King Brady and Young King Brady. Old King Brady first appeared in Francis W. Doughty's "Old King Brady the Sleuth-Hound," New York Detective Library #154, November 14, 1885. Young King Brady (no blood relation) first appeared in an NYDL *issue in 1895. Their last appearance was in 1912, but they've clearly been working since then. When Old King first appeared he was 40, which would*

make him 79 in this issue—old, but not decrepit and still capable, so this must be the real Old King Brady. Ted Strong first appeared in "Ted Strong's Rough Riders; or, The Boys of Black Mountain," Rough Rider Weekly #1, April 23, 1904. Ted Strong was a cowboy and veteran of the Spanish-American War. In New Nick Carter Weekly #525 (January 15, 1907) Strong and the Rough Riders teamed up with Nick Carter. Nick Carter first appeared in "The Old Detective's Pupil; or, The Mysterious Crime of Madison Square," New York Weekly, September 18, 1886. He was still appearing in 1924, although he'd have been in his fifties at that point. At some point, likely in the 1920s, Nick probably retired and was replaced by his son, Chickering Carter, who probably took the name "Nick Carter" for professional reasons. But I think this is a reference to the original Nick and not Chick. Frank Reade, Jr., first appeared in Luis Senarens' "Frank Reade Jr. and His Steam Wonder," Boys of New York #338, February 4, 1879. Frank is about 14 in his first appearance, but is middle-aged in "Young Frank Reade and his Electric Air Ship; or, a 10,000 Mile Search for a Missing Man," Happy Days #261, October 4, 1899, the first (and only) story to feature "Young Frank Reade," who is explicitly described as Frank Reade, Jr.'s son. So I posit that the "Frank Reade, Jr." in "Frank Merriwell vs. Fred Fearnot" must be the grown-up "Young Frank Reade." Frank Jr. would have been at least in his mid 50s, if not older, in this story, while Young Frank would have been in his mid-thirties-prime of life, in other words, and quite capable of assisting Nick Carter. The Three Chums first appeared in "Three Chums at School; or, All for One and One for All," Three Chums #1, November 10, 1899. They appeared in 60 stories, the last in December 1900. Young Klondike first appeared in Francis W. Doughty's "Young Klondike; or, Off for the Land of Gold," Young Klondike #1, March 10, 1898. His last appearance was in 1899. Klondike Kit first appeared in William Wallace Cook's "Klondike Kit; or, A Freeze-Out in the Chilkoot Pass," Klondike Kit Library #1, May 28, 1898. His last appearance was in 1899. Old Broadbrim first appeared in "Old Broadbrim, the Quaker Detective; or, The Strangest Trail of Crime on Record," Old Cap Collier Library #92, May 2, 1884. Old Cap Collier first appeared in T.C. Harbaugh's "Old Cap Collier, Chief of Detectives; or, 'Piping' the New Haven Mystery" Old Cap Collier Library #1, April 9, 1883. I haven't been able to find bibliographic information on Cap'n Wiley, but I know he was a real dime novel character. Graham McNamee was the first major baseball radio broadcaster, beginning his work in 1923. Frank Manley first appeared in Harrie Hancock's "Frank Manley's Start in Athletics; or, The 'Up and at 'Em Boys," Young Athlete's Weekly #1, January 27, 1905. His last appearance was in 1906. Dick Daresome first appeared in 'Dick Daresome's Schooldays; or, The Victory of the New Boy," Wide Awake Weekly #137, November 28, 1908. His last appearance was in 1909. Bowery Billy first appeared in "Bowery Billy, the Street Vagabond; or, A Boy Hero in Rags," Bowery Boy Weekly #1, October 21, 1905. His last appearance was in 1907.

Summer. The first case of the Hardy Boys, *The Tower Treasure*, as told by Franklin W. Dixon.

July 1924-July 1925
THE BIG FOUR

Hercule Poirot and Captain Hastings battle an international crime conspiracy to rule the world, headed by a mysterious group known as "The Big Four." The Big Four are Li Chang Yen (Number One); a Chinese mandarin; American millionaire Abe Ryland (Number Two); the French scientist Madame Olivier (Number Three); and Claude Darrell (Number Four, aka "the destroyer"), a murderous master of disguise. Among those aiding Poirot in the battle is an American Secret Service agent, Captain Kent.

Novel by Agatha Christie. Rick Lai, in his article "Partners in Crime: Fu Manchu and Carl Peterson," convincingly posits that not only were Li Chang Yen and Claude Darrell intended to be pastiches of Fu Manchu and Carl Peterson, but that for purposes of literary archaeological research, these characters actually are the Devil Doctor and Bulldog Drummond's nemesis. Based on this, "Captain Kent" can be interpreted as being Kent Allard, who later became The Shadow. "Partners in Crime" can be read at The Wold Newton Universe *website, or in* Rick Lai's Secret Histories: Criminal Masterminds, *Altus Press, 2009.*

August
THE LANGUAGE OF BEES

Mary Russell considers, and then dismisses, consulting with a noted amateur detective.

Autobiographical account by Mary Russell Holmes, edited by Laurie R. King, Bantam Books, May 2009. Given prior references in the Mary Russell books, the amateur detective can only be Lord Peter Wimsey.

Summer 1924-1928
KINGSLEY—GENTLEMANTYVEN

Nat Pinkerton hunts Lord Kingsley, a gentleman thief in the mold of Raffles and Lupin.

Danish pulp Lord Kingsley—Gentlemantyven *#1-133, 1925-1929, by Niels Meyn.* Jess Nevins notes, "As far as I can tell, Pinkerton appears in roughly three quarters of the stories, pursuing (almost always fruitlessly) Kingsley or (on the odd occasion) working with him against some greater evil. It's not a one-shot—Pinkerton is part of the regular cast." The connection with Nat Pinkerton places Lord Kingsley in the Crossover universe.

Autumn. J.G. Reeder's first case, as documented by Edgar Wallace in Room 13.

Autumn. Events of *The Pimpernel and Rosemary* by Baroness Orczy, featuring the adventures of Peter Blakeney, the great-great-grandson of Sir Percy Blakeney (The Scarlet Pimpernel).

Autumn. Novelist and amateur detective Roger Sheringham's first case, *The Layton Court Mystery*, as told by Anthony Berkeley.

Late October
LEGACIES

At the Soviet Embassy in Paris, Arsène Lupin, Rouletabille, Baron Karl, the White Russian Countess, the Countess of Cagliostro, the Marquis de Saint-Loup, the Prince of Guermantes, Commissar Varishkin, and Lady Diana Wyndham are mixed up in intrigue concerning the Romanov jewels. Lupin's nemesis Inspector Ganimard, now retired, also appears. Lupin also refers to Constance Bakefield.

Short story by Jean-Louis Trudel in Tales of the Shadowmen Volume 2: Gentlemen of the Night, *Jean-Marc and Randy Lofficier, eds., Black Coat Press, 2006; reprinted in French in* Les Compagnons de l'Ombre (Tome 3), *Jean-Marc and Randy Lofficier, eds., Rivière Blanche, 2009. Lupin, Ganimard, Constance Bakefield, and the Countess of Cagliostro are from the stories by Maurice Leblanc. Rouletabille is the reporter and detective Joseph Josephin created by Gaston Leroux. Baron Karl is meant to be Baron von Hessel from Philip José Farmer's Doc Savage novel* Escape from Loki. *Baron Karl from the Doc Savage novel* Fortress of Solitude *was first identified with Farmer's Baron von Hessel in Christopher Paul Carey's essay "They Green Eyes Have It—Or Are They Blue?" (*Myths for the Modern Age: Philip José Farmer's Wold Newton Universe*). Based on Carey's research and theory, I used the name "Baron Karl von Hessel" in the essay "Who's Going to Take Over the World When I'm Gone?" (*Myths for the Modern Age: Philip José Farmer's Wold Newton Universe*). The White Russian Countess is intended to be Lili Bugov, the Countess Idivzhopu from* Escape from Loki. *Lady Diana Wyndham and Commissar Varishkin ("Varichkine" in the Wyndham tales) are from stories by Maurice Dekobra, and this crossover links them into the CU. The Marquis de Saint-Loup and the Prince of Guermantes are from the works of Marcel Proust.*

Late Autumn
BEHIND A LOCKED AND BOLTED DOOR
   Rita Yarborough of Company Z encounters Captain Henry Arthur Milton, aka the Ringer.
   A short story found in More J.T.'s Ladies. The Ringer *is by Edgar Wallace. J.T. Edson suggests that the Ringer was in fact an early member of the "Double O" section of the British Secret Service.*

1925

Winter
SCREAM FOR JEEVES
   Bertie Wooster and his manservant Jeeves have several close encounters with a variety of Cthulhuoid horrors.
   This slim volume contains three short stories: "Cats, Rats and Bertie Wooster," "Something Foetid," and "The Rummy Affair of Young Charlie," and is also found in Peter Cannon's volume The Lovecraft Papers. *Jeeves and Wooster are the characters in a humorous series of books by P.G. Wodehouse, and this Cthulhu connection cements their link to the Crossover Universe.*

MAGYAR NICK CARTER
   A Hungarian consulting detective calls himself "Nick Carter" and, following the methods of Carter and Sherlock Holmes, sets up a practice in Budapest.
   Urania Kvny's Magyar Nick Carter *#1-4, 1926.*
   April. Sherlock Holmes crosses paths with H.P. Lovecraft, Frank Belknap Long, and Harry Houdini. (*Pulptime,* a novella written by Frank Belknap Long, Jr., and edited by Peter Cannon, found in Cannon's volume *The Lovecraft Papers,* Guild America Books. Holmes also met Houdini in 1910 and 1922.)
   Spring. Jules de Grandin's first recorded case, "Terror on the Links," by Seabury Quinn
   Spring. The affair of *The Abominable Dr. Phibes.*
   Spring. Chinese detective Huo Sang clashes with Chinese gentleman thief Lu Ping for the first time. ("Huo Sang Versus Lu Ping" by Sun Liahong.)

Spring
ŞERLOK HOLMES'E KARSI CINGÖZ RECAI (SHERLOCK HOLMES VERSUS WILY RECAI)
Turkish thief Recai versus Sherlock Holmes.
1926 story. Later in his career, Recai would joust with Arsène Lupin.

DEN MYSTISKE LORD X
Gentleman thief Lord Kingsley encounters Lord X, a tuxedo-clad occult detective.
Story by Niels Meyn in Lord Kingsley *#74, 1926. Jess Nevins adds, "Niels Meyn then went on to write* Den Gadefulde Dr. X *#1-? (1940?), and* Den Mystiske Mr. X *#1-76 (1943-1944), starring a tuxedo-clad occult detective, variously Dr. X and then Mr. X. His adventures seem to have been fully as entertaining and imaginative as those of, say, Sâr Dubnotal, ranging from the possibly Satanic femme fatale Lady Devil to mummies, cannibals, pirates, androids, vampires, and Leopard-Men."*

May
BELPHÉGOR
The detective Chantecoq and his reporter friend Bellegarde investigate a ghostly presence haunting the Louvre. The Celeritas Detective Agency also appears.
French serial in four episodes, written by Arthur Bernède, 1927; the novelization is called Le Mystère du Louvre *(*The Mystery of the Louvre*). The Celeritas Detective Agency also appeared in the serial* Judex, *which takes place in the CU. According to Jean-Marc Lofficier, "Chantecoq, the 'King of Detectives,' first appeared in 1912 in Bernède's* Coeur de Française *as a French secret service agent, then in* L'Espionne de Guillaume *(1915), and* Chantecoq *(1916), and became a detective after World War I."*

Summer. Charlie Chan's first case, *The House Without a Key*, as related by Earl Derr Biggers.

Summer. Birth of Llana of Gathol, daughter of Tara of Helium and Gahan of Gathol, granddaughter of John Carter and Dejah Thoris.

Summer. Birth of "Shrinking" Violet Holmes, daughter of British spymaster Mycroft Holmes (see my "The Eye of Oran," *Tales of the Shadowmen Volume 2: Gentlemen of the Night*, Black Coat Press, 2006).

Summer. Ruven van Helsing joins the McReady expedition, as told in Jean-Marc Lofficier's *Crépuscule Vaudou* aka *The Katrina Protocol*).

Summer
WHO GOES THERE? AKA THE THING FROM ANOTHER WORLD
McReady, "a bronze giant of a man," joins an Antarctic expedition as meteorologist and second-in-command. He and the other members of the expedition must fight for their lives when they discover a Thing (from another world).

Novella by John W. Campbell, Jr., most recently published in the collection The Antarktos Cycle, *Chaosium, 1999, as* The Thing from another World. *The theory that McReady is Clark Savage, Jr., thinly disguised, was first proposed by Albert Tonik in "A Doc Savage Adventure Rediscovered," published in* Doc Savage Club Reader *#4, 1978. Savage does not have his M.D. yet (according to Farmer, he got his M.D. in 1926); hence, the 1925 date.*

TARZAN VS. THE MOON MEN
Tarzan and Korak travel to the 24th century to battle invaders from the Moon.

Story by Tim Truman, Thomas Yeates, and Al Williamson, in Tarzan *#17-20, Dark Horse Comics. Tarzan crosses-over with another Edgar Rice Burroughs creation, the Moon series, which detailed the history of Earth's battle with the Moon Men from the 20th through the 24th century. The future depicted here is that of Earth's counterpart in an alternate future timeline.*

THE NAILS IN MR. CAYTERER
Detective Robin Thin reads about bounty on the Dis-and-Dat Kid, who has just escaped from Leavenworth.

Story by Dashiell Hammett, Black Mask, *January 1926. The Dis-and-Dat Kid would be mentioned in a Continental Op story, thus putting Robin Thin in the CU.*

DR. Z
Dr. Joseph Zimmertür, an eccentric Jewish psychoanalyst active in Stockholm as a therapist and crime-solver, admits to a friend that he is indebted to Mycroft Holmes for his methods.

A novel by Frank Heller, the first of five Dr. Zimmertür novels.

Autumn
CODE OF THE WOOSTERS
Bertie Wooster makes reference to Blandings Castle.

P.G. Wodehouse crosses-over two of his series, the Jeeves and Wooster stories, and the Lord Emsworth/Blandings Castle stories. This story takes place sometime after 1921, and after Mussolini has come to power, but before Hitler does (therefore, between 1924 and 1933). Art Bollmann adds, "Some of the minor characters in the Jeeves books turn up elsewhere. Barmy Phipps for example features in 'Barmy in Wonderland.' Also Bingo Little appears in many of the Drones stories, while Sir Roderick Glossop turns up in 'Uncle Fred in the Springtime.'"

ANGEL DOWN, SUSSEX
Edwin Winthrop and Catriona Kaye continue their work on behalf of the Diogenes Club, which is becoming the occult investigative arm of the British Secret Service, dealing with the apparently inexplicable. Charles Beauregard is still in charge of the Diogenes Club section of the BSS. Catriona mentions Dr. Martin Hesselius and Dr. Silence. Sir Arthur Conan Doyle and Aleister Crowley also figure in the case, which involves "Little Grey People" and mysterious undertakers who appear out of nowhere, all dressed in black with tops hats and smoked glasses covering their eyes.

A short story by Kim Newman in the U.K. anthology Seven Stars, *Pocket Books, 2000; reprinted in Newman's collection* Dead Travel Fast, *Dinoship Books, 2005; reprinted in Newman's collection* The Secret Files of the Diogenes Club, *MonkeyBrain Books, 2007. Dr. Hesselius was a German psychic physician introduced in J. Sheridan Le Fanu's "Green Tea," first published in the periodical* All the Year Round *(1869). Algernon Blackwood created and wrote the stories featuring the occult investigator Dr. John Silence. This crossover brings both characters into the CU. The Diogenes Club appeared in Doyle and Watson's tales of Sherlock Holmes. It is specifically stated that Sherlock Holmes and Mycroft Holmes are real people in relation to the man who brought their stories to the public, Sir Arthur Conan Doyle. The Little Grey People are possibly "gray" aliens as depicted in* The X-Files *and elsewhere. If so, then the "grays" visited Earth much earlier than 1947 (the Roswell incident). The undertakers are also seen in Newman's "Sorcerer Conjuer Wizard Witch."*

ALLEYS OF PERIL
Sailor Steve Costigan encounters the White Tigress.
Story by Robert E. Howard. The White Tigress had also encountered John Gorman in 1913, thus linking Sailor Steve Costigan into Crossover Universe continuity.

October
GHOSTS OF DRACULA
Séance-buster Harry Houdini becomes involved with Count Dracula, who seeks to contact the spirit of his late beloved Lucy Westenra. Meanwhile, Sher-

lock Holmes turns down Dr. Abraham Van Helsing's plea to help track down a particularly gruesome serial killer in London.

Five-issue comic book miniseries by Martin Powell and Seppo Makinen, Eternity Comics, 1991. Houdini met Holmes, as well as Dr. Watson's literary agent, Sir Arthur Conan Doyle, on several other occasions. Please see Chuck Loridans' MONSTAAH *website for the full history of Count Dracula and the Van Helsings in the Crossover Universe.*

1926

Winter. Events of Sir Arthur Conan Doyle's *The Maracot Deep*, in which a scientist, Maracot, leads an expedition that apparently discovers Atlantis.

Winter. Events of "Pickman's Model," by H.P. Lovecraft.

Winter
ISTANBUL'UN ARSEN LUPIN'I ELEGECMEZ KADRI'NIN SERUVENLERI

Master thief Kadri becomes known as "the Arsène Lupin of Istanbul" based on a daring series of thefts across Istanbul and the Ottoman Empire.

From Istanbul'un Arsen Lupin'i Elegecmez Kadri'nin Seruvenleri *#1-31, 1927, written by Iskender Fahrettin Sertelli.*

THE DEVIL IN THE BELFRY (AKA HEROD'S PEAL)

Macauley of Scotland Yard solves a series of murders which occur in several villages in Kent, including Dullchester and Dymchurch.

Novel by Russell Thorndike, 1932. Macauley was first seen in Thorndike's novel The Slype. *Dymchurch is a real place, and is the home of Thorndike's Dr. Syn. However, Dullchester is a fictional village, and thus serves as a connection bringing Macauley into the Crossover Universe.*

Spring. The events of Thorne Smith's novel *Topper*.

Spring. Marriage of Nick and Nora Charles.

Spring. Nancy Drew's first adventure, *The Secret of the Old Clock*, as recounted by Carolyn Keene.

Spring
THE TERROR
   Superintendent Hallick of Scotland Yard is trying to find a master criminal, Leonard O'Shea. Inspector Elk discusses the O'Shea case with Hallick, mentioning that it's unfortunate that Inspector Bradley, the man most familiar with the O'Shea case, is on vacation. The conclusion reveals that Bradley has secretly assumed a false identity and gone undercover to find O'Shea.
   Novel by Edgar Wallace crossing over two of his detectives, Hallick and Elk. Inspector Bradley may be the same character seen in Wallace's The Flying Squad.

THE ALIEN JUNGLE
   Korak is kidnapped by aliens who are visiting Earth collecting biological specimens.
   Story by Gaylord Dubois and Russ Manning in Korak, Son of Tarzan #21, *Gold Key Comics, February 1968. The aliens are the same ones seen in Manning's series Captain Johner and the Aliens, which ran as a backup feature in* Magnus, Robot Fighter *in the 1960s.*

THE BIG KNOCKOVER
   The Dis-and-Dat Kid gets double-crossed and murdered.
   Story by Dashiell Hammett, Black Mask, February 1927, featuring the Continental Op. The Dis-and-Dat Kid was previously mentioned in a Robin Thin story by Hammett.

Summer. Birth of Bob Morane.

Summer. Aviator Ted Scott flies *Over the Ocean to Paris, or, Ted Scott's Daring Long Distance Flight*, as told by Franklin W. Dixon.

Summer
ALL'S WELL WITH BINGO
   At the Hotel Magnifique in Nice, the guests include the "Prince and Princess of Graustark" and the "ex-king of Ruritania."
   A tale in the Drones Club series by P.G. Wodehouse in Tales from the Drones Club. *The story's protagonist, Bingo, was originally a supporting character in Wo-*

dehouse's Jeeves series, which takes place in the CU. Ruritania (from The Prisoner of Zenda) is a country in the CU and this crossover also confirms that the Graustark novels of George Barr McCutcheon take place in the CU.

Late October. Arthur Conan Doyle, Harry Houdini, Charles Fort, and H.P. Lovecraft come together to fight the menace of the Great Old Ones, who have connected to Houdini after he has ventured into the Dreamlands in an attempt to discover the secrets of the afterlife. The Old Ones use a branch of the Illuminati as their earthly agents. (*Necronaughts*, a graphic novel by Gordon Rennie and Frazer Irving, published by 2000 AD, 2003.)

Late Autumn
X ESQUIRE
Terry Mannering is the vigilante hero who, as "X Esquire," kills criminals who are planning mass murder with poison cigarettes. At the conclusion, Mannering receives a full pardon, retires, and plans to marry. Assistant Commissioner Bill Kennedy of Scotland Yard appears; Kennedy's subordinates are Henderson and Peters.

Novel by Leslie Charteris, 1927. Henderson, Peters, and Kennedy are also variously mentioned in The Saint Meets His Match *(aka* She Was a Lady, *aka* Angels of Doom), The Saint vs. Scotland Yard *(aka* The Holy Terror) *and* The Saint and Mr. Teal *(aka* Once More the Saint). *In* The Saint Closes the Case *(aka* The Last Hero), *Simon says that Patricia Holm is "Spending a couple of days in Devonshire with the Mannerings." All these references place Terry Mannering in the CU.*

1927

January-February
THE ADVENTURE OF THE CLUBS AKA THE TERROR OVER LONDON
Solar Pons' raconteur, Dr. Parker, refers to Pons as the greatest detective ever, other than the "late Sherlock Holmes." The murder of Lord Cantlemere is mentioned.

A Solar Pons novella by Dr. Lyndon Parker, and edited by August Derleth, published in The Final Adventures of Solar Pons, *Mycroft and Moran Books, 1998. Parker, of course, is covering for the fact that Sherlock Holmes is still alive. Rick Lai points out, "Lord Cantlemere was the rude overbearing government official in Doyle's 'The Adventure of the Mazarain Stone' (Baring-Gould puts the story in 1903). It could be that the two Cantlemeres are the same person, or that the Lord Cantlemere of the 1920s was the son of the nobleman encountered by Holmes."*

February
ROUGH NIGHT IN INNSMOUTH
A sailor named Dorgan helps an old buddy in Innsmouth.
Short story by Ron Shiflet in Nightscapes, *December 1999. Matthew Baugh notes that "It takes place the year before the assault on Innsmouth by the U.S. government, as mentioned in 'The Shadow over Innsmouth' by H.P. Lovecraft. In the story, Steve Costigan is referred to as Dorgan, which suggests that his friend Max Peaster did not write it down until after 1933 when Steve was using the Dorgan alias for all his stories. Alternatively, the Dorgan of the story may not be Steve at all but another tough sailor character of Robert E. Howard's named Mike Dorgan."*

Winter. The first case of Richard William Chandos, Blind Corner, as documented by Dornford Yates.
Winter. Publication of Trader Horn, an autobiographical account by African explorer Alfred Aloysius "Trader" Horn. Horn, seventy-three years of age at publication, was in his lifetime an animal collector, gold prospector, Scotland Yard detective, artist, archeologist, and blood-brother of cannibals. A fictionalized film version was released in 1931.

Winter
THE CASE OF THE CURIOUSLY COMPETENT CONJURER
Dr. Anton Zarnak receives a telepathic message from Dr. Phibes, who is resting in his tomb. It is also stated that that Zarnak trained with Spratt at St. Swithen's. The Orlac case, in which an organ transplant leads to horrible results, is mentioned. Zarnak sends telegrams to a New York neurologist and to occultists in New Orleans and New Hampshire.

A Dr. Zarnak short story by James Ambuehl and Simon Bucher-Jones, in Lin Carter's Anton Zarnak Supernatural Sleuth. *Since Zarnak is in the Crossover Universe, so is Dr. Phibes. According to Rick Lai, "The first Dr. Phibes film,* The Abominable Dr. Phibes, *was set in 1925. Mrs. Phibes died during an operation in 1921 (see the year on her coffin in the mausoleum), and Dr. Vesalius reminded Nurse Allen that the operation was four years ago. The second Dr. Phibes movie,* Dr. Phibes Rises Again, *happens three years later (1928)." Lai continues, "Sir Lancelot*

Spratt taught surgery at St. Swithin's (called 'St. Swithens' in the Zarnak story) in Richard Gordon's Doctor in the House series. Spratt would have been too young to have been a teacher at St. Swithin's when Zarnak attended there, and would more likely have been a fellow student. The neurologist is Dr. Lowell from A. Merritt's Burn, Witch, Burn *and* Creep, Shadow, Creep. *The New Orleans occultist is Etienne de Marginy from the Lovecraft/Price collaboration, 'Through the Gates of the Silver Key.'"* Simon Bucher-Jones has responded, "Very pleased to have my work noticed, however as the Spratt in the story is not given a forename could he not in fact be Lancelot Spratt's father? That's my cop-out and I'm sticking to it!" Chuck Loridans points out that the Orlac reference is to The Hands of Orlac *(directed by Robert Wiene, 1924, based on the book* The Hands of Orlac *by Maurice Renard), the story of a classical pianist whose hands are crushed in a train accident. When a scientist replaces Orlac's hands with those of a killer, the results are murderous.*

Spring. Silver John is born in Moore County, NC.

Spring
THE SHADES OF PEMBERLEY

At the behest of Edith, the Dowager Duchess of Holderness, and her secretary, Augustus Moran, Sexton Blake and his assistant Tinker investigate the case of the ghost of Bess d'Arcy of Pemberley, who is haunting Pemberley House. Blake places a call to Sherlock Holmes to discuss Holmes prior dealings with the 6th Duke of Holderness during the Priory School case; he also speaks with Russell, and Holmes' niece Violet is mentioned. Holmes reminds Blake that the late 6th Duke's son is not now the 7th Duke, but does not further explain this cryptic remark. It is also noted that Blake has worked with Nelson Lee, Sir Eric Palmer, and Erast Fandorin. Captain John Caldwell-Grebson is mentioned as having been involved with the d'Arcys in the late 1500s, and that the d'Arcy and the Caldwell-Grebson families joined years later when Ursula d'Arcy married Ralph Arthur Caldwell-Grebson in 1667. Blake says that normally he'd pass the case on to Carnacki or Dickson, but that he'll keep it since years back, in 1904, he did a bit of work for the 6th Duke after Holmes' involvement in the Priory School affair, tracking down the whereabouts of the Duke's illegitimate son, James Wildman. On their way to Pemberley House, Blake and Tinker pass through the village of Lambton, as well as the Lower Gill Moor and the Fighting Cock Inn. At Pemberley House, they see portraits of Fitzwilliam Darcy and his wife, Elizabeth Bennet Darcy. The Duchess mentions her adopted son, Carlo Deguy, and her late husband's uncle, Sir William Clayton. She says that her son, the 7th Duke, has refused to see her for almost twenty years. Moran recites much family history of Darcys and of the Dukes of Holderness, the Claytons, including rumors of a surviving feral child after the wreck of the ship *Fuwalda*, but it is all passed off to rumor. However, Blake knows, via one of Holmes' secret case files from 1916, that there was a *Fuwalda* survivor, who was raised by apes; this man resembled his cousin, the 7th Duke, so much that when the 7th Duke died, the ape-man took the 7th Duke's place, although he was entitled to a lordship anyway. He did so to avoid publicity, and thus refused to ever see the late 7th Duke's mother, Edith, as she was the only one who might pierce the façade. Blake identifies Augustus Moran as the grandson of the infamous Col. Sebastian Moran, and then recruits Dr. Francis Ardan, who is about to mount a Far East expedition, to help on the case. It turns out that Ardan is the son of James Wildman, the illegitimate son of the late 6th Duke. Wildman was known to use aliases such as Savage and Ardan, and is credited with opening up British Hidalgo. It is noted that the younger Ardan is a veteran of a 1925 Antarctic expedition, and that his father explored the Lost World with Hareton Ironcastle. Professor Challenger and Lord John Roxton are also mentioned. In the end, Ardan refuses to help break the curse of Bess of Pemberley. Blake calls one of his operatives, Baron St. John-Orsini, who discovers that the Duchess' "adopted" son is really her biological child by the self-styled "Comte de Guy." Blake finally solves the Duchess' ghost problem, and she refuses to pay him, until Blake mentions the case of the unsolved murder of Charles Augustus Milverton.

Short story in two parts by Win Scott Eckert in Farmerphile: The Magazine of Philip José Farmer *#8 (April 2007) and 9 (July 2007), Christopher Paul Carey and Paul Spiteri, eds. The story serves as a prequel to Philip José Farmer and Win Scott Eckert's novel,* The Evil in Pemberley House *(Subterranean Press, 2009), and is incorporated into that novel as a tale that the protagonist, Patricia Wildman, reads. Sexton Blake, Tinker, and their housekeeper Mrs. Bardell are from the long-running series of Sexton Blake novels begun by Harry Blyth and continued by countless others. The late 6th Duke of Holdernesse; the Dowager Duchess of Holdernesse; their kidnapped son (the short-lived 7th Duke); the illegitimate son of the 6th Duke, Mr. James Wildman (as Farmer identified him in* Tarzan Alive *and* Doc Savage: His Apocalyptic Life; *Doyle and Watson called him "James Wilder"); the Fighting Cock Inn; the villain Hayes; and the Lower Gill Moor are all from Doyle and Watson's Sherlock Holmes story, "The Adventure of the Priory School." The blackmailer Charles Augustus Milverton is from Doyle and Watson's "The Adventure of Charles Augustus Milverton." The Lost World, Professor Challenger, and Lord John Roxton are from Doyle's* The Lost World. *Pemberley House, the village of Lambton, Fitzwilliam Darcy, and Elizabeth Bennet are from Jane Austen's* Pride and Prejudice. *Doctor Francis Ardan and his expedition to the Far East are from Guy D'Armen's* Doc Ardan: City of Gold and Lepers. *Jean-Marc Lofficier originally made the identification between Doc Ardan and Doc Savage (aka Clark Savage, Jr., aka James Clarke Wildman, Jr.). The Central American country of Hidalgo is from the Doc Savage pulp novels by Lester Dent, but British Hidalgo is from the Limekiller stories by Avram Davidson. The two Hidalgos, here, are meant to be the same country. Many of the crossover connections come from the Wold*

Newton mythos of Philip José Farmer: Doc Savage (real name: James Clarke Wildman, Jr.) as the son of James Wilder (real name: James Clarke Wildman) and grandson of the 6th Duke (Doc Savage: His Apocalyptic Life); the Dukes of Holdernesse = the Dukes of Greystoke (Tarzan Alive); Holdernesse Hall = Pemberley House (Tarzan Alive); Captain John Caldwell-Grebson, Ralph Arthur Caldwell-Grebson, Ursula d'Arcy, Fitzwilliam Bennet Darcy, Athena Darcy, Sir Gawain Darcy (Tarzan Alive); the Greystokes as descendants of the Darcys (Tarzan Alive); Bess of Pemberley, the Pemberley Curse, and Augustus Moran (The Evil in Pemberley House); Sexton Blake's 1904 investigation into the whereabouts of James Wilder, the illegitimate son of the 6th Duke (Doc Savage: His Apocalyptic Life); Sir William Clayton (Doc Savage: His Apocalyptic Life); Edith, the Duchess of Holdernesse/Greystoke as the murderess of Charles Augustus Milverton (Tarzan Alive and The Evil in Pemberley House); the duchess' illegitimate son, --- Deguy, by the "Comte de Guy" (The Evil in Pemberley House); the duchess as a descendant of the Darcys (The Evil in Pemberley House, implied); the kidnapped son of the Duke and Duchess from "Priory House" as the 7th Duke of Greystoke (Tarzan Alive); Holmes and Watson's 1916 African adventure (The Adventure of the Peerless Peer); the 8th Duke, Tarzan assuming the identity of his look-alike cousin, the 7th Duke, upon the 7th Duke's death in 1910, in order to avoid publicity surrounding status as a feral child raised by "apes" (Tarzan Alive and The Adventure of the Peerless Peer); and the deaths of John and Alice Clayton off French Congo, and the wreck of the Fuwalda off St. Helena (Edgar Rice Burroughs' Tarzan of the Apes and Farmer's Tarzan Alive). The "Comte de Guy" is Carl Peterson from H.C. "Sapper" McNeile's Bulldog Drummond novels. Hareton Ironcastle's expedition to the Lost World with Doc Savage's father is from Ironcastle by J.-H. Rosny and Philip José Farmer. Russell is Mary Russell, Holmes' wife from Laurie R. King's long-running series of novels. Sir Eric Palmer, the king of detectives, is from Felifax, the Tiger Man by Paul Féval, Fils. Nelson Lee is from the dime novels by Maxwell Scott and various others. Erast Petrovich Fandorin is the Russian detective from the series of novels by Boris Akunin. Carnacki is William Hope Hodgson's Thomas Carnacki, the "ghost finder." Harry Dickson is from the stories by Jean Ray and various others. Baron St. John-Orsini is meant to be the grandfather of Baron Reynaldo

St. John-Orsini from *The Baroness* series of 1970s thrillers by Paul Kenyon. Violet Holmes, co-created by Matthew Baugh and Eckert, is Sherlock Holmes' niece from Eckert's story "The Eye of Oran," Tales of the Shadowmen, Volume 2: Gentlemen of the Night. The identification of Augustus Moran as the grandson of Col. Sebastian Moran, and the Christian name of the Duchess' illegitimate son, Carlo, are Eckert's.

GUNS OF THE DRAGON
Bat Lash, Hans von Hammer, and Biff Bradley go on a mission to save China and get more than they bargained for when they encounter the dinosaurs of Dragon Island. Lash also mentions his acquaintance, the legendary gunfighter Jonah Hex. "Chop-Chop" and Miss Fear, in their pre-Blackhawk days, also make appearances, as do the ninja shapeshifter Major Kung and an immortal villain who is called Vandal Savage in this story.

1998 DC Comics miniseries by Tim Truman, who manages to defuse the ethnic stereotyping inherent in the "Chop-Chop" character. There is already a CU version of Blackhawk (see the Batman and Captain America *crossover). This adventure integrates the CU versions of Lash, Von Hammer, Hex, and Kung, as well as Miss Fear, who would go on to many appearances as an ally of the Blackhawks. Von Hammer's descendant, Heinrich Franz, later met The Batman. And Biff Bradley's younger brother, Slam, later opened his own detective agency and worked on an important case with The Batman and Sherlock Holmes.*

LE PIÈGE MACHIAVÉLIQUE (THE MACHIAVELLIAN TRAP)
Harry Dickson works with Belgian detective Hercule Poirot.
#5 of Harry Dickson *(German series); Dutch series #73.*

Summer. Although Harry Houdini is believed to have died the previous year, on October 31, 1926, Sherlock Holmes is once again involved in his affairs. In the course of their investigation, Holmes and Watson interview Houdini's friend, Walter B. Gibson. It is unclear why the editor attributed a fictional statement to Gibson, to the effect that Gibson was thinking about creating a character for radio and the pulps called "The Shadow." (Sherlock Holmes and the Houdini Birthright, Part Two, novel by Dr. Watson, edited by Val Andrews, Breese Books, 1995. Gibson, of course, was Kent "The Shadow" Allard's primary biographer and wrote of his exploits under the pen name of Maxwell Grant in *The Shadow Magazine* from 1931 to 1949. Gibson's alleged statement is clearly fictional since The Shadow is a real person.)

Summer. Birth of Adélaïde Lupin, daughter of Arsène Lupin and American reporter Patricia Johnston (see "The Eye of Oran," *Tales of the Shadowmen Volume 2: Gentlemen of the Night*, Black Coat Press, 2006; and the Wold Newton novel *The Evil in Pemberley House*).

Summer-Fall
DOC ARDAN: CITY OF GOLD AND LEPERS
   Doctor Francis Ardan and Doctor Louise Ducharme battle the evil Doctor Natas. Ardan was born in 1901, has his M.D. from Johns Hopkins, his Ph.D. in other scientific fields, and is described as having bronze skin. Dr. Natas (Satan spelled backwards) is an Asian megalomaniac with green eyes, or at least green flecks in his eyes. There are also references to a metal from Wakanda and the Mi-Go.

   La Cite de l'Or et de la Lèpre is a 1928 novel by Guy d'Armen adapted and retold by Jean-Marc and Randy Lofficier, Black Coat Press, August 2004. The description of Doc Ardan easily could be that of a young Doc Savage. In fact, the details of Doc Ardan's birthdate and medical education come directly from Philip José Farmer's Doc Savage: His Apocalyptic Life. *Doc could be using the alias "Francis Ardan"; as the Lofficiers point out in their introduction, "The name Ardan, or more properly Ardent (the last t is silent in French), means fierce, fiery, wild, or savage..." Likewise, Dr. Natas could be Dr. Fu Manchu, who was described as having a face like Satan. So for crossover purposes, this is very likely a battle between Doc Savage and the Devil Doctor. Ducharme was first seen as Fu Manchu's concubine in the early 1970s in Marvel Comics'* Master of Kung Fu. *Perhaps the Ducharme in* Master of Kung Fu *is the descendant of Louise Ducharme. The remote African kingdom of Wakanda is from Marvel Comics, so a version of Wakanda must exist in the CU. In the Cthulhu Mythos, the Mi-Go are the source of the legends of the Yeti of Tibet.*

Late Summer
CLUBLAND HEROES
   Edwin Winthrop enlists his lover, Catriona Kaye, to take on a murder investigation on behalf of the Diogenes Club. Charles Beauregard is part of the Ruling Cabal of the Diogenes Club, along with Sir Henry Merrivale and others. Maple White Land is mentioned, as is Doctor Shade.
   A short story by Kim Newman in the anthology Retro Pulp Tales, *Joe R. Lansdale, editor, Subterranean Press, 2006; reprinted in Newman's collection* The Secret Files of the Diogenes Club, *MonkeyBrain Books, 2007. Merrivale*

solved cases chronicled by John Dickson Carr writing as Carter Dickson. Maple White Land is from Doyle's The Lost World. *Doctor Shade is Newman's own take on the 1930s pulp vigilante.*

Autumn. First recorded adventure of British spy "James Nobody." (*The Red Virgin of the Kremlin* by Charles Lucieto.)

Autumn. Miss Marple's first case, *Murder at the Vicarage* by Agatha Christie.

Autumn
THE WHITE RIDER

Peter Lestrange is supposedly a crook, but he's eventually revealed to be a kind of Secret Service agent for the Foreign Office. He is also planning to marry a girl named Marion.

Novel by Leslie Charteris, 1928. In "The Gold Standard" (from The Saint and Mr. Teal*), Patricia Holm states "I met Marion Lestrange in Bond Street yesterday, and I promised to drop in for a cocktail this evening." The connection to The Saint places Lestrange in the CU.*

Late Summer 1927-1928
TARZAN AT THE EARTH'S CORE

Tarzan meets Jason Gridley and travels to the inner world of Pellucidar.

In this novel, Edgar Rice Burroughs crosses-over two of his own creations, Tarzan and Pellucidar. The date is derived from Farmer's Tarzan Alive. *The character Jason Gridley is also mentioned in Burroughs' John Carter of Mars series. It should be noted here that, although in* Tarzan Alive *Philip José Farmer considered Pellucidar and this novel to be completely fictional in relation to the "real" Tarzan stories, he nevertheless provided a date for this adventure in his Tarzan chronology. Additionally, after he wrote* Tarzan Alive, *Farmer gave permission to Western and adventure writer J.T. Edson to use and refer to the Wold Newton concepts in his books. Several of Edson's books referred to Tarzan and family relocating to Pellucidar in the 1970s. Farmer never objected to Edson's reintroduction of Pellucidar into the Wold Newton mythos. I think that Pellucidar is a real location in the CU, although its true nature has not been fully revealed (perhaps it is more accurately a grand series of underground caverns, as depicted in "Black as the Pit, From Pole to Pole") and that Tarzan and others really did travel there in* Tarzan at the Earth's Core.

Autumn 1927-1928
FELIFAX, L'HOMME TIGRE

A hybrid tiger-man created by a mad scientist vs. a great British detective, Sir Eric Palmer: "Sir Eric Palmer had a worldwide reputation, not only because his abilities as a doctor had advertised themselves in marvelous cures, but because numerous complicated police cases owed their elucidation to him. Much like Doctor Watson, the friend of the great Sherlock Holmes, he had begun by collaborating with two or three notable detectives. Then, his own methods being in flagrant contradiction to those of the police, he had undertaken to interest himself personally, working alone on several mysterious cases in which he had succeeded where others had failed." Deep in the case, Sir Eric tells the head of Scotland Yard: "The master of us all, the great Sherlock Holmes, often acted without the support of your services." Regarding a rich divorcée's country house, it is said, "The musketeer D'Artagnan and Cyrano de Bergerac stayed there when they came to England to save the son of Anne of Austria." In an open letter, a journalist urges the divorcée not to "…play the part of a petty Marguerite de Bourgogne."

Novel by Paul Féval fils, 1929, translated and adapted by Brian Stableford, Black Coat Press, 2007. The crossover references to Holmes and Watson place Felifax and Sir Eric Palmer in the Crossover Universe. The incident involving D'Artagnan and Cyrano de Bergerac is recorded in another crossover novel by Féval fils, the four-volume novel D'Artagnan contre Cyrano de Bergerac, *1925, although of course the novel involves the fictional versions of D'Artagnan and de Bergerac rather than the historical characters. Féval fils also wrote several pastiche sequels to both Dumas'* The Three Musketeers *and Edmond Rostand's 1897 play recounting the exploits of Cyrano de Bergerac. Marguerite de Bourgogne is from Dumas père's play* La Tour de Nesle, *which is thus linked into the Crossover Universe.*

1928

Winter
A FIGHTING MAN OF MARS
    Jason Gridley is in Pellucidar during the time period that this John Carter of Mars novel takes place.
    Novel by E.R. Burroughs. The date is derived from Farmer's Tarzan Alive *and John Flint Roy's* A Guide to Barsoom.

February
THE CASTLEMAINE MURDERS
  Phryne Fisher, a female private detective in Melbourne, Australia, notes, "Someone had married Lord Greystoke, admittedly, but he was just a large ape."
  Novel by Kerry Greenwood, Poisoned Pen Press, 2006. Loki Carbis notes that the context makes it clear that Phryne is referring to a real person. This places the Phryne Fisher stories in the Crossover Universe.

  March-May. "The Dreams in the Witch-House," as chronicled by H.P. Lovecraft.
  March 19. Birth of secret agent John Drake (*Danger Man*, *The Prisoner*).
  Spring. The first case of Mrs. Adela Lestrange Bradley, Home Office psychologist and amateur criminologist, as recounted in *Speedy Death* by Gladys Mitchell.

Spring
BACK TO THE STONE AGE
  Tarzan's expedition of a year ago is mentioned in this Pellucidar novel.
  Novel by E.R. Burroughs. The date is derived from Farmer's Tarzan Alive.

EL SHERIFF

Sheriff "Arizona Jim" first fights crime in the American Southwest, but soon takes the fight all over the world, confronting the minions of Fu Manchu and capturing Captain Nemo's *Nautilus*. After his death, Arizona Jim comes back to life to continue the fight against evil, aiding his former sidekick Pete.

From El Sheriff *#1-200, 1929-1935, and* Pete *#1-?, 1935-? The references to Fu Manchu and Captain Nemo place Arizona Jim and Pete in the CU.*

May. First adventure of mail pilot and daredevil barnstormer Tailspin Tommy Tompkins.

Summer. Detective Ellery Queen's first published case, *The Roman Hat Mystery*, written by "Ellery Queen." (Although we are told that Queen and his father, retired police Inspector Richard Queen, were major cogs in the New York police force between 1910 and 1930, Julian Symons has concluded that this is obfuscation on the narrator's part. The characters speech and behavior clearly indicate that the mysteries take place near their publication dates, e.g., the late 1920s and early 1930s. See Symons' *The Great Detectives: Seven Original Investigations*. Symons also makes a convincing case that, after the tenth Ellery Queen novel, the novels and stories actually recount the mystery-solving exploits of Ellery's younger brother, Dan Queen.)

Summer. Inspector Jules Maigret's "first" case, *Pietr-le-Letton* (*The Case of Peter the Lett*), as told by Georges Simenon. Actually, Simenon's novel *Train de Nuit* (*Night Train*), written under the under the pseudonym Christian Brulls, was the first to feature police detective Maigret. Maigret's role in the novel is a small one, but Simenon wrote (under the pseudonyms Christian Brulls and Georges Sim) three more novels featuring police detective Maigret, before the introduction of Inspector Maigret.

Summer. First recorded exploit of Ken King, South Seas trader and adventurer. ("King of the Islands" by Charles Hamilton.)

Summer
PIRATES OF VENUS

Carson Napier, "Carson of Venus," departs for Barsoom (Mars), but arrives instead on Amtor (Venus), just after the events of *Back to the Stone Age*, a Pellucidar novel.

The first novel in the Venus series by Edgar Rice Burroughs. At this point, we can conclude that all of Burroughs' major creations, Tarzan, Pellucidar, John Carter of Mars, and Carson of Venus, all start out in the Crossover Universe, although some of the characters who start out in this universe end up in a parallel universe, which I will call the "The Edgar Rice Burroughs Alternate Universe." The remaining novels of the Venus series are: Lost on Venus, Carson of Venus, Escape on Venus, *and* The Wizard of Venus.

THE RELUCTANT PRINCESS
Doctor Francis Ardan liberates a Princess who is unenthusiastic about being rescued. The Princess later becomes the heroine Phantom Angel, batting evildoers such as the anarchist Azzef, her exploits recounted by the prominent journalist Joseph Rouletabille.

Short story by Randy Lofficier in Tales of the Shadowmen Volume 4: Lords of Terror, *Jean-Marc and Randy Lofficier, eds., Black Coat Press, 2008; reprinted in French in* Les Compagnons de l'Ombre (Tome 2), *Jean-Marc and Randy Lofficier, eds., Rivière Blanche, 2008; and in the Lofficiers' collection* Pacifica, *Black Coat Press, 2010. Ardan is from Guy d'Armen's* Doc Ardan: City of Gold and Lepers, *in which he was identified as Doc Savage in the Loffciers' translation. The Princess is Charles Perrault's Sleeping Beauty. Rouletabille is Gaston Leroux's hero, while Azzef the Anarchist is historical but also the archfoe of the Sâr Dubnotal. The Phantom Angel is Randy Lofficier's creation.*

DAREDEVIL
Terry Mannering, a friend of hero Christopher "Storm" Arden, briefly appears. Inspector Teal also appears. At the conclusion of the case, Arden assumes the title of Lord Hannassay and the impression is given that he will marry the heroine.

Novel by Leslie Charteris, 1929. Inspector Teal is the Saint's nemesis. Terry Mannering is from Charteris' X Esquire. *In* The Saint Closes the Case *(aka* The Last Hero*), Patricia Holm tells Simon Templar, "Darling Simon...you know we'd promised to have dinner with the Hannassays." Since the Saint's exploits take place in the CU, so do the events of this novel.*

THE INDIA-RUBBER MAN
Inspector John Wade of Scotland Yard works with Inspector Elk.

A novel in the Inspector Elk series by Edgar Wallace. Wade appeared in J.T. Edson's Cap Fog, Texas Ranger Meet Mr. J.G. Reeder. *This link places Inspector Elk in the CU. Other novels in the series are* The Fellowship of the Frog, The Joker, The Twister, *and* White Face.

JOURNEY TO THE CENTER OF CHAOS
In Tibet, Professor Whateley of Miskatonic University and his companion, John Green, seek the Crown of Genghis. Meldrum Strange has financed the expedition. Robur and his cohort, Sâr Dubnotal, also seek the Crown, to prevent it from falling into the wrong hands. "John Green" is later revealed to by James Schuyler Grim, aka Jimgrim. The Iron Temple in London is mentioned. Other references are "the Hideous Strength," Orichalcum, Ys, and Robur's friend Seaton. References connected to the Cthulhu Mythos are: Yog-Sothoth, the "Crawling Chaos"; the Dyzan; K'n-yan; Mi-Go; Yian-Ho; and the Heart of Ahriman, aka the Heart of Azathoth.

Short story by Jean-Marc and Randy Lofficier in Tales of the Shadowmen Volume 1: The Modern Babylon, *Jean-Marc and Randy Lofficier, eds., Black Coat Press, 2005; reprinted in French in* Les Compagnons de l'Ombre (Tome 3), *Jean-Marc and Randy Lofficier, eds., Rivière Blanche, 2009; and in the Lofficiers' collection* Pacifica, *Black Coat Press, 2010. Miskatonic University is from the tales of H.P. Lovecraft. Meldrum Strange is an American millionaire from Talbot Mundy's tales including* Jimgrim *and* The Gray Mahatma. *Robur is from Jules Verne's novel* Robur the Conqueror *and its sequel* Master of the World, *while Sâr Dubnotal appeared in French pulp stories by an anonymous creator. The Iron Temple is from a Harry Dickson novel confirming the "American Sherlock Holmes" in the CU. "The Hideous Strength," is from C.S. Lewis' Space Trilogy. Orichalcum is from Plato's accounts of Atlantis. Ys is a magical land in Breton folklore. Seaton is Richard Seaton from E.E. "Doc" Smith's Skylark books; since the Skylark series involves the discovery of alien beings and societies on a large scale in the 1920s-30s, it's assumed that the series take place in an alternate timeline to the CU; the Seaton in this tale is the Crossover Universe version of the character. References connected to the Cthulhu Mythos: the "Crawling Chaos" is from Lovecraft's "The Dream-Quest of Unknown Kadath"; the Dzyan are from* The Book of Dzyan; *the K'n-yan are a subterranean people from "The Mound" by H.P. Lovecraft and Zealia Bishop; Mi-Go is another name for the Yeti of Tibet; Yian-Ho is either an eldritch place accessible through a dimensional portal or an Asian locale associated with the Plateau of Leng. The Heart of Ahriman is from Robert E. Howard's Conan novel* The Hour of the Dragon, *aka* Conan the Conqueror. *In this story, the Heart of Ahriman is associated with the Heart of Azathoth; in Lovecraft's Cthulhu Mythos, Azathoth is Outer God known as the Primal Chaos.*

TARZAN AND THE CULT OF THE MAHAR (aka THE MAHAGGA)

Tarzan encounters a Mahar from Pellucidar.

This comic story by Russ Manning originally ran in the daily Tarzan *newspaper strip (March 12, 1971-July 31, 1971); a reprint can be found in #235 of the DC Comics* Tarzan *series (March 1975).*

Autumn. Simon Templar, aka The Saint, has his first exploit, as recorded by Leslie Charteris in *Meet—The Tiger!*

Autumn. Birth of Richard Grayson (Robin, and later, the second Batman).

Autumn
KORAK AT THE EARTH'S CORE (aka RETURN TO PELLUCIDAR/ESCAPE FROM PELLUCIDAR)
Tarzan and his son Korak are in Pellucidar.
Russ Manning's daily newspaper strip tale *(November 22, 1971-July 29, 1972)* is reprinted in #238 of the DC Comics Tarzan series *(June 1975)* and concludes in #60 of DC's Tarzan Family *(December 1975).*

CADAVRES EXQUIS
As Fascinax (George Leicester, M.D.) heads to his latest duel with his archnemesis, the diabolical Numa Pergyll, he recalls the events of a year ago in Paris, when he and Jules de Grandin stopped Pergyll's most recent scheme.
Short story by Bill Cunningham in Tales of the Shadowmen Volume 1: The Modern Babylon, *Jean-Marc and Randy Lofficier, eds., Black Coat Press, 2005* reprinted in French in Les Compagnons de l'Ombre (Tome 5), *Jean-Marc and Randy Lofficier, eds., Rivière Blanche, 2009. Fascinax is Dr. George Leicester, an occult investigator with supreme mental powers, conferred upon him by a mystic in the Philippines. The French* Fascinax *series was published by the Librairie des Romans Choisis in 1921. In 1924, the series was reprinted and translated into Italian. The author or authors remain anonymous. The reference to de Grandin places Fascinax in the CU.*

THE ENGLISH GENTLEMAN'S BALL
THE SPEAR OF DESTINY
Master criminal Belphégor marries the wealthy Gregor Mac Duhl and becomes stepmother to Sylvie. The heroine Phantom Angel defeats Belphégor's plan, with an assist from Jeeves and Bertie Wooster. The Phantom Angel then, on Rouletabille's recommendation, consults Parisian attorney Gaston Sainclair for his help in securing a small house in the off-the-beaten-path village of Chalabre. The Phantom Angel intends to hide the recently discovered Spear of Destiny there, to that her arch-enemy Belphégor cannot locate it.
"The English Gentleman's Ball" is a short story by Randy Lofficier in Tales of the Shadowmen Volume 5: The Vampires of Paris, *Jean-Marc and*

Randy Lofficier, eds., *Black Coat Press, 2009; reprinted in French in* Les Compagnons de l'Ombre (Tome 5), *Jean-Marc and Randy Lofficier, eds., Rivière Blanche, 2009; and in the Lofficiers' collection* Pacifica, *Black Coat Press, 2010.*

"The Spear of Destiny" is a short story by Randy Lofficier in Tales of the Shadowmen Volume 6: Grand Guignol, *Jean-Marc and Randy Lofficier, eds., Black Coat Press, 2010; reprinted in French in* Les Compagnons de l'Ombre (Tome 6), *Jean-Marc and Randy Lofficier, eds., Rivière Blanche, 2010.*

The Phantom Angel is Randy Lofficier's creation, based on the Princess from Charles Perrault's "Sleeping Beauty." Belphégor *is a French serial in four episodes, written by Arthur Bernède, 1927; the accompanying novelization is* Le Mystère du Louvre *(*The Mystery of the Louvre*).* Gregor Mac Duhl and Sylvie Mac Duhl are from Jean de La Hire's Nyctalope series. Jeeves and Bertie Wooster are from the popular stories by P.G. Wodehouse. The tale is a play on "Cinderella." *Rouletabille and Maître Gaston Sainclair are from Gaston Leroux's* Le Mystère de la Chambre Jaune (Rouletabille and the Mystery of the Yellow Room).

October
THE MURDER OF RANDOLPH CARTER

Hercule Poirot investigates the recent death of Randolph Carter. The murder weapon is an Arumbaya fetish. Charles Dexter Ward is one of the suspects, as are Lavinia Whateley (a cousin of Wilbur Whateley and Randolph Carter) and David Marsh. The murder centers on a copy of Quentin Moretus Cassave's renowned Flemish translation of the *Necronomicon*. The copy comes from the Comte d'Erlette's collection. A fearless reporter with a tuft of hair is mentioned. The cat at the hotel where the murder occurs is named Murr. The hotel turns out to be the house once known as Malpertuis, now called Pension Doucedame.

Short story by Jean-Marc Lofficier *in* Tales of the Shadowmen Volume 3: Danse Macabre, *Jean-Marc and Randy Lofficier, eds., Black Coat Press, 2007; reprinted in French in* Les Compagnons de l'Ombre (Tome 1), *Jean-Marc and Randy Lofficier, eds., Rivière Blanche, 2008; and in the Lofficiers' collection* Pacifica, *Black Coat Press, 2010.* Randolph Carter is from H.P. Lovecraft's "The Statement of Randolph Carter," "The Silver Key," and others. Peter Cannon's "The Chronology Out of Time" places the death of Wilbur Whateley on 3 August 1928; since Lavinia is trying to preserve her inheritance in the wake of Wilbur's death, "The Murder of Randolph Carter" must take place sometime after that. Lavinia Whateley was Wilbur's late mother in Lovecraft's "The Dunwich Horror." Here, she is Wilbur's cousin, so Lavinia must be a family name. Lovecraft's "The Case of Charles Dexter Ward" ends in April 1928, but perhaps when Curwen dissolved into dust, the maddened Ward was still alive. Cannon's "Chronology" had Carter disappearing from the sight of men on 7 October 1928, thus placing this tale shortly thereafter. The Comte d'Erlette wrote the

Cultes des Goules *and first appeared in Robert Bloch's Cthulhu Mythos tale "The Suicide in the Study." The Comte's name is based on Mythos author August Derleth. David Marsh is a member of the Marsh family seen in Lovecraft's "The Shadow over Innsmouth." Quentin Moretus Cassave is a warlock from Jean Ray's* Malpertuis, *placing the events of that novel (and 1971 film by Belgian filmmaker Harry Kümel) in the CU. Malpertuis itself is the ancient house where Cassave has trapped the aging gods of Olympus inside the "skins" of ordinary Flemish citizens. Doucedame the Elder and Doucedame the Younger are two of the narrators of* Malpertuis. *The Arumbaya fetish is from Hergé's* Tintin, *who also happens to be the fearless reporter with a tuft of hair. Murr is from E.T.A. Hoffmann's* The Life and Opinions of the Tomcat Murr.

November
THE MALTESE FALCON

Sam Spade's most famous case. Brigid O'Shaughnessy tells Spade that one of the cops who questioned her at police headquarters was named O'Gar.

*Novel by Dashiell Hammett. According to Philip José Farmer, Spade is a Wold Newton Family member, the grandson of Ned Land (*20,000 Leagues under the Sea*) and grand-nephew of Johnny Shawnessy (*Raintree County*). O'Gar also appeared in several Continental Op stories by Hammett, most notably the novel* The Dain Curse. *Therefore the Op's tales also take place in the CU.*

Late Autumn
FOOL ME ONCE...

Baker Street detective Harry Dickson (aka "Hunter") is called in by M of Her Majesty's Secret Service to investigate the case of gruesome murders of three women. Fascinax also enters the case. Mentioned are: Griffin's bandages and glasses; a U.S. Cavalry Officer's sword; Belphégor; Blake's damn albino; Flax; Seward's Sanitarium; Fantômas; Numa Pergyll; Leonid Zattan; Dorje; Benedict Stark; Dr. Natas; Dr. Mabuse; and Roxor.

Short story by Bill Cunningham in Tales of the Shadowmen Volume 4: Lords of Terror, *Jean-Marc and Randy Lofficier, eds., Black Coat Press, 2008; reprinted in French in* Les Compagnons de l'Ombre (Tome 4), *Jean-Marc and Randy Lofficier, eds., Rivière Blanche, 2009. Harry Dickson is from the stories by Jean Ray and various others. M must be a head of the Secret Service who served between the tenures of Mycroft Holmes and Admiral Sir Miles Messervy.*

Fascinax is George Leicester, M.D., an occult investigator with heightened senses and supreme mental powers. Hunter was the code name of Callan's section head in the British television series Callan. *Griffin's bandages and glasses are from Wells'* The Invisible Man. *The U.S. Cavalry Officer's sword is probably that of Captain John Carter. Belphégor is from* The Phantom of the Louvre. *Blake's damn albino is Sexton's Blake's nemesis, M. Zenith. Flax is Dickson's own adversary, Professor Flax, who also fought Sherlock Holmes. Seward's Sanitarium is based on Dr. John Seward from Stoker's* Dracula. *Fantômas needs no further introduction at this point. Numa Pergyll is Fascinax's primiary nemesis. Leonid Zattan battled the heroic Nyctalope. Dorje is an agent of Talbot Mundy's* Nine Unknown. *Benedict Stark is a recurring nemesis of The Shadow. Doctor Natas is from Guy d'Armen's* Doc Ardan: City of Gold and Lepers, *and was identified as Sax Rohmer's Doctor Fu Manchu by Jean-Marc Lofficier. Doctor Mabuse is from the series of German films by Fritz Lang and fiction by Norbert Jacques. Roxor is the villain from the 1932 film* Chandu the Magician.

CAP FOG, TEXAS RANGER MEET MR. J.G. REEDER
THE RETURN OF RAPIDO CLINT AND MR. J.G. REEDER
RAPIDO CLINT STRIKES BACK

Alvin Fog works with J.G. Reeder and they encounter Inspector John Wade, Leopold Moran, and Oliver Rater. Fog and Reeder also meet Albert Henry "Bert the Jump Up" Fredricks. References are made to Albert Campion and Nicholas Ramage.

Three novels in the Alvin Dustine "Cap" Fog series by J.T. Edson. John Wade, Leopold Moran, and Oliver Rater are from The India-Rubber Man, The Clue of the Silver Key, *and* The Orator, *respectively, all by Edgar Wallace. Albert Henry "Bert the Jump Up" Fredricks is from* Underworld Nights *by Charles Raven. Albert Campion is Margery Allingham's detective, and Nicholas Ramage is from the Ramage naval series by Dudley Pope.*

1929

January-May
TARZAN THE INVINCIBLE
Tarzan returns to Opar.
Another Burroughs novel, wherein Tarzan revisits Opar. Date derived from Farmer's Tarzan Alive.

Winter. Teenaged Belgian reporter Tintin begins a lifetime of adventure. (*Tintin In the Land of the Soviets* by Hergé.)
Winter. Parisian Magistrate M. Froget solves a series of brutal crimes in Paris. (Thirteen stories collected in *The 13 Culprits* [*Les 13 Coupables*] by Georges Simenon.)

Winter
TURK SERLOK HOLMESI ATES AHMET
Consulting detective Ates Ahmet becomes known as "the Turkish Sherlock Holmes" after solving a series of difficult crimes.
From Turk Serlok Holmesi Ates Ahmet *#1-5, 1930. The detective Avni was the first "Turkish Sherlock Holmes."*

THE EYE OF BLACK A'WANG
Malay Collins, the Master Thief of the East, is to "the nimble fingered thieves of Shanghai, of Singapore, of Lahore, and of Kandy as Arsène Lupin to the youth of Europe. He was an ideal, a pattern, a veritable hero of the illicit."
*A short story by Murray Leinster (*nom de plume *for William F. Jenkins) in* Short Stories *magazine, January 1930. According to another story, "The Emerald Buddha," Malay Collins is a Caucasian, apparently orphaned in the East at age eight: "Owning to the stupidity of certain white folk who did not recognize his race as a child, Collins was raised by a benevolent Oriental master thief to be his assistant in the business." The comparison to Lupin, a Wold Newton Family member, brings Collins into the Crossover Universe.*

THE ADVENTURE OF THE LOGICAL SUCCESSOR
Sherlock Holmes meets another brilliant detective, Ellery Queen, to whom he bequeaths his methods and his philosophy.
A story by, J. Randolph Cox, in The Baker Street Journal, *v32, #2, September 1982.*

THE CHILDREN OF THE NIGHT
Among occultist/adventurer John Kirowan's friends is one named Taverel. This may be Sir Rupert Taverel. There is also a possible connection to the noble Tafaral family who are aided by Solomon Kane. The books *Unspeakable Cults* by Von Juntz and the dread *Necronomicon* are mentioned, as are the beings Cthulhu, Yog-Sothoth, Tsathoggua and Gol Goroth, and a modern cult devoted to Bran Mak Morn.
The Lovecraftian references in this Robert E. Howard story (found in Beyond the Borders, *Baen Books, 1996;* Pigeons from Hell, *Ace Books, 1979; and* Bran Mak Morn: The Last King, *Del Rey Books, 2005) and the reference to Howard's fantasy hero Bran Mak Morn, place John Kirowan in the CU. The creatures featured in this tale are the same beings seen in Howard's "Worms of the Earth" and "People of the Dark." The story "Taverel Manor," featuring the death of Sir Rupert Taverel, is also by Robert E. Howard. The Solomon Kane story featuring the Tafarals is "Moon of Shadows." The spelling of the names Taverel and Tafaral are slightly different, but that is not unusual over several hundred years, and the fact that both the Taverels of "Taverel Manor" and the*

Tafarals are menaced by survivors of ancient Atlantis makes this possibility too intriguing to ignore. Bran Mak Morn was the last great king of the Picts (Howard's fictional Picts, not the genuine, historical Pictish folk). Although he died in a great battle in which the Romans were forced back across the British Isles, Bran Mak Morn's soul entered a statue carved in his likeness by a wizard. This statue is seen in the Turlogh O'Brien story "The Dark Man."

Spring. Kent Allard creates the identity of The Shadow and begins gathering agents worldwide in his quest against evil.

April
THE ADVENTURE OF THE PRAED STREET IRREGULARS
Solar Pons and Fu Manchu meet again.
In The Reminiscences of Solar Pons *(book 5) by August Derleth.*

Spring
RAMA SAHIB, LA TIGRE DELLA JUNGLA NERA
The Indian Rama Sahib begins fighting crime in the Black Jungle.
Rama Sahib, La Tigre della Jungla Nera. *The "Black Jungle" is the setting of the Sandokan stories by Emilio Salgari, thus placing Rama Sahib in the Crossover Universe.*

AT THE PALACE DA NOSTRA
Paul Harley cables Gaston Max for information.
A short story by Sax Rohmer published in 1930 and reprinted in the American edition of the collection Tales of East and West. *Since Gaston Max is in the CU, so is Paul Harley, a private detective who tracks down master criminals. At this point it is not difficult to conclude that most, if not all, of Rohmer's stories and novels take place within the same connected universe, and thus within the CU.*

THE EVILS AGAINST WHICH WE STRIVE
In New York, visiting Judge Keith Hilary Pursuivant, the Sâr Dubnotal ends up teaming with The Shadow to fight the ghost of Ligeia.
Short story by Roman Leary in Tales of the Shadowmen Volume 4: Lords of Terror, *Jean-Marc and Randy Lofficier, eds., Black Coat Press, 2008; reprinted in French in* Les Compagnons de l'Ombre (Tome 4), *Jean-Marc and*

Randy Lofficier, eds., Rivière Blanche, 2009. Judge Pursuivant's tales were told by Manly Wade Wellman. Sâr Dubnotal was an anonymously created mystical hero. Ligeia was created by Edgar Allan Poe in the eponymous story.

June 8-9
ANIMAL CRACKERS
After the theft of a valuable painting at the Rittenhouse mansion, Arabella Rittenhouse says to her boyfriend, John Parker, "Just think, whoever took it was right in the room with us! Just like Raffles!" Later on, an Italian man currently using the alias Emanuel Ravelli tells another mustachioed man using the name Capt. Geoffrey T. Spaulding, "In-a case like-a this that's-a so mysterious, you gotta get-a the clues. You gotta use-a the Sherlock-a Holmes-a method."

The second film featuring The Marx Brothers, 1930. These comments could be interpreted as referring to the fictional characters Raffles and Holmes. However, it has been shown that the man with the mustache, the Italian, and their companion, the innocent mute, exist in the CU, as seen in Marvel Comics' Shang Chi: Master of Kung Fu *series. Therefore, the references must be to the real Wold Newton Family members Holmes and Raffles.*

Summer. In Gotham City, The Shadow captures a group of gunmen and saves the lives of Thomas Wayne and his son Bruce ("The Night of the Shadow," *Batman #259*).

July
THE ADVENTURE OF THE ANCIENT GODS
Sherlock Holmes, visiting Arkham, Massachusetts, again encounters writer H.P. Lovecraft, along with further Cthulhuoid horrors, after being asked to investigate the disappearance of Randolph Carter.

Holmes once again shares the stage with the Cthulhu Mythos in this short story by Ralph Vaughan, Gryphon Publications, 1990. Randolph Carter figures in several of Lovecraft's works, including "The Statement of Randolph Carter," "The Silver Key," and "The Dream-Quest of Unknown Kadath." Vaughan places these events in 1927. However, this story is set after the disappearance of Randolph Carter, which is given in "Through the Gates of the Silver Key" as October 1928.

BLOOD MONEY AND HUMAN BONDAGE
Tarzan returns to Pellucidar. The villainous Abdul Al-Hazred, who also calls himself "the Mad Arab," is clearly not the same Mad Arab who authored the *Necronomicon* in centuries past; he is a lowly, thieving lieutenant in a band of Arab slavers, until a chance encounter with energy from a device created by the Mahars of Pellucidar alters him. Likewise, the African princess Ayesha is

obviously not the same person as the immortal Ayesha, She-who-must-be-obeyed.

Comic story in Marvel Comics' Tarzan, #15-24, written by David A. Kraft, Bill Mantlo, John Buscema, Klaus Janson, Sal Buscema, Bob Hall, Rudy Nebres, Jim Mooney, and Pablo Marcos. The original Abdul Al-Hazred is from H.P. Lovecraft's Cthulhu Mythos tales, while the original Ayesha is featured in a series of novels by H. Rider Haggard.

Late Summer
OUGON KAMEN (THE GOLDEN MASK)
The infamous gentleman burglar, Arsène Lupin, travels to Japan to steal a priceless relic. While there, he matches wits with Japan's greatest detective, Kogoro Akechi.

*Ougon Kamen (*The Golden Mask, *1930-31) is a pastiche by "Edogawa Rampo" (pseudonym for Taro Hirai), the father of the Japanese detective story, placing Akechi in the CU. This pastiche combines classical aspects of Arsène Lupin with "Le roi au masque d'or" (1892), by Marcel Schwob and Edgar Allan Poe's "The Masque of the Red Death." Several episodes of the* Kogoro Akechi *television series were based on this pastiche. Kadzuwo J. Shimidzu has speculated that Lupin III is the grandson of Lupin (of course) and Fujiko Otori from* Ougon Kamen. *Shimidzu continues: "If so, it is natural that he has a Japanese appearance, because he is a quarter-breed. This is the reason that he calls himself 'Lupin III' not 'Arsène III.'" The 1929 time frame allows just enough time for Lupin II (b. 1930) to grow up and have a son Lupin III (b. circa 1946), whose adventures started in 1966.*

LE PROFESSEUR FLAX, MONSTRE HUMAIN
Harry Dickson, "the American Sherlock Holmes," first clashes with the wicked Professor Flax.
Story by Jean Ray in Harry Dickson *#18, 1930.*

October. Birth of Spencer Holmes (probable son of Nero Wolfe). The date is conjecture.
October 1929-February 1930. Ruven van Helsing is part of the Mountains of Madness expedition. (*Crépuscule Vaudou* aka *The Katrina Protocol*, Jean-Marc Lofficier.)

October 1929-February 1930
AT THE MOUNTAINS OF MADNESS
The leader of the Miskatonic University expedition to Antarctica, Professor Dyer, and Professor William Harper "Johnny" Littlejohn, one of Doc Savage's five assistants, are probably one and the same person.

This is a novel by H.P. Lovecraft, originally published in the 1930s; reprinted by Del Rey Books, 1985; reprinted in the anthology The Antarktos Cycle, *Chaosium, 1999. It is Farmer's hypothesis that the expedition's leader was Johnny, which would bring Lovecraft's Cthulhu Mythos into the Crossover Universe. The date is derived from Farmer's* Doc Savage: His Apocalyptic Life.

October
FROM A DETECTIVE'S NOTEBOOK
Mr. Mulliner's nephew, Adrian Mulliner, is a private detective who informs friends that he has investigated the recorded cases of Sherlock Holmes and has reached the conclusion that Moriarty and Holmes were the same man.

A story by P.G. Wodehouse in The World of Mr. Mulliner. *Adrian Mulliner, who first appeared in "The Smile That Was," was obviously mistaken about Holmes and Moriarty.*

November
IRON AND BRONZE
Hareton Ironcastle and his companion N'desi, bearer of the Reaver of Worlds, arrive at Queen Antinea's African outpost in the Hoggar Mountains, the Mountain of Evil Spirits, only to find Harry Killer in charge. Killer was formerly the ruler of the criminal outpost Blackland before its destruction, and is now served by the beast-like ape-men called Wandarobo. He seeks the secret of Antinea's immortality, which lies in the crystalline roots of what Antinea calls the Tree of Dreams. Antinea has called upon Doctor Francis "Doc" Ardan to battle Killer. When Ardan touches the root of the Tree of Dreams, he has visions of his past battle with Doctor Natas, as well as of an infant, a woman in a plane flying over the Arctic, and subterranean adventure in which he sees an other version of himself across a mirror-like threshold. At the conclusion, Ironcastle, N'desi, Ardan, and

Antinea think that Killer is dead, but he's actually survived, the cursed native word "Xanigew" ringing in his brain, experiencing visions of his own, which include a laughing man in a slouch hat with blazing twin .45s. There are also references to Hâjî Abdû, Gondokoro, and *taduki*.

Short story by Christopher Paul Carey and Win Scott Eckert in Tales of the Shadowmen Volume 5: The Vampires of Paris, *Jean-Marc and Randy Lofficier, eds., Black Coat Press, 2009; reprinted in French in* Les Compagnons de l'Ombre (Tome 6), *Jean-Marc and Randy Lofficier, eds., Rivière Blanche, 2010. Hareton Ironcastle is the famed explorer from J.-H. Rosny aîné's* L'Étonnant Voyage d'Hareton Ironcastle *(1922), which was translated and revised by Philip José Farmer for publication in English as* Ironcastle *(DAW Books, 1976). Gondokoro is also from Rosny aîné's* Ironcastle; *the dendroid and its crystalline roots are meant to be extensions of the star-shaped mineral-vegetable king from Rosny aîné's novel and related to the Crystal Tree of Time from* The Dark Heart of Time *by Philip José Farmer (based on ideas from "Crystal Corridors in the Farmerian Monomyth," presentation by Christopher Paul Carey and Dennis E. Power, FarmerCon III, Peoria, Illinois, July 26, 2008). N'desi is meant to be a grandson of the witchdoctor Mavovo from* Allan and the Holy Flower *by H. Rider Haggard. N'desi's square-ended, slightly curving iron sword is meant to be an ancient Khokarsan* tenu *(sword) from Philip José Farmer's Ancient Opar series. Harry Killer and Blackland are from Jules and Michael Verne's* L'Étonnante Aventure de la mission Barsac *(*The Barsac Misson*). Antinea and her African outpost of Atlantis are from Pierre Benoit's* L'Atlantide. *Doc Ardan is from Guy d'Armen's* Doc Ardan: City of Gold and Lepers, *in which he battled Doctor Natas. In the English translation by Jean-Marc and Randy Lofficier, Ardan was identified as Doc Savage (who is also known as Dr. James Clarke Wildman, Jr.) and Natas was identified as Fu Manchu. Ardan's visions of the infant and the woman in the plane are of his future daughter, Patricia Wildman, and wife, Adélaïde Lupin Wildman, as seen in* The Evil in Pemberley House *by Philip José Farmer and Win Scott Eckert. Ardan/Wildman's vision of the other in the mirror is of a future encounter with his alternate universe counterpart, Doc Caliban, as seen in Farmer's unfinished* Down to Earth's Centre/The Monster on Hold. *Hâjî Abdû is meant to be Hâjî Abdû El-Yezdi, the author of* The Kasidah of Hâjî Abdû El-Yezdi, *who is identified as one of Doc Savage's tutors in Farmer's* Escape from Loki. *The Wandarobo are from the Ki-Gor pulp novels by John Peter Drummond, and are an offshoot of the beast-men of Opar from the Tarzan novels of Edgar Rice Burroughs. The Reaver of Worlds is fashioned from a fragment of the Axe of Victory from* Allan and the Ice-Gods *and other novels by H. Rider Haggard, as well as Philip José Farmer's Ancient Opar series (see especially* The Song of Kwasin *by Philip José Farmer and Christopher Paul Carey). Taduki is from the Allan Quatermain novels by H. Rider Haggard. The native word "Xanigew" gives Harry Killer his new name, Zanigew, a nemesis of The Shadow, as postulated by Rick Lai in his essay "Zanigew the Killer"* *(see* The Wold Newton Universe *website and* Rick Lai's Secret Histories: Criminal Masterminds, *Altus Press, 2009); the laughing man in a slouch hat with blazing twin .45s is The Shadow.*

November. Murder of Thomas and Martha Wayne. Their son, Bruce, is spared, and swears on the spirits of his parents to avenge their deaths by spending the rest of his life warring on all criminals.

November 1929-May 1936
THE BAT

A man named Wesley Sharp witnesses the brutal murder of a man and a woman, and comforts their surviving son. Wishing he could have done more, the incident inspires Sharp to change his life and he embarks on a cruise around the world. Upon his return, Sharp adopts the guise of a masked vigilante, The Bat. On his first mission, Dracula appears to The Bat and gives him a ring. On his final mission, in 1936, The Bat is shot full of holes by gangsters, but the power of Dracula's ring, combined with a similar amulet, brings The Bat back to life so that he can exact revenge upon his killers. Once that final task is complete, he removes the ring and the amulet and dies, his soul exiting his body in the form of a bat. The bat flies in an open window of a gothic mansion, and a voice exclaims, "A bat! That's it! An omen! I shall become a bat!"

One-shot by Rick Shanklin, Mark Wheatley, and Neil Vokes, Apple Comics, Spring 1990. The murdered man and woman are Thomas and Martha Wayne, and the survivor is their son, Bruce Wayne. The voice exclaiming about the bat flying in the window is that of Bruce Wayne, and the dialogue is from Detective Comics *#33, November 1939, which provides The Batman's origin and inspiration.*

Late November. The Shadow's first recorded case *(The Living Shadow* by "Maxwell Grant" [Walter Gibson]*).*

December 31, 1929-January 2, 1930
THE DRUMS OF DAMBALLAH

Jules de Grandin remarks about a voodoo worshipper with incredible agility: "Only the apes of Tarzan could have gained a vantage-point to hurl the fatal knife, then effect escape from immediately beneath our noses."

Story by Seabury Quinn in Weird Tales, *March 1930. The reference is in a context that suggests that the French occultist was coexistent with Edgar Rice Burroughs' jungle adventurer. Rick Lai adds: "According to Seabury Quinn, de Grandin visited both the French and Belgian Congo. De Grandin probably heard rumors of the Mangani, the apes that raised Tarzan, during his 1905-1907 experiences in Africa."*

1930

Winter. Nero Wolfe buys an old brownstone on West 35th Street in New York City, hires his nephew Archie Goodwin as his right-hand-man, and begins his career as a private detective.

Winter. First known case of Henri Bencolin, juge d'instruction of the Paris police. (*It Walks By Night* by John Dickson Carr.)

Winter
THE SILVER HAIR CRIME
"Gaston Dupont," France's greatest thief, returns to America for another bout with Nick Carter.
By "Nick Carter," in New Magnet Library *#1282. Nick Carter expert Jess Nevins notes that "Dupont" is obviously a pseudonym for Arsène Lupin.*

MURDER ON CAPE COD
New York Police Inspector Dan Doner tells his Watson, *New York Globe* reporter George Holt, some privileged information about a murder: "Keep it away from Philo Vance and I'll tell you."
Novel by Frank Shay, 1931. This comment could be taken either way, so I'll opt in favor of inclusion of Doner and Holt.

March 10
DIG ME NO GRAVE
The dying John Grimlan mentions several Lovecraftian deities, including Yog-Sothoth and Kathulos.
This John Kirowan story by Robert E. Howard is in Beyond the Borders, *Baen Books, 1996; in* Pigeons From Hell, *Ace Books, 1979; and in* Cthulhu: The Mythos and Kindred Horrors, *Baen Books, 1987. The deities mentioned are probably only variant spellings of Yog-Sothoth and Cthulhu, but it is interesting to note that the villain of Howard's story "Skull-Face" is a priest of ancient Atlantis named Kathulos. Possibly this is the Atlantean version of the Great Old One's name and the priest adopted the name of his deity, much as Zhar-nak did. Grimlan is also mentioned in Lin Carter's story "Dope War of the Black Tong," connecting John Kirowan with Anton Zarnak and Steve Harrison.*

March
PROWLER: THE OFFICIAL ACCOUNT
Leo Kragg turns vigilante as the Prowler. On his first case, he defeats zombie master Murder Legendre.

A tale in #2-4 of the miniseries Prowler by Michael H. Price, Timothy Truman and Graham Nolan, Eclipse Comics, 1987. Voodoo priest Murder Legendre is from the 1932 film, White Zombie, *and is in the CU through a reference in Jeff Rovin's novel* Return of the Wolf Man. *Therefore the Prowler is also in the CU. The Prowler battled Legendre several more times in the comics, including the one-shot* The Prowler in White Zombie.

Spring. The events of Talbot Mundy's *Jimgrim and the King of the World*, featuring James Schuyler Grim, Jeff Ramsden, and Chullunder Ghose, and wherein Grim perishes defeating the evil mastermind Dorje.

Spring. River Patrolmen Nick Kennedy and his Night Patrol wage a never-ending war against Fang Wu and the Red Shadow Tong. (The Kennedy of the River Patrol series of short stories in *Bullseye*.)

Spring. First recorded cases of Dutch consulting detective Myneer Amayat. (*The Tales of Mynheer Amayat*, collection of short stories by H. De Vere Stacpoole.)

Spring
BACHELORS ANONYMOUS
Hollywood mogul Ivor Llewellyn, suffering from a compulsive urge to marry, hides from a local actress who is pursuing him by admitting himself to a London hospital, St. Swithin's. The novelist Rosie M. Bank is mentioned. Joe Pickering is employed by the law firm of Shoesmith, Shoesmith, Shoesmith, and Shoesmith.

Novel by P.G. Wodehouse. St. Swithin's from Richard Gordon's Doctor in the House series. This is the same hospital that appeared under a slightly different spelling (St. Swithen's) in an Anton Zarnak story. Ivor Llewellyn had appeared earlier in two of Wodehouse's Monty Bodkin novels, The Luck of the Bodkins *and* The Plot that Thickened. *The law firm appeared earlier in* Money in the Bank, Ice in the Bed Room, *and* Biffen's Millions. *Rosie is the wife of Bingo Little, and appears in both the Jeeves/Wooster series and the Drones Club stories.*

WHAT HO, GODS OF THE ABYSS
Bertie Wooster and his manservant Jeeves once again run afoul of various Lovecraftian horrors, and the day is saved by Mina Murray, Allan Quatermain, Jr., Orlando, and Thomas Carnacki.

Short story by the Rt. Hon. Bertram Wooster, edited for publication by Alan Moore, in The League of Extraordinary Gentlemen: Black Dossier, *America's Best Comics, 2007.*

MEISTER DETEKTIV VS MEISTER DIEB
John Baxter, the world-traveling detective, clashes yet again with his old foe, Lord Lister.
Story in John Baxter Der Detektiv *#38, 1931. This confirms that the German John Baxter is the same John Baxter who fought so long with Lord Lister. Baxter also attended Nic Pratt's wedding (*John Baxter der Detektiv *#33, 1931). John Baxter's magazine ran for 50 issues from 1929 to 1932.*

Summer. Sir John Saumarez's first case, Enter Sir John, as chronicled by Helen Simpson. According to Jess Nevins, "Sir John is a prominent, older actor in London who solves crimes in his spare time."

Summer. Flash Gordon and Dale Arden disappear during the Rogue Planet Crisis of 1930. They go on to have many bizarre adventures on the planet Mongo. Sometime later in their adventures, Flash and company would meet the cast from the news strip *Secret Agent X-9/Secret Agent Corrigan*, thus placing Agent Phil Corrigan in the CU. There was also a 26-episode radio series, *The Amazing Interplanetary Adventures of Flash Gordon*, which adapted the comic strip adventures, except for the last two episodes, in which Flash, Dale, and Dr. Zarkov returned to earth in their rocketship and crash-landed in Africa. Flash and Dale got married on Earth, in the African jungle, in 1933. Among the attendees was "Jungle" Jim Bradley. The radio series then carried on with *The Adventures of Jungle Jim*, thus placing the Jungle Jim radio series and news strip adventures in the CU.

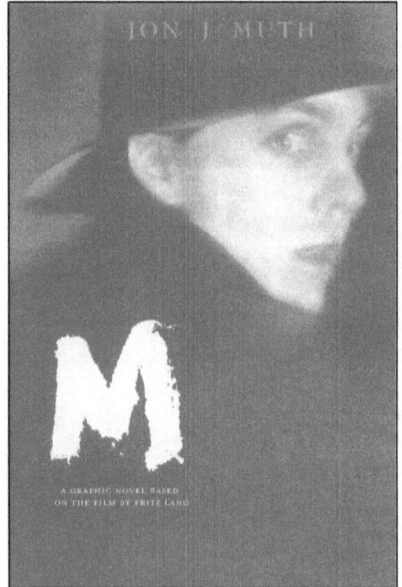

Summer. Inspector Karl Lohmann investigates a serial child-murderer in Fritz Lang's 1931 film *M*.

Summer
TIT, EL HIJO DE SHERLOCK HOLMES
"Tit," the "son of Sherlock Holmes," begins solving crimes.
From Tit, El Hijo de Sherlock Holmes, Aventuras Emocionantes del detective pequeño mas valiente del mundo, *#1-8, 1931. Written by "Hugo Reyd." Tit is probably not really the son of Holmes.*

PEOPLE OF THE DARK
The Black Stone appears again in this tale, which also features the Children of the Night. Intriguingly, the narrator, John O'Brien, after a knock on the head, believes himself to be the reincarnation of an individual called Conan of the reavers. Substantiating his belief, his companion Eleanor Bland seems to share his experience.

Robert E. Howard story, reprinted in Cthulhu: The Mythos and Kindred Horrors, Baen Books, 1987; *and in* Pigeons From Hell, Ace Books, 1979. *The Black Stone which sits on the altar of stones is the same as that in "Worms of the Earth." The creatures featured in this tale are the same beings seen in Howard's "The Children of the Night" and "Worms of the Earth." Regarding Conan of the reavers, O'Brien says this occurred 3,000 years ago, which is not Conan the Barbarian's time. However, this could be hyperbole; how would O'Brien know how far back in time this experience was?*

Matthew Baugh writes: "I believe that 'People of the Dark' was actually written before any of the Conan stories. I believe that the hero of that story (who mentions having lived in the American southwest) was a friend of Howard's. He told him about his experience, which actually revolved around the Cimmerian's participation in the raid on the outpost of Venarium when he was only 17 or 18 years old. Howard loved the story, but doubted people would accept the 'age undreamt of by man' angle. He fictionalized it as having taken place in the bronze-age British Isles. He only had to make minor changes because these were the same countries in the Hyborian Age; they just hadn't broken loose from the mainland yet. Also, the Cimmerians and the people of Venarium were, according to Howard, the ancestors of the Irish Celt and the Britons. Howard's friend continued to remember more and more about his past life, and to resemble Conan more and more strongly. He contacted Howard often to tell him new stories of his old life he remembered. This is how Howard came up with such detailed information about the life of a man dead for 12,000 years."

DER MANN AUS DER BAKER STREET (THE MAN FROM BAKER STREET)
John Kling, an extraordinary German detective, teams up with Sexton Blake on a case.
A story by Paul Pitt in John Kling's Abenteuer *(*John Kling's Adventures*) #501, 1931.*

KING KONG: THE ISLAND OF THE SKULL
A dying native girl from Skull Island murmurs in her own language "Ka-neh, ry-leh nah."
A novel by Matthew Costello, Pocket Books, November 2005. The novel is a prequel to Peter Jackson's 2005 remake of King Kong. *R'lyeh is a sunken city in the southern Pacific built by Cthulhu and his followers millions of years ago. Perhaps the sunken city of R'lyeh, which mysteriously surfaces from time to time, is somehow associated with Skull Island.*

OSCAR-BILL LE ROI DES DETECTIVES DANS SES EXPLOITS EXTRAORDINAIRES
The French detective "Oscar-Bill" begins his career solving crimes, and becomes world-renowned, being describes as "omniscient as Nick Carter."
The Oscar-Bill stories by Érik, aka André René Jolly, in Oscar-Bill le roi des détectives dans ses exploits extraordinaires *#1-26, 1931.*

September
THE PLAGUE COURT MURDERS
Sir Henry Merrivale's first recorded case, in which it is revealed that Sir Henry ("H.M.") is a member of the Diogenes Club. H.M. was also the former head of British Counter Espionage, where his nickname was Mycroft. Dr. Fu-Manchu calls upon Merrivale, but Merrivale declines to see him.
This case was recorded by John Dickson Carr writing as Carter Dickson. These links to the Sherlock Holmes canon place H.M. in the CU. H.M. also ap-

peared in Farmer's The Adventure of the Peerless Peer, *as an assistant to Mycroft Holmes. Rick Lai's essay, "Secrets of Sir Henry Merrivale," explains that this really was Rohmer's character Fu Manchu who paid a visit to Merrivale (Rick Lai's* Secret Histories: Daring Adventurers, *Altus Press, 2008).*

October
THE ADVENTURE OF THE SIX SILVER SPIDERS
Solar Pons investigates a case with several Cthulhu references, including Abdul Al Hazred's *Necronomicon* and Miskatonic University in Arkham, Massachusetts.
This short story by August Derleth is in the third Pons volume, The Memoirs of Solar Pons. *Surely Solar Pons was dissembling when he dismissed these references as fictional. After all, he did count among the many monographs he authored, "An Inquiry Into the Nan-Matal Ruins of Ponape" and "An Examination of the Cthulhu Cult and Others." Derleth, of course, was a major contributor to Lovecraft's universe and coined the phrase "Cthulhu Mythos."*

Autumn
THE ADVENTURE OF THE SNITCH IN TIME
Solar Pons refers to the events at Reichenbach Falls (the Holmes-Moriarty confrontation of 1891) and makes it clear that he would like to take on Moriarty. An astute attorney named Randolph Mason is discussed. But in the end, Pons refers his client to other legal counsel, an attorney practicing in Los Angeles, California, also named Mason.
It is unclear whether the Moriarty referred to in this story is the first Professor (who survived Reichenbach), the second Professor who took his place (see The Second War of the Worlds*), or a completely different Moriarty from an alternate universe. In any event, this story by August Derleth and Mack Reynolds features Erle Stanley Gardner's Perry Mason, and thus links Melville Davison Post's Randolph Mason into the Crossover Universe. The short story can be found in* The Misadventures of Sherlock Holmes, *Sebastian Wolfe, ed., Citadel Press, 1991.*

December
THE MOST EXCITING GAME
New York police Sergeant Purley Stebbins and D.A. John F.-X. Markham inspect the carnage in a newly arrived ship, the *Karaboudjan,* and Markham indicates he has no interest in consulting Vance on the case, instead heading for Lamont Cranston's Cobalt Club, where he meets Margo Lane. Markham hopes that Cranston may put him in touch with The Shadow. Margo mentions her little sister Lois, and introduces Markham to Count Zaroff, who in turn mentions that he's come to the Cobalt Club seeking his old friend Kent Allard. Margo thinks to herself that Cranston may as well be in Shangri-La. Zaroff is stating at the lo-

cal branch of the Gun Club, which in its time has boasted members such as Allan Quatermain, Hareton Ironcastle, Lord John Roxton, and Colonel Sebastian Moran. Zaroff has also engaged the services of a law firm, Morrison, Morrison, & Dodd. The Serpent Men of Valusia, from the time of King Kull, are mentioned. The famous gunsmith Von Herder is also mentioned. Zaroff utters a command taught him by Greystoke and then recites Captain Marsh's prayer as he battles the Serpent Man. The Ceintras/de Venasque polar expedition is mentioned.

Short story by Xavier Maumèjean in Tales of the Shadowmen Volume 5: The Vampires of Paris, *Jean-Marc and Randy Lofficier, eds., Black Coat Press, 2009; reprinted in French in* Les Compagnons de l'Ombre (Tome 5), *Jean-Marc and Randy Lofficier, eds., Rivière Blanche, 2009. The* Karaboudjan *is from Hergé's* Tintin *series. Purley Stebbins is from Rex Stout's Nero Wolfe novels and stories. John F.-X. Markham and Vance are from S.S. Van Dine's Philo Vance novels. Kent Allard (The Shadow), Lamont Cranston (an alias The Shadow often uses, although there is also a real Lamont Cranston), the Cobalt Club, and Margo Lane are all from The Shadow novels by "Maxwell Grant" (Walter B. Gibson and others). Although Margo is not yet an agent of The Shadow, she does know Cranston by this time. For an overview of Kent Allard and the various Cranstons, see "The Shadow Chronology, or, The Adventure of the Five Lamont Cranstons, or, Too Many Cranstons," available on the* Wold Newton Universe *website. The theory that Lois Lane is Margo Lane's sister was proposed, tongue-in-cheek, by Philip José Farmer in his* Doc Savage *biography. It has been expanded upon in "The Amazing Lanes," available on Mark Brown's* Wold Newton Chronicles *website. Shangri-La is from James Hilton's* Lost Horizon. *The Gun Club is from Jules Verne's* From the Earth to the Moon *and* Round the Moon. *Allan Quatermain is from the novels and stories by H. Rider Haggard. Hareton Ironcastle is from J.-H. Rosny aîné's* L'Étonnant Voyage d'Hareton Ironcastle *(1922), translated and revised by Philip José Farmer for publication in English as* Ironcastle *(DAW Books, 1976). Lord John Roxton is from Sir Arthur Conan Doyle's* The Lost World, *while Moran is from Doyle and Watson's Sherlock Holmes tales. Morrison, Morrison, & Dodd is from the Holmes story "The Sussex Vampire." The tales of King Kull, and his battles against the Serpent Men of Valusia, were told*

by Robert E. Howard. Von Herder is from the Holmes story "The Empty House." Greystoke is Edgar Rice Burroughs' Tarzan. Captain Marsh is from H.P. Lovecraft's "The Shadow over Innsmouth." The Ceintras/de Venasque polar expedition is from *The People of the Pole by Charles Derennes (1907), translated by Brian Stableford and published by Black Coat Press, 2008. Count Zaroff is from "The Most Dangerous Game" (1924) by Richard Connell. Mauméjean's tale presents a chronological conundrum, as Zaroff must have purchased his Caribbean island and held manhunts before the 1924 publication of Connell's tale, and yet in Mauméjean's story, Zaroff has come to New York City to purchase his island. It's implied that Zaroff died at the conclusion of Connell's tale, but perhaps he survived to repeat his depredations.*

December 31, 1930-January 1931
DEVIL'S THOUGHTS
Johnny Littlejohn, one of Doc Savage's five assistants, is an archaeology professor at Miskatonic University in Arkham, Massachusetts.

This Doc Savage comic book miniseries by Charles Moore, Mark Ellis, and Steve Stiles, Millennium Comics, 1991, further cements the notion that the expedition's leader in At the Mountains of Madness *was Johnny Littlejohn, while confirming the presence of the Cthulhu Mythos in the Crossover Universe. Although the story states it takes place in 1931-1932, the tale has been moved back one year in this chronology to accommodate other events.*

1931

January-October. The events of *King Kong* (novelization of the 1933 film by Delos W. Lovelace, Ace Books, 1976). At the conclusion, Kong climbs to the top of the Empire State Building. The 86th floor of the Empire State Building houses Doc Savage's headquarters, although Doc and his men are probably not there at the time. The following is excerpted from an article entitled "The Life Story of King Kong" by Jim Harmon, *Monsters of the Movies* magazine #1, Magazine Management Co., June 1974: "Yes, there were airplanes coming after Kong—primitive bi-planes looking much like they did in the First World War. Who were flying those planes? They are only unnamed 'Army pilots from Roosevelt Field'—but who were they really? One story has it that Merian C. Cooper, producer of the picture, is in the cockpit of the lead plane. But that is only in the motion picture re-enactment. Who was flying those planes when the actual events occurred? Does it stand to reason that so great a figure as King Kong could be slain by just an anonymous pilot? Not to me. I can't prove it but I know who must have been the leader of that squadron. Only one man could have done the job. During the First World War, he had been known only as G-8. Together with his Battle Birds, G-8 had fought other menaces, some nearly as great as King Kong. A man who can fight a horde of giant bats can move to fighting a giant ape more easily than those with less experience. Of course the war was over now. G-8 had added '4' to his name in honor of four fallen comrades. He was now Twelve, or more specifically, Midnight—Captain Midnight. (There were vicious rumors that this man had taken to wearing a cloak and shooting people in the dark of night, but they were only rumors. He had always flown high and clear. He did not hide in the shadows like some creeping spider. [*This is true. The Spider, Richard Wentworth, was the half-brother of G-8/Captain Midnight. -WSE.*]) So it was Captain Midnight, and the men who flew with him, who attacked King Kong. They were good men—Jack Martin, Jimmie Allen, Tommy Tompkins—some of them were young, but they had the skill and the courage of born fliers. Their tiny biplanes dropped to do combat  with the mightiest monster the world had ever known!" Jack Martin is Smilin' Jack Martin and Tommy Tompkins was also known as Tailspin Tommy. They, along with Jimmie Allen, were famous aviators from radio, the comics, and the pulps.

There have been several sequels and even prequels to *King Kong*, both in prose and film, as well as remakes. These include: *Son of Kong*, feature film, 1933; "The Menace of the Monsters," John Hunter, *The Boys' Magazine* #609, November 4, 1933; *King Kong vs. Godzilla*, feature film, 1962; *King Kong Escapes*, feature film, 1967; *King Kong*, feature film (remake), 1976; "After King Kong Fell," Philip José Farmer, *The Grand Adventure*, Berkley Books, 1984; *King Kong Lives*, feature film (sequel to 1976 remake), 1986; *Kong: King of Skull Island*, Joe DeVito, and Brad Strickland, DH Press, December 2004; *King Kong*, feature film (remake), 2005; *King Kong: The Island of the Skull*, Matthew Costello, Pocket Star Books, November 2005; and *Kong Reborn*, Russell Blackford, iBooks, September 2005. Intrepid creative mythographer John Allen Small has examined and reconciled the various stories, in his tour-de-force piece "The Beast," *Glimmerglass: The Creative Writer's Annual, Volume 1*, John Allen Small, ed., 2009.

Winter
THE SECRET OF THE SEA

Olaf Abelsen, a Swede framed and on the run, travels through a Russian-dug tunnel and finds an undersea passage into the Lidenbrock Sea.

Story by Walther Kabel in Olaf Karl Abelsen—Abseits der Alltagswege #37, 1932. *The Lidenbrock Sea is from Jules Verne's* Journey to the Centre of the Earth. *The crossover with Verne's novel brings Abelsen into the CU.*

THE RISE OF MINA NODSTROM
The "ex-King of Ruritania" is a guest at a Hollywood's executive's dinner.

A Mr. Mulliner story by P.G. Wodehouse in The World of Mr. Mulliner. *The story takes place during the talkie era in Hollywood and during Prohibition. Ruritania is the locale of* A Prisoner of Zenda, *which takes place in the CU. Therefore, this tale also occurs in the CU.*

March-April. Doc Savage and his five associates begin their fight against the forces of evil (*The Man of Bronze* by "Kenneth Robeson" [Lester Dent]).

Spring. Events of the film *White Zombie*, about voodoo priest Murder Legendre.

Spring. The first adventure of Tiger Standish, as told by Sydney Horler.

Spring. Judy Bolton's first case, *The Vanishing Shadow*, as recounted by Margaret Sutton.

May. Main events of James Hilton's *Lost Horizon*.

Spring
EX CALCE LIBERATUS
The French police team with Japanese detective Kogoro Akechi in a case of missing swords of historical import. Of course Asène Lupin is involved. Appearing or mentioned are: Inspectors Ganimard and Folenfant, *L'Écho de France*, District Attorney Kasamori, Fumiyo, Philippe Guérande, Oscar Mazamette, Irma Vep, Le Mondial, *La Capitale*, Cyrano de Bergerac, Kegan Van Roon, Louis de Bussy d'Amboise, D'Artagnan, Le Chevalier de Lagardère, Agnes de Chastillon, Jirel of Joiry, La Demoiselle Grise, André-Louis Moreau, The Prince, Cordell Fennevall, the zantetsuken, the blind swordsman Ichi, Yu'an Hee See, the "statue drug," Doctor Natas, and Sir Lancelot du Lac.

Short story by Matthew Baugh in Tales of the Shadowmen Volume 2: Gentlemen of the Night, *Jean-Marc and Randy Lofficier, eds., Black Coat Press, 2006; reprinted in French in* Les Compagnons de l'Ombre (Tome 3), *Jean-*

Marc and Randy Lofficier, eds., Rivière Blanche, 2009. Arsène Lupin, Inspectors Ganimard and Folenfant, and L'Écho de France *are from the Arsène Lupin stories of Maurice Leblanc. Kogoro Akechi, District Attorney Kasamori, and Fumiyo are from the Akechi Kogoro stories by Edogawa Rampo. Philippe Guérande, Oscar Mazamette, Irma Vep, and* Le Mondial *are from* Les Vampires *by Louis Feuillade.* La Capitale *is the newspaper that employed Jerome Fandor in the Fantômas stories of Marcel Allain and Pierre Souvestre. Cyrano de Bergerac is a historical figure whose adventures have often been used as sources for fiction. Kegan Van Roon is from* The Return of Dr. Fu Manchu *by Sax Rohmer. Louis de Bussy d'Amboise is from* La Reine Margot *by Alexandre Dumas. D'Artagnan is the hero of* The Three Musketeers *and several sequels by Alexandre Dumas. Le Chevalier de Lagardère is from* Le Bossu *by Paul Féval. Agnes de Chastillon is the heroine of several stories by Robert E. Howard which have been collected in* The Sword Woman. *Jirel of Joiry is the heroine of a series of stories by C.L. Moore which are mostly collected in* Jirel of Joiry. *La Demoiselle Grise (or the Grey Maiden) is featured in a number of stories by Arthur D. Howden Smith. These are collected in* The Grey Maiden, the Story of a Sword Through the Ages. *André-Louis Moreau is the hero of* Scaramouche *by Rafael Sabatini. The Prince is Prince Valiant from Hal Foster's comic strip* Prince Valiant in the Days of King Arthur. *("Prins Hugrakkurssaga" is Icelandic for "Prince Valiant's Saga.") Cordell Fennevall is one of the aliases used by Prince Corwin of Amber during his long stay on Earth. Corwin appears in the Amber series by Roger Zelazny beginning with the novel* Nine Princes in Amber. *The zantetsuken is the sword used by Goemon in the anime series* Lupin III. *The blind swordsman, Ichi, is from the Zatoichi series of movies. Yu'an Hee See is from* Yu'an Hee See Laughs *by Sax Rohmer. The "statue drug" is from* The Trail of Fu Manchu *by Sax Rohmer. Doctor Natas is from Guy d'Armen's* Doc Ardan: City of Gold and Lepers, *and was identified as Sax Rohmer's Doctor Fu Manchu by Jean-Marc Lofficier. Sir Lancelot du Lac (Père Dulac) is a character from Arthurian romance. His first known appearance is in* Le Chevalier de la Charette *by Chrétien de Troyes.*

RED KELSO

Two of Ulysses "Red" Kelso's associates are Percival "Pongo" Challenger, the nephew of Professor Challenger, and Lord Jack Roxton, the son of Lord John Roxton. In a December 31, 1930 flashback, Red Kelso's half-sister, Ann Sauvage, has a bumpy landing putting down her auto-gyro on the deck of a ship. The ship's captain rails at her, "Just who in Sam Hill do you think you are—Athena Voltaire?!" Ann responds, "Well, she did teach me 'ow to fly ziss machine."

A Red Kelso web comic by Gary Chaloner and Jake Chaloner. Brad Mengel discusses Pongo Challenger and Lord Jack Roxton in his essay "The Challenging Rutherfords" on The Wold Newton Universe: A Secret History *website.*

Lord Jack Roxton would be a younger half-brother to Richard Wentworth, The Spider. Perhaps Jack Roxton took the Lordship upon the abdication of his elder half-brother, when Wentworth chose to become an American citizen. Stunt pilot and adventuress Athena Voltaire has further connections to the CU, as demonstrated in a later entry.

June
ASK A POLICEMAN
Lord Peter Wimsey, Mrs. Bradley, Sir John Saumarez, and Mr. Roger Sheringham all engage in parts of a mystery.
Round-robin novel by Dorothy L. Sayers, Gladys Mitchell, Helen Simpson, Anthony Berkeley, Millward Kennedy, and John Rhode, 1933 (reprinted by Berkley Books, June 1987). Interestingly, Sayers, Berkeley, Mitchell, and Simpson wrote the chapters for each others' detectives. Since Lord Peter is a Wold Newton Family member, as established by Farmer's Tarzan Alive, *Mrs. Bradley, Sir John Saumarez, and Mr. Roger Sheringham all exist in the CU.*

Summer. Detective Wade Hammond begins taking on weird cases that others won't, in "Satan's Shrine," *Detective-Dragnet Magazine*, March 1932.
Summer. The Invisible Man Returns, in which Dr. Frank Griffin gives the invisibility formula to Geoffrey Radcliffe, in order to help Radcliffe escape from prison, after Radcliffe has been framed for murder. Dennis E. Power's article, "The Invisibles," proposes that Dr. Frank Griffin is the brother of Jack Griffin, and the second son of John Hawley Griffin.
Summer. Events of Ernest Hemingway's "The Snows of Kilimanjaro."

Summer
TARZAN IN SAVAGE PELLUCIDAR
Tarzan travels to Pellucidar in a submarine down via the bottom of Loch Ness. He battles Hooja the Sly One, the Sagoths, and the Mahars.
Tarzan graphic novel by Mike Royer and Russ Manning, 1975.

THE ORATORS: AN ENGLISH STUDY
"The Airman," an aviator and spy despairing of his work and the condition of England, utters a prayer to the Four Just Men, Dixon Hawke, Sexton Blake, Bulldog Drummond, Ferrers Locke, Panther Grayle, Hercule Poirot, and Sherlock Holmes, asking them to "spare us" and "deliver us."
A long-form poem by W.H. Auden, 1932. Jess Nevins notes, "Only Panther Grayle (a British consulting detective modeled on Craig Kennedy) is new, but it's nice to have all of those names dropped at once. Panther Grayle was created by Alfred Edgar, writing as 'Howard Steel,' and appeared in the Champion, *1922-1930."*

THE SINISTER RAY
Scientific detective Lynn Lash, a consulting expert for the Police Department, is called "… all Sherlock Holmes was and a lot Sherlock wasn't."

The first Lynn Lash story by Lester Dent appeared in Detective Dragnet, *March 1932. Holmes is referred to as a real person.*

Autumn. The events of the film *Chandu the Magician.*

October. Dick Tracy begins his never-ending battle against hoodlums and mobsters, as chronicled by Chester Gould.

October
AFTER KING KONG FELL
Doc Savage, his five assistants, and The Shadow and Margo Lane witness the aftermath of Kong's plunge from the Empire State Building. A young man who is visiting New York and witnesses Kong's fall is one Tim Howller of Peoria, Illinois, age thirteen.

Story by Philip José Farmer in The Grand Adventure, *Berkley Books, 1984.* Although Margo Lane was not yet operating as one of The Shadow's agents at this time, she did know Lamont Cranston. Tim Howller also appears in Farmer's short story, "The Face that Launched a Thousand Eggs."

BEAUTY AND THE BEAST
Adventurer Rex Solomon and his pal Moses "Moe" Marx return from an escapade and receive a call from a woman named Ruth. Unfortunately, just as Rex is taking the call, he and Moe are attacked by an assassin. Ruth is trying to give Rex some info on an "odd occurrence" which he might be interested in, but they get disconnected and she hangs up in a miff, complaining about "Men!" Another woman, in tattered and torn clothing, agrees with her as they look upon the gigantic corpse of King Kong.

Story by J. Morgan Neal, Gregg W. Noon, Kieran McKeown, Michelle Coulter, and Sean Taylor, Shooting Star Comics Anthology #3, *Winter 2004. The connection to King Kong brings Rex Solomon into the Crossover Universe.*

November. Following the events of King Kong, "Red Albright" (aka G-8, aka Bruce Hagin Rassendyll) goes into regular action as Captain Midnight in order to foil the plans of the evil Ivan Shark and his daughter Fury. He is assisted by Chuck Ramsay, Patsy Donovan, and Joyce Ryan, members of his Secret Squadron. Midnight is also joined by mechanic Ichabod Mudd, possibly an ancestor of one Harcourt Fenton Mudd.

November 1931-November 1932. Events of *The Son of Kong*.

1932

Winter. Perry Mason's first mystery, *The Case of the Velvet Claws*, as revealed by Erle Stanley Gardner.

Winter. First recorded story of the Black Moon café, "The Mark of the Black Hand" (*Bullseye*, April 9, 1932).

Winter
THE MUMMY

Sir Joseph Whemple is killed, but his son Frank ultimately triumphs over the mummy Imhotep. The Scroll of Thoth figures largely in this adventure.

Feature film from Universal Pictures. The Scroll of Thoth also appears in Richard Tierney's tales of Simon of Gitta.

DRACULA VS. THE MUMMY

During the events of *The Mummy*, Dracula and Imhotep have a brief skirmish.

A short story in the Universal Monsters Kombat series by "Professor Anton Griffin," Scary Monsters Magazine *#52, Dennis Druktenis Publishing, September 2004; reprinted in* The Midnight Shadow Show: Prof. Griffin Journals *by Joseph Fotinos, 2005. The tale is accompanied by an illustration of the monstrous battle by Chuck "The Savage Chuck" Loridans of the* MONSTAAH *website.*

THE PLAGUE OF THE ONION MEN

"Aristide Dupin," France's greatest thief and the "Laughing Cavalier" of crime, jousts with London detective Sexton Blake as part of the conspiracy of the Onion Men.

By Gwyn Evans, in Union Jack *#1493, May 28, 1932. Jess Nevins notes that Dupin is clearly meant to be Wold Newton Family member Arsène Lupin. Rick Lai adds, "The League of Onion Men is a Royalist conspiracy whose leader claimed to be a descendant of Louis XVII (the Dauphin who in conflicting accounts was rescued by Orczy's Scarlet Pimpernel, Sabatini's Baron de Batz and*

Wheatley's Roger Brook). *The League's leader was known as Louis de Rais and may also be a descendant of Gilles de Rais, the historical follower of Joan of Arc who became a Satanic mass murderer. The League of Onion Men was seeking the Five Keys of Gilles de Rais, supposedly magical talismans. Also seeking the Five Keys for unstated reasons was Aristide Dupin, the 'Laughing Cavalier' of crime and the greatest thief of France. Dupin/Lupin was a master of disguise. The Plague of Onion Men was not the final episode in the Onion Man series. This episode ended with Aristide Dupin outwitting Blake and stealing three keys successfully from the British sleuth. I have no idea how this epic struggle ended. I (and possibly Jess as well) am only aware of The Plague of the Onion Men because it was reprinted in one of the Sexton Blake hardcover collections. Unfortunately, no further information was given about this ongoing duel when the story was reprinted." Jess Nevins provides the titles for the whole saga:* "The League of Onion Men, The Mystery of Bluebeard's Keys, Fear-Haunted, The Plague of the Onion Men, *and* The Fifth Key."

BLACK BIRD—DER SCHWARZE VOGEL VON SCOTLAND YARD

The detective known as "Black Bird" begins his career in London. Later in the year he solves a crime at the home of the "late Sherlock Holmes."

Stories by "Harald West" (Elisabeth von Aspern) in Black Bird—der schwarze Vogel von Scotland Yard *#1-33, 1933. Of course, Sherlock Holmes was not "late" in 1932, but he no longer lived permanently at 221B Baker Street, although he may have still used it as a base of operations when visiting London. Perhaps by this point Holmes owned 221B outright and detective Harry Dickson was his tenant.*

ROLF TORRING ALS RETTER (ROLF TORRING AS A RESCUER)

In Africa, Jörn Farrow is rescued by Rolf Torring.

A tale in Rolf Torring *#100. This brings Rolf Torring into the Crossover Universe because Farrow met Captain Mors. Rolf Torring also met Hans Farrow (*Rolf Torring *#92), when it was revealed that after the Great War, Hans Farrow and his U-boat wandered the world's oceans until they discovered the South Seas atoll where Captain Nemo used to re-supply the* Nautilus. *They established a base there and continued to aid Germany against its enemies.*

THE SNAKE HEAD OF THE MEDUSA

The Three Vigilantes, friends of Olaf Abelsen's, strike out on their own and begin fighting those criminals the law cannot touch.

Story by Walther Kabel in Der Drei Von Der Feme *#1, 1933. Since Abelsen is in the CU, so are the Three Vigilantes.*

March
KNOCK-OUT (aka BULLDOG DRUMMOND STRIKES BACK)
Ronald Standish, an amateur sleuth with high government connections, and his friend Bill Leyton team with Hugh "Bulldog" Drummond and his pal Peter Darrell. Together, they investigate the murder of a high-up in British Intelligence, Sanderson, and end up fighting a supervillain named Demonico.
The eighth Bulldog Drummond novel by H.C. "Sapper" McNeile. Standish was another of Sapper's series characters and this novel places him in the CU. This Drummond novel also marks a transition from Drummond's status as a vigilante to a sanctioned sometime-operative for Scotland Yard and the government.

Spring. Alexander Waverly accepts a post in Department Z, a supersecret counterespionage arm of British Intelligence commanded by Gordon Craigie (John Creasey's *The Death Miser*; David McDaniel's *The Rainbow Affair*). Employing a varied group of agents, Department Z guards England's security before and during World War II.
Spring. Pete Rice begins a long and successful career enforcing the law in Trinchera County, Arizona. (*The Sheriff of Buzzard Gap* by Ben Conlon, *Pete Rice Magazine* v1, #1, November 1933.)

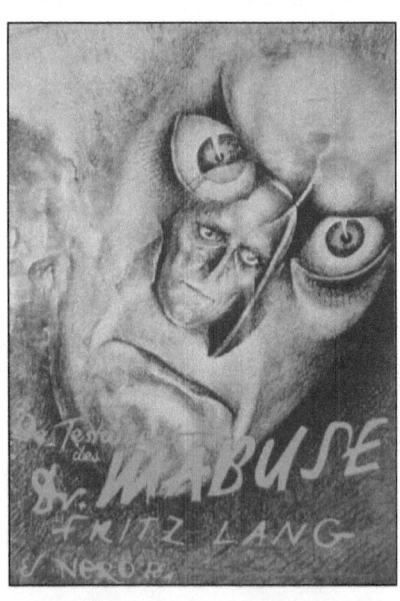

Spring
THE TESTAMENT OF DR. MABUSE (DAS TESTAMENT DES DR. MABUSE)
Inspector Lohmann, a Berlin policeman, investigates a case in which all the clues point toward Dr. Mabuse, who has been committed to an asylum for many years.
1933 German film directed by Fritz Lang, a sequel to 1922's Dr. Mabuse, der Spieler. *Rudolf Klein-Rogge played Mabuse in both films. Lohmann was played by Otto Wernicke, who originated the role in Lang's* M. *Mabuse was incorporated into the Crossover Universe in various stories by Rick Lai in the* Tales of the Shadowmen *series. This crossover brings Inspector Lohmann into the CU. There is a series of Inspector Lohmann novels by Jack Gerson which appear to be about the same character:* Death's Head Berlin, Death Squad London, *and* Deathwatch '39.

KAPITÄN MORS (CAPTAIN MORS)

Jörn Farrow, a Captain Mors-like submarine commander, meets Captain Mors himself.

A story by Hans Reinhard in Jörn Farrow's U-Boot-Abenteuer *(*Jörn Farrow's U-Boat Adventures*)* #61, 1933. This tale brings Jörn Farrow, who must be the son of Hans Farrow, into the CU.

AROUSED, THE DOMINO LADY

After the murder of her father, socialite and world-traveler Ellen Patrick dons the mask and slinky evening dress (and not much else) of the Domino Lady. She avenges herself upon her father's killers, arranging their downfall by setting them against one another. In her late father's library, Ellen reminisces that, "He had a special affection for adventure yarns and read them regularly to his daughter, including her favorite: Johnston McCulley's swashbuckling swordsman, Zorro. Maybe it was that the Curse of Capistrano battled his enemies in the same Southern California hills that surrounded her home." Assisting Ellen is her father's former helper, Nick Wheeler, who asks Ellen if she's going to put on a mask and carry a gun like Zorro.

Short story by Jim Steranko in Domino Lady: The Complete Collection—The Steranko Edition, *Vanguard Productions, August 2004. Steranko's tale provides an origin for the Domino Lady, whose stories were first told by Lars Anderson in the pulp pages of* Saucy Romantic Adventures *and* Mystery Adventure Magazine. *The reference to Zorro's hills of California, taken alone, would probably not be sufficient to place the Domino Lady in the CU. However, Wheeler's apparent error in stating that Zorro carried a gun actually makes a connection to the CU more likely. Wheeler must have been referring to the latest Zorro, James Vega, who was seen in* Zorro Rides Again *(as outlined in Matthew Baugh's "The Legacy of the Fox: Zorro in the Wold Newton Universe,"* Myths for the Modern Age: Philip José Farmer's Wold Newton Universe, Monkey-Brain Books, 2005). *The most recent Zorro, James Vega, was actually much less well-known than his famous ancestor, Don Diego Vega, who did not carry a gun. The fact that Wheeler refers to Zorro as carrying a gun makes it much more likely that he is referring to a real person in the CU, the less well-know James Vega/Zorro, rather than a pop-culture reference to a fictional Zorro. Matthew Baugh adds that "The reference doesn't need to be to James Vega. The*

heroes of The Son of Zorro *and* The Ghost of Zorro *both carried pistols rather than swords and operated in the mid 1860s. The Domino Lady reference could be to either of them."*

ALASKA JIM
   Sun Koh, the inheritor of the legacy of "Atlantis," meets a very old but still spry Alaska Jim.
   From Paul Alfred Müller-Murnau's Sun Koh, Die Erbe von Atlantis *#49, 1933. This brings Sun Koh into the CU.*

Summer
VAMPIRE MEAT
   The Prowler becomes involved in a mysterious case of vampire bat attacks that seem to be connected to Dr. Otto von Niemann. In the end, it is revealed that the Prowler's archnemesis, Murder Legendre, was also involved.
   A story in #1 of the miniseries Revenge of the Prowler *by Michael H. Price and Graham Nolan, Eclipse Comics, 1988. The story integrates the Prowler and Legendre into the events of the 1933 Majestic Pictures film* The Vampire Bat. *Since* The Vampire Bat *takes place in the village of Klineschloss, it is possible that Dr. von Niemann and the simple-minded Herman Gleib somehow escaped, and than von Niemann continued his experiments anew in New York City.*

LA BANDE DE L'ARAIGNÉE
   Harry Dickson first fights against Georgette Cuvelier, "the Spider," the daughter of Professor Flax.
   Story by Jean Ray in Harry Dickson *#85.*

THE SURVIVOR'S SECRET
   Sexton Blake befriends Arthur Stukeley Pennington, aka "R.S.V.P.," aka "A.S.P.," and the two solve a case together.
   Story by John G. Brandon in Sexton Blake Library, *Second Series, #365, January 1933. This team-up brings Arthur Stukeley Pennington into the CU. Pennington went on to team up with Detective Inspector Patrick Aloysius McCarthy several times, placing McCarthy in the CU as well. Jess Nevins notes,*

"The character Ronald Sturges Vereker Purvale, aka the Honorable R.S.V.P., was created by John G. Brandon and appeared in various Sexton Blake stories and then later in his own series of stories. Brandon changed Purvale's name to Arthur Stukeley Pennington ('A.S.P.') and wrote a series of novels about him. Both R.S.V.P. and A.S.P. had the same manservant, 'Flash' George Wibey, and the same chauffeur, Big Bill Withers. It turns out that Brandon was given to recycling more than just his characters. Some of Brandon's Blake stories were lifted wholesale, by Brandon, and reprinted, with minimal revision, as A.S.P. stories. This is of interest because in a 1939 story R.S.V.P.'s father and grandmother are named: Viscount Ebdale, K.G., and the Dowager Duchess of Faulkside. In Brandon's Murder in Pimlico, A.S.P.'s father and grandmother are named: Viscount Ebdale and the Duchess of Faulkside. So either R.S.V.P. and A.S.P. are the same character, or they're brothers. A.S.P. also fought two villains, the Wallflower and Mme. Osaki du Chane, who fought Blake and R.S.V.P."

Summer 1932
THE HEIR OF DRACULA

Harry Dickson and Tom Wills track down a brutal vampire who is said to be a descendent of Count Dracula.

Originally published as Le Vampire aux Yeux Rouges *in* Harry Dickson *#81, January 1933; translated by Jean-Marc and Randy Lofficier and collected in* Harry Dickson: The Heir of Dracula, *Black Coat Press, 2009.*

September
ABOUT MAIGRET AND THE STOLEN PAPERS

Inspector Maigret pursues a packet of stolen diplomatic papers and crosses paths with a self-described "...consulting detective. The greatest in the world." The detective, Hercule Poirot, applies his "little grey cells" to the problem at hand.

A tale by Julian Symons in The Great Detectives: Seven Original Investigations, *confirming Georges Simenon's Maigret into the CU.*

Autumn. Drury Lane's first case, *The Tragedy of X*, as told by Ellery Queen, writing as Barnaby Ross.

Autumn. Richard Curtis Van Loan's first case as The Phantom Detective, as told by G. Wayman Jones in *The Emperor of Death* (*Phantom Detective* v1, #1, February 1933).

Autumn. Royston Aylett, an English big game hunter and fighter for good, meets his future wife Joan and battles evil fakirs, led by Ashraf Daiye, in Africa. ("The Devils' Drums" by Vivian Meik.)

Autumn. The Moon Man's first case, "The Sinister Sphere," by Frederick C. Davis (*Ten Detective Aces*, May-June 1933).

Autumn
MENACE OF THE MONSTERS
   Carl Denham returns to The Isle of Mists (later called "Skull Island") and loads various dinosaurs onto his ship. Unfortunately, the ship is wrecked on the English coast, and the dinosaurs are set loose in England. Some of them reach England, causing great chaos, with a brontosaurus wrecking the London Bridge. Eventually all of the dinosaurs are hunted down and killed.
   Story by John Hunter in The Boys' Magazine *#609, November 4, 1933. The Boys' Magazine #608 published the official ("By Special Permission of Radio Pictures Ltd.") short story adaptation of King Kong. #609 was the official sequel to the short story adaptation, although the destructive events of the sequel are obviously exaggerated.*

MR. DEXTER'S MYSTERY FIELD
   Dixon Hawke clashes with Waldo the Wonder Man.
   Story written by Edward Searles Brooks, Dixon Hawke Library *#366, December 9, 1933. Since Waldo the Wonder Man is in the CU, so is Dixon Hawke.*

October. Harry Dickson battles monstrous creatures in a futuristic lair deep beneath London in *Le Temple de Fer* (*The Iron Temple*), *Harry Dickson* #93, July 1933; translated and adapted by Jean-Marc and Randy Lofficier in the collection *Harry Dickson: The Heir of Dracula*, Black Coat Press, November 2009.
   November 22. Future U.N.C.L.E. agent Napoleon Solo is born in Montréal.
   December 1932-September 1933. Hard-boiled private eye Nate Heller meets Eliot Ness. (*True Detective*, novel by Max Allan Collins. Ness knew Indiana Jones in 1920.)

1933

January 6
SHERLOCK HOLMES OUT WEST
   Sherlock Holmes comes out West to visit Tom Mix for their birthdays and they solve a minor mystery together. It is mentioned that Holmes has visited Mix in the past, usually traveling under the name "Mr. Mycroft." A tall man

wearing dark glasses, a semi-retired Texas Ranger who's obliged to keep his identity secret, also attends the birthday party.

Short story by Jim Harmon in It's That Time Again, Volume 4, *Jim Harmon, ed., BearManor Media, 2009. The tale placed the Old Time Radio version of Tom Mix (not the historical Tom Mix) in the Crossover Universe. The semi-retired Texas Ranger wearing dark glasses is a very elderly Lone Ranger.*

January-April. James Bond enters Eton mid-term. A short while later, on holiday at his Uncle Max's cottage in Scotland, Bond becomes embroiled in a quest to defeat the plans of the sinister Lord Hellebore, and receives the distinctive scar on his cheek (*SilverFin* by Charlie Higson). It should be observed that Higson's account of young Bond's life in SilverFin differs slightly from that of John Pearson's *James Bond: The Authorized Biography of 007*. Pearson states that James had a brother one year older, named Henry Bond, while Higson portrays James as an only child. Pearson also explains that Bond entered Eton in Autumn 1933, while Higson has Bond entering Eton mid-term in January 1933. And Pearson states that Bond was born in Wattenscheid, while *SilverFin* establishes that Bond was born in Vienna. Finally, it bears note that young Bond was the victim of some relentless harassment upon his entry to Eton, whereas Tim Heald's John *Steed: An Authorized Biography, Volume 1: Jealous In Honour* has it that Bond was a bully. Dennis E. Power notes, "Both could be true. Steed was a couple of years younger than Bond. It is one of the 'traditions' of the English public school system that the upperclassmen bully the lower classmen. So when Bond was younger he was bullied and as he became older he in turn bullied the younger students."

Winter. Philip Marlowe opens his private investigation practice in Los Angeles. Philip José Farmer has placed Marlowe in the Wold Newton Family as the grandson of Ned Land.

Winter. British secret service agent Colin Gray begins fighting for the empire in Central Asia. (*King Cobra* by Mark Channing.)

Winter
VEILS OF FEAR

In this tale about Royston and Joan Aylett, a journalist, and a padre facing off against an evil fakir, there is the following exchange: "Then how had Aylett become Noorali? Some queer trick of near-metamorphosis, like the 'man of forty faces' at home, who had been able, as Scotland Yard had proved, to remould his features beyond recognition by muscular action alone." During the adventure Joan Aylett refers to the events of Dornford Yates' *The Stolen March*.

A novel by Vivian Meik, 1934. This novel takes place in the CU through the reference to Yates' The Stolen March, *which although dismissed here as "lovely fairy-tale," can be shown to have actually occurred in the CU (see the entry for*

Combined Forces). *The "man of forty faces"* is Hamilton Cleek, so this reference also adds Cleek to the CU.

Spring. Richard Wentworth begins his one-man-war against crime as *The Spider* in *The Spider Strikes!* as told by R.T.M. Scott (*The Spider*, October 1933). Wentworth is the half-brother of The Shadow and G-8.

Spring. Scotland Yard Inspector Roderick Alleyn's first mystery, *A Man Lay Dead* by Ngaio Marsh.

Spring. French Great War veteran Gil Benoit begins fighting German spies as a member of the Deuxième Bureau. (*Ceux de S.R.* by Charles Robert-Dumas.)

Spring. Sisters Jean and Louise Dana solve their first mystery, *By the Light of the Study Lamp*, as told by Carolyn Keene.

April
DOOM ON THUNDER ISLAND
As Doc Savage and the boys get into underwater gear, Monk asks, "Are you sure Captain Nemo got started this way?"
Marvel Comics' Doc Savage *magazine # 1, August 1975, by Doug Moench, John Buscema, and Tony DeZuniga.*

May
THE ADVENTURE OF THE CAMBERWELL BEAUTY
London detective Solar Pons and Fu Manchu match wits again.
In The Return of Solar Pons *(book 6) by August Derleth, Pinnacle Books.*

May-June. The events of Edgar Rice Burroughs' *Tarzan's Quest*, in which Tarzan, Jane, and a few others acquire Kavuru immortality pills. Philip José Farmer discovered that after this adventure, Tarzan sent a sample to his cousin, Doc Savage, for analysis. Savage was able to synthesize the compound, after which both Tarzan and Savage had access to an unlimited supply for themselves, their families, and comrades.

June
THE SINISTER CHEESECAKE
Holmes is in America, attempting to prevent sabotage at the League of Nations. Nathan Detroit is mentioned, as are the Lemon Drop Kid, Harry the Horse, and Nicely Nicely Johnson.

Short story by Craig Shaw Gardner, in the anthology The Game is Afoot. *Nathan Detroit is a character in* Guys and Dolls; *the Lemon Drop Kid was a character in a Damon Runyan story that was made into a film with Bob Hope. Most of Runyan's stories are interconnected, with one character referring to another, and so on.*

MURDER MUST ADVERTISE

A carbonated beverage called "Brotherhood's Sparkling Pomayde" appears.

A Lord Peter Wimsey novel by Dorothy Sayers. Brotherhood's Sparkling Pomayde also appeared in Sayers' Montague Egg stories, thus placing the mysteries featuring Egg, a traveling wine salesman, in the CU.

THE DRONE

Several members of the Explorer's Club, including one Martin Hewitt, a botanical researcher, recount their various experiences with werewolves, vampires, foxwomen, and similar superstitions.

A short story by Abraham Merritt in Fantasy Magazine, *September 1934; reprinted in* The Fox Woman and Other Stories. *Martin Hewitt was a lawyer and private investigator in 1890s London. The Hewitt seen here must be his son; this is made more likely by the first words he utters in the story: "Will the opposing counsel kindly shut up and listen to expert testimony."*

Summer. The events of the film *The Return of Chandu.*

Summer. Secret Agent X's first adventure, *The Torture Trust* by Paul Chadwick writing as Brant House (*Secret Agent X* v1, #1, February 1934).

Summer. Albert Campion's first case, *Sweet Danger* (U.S. title *Kingdom of Death*), as recounted by Margery Allingham.

Summer. The Masked Invasion, the first recorded adventure of Jimmy Christopher, Secret Service Operator #5, as told by Frederick C. Davis, writing as Curtis Steele (*Operator #5* v1, #1, April 1934).

Summer. The first case of Dr. Gideon Fell, *Hag's Nook* by John Dickson Carr.

Summer
SORCERER CONJURER WIZARD WITCH

Charles Beauregard, the current Chairman of the Ruling Cabal of the Diogenes Club, becomes involved with the four "ravens" guarding London, although one may be secretly helping a mage incite a Wizard's War. Beauregard pays a visit to rival agency the Undertaking. Both agencies are secret arms of British Intelligence. Edwin Winthrop is the top agent, the "Most Valued Member," of the Diogenes Club. Mentioned or appearing: Mycroft Holmes; the "Unnameables" section of the American federal government; Innsmouth, the Esoteric Order of Dagon, and the Deep Ones; Captain Geoffrey Jeperson; Isadora Persano; Egdon Heath; the Angel Down Changeling; the Mi-Go; Abraham Van Helsing and Dracula; Geneviève Dieudonné; Kate Reed; Carnacki; Dr. Nikola; the Tong of Weng-Chiang; the Si-Fan; Dravot; Catriona Kaye; Colonel Zenf; Margery Device; Professor Moriarty; the Great Old Ones; Oliver Haddo; Declan Mountmain; Adrian Marcato; Anselm Oakes; Hjalmar Poelzig; Julian Karswell; Hallward; the Duke of Emsworth; Rodger Baskerville; Sir Francis Varney; Sir Henry Merrivale; Hugh Drummond; Dr. Jonathan Chambers; Dennis Rattray; Michael Bellamy; Simon Templar; Zenith the Albino; Pandora Reynolds; Roderick Spode; Roger Ackroyd; Rebecca DeWinter; Lord Peter Wimsey; the appalling American upstart Vance; Leo Dare; Nicholas Goodman, Eithne Orfe, and Mildew Manor; the Yard's Department of Queer Complaints; the Lord of Strange Deaths; Martin Hesselius; Millie Karnstein; Lord Ruthven; Colonel Sebastian Moran; the Splendid Six; Sir Denis Nayland-Smith; Jane Marple; Constable Ottermole; the Drones Club; the Criterion Bar; Granite Grant; Frank "Chandu" Chandler; the Duc de Richlieu; Fantômas; Arsène Lupin; the Purfleet sanatorium; Dr. Silence; Morris Klaw; Harry Dickson; Taverner; Chard; and Scarfe.

A Diogenes Club story by Kim Newman in the anthology A Book of Wizards, *edited by Marvin Kaye, Science Fiction Book Club, April 2008. "Sorcerer Conjurer Wizard Witch," like the rest of the Diogenes Club stories, takes place in the Crossover Universe. Mycroft Holmes, the Diogenes Club, the Criterion Bar, Colonel Sebastian Moran, and Professor Moriarty are from Doyle and Watson's Sherlock Holmes tales. Beauregard, Winthrop, Geneviève Dieudonné, Catriona Kaye, and Kate Reed appear in many of Newman's Diogenes Club tales, and have alternate universe counterparts in the Anno Dracula novels and stories. The "Unnameables" section is from Newman's "The Big Fish." Innsmouth, the Deep Ones, and the Esoteric Order of Dagon are from H.P. Lovecraft's "The Shadow over Innsmouth." Captain Geoffrey Jeperson is the adoptive father of Richard Jeperson, a member of the 1960s-1970s Diogenes Club. Isadora Persano is from Doyle and Watson's "The Problem of Thor Bridge." Egdon Heath is from Evelyn Waugh's* Decline and Fall *and Thomas Hardy's* Return of the Native. *The Angel Down Changeling is from Newman's "Angel Down, Sussex." The Mi-Go and the Great Old Ones are from H.P. Lovecraft's Cthulhu Mythos. Van Helsing is from Bram Stoker's Dracula. Carnacki is William Hope Hodgson's "ghost finder." Dr. Nikola's stories were chronicled by Guy Boothby. The Tong of Weng-Chiang is from the* Doctor Who *program "The Talons of Weng-Chiang" and substantiates a version of the Doctor in the Crossover Universe. The Si-Fan organization is from Sax Rohmer's Fu Manchu novels. Dravot is Daniel Dravot from "The Man Who Would Be King." Colonel Zenf also appears, and Leo Dare is mentioned, in Newman's "Cold Snap." Margery Device also appears in Newman's "Moon Moon Moon." Oliver Haddo is from W. Somerset Maugham's 1908 novel* The Magician.

Declan Mountmain is from Newman's Seven Stars. Adrian Marcato is mentioned in the 1968 film Rosemary's Baby. Anselm Oakes is from Christopher Isherwood's story "A Visit to Anselm Oakes." Hjalmar Poelzig is from the 1934 film The Black Cat. Julian Karswell is from M.R. James' "Casting the Runes." Hallward is Basil Hallward from Oscar Wilde's The Picture of Dorian Gray. The Duke of Emsworth is from P.G. Wodehouse's Blandings Castle saga. Rodger Baskerville is from Doyle's The Hound of the Baskervilles. Sir Francis Varney is from James Malcolm Rymer's Varney the Vampyre; or, The Feast of Blood. Sir Henry Merrivale is from mysteries by Carter Dickson (John Dickson Carr). Hugh Drummond is from H.C. "Sapper" McNeile's Bulldog Drummond books. Dr. Jonathan Chambers is from Newman's  "The Original Dr. Shade" and The Quorum. Dennis Rattray is "Blackfist" from Newman's "Clubland Heroes." Michael Bellamy is the title character in Edgar Wallace's 1923 novel The Green Archer. Simon Templar is Leslie Charteris' legendary hero, The Saint. Zenith the Albino is one of Sexton Blake's primary nemeses. Pandora Reynolds is from the 1951 film Pandora and the Flying Dutchman. Roderick Spode is from P.G. Wodehouse's Jeeves and Wooster stories. Roger Ackroyd is from Agatha Christie's 1926 Hercule Poirot novel The Murder of Roger Ackroyd. Rebecca DeWinter is from Daphne du Maurier's 1938 novel Rebecca. Lord Peter Wimsey is Dorothy Sayers' famous amateur detective. Vance is S.S. Van Dine's Philo Vance. Nicholas Goodman, Eithne Orfe, and Mildew Manor are from Newman's "Mildew Manor, or The Italian Smile." The Department of Queer Complaints is from Carter Dickson's 1940 collection of the same name. The Lord of Strange Deaths is Doctor Fu Manchu. Sir Denis Nayland-Smith is Fu Manchu's primary adversary. Dr. Martin Hesselius is from J. Sheridan Le Fanu's "Green Tea" (1872). Millie Karnstein is Le Fanu's "Carmilla." Lord Ruthven is from John Polidori's The Vampyre. The Splendid Six are from Newman's "Clubland Heroes." Jane Marple is Agatha Christie's mystery solver, better known as Miss Marple. Constable Ottermole is from "The Hands of Mr. Ottermole" in Thomas Burke's 1931 collection The Pleasantries of Old Quong. The Drones Club appears in a series of short stories by P.G. Wodehouse. Granite Grant is James "Granite" Grant, a British Secret Service agent who appeared in several Sexton Blake stories throughout the 1920s.

Frank "Chandu" Chandler is otherwise known as Chandu the Magician, from two films and a radio series. The Duc de Richlieu is from novels by Dennis Wheatley. Fantômas and Arsène Lupin should need no further introduction at this point. The Purfleet sanatorium is Dr. John Seward's from Bram Stoker's Dracula. Dr. Silence is an occult investigator in stories by Algernon Blackwood. Morris Klaw is a supernatural detective from Sax Rohmer's The Dream tive. The tales of Harry Dickson, the American Sherlock Holmes, were told by Jean Ray and others. Taverner is from Dion Fortune's The Secrets of Dr. Taverner (1926). Chard and Scarfe are Francis Chard and Derek Scarfe from Alfred McLelland Burrage's collection Some Ghost Stories (1927).

Mid-July
THE ADVENTURE OF THE TOTTENHAM WEREWOLF
Solar Pons and Lyndon Parker dine at Mycroft Holmes' club, the Diogenes Club.

Short story by August Derleth in the third volume, The Memoirs of Solar Pons.

Late Summer
A CASE OF TOMFOOLERY
Campion has recently finished his first case, recorded as *Sweet Danger*. After Campion's butler Lugg reads an account of Lord Peter Wimsey's solving of the "belfry case," Lugg comments on both Campion and Wimsey, complaining that the aristocracy is "carrying on like second-rate Sexton Blakes." In order to annoy Lugg, Campion praises Wimsey's butler, Bunter. Lugg then makes the charge that Bunter is a womanizer. Lugg claims that he and Bunter belong to the same servants' club, and that Bunter has been reprimanded there for "his conduct with young ladies." In the conclusion of this story, Campion expresses the desire to be "canonized alongside Sherlock Holmes and Sexton Blake."

A pastiche by Spencer Lodge in The Albert Memorial: A 100th Birthday Tribute to Mr. Albert Campion, *edited by Roger Johnson and B. A. Pike. This story links together Margery Allingham's Albert Campion to Lord Peter Wimsey, Sexton Blake, and Sherlock Holmes. The "belfry case" refers to Dorothy Sayers' Lord Peter mystery,* The Nine Tailors. *It should be noted that Lugg is not always a reliable source in Allingham's novels, and his comments could be wild accusations spurred by jealousy.* The Albert Memorial: A 100th Birthday Tribute to Mr. Albert Campion *also contains a short piece called "My Advice to Mr. Campion" by Sherlock Holmes (edited by Matthew Coniam), which is excerpted from* Reflections Upon the Methods and Achievements of Other Detectives, *a posthumous work found among the papers of Sherlock Holmes after the great detective allegedly died in 1957 (this date is from Baring-Gould's biography). Holmes praised Campion's method and acclaimed him "the most effective skilled, inventive, and effective of all the detectives whose methods and* achievements I have studied in these pages." The names of the other detectives besides Campion are not mentioned with the exception of Dupin (Holmes' opinion hasn't changed since A Study in Scarlet). Of course Holmes did not pass this mortal veil in 1957, but perhaps he did fake his death at that time, as he was later sighted under the name "William Escott."

FLASH, DALE, AND DR. ZARKOV CRASH IN ROCKET/FLASH AND DALE ARE MARRIED IN THE JUNGLE

Flash Gordon, Dale Arden, and Dr. Zarkov return to Earth from Mongo and crash in the jungle. Flash and Dale get married, with Jungle Jim Bradley in attendance.

Episodes of the radio series The Amazing Interplanetary Adventures of Flash Gordon, *which actually transitioned in the final two episodes to a new title,* The Adventures of Flash Gordon and Jungle Jim.

Sept. 19. Illya Nickovetch Kuryakin is born in the Ukraine, U.S.S.R.

Autumn. Events of the film *The Wolf Man*, chronicling the transformation of Lawrence Stewart Talbot. Lawrence Stewart Talbot's adventures continue in *Frankenstein Meets the Wolf Man, The House of Frankenstein, House of Dracula, Abbott and Costello Meet Frankenstein,* and the novel *Return of the Wolf Man*.

Autumn. Dr. Vitas Verdegast engages in a chess game for human lives against Satan worshipper Hjalmar Poelzig in *The Black Cat*.

Autumn. Dan Turner solves his first case, "Murder by Proxy," as told by Robert Leslie Bellem (*Spicy Detective Stories*, June 1934).

Autumn. Rick and Evelyn O'Connell, and their son Alex, once again battle the evil mummy Imhotep (*The Mummy Returns*).

Autumn. Nick and Nora Charles are mystery-solvers in *The Thin Man*, as told by Dashiell Hammett.

Autumn
WALDO'S WONDER TEAM
    Nelson Lee encounters Waldo the Wonder Man at St. Frank's. Boys' Friend Library, *Second Series, #445, September 1934.*

Autumn 1933-Autumn 1934
THE RED SILK SCARF
   Harry Dickson falls in love, briefly, with Kanoto Yoshimuta, and also encounters John Ashenden. Also appearing is Dr. Daisuke Serizawa, while Dr. Francis Ardan is mentioned.
   Story by Michel Stéphan in Tales of the Shadowmen Volume 6: Grand Guignol, *Jean-Marc and Randy Lofficier, eds., Black Coat Press, 2010; published in French in* Les Compagnons de l'Ombre (Tome 5), *Jean-Marc and Randy Lofficier, eds., Rivière Blanche, 2009. Kanoto Yoshimuta is the future Madame Atomos, from the novels by André Caroff, while Ashenden is from W. Somerset Maugham's* Ashenden; or the British Agent. *Dr. Daisuke Serizawa is from the 1954 Japanese film* Gojira *(*Godzilla*). The events of* Godzilla *and its multitudinous sequels did not occur in the Crossover Universe, but that does not prevent the presence of a CU-specific version of Serizawa. Dr. Francis Ardan, Jr. is from Guy d'Armen's* Doc Ardan: City of Gold and Lepers, *and has been identified as Lester Dent's Doc Savage.*

December
DOUBLE OR DIE
   One of James Bond's messmates at Eton, Tommy Chong, mentions that King Kong was a secret "until they found him on Skull Island."
   Novel by Charlie Higson, Puffin Books, 2007. Chong's statement could certainly be interpreted as a reference to the recently released film King Kong. *On the other hand, Philip José Farmer established that King Kong and James Bond coexist in the same continuity, so there is no reason not to interpret this as a valid crossover link.*

1934

1934-1936. Events of the French film *Pépé le Moko*, based on the novel by Henri La Barthe.
   Winter. Birth of Mack Bolan, son of Richard Wentworth (The Spider) and Nita van Sloan. Bolan became a veteran of the Korean and Vietnam wars. It is likely that he was placed with the Bolans, relatives of Nita's family.

Winter
INDIANA JONES AND THE HOLLOW EARTH
   Shangri-La is mentioned.
   Indiana Jones novel by Max McCoy. The Shangri-La of James Hilton's Lost Horizon *was also visited by Tarzan at some point, as he mentioned in Russ Manning's* Tarzan in the Land That Time Forgot *and* The Pool of Time.

SERVANTS OF THE SKULL

Secret Agent X, being escorted through a labyrinthine hideout, asks, "What's all the mystery about? You'd think the Skull was another Fu Manchu with all these secret passages and things."

Secret Agent X pulp novel by Brant House, November 1934.

THE YESTERDAY CONNECTION

In 1934, Doc Savage and his men encounter a strange woman from a parallel dimension, who seeks his help in vanquishing another strange, violent being, also from her dimension. Doc succeeds in sealing the creature into the cornerstone of a building under construction, but has a weird feeling that the case is somehow unfinished. In 1974, the building is about to be demolished. The other-dimensional woman seeks Spider-Man's assistance in preventing the creature's escape. Instead, Spidey senses something wrong and demolishes the cornerstone with a jackhammer, freeing the creature. It turns out that the woman had tricked Doc into unjustly imprisoning the creature, and Spidey was able to right an ancient wrong.

Giant-Size Spider-Man # 3 *by Gerry Conway, Ross Andru, and Mike Esposito, Marvel Comics, January 1975. This crossover features the Crossover Universe version of Spider-Man, rather than the "mainstream" Spidey of the Marvel Comics Universe.*

THE BAT FLIES LOW

"Captain Rorke crossed to the fire, tossing the end of a cigarette in among the burning logs. While a physiognomist might have been mistaken in the temper and make-up of the man, the lamented Sherlock Holmes could not have failed to note his hands. Although well cared for, they were significantly muscular with a predominance of thumb which told its own story."

*Novel by Sax Rohmer. The reference to Holmes implies that he is a real person, not just a fictional character. The use of the word "lamented" implies that Holmes was dead by the time of this novel, but his retirement to Sussex may have led many people to falsely assume that he had died. Rick Lai observes that "*The Bat Flies Low *features an Egyptian character, Hassan es-Sugra, who acts as a guide and headman for archaeological expeditions. The same character* *appears in two other works by Rohmer, 'The Death-Ring of Sneferu' from* Tales of Secret Egypt *and the novel* She Who Sleeps.*"*

Spring. Birth of Cordwainer Bird. According to Philip José Farmer, Bird is the nephew of both The Shadow and G-8. He is also the great grandson of Leopold Bloom (see James Joyce's *Ulysses*).

Spring. Savile Row tailor Horace Treadgold begins solving crimes. (*Footsteps at Night* by Valentine Williams, *The American Magazine*, June-November 1935.)

Spring
THE DEVIL RIDES OUT

The Duke de Richlieu mutters "the last two lines of the dread Sussamma ritual" as protection against a supernatural entity, which is described as "a Saiitii manifestation" and "an ab-human monster from the outer circle."

Novel by Dennis Wheatley. Although Wheatley changed the name of the ritual from Saaamaaa to Sussamma, it is clearly the same ritual seen in several Carnacki stories by William Hope Hodgson ("The Gateway of the Monster," "The House Among the Laurels," and "The Whistling Room") because Carnacki also mentioned the Saiitii in "The Whistling Room." Since Carnacki is in the CU, so is the Duke de Richlieu. Rick Lai observes that "The Saaamaaa ritual became part of the Cthulhu Mythos in Ramsey Campbell's 'The Stone on the Island,' first published in August Derleth's anthology, Over the Edge *(1964), and reprinted in Campbell's Mythos collection,* Cold Print *(the expanded British edition, Headline, 1993). Supposedly the Saaamaaa Ritual can be used as protection against the Great Old Ones and their servants."*

THE CASE OF THE DEATH BARQUE

Sir Ronald, a mad scientist, performs brain-enhancing experiment on giant rats from Sumatra. One of the rats escapes and seeks refuge on a ship, the *Matilda Briggs*. Using the ship as a nest, the rat goes out at night and fatally attacks humans. "Sir Ronald, the brain specialist, lies with his throat ripped away, victim of his own experiments with the Giant Rats of Sumatra."

Story by H. Bedford-Jones, Argosy, *February 9, 1935. The reference to the Giant Rats of Sumatra was originally from Doyle and Watson's Holmes tale, "The Sussex Vampire," and these events must constitute a sort-of sequel to the events involving Holmes and the Giant Rats, thus bringing pulp adventurer John Solomon into the CU.*

Summer. The villainous Doctor Satan begins his mad schemes, and is opposed by brilliant criminologist Ascott Keane and his faithful secretary and companion, Beatrice Dale, as told in stories in *Weird Tales* by Paul Ernst.

Summer. Terry Lee and Pat Ryan go adventuring in the Far East, in *Terry and the Pirates*, as told by Milton Caniff, and later, George Wunder.

Summer 1934-1935. After discovering Radium-X in a fallen meteor, Dr. Janos Rukh starts glowing and kills with a mere touch. He eventually goes completely insane in *The Invisible Ray*.

Summer
KAPITÄN HOLM

Rolf Torring, a Great White Hunter, encounters Captain Holm, the modern descendant of the 18th-century seaman Captain Axel Holm.

From Hans Warren's Rolf Torring's Abenteuer *(Rolf Torring's Adventures) #330, 1935, placing Captain Axel Holm in the CU.*

EL INSPECTOR DAN CONTRA FU MANCHU (INSPECTOR DAN VS. FU MANCHU)

Inspector Dan of the Flying Patrol goes up against Dr. Fu Manchu.

Spanish comic story in Revista Campeón, *1948. Inspector Dan was a Scotland Yard investigator who was involved in many paranormal cases, going up against mummies, vampires, werewolves, mad scientists, etc. His secretary was named Stella and he was under the orders of Colonel Higgins, a character similar in style to Sir Henry Merrivale. Roberto Lionel adds, "There is also a Spanish comic which pits Fah Lo Suee, the daughter of Fu Manchu, against the Copperhead, the hero of the serial* The Mysterious Dr. Satan.*"*

September
THE CLAWS OF THE CAT

Ellen Patrick (The Domino Lady), mentions having lunch with her former sorority sister, Delores Colquitt. Delores is in Los Angeles with her boyfriend, Jim Anthony, the super-detective, because several studios are interested in making a serial cliff-hanger based on his adventures.

Short story by Ron Fortier in Domino Lady: Sex as a Weapon, *edited by Lori Gentile, Moonstone Books, 2009. The first Jim Anthony adventure was published in October 1940. This crossover demonstrates that he began his adventuring career several years before that.*

Autumn. The first known escapade of Mandrake the Magician, as related by biographer Lee Falk.

Autumn. While in Tibet, British botanist Wilfred Glendon is attacked by a werewolf. Back in England, he becomes the Werewolf of London.

Autumn
JOHN STEED: AN AUTHORIZED BIOGRAPHY, VOLUME 1: JEALOUS IN HONOUR

In chapter four, "Eton 1934-6," we discover that during Steed's first year at Eton (1934), he encounters a young James Bond: "One factor which seems to have contributed to John's unhappiness at this time was the bullying which was an unfortunate feature of life in the school—or at least in those circles in which Steed moved. The main bully was a boy called Bond, later to achieve a certain notoriety in a career not totally unlike Steed's. Indeed their paths were to cross several times in adult life, seldom with profitable results. Although Bond was only two or so years older than Steed (a fact which will doubtless be disputed by Bond and his cronies) he was a great deal bigger. One of his fetishes was to make smaller boys stir his evening mug of cocoa for him, just as in later life he was to make a laughable affectation out of his insistence on dry martini cocktails being stirred rather than shaken. One day he demanded that Steed perform this service. Steed refused. Bond again insisted. 'Who the hell do you think you are?' enquired Steed, suggesting at the same time that he should pick on someone his own size. 'Bond, James Bond,' replied the bully, clearly expecting young Steed to fall groveling at his feet. 'Well, Bond,' said Steed evenly, 'if you'd like to present yourself behind the Fives Courts by Jordan in half an hour's time I'll show you in the only language you apparently understand, precisely why I have no intention of stirring your rotten cocoa.' Alas, poor Bond! He had never heard of the Bodger business at Lyeard Lodge. Thirty minutes later he was waiting behind the fives court, aglow with cocky truculence. Thirty-five minutes later he was being half dragged home by two of his familiars, his jaw and his ego both equally badly bruised."

By Tim Heald, published in hardcover by Weidenfeld & Nicolson, 1977. However, see the previous notes on young James Bond's first adventure, Silver-Fin.

THE HAUNTER OF THE RING

The sorcerous ring used by Vrolok is none other than the Serpent Ring of Set worn by Conan's archfoe, Thoth-Amon.

This John Kirowan story by Robert E. Howard can be found in Beyond the Borders, Baen Books, 1996. The Ring was seen in the Conan tale "The Phoenix on the Sword." The Ring also appears in "The Ring of Set," one of the Simon of Gitta stories by Richard Tierney. Though the description differs somewhat, this may be the same ring used by the magician Roger Simeon in the Solomon Kane story "The Right Hand of Doom."

DAS GEHEIMNIS DER MORS (THE SECRET OF MORS)

Four heroic German airmen calling themselves "The Four Musketeers" battle evil around the world, using technology from Captain Mors.

Story in Die Vier Musketiere #5, 1935. This brings the Four Musketeers into the CU.

THE SEVENTH VICTIM

Dr. Louis Judd, a psychiatrist, tries to protect a woman, Jacqueline Gibson, from a vengeful group of Satanists.

Feature film written by DeWitt Bodeen and Charles O'Neal, directed by Mark Robson, and produced by Val Lewton, 1943. In The Seventh Victim, Dr. Judd claims to no longer treat patients in private practice. However, by the time of the events of Lewton's Cat People, he must have reversed this decision.

1935

January. Indiana Jones meets aviatrix Amelia Earhart. (*Indiana Jones and the Shrine of the Sea Devil*, serialized comic book story by Gary Gianni in the anthology series Dark Horse Comics, #3-6, 1992-1993.)

Winter. Sir John Appleby's first recorded case, *Death at the President's Lodging*, as told by Michael Innes.

Winter. First recorded case of Parisian policeman Charles C.M. Carlier. (*The Mystery of St. Eustache*.)

Winter. Events of the feature film *Son of Dracula*.

March
RASPUTIN RETURNS

The Shadow battles Moriarty's son, Rasputin.

Comic story by Gerard Jones and Eduardo Barreto, in #1-4 of DC Comics' third Shadow series, The Shadow Strikes! *This crossover reinforces Rasputin's place in the Crossover Universe. Rasputin was established as the son of the first Professor Moriarty in John T. Lescroart's novel* Rasputin's Revenge.

April. Val Kildare and Jerry Hazard go up against the mysterious Wu Fang in *The Case of the Six Coffins* by Robert J. Hogan (*The Mysterious Wu Fang* v1, #1, September 1935). Jerry Hazard is likely a member of the same family as Captain Kevin Douglas Rex Hazard. (In his pulp appearances, Captain Hazzard's surname was spelled with a double-Z.) Jerry Hazard is also probably the brother of Mark Hazard who worked with Nayland Smith and provided a first-person narrative of the adventure, which Sax Rohmer entitled *President Fu Manchu*. Val Kildare must be related to a famous young doctor whose story was recounted by Max Brand.

April
THE CONFLAGRATION MAN

Doc Savage's first meeting with The Shadow. The Shadow, disguised, as a criminal, goes into a bar in which some patrons in the background are discussing a "crap game in the Biltmore basement." Later, when Doc and The Shadow are fighting, The Shadow uses a grip on Doc, which Doc breaks. The Shadow states, "I thought only the man who created the martial art of Baritsu and I knew the secret to breaking that hold—and he would not teach it to one he deemed unworthy!" Doc replies, "That's exactly what I was thinking."

Comics story in four parts by Mike W. Barr, Gerard Jones, Rod Whigham, and Eduardo Barreto, DC Comics, 1989-1990. Two parts were published in DC's Doc Savage *ongoing series, #17 and 18; the remaining two parts were published in* The Shadow Strikes! *#5 and 6. In the musical* Guys and Dolls, *Nathan Detroit runs a nightly floating craps game, but he needs a thousand dollars to hold his game in the Biltmore garage. Regarding Baritsu, there is only one other known practitioner: Sherlock Holmes. From Philip José Farmer, we know that Doc trained with Holmes. Therefore, Holmes must have taught the art of Baritsu to both The Shadow and Doc Savage. Rick*

Lai notes that Doc Savage and The Shadow also met in 1940s comics: "Doc's comic book adventures from the 1940s are contradictory to the pulps (Monk is bald, etc.). One issue has a crossover with The Shadow whose comic book incarnation can really turn invisible. The Shadow leaves New York to go on a secret mission to Japan. In his absence, an invisible crook frames The Shadow for a series of crimes. Doc catches the crook and clears The Shadow's name. I would consider this an alternate universe story."

THE VOLCANO
Private detective Curtius Parry receives a tip on a case from his friend, *Globe* reporter Edward Malone.
"The Volcano" is a short story by Paul Chapin, edited by Philip José Farmer. It is found in Riverworld and Other Stories, *Berkley Books, 1979; reprinted in* Venus on the Half-Shell and Others, *Christopher Paul Carey, ed., Subterranean Press, 2008. Writer Paul Chapin once met Wold Newton Family member Nero Wolfe, in Archie Goodwin and Rex Stout's* The League of Frightened Men. *Reporter Edward Malone is likely the same Malone from Sir Arthur Conan Doyle's Professor Challenger stories.*

Spring. Japanese secret agent Mr. Moto's first recorded adventure, *Your Turn, Mr. Moto*, as told by John P. Marquand. Farmer proposed that Mr. Moto was a Wold Newton Family member in Doc Savage.

Spring. "Crash" Corrigan, a naval officer, accompanies Professor Norton on a submarine expedition, where they discover what appears to be the lost city of Atlantis. The underwater ruler, Unga Khan, wants to conquer the upper world with robots and death rays, but Corrigan defeats him (film serial *Undersea Kingdom*).

Spring. Gotham Police Commissioner James "Wildcat" Gordon starts his battle against crime as The Whisperer in "The Dead Who Talked," as told by Clifford Goodrich (pseudonym for Laurence Donovan) in *The Whisperer* #1, Fall 1936. Gordon is the grandson of former Secret Service agent Artemus Gordon, as revealed in Mark Brown's "The Magnificent Gordons," *Myths for the Modern Age: Philip José Farmer's Wold Newton Universe.*

Late May. Dr. Yen Sin vs. Michael Traile, "The Man Who Never Sleeps," in *The Mystery of the Dragon's Shadow* by Donald E. Keyhoe (*Doctor Yen Sin* v1, #1, May 1936).

June
MASTER OF THE DEATH MADNESS
Richard Wentworth (The Spider) makes a fool of a "youngish, broad-faced man named Christopher, who represented the Secret Service."
The Spider, August 1935 issue, written by Norvell Page (writing as Grant Stockbridge). The Christopher mentioned must be Jimmy Christopher, Secret Service Operator #5. As to why Wentworth would be unkind to a fellow crime-fighter, we can only speculate that perhaps Christopher had unwittingly interfered in one of Wentworth's investigations. Operator #5 is in the CU, but only the stories from April 1934 through approximately early 1935 (which marks the start of World War II in the Christopher novels). At this point, the Operator #5 novels diverge into an alternate universe. The remainder of the Jimmy Christopher novels take place in this alternate universe, including the Purple Invasion saga. We may postulate that Operator #5's remaining adventures in the CU were of a somewhat less apocalyptic nature than those chronicled in the pulp novels of 1935-1939.

THE ADVENTURE OF THE DEFEATED DOCTOR
Solar Pons and Fu Manchu go head-to-head once more.
Short story found in the ninth volume, The Further Adventures of Solar Pons *by Basil Copper. The 1935 date is conjectural.*

Summer. Lemmy Caution's first case, *This Man is Dangerous*, as recounted by Peter Cheyney.
Summer. Aerial ace Lance Star—Sky Ranger's first adventure.
Summer. G-Man Dan Fowler's first case, "Snatch!" by "C.K.M. Scanlon" (George Fielding-Eliot), *G-Men Detective*, October 1935.

Summer 1935-1936
CAT PEOPLE
Dr. Louis Judd attempts to treat Irena Dubrovna for alleged delusions that she is a were-cat.
Feature film written by DeWitt Bodeen, directed by Jacques Tourneur, produced by Val Lewton, 1942. Cat People *spawned a sequel,* The Curse of the Cat People *(1944). Dr. Judd also appeared in Lewton's* The Seventh Victim *(1943). Since Judd dies in* Cat People, *it must take place after* The Seventh Victim.

Summer
BIGGLES, AIR COMMODORE
    Biggles tracks down a submarine that is destroying British ships in the Indian Ocean. Biggles' cousin and partner, Algy Lacey, is traveling through a Southeast Asia jungle: "For a while he scrambled desperately, often dangerously, from branch to branch after the manner of the renowned Tarzan of the Apes, but he quickly discovered that this method of progress was much easier to imagine than put into practice, as the palms of his hands testified."
    Novel by Captain W. E. Johns, 1937. A recurring character in the Biggles novels is Major Raymond, who also appears in W.E. Johns' Steeley novels. Steeley was a Great War veteran and air ace turned modern Robin Hood, a la The Saint. Major Raymond also appears in several of Johns' novels and stories about Worrals of the W.A.A.F. (Woman's Auxiliary Air Force). "Worrals" is eighteen-year-old pilot Joan Worralson.

MONKEYSHINES
    In Toronto, The Red Panda and his trusty sidekick, The Flying Squirrel (the lovely Kit Baxter), go up against the sinister simian known as The Mad Monkey. The Mad Monkey was formerly known as Anton Creswell, who was stranded in Africa and lived among the baboons of the savannah for six years after a plane crash. After his rescue, Creswell claimed to be able to communi-

cate with the baboons, and went on a speaking tour. However, Creswell's speaking tour was cut short amidst publicity about an orphaned English Lord who could speak to apes, and a boy in India who was raised by wolves, and Creswell faded into oblivion, lost in the shuffle of wild men.

Episode #20 of The Red Panda Adventures *by Gregg Taylor, available via the* Decoder Ring Theater *website. The Red Panda is an unnamed playboy millionaire who fights crime as a masked mystery man. He uses many scientific gadgets and is a master of hypnosis. His sidekick is his streetwise, tough as nails lady chauffeur, Kit Baxter, aka The Flying Squirrel. The orphaned English Lord who could speak to apes is Edgar Rice Burroughs' Tarzan. The boy in India who was raised by wolves is Mowgli from Rudyard Kipling's* The Jungle Book (1894). *Interestingly,* Dennis E. Power's "*Jungle Brothers, Or, Secrets of the Jungle Lords*" (*in* Myths for the Modern Age: Philip José Farmer's Wold Newton Universe) *postulated that Tarzan and Mowgli were half-brothers. The connections to Tarzan and Mowgli place The Red Panda and The Flying Squirrel squarely in the Crossover Universe.*

Autumn. The Invisible Man's Revenge, in which Robert Griffin is provided with an invisibility formula by Dr. Peter Drury. Dennis E. Power has proposed that Robert Griffin is the third son of John "Jack" Hawley Griffin, and brother to Jack Griffin and Frank Griffin.

Autumn. Spenser is born in Laramie, Wyoming. It has been suggested that he is the nephew of Philip Marlowe.

Autumn. Britt Reid and Ikano Kato go to work busting crime as The Green Hornet and Kato. *The Green Hornet* radio series debuted on Detroit station WXYZ on January 31, 1936, replacing *Warner Lester, Manhunter* and *Dr. Fang*. Both of those series ended with heroic Warner Lester in a final battle to the death with the nefarious Dr. Fang. Warner Lester's sidekick, Mike Axford, went on to appear in *The Green Hornet*. This means that *Warner Lester, Manhunter* and *Dr. Fang* take place in the CU.

Autumn
EL REY DE LA SELVA Y EL JUDÍO ERRANTE (THE KING OF THE FOREST AND THE WANDERING JEW)
　　Tarzan encounters the Wandering Jew.
　　Story by J.A. Brau Santillana in an Argentinean series of Tarzan tales.

THE ORB OF ATAN

The *Book of Thoth* is featured in this episode of the continuing battle of Rick and Evelyn O'Connell, and their son Alex, against the evil mummy Imhotep.

Sixth episode of the animated television series, The Mummy. *The* Book of Thoth *also features in Richard Tierney's tales of Simon of Gitta, which in turn relate back to Conan's old adversary, Thoth-Amon. Since Conan and Simon of Gitta are in the Crossover Universe, so are the events of* The Mummy *animated series, which in turn is a spin-off of 1999's* The Mummy *and the sequels* The Mummy Returns *and* The Mummy: Tomb of the Dragon Emperor. *The* Scorpion King *prequels would also be included. The Imhotep in this series is different from the mummy Imhotep that the Whemples encountered in the 1932 film* The Mummy.

December
THE STRANGE CASE OF THE DOMINO LADY AND MR. HOLMES

The Domino Lady is in London on a mission, but when the last vial of the notorious Dr. Jekyll's serum is stolen from a museum, an elderly Sherlock Holmes recruits her to help nab the perpetrator.

Short story by Nancy Holder in Domino Lady: Sex as a Weapon, *edited by Lori Gentile, Moonstone Books, 2009. The story makes it clear that although Holmes has long since "retired" to the country, he still maintains his digs at 221B Baker Street, for when he is needed in London. This is consistent with other Holmes pastiches set in this general time frame. Since detective Harry Dickson is the new permanent resident at 221B, he must not be averse to sharing quarters with his mentor when the older detective comes into town. Watson is referred to as having passed on, but clearly this is a cover for the longevity elixir to which he and Holmes have access. Ellen Patrick has been active as The Domino Lady for three years, placing this case in 1935.*

Late December
DOC SAVAGE AND THE CULT OF THE BLUE GOD

After receiving a telegram from Doc Savage, Sherlock Holmes, in retirement in Sussex, refers to Doc as the greatest student of detection he ever had. Holmes and Watson continue their reminiscences, remembering that they first encountered Doc's father, Savage, Sr., during the case which Watson recorded as "The Adventure of the Priory School," which case unfortunately resulted in Savage, Sr.'s expedient flight from England. In Abyad, Maghreb, Doc sees a man who looks like French gangster and thief Pépé le Moko.

Screenplay by Philip José Farmer for the second, unmade Doc Savage feature film, published in the collection Pearls from Peoria, *Paul Spiteri, ed., Subterranean Press, 2006. Although Farmer's screenplay dates these events during*

Christmastime, 1936, this does not fit into Farmer's own Chronology from Doc Savage: His Apocalyptic Life. *Therefore I have placed the events during Christmastime, 1935.* Pépé le Moko *is from the 1937 film of the same name, remade as* Algiers *in 1938 and* Casbah *in 1948. Of note, Monk and Ham enter a nightclub that looks exactly like Rick's from* Casablanca, *but the timing and Abyad location argue against this being a valid crossover.*

1936

January 29. Future U.N.C.L.E agent Mark Slate is born in London.

Winter. First recorded exploit of Colonel Dubois, head of French counter-intelligence. (*The Two Crimes on the Maginot Line* by Andre Brouillard.)

Winter. The 20th Phantom begins his crime-fighting activities after the death of his father, the 19th Phantom. This is the Phantom who will eventually marry Diana Palmer. They will have two children, Kit and Heloise. Many chronicles of this Phantom indicate that he is the 21st. His activities are documented starting in the mid 1930s all the way through the 1990s. However, there is no indication that any of the Phantom line ever had access to age-delaying elixir. It is unlikely that this Phantom's career lasted sixty years. It is more likely that, over the years, Phantom biographer Lee Falk had access to the histories of both the 20th and 21st Phantoms. He documented the careers of both men and merged them into one Phantom, calling him the 21st. The 20th Phantom was most likely killed in the 1960s and his son took over, operating until his death in 1989. The Phantom who began operating in 1989 is also mistakenly called the 21st Phantom (see *The Ghost Who Walks*, Marvel Comics, 1995). It would be unlikely that the 21st Phantom, as a man in his mid 20s in the mid 1990s, would have an adult grandson operating as the 23rd Phantom in the mid 2010s through the early 2020s (see *Phantom 2040*). Additionally, the mother of 1990s Phantom is called Jane, not Diana. He cannot be the son of the 20th Phantom, whose wife was Diana Palmer. He must be the grandson, and thus, the 22nd Phantom. The son of the 22nd Phantom took over as the 23rd in the mid 2010s and had a very short-lived career, dying in 2024. His son assumed the mantle of the Phantom in the year 2040.

Winter
TARGET: DOMINO LADY

Ellen Patrick (The Domino Lady) makes passing reference to attending a charity air show on Long Island in a few weeks. Gotham City is also briefly mentioned.

Short story by Bobby Nash in Domino Lady: Sex as a Weapon, *edited by Lori Gentile, Moonstone Books, 2009. The Gotham City reference links The Domino Lady to Batman. The annual air show in Long Island is a staple of the Lance Star pulp stories.*

RAIDERS OF THE LOST ARK
The hieroglyphic inscriptions in the Well of Souls, where Indiana Jones and Sallah discover the fabled Ark of the Covenant, seem to depict anachronistic robots.

Feature film from Paramount Pictures, 1981. The robots look exactly like the "droids" R2-D2 and C-3PO, from the Star Wars Universe. Perhaps there is a wormhole or tear in space that connects the Milky Way galaxy with the Star Wars galaxy, and the two droids once ended up on Earth in ancient times, in an adventure yet to be revealed.

BLOODED
The Domino Lady and Sherlock Holmes cross paths once more, when he comes to California on a mission to rescue Xian Wu, the daughter of an old friend who was kidnapped in London by a villain called Chang Kai-Fong. Chang Kai-Fong wants Holmes to locate a statue called the Jade Dragon in exchange for Xian Wu's life.

Comic story in Domino Lady #1 by Nancy Holder and Danny Sempere, Moonstone Comics, 2009. This is the second meeting of Holmes and the Domino Lady; the first occurred on Holder's prose story "The Strange Case of the Domino Lady and Mr. Holmes" in Moonstone's anthology Domino Lady: Sex as a Weapon. Holmes is not depicted as terribly elderly, although he is eighty-two years old. Perhaps the Royal Jelly bee pollen life-extension elixir actually retards aging to a certain degree.

March
THE REVENGE OF SHIWAN KHAN
This tale reveals that Terry Lee and Pat Ryan are The Shadow's agents in China. Their nemesis, the Dragon Lady, also appears. Later, agent Harry Vincent meets up with two ramblers, Wash Tubbs and Captain Easy. Shiwan Khan is currently in possession of the Maltese Falcon. In China, an adventurer named Roy Andrews also briefly meets with The Shadow and Vincent. Versions of Popeye and Daddy Warbucks also appear.

Story arc by Gerard Jones, Rod Whigham, Gerry Fernandez, and John Beatty, in DC Comics' The Shadow Strikes! #21-27; the key issues here are 25 *and 27, bringing the comic strip perennials* Terry and the Pirates *and* Wash Tubbs and Captain Easy *into the Crossover Universe. The Falcon appears in #26, page 12, panel 4. Roy Chapman Andrews was an explorer-adventurer who mounted a series of Central Asiatic expeditions in the 1930s, in which he found many caches of fossilized dinosaurs and extinct mammals, adding significantly to the paleontological record. If Popeye really does exist in the CU, then clearly his comic strip adventures were greatly exaggerated. The Warbucks seen here does not appear to be in character with his portrayal with the* Little Orphan Annie *strip.*

March. Vladimir Nabokov's *The Real Life of Sebastian Knight.*

April. The Shadow meets Amelia Earhart. ("Aloha," a story by Gerard Jones and Steve Leialoha in #28 of DC Comics' *The Shadow Strikes!* Indiana Jones met Earhart one year ago in *Indiana Jones and the Shrine of the Sea Devil,* and a woman purporting to be Earhart was seen in *Doc Dare* in 1939.)

Spring
FEAR ITSELF

In New York, The Spider (Richard Wentworth) encounters Serpent-men from the cult of Set seeking the Cobra Crown. Wentworth is assisted by a supernatural expert, Professor Guicet.

Short story by Joel Frieman and C.J. Henderson, The Spider Chronicles, *Moonstone Books, 2007. The Cobra Crown is from the universe of Robert E. Howard's King Kull and Conan, and appeared in* Conan the Buccaneer *by L. Sprague de Camp and Lin Carter, in which it was destroyed. For its appearance in "Fear Itself," it was reconstituted or there are least two Cobra Crowns. Rick Lai ads: "In Henderson's 'Admission of Weakness,' Anton Zarnak's predecessor as an agent of Tibetan mystics was Professor Guicet. Guicet disappeared in 1922, and was revealed to be in some other dimension in Henderson's Teddy London/Anton Zarnak story, 'The Door.' One possible theory to explain Guicet's appearance in 'Fear Itself' is that he is really Anton Zarnak, pretending to be his predecessor (Guicet is never really described in detail)."*

THE MAN FOR THE JOB

A man named Carson interviews Mr. Piper, who once worked in Hamelin, Germany, for assistance with a problem. Piper recites his accomplishments, which include: working for a firm called Morrison, Morrison & Dodd and teaming with a British detective on an island near Sumatra; handling the Delapore case at Exham Priory in England; the Willard Stiles case in the U.S.; and helping the British Minister of Health, Mr. Foskins, to save London. Carson offers Piper the job, which involves his house and a curse dating back to the first occupant, Abigail Prim. Piper takes the case, saying he must first deal with Monsieur Skinner's Restaurant Gusteau in Paris.

Short story by Xavier Maumèjean in Tales of the Shadowmen Volume 6: Grand Guignol, Jean-Marc and Randy Lofficier, eds., Black Coat Press, 2010; printed in French in Les Compagnons de l'Ombre (Tome 5), Jean-Marc and Randy Lofficier, eds., Rivière Blanche, 2009. Mr. Piper is the Pied Piper of Hamelin. Morrison, Morrison & Dodd is from the Sherlock Holmes story "The Sussex Vampire." The British detective is Holmes and the island near Sumatra refers to the "untold" Holmes case "The Giant Rat of Sumatra." The Delapore case at Exham Priory refers to H.P. Lovecraft's tale "The Rats in the Walls" (Weird Tales, March 1924). Willard Stiles is from Willard, a 1971 horror film. Mr. Foskins is from James Herbert's 1974 novel The Rats. Monsieur Skinner and the Restaurant Gusteau in Paris are from the 2007 film Ratatouille. Carson and Abigail Prim (who is meant to be Abigail Prinn) are from Henry Kuttner's "The Salem Horror" (Weird Tales, May 1937).

Early May. Bruce Wayne's first case as The Bat-Man, "The Case of the Chemical Syndicate" (*Detective Comics* #27 by Bob Kane, DC Comics, May 1939). The Shadow had a very similar investigation in the pulp novel *Partners in Peril*, and one can postulate that The Bat-Man and The Shadow worked on the same case, although they didn't cross paths.

Summer. First case of Gregory George Gordon (aka "Gees") as chronicled by Jack Mann in *Gees' First Case.*

Summer. Miss Maud Silver's first full-fledged case, *The Case is Closed,* as related by Patricia Wentworth. Miss Maud Silver first appeared as a minor character in Wentworth's *Grey Mask* (1928). Wentworth also chronicled the cases of Miss Maud Silver's Scotland Yard contact, Chief Inspector Lamb.

Summer
THE BLACK COAT AND ATHENA VOLTAIRE: ATHENA VOLTAIRE AND THE ISLE OF THE DEAD

Athena Voltaire is hired to locate the shipwreck which occurred when The Black Coat battled pirates back in 1767. Her client's real goal is the shipment of waters from the Fountain of Youth.

One-shot comic, story by Steve Bryant, Ape Entertainment, February 2009. There are many links placing Athena Voltaire in the Crossover Universe; thus, The Black Coat's exploits take place *in the CU as well.*

BLACK SUN LIVES!

In 1936, Doc Savage, Monk Mayfair, and Renny Renwick receive a visit from Mrs. Raymond Lightner, a prominent astronomer. Dr. Lightner is going insane, and has a scheme to harness the power of the stars and focus it on himself. As the city blacks out, Doc, Monk, and Renny rush to Lightner's laboratory. "Meanwhile," in 1976, The Thing (Ben Grimm), and the Human Torch (Johnny Storm), receive a visit from Janice Lightner, the daughter of the 1930s Lightners. She tells them of her brother's mad scheme to recreate their father's doomed, insane experiments, and they rush to Lightner's laboratory. In both time periods, both groups are caught in the experiment's star-beam, and Doc and the boys are thrown into the future. Both Dr. Raymond Lightner and his son, Tom, are fused together to create the being called "Black Sun." With Black Sun's defeat, the temporal field returns Doc and the boys to 1936.

Marvel Two-In-One *#21, November 1976,* by Bill Mantlo, Ron Wilson, and Pablo Marcos. *This story brings parallel universe versions of the "Fantastic Four" characters into Crossover Universe continuity; it does not incorporate Marvel Comics Universe continuity. Tony Stark is mentioned in a flashback and Dr. Don Blake is also mentioned. However, appearances or cameos of a superhero's alter ego are sufficient to place that alter ego in the CU, but are not enough to substantiate the presence of the actual superhero.*

THE BEST SOLUTION

Dr. Anton Zarnak consults Dr. Seward's book on vampires. He also makes reference to a vampire named Tepes (Dracula's historical title). The story also mentions Ruthven.

By John L. French. Found in Crypt of Cthulhu *#100; reprinted in Lin Carter's* Anton Zarnak, Supernatural Sleuth, *Robert Price, ed., Marietta Publishing, 2002. These links both set Zarnak squarely in the same universe as Dracula. Lord Ruthven is from John Polidori's* The Vampyre.

LE TIGRI DELL'ATLANTICO
Italian policeman John Mauri starts his career. Shortly thereafter, he clashes with a gang of Moroccan Thugs in northwest Africa. They are an African branch of the Thugs who Sandokan battled in the 19th century.

Gianluigi Bonelli's John Mauri novels, beginning with Le Tigri dell'Atlantico, *1937. The link to the Sandokan series brings Mauri into the Crossover universe.*

THE BLACK-EYED BLONDE
Philip Marlowe receives a phone call from a Mrs. De Ruse, whose maiden name is Francine Levy. Her husband is gambler Johnny De Ruse, who recently took over Benny Cyrano's joint. Francine suspects her husband of adultery, and wants Marlowe to follow him. Marlowe was recommended by private eye Ted Carmady, who doesn't take as many cases since he became "hooked up" with a woman named Jean Adrian. Marlowe, who doesn't like divorce work, turns down the case.

Short story by Benjamin M. Schultz in the anthology Raymond Chandler's Philip Marlowe, *Byron Preiss, ed., 1988. The characters mentioned here are from two non-Marlowe stories by Chandler. Johnny De Ruse and Francine Levy are from "Nevada Gas," while Ted Carmady, Jean Adrian, and Benny Cyrano are from "Guns at Cyrano's." Both were published in the Chandler collection,* Pickup on Noon Street. *This crossover brings private eye Ted Carmady into the CU.*

August 8. Death of Robert Blake in an old abandoned church on Federal Hill in Providence, Rhode Island, as told in H.P. Lovecraft's The Haunter of the Dark.

September
THE SKY STEALERS
Johnny Littlejohn mentions that Dr. Petrie, the father of modern archaeology, was a large inspiration in his studies. The *Scroll of Thoth* also figures in the story. Finally, Ham compares Monk to a "dwarf edition of King Kong."

Marvel Comics' Doc Savage *magazine #6, October 1976, by Doug Moench and Tony DeZuniga. Dr. Petrie, the archaeologist, does have a close connection to the Crossover Universe (see "Who's Going to Take Over the World When I'm Gone?"* Myths for the Modern Age: Philip José Farmer's Wold Newton Universe*). The* Scroll of Thoth *also features in Richard Tierney's tales of Simon of Gitta, which in turn relate back to Conan's old adversary, Thoth-Amon. The Kong comparison is especially apt, given that Doc and his men actually witnessed the aftermath of Kong's rapid descent from the top of the Empire State Building (Farmer's "After King Kong Fell," which took place in October 1931).*

THE HAND IN THE GLOVE
   Dol Bonner, sometime Nero Wolfe assistant, solves her own case.
   Novel by Rex Stout. The connection between Wolfe, a Wold Newton Family member, and Dol Bonner, places Bonner in the CU.

   Autumn. Private eye Slam Bradley, the younger brother of Biff Bradley, receives his license and goes into business with partner Samuel "Shorty" Morgan (DC Comics' *Detective Comics* #1, March 1937).

Autumn
ATOMFEUER AUF GRONLAND (ATOMIC FIRE IN GREENLAND)
   Sun Koh assists Jan Mayen, an adventurer and pilot of an atom-powered aircraft, on a case in Greenland.
   From Paul Alfred Müller-Murnau's Jan Mayen *#106. This brings Jan Mayen into the CU because Sun Koh met Alaska Jim, and Alaska Jim met Captain Mors. Jess Nevins notes, "Mayen ends up assisting Sun Koh on a number of occasions and, after Sun Koh has assumed power in 'Atlantis,' helps Sun Koh transform parts of Greenland into arable territory. (Paul Alfred Müller-Murnau's* Jan Mayen, der Herr der Atomkraft *#1-120, 1936-1938). The events detailed in the Sun Koh and Jan Mayen stories are, of course, greatly exaggerated by their individual biographers. While most of the individual chapters of their biographies were based on real events, the world-changing and apocalyptic events described are fiction, written to appeal to the German audience." Presumably Sun Koh's assumption of power in Atlantis and transformation of Greenland are included in these fictional exaggerations.*

RAFFLES VS. SEXTON BLAKE
   A.J. Raffles and Sexton Blake clash for the first time, when Raffles pursues a bracelet called the "Fetter of Buddha."
   This crossover is by Barry Perowne in The Sexton Blake Library, *Second Series, #577, June 1937. Both Baker Street detective Sexton Blake and the notorious thief A.J. Raffles are mentioned in Philip José Farmer's Wold Newton works. However, this may in truth be a tale of R.J. Raffles rather than A.J. Raffles.*

MASKS OF MADNESS
   The Domino Lady meets The Phantom in his jungle home, the Deep Woods.

She learns he has additional information about her father's death, and they then travel separately to St. Paul, Minnesota, where she prepares to exact her revenge.

Short story by Martin Powell in Domino Lady: Sex as a Weapon, *edited by Lori Gentile, Moonstone Books, 2009. In Jim Steranko's tale "Aroused, the Domino Lady," which takes place in 1932, Ellen Patrick discovers her father's murderers. The perpetrator in this tale must have been an additional conspirator who went undiscovered for several years.*

1937

January
THE TWILIGHT AVENGER: THE CENTIPEDE CRAWLS

In Tulsa, Oklahoma, after criminals run down his fiancée, Randolph College football star and honor student Reece Chambers becomes The Twilight Avenger, emerging under cover of darkness to fight evil. Joining him in his battle is Professor Milton Herth, father of Reece's fiancée Delores. Professor Herth provides the latest scientific weaponry that modern technology can devise. Meanwhile, as Delores lies comatose in the hospital, reporter Joan Casey, who mentions celebrated New York detective Philo Vance, discovers The Twilight Avenger's true identity and begins sharing his adventures.

The Twilight Avenger *was created and written by John Wooley and Terry Tidwell. Parts one and two of* The Twilight Avenger *were published in 1986 by Elite Comics; the final, double-length chapter of this particular story was not published until 1996 by Miracle Comics.* The Twilight Avenger *also ran for eight issues, published by Eternity Comics from 1988-1990, with stories that take place after this one. Philo Vance is already included in the CU. Lots of straightforward pulp hero adventure, leavened with a good dose of horror and "good girl" (and bad girl) art, akin to* The Rocketeer.

Winter
WARRANT FOR X

Detective Anthony Gethryn "...wished that he were Dr. Thorndyke—and then, with an excitement such as he had not felt for years, felt suddenly, if not like Dr. Thorndyke, at least like Inspector French."

One in a series of novels by Philip MacDonald about detective Anthony Gethryn. Dr. Thorndyke is already in the CU so this reference brings in both Gethryn and Freeman Wills Crofts' Inspector French.

March. Pulpsters Lester Dent and Walter Gibson investigate the murder of H.P. Lovecraft, and foil a fiendish plot in New York's Chinatown, with a lot of help along the way from Lester's wife Norma, L. Ron Hubbard, and Robert

Heinlein. Orson Welles makes a cameo appearance. (*The Chinatown Death Cloud Peril* by Paul Malmont.)

March
CAPTAIN MIDNIGHT AT ULTIMA THULE

The Americans discover an intra-atomic energy source called "Metal X," which turns out to be the same substance known as *vril*, first discovered by an antediluvian race called the Vril-ya. The destruction of the German zeppelin *Krueger* is witnessed by a tourist from Peoria named Tim Howller. Reporter Patricia Johnston writes about the disaster in the newspaper *L'Echo de France*. In New York's Chinatown, Captain Midnight receives help from an ingénue named Madame Inga. Midnight ends up battling Sun Koh, "the Inheritor of Atlantis," putting to the test all of the Baritsu lessons that he received from the Great Detective. Sun Koh swears by Resu and has a strange map tattooed on his back depicting something resembling the African continent with two huge inland seas.

Short story by Win Scott Eckert in the anthology Captain Midnight Chronicles, *Christopher Mills, ed., Moonstone Books, 2010. Metal X is from E.E. "Doc" Smith's* The Skylark of Space *(1928) and follow-up novels in the Skylark series. The Skylark series must take place in an alternate timeline where Seaton's discovery of Metal X took place in the late 1920s. Conversely, in the Crossover Universe his discovery takes place in the late 1930s and presumably he does not go on to interplanetary adventures as he does in the Skylark timeline. The Vril-ya and vril are from Edward Bulwer-Lytton's* The Coming Race. *The theosophist William Scott-Elliot described the aircraft of Atlantis as being powered by* vril-*force. Sun Koh, "the Nazi Doc Savage," was the protagonist of German pulp stories written by Paul Alfred Müller-Murnau, 1933-1936. Jess Nevins has described the advent of Sun Koh thusly: "A man falls out of the sky one rainy night and lands in front of a group of amazed bystanders in London. He is tall, muscular, and has bronzed skin; on his back is tattooed a strange map. But he has total amnesia. This does not prevent him from quickly gathering a group of friends and fighting evil as the city of 'Atlantis' rises from its watery grave at the center of the hollow earth. The man, who eventually learns that he is German and that his name is 'Sun Koh,' ultimately claims power over Atlantis and begins preparing for the ice age which is about to engulf the Earth." The zeppelin* Krueger *is named after G-8's archenemy from the Great War, Herr Docktor Krueger. Madame Inga also appeared in the Lance Star—Sky Ranger story "Shadows Over Kunlun" and is meant to be Fah Lo Suee, the daughter of Fu Manchu. The newspaper* L'Echo de France *is from the Arsène Lupin stories by Maurice Leblanc; reporter Patricia Johnston is specifically from Leblanc's* Les Milliards d'Arsène Lupin. *Tim Howller of Peoria is from Philip José Farmer's "After King Kong Fell" and "The Face that Launched a Thousand Eggs." The Great Detective, the world's greatest practitioner of Baritsu, is of course Sherlock Holmes. Resu is the Flaming God of Ancient Opar in two novels* by Philip José Farmer, Hadon of Ancient Opar *and* Flight to Opar. *In the Ancient Opar books, Opar's religion of the Flaming God is derived from the Tarzan novels of Edgar Rice Burroughs, and Opar is a kingdom in the larger civilization of Khokarsa, which can be equated with Atlantis. The map tattooed on Sun Koh's back depicts the land and seas of Khokarsa, circa 12,000 BCE. These various clues solve the mystery of Sun Koh's otherwise very odd name: "Sun" is indicative of his worship of the ancient sun god, Resu, and "Koh" is a bastardization of the name Khokarsa, otherwise known as Atlantis.*

THE FACE THAT LAUNCHED A THOUSAND EGGS

This story features nineteen-year-old Tim Howller, who attends the University of Shomi.

Story by Philip José Farmer in Farmerphile: The Magazine of Philip José Farmer *#1, July 2005, edited by Christopher Paul Carey and Paul Spiteri, and published by Michael Croteau; reprinted in* Up From the Bottomless Pit and Other Stories, *Christopher Paul Carey, ed., Subterranean Press, 2007. This is undoubtedly the same Tim Howller from "After King Kong Fell," and what's more, "The Face that Launched a Thousand Eggs" is semi-autobiographical. The inescapable conclusion is that Philip José Farmer himself witnessed Kong's plunge from the Empire State Building. And if that doesn't enhance our understanding of the intertangled history behind the Crossover Universe, then I don't know what does.*

Mid April
RAFFLES' CRIME IN GIBRALTAR

A.J. Raffles, on the lam in Gibraltar, again matches wits with the detective of Baker Street, Sexton Blake.

Novel by Barry Perowne in The Sexton Blake Library, *Second Series, #601, December 1937. It was reprinted in 1968 by Dean & Son, Ltd., and provides further confirmation that Raffles and Blake exist in the same universe. The prologue in New York takes place on January 15, 1937. Again, the Raffles seen here could be R.J. rather than A.J.*

Spring
MERRIDEW OF ABOMINABLE MEMORY
Dr. John Watson recounts a case which occurred in 1889 to another doctor, mentioning that on a recent visit to London he'd stopped by his old Baker Street digs, but they were now occupied by a detective named Blake. During the course of the case, Holmes refers to Ireneo Funes.

Story by Chris Roberson in Gaslight Grimoire, J.R. Campbell and Charles Prepolec, eds., Edge Science Fiction and Fantasy Publishing, 2008. The detective Blake is Sexton Blake. But although Blake's digs are on Baker Street, they are not at 221B; Harry Dickson actually took over the spot at 221B. Watson must have been confused. Ireneo Funes is the titular character from Jorge Luis Borges' "Funes the Memorious."

Spring. Marine Lts. Tom Grayson and Frank Corby battle a masked villain bent on dominating the world in the serial *The Fighting Devil Dogs*.

May 3-6. Author Leslie Charteris, the raconteur of The Saint's exploits, solves a mystery of his own in *The Hindenburg Murders*, as related by Max Allan Collins.

May 1937. Captain Kevin Douglas Rex Hazzard's first recorded adventure, Python Men of the Lost City, as told by "Chester Hawks" (pseudonym for Paul Chadwick), *Capt. Hazzard*, May 1938. An expanded version of the novel is now available by Ron Fortier and Chester Hawks, Wild Cat Books, 2006.

May-June. The Avenger, Richard Henry Benson, begins gathering agents and starts *Justice, Inc.* (September 1939), first in a series pulp novels by Paul Ernst, writing as "Kenneth Robeson."

May 1937-1938
FRANKENSTEIN MEETS THE WOLF MAN
Lawrence Talbot (The Wolf Man) is revived and seeks the secrets of the Frankensteins in order to end his existence. However, he can only locate Elsa Frankenstein, the daughter of Dr. Ludwig Frankenstein. In the course of the adventure, the Frankenstein Monster created by Elsa's grandfather, Dr. Henry Frankenstein, is revived.

Feature film, Universal, 1943. The full cycle of adventures of this particular Frankenstein Monster is as follows: Frankenstein, Bride of Frankenstein, The Shadow of Frankenstein (*a novel by Stefan Petrucha*), The Son of Frankenstein, The Ghost of Frankenstein, Frankenstein Meets the Wolf Man, The House of Frankenstein, House of Dracula, Abbott and Costello Meet Frankenstein, Return of the Wolf Man (*a novel by Jeff Rovin*), The Devil's Brood (*a novel by David Jacobs*), *and* The Devil's Night (*a novel by David Jacobs*).

May

MONSTER MANSION

Reporter Joan Casey, while investigating a mansion museum to horror films, observes a portrait of actor Hamilton Wynde.

#6 of The Twilight Avenger *by John Wooley and Terry Tidwell, Eternity Comics, May 1989. Hamilton Wynde is a member of the Miracle Squad.*

THE CASE OF THE SHRIEKING SKELETONS

The Shadow and Doc Savage team again. Dr. Reinstein is working on pioneering research into chemically enhancing human physique and intelligence.

Comic book miniseries by Steven Vance, Stan Manoukian, and Vince Roucher, Dark Horse Comics, 1995. Dr. Reinstein is from the first issue of Timely Comics' (later Marvel Comics) Captain America, *published in 1941.*

TARZAN AND THE SILVER GLOBE

Tarzan returns to Opar.

This novel was the first in a new series of unauthorized Tarzan books by Barton Werper, published by Gold Star Books in 1964. Remaining titles in the series are Tarzan and the Cave City, Tarzan and the Snake People, Tarzan and the Abominable Snowmen, *and* Tarzan and the Winged Invaders.

June
SATAN'S SISTERS

Joan Casey, while poking fun at her crimefighting partner, The Twilight Avenger, refers to Tailspin Tommy Tompkins.

The eighth and unfortunately final issue of The Twilight Avenger *by John Wooley and Terry Tidwell, published by Eternity Comics. Researcher Greg Gick suggests that Joan Casey is the sister of Flashgun Casey, a pulp character created by George Harmon Coxe.*

Summer. The Great Merlini solves his first case in *Death from a Top Hat* by Clayton Rawson.

Summer. Nestor Burma hangs out his shingle as a private eye in Paris.

Summer. First recorded adventure of Ki-Gor in *Ki-Gor, King of the Jungle* by John Murray Reynolds, *Jungle Stories*, Winter 1938.

Summer
NO GREATER LOVE
This tale, in which Nowell Ffoulkes appears, is set in England and Russia. Ffoulkes is the great-great-grandson of Sir Andrew Ffoulkes: "I have heard it said that he was an intimate friend of Sir Percy Blakeney, who was believed in his day to have been the Scarlet Pimpernel."
Novel by Baroness Orczy, 1938.

THE CITADEL OF FEAR
Capt. Hazzard battles The Green Dragon, whose crimes are linked to Dr. Yu Sun. Yu Sun's nemesis was Matt Hale, a man with a "tireless constitution." Hale battled Yu Sun a dozen times before the criminal's apparent death, and was assisted by FBI agent Ernest Grogan.
Novel by Ron Fortier and Martin Powell, Wild Cat Books, 2006. Rick Lai notes, "Dr. Yu Sun is a thinly disguised version of Dr. Yen Sin from the pulps. In the pulp novels by Donald Keyhoe, Dr. Yen Sin was opposed by Michael Traile, the Man Who Could Not Sleep. Traile was assisted by Eric Gordon. However, Gordon was a reporter and not an FBI agent. The FBI did play a large role in assisting Traile. Perhaps Eric Gordon decided to formally join the Bureau as an agent sometime after the third battle between Traile and Yen Sin." This story strengthens Dr. Yen Sin's link into the Crossover Universe.

July
RED THREADS
Inspector Cramer teams with a young fashion designer to solve the murder of a millionaire.
A novel by Rex Stout. Cramer often needs Nero Wolfe's assistance to solve his cases, but this time he manages on his own.

August
THE DOOR IN THE HOUSE OF THE NEVER SLUMBERING DEMONS
Dr. Zarnak meets John O'Dare and helps him return to the magical world of Sgra Astdaparl. Jules de Grandin and Dr. Trowbridge are also mentioned.
Short story by Joseph S. Pulver, Sr., Lin Carter's Anton Zarnak, Supernatural Sleuth, Marietta Publishing, 2002. John J. O'Dare is a novelist who had Burroughs-style adventures in Sgra Astdaparl before returning to Earth. He appeared in a fragment by Robert E. Howard called "The Door to the World." Pulver completed this fragment in a Chaosium collection of Howard's' Mythos fiction, Nameless Cults.

FORTRESS OF SOLITUDE
Doc Savage and his crew face their most difficult villain yet, when they go up against John Sunlight. Baron Karl compares John Sunlight to a host of historical personages, as well as to Dracula and Frankenstein. Sunlight replies, "Those were very bad people."
A novel in the Doc Savage series by "Kenneth Robeson" (Lester Dent), further cementing Dracula and Frankenstein in the CU. A theory that Sunlight is the son of Doc Savage is explained elsewhere in this Chronology.

Autumn. Cary Adair goes into battle against crime as Captain Satan in *The Mark of the Damned* by William O'Sullivan (*Captain Satan*, March 1938).

Autumn. Clark Kent moves to Metropolis, starts working for the *Daily Star* newspaper, and makes his first appearance as Superman (*Action Comics* #1 by Jerry Siegel and Joe Shuster, DC Comics, June 1938; *The Adventures of Superman* by George Lowther, 1942). Throughout his career, Superman ensures that he reveals his extraterrestrial origins only to those he trusts implicitly, such as his wife, Lois Lane, and his close friend, Bruce Wayne.

Autumn
THE FANTASTIC CASE OF THE FOUR SPECIALISTS
Sherlock Holmes, Philo Vance, Hercule Poirot, and Father Brown work together on a case.
Australian radio play by writer and radio actor Max Afford, 1938.

DEATH AT THE BANK
Scotland Yard Detective-Sergeant Paul Dean says, "Nothing much in the way of clues, sir, is there? None of those beautiful things our old friend Sexton Blake used to find on a job of this sort."
Novel by Basil Francis, 1938, the first of five books in the Sergeant Dean series. The reference to Blake as a fellow detective brings Dean into the CU.

THE HOUNDS OF HELL
Doctor Satan versus Ascott Keane and the Moon Man!
Novel by Ron Fortier and Gordon Linzner, with accompanying art by Rob Davis and Bradley Walton, originally serialized on the Modern Pulp *website,*

published by Wild Cat Books, 2005. Since the Moon Man is in the CU, so is the nefarious Doctor Satan and the Doctor's nemesis, criminologist Ascott Keane. Keane's secretary and companion was Beatrice Dale, the daughter of Jimmie Dale, the Gray Seal. Beatrice's twin sister was reporter Betty Dale, companion to Secret Agent X. (See "The Amazing Lanes" on The Wold Newton Chronicles *website.)*

October. The events of *The Devil Genghis*, featuring the second appearance of John Sunlight, as related by Lester Dent.

October
GROUCHO MARX, MASTER DETECTIVE

Actor and comedian Julius "Groucho" Marx solves the murder of a young actress in Hollywood. The narrator, Frank Denby, says, "But from the late 1930s, trust me, Groucho was giving such West Coast sleuths such as Philip Marlowe, Sam Spade, and Dan Turner some stiff competition." Groucho also quips, "My sleuthing turned Sherlock Holmes green with envy. Or maybe that was only because we left him out in the rain too long."

A mystery novel by Ron Goulart, St. Martin's Press, 1998. Groucho Marx, of course, along with his brothers, immortalized in film the antics of a group of rather notorious con men and tricksters. One of these con men, while using the name Rufus T. Hackstabber, once met Fu Manchu's son Shang Chi while posing as a New York cabbie. Per Farmer, Philip Marlowe and Sam Spade are Wold Newton Family members. This crossover brings Dan Turner, "Hollywood Detective," into the Crossover Universe. There are also various Sherlockian references throughout the novel, such as, "The game is afoot."

November. Crime Busters, the first recorded adventure of inventor Clickell Rush, "The Gadget Man," as told by "Kenneth Robeson" (Lester Dent).

November
RAFFLES AND THE KEY MAN (aka SCUTTLER'S CACHE)

Raffles goes up against "criminologist" J.R. (Rick) Leroy. Raffles and Leroy have tangled twice before. The first time had been over a missing bracelet called the "Fetter of Buddha." The second time was a game of cat-and-mouse in Gibraltar in which they never actually met face-to-face, which occurred seven months ago, as documented in Raffles' Crime in Gibraltar.

Novel by Barry Perowne, J.B. Lippincott Company, 1940. This is a bit of a story behind this crossover. Perowne's Raffles' Crime in Gibraltar *took place seven months ago, in April 1937. However, Raffles' nemesis was Sexton Blake, not J.R. Leroy. Unfortunately, I have been unable to secure a copy of the first Raffles/Sexton Blake crossover by Perowne,* Raffles vs. Sexton Blake, *but it does involve a missing bracelet called the "Fetter of Buddha." There is also a* version of *Raffles'* Crime in Gibraltar *that features Leroy rather than Blake, called* They Hang Them in Gibraltar. *To further confuse matters,* Raffles and the Key Man *was originally serialized under the title* Raffles—Sea Thief, *and it also appeared in the* Sexton Blake Annual #1 (1938), *as a three-part tale,* Scuttler's Cache *(comprised of "Scuttler's Cache," "The House in Berkeley Square," and "The 'Shanghai' Ship.") Clearly,* Scuttler's Cache *was the original story, featuring Sexton Blake, and when it was released as a book, it was rewritten to make it a Leroy adventure. Despite my general aversion to conflation of characters, it would seem warranted in this case to say that any Leroy story by Perowne is really a Sexton Blake story. However, Perowne published his first Leroy story in the early 1930s. This is several years before he started writing any Blake pastiches. So Leroy seems to have at least started out as an independent character. Perowne wrote several Blake/Raffles crossovers for* The Sexton Blake Library, *and then revised them as Leroy/Raffles crossovers for his own J.R. Leroy series. Giving the original versions of the stories primacy, I am treating* Raffles and the Key Man *as a third meeting between Raffles and Blake, rather than a Leroy/Raffles crossover.*

THE DEVIL'S MOUTHPIECE
　　Deputy Commissioner Barth is mentioned.
　　Short story by Martin Powell in the anthology The Avenger Chronicles, *Joe Gentile and Howard Hopkins, eds., Moonstone Books, 2008. The Deputy Commissioner must be Wainright Barth from The Shadow novels.*

　　Late Autumn. The Grapes of Wrath *by John Steinbeck.*

Late Autumn 1937-Early 1938
THE MIRACLE SQUAD: BLOOD AND DUST
　　The members of The Miracle Squad raise Cliff Secord's ire while drooling over his girlfriend, Betty Page. Additionally, while the Squad's star cowboy-actor is traveling through Oklahoma, he picks up hitchhiker Tom Joad, who has just gotten out of jail for murder. In a sheriff's office in Oklahoma, there is a wanted poster for The Twilight Avenger. Philo Vance is briefly mentioned.

Comic book miniseries written by John Wooley and Terry Tidwell, Apple Press, 1989, bringing the pulp-style adventures of The Miracle Squad, a small group of actors, detectives, stuntmen, etc., who work for a tiny B-movie studio, into the Crossover Universe. Tom Joad is from Steinbeck's The Grapes of Wrath. *S.S. Van Dine wrote the Philo Vance mysteries. The Twilight Avenger is a pulp-style hero in comics written by Wooley and Tidwell.*

1938

Winter. First adventure of the spy known as The Eagle, in "Storm over the Americans" by Norman A. Daniels, *Thrilling Spy Stories*, Fall 1939.

Winter. A child is born to La of Opar. The child is orphaned and eventually grows up to become known as Modesty Blaise (see Chuck Loridans' "The Daughters of Greystoke," *Myths for the Modern Age: Philip José Farmer's Wold Newton Universe*).

Winter. Famous British mansion Manderley burns to the ground. (*Rebecca* by Daphne du Maurier.)

Winter. Scatterbrained Gracie Allen meets detective Philo Vance and together they solve a mystery. (*The Gracie Allen Murder Case*, a Philo Vance novel by S.S. Van Dine also made into a movie.) Gracie Allen's husband was George Burns. Burns' best friend was the miserly Jack Benny, whose butler was named Rochester. Rochester, for a short time also worked for Cosmo Topper (see *Topper Returns*). Since Philo Vance is part of CU continuity, so is Topper.

A MAN AND A MESS
Click Rush, the Gadget Man, pays a visit to the Los Angeles office of the Continental Detective Agency.

This story by Lester Dent, in Crimebusters, *July 1938, is an obvious homage to Dashiell Hammett's Continental Op stories, and confirms the Continental Op into the Crossover Universe. Click Rush is already in the CU since he is mentioned in one of Ron Goulart's Avenger novels,* Dr. Time.

THE ADVENTURES OF CREIGHTON HOLMES
Sherlock Holmes' grandson continues the family tradition of mystery-solving.

A collection of short stories by Ned Hubbell, Popular Library, 1979. The histories provided both in this book and in R. Holmes & Co. are not inconsistent and it is therefore probable that Creighton Holmes is the son of Raffles Holmes.

THE PLAGUE DOCTOR
Secret Agent X comes to the steel city, Graytown, to combat the menace of the dreaded Black Death. Hazzard Laboratories is mentioned. It is revealed that Secret Agent X once learned the secrets of rudimentary communication with an-

imals from an English Lord living in Africa. The Plague Doctor asks Agent X, "Who are you? The Phantom Detective? The Eagle? Hammond? No? Not going to say? Well, I suppose it doesn't matter." Al Vittoro thinks that Agent X is Operator #5.

Short story by G.L. Gick in Secret Agent X, Volume 2, *Ron Fortier, ed., Wild Cat Books, 2007. Hazzard Laboratories is from the Captain Hazzard pulp novels. The English Lord from Africa is Tarzan. This story confirms the Phantom Detective and Operator #5 in the Crossover Universe, while linking in The Eagle, American Secret Agent (a spy character who appeared in stories by Norman Daniels and Kerry McRoberts), and detective Wade Hammond (from 1930s pulp tales written by Paul Chadwick).*

CURSE OF THE CRIMSON HORDE
    Tyler Randall, (here called "Crandall"), Captain Hazzard's ace pilot, works with Secret Agent X.
    Story by Brant House, Secret Agent X, *September 1938.*

THE A.R.P. MYSTERY
    Sexton Blake and Raffles joust once more.
    Novel by Barry Perowne in *The Sexton Blake Library,* Second Series, #669, May 1939. The fourth and final Blake/Raffles crossover.

MR. MOTO'S GAMBLE
    Mr. Moto, assisted by Charlie Chan's son Lee Chan, must discover who poisoned a fighter in the boxing ring.
    This movie began as Charlie Chan at the Ringside, *but Warner Oland died during the filming so it was changed to a Mr. Moto film, thus connecting Charlie Chan to the CU.*

SEX SLAVES OF THE DRAGON TONG
    The Mandarin of San Francisco's Chinatown, a doctor with green eyes who employs dacoits, intervenes after members of the Dragon Tong kidnap a red-haired little girl whose incredibly rich father is named Oliver. The girl's sandy-haired dog is shot, but survives. The green-eyed Chinaman and Oliver have an undisclosed history.

A short story by F. Paul Wilson in the anthology Retro Pulp Tales, *Joe R. Lansdale, editor, Subterranean Press, 2006. The Mandarin is clearly Doctor Fu Manchu. The red-haired girl is "Little Orphan Annie" and her father is Oliver "Daddy" Warbucks.*

Spring. Miami private investigator Mike Shayne's first recorded case, *Dividend on Death*, as told by Brett Halliday.

Spring. Joshua Jones discovers the alien Element 155 in the Mayan ruins at Chichen Itza, Mexico, and uses it to fight a Nazi plot as Captain Gravity. (*Captain Gravity* by Stephen Vrattos and Keith Martin, Penny-Farthing Press, 1999. Subsequent Captain Gravity tales indicate that his gravity-defying powers are really derived from the *vril*.)

Spring. Professor Gibbs provides Kitty Carroll with an invisibility formula in the film *The Invisible Woman*.

April
GROUCHO MARX, PRIVATE EYE

Groucho's sidekick, Frank Denby, describes himself as, "A sort of Archie Goodwin to his Nero Wolfe." Contemporary investigators Perry Mason and the Lone Wolf are also mentioned.

The second Groucho mystery novel is by Ron Goulart, St. Martin's Press, 1999. Wolfe and Goodwin are both in the Crossover Universe, as is Perry Mason. The Lone Wolf was Michael Lanyard, a suave ex-jewel thief turned gentleman benefactor created by Louis Vance. He appeared in a series of books from 1914-1934. His exploits were then documented in a series of movies from 1917-1949. The next Groucho novel, Elementary, My Dear Groucho, *involves a murder on the set of a Sherlock Holmes film.*

THE ROCKETEER

The Rocketeer (Cliff Secord) meets Doc Savage after the former finds the latter's experimental rocket pack.

Five comics by Dave Stevens released over several years by various publishers, compiled in graphic novel format by Eclipse Books; collected as The Rocketeer: The Complete Adventures, *IDW Publishing, October 2009. It should be noted that the film version deviated significantly from this original story, both in its omission of Doc Savage and in its depic-*

tion of the lead female protagonist, Betty Page. The graphic novel is a wonderful comic experience, not to be missed.

THE ROCKETEER: DEATH STALKS THE MIDWAY
The Rocketeer meets The Shadow.
Three comics by Dave Stevens released over several years by various publishers, compiled in graphic novel format by Dark Horse Comics; collected as The Rocketeer: The Complete Adventures, *IDW Publishing, October 2009.*

May
THE MONARCH OF ARMAGEDDON
Doc Savage's aides refer to the kid who recently stole Doc's rocket pack, meaning The Rocketeer. John Sunlight and Princess Monja also appear in this adventure.
A Doc Savage comic book miniseries by Mark Ellis, Darryl Banks, and Robert Lewis, Millennium Comics, 1991.

CARIBBEAN BLUES
Private eyes Nate Heller, Dr. Philip d'Artagnan Phlem, Andy Baltimore, Devlin "Trace" Tracy and his girlfriend Michiko "Chico" Mangini, Leslie Dither, and Jack Miles come together to solve a mystery on the high seas during a Caribbean cruise. Dither allegedly comes from a long line of detectives who trace their history back to before Sherlock Holmes.
A collaborative novel by Mary Higgins Clark, Molly Cochran, Max Allan Collins, Gregory Mcdonald, Richard Meyers, Warren Murphy, and Robert J. Randisi, PaperJacks Books, March 1988. Since Heller is already in the Crossover Universe, so are the rest of these detectives. The Jack Miles chapters are written by Randisi. A similarity in names leads one to the conclusion that the Jack Miles character is an allusion to Randisi's modern detective Miles Jacoby. "Jack Miles" was probably Miles Jacoby Sr. and the modern Jacoby, whose career began in the mid 1970s, is his grandson.

Summer
THE ADVENTURE OF THE ORIENT EXPRESS
Solar Pons and Dr. Lyndon Parker meet Simon Templar (The Saint) and Hercule Poirot aboard the Orient Express. The British spy Ashenden is also featured, as is a German spy master with a clubfoot.
Short story by August Derleth in The Chronicles of Solar Pons *(book 2). Ashenden is from* Ashenden; or the British Agent *by W. Somerset Maugham, first published in 1928. The German spy with the clubfoot is Valentine Williams' Clubfoot, the villain of a series of books that take place before the Great War. It's worth noting that Clubfoot also battled Bob Harder, a Norwegian Nick Carter type, in the early 1940s, in the Norwegian pulp Den Berømte Engelske*

Kriminal-Serie Bob Harder (The Famous English Detective Series Bob Harder) #16, Manden med Klumpfoden. "H. Wayne & R. Patricks" wrote Harder's adventures, in which he also apparently met The Shadow (#13, Hævneren) and wrangled with Fu Manchu (#24, Djævledoktoren).

THE TERROR IN TIBET
    Athena Voltaire stops in Casablanca and consults "Ferrani," a dealer in information. Beforehand, she passes a group of three men who look like Red Kelso, Pongo Challenger, and Jack Roxton. Athena races the Nazis to reach Tibet, with the goal of contacting the Vril-ya, among whom are good and evil factions. Athena is assisted in this exploit by a man named Harcourt Templeman.
    An Athena Voltaire story by Paul Daly, Steve Bryant, and Chad Fidler, Athena Voltaire: The Collected Webcomics, *Ape Entertainment, 2006. "Ferrani" is an alias for Ferrari, Sydney Greenstreet's character from* Casablanca. *Kelso, Challenger, and Roxton are from Gary Chaloner's* Red Kelso *strip. The Vril-ya are the underground denizens of Edward Bulwer-Lytton's* The Coming Race. *Templeman looks like actor Roger Moore and calls his adversaries "the ungodly," leading one to believe that Templeman is meant to be an alias of Simon Templar, The Saint. All these connections place adventuress Athena Voltaire in the CU.*

OUT OF THE SILENT PLANET
    Dr. Elwin Ransom is abducted and taken on a secretly developed spaceship to the planet Malacandra, which appears to be Mars. While on Malacandra, Ransom recalls how Professor Cavor met his end on the Moon.
    Novel by C.S. Lewis, the first part of the Space Trilogy. *(Subsequent volumes are* Perelandra *and* That Hideous Strength). *Based on references in the* Star Trek *novel* The Wounded Sky, *Dr. Ransom appears to be a real person in the Crossover Universe, and the existence of the planet Malacandra seems to be common knowledge, at least by 2272. Although Malacandra appears to be an analogue of Mars, it does not seem to be the real Mars of our universe. Likewise, it also does not appear to be the parallel Mars known as Barsoom; it may exist in a yet*

different parallel plane. However, The League of Extraordinary Gentlemen II *clearly equates Malacandra with Barsoom, as well as other versions of Mars.*

Just as Lewis and Ransom elected to publish Ransom's adventures in the guise of fiction, Ransom may not have known that the exploits of Professor Selwyn Cavor, as depicted in H.G. Wells' The First Men in the Moon, *also had a basis in reality.* Out of the Silent Planet *was published in 1939. The sequel,* Perelandra, *with references to black-outs and raids, clearly takes place during World War II.*

October. Newspaper publisher Lee Travis dons the cloak and mask of the Crimson Avenger (as told by Roy and Dann Thomas, Gene Colan, and Mike Gustovich in *Secret Origins* #5, DC Comics, August 1986).

Mid-October. Philip Marlowe's case, *The Big Sleep*, as related by Marlowe and edited by Raymond Chandler. Marlowe continues in a long career as a private detective in novels by edited Chandler and Robert B. Parker.

October 27-30
THE WAR OF THE WORLDS MURDER

The Shadow's primary biographer and sometime agent, Walter Gibson ("Maxwell Grant"), investigates a murder during radio legend Orson Welles' broadcast of *The War of the Worlds*. New York Police Inspector Kramer arrives at the radio studio, chomping his unlit cigar, in the aftermath of the broadcast.

A novel told by Gibson to Max Allan Collins, Berkley Books, July 2005. "Kramer" is clearly intended to be Inspector Cramer from Rex Stout's Nero Wolfe mysteries.

October 30
WAR BETWEEN TWO WORLDS

A "Man of Action," who in everyday life is a mild-mannered reporter, rushes to the site of an alien invasion. He makes a valiant effort against the invaders, but toward the end their numbers prove too great even for him. At the last possible minute, the invaders stand down, and a cursory medical examination reveals that they were laid low by a common Earth bacteria to which they have no immunity.

Short story by Ricky Louis Phillips in It's That Time Again 3: Even More New Stories of Old-Time Radio, *Jim Harmon, ed., BearManor Media, 2006. The "Man of Action" is clearly meant to be Superman, right down to the superhuman strength, colorful costume, and cape, as well as the glasses which preserve his secret identity. The invaders are the Martians depicted in Orson Welles' broadcast of* The War of the Worlds. *This would constitute a follow-up attempt to invade Earth, the first being the Martian Invasion of 1898 as seen in H.G. Wells' novel* The War of the Worlds. *The story provides a clear connection placing a version of the Golden Age Superman in the Crossover Universe.*

Autumn. The first appearance of Prince Namor, the Sub-Mariner (Timely's *Marvel Comics* #1, October 1939). Although Namor is initially bent on revenge against land-dwellers for the destruction of his undersea home and deaths of his people, he eventually works with the Allies during World War II to defeat the Axis powers.

Autumn
LUNAR LEAGUE
Secret Agent X and his companion, reporter Betty Dale, are in Great City for a newspaper conference when the Lunar League, a criminal gang claiming to operate under the auspices of the Moon Man, strikes. Secret Agent X and the real Moon Man team up to shut down the gang. The head gang member disguises himself as the Moon Man, and goes out in a hail of police bullets. The police, believing the gang member to have always been the Moon Man since he first appeared in the early 1930s, close the ongoing cases against the Robin Hood-like vigilante. The real Moon Man, police sergeant Steve Thatcher, takes the opportunity to retire as the Moon Man and marries his sweetheart, Sue McEwen. The Moon Man's underworld assistant, ex-boxer Ned "Angel" Dargan, accompanies Secret Agent X and Betty Dale to New York City, where X gets Dargan a new identity, "Sam Daniels," and job at Jim Hobart's Detective Agency.
Novella by Lance Curry in Tales of Masks and Mayhem, *Mystic Toad Press, 2005. This would seem to constitute the Moon Man's last appearance; however, he must have come out of retirement many years later, as seen in Philip José Farmer's* Greatheart Silver. *Jim Hobart's Detective Agency appears in the Secret Agent X stories.*

THE FRANKENSTEIN MONSTER VS. THE WOLF MAN
The Frankenstein Creature and The Wolf Man have a brief rematch.
A short story in the Universal Monsters Kombat series by "Professor Anton Griffin," Scary Monsters Magazine *#51, Dennis Druktenis Publishing, June 2004; reprinted in* The Midnight Shadow Show: Prof. Griffin Journals *by Joseph Fotinos, 2005. The Creature in this story is the one created by Henry Frankenstein.*

BLACK PEARL

Bon Chance Louie tells Jake Cutter that he has been to a Viking funeral, when he served in the Legion at Fort Zinderman.

An episode of the television program Tales of the Gold Monkey, *referring to* Beau Geste *by Percival Christopher Wren. Fort Zinderneuf (not "Zinderman") was where Beau Geste served in Le Legion Etranger. When Beau died, his brother Digby rigged an impromptu Viking funeral for him by laying him on a bed with his weapons, setting fire to the room, and leaving the body of the villain at his feet. (A true Viking funeral calls for a dog at the warrior's feet, but Digby concluded that the villain lived like a dog and so fit the bill.) The names Fort Zinderneuf and Fort Zinderman, and the described circumstances, are similar enough that it's highly unlikely this reference is coincidental. Since Beau Geste is the CU, so are Cutter and company.*

DOPE WAR OF THE BLACK TONG

Steve Harrison has a major role in this Anton Zarnak adventure, as does the cat-headed fetish once wielded by Solomon Kane. The late John Grimlan is also mentioned.

Story by Robert M. Price collected in Disciples of Cthulhu, *1997; reprinted in Lin Carter's Anton Zarnak, Supernatural Sleuth. Grimlan is also mentioned in Robert E. Howard's "Dig Me No Grave," thus connecting John Kirowan with Anton Zarnak.*

THE MYSTERY OF THE MALI IBEX

In Casablanca, the 20th Phantom encounters the Prefect of Police, Captain Louis Renault.

#70 of Charlton Comics' The Phantom, *published in 1976 and beautifully illustrated by Don Newton. The story is a visual tribute to several Humphrey Bogart movies, including* Casablanca, The Big Sleep, The African Queen, *and* The Treasure of Sierra Madre. *The characters are drawn to resemble characters from those films. The Bogie character is called Rick Clifford. Betty Ingred is played by Lauren Bacall. Max Grossman is portrayed by Sydney Greenstreet. Peter Lorre appears as a hired gun, Slink. Interestingly, the Claude Rains character, in a French policeman's uniform, is only referred to as "Captain." Thus, we may infer that this really is Captain Louis Renault, and that the events of* Casablanca *and its novel sequel,* As Time Goes By, *take place in the Crossover Universe. The story also contains an epilogue, which takes place in 1976. The supposition that two different Phantoms, the 20th and the 21st, operated over this time-span is confirmed, as it is made clear that the Phantom in 1976 is the son of the Phantom who had the Ibex adventure.*

December
THE NIGHT OF THE AVENGER

The Shadow and The Avenger fight against one of The Shadow's greatest villains, Shiwan Khan.

Story by Michael Uslan and E.R. Cruz in DC Comics' first ongoing Shadow series, The Shadow #11, *June-July 1975 (not to be confused with DC Comics' third series, called* The Shadow Strikes!, *published in the 1990s).*

THE DARK CROSS CONSPIRACY

The Crimson Avenger, otherwise known as "The Crimson," and his partner, Wing, battle a vicious gang of arms dealers. One of them, based in San Francisco, is called Wu Fang.

The Crimson Avenger *miniseries is by Roy and Dann Thomas, Greg Thomas, and Mike Gustovich, DC Comics, 1988. Although there are several "Wu Fangs" from which to choose, this one is probably "The Mysterious Wu Fang" who fought against Val Kildare and Jerry Hazard a few years earlier, as documented in pulp novels by Robert J. Hogan. Hogan's Wu Fang was also known as the "Dragon Lord of Crime," while in "The Dark Cross Conspiracy" the crime lord is headquartered at Wu Fang's Dragon Palace. The archcriminal must have relocated from New York to San Francisco in the intervening years. Note that characters in this tale also make reference to the Lone Ranger, the Green Hornet, and so forth, but these references are more wisecracks than allusions to real people. However, the Wu Fang connection is solid.*

1939

January. Blinded D.A. Tony Quinn begins his battle against the underworld as The Black Bat (*Brand of the Black Bat* by "G. Wayman Jones" (Norman A. Daniels) in *Black Book Detective*, July 1939).

Winter. French heroic thief Sigono's first recorded exploit. (*Sigono Versus the Police* by Edward Brooker.)

Winter. Mystery man The Sandman (Wesley Dodds) dons gasmask and overcoat, going into action in *Adventure Comics* #40 (July 1939) and the 1939 *New York World's Fair Comics*.

January

THE POLTERGEIST OF SWAN UPPING

Jules de Grandin consults Judge Keith Hilary Pursuivant's *The Unknown That Terrifies* concerning the use of silver against the supernatural.

Story by Seabury Quinn in Weird Tales, *February 1939. According to Rick Lai and Matthew Baugh, "Pursuivant was the creation of fellow Weird Tales writer Manly Wade Wellman, and the Judge's book is mentioned in Wellman's 'The Black Drama.' Wellman also had references to de Grandin and Trowbridge in the Pursuivant stories, and in the tales about fellow occult detective John Thunstone. There are also references to Thunstone in later de Grandin stories. In fact, Manly Wade Wellman himself would also be treated as a friend of de Grandin and Trowbridge."*

Winter
RETURN TO MARS

Dr. Alan Kane teams up with Jack Armstrong.

Serialized story by Carl H. Claudy in The American Boy, *September-December 1939. Claudy wrote a series of twenty stories starring adventurers Alan Kane and Ted Dolliver. Since Jack Armstrong is in the CU, so are Kane and Dolliver.*

Spring. Cherry Ames' first case in *Cherry Ames, Student Nurse,* as told by Helen Wells.

Spring-September 1, 1939. The events of the film *Pimpernel Smith.*

Late March
FAREWELL, MY LOVELY

Ann Riordan says, "You ought to have given a dinner party...and you at the head of the long table telling all about it, little by little, with your charming light smile and a phony English accent like Philo Vance."

The second Philip Marlowe novel by Raymond Chandler. Ann Riordan could have actually sat through such a dinner with Vance.

April
THE ORDER OF BEASTS

When it is revealed that The Batman is in London, investigating a murder, Alfred tells Bruce Wayne that *The Times* has compared him to the great Sherlock Holmes. Wayne replies that his need to depart crime scenes quickly makes him sound more like Moriarty than Holmes. The Batman is working with Scotland Yard Inspector Frank Constantine on the case. Constantine indicates that he is the "white sheep" of the family.

"Elseworlds" graphic novel by Eddie Campbell, Daren White, and Michael Evans, DC Comics, 2004. The Holmes reference can definitely be interpreted as to a real person within The Batman's universe. Inspector Frank Con-

stantine must be a relative of DC Comics' John Constantine (Hellblazer), thus bringing a version of Constantine into the CU.

Spring
MASTER OF MADNESS
Secret Agent X tries to hail a taxi: "Outside the place the Agent hailed a hack. The small-built, tough-looking cabbie whizzed by him so quickly that X caught only a glimpse of the man's surname, 'Shrev-something-or-other,' written on the door, and the man was out of sight."
Story by "Brant House" in Double Danger Tales #1-3, Fading Shadows, February-April 1997. Since the Agent almost had an encounter with The Shadow's Moe Shrevnitz, the Agent's adventures take place in the CU.

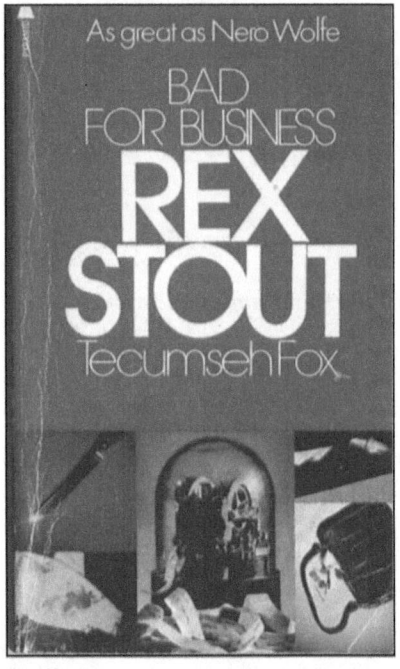

BAD FOR BUSINESS
Amy Duncan, an operative for Dol Bonner's detective agency, becomes involved in a case with private detective Tecumseh Fox. The restaurant Rusterman's is also mentioned.
Novel by Rex Stout, 1940. Since Dol Bonner occasionally works for Wold Newton Family member Nero Wolfe, Fox must also exist in the CU. Rusterman's is operated by Wolfe's brother Marko Vukcic.

THE TALE OF THE GREEN LANTERN
Alan Scott is saved from a train wreck by a mystical railroad lantern formed from a huge green meteorite which fell in China hundreds of years ago. The lantern mentally instructs Scott to form a ring from the lantern, giving him the power of the lantern for twenty-four hour time periods, and he adopts the identity of the "The Green Lantern." The lantern's history reveals that, in its previous incarnation as a Chinese lamp, the lamp/lantern was discovered in the mid 1930s by three adventurers tracking China Seas pirates. The three adventurers were Pat Ryan, Terry Lee, and Connie.
This story is by Roy Thomas, George Freeman, and Anthony Tollin in DC Comics' Secret Origins #18, September 1987. It is based on the original tale, "The Green Lantern," and other material by Mart Nodell and Bill Finger, appearing in All-American Comics #16-18, 1940. Terry Lee, Pat Ryan, and Con-

nie are from the classic newspaper strip Terry and the Pirates by Milton Caniff. They are not named in "The Tale of the Green Lantern," but the artistic depiction clearly indicates that it is Terry, Pat, and Connie. In DC Comics' The Shadow Strikes! #25, it is revealed that Terry and Pat are agents of The Shadow in China. One cannot help but wonder whether The Shadow had a hand in Pat, Terry, and Connie's discovery of the mystic Chinese lamp, and its eventual journey into Alan Scott's hands. Christopher Paul Carey adds that The Shadow may have located the lamp because he knew about the effects of the Wold Newton meteorite.

THE ADVENTURE OF NAPOLEON'S RAZOR
Ellery Queen meets a Frenchman named Dubois, who says, "In my native France, you are much admired. Next to Hercule Poirot, le petite Belge, you are my favorite detective."

An Ellery Queen *radio play broadcast on July 9, 1939, published in* The Adventure of the Murdered Moths and Other Radio Mysteries *by Ellery Queen, Crippen & Landru, 2005. The comments of Dubois treat Poirot as a contemporary of Ellery. The New York World's Fair is open at the time of the story, so it is set in either the spring or summer of 1939.*

June
THE NECKLACE OF ATLANTIS
An unnamed volcanic island in the Pacific, supposedly cursed, is mentioned. The island has since vanished beneath the sea.

Short story by Clay and Susan Griffith in the anthology The Avenger Chronicles, *Joe Gentile and Howard Hopkins, eds., Moonstone Books, 2008. The island is probably H.P. Lovecraft's R'lyeh.*

Summer. Upon the death of his Uncle Max, Tom Mayflower takes over as The Escapist (*Amazing Midget Radio Comics* #1, Empire Comics, January 1940).

Summer. Nick Terry and Belle Wayne fly into action as the costumed vigilantes The Owl and Owl Girl (*Crackajack Funnies* #25, Dell, July 1940).

Summer. The events of the film *The Phantom Creeps*, featuring the evil Dr. Alexei Zorka.

Summer. Jeff Troy and Haila Rogers

team up to solve murder on Broadway (*Made Up to Kill* by Kelley Roos.) They marry, on go on to solve several more mysteries as a husband-and-wife sleuthing team.

Summer. First appearance of sailor Lance O'Casey (*Whiz Comics* #2, Fawcett *Comics*, February 1940).

Summer. George Chance's first case, *Calling the Ghost* by "George Chance" (G.T. Fleming-Roberts), The Ghost v1, #1, January 1940.

Summer. Doctors Malinsky and Hale create the Purple Zombie (*Reg'lar Fellers Heroic Comics* #1, August 1940, by Tarpé Mills).

Summer. The Batman duels with the diabolical Dr. Hugo Strange for the second time. This time Strange is aided by a gang of thugs who have been scientifically transformed into giants. (*Batman* #1, Spring 1940.) This was probably accomplished through the use of the same formula used against Doc Savage in the pulp novel *The Monsters* (April 1934).

Summer
CAPTAIN SPECTRE

When a bunch of kids in Omaha, Nebraska discover that their radio hero, Captain Spectre, is a real person, they speculate that perhaps Edgar Rice Burroughs is really writing about real people, and that he got the Tarzan stories from the real Lord Greystoke. They go on to speculate that John Carter of Mars, Doc Savage, The Shadow, and The Spider are also real people. Later, a man named Clark places a call to one of Captain Spectre's assistants, Patch, ordering him to attend a session of the "Conclave." The Conclave is unhappy about Captain Spectre's decision to go public. Attending the Conclave, held on the 86th floor of a skyscraper in New York City, are Clark, Kent, Red, Dick, and Britt. A man named Kato serves drinks, and Red offers Patch a place in his Squadron. Meanwhile, Captain Spectre crashes his rocket pack in darkest Africa. Holing up on a tree branch, he wonders to himself how Greystoke sleeps like this, anyway.

Online Captain Spectre *comic strip by Tom Floyd. Of course, in addition to Captain Spectre, Tarzan (Lord Greystoke), John Carter, Doc Savage, The Shadow, and The Spider are real people in the Crossover Universe. "Clark" is Dr. Clark "Doc" Savage; "Kent" is Kent Allard, The Shadow; "Red" is Red Albright, Captain Midnight; "Dick" is Richard Wentworth, The Spider; and "Britt" is Britt Reid, The Green Hornet. Kato is The Green Hornet's assistant. The Squadron is Captain Midnight's Secret Squadron.*

DARK CONTINENT

Ki-Gor, the jungle lord, battles Doctor Satan, who has come to the jungle in search of ancient tribal magic.

Short story by Wayne Skiver in Lost Sanctum *magazine #3, Wild Cat Books, 2007. This crossover links the pulp jungle hero, Ki-Gor of the Jungle, into the Crossover Universe.*

AND SO TO MURDER

Mrs. Colonel Granby is mentioned.

A novel in the Sir Henry Merrivale series by Carter Dickson (John Dickson Carr). Francis Beeding wrote a series of espionage novels featuring the married Colonel Granby. This reference brings Colonel Granby into the CU.

THE WRATH FROM THE TOMB

Athena Voltaire battles Dracula's daughter, Countess Franziska Doraku-ra, who awakens from a long sleep more than forty years after her father's destruction by Van Helsing and company, against whom Franziska seeks revenge. Franziska has a servant named Shandor. St. Leger, a vampire hunter trained by Abraham Van Helsing, claims that Dracula's vampirism resulted from a deal with evil members of the Vril-ya. The Rocketeer's helmet is seen in Lord Godalming's study.

An Athena Voltaire story by Paul Daly, Steve Bryant, and Chad Fidler, Athena Voltaire: The Collected Webcomics, *Ape Entertainment, 2006. Countess Franziska Dorakura is a different daughter from Countess Marya Zaleska, who was seen in Universal Pictures'* Dracula's Daughter. *Shandor looks just like the character Sandor from* Dracula's Daughter. *While we don't learn Abraham Van Helsing's fate, it is revealed that Dr. Seward died from a drug overdose, possibly suicide, before Franceska's reprisal. It is also revealed that Mina Harker disappeared; this is a possible reference to* The League of Extraordinary Gentlemen. *Jonathan Harker is still alive in the 1930s with two daughters, but there is no reference to son Quincey Harker. St. Leger might be John St. Leger from T. Mullett Ellis'* Zalma *(1895). Jess Nevins comments, "Zalma is a femme fatale with implied vampiric powers, and St. Leger is her enemy and an agent of the Crown." While the connection to the Vril-ya of Bulwer-Lytton's* The Coming Race *is interesting, the true origin of Dracula's vampirism is doubtlessly more complicated than this. The Rocketeer's helmet may be the original or a duplicate.*

GROUCHO MARX AND THE BROADWAY MURDERS

Groucho at first refuses to take a case, saying, "You might try Philip Marlowe, Dan Turner, or some other Hollywood shamus." Groucho's secretary also pins her breakups with two stage magicians, Yarko the Great and the Amazing El Carim, on Groucho. Groucho calls Frank Denby's wife Nancy Drew. Groucho refers to Crash Corrigan as "an old chum."

This fourth Groucho mystery novel is by Ron Goulart, St. Martin's Press, 2001. Philip Marlowe is a Wold Newton Family member and Dan Turner is already in the CU though an earlier Groucho novel. El Carim and Yarko were both very obscure comic book magicians who appeared in Master Comics *and* Wonder Comics, *respectively. Groucho may know about the Nancy Drew books, or perhaps he actually knows the girl detective. Crash Corrigan is from the serial* Undersea Kingdom; *although Crash was played by Ray Corrigan in the serial, we can assume that this reference is to the naval officer, not the actor.*

FLIGHT OF THE FALCON
Athena Voltaire is called upon by Hong Kong antiquities dealer Nathan Cairo to search for an ancient artifact which may have the power to open access points to the Inner World. It is implied that the artifact is the Maltese Falcon. There are also references to the Nine Unknown and the Vril-ya, and man wearing a fedora complains about the occasional loss of artifacts before heading back to his university.

Athena Voltaire miniseries by Paul Daly, Steve Bryant, and Chad Fidler. The first issue was published by Speakeasy Comics, 2006, and then the series moved to Ape Entertainment, where the first issue was reprinted, along with the remainder of the series. Nathan Cairo may be the brother of Joel Cairo from Hammett's The Maltese Falcon. *The Nine Unknown are from Talbot Mundy's Jimgrim novel of the same name, while the Vril-ya are from Edward Bulwer-Lytton's* The Coming Race. *The man with the fedora is Indiana Jones.*

THE PHANTOM MEETS ZIGOMAR
The Phantom works with a Serbian hero named Zigomar.

Zigomar is a pre-WW II Serbian masked hero. Zigomar appeared in the Serbian magazine Mikijevo carstvo, *and was created by Nikola Navojev and Branko Vidic. The original Zigomar was a masked villain in French pulp fiction circa 1909-1910. Zigomar II was actually a hero, "heavily influenced" by the Phantom.*

July
DOOM DYNASTY
Doc Savage fights against the evil villain Dr. Nikola. Monk mentions that Johnny is at that weird University in Massachusetts.

Doc Savage comic book miniseries by Terry Collins, Mark Ellis, Mike Wieringo, and Marcus Rollie, Millennium Comics, 1991. The weird University is Miskatonic University. Dr. Nikola was an evil genius created by writer Guy Boothby, appearing in five books from 1895 to 1901, including A Bid for Fortune (or, Dr. Nikola's Vendetta) *(1895),* Dr. Nikola *(1896),* The Lust of Hate *(1898),* Dr. Nikola's Experiment *(1899), and* Farewell, Nikola *(1901).*

Early August-December
DOCTOR DARE: THE SPEAR OF DESTINY

Scientist Joanna Dare works on duplicating a formula invented by a Colorado scientist, Abednego Danner. The project is called "Project: Gladiator." Danner's original formula was meant to be injected into a prenatal embryo, and Doctor Dare is trying to determine how to make it work in a grown man. However, before she can complete her research, Nazis break in looking to steal the formula. Joanna manages to drink a test batch of the serum in a desperate measure to save herself. The serum unlocks the human body's vast potential, but thanks to the Nazi attack, she is its only recipient. An interesting side effect of this version of the formula is that its strength- and invulnerability-enhancing effects only take place after she has sex. A filing cabinet seen in a secret government warehouse reveals files not only on Dr. Dare, but on Dr. C. Savage, and Dr. I. Jones. Franklin and Eleanor Roosevelt also appear, as does Winston Churchill. Doc Dare also apparently solves the mystery of the disappearance of Amelia Earhart. In Africa, she discovers the hidden Roman city of Prestor John, where the Spear of Destiny is kept. Charlie Allnut briefly appears. In Casablanca, a man poses as a doctor named LaBeau, but in the future he will be known as Ugarti. Similarly, a fat man in Casablanca calls himself Kurt Wasserman, but is better known as Signor Ferrari. Rick Blaine, Sam, and Captain Louis Renault also appear. In Rick's Cafe Americain, a man known by various identities such as Mr. Hammer, Capt. Geoffrey T. Spaulding, Professor Quincy Adams Wagstaff, Rufus T. Firefly, Otis P. Driftwood, Hugo Z. Hackenbush, Gordon Miller, J. Cheever Loophole, Wolf J. Flywheel, Ronald Kornblow, Sam Grunion, and Rufus T. Hackstabber, is briefly seen with his two associates, the mute and the Italian.

In addition to the saga The Spear of Destiny, *this graphic novel by George Caragonne and Gray Morrow includes the little-seen origin prologue. First published in* Penthouse Comix *#1-7; republished by Eros, 1999. This crossover not only provides the best evidence that Doc Savage and Indiana Jones coexisted in the same universe, but it also brings in the characters from Philip Wylie's novel* Gladiator, *Abednego Danner and, by implication, Hugo Danner. Doctor Dare also makes a*

worthy addition to the Crossover Universe. *The Roosevelts met Sherlock Holmes in 1905. Churchill also met Holmes, and Indiana Jones. Given the multiple "solutions" of the Earhart mystery in the CU, it is possible that the Earhart seen here is an impostor or some kind of double. Indiana Jones would also have an adventure involving the Spear of Destiny, in 1945. A mystery regarding the Spear's status in the CU remains, as the series of generational heroines called "The Magdalena" has been said to possess it throughout history. The appearance of Charlie Allnut confirms the events of* The African Queen *in the CU; likewise the appearance of Blaine, Sam, Renault, Ferrari, and Ugarti and the events of* Casablanca. *Hackstabber was also seen in the comic book series* Shang Chi: Master of Kung Fu.

August 17
THE DEADLY DESERT GNOME
Doctor Omega and his granddaughter Suzette travel to the New York premiere of film *The Wizard of Oz*, but they find a dead city, the victim of a calamity several years in the past. The Doctor investigates the Empire State Building and starts to piece together that a particular important crimefighter of the 1930s was absent during this calamity, allowing two of his greatest enemies to destroy New York. The Doctor reads newspaper headlines from 1933 referring to Merchants of Death and Emperor Cadwiller. In the course of solving the mystery and repairing the timeline, the Doctor and Suzette encounter another time traveler with a pocketwatch, and Whimsies and Wheelers on Broadway, and then travel to Oz for a confrontation with the Nome King. Doctor Omega mentions the Andromeda Strain, the Eddorians, and the Gamma Quadrant 100. Doctor Omega and Suzette finally achieve their goal, saving Francis Ardan, Sr. (aka James Clarke Wildman, Sr.) and returning him to the Australian desert in 1901.

Short story by Dennis E. Power in Glimmerglass: The Creative Writer's Annual, Volume 1, *John Allen Small, ed., 2009. Doctor Omega is from the novel by Arnould Galopin, adapted and retold by Jean-Marc and Randy Lofficier. Doctor Omega is the Crossover Universe version of Doctor Who, specifically the First Doctor. Suzette, his granddaughter, is otherwise known as Susan. Emperor Cadwiller is Cadwiller Olden from the pulp novel* Repel, Doc Savage Magazine, *October 1937, The Merchants of Death, aka The Merchants of Disaster, are from the novel* The Merchants of Disaster, Doc Savage Magazine, *July 1939. The time traveler with the pocketwatch is Phineas Bogg from* Voyagers, *a 1982-1983 television series. The Wheelers are from* Ozma of Oz, Reilly and Britton, 1907. *The Whimsies and Roquat, the Nome King, are from* The Emerald City of Oz, Reilly and Britton, 1910. *The Eddorians are from E.E. "Doc" Smith's Lensman series. The Gamma Quadrant 100 are from the television series* Star Trek: Deep Space Nine. *The Andromeda Strain is a novel by Michael Crichton, with a subsequent feature film adaptation. Although there are multiple Ozs which exist parallel to the Crossover Universe, the one visited here is most* likely the one created by L. Frank Baum, which can be referred to as "Oz-Prime." Francis Ardan, Sr. (aka James Clarke Wildman, Sr.) is the father of the 1930s crimefighter who was absent in the alternate timeline. Doctor Francis Ardan, Jr. (not seen in this tale, but implied) is from Guy d'Armen's Doc Ardan: City of Gold and Lepers, and was identified as Lester Dent's Doc Savage by Jean-Marc Lofficier.

August
NIGHT OF NEPTUNE'S DEATH

The Shadow begins a case, which will be concluded by The Avenger.

Story in DC Comics' first The Shadow *series, #5, by Denny O'Neil and Frank Robbins.*

September
THE MONSTER BUG

The Avenger finishes a case begun by The Shadow.

Story in DC Comics' Justice, Inc., *#3 by Denny O'Neil and Jack Kirby.*

Autumn
ADELITA Y LA GUERRILLAS

Adelita, an independent and headstrong Mexican woman, and Nancy, a detective from Mexico City, are both investigating a gang of bandits in northern Mexico when Adelita is captured, bound and gagged, and her car sent hurtling over a cliff. Superman appears at the last moment and rescues Adelita.

Story in the Mexican comic book Pepin, *#409, March 24, 1940, bringing the exploits of Adelita and Nancy, a pair of realistic adventurers, into the CU.*

Early October
THE MINDLESS MONSTERS

A quote appears from a New York newspaper called *The Classic*.

A Doc Savage pulp novel written by Alan Hathway under the Kenneth Robeson house name, September 1941. One of The Shadow's agents, Clyde Burke, was a reporter for The Classic.

October 30-November 10, 1939
GROUCHO MARX, SECRET AGENT

Groucho retorts to Zeppo that he doesn't think he's Sherlock Holmes. Frank Denby's wife, Jane, asks him, "Who's the fat detective who never goes out and just sits around and solves things?" Frank, of course, knows that this is Nero Wolfe. Jane later refers to Frank's burgeoning Nero Wolfe abilities.

This is the fifth Groucho mystery novel by Ron Goulart, St. Martin's Press, 2002. Holmes and Wolfe are Crossover Universe mainstays. The sixth Grouch novel is called Groucho Marx, King of the Jungle.

November
BATMAN AND TARZAN: CLAWS OF THE CAT-WOMAN

The Batman (Bruce Wayne) and Tarzan, Lord Greystoke, meet in Gotham City and begin working together on a case involving treasures stolen from the hidden city of Memnon in Africa. An object is seen in the Gotham Museum, which just might be the legendary Maltese Falcon.

Comic book miniseries by Ron Marz and Igor Kordey, DC Comics and Dark Horse Comics, 1999, providing the best substantiation of the existence of the Crossover Universe version of Batman. The "Cat-Woman" of the title is not Selina Kyle; Wayne has yet to encounter her. This exploit takes place before Dick Grayson joins Wayne as a crime-fighting partner. Furthermore, although there is no textual evidence, notes to the artist's sketches in issues 1 and 3 indicate the date is 1939.

December. Bruce Wayne adopts orphaned Dick Grayson and young Grayson begins his training to become Robin (*Detective Comics* #38, April 1940).

December 1939-January 1940
THE CURSE OF THE NIBELUNG
Winston Churchill enlists (the very elderly) Sherlock Holmes and Dr. Watson to uncover a secret Nazi plot. Watson calls Hercule Poirot an upstart, who "uses your methods and claims them as his. Same with Father Brown, plagiarists all."

A novel by Sam North, published by Lulu Press, 2006; previously published in 1981 under the pen name "Marcel D'Agneau." Holmes is referred to as a lord, while Watson is now Sir John Watson. These are most likely fictionalizations, as neither man would be likely to accept such honors.

To be continued in Crossovers Volume Two: 1940-The Future

Addendum 1:
The Night of the Television Crossovers That Wouldn't Die!

The astute reader has discovered by now that, while I have a few relevant examples listed in the main Crossover Chronology, by and large I have not devoted much space to crossovers between television shows, especially sitcoms and straight dramas. I'm much more interested in crossovers which appear in genres such as mystery, espionage, and science-fiction. The animated comedies *The Simpsons* and *Futurama* merit a universe all their own. Additionally, while many television programs are listed on the main Chronology, they are generally in the context of references in novel or comic tie-ins, as with *The Man From U.N.C.L.E.*, *The Prisoner*, and *Star Trek*. This is not a hard-and-fast rule, but is typically true, and again arises mostly from my lack of interest in placing sitcoms or straight dramas on the main Chronology. So here is a listing of some further inter-television crossovers that take place in the Crossover Universe.

For this Addendum I'd like to acknowledge the contributions of Matthew Baugh, Fabio Blanco, Mark Brown, Greg Gick, Thom Holbrook, Rick Lai, Brad Mengel, Lou Mougin, Kim Newman, *Toby O'Brien,* Dennis E. Power, John Small, Mark Suggs, and Chris Wike. I would also note that this list barely scratches the surface of inter-television crossovers. I don't pretend that this is a complete list, and for further investigation, the interested reader should consult Thom Holbrook's masterfully complete *Crossovers and Spin Offs Master Page* on the Internet.

Since *The X-Files*, *Millennium*, *Special Ops Force*, *Alias*, and *Lost* take place in the Crossover Universe, the shows in the following chain of crossovers are also included:

- *The X-Files* & *Millennium*: A character, writer Jose Chung, is featured on both of these shows. Furthermore, the final episode of *Millennium*'s second season features a scene in which a character finds the butt of a Morley cigarette, the brand of choice of *The X-Files*' Cigarette Smoking Man. Finally, a 1999 *X-Files* episode entitled "*Millennium*" provides a wrap-up for that now-defunct show.
- *The X-Files* & *Millennium* & *Special Ops Force* & *The Pretender* & *That Girl* & *Grosse Point* & *Renegade* & *Pacific Blue* & *3rd Rock from the Sun* & *Married...with Children* & *Family Guy* & *That '70s Show* & *CSI* & *Rules of Engagement* & *Lost* & *Supernatural* & *In Case of Emergency* & *Kyle XY*: *Playpen* magazine appears on or is mentioned on all of these shows.

- *The X-Files & Strange Luck*: A short-lived Fox show called *Strange Luck* has the main character's brother work for the FBI where he knows a guy named "Fox," a link to *The X-Files*.
- *The X-Files & Picket Fences*: One of the shows has at least one line referring to events on the other.
- *The X-Files & The Lone Gunmen*: *The Lone Gunmen* is a spin-off from *The X-Files*.
- *The X-Files & Homicide: Life on the Street*: In the *X-Files* episode "Unusual Suspects," Detective Munch arrests the *X-Files* computer nerds, the Lone Gunmen.
- *Homicide: Life on the Street & Law and Order*: These two series have several crossover episodes. *Law and Order* has numerous spin-offs.
- *Law and Order & Law and Order: Criminal Intent & Law and Order: Special Victims Unit & Law and Order: Trial by Jury & Conviction & Deadline & New York Undercover & The Beat:* These shows all take place in a shared universe. Detective Munch from *Homicide: Life on the Street* is also a regular character on *Law and Order: Special Victims Unit* and also appears on *The Beat* and *Arrested Development*. (It's worth noting that Munch also makes an unnamed appearance in the film *A Very Brady Sequel;* the film implies that Carol Brady's first husband was the Professor from *Gilligan's Island*, while Mike Brady's first wife was Jeannie from *I Dream of Jeannie*. Extending the chain brings in *The Brady Kids* cartoon, as well as *The New Adventures of Gilligan, The Harlem Globetrotters on Gilligan's Island*, and *Gilligan's Planet*. Thank you, Det. Munch.)
- *Homicide: Life on the Street & Chicago Hope*: A heart is harvested from a shooting victim in Baltimore during an episode of *Homicide: Life on the Street* and rushed by helicopter to *Chicago Hope* Hospital where Dr. Jeffrey Geiger receives it and rushes into surgery.
- *Picket Fences & Chicago Hope*: These two shows cross-over when a character from *Picket Fences* goes to the hospital in *Chicago Hope*.
- *Chicago Hope & Early Edition:* Characters from these two programs interact on an episode of *Early Edition*, when that show's hero, Gary Dobson, takes a sick friend to *Chicago Hope* Hospital.
- *Early Edition & Martial Law:* Special Investigator Sammo Law travels from California to Chicago to track down a stolen Oriental artifact and works alongside Gary Dobson in an episode of *Early Edition*.
- *Martial Law & Walker, Texas Ranger:* There is a two-part episode in which Walker and Sammo Law team up (first in L.A. and then in Dallas) to take down a David Koresh-like megalomaniac whose efforts to launch a militia movement to overthrow the U.S. government result in the deaths of several Texas Rangers and a female military intelligence officer in California.

- *Walker, Texas Ranger & Sons of Thunder:* The short-lived but entertaining spin-off of *Walker, Texas Ranger* is *Sons of Thunder*, in which two of Walker's former protégés set up their own private investigation agency.
- *Homicide: Life on the Street & St. Elsewhere*: In an episode of *Homicide*, actress Alfre Woodard reprises her *St. Elsewhere* role.
- *St. Elsewhere & The Bob Newhart Show*: The neurotic character of Mr. Carlin (a regular on *Bob Newhart*) appears on several episodes of *St. Elsewhere* as a patient. He refers (though not by name) to Newhart's character, Dr. Robert Hartley.
- *The Bob Newhart Show & Murphy Brown*: Carol Bondurant moves to Washington D.C. and works for Murphy Brown as her secretary, proving to be the best secretary Murphy ever had, until Dr. Hartley comes down to fetch her back, saying that Jerry is sorry for what he said. Trying to hang on to Carol, Murphy engages in a war of words with Bob.
- *St. Elsewhere & Cheers*: In an episode of *St. Elsewhere,* several characters go to the bar where they interact with Norm, Carla, and other Cheers regulars. On an episode of *Cheers*, Sam directs characters to take an ailing patron to St. Elegius hospital.
- *St. Elsewhere & The White Shadow:* A character from *The White Shadow* becomes a regular on *St. Elsewhere*.
- *St. Elsewhere & Oz*: The Weigert Medical Corporation appears in both shows.
- *St. Elsewhere & Tattinger's/Nick and Hillary*: A guest character on *Tattinger's/Nick and Hillary* with the last name Axelrod bemoans the death of his cousin Elliot from Boston. Dr. Elliot Axelrod died on the series *St. Elsewhere*.
- *St. Elsewhere & M*A*S*H*: On *St. Elsewhere*, a character mentions his friend B.J. Hunnicut from the series *M*A*S*H*.
- *M*A*S*H & AfterMASH & Trapper John, M.D.*: The latter two shows are spin-offs of *M*A*S*H*.
- *Cheers & Wings*: These shows cross-over when Frasier and Lilith visit the *Wings* gang.
- *Cheers & Frasier*: *Frasier* is a spin-off of *Cheers*.
- *CSI & CSI: Miami & CSI: New York*: *CSI: Miami* and *CSI: New York* are spin-offs of *CSI*.
- *CSI: New York & Cold Case*: These two shows cross-over.
- *CSI & Without a Trace*: A two-part crossover begins on an episode of *CSI* and concludes on *Without a Trace*.
- *Lost & Heroes & Nip/Tuck*: Identical brochures for Gannon Car Rentals appear in all three shows.
- *Heroes & Las Vegas*: Characters from *Heroes* stay at the Montecito, the hotel and casino featured in the series *Las Vegas*.

- *Las Vegas* & *Crossing Jordan*: These two shows cross-over.
- *Las Vegas* & *The Office* (U.S.): A character on *Las Vegas* refers to a convention of the Dunder-Mifflin paper company from the U.S. version of the comedy *The Office*.

Since *Kojak* takes place in the Crossover Universe, the following shows do also:

- *Magnum P.I.* & *Columbo* & *Kojak* & *The Streets of San Francisco*: An episode of *Magnum, P.I.* features television cops Columbo, Kojak, and Detective Mike Stone (*The Streets of San Francisco*) attending a convention.
- *Magnum P.I.* & *Simon and Simon*: These shows have frequent crossovers.
- *Magnum P.I.* & *Murder, She Wrote:* These shows also cross-over.
- *Murder, She Wrote* & *The Law and Harry McGraw:* The Law and Harry McGraw is a spin-off of Murder She Wrote.
- *Magnum P.I.* & *Hawaii 5-O*: In one show, Magnum gets on the radio and impersonates Steve McGarrett, thus bringing *5-O* into the Crossover Universe.
- *Simon and Simon* & *Whiz Kids*: Simon and Simon cross-over with this short-lived television series involving teenage computer hackers.

ns: Impossible* is in the Crossover Universe, thereby bringing in the following chain of shows:

- *Mission: Impossible* & *Diagnosis Murder*: The Dick van Dyke murder mystery show features Cinnamon Carter, from the original *Mission: Impossible*, in a 1997 episode, "Discards."
- *Diagnosis Murder* & *Jake and the Fatman*: *Diagnosis Murder* is a spin-off of *Jake and the Fatman*.
- *Diagnosis Murder* & *Mannix*: Mike Conners reprises his Mannix role on and episode of *Diagnosis Murder*.
- *Mannix* & *Here's Lucy*: Mannix appears on an episode of *Here's Lucy*.
- *Here's Lucy* & *Love That Bob*: Bob Collins of *Love That Bob* appears on *Here's Lucy*.
- *Diagnosis Murder* & *Matlock*: Andy Griffith reprises his *Matlock* role on *Diagnosis Murder*.
- *Diagnosis Murder* & *Promised Land:* Episodes of these two shows share a guest character.
- *Touched by an Angel* & *Promised Land: Touched by an Angel* is the parent series of *Promised Land*.

***Have Gun, Will Travel, Bonanza, Cheyenne, Bronco, Kung Fu, Kung Fu: The Legend Continues*, and *Maverick* are in the Crossover Universe, thus bringing in the following Westerns and other shows:**

- *The Gambler Returns: Luck of the Draw:* This television movie features Kenny Rogers as his character Brady Hawks, who was established in several earlier productions. There are many Western appearances:
    o Bart Maverick from *Maverick*.
    o Wyatt Earp from *The Life and Legend of Wyatt Earp*.
    o Bat Masterson from *Bat Masterson*.
    o Cheyenne Bodie from *Cheyenne*.
    o Kwai Chang Caine from *Kung Fu* (which also pulls in *Kung Fu: The Legend Continues*, in which the character Cheyenne Bodie also appears again).
    o Lucas McCain from *The Rifleman*.
    o "Wishbone" the chuck wagon cook from *Rawhide*.
    o Two cowboys played by James Drury and Doug McClure are obviously Trampas and the Virginian from *The Virginian*, although their names are not used.
    o The movie comes to a climax at a high stakes poker tournament in San Francisco in a hotel owned by the late gunfighter Paladin of *Have Gun, Will Travel*.
    o It also features Brian Keith as *The Westerner*. There is also a detail which allows us to precisely date the action. In the middle of the story the characters pass through Virginia City on the day John L. Sullivan loses his boxing title to Gentleman Jim Corbett. The fight happened on September 7, 1892, though in "our" universe it was held in New Orleans. However, references to the San Francisco earthquake probably place this story in 1906.
- *Maverick & The Lawman & Cheyenne & Bronco & Sugarfoot & Colt .45 & 77 Sunset Strip:* In the *Maverick* episode "Hadley's Hunters," Bart Maverick meets Marshall Dan Troop and Deputy Johnny McKay from *The Lawman*, Cheyenne Bodie from *Cheyenne*, Bronco Layne from *Bronco*, and the *Sugarfoot* lawyer Tom Brewster. Bart also stops in the office of *Colt .45* but finds that Christopher Colt isn't around. Matthew Baugh notes, "The strangest crossover character in this episode is Gerald Lloyd 'Kookie' Kookson from *77 Sunset Strip*, a detective show set in the early 1960s. Kookie in the 1870s is a quandary, but the most logical scenario is to assume that Bart actually meets Gerald Lloyd Kookson I, the grandfather of the more familiar Kookie."
- *Maverick & Sugarfoot*: Bret Maverick appears an episode of *Sugarfoot* called "Misfire."

- *Maverick & Gunsmoke & Have Gun, Will Travel*: A 1959 episode of *Maverick* called "Gun-Shy" is actually a spoof of *Gunsmoke* featuring a character named Mort Dooley (a parody of Matt Dillon), who is the Marshall of a town called Ellwood. At one point, Dooley remarks: "We've been getting some strange breeds in Elwood lately. Remember that gunman who came through last week passing out business cards?" This refers to Paladin from Have Gun, Will Travel.
- *Maverick & Bonanza*: On an episode of Maverick, Bart runs across the "Wheelwright" family at the "Subrosa" Ranch, whose members include "Henry," "Moose," and "Small Paul." The Wheelwrights are obviously thinly disguised versions of the Cartwrights (the names have apparently been changed to protect the innocent).
- *Maverick & Bret Maverick & Young Maverick*: *Bret Maverick* and *Young Maverick* are spin-offs of *Maverick*.
- *Have Gun, Will Travel & Gunsmoke*: In an episode of *Have Gun, Will Travel*, "The Protégé," a gunfighter claims to have been a deputy for five years for Matt Dillon (from *Gunsmoke*) in Austin. Paladin calls his rival a liar because Dillon was never assigned to Austin.
- *Sugarfoot & Colt .45:* Christopher Colt guests on *Sugarfoot* several times.
- *Sugarfoot & Bronco & Cheyenne & Maverick*: Tom "Sugarfoot" Brewster appears once each on *Bronco*, *Cheyenne*, and as noted above, *Maverick*.
- *The Lawman & Sugarfoot & Colt. 45 & Maverick*: These shows cross-over when Deputy Johnny McKay (from *The Lawman*) testifies on Sugarfoot. The same episode has a guest appearance by Christopher Colt of *Colt. 45* and Bret Maverick appears on a "Wanted" poster.
- *77 Sunset Strip & Hawaiian Eye*: Stuart Bailey of *77 Sunset Strip* appears on the first episode of *Hawaiian Eye*. Both Stu Bailey and his partner Jeff Spencer (again of *77 Sunset Strip*) appear on a later episode of *Hawaiian Eye*. Tom Lopaka of *Hawaiian Eye* also appears on two episodes of *77 Sunset Strip*. And *77 Sunset Strip's* Kookie Kookson appears on two episodes of *Hawaiian Eye*.
- *Bourbon Street Beat & 77 Sunset Strip:* Rex Randolph of the short-lived *Bourbon Street Beat* becomes a regular on *77 Sunset Strip*.
- *Bourbon Street Beat & Surfside 6*: Kenny Madison of *Bourbon Street Beat* becomes a regular on *Surfside 6*.
- *77 Sunset Strip & Surfside 6*: *Surfside 6* characters Sandor "Sandy" Winfield II and Ken Madison appear once on *77 Sunset Strip*. Kookie Kookson and Jeff Spencer of *77 Sunset Strip* later appear on *Surfside 6*.
- *Wyatt Earp & Bat Masterson & Paradise*: The actors from *Wyatt Earp* and *Bat Masterson* reprise their characters in an episode of a 1980s Western television show called *Paradise*.
- *Kung Fu & Kung Fu: The Legend Continues & Cheyenne*: *Kung Fu* (featuring Kwai Chang Caine in the Old West) is the parent series of *Kung Fu:*

The Legend Continues (featuring the 1990s grandson of the original Kwai Chang Caine). In one episode, the original Caine comes forward time and swaps places with his grandson, who goes back in time and meets Cheyenne Bodie from *Cheyenne*.

- *Cheyenne & Bronco & The Dakotas*: *Bronco* and *The Dakotas* are spin-offs of *Cheyenne*.
- *The Rifleman & Dick Powell's Zane Grey Theater & Law of the Plainsman*: *The Rifleman* series originates as an episode of the anthology series *Dick Powell's Zane Grey Theater*. *Law of the Plainsman* then spins-off from *The Rifleman*.
- *The Virginian & Laredo & The Men from Shiloh & Decision*: *Laredo* and *The Men from Shiloh* are spin-offs of *The Virginian*. *The Virginian* first appears on television as an episode of the anthology series *Decision* before becoming an ongoing series.

Dragnet takes place in the Crossover Universe, thereby bringing in the following chain of shows:

- *Dragnet & Adam-12*: *Adam-12* is a spin-off of *Dragnet*.
- *Adam-12 & Emergency*: These two shows crossed-over.
- *Emergency & Sierra*: These two shows crossed-over.
- *Dragnet & The New Dragnet* (aka *Dragnet: The Nineties*): *The New Dragnet* is a spin-off of *Dragnet*.
- *Dragnet & L.A. Dragnet*: *L.A. Dragnet* is a spin-off of *Dragnet*.

About the Author

Win Scott Eckert is the editor of and a contributor to *Myths for the Modern Age: Philip Jose Farmer's Wold Newton Universe*, a 2007 *Locus* Awards finalist. He has written numerous short stories for Black Coat Press' *Tales of the Shadowmen* series, as well as tales for Moonstone Books about The Avenger, The Phantom, Zorro, Captain Midnight, and The Green Hornet. He contributed the Foreword to Philip José Farmer's seminal "fictional biography," *Tarzan Alive* (Bison Books, 2006), and co-authored with Farmer the Wold Newton novel *The Evil In Pemberley House*, about Patricia Wildman, the daughter of a certain bronze-skinned pulp hero.

CROSSOVERS 2
A Secret Chronology of the World

Win Scott Eckert

www.ingramcontent.com/pod-product-compliance
Lightning Source LLC
Chambersburg PA
CBHW021753230426
43669CB00006B/64